Fodor's

BARCELONA

3rd Edition

Fodor's Travel Publications New York, Toronto, London, Sydney, Auckland
www.fodors.com

Be a Fodor's Correspondent

Your opinion matters. It matters to us. It matters to your fellow Fodor's travelers, too. And we'd like to hear it. In fact, we need to hear it.

When you share your experiences and opinions, you become an active member of the Fodor's community. That means we'll not only use your feedback to make our books better, but we'll publish your names and comments whenever possible. Throughout our guides, look for "Word of Mouth," excerpts of your unvarnished feedback.

Here's how you can help improve Fodor's for all of us.

Tell us when we're right. We rely on local writers to give you an insider's perspective. But our writers and staff editors—who are the best in the business—depend on you. Your positive feedback is a vote to renew our recommendations for the next edition.

Tell us when we're wrong. We're proud that we update most of our guides every year. But we're not perfect. Things change. Hotels cut services. Museums change hours. Charming cafés lose charm. If our writer didn't quite capture the essence of a place, tell us how you'd do it differently. If any of our descriptions are inaccurate or inadequate, we'll incorporate your changes in the next edition and will correct factual errors at fodors.com immediately.

Tell us what to include. You probably have had fantastic travel experiences that aren't yet in Fodor's. Why not share them with a community of like-minded travelers? Maybe you chanced upon a beach or bistro or B&B that you don't want to keep to yourself. Tell us why we should include it. And share your discoveries and experiences with everyone directly at fodors.com. Your input may lead us to add a new listing or highlight a place we cover with a "Highly Recommended" star or with our highest rating, "Fodor's Choice."

Give us your opinion instantly at our feedback center at www.fodors.com/feedback. You may also e-mail editors@fodors.com with the subject line "Barcelona Editor." Or send your nominations, comments, and complaints by mail to Barcelona Editor, Fodor's, 1745 Broadway, New York, NY 10019.

You and travelers like you are the heart of the Fodor's community. Make our community richer by sharing your experiences. Be a Fodor's correspondent.

Happy Traveling!

Tim Jarrell, Publisher

FODOR'S BARCELONA

Editor: Maria Teresa Hart
Editorial Contributors: George Semler, Erica Duecy, Helio San Miguel

Production Editor: Astrid deRidder
Maps & Illustrations: Mark Stroud and Henry Colomb, Moon Street Cartography; David Lindroth, *cartographers;* Bob Blake, Rebecca Baer, *map editors;* William Wu, *information graphics*
Design: Fabrizio La Rocca, *creative director;* Guido Caroti, Siobhan O'Hare, *art directors;* Tina Malaney, Chie Ushio, Ann McBride, Jessica Walsh, *designers;* Melanie Marin, *senior picture editor*
Cover Photo: Park Güell by Antoni Gaudi: Ken Welsh/easyFotostock/age fotostock
Production Manager: Angela L. McLean

3rd Edition

ISBN 978–1–4000–0423–2

ISSN 1554–5865

SPECIAL SALES

This book is available at special discounts for bulk purchases for sales promotions or premiums. Special editions, including personalized covers, excerpts of existing books, and corporate imprints, can be created in large quantities for special needs. For more information, write to Special Markets/Premium Sales, 1745 Broadway, MD 6-2, New York, New York 10019, or e-mail specialmarkets@randomhouse.com.

AN IMPORTANT TIP & AN INVITATION

Although all prices, opening times, and other details in this book are based on information supplied to us at press time, changes occur all the time in the travel world, and Fodor's cannot accept responsibility for facts that become outdated or for inadvertent errors or omissions. So **always confirm information when it matters,** especially if you're making a detour to visit a specific place. Your experiences—positive and negative—matter to us. If we have missed or misstated something, **please write to us.** We follow up on all suggestions. Contact the Barcelona editor at editors@fodors.com or c/o Fodor's at 1745 Broadway, New York, NY 10019.

PRINTED IN SINGAPORE

10 9 8 7 6 5 4 3 2

CONTENTS

MAPS

ABOUT THIS BOOK

Our Ratings

Sometimes you find terrific travel experiences and sometimes they just find you. But usually the burden is on you to select the right combination of experiences. That's where our ratings come in.

As travelers we've all discovered a place so wonderful that its worthiness is obvious. And sometimes that place is so unique that superlatives don't do it justice: you just have to be there to know. These sights, properties, and experiences get our highest rating, **Fodor's Choice** indicated by orange stars throughout this book.

Black stars highlight sights and properties we deem **Highly Recommended** places that our writers, editors, and readers praise again and again for consistency and excellence.

By default, there's another category: any place we include in this book is by definition worth your time, unless we say otherwise. And we will.

Disagree with any of our choices? Care to nominate a place or suggest that we rate one more highly? Visit our feedback center at www.fodors.com/feedback.

Budget Well

Hotel and restaurant price categories from ¢ to $$$$ are defined in the opening pages of their respective chapters. For attractions, we always give standard adult admission fees; reductions are usually available for children, students, and senior citizens. Want to pay with plastic? **AE, D, DC, MC, V** following restaurant and hotel listings indicate whether American Express, Discover, Diners Club, MasterCard, and Visa are accepted.

Restaurants

Unless we state otherwise, restaurants are open for lunch and dinner daily. We mention dress only when there's a specific requirement and reservations only when they're essential or not accepted—it's always best to book ahead.

Hotels

Hotels have private bath, phone, TV, and air-conditioning and operate on the European Plan (aka EP, meaning without meals), unless we specify that they use the Continental Plan (CP, with a Continental breakfast), Breakfast Plan (BP, with a full breakfast), or Modified American Plan (MAP, with breakfast and dinner) or are all-inclusive (AI, including all meals and most activities). We always list facilities but not whether you'll be charged an extra fee to use them, so when pricing accommodations, find out what's included.

Listings

★	Fodor's Choice
★	Highly recommended
⊠	Physical address
✛	Directions or Map coordinates
⬚	Mailing address
☎	Telephone
🖷	Fax
⊕	On the Web
✉	E-mail
⬚	Admission fee
☉	Open/closed times
Ⓜ	Metro stations
▤	Credit cards

Hotels & Restaurants

🏨	Hotel
⇗	Number of rooms
⚲	Facilities
⅋Ⓞⅼ	Meal plans
✕	Restaurant
⬿	Reservations
⋔	Dress code
⌇	Smoking
🍸	BYOB

Outdoors

⚘	Golf
⛺	Camping

Other

☻	Family-friendly
⇨	See also
⊠	Branch address
☞	Take note

Experience
Barcelona

BARCELONA TODAY

Capital of an ever-more-autonomous Catalonia, Barcelona continues to thrive as a bilingual (Catalan and Spanish) city in love with everything avant-garde.

A Tale of Two Cities

Having languished for centuries in official "second-city" status in the shadow of Madrid, Barcelona's drive to excel, create, innovate, and improvise is largely a result of its ongoing obsession with eclipsing its eternal rival. Even within Barcelona, a healthy sense of national identity goads designers, architects, merchants, and industrialists to ever higher levels of originality and effectiveness. Ever since 1990, when the International Olympic Committee announced that the 1992 Olympic Games were to be held in the Catalan capital, Barcelona has been booming with pride and confidence in its ever brighter future as (finally!) a bona fide European capital recognized on its own merits.

Design, Architecture, Fashion, Style

Now that the city's haute couture status is increasingly seen as biting at the heels of more established design superstars such as Paris and Milan, present-day Barcelona more and more resembles a carousel of postmodern visual surprises, from "cool hunter" Brandery fashions to dizzying architecture—Jean Nouvel's Torre Agbar gherkin, Norman Foster's giant erector-set communications tower on the Collserola skyline, or Ricardo Bofill's Hotel Vela (Sail), the W hotel's nickname, looming over the waterfront.

Cuisine: Haute and Hot

Ever since Ferran Adrià and his restaurant El Bulli became synonymous with the planet's most innovative avant-garde culinary phenomenon in Northern Catalonia's Roses, the spin-off chef d'auteur successes, especially in Barcelona, have exponentially proliferated. With more than a dozen superb restaurants winning international awards and more on the way, keeping abreast of the city's gastronomic rock stars can be a dizzying pursuit. Direct Adrià disciples such as Sergi Arola at the Hotel Arts and Carles Abellán at Comerç 24 join Adrià precursors such as Jean Louis Neichel or old pals like Fermí Puig at the Hotel Majestic's Drolma, along with relative newcomers such as Jordi Artal of Cinc Sentits or Jordi Herrera of Manairó, in a glittering galaxy of gastronomical creativity. Meanwhile, carpetbaggers like the Roca brothers from Girona or Martin Berasategui from even farther afield in San Sebastián have opened award-winning hotel restaurants

WHAT WE'RE TALKING ABOUT

Can FC Barcelona do it again? The chance to win a second consecutive Champions title in Madrid's Bernabeu stadium where the final is scheduled to be held in May of 2010 is unadulterated *fútbol* aphrodisiac to Catalans.

The new Mandarin Hotel opening in 2010 in midtown Barcelona will star Carme Ruscalleda, Spain's most important female restaurateur, guiding the hotel restaurant with her son at the burners—another great leap forward for the pixie-ish Sant Pol de Mar master chef.

The W Hotel, also known as Hotel Vela, a huge sail-shaped skyscraper over the Barcelona waterfront, is causing a stir. While Barcelona's movers and shakers celebrate this iconic new monolith, residents of La Barceloneta protest the loss of the fishing quarter's salty character and identity.

in, respectively, the Omm (Moo) and the Condes de Barcelona (Lasarte) even as younger and smaller restaurants such Saüc, Ot, and Hisop are producing creative and streamlined cuisine at less than bank-breaking prices.

Fútbol Nirvana

Barcelona's always amazing FC Barcelona soccer juggernaut seemed as if it had peaked in 2006 when a hirsute athlete with an overbite named Ronaldinho led the team to its second European title . . . but the best was yet to come. Former star midfielder Pep Guardiola and a largely homegrown team of stars dazzled the world in 2009, winning the *triplete*, or the trifecta: the Spanish Liga, the King's Cup, and the Champions League European title. With star player Leo Messi still in his early 20s and the farm system producing a steady supply of new players committed to Barcelona's razzle-dazzle style of attacking, esthetically stunning play, 2010 could be even more apotheosic than 2009. What is certain, with or without titles, the creative choreography and the dedication to exciting, offensive soccer is here to stay.

New Toys

With a new airport terminal, a new waterfront monolith towering over the Mediterranean, the new AVE high-speed train connection making once remote Madrid into a little more than a Barcelona suburb, Barcelona is once again on the move. City planners predict that the new AVE terminal at Plaça de les Glòries will shift the city center eastward, and that the new Barcelona hub will surround the Torre Agbar and the Fòrum at the Mediterranean end of the Diagonal.

Political Progress

The approval of Catalonia's controversial new Autonomy Statute ushered in a wave of change in Catalonia. Bitterly opposed by the right-wing Partido Popular, the new autonomy agreement gives Catalonia a larger slice of local taxes and more control of its own infrastructure, such as ports, airports, and the high-speed AVE train. Perhaps more importantly, the new statute reinforces the use of the Catalan language and formally establishes Catalonia as one of the most progressive pockets in Europe, with special provisions safeguarding human rights on same-sex marriage, euthanasia, and abortion that would win scant support in other more traditional regions of Spain.

Catalonia's ongoing campaign to reinforce an identity distinct from that of Spain—comparable to Ireland distinguishing itself from England—is poised to lower the boom on bullfighting. The Parliament of Catalonia, pressured by animal rights groups and Catalan nationalists, is about to vote on the abolition of bullfighting, though in business-minded Catalonia the bottom line will probably be . . . the bottom line.

Gaudí's Sagrada Família has been placed on the World Monuments Fund's endangered monument Watch List as a result of ongoing construction of a high-speed train line under the site. The Madrid-based train tunnel project managers and Barcelona's Sagrada Família architects do not agree on the degree of danger the excavation entails.

BARCELONA PLANNER

When to Go

For optimal weather, fewer tourists, and a sense of local life as it is, the best times to visit Barcelona, Catalonia, and Bilbao are April–June and mid-September–mid-December. Catalans and Basques themselves vacation in August, causing epic traffic jams at both ends of the month. Major cities are relaxed and, except for tourists, empty in August, though Gràcia's Festa Major in Barcelona and Semana Grande in Bilbao keep these two cities very much alive during the festivities. Small shops and some restaurants shut down for the entire month, musical venues are silent, but museums remain open.

Summers in Barcelona, though occasionally very hot, are usually not too steamy for comfort. Temperatures rarely surpass 100°F (38°C), and air-conditioning is becoming more widespread. In any case, dining alfresco on a warm summer night is one of northern Spain's finest pleasures. Bilbao's legendary *siri-miri* (drizzle) keeps the city cool in summer, though winters can be irritatingly wet. All in all, spring and fall offer the best weather and temperatures at both ends of the Pyrenees. Barcelona winters are chilly enough for overcoats, but never freezing: ideal for walking, fireside dining, and hearty winter cuisine.

Getting Around

The best way to get around Barcelona is on foot, though a combination of subways, taxis, tramways, and walking will be required for covering the entire city. The central FGC (Ferrocarril de la Generalitat de Catalunya) train that runs between Plaça Catalunya and Sarrià is comfortable, air-conditioned, and leaves you within a 20- to 30-minute walk of nearly everything. (The metro and the FGC close at 11:45 weekdays and Sunday and run all night Friday and Saturday.) The main attractions requiring taxis or the metro are Montjuïc (Miró Foundation, MNAC, Mies van der Rohe Pavilion, Caixaforum, and Poble Espanyol), most easily accessed from Plaça Espanya; Park Güell above Plaça Lesseps; and the Auditori at Plaça de les Glories. Gaudí's Sagrada Familia is served by two metro lines (2 and 5), but the walk from the FGC's Provença stop is an enjoyable half-hour jaunt that passes three major Moderniste buildings: Palau Baró de Quadras, Casa Terrades (les Punxes), and Casa Macaia.

Sarrià and Pedralbes are easily explored on foot, though (depending on hiking ambition and footwear choice) the Torre Bellesguard or the Colegio de les Teresianas might require taxi hops. Walking from Sarrià down through the Jardins de la Vil.la Cecilia and Vil.la Amèlia to the Cátedra Gaudí is a pleasant stroll, while from there to the Futbol Club Barcelona you can cut through the Jardins del Palau Reial de Pedralbes and the university campus or catch a two-minute taxi.

All of Ciutat Vella (Barri Gòtic, Rambla, Raval, Ribera-Born, and Barceloneta) is best explored on foot, though an after-dinner taxi from Barceloneta to your hotel (usually not more than €10) is best called from your restaurant by radio taxi.

The city bus system is also a viable option, allowing a better look at the city as you travel, but the metro is faster and more comfortable. The tramway is a verdant and quiet ride down grassy tracks if you're headed from Plaça Francesc Macià out the Diagonal to the Futbol Club Barcelona, or from behind the Ciutadella Park out to Glòries and the Fòrum at the east end of the Diagonal.

Leave Barcelona with Everything You Brought—or Bought

Although muggings are practically unheard of in Barcelona, petty thievery is common. Handbags, backpacks, camera cases, and wallets are favorite targets, so tuck those away. Coat pockets with zippers work well for indispensable gear, while cash and a few credit cards wedged into a front trouser pocket are almost unassailable. Handbags hooked over chairs, on the floor or sidewalk under your feet, or dangling from hooks under bars are easy prey. Even a loosely carried bag is tempting for bag-snatchers. Should you carry a purse, use one with a short strap that tucks tightly under your arm without room for fleet hands to unzip. A plastic shopping bag for your essentials will attract even less attention.

Catalan for Beginners

Anyone who questions how different Catalan and Spanish are need only have a look at the nonsensical Catalan tongue twister "Setze jutges d'un jutjat menjen fetge d'un penjat" (Sixteen judges from a courthouse eat the liver of a hanged man) in Spanish: "Dieciseis jueces de un juzgado comen el higado de un ahorcado." Catalan is derived from Latin and Provençal French, whereas Spanish has a heavy payload of Arabic vocabulary and phonetics. For language exchange (intercambios), check the bulletin board at the Central University Philosophy and Letters Faculty on Gran Via or any English bookstore for free half-hour language exchanges of English for Catalan (or Spanish). It's a great way to get free private lessons, meet locals, and, with the right chemistry, even begin a cross-cultural fling. Who said the language of love is French?

Top Festivals and Events

Carnaval dances through Barcelona in February just before Lent, most flamboyantly in Sitges, though Barcelona's Carnestoltes are also wild and colorful.

Semana Santa (Holy Week), the week before Easter, is Spain's most important celebration everywhere but Barcelona, where the city empties.

La Diada de Sant Jordi is Barcelona's Valentine's Day, fused with International Book Day, celebrated on April 23 to honor the 1616 deaths of Miguel de Cervantes and William Shakespeare.

La Fira de Sant Ponç brings farmers to town with produce and natural remedies on May 11.

La Verbena de Sant Joan celebrates the summer solstice and Midsummer's Eve with fireworks and all-night beach parties on the night of June 23.

La Festa Major de Gràcia Barcelona's village-turned-neighborhood, Gràcia celebrates its fiesta in honor of Santa Maria with street dances and concerts in mid-August.

Festes de La Mercé celebrates Barcelona's patron saint, Nostra Senyora de la Mercé (Our Lady of Mercy) for a wild week beginning September 24.

WHAT'S WHERE

1 The Rambla. This is the city's most emblematic promenade, once a seasonal watercourse that flowed along the outside the 13th-century city walls. A stroll on the Rambla—pickpockets, buskers, scammers, street theater, and all—passes the Boqueria market, the Liceu opera house, and, at the port end, Drassanes, the medieval shipyards. Just off the Rambla is Plaça Reial, a popular neoclassical square, while off the other side is Gaudí's masterly Palau Güell.

2 The Barri Gòtic. The medieval Gothic Quarter surrounds the Catedral de la Seu on the high ground the Romans settled in the 1st century BC. The medieval Jewish quarter, the antiquers' row, Plaça Sant Jaume, and the Sant Just neighborhood are quintessential Barcelona.

3 The Raval. Once a rough-and-tumble slum, this area west of the Rambla has brightened considerably, thanks partly to the Barcelona Museum of Contemporary Art, designed by Richard Meier. Behind the Boqueria market is the stunning Antic Hospital de la Santa Creu, with its high-vaulted Gothic Biblioteca de Catalunya reading room. Sant Pau del Camp, Barcelona's earliest church, is at the far corner of the Raval, while the Espanña hotel and Gaudí's Palau Güell are nearer the Rambla.

4 Sant Pere, La Ribera, and El Born. Northeast of the Rambla, Sant Pere is the city's old textile neighborhood. La Ribera and the Ribera-Born neighborhood is filled with shops, restaurants, tiny medieval streets, and the Picasso Museum. Passeig del Born, once the medieval jousting ground, draws crowds to its shops by day and to its saloons by night.

5 Barceloneta. This neighborhood, just east of the Born-Ribera neighborhood, was open water until the mid-18th century, when it was landfilled. Laundry-festooned streets and the city's best seafood and rice restaurants make Barceloneta a city favorite for Sunday-afternoon paella gatherings.

6 The Eixample. The Eixample is the post-1860 grid square of city blocks uphill from Ciutat Vella containing most of Barcelona's Moderniste (Art Nouveau) architecture, including Gaudí's work-in-progress, the Sagrada Família church. Passeig de Gràcia is the city's premier shopping street. It also offers more Gaudí at Casa Batlló, Casa Milà (La Pedrera), and Casa Calvet.

C. de Provença
Casa Milà
C. de Mallorca

C. de Gràcia
C. de Pau Claris
C. de Roger Llúria

C. de València

Av. Diagonal

EIXAMPLE

Rambla de Catalunya

Passeig de Gràcia

Passeig de S. Joan

C. de Roger de Flor

Temple Expiatori de la Sagrada Familia

C. de Balmes

C. Consell de Cent

6

C. de Napoles
C. de Sicília
C. de Sardenya

C. d'Aragó

C. de la Diputació

Plaça Universitat

Plaça Tetuán

Gran Via de les Corts Catalanes

Casa Calvet

C. del Bruc
C. de Girona
C. de Bailén

C. de Casp

C. d'Ausias Marc

C. de Ribes

Barcelona Museum of Contemporary Art

Plaça de Catalunya

i

C. Sta. Anna

Ronda S. Pere

Arc del Triomf

C. de Tànger

P. de Cartes I

BARRI GÒTIC

Jongueres
S. Pere Més Alt

2

C. del Carme

La Boqueria

C. de la Palla

Via Laietana

S. Pere Més Baix

SANT PERE

C. dels Almogàvers

Avda. de la Meridiana

1

RAMBLA

Avda. Catedral
Cathedral

Passeig de Lluís Companys

C. de Sancho de Avila

Gran Teatre del Liceu

C. Ferran

Plaça del Rei

C. del Comerç

Passeig Pujadas

7
Pl. St. Jaume

C. Princesa

LA RIBERA

4

Pg. Picasso

Passeig de Cartes I

Palau Güell

Plaça Reial

C. Ciutat

EL BORN

Picasso Museum

Parc de la Ciutadella

C. de Wellington

C. Ample

Passeig del Born

Pl. d'Antoni López

Estació de França

Plaça Portal de la Pau

Pg. de Colom

Avda. d'Icària

Rambla de Mar

Moll de Barceloneta

Passeig Joan de Borbó

BARCELONETA

5

Vila Olímpica

Avda. Litoral Costat Muntanya

Parc de Mar

Moll d'Espanya

Passeig Marítim

Mediterranean Sea

WHAT'S WHERE

7 Gràcia. The former outlying village of Gràcia begins at Gaudí's playful Parc Güell and continues down past his first house, Casa Vicens, through two markets and various pretty squares such as Plaça de Rius i Taulet and Plaça del Sol. Carrer Gran de Gràcia, though narrow and noisy, is lined with buildings designed by Gaudí assistant Francesc Berenguer.

8 Sarrià and Pedralbes. Sarrià is a country hamlet within the burgeoning metropolis. A wander through these peaceful streets reveals several interesting buildings, antiques shops, boutiques, and a handful of fine-dining opportunities. Nearby is the Monestir de Pedralbes, a 14th-century architectural gem with a rare triple-tiered cloister; not far away are Gaudí's Colegio de les Teresianas and his Torre Bellesguard.

9 Tibidabo, Vallvidrera, and the Collserola Hills. Tibidabo, Barcelona's perch is generally a place to avoid unless you're seduced by Ferris wheels and amusement-park kitsch. The square at the funicular up to the amusement park, however, has restaurants with terrific views over the city, and the Gran Hotel la Florida up above it all is a tour de force. Even better is the Collserola forest and natural park on the far side of the hill, accessible by the FGC train out to the Baixador de Vallvidrera. Meanwhile, Vallvidrera is a sleepy village with a good restaurant (Can Trampa), a Moderniste funicular station, several quirky villas, and views west to the Montserrat massif.

10 Montjuïc. Montjuïc may seem dull compared to the electric street scene in the rest of Barcelona, but the Museu Nacional d'Arte de Catalunya (MNAC) in the Palau Nacional holds great art, as does the Joan Miró Foundation.

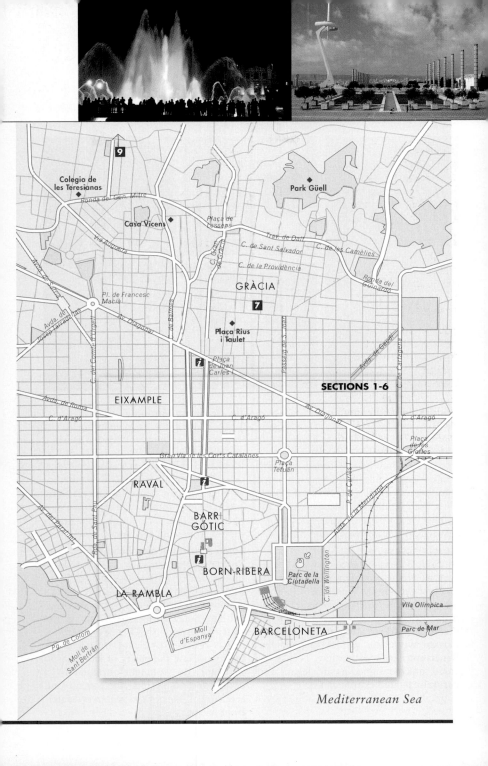

9

Colegio de
les Teresianas

Park Güell

Ronda del Gen. Mitre

Casa Vicens

Plaça de
Lesseps

Trav. de Dalt

C. de Sant Salvador

C. de les Camèlies

C. Gran de Gràcia

C. de la Providència

Ronda del
Guinardó

GRÀCIA

7

Pl. de Francesc
Macià

Plaça Rius
i Taulet

7

Plaça
de Joan
Carles I

SECTIONS 1-6

EIXAMPLE

Av. Diagonal

Avda. de Roma

C. d'Aragó

C. d'Aragó

C. d'Aragó

Plaça
de les
Glòries

Gran Via de les Corts Catalanes

Plaça
Tetuán

7

RAVAL

BARRI
GÓTIC

7

BORN-RIBERA

Parc de la
Ciutadella

Vila Olímpica

LA RAMBLA

BARCELONETA

Parc de Mar

Pg. de Colom

Moll
d'Espanya

Moll de
Sant Beltrán

Mediterranean Sea

BARCELONA TOP ATTRACTIONS

Gaudí's Sagrada Família

(A) The city's premier icon, Gaudí's gargantuan unfinished Temple Expiatori de la Sagrada Família (Expiatory Temple of the Holy Family) is entering its 125th year of construction. The peculiar pointed spires, with organic shapes that resemble a honeycombed confection, give the whole place a sort of fairy-tale quality that would suit a Harry Potter film.

Museu Picasso

(B) Pablo Picasso's connection to Barcelona, where he spent key formative years and first showed his work in 1900, eventually bore fruit when his manager Jaume Sabartés donated his collection to the city in 1962. Nearly as stunning as the 3,500 Picasso works on display are the five Renaissance palaces that have been renovated and redesigned as an elegant and naturally lighted exhibit space.

The Boqueria Market

(C) The oldest mid-city, open-air market of its kind in Europe, the Boqueria market, a jumble of color and aromas just off the Rambla, is the heart, as well as the stomach, of the city. As Barcelona's culinary fortunes soar, the Boqueria is increasingly assuming its pivotal role as the prime supplier of the fish, foul, meats, wild mushrooms, fruits, and vegetables.

Santa Maria del Mar Basilica

(D) For peace, symmetry, and Mediterranean Gothic at its classical best, Santa Maria del Mar is the Sagrada Família's polar opposite. Burned back to its original bare-bones structure by a fire at the start of the Spanish Civil War in 1936, it was restored by post-Bauhaus architects who saw the purity of stonemason Berenguer de Montagut's original 1329 design and maintained the elegant and economical lines of the seafarers' waterfront basilica.

Palau de la Música Catalana

(E) Often described as the flagship of Barcelona's Modernisme, this dizzyingly ornate tour de force designed by Lluís Domènech i Montaner is a catalog of Art Nouveau crafts and recourses, including ceramics, sculpture, stained glass, paintings, and a plethora of decorative techniques. Much criticized during the aesthetically somber 1939–75 Franco regime, the city's long-time prime concert venue is an exciting place to hear music.

Casa Batlló and the Manzana de la Discòrdia

(F) The Manzana de la Discòrdia (Apple of Discord) on Passeig de Gràcia is so called for its row of eye-knocking buildings by the three most famous Moderniste architects—Domènech i Montaner, Puig i Cadafalch, and Gaudí. Of the three, Gaudí's Casa Batlló, with its undulating dragon-backed roof, multicolor facade, skull-and-bones balconies, and underwater interior, is the most remarkable and the only one open to the public.

Park Güell

(G) Gaudí's light and playful park in the uppermost reaches of the village of Gràcia was originally developed as a garden community for Count Eusebi Güell and his closest friends. The flower-choked hillside contains a series of Moderniste gems ranging from the undulating ceramic bench around the central square to the gingerbread gatehouses.

Museu Nacional d'Art de Catalunya (MNAC)

(H) Barcelona's answer to Madrid's Prado hulks grandly atop the stairway leading up from Plaça Espanya. MNAC houses nearly all of Catalonia's art, from Romanesque altarpieces to Art Nouveau masters like Casas.

FLAVORS OF BARCELONA

Long before the molecular gastronomy craze made Catalonia a culinary funhouse, Barcelona and its surrounding hinterlands had their own lush tastes and textures, including sausages and charcuterie, wild mushrooms, spring onions with romescu sauce, and acorn-fed hams from southwestern Spain, all happily irrigated with sparkling wines from the Penedès. These items below represent the "must eats" that every visitor should try—the quintessential flavors of this city.

Calçots

One of Catalonia's most beloved and authentic feasts is the winter calçotada, with the *calçot* (a sweet, long-stemmed, twice-planted spring onion) as the star of the show. Originally credited to a 19th-century farmer named Xat Benaiges who discovered a technique for extending the scallion's edible portion by packing soil around the base, giving them stockings or shoes (*calçat*), so to speak, Valls and the surrounding region now produce upwards of five million calçots annually. Calçotades (calçot feasts) take place in restaurants and homes between January and March, though the season is getting longer on both ends. On the last weekend of January, the calçot capital of Valls holds a public calçotada, hosting as many as 30,000 people who come to gorge on calçots, sausage, lamb chops, and young red wine. During the festival, you can learn how to grow calçots, how to make the accompanying salbitxada sauce (romescu) and, most important, how to eat them. The culminating event is the calçot-eating competition, when burly competitors from all over Catalunya swallow as many as 300 calçots in a 40-minute contest as the crowd cheers them on. Once the winner is decided, large grills set up all over town roast calçots over sarmientos (grape vine clippings), as red wine and cava are splashed from long-spouted porrons.

Wild Mushrooms

Wild mushrooms are a fundamental taste experience in Catalan cuisine: the better the restaurant, the more chanterelles, morels, black trumpets, or 'shrooms of a dozen standard varieties are likely to appear on the menu. Wild mushrooms (in Spanish *setas*, in Catalan *bolets*) are valued for their aromatic contribution to gastronomy, a defining element in the olfactory taste process. While the black (or white) truffle is a delicious and extreme example, the musty, slightly gamey taste of the forest floor, the dark flavor of decay, is the aroma (hence, taste) that the wild mushroom imparts to the raw materials such as meat or eggs with which they are typically cooked. Most barcelonins are proficient wild mushroom stalkers and know how to find, identify, and prepare up to half a dozen kinds of bolets, from *rovellones* (*Lactarius deliciosus*) sautéed with parsely, olive oil, and a little garlic, to *camagrocs* (*Cantharellus lutescens*) scrambled with eggs. Wild mushrooms flourish in the fall, but different varieties appear in the spring and summer, and dried and reconstituted mushrooms are available year round. Pan-like Llorenç Petràs and his Fruits del Bosc (Forest Fruits) stall at the back of the Boqueria market is the place to go for a not-so-short course in mycology. Petràs supplies the most prestigious chefs in Barcelona and around Spain with wild mushrooms. If morels are scarce in the hinterlands of Catalonia but abundant in, say, Wisconsin, Petràs will have them. His book *Cocinar con Setas* (Cooking with Wild Mushrooms) is a runaway best seller presently in its 10th edition.

Sausage

Catalonia's variations on this ancient staple cover a wide range of delicacies. Typically ground pork is mixed with black pepper and other spices, stuffed into sterilized intestines, and dried to create a protein-rich, easily conservable meat product. If Castile is the land of roasts and Valencia is the Iberian rice bowl and vegetable garden, Catalonia may produce the greatest variety of sausages. Below are some of the most common:

Botifarra: pork sausage seasoned with salt and pepper. Grilled and served with stewed white beans and *allioli* (garlic mayonnaise). Variations include botifarra with truffles, apples, wild mushrooms, and even chocolate.

Botifarra Blanca: typical of El Vallès Oriental just north of Barcelona, made of tripe and pork jowls, seasoned and boiled. Served as a cold cut.

Botifarra de Huevo: Egg sausage with ingredients similar to botifarra but with egg yolks added.

Botifarra de perol: made with head meat boiled before stuffing.

Botifarra Catalana Trufada: a tender, pink-hued sausage, seasoned and studded with truffles.

Botifarra dolça: cured with sugar instead of salt and seasoned with spices such as cinnamon and nutmeg, served as a semi-dessert, this sausage is typical of the Empordà region.

Botifarra negra: Catalan blood sausage made with white bread soaked in pig blood with fat, salt, and black pepper.

Fuet: means "whip" for its slender shape, made of 60/40 lean meat to fat, also known as *secallona, espetec,* and *somalla.*

Ibérico Ham

The ham of the Ibérico pig, a descendant of the *Sus mediterraneus* that once roamed the Iberian Peninsula, has become Spain's modern-day caviar. *Jamón ibérico de bellota* (acorn-fed Ibérico ham) is dark, red, myoglobin-rich muscle tissue striated with fat, and tastes entirely of the acorns, grasses, roots, herbs, spices, tubers, and wild mushrooms of southwestern Spain. The defining characteristic of this free-range pig is its ability to store monounsaturated fats from acorns in streaks or marbled layers that run through its muscle tissue. This is one of the few animal fats scientifically proven to fight the cholesterol that clogs arteries. Also the taste and aromas, after two years of aging, are complex, and so nutty, buttery, earthy, and floral that Japanese enthusiasts have declared Ibérico ham *umami,* a word used to describe a fifth dimension in taste, in a realm somewhere beyond delicious. In addition, jamon ibérico de bellota liquefies at room temperature, so it literally melts in your mouth.

Caveats: *Jamón serrano* refers to mountain (*sierra*)-cured ham and should never be confused with *jamón ibérico de bellota.* What is commercialized in the U.S. as Serrano ham comes from white pigs raised on cereals and slaughtered outside of Spain. *Pata negra* means "black hoof." Not all ibérico pigs have black hooves, and some pigs with black hooves are not purebred ibéricos. *Jabugo* refers only to ham from the town of Jabugo in Huelva in the Sierra de Aracena. The term has been widely and erroneously applied to jamón ibérico de bellota in general.

LIKE A LOCAL

If you want to get a sense of local Barcelona culture and indulge in some of the pleasures treasured by barcelonins, start by familiarizing yourself with the rituals of daily life. These are a few highlights—activities and events you can take part in along with Barcelona's rank and file.

Grazing: Tapas and Wine Bars

Few pastimes in Barcelona are more satisfying than wandering, tippling, and tapas-hunting. Whether during the day or after dark, meandering through the Gothic Quarter, Gràcia, Barceloneta, or the Born-Ribera district offers an endless selection of taverns, cafés, bars, and restaurants where wines, beers, or *cava* (Catalan sparkling wine), accompany little morsels of fish, sausage, cheese, peppers, wild mushrooms, or *tortilla* (potato omelet). If you find yourself stuck on Passeig de Gràcia or the Rambla in bars that serve microwaved tapas, know this: you're missing out. The areas around Passeig del Born, Santa Maria del Mar, Plaça de les Olles, and the Picasso Museum are the prime *tapeo* (tapa-tasting) and *txikiteo* (tippling) grounds.

Openings, Presentations, Lectures, and Musical Events

Check listings in the *Guía del Ocio* or in the daily newspapers *El País* or *La Vanguardia* to find announcements for art gallery openings, book presentations, and free public concerts. Often serving cava and canapés, these little gatherings welcome visitors (if it's announced in the papers, you're invited). Famous authors from Richard Ford or Michael Chabon to Martin Amis or local stars such as Javier Marías or Carlos Ruiz Zafón may be presenting new books at the British Institute or at bookstores such as La Central. Laie Libreria holds jazz performances in its café, while the travel bookstore Altair has frequent book signings and talks by prominent travel authors. Events in the town hall's Saló de Cent are usually open to the public.

Sunday Sardanas, Puppets, and Castellers

The Sunday-morning papers carry announcements for local neighborhood celebrations, flea markets and produce fairs, puppet shows, storytelling sessions for children, *sardana* dancing (Catalonia's national dance), bell-ringing concerts, and, best of all, *castellers*. The castellers, complex human pyramids sometimes reaching as high as 10 stories, are a quintessentially Catalan phenomenon that originated in the Penedés region west of Barcelona and are performed regularly at neighborhood fiestas or key holidays. Most Sunday-morning events are over by two o'clock, when lunchtime officially reigns supreme, so an early start is recommended. The Barcelona town hall in Plaça Sant Jaume is a frequent castellers and sardanas venue, as is Plaça de la Catedral.

Soccer: FC Barcelona

As FC Barcelona's soccer fortunes soar, sports bars proliferate throughout the city. Though the pubs showing soccer near the Rambla are usually heavily populated by foreign tourists, the taverns and cafés in Barceloneta, El Raval, Gràcia, and Sarrià are generally local *penyas* (fan clubs), where passions run high. For the real thing, there is the Camp Nou stadium; strangely, the stadium, though beautiful, often seems soporific compared to the taverns and bars where 90% of Barcelona's soccer fans get their weekly hit of "the opium of the masses."

GREAT ITINERARIES

Ciutat Vella, Quintessential Barcelona
Stroll the Rambla and see the colorful Boqueria market before cutting over to the Catedral de la Seu in the city's hushed and resonant Gothic Quarter. Detour through stately Plaça Sant Jaume where the Palau de la Generalitat, Catalonia's seat of government, faces the town hall. The Gothic Plaça del Rei and the neoclassical Plaça Reial (not to be confused) are short walks from Plaça Sant Jaume. The Museu Picasso is five minutes from the loveliest example of Catalan Gothic architecture, the basilica of Santa Maria del Mar. An evening concert at the Palau de la Música Catalana after a few tapas and before a late dinner is an unsurpassable way to end an epic day in Barcelona.

The Raval, behind the Boqueria, holds the Museu d'Art Contemporani de Barcelona, the medieval Antic Hospital de la Santa Creu, the Sant Pau del Camp church, and the medieval shipyards at Drassanes Reiales. Palau Güell, just off the lower Rambla, is a key Gaudí visit. A short hike away, the waterfront Barceloneta neighborhood is one of Barcelona's most characteristic and picturesque districts, as well as a prime place for a paella on the beach.

The post-1860 Checkerboard Eixample
A morning touring the Eixample begins at Gaudí's still-in-progress magnum opus, the Temple Expiatori de la Sagrada Família. On the way back to the Eixample's vertebral Passeig de Gràcia, swing past Moderniste architect Puig i Cadafalch's Casa Terrades as well as his Palau Baró de Quadras. Spend the afternoon in the Eixample touring the undulating facades and stunning interiors of Casa Milà and Casa Batlló. Other Eixample architecture includes Gaudí's Casa Calvet, not far from Plaça Catalunya, the Fundació Tàpies, and more far-flung Moderniste gems such as Casa Golferichs, or Casa de la Papallona out toward Plaça de Espanya. Rambla Catalunya's leafy tunnel is a cool and shaded promenade lined with shops and sidewalk cafés.

Upper Barcelona: Gràcia and Sarrià
For a more rustic and restful urban excursion, try the formerly outlying towns of Gràcia and Sarrià. Gràcia is home to Gaudí's first house, Casa Vicens, and his playful Parc Güell above Plaça Lesseps, while the tree-lined lower reaches of this intimate neighborhood are filled with houses by Gaudí's right-hand man, Francesc Berenguer. Sarrià is a village stranded in the ever-expanding metropolis, with diminutive streets, shops and restaurants, and the Monestir de Pedralbes, a venerable monastery with a superb Gothic cloister. Also in Sarrià are Gaudí's Torre Bellesguard and the Colegio de les Teresianas.

Art in Montjuïc
Montjuïc offers various art collections at the Museu Nacional d'Art de Catalunya, while the nearby Fundació Miró features Catalan artist Joan Miró's colorful paintings and a stellar Calder mobile. Down the stairs toward Plaça Espanya are the Mies van der Rohe Barcelona Pavilion and the restored Casaramona textile mill, now the Caixaforum cultural center and gallery.

A WALK AROUND LA RAMBLA

La Rambla is a live wire of energy, spilling over with people, markets, and cafés. Meander down this main artery, with a loop through the Boqueria into the Raval and back out to the Rambla, and you'll understand the city's twin passions for great food and gorgeous architecture, both considered vital to barcelonins.

LA RAMBLA: RIVER OF LIFE

Starting from the top of the Rambla at **Plaça de Catalunya,** jump into the stream of humanity. Each section of the Rambla has its personality, from the **Rambla de Canaletes** with its magic fountain, through the **Rambla dels Ocells** with its bird vendors, past the ceramic representation of the 14th-century Rambla at the opening into Carrer de Portaferrissa, and through the flower stalls along the **Rambla de les Flors.** The **Boqueria market** opens up off the Rambla de les Flors, while farther down the Rambla the **Liceu opera house** overlooks street performers and human statues stretching down through the Rambla de Santa Mónica to the Mediterranean.

THE BOQUERIA: HORN OF PLENTY

Halfway down the Rambla is the Mercat de Sant Josep, popularly known as **La Boqueria.** Famous chefs and hurried housewives browse through their favorite stands. Highlights are **Pinotxo,** the legendary dozen-stool gourmet counter, **Quim de la Boqueria** with its famous *ous esclafats amb llanqueta* (eggs with tiny fish), **Petràs,** the world-renowned wild mushroom czar, and the farmers market out at **Plaça de Sant Galdric** at the upper side of the square.

THE MEDIEVAL HOSPITAL: GOTHIC SPLENDOR

Behind the Boqueria and through Plaça de la Gardunya is the medieval **Hospital de la Santa Creu,** founded in the 13th century by King Martí l'Humà (Martin the Humane), famed for spending treasure on health care rather than warships. Starting at the Casa de la Convalescencia off Passatge de l'Hospital, look for the ceramic tiles in the vestibule portraying the life of Saint Paul and look through the Renaissance patio inside. The courtyard of the hospital, now the Biblioteca de Catalunya, leads through an orange grove to the library up the stairs to the right. The breathtaking Gothic stone arches allow abundant light to flood into what was once Europe's most complete medical center.

MODERNISTE RAVAL: GAUDÍ AND DOMÈNECH I MONTANER

From the medieval Hospital, walk back along the Carrer Hospital to Plaça de Sant Agustí, with the rough unfinished façade of the Sant Agustí church looming overhead. Cut through Carrer de l'Arc de Sant Agustí to the **Hotel Espanya,** a Moderniste masterpiece by architect Lluís Domènech i Montaner. The mermaid murals and the marble fireplace are highlights. Cut from Carrer Sant Pau through the **Liceu opera house shop,** filled with musical gifts. Back out on the Rambla, the first street to the right is Carrer Nou de la Rambla, with Antoni Gaudí's **Palau Güell** just 50 yards down the street. The neoclassical **Plaça Reial** is directly across the Rambla from Carrer Nou de la Rambla.

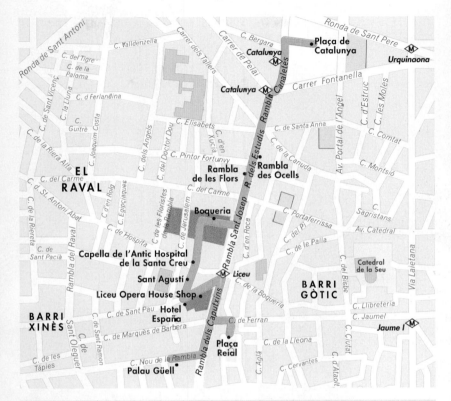

Highlights:	Canaletas fountain, Rambla de les Flors, La Boqueria, the ceramic life of Saint Paul, Hotel Espanya, the Liceu opera house shop, Palau Güell, Plaça Reial.
Where to Start:	Top of the Rambla at Plaça Catalunya.
Length:	3 hours with time for browsing through the Boqueria. 2 mi in all.
Where to Stop:	Plaça Reial.
Best Time to Go:	Before 2 PM when everything is open and the market is raging.
Worst Time to Go:	Between 2 PM and 4 PM when the market starts to slow down and Palau Güell closes.
Where to Refuel:	Café Viena for the famous flautas de jamón iberico (Iberico ham sandwiches); Bar Pinotxo and Quim de la Boqueria in La Boqueria; La Taxidermista in Plaça Reial.

GAUDÍ
ARCHITECTURE
THROUGH
THE LOOKING
GLASS

(left) The undulating rooftop of Casa Batlló. (top) Construction continues on la Sagrada Família.

Before his 75th birthday in 1926, Antonio Gaudí was hit by a trolley car while on his way to Mass. The great architect—initially unidentified—was taken to the medieval Hospital de la Santa Creu in Barcelona's Raval and left in a pauper's ward, where he died two days later without regaining consciousness. It was a dramatic and tragic end for a man whose entire life seemed to court the extraordinary and the exceptional.

Gaudí's singularity made him hard to define. Indeed, eulogists at the time, and decades later, wondered how history would treat him. Was he a religious mystic, a rebel, a bohemian artist, a Moderniste genius? Was he, perhaps, all of these? He certainly had a rebellious streak, as his architecture stridently broke with tradition. Yet the same sensibility that created the avant-garde benchmarks Park Güell and La Pedrera also created one of Spain's greatest shrines to Catholicism, the *Temple Expiatori de la Sagrada Família* (Expiatory Temple of the Holy Family), which architects agree is one of the world's most enigmatic structures; work on the cathedral continues to this day. And while Gaudí's works suggest a futurist aesthetic, he also reveled in the use of ornamentation, which 20th century architecture largely eschewed.

What is no longer in doubt is Gaudí's place among the great architects in history. Eyed with suspicion by traditionalists in the 1920s and 30s, vilified during the Franco regime, and ultimately redeemed as a Barcelona icon after Spain's democratic transition in the late 70s, Gaudí has finally gained universal admiration.

THE MAKING OF A GENIUS

Gaudí was born in 1852 the son of a boilermaker and coppersmith in Reus, an hour south of Barcelona. As a child, he helped his father forge boilers and cauldrons in the family foundry, which is where Gaudí's fascination with three-dimensional and organic forms began. Afflicted from an early age with reoccuring rheumatic fever, the young architect devoted his energies to studying and drawing flora and fauna in the natural world. In school Gaudí was erratic: brilliant in the subjects that interested him, absent and disinterested in the others. As a seventeen-year-old architecture student in Barcelona, his academic results were mediocre. Still, his mentors agreed that he was brilliant.

Unfortunately being brilliant didn't mean instant success. By the late 1870s, when Gaudí was well into his twenties, he'd only completed a handful of projects, including the Plaça Reial lampposts, a flower stall, and the factory and part of a planned workers' community in Mataró. Gaudí's career got the boost it needed when, in 1878, he met Eusebi Güell, heir to a textiles fortune and a man who, like Gaudí, had a refined sensibility. (The two bonded over a mutual admiration for the visionary Catalan poet Jacint Verdaguer.) In 1883 Gaudí became Güell's architect and for the next three decades, until Güell's death in 1918, the two collaborated on Gaudí's most important architectural achievements, from high-profile endeavors like Palau Güell, Park Güell, and Pabellones Güell to smaller projects for the Güell family.

(top) Interior of Casa Batlló. (bottom) Chimneys on rooftop of Casa Milà recall helmeted warriors or veiled women.

GAUDÍ TIMELINE

1883–1884

Gaudí builds a summer palace, *El Capricho* in Comillas, Santander for the brother-in-law of his benefactor, Eusebi Güell. Another gig comes his way during this same period when Barcelona ceramics tile mogul Manuel Vicens hires him to build his town house, *Casa Vicens*, in the Gràcia neighborhood.

El Capricho

1884–1900

Gaudí whips up the Pabellones Güell, Palau Güell, the Palacio Episcopal of Astorga, Barcelona's Teresianas school, the Casa de los Botines in León, Casa Calvet, and Bellesguard. These have his classic look of this time, featuring interpretation of Mudéjar (Moorish motifs), Gothic, and Baroque styles.

Palacio Episcopal

BREAKING OUT OF THE T-SQUARE PRISON

If Eusebi Güell had not believed in Gaudí's unusual approach to Modernisme, his creations might not have seen the light of day. Güell recognized that Gaudí was imbued with a vision that separated him from the crowd. That vision was his fascination with the organic. Gaudí had observed early in his career that buildings were being composed of shapes that could only be drawn by the compass and the T-square: circles, triangles, squares, and rectangles—shapes that in three dimensions became prisms, pyramids, cylinders and spheres. He saw that in nature these shapes are unknown. Admiring the structural efficiency of trees, mammals, and the human form, Gaudí noted ". . . neither are trees prismatic, nor bones cylindrical, nor leaves triangular." The study of natural forms revealed that bones, branches, muscles, and tendons are all supported by internal fibers. Thus, though a surface curves, it is supported from within by a fibrous network that Gaudí translated into what he called "ruled geometry," a system of inner reinforcement he used to make hyperboloids, conoids, helicoids, or parabolic hyperboloids.

These tongue-tying words are simple forms and familiar shapes: the femur is hyperboloid; the way shoots grow off a

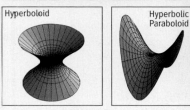

Hyperboloid

Hyperbolic Paraboloid

The top of the gatehouse in Park Güell at the main entrance; note the mushroom-like form.

branch is helicoidal; the web between your fingers is a hyperbolic paraboloid. To varying degrees, these ideas find expression in all of Gaudí's work, but nowhere are they more clearly stated than in the two masterpieces La Pedrera and Park Güell.

1900-1917

Gaudí's Golden Years—his most creative, personal, and innovative period. Topping each success with another, he tackles Park Güell, the reform of Casa Batlló, the Güell Colony church, Casa Milà (La Pedrera), and the Sagrada Família school.

Casa Batlló's complex chimneys

1918-1926

A crushing blow: Gaudí suffers the death of his assistant, Francesc Berenguer. Grieving and rudderless, he devotes himself fully to his great unfinished opus, la Sagrada Família—to the point of obsession. On June 10th, 1926, he's hit by a trolley car. He dies two days later.

La Sagrada Família

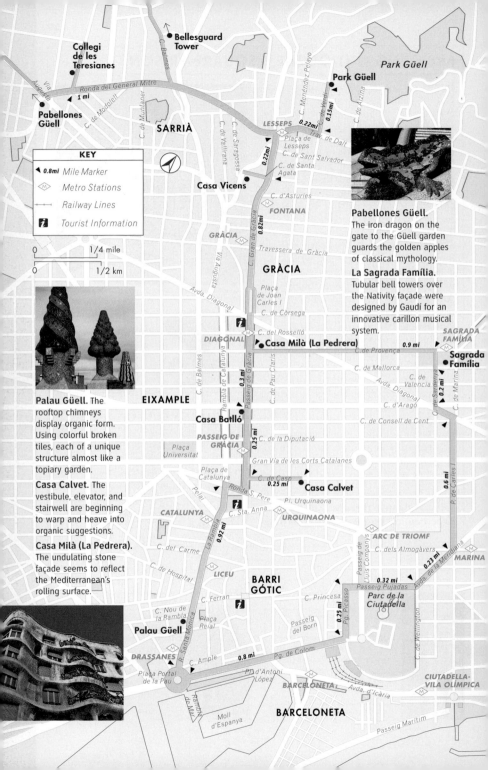

Collegi de les Teresianes

Bellesguard Tower

Park Güell

Pabellones Güell

Ronda del General Mitre

1 mi

SARRIÀ

LESSEPS

Plaça de Lesseps

C. de Sant Salvador

C. de Santa Agata

Casa Vicens

FONTANA

C. d'Asturies

GRÀCIA

Travessera de Gràcia

GRÀCIA

Plaça de Joan Carles I

C. de Còrsega

KEY

◀ 0.8mi Mile Marker

Ⓜ Metro Stations

┼ Railway Lines

ℹ Tourist Information

0 ____ 1/4 mile
0 ____ 1/2 km

DIAGONAL

C. del Rosselló

● Casa Milà (La Pedrera)

C. de Provença 0.9 mi

SAGRADA FAMÍLIA

● Sagrada Família

C. de Mallorca

Avda. Diagonal

C. de Pau Claris

0.3 mi

EIXAMPLE

Casa Batlló

PASSEIG DE GRÀCIA

Plaça Universitat

C. de la Diputació

0.25 mi

Gran Via de les Corts Catalanes

Plaça de Catalunya

Ronda S. Pere

C. de Casp
0.25 mi ● Casa Calvet

CATALUNYA

C. Sta. Anna

Pl. Urquinaona

URQUINAONA

0.92 mi

ARC DE TRIOMF

C. dels Almogàvers

MARINA

0.23 mi

LICEU

BARRI GÒTIC

C. Ferran

C. Princesa

Passeig del Born

Parc de la Ciutadella

0.32 mi

Passeig Pujades

0.25 mi

Palau Güell

DRASSANES

C. Ample 0.8 mi

Pg. de Colom

Pl. d'Antoni López

BARCELONETA

CIUTADELLA-VILA OLÍMPICA

Plaça Portal de la Pau

Moll d'Espanya

BARCELONETA

Passeig Marítim

Pabellones Güell. The iron dragon on the gate to the Güell garden guards the golden apples of classical mythology.

La Sagrada Família. Tubular bell towers over the Nativity façade were designed by Gaudí for an innovative carillon musical system.

Palau Güell. The rooftop chimneys display organic form. Using colorful broken tiles, each of a unique structure almost like a topiary garden.

Casa Calvet. The vestibule, elevator, and stairwell are beginning to warp and heave into organic suggestions.

Casa Milà (La Pedrera). The undulating stone façade seems to reflect the Mediterranean's rolling surface.

HOW TO SEE GAUDÍ IN BARCELONA

Few architects have left their stamp on a major city as thoroughly as Gaudí did in Barcelona. Paris may have the Eiffel Tower, but Barcelona has Gaudí's still unfinished masterpiece, the **Temple Expiatori de la Sagrada Família,** the city's most emblematic structure. Dozens of other buildings, parks, gateways and even paving stones around town bear Gaudí's personal Art Nouveau signature, but the continuing progress on his last and most ambitious project makes his creative energy an ongoing part of everyday Barcelona life in a unique and almost spectral fashion.

In Barcelona, nearly all of Gaudí's work can be visited on foot or, at most, with a couple of metro or taxi rides. A walk from **Palau Güell** near the Mediterranean end of the Rambla, up past **Casa Calvet** just above Plaça Catalunya, and on to **Casa Batlló** and **Casa Milà** is an hour's stroll, which, of course, could take a full day with thorough visits to the sites. **Casa Vicens** is a half hour's walk up into Gràcia from **Casa Milà. Park Güell**

(top) The serpentine ceramic bench at Park Güell, designed by Gaudí collaborator Josep Maria Jujol, curves sinuously around the edge of the open square. (bottom) Sculptures by Josep María Subirachs grace the temple of the Sagrada Família.

is another thirty- to forty-minute walk up from that. **La Sagrada Família,** on the other hand, is a good hour's hike from the next nearest Gaudí point and is best reached by taxi or metro. The **Teresianas** school, the **Bellesguard Tower,** and **Pabellones Güell** are within an hour's walk of each other, but to get out to Sarrià you will need to take the comfortable Generalitat (FGC) train.

MAKING THE MOST OF YOUR EUROS

Barcelona is in the same league as other major European destinations in terms of cost. And depending on where the euro is, that exchange rate can take a bite. But remember that there are such things as discounts, and if you can live like a local you save like a local.

Although your pocket might feel the pinch, greenbacks can punch above their weight with a few well-chosen tips. Travelers posting on the Travel Talk forums at Fodors.com recommend the following budget-saving tips:

Save with a Card

■TIP➜ The T10 card, the ArticketBCN card, and the Barcelona card all offer bundled discounts for museum passes, transit, and more.

"I found the T10 card very useful. I was in Barcelona for only three and a half days but I knew I would use the train to and from the airport as well as going to Montjuïc and Park Güell—so six trips made it worth my while and I used it two more times." —Mara

"If you are interested in the major art museums, the ArticketBCN is a good buy since it gives you free (not just discounted) admissions." —QueScaisJe

"[The ArticketBCN is] a decent buy at 20 euros *provided* that you are indeed interested in, and have time for, at least four of the following 7 museums: Picasso, Fundació Miró, Fundació Tàpies, La Pedrera, MACBA, CCCB, MNAC." —Maribel

Walk and use Pubic Transportation

■TIP➜ Barcelona is definitely a city to explore on foot. Take the opportunity to stroll through the central neighborhoods, and when your feet get tired, take the metro instead of a taxi.

"Barcelona is very walkable, but you'll probably want to use the metro to go to the Sagrada Família or over to the Montjuïc funicular. You'll save a little by buying a 10-trip ticket." —martytravels

"I am personally a fan of staying in the Barri Gòtic as you can reach many areas on foot. The only attraction that would require transportation is if you want to see the Sagrada Família (which I highly recommend) or Park Güell. The city has a good Web site for public transportation and you can enter your starting and ending destinations." —Cristina_C

Hit Museums on Free Nights

■TIP➜ Nothing beats "free," so if you're a culture buff on a budget, plan your visits around the various free nights offered by local museums.

"[Many museums] have a free day during the week . . . In Barcelona the National Museum of Catalan Art is free the first Sunday of the month; good timing, proper planning, and careful research is all it takes." —Viajero2

Fill Up Like a Local

■TIP➜ There are so many ways to eat well in Barcelona and still save money: tapas, wine bars, and cafés all offer terrific casual foods that satisfy your taste buds and your wallet. And don't forget to capitalize on a big, less expensive lunch to save money at dinnertime.

"Make the midday meal your main meal of the day and patronize *tabernas* that post their *menú del día* on a chalkboard just outside the door." —NEDSIRELAND

Exploring Barcelona

WORD OF MOUTH

"The Sagrada Família is spectacular; even if you've seen pictures you won't believe it in real life. I would describe it as surreal. I loved the use of color and mosaics, and found it very unusual and uplifting. "

—kireland

By George
Semler

The thronging Rambla, the reverberation of a flute in the medieval Gothic Quarter, bright ceramic colors splashed across Art Nouveau facades, glass and steel design over Roman stone: one way or another, Barcelona will find a way to get your full attention.

The Catalonian capital has barnstormed into the new millennium in the throes of a cultural and industrial rebirth comparable only to the late-19th-century Renaixença (Renaissance) that filled the city with its flamboyant Moderniste (aka Art Nouveau) architecture. Today new architecture and design—including some of Europe's hottest new fashions in hip boutiques—provide the city with an exciting effervescent edge. Wedged along the Mediterranean coast between the forested Collserola hills and Europe's busiest seaport, Barcelona has catapulted to the rank of Spain's most-visited city, a 2,000-year-old master of the art of perpetual novelty.

The city's palette is vivid and varied: the glow of stained glass in the penumbra of the Barri Gòtic; Gaudí's mosaic-encrusted, undulating facades; the chromatic mayhem at the Palau de la Música Catalana; Miró's now universal blue and crimson shooting stars. Then, of course, there is the physical setting of the city, crouched catlike between the promontories of Montjuïc and Tibidabo, between the Collserola woodlands and the 4,000-acre port. Obsessed with playful and radical interpretations of everything from painting to theater to urban design and development, Barcelona consistently surprises.

Barcelona is wired with a vitality that somehow stops short of being intimidating. Just about the time you might begin to drop into a food- and wine-induced slumber at two in the morning, barcelonins are just heading out, when the city's night scene begins to kick in for real. Irrepressibly alive, creative, acquisitive, and playful in about equal doses, the city never stops. Regardless of outside governmental regimes that once tried to hold the reins, Catalans just kept on working, scheming, playing, and building. Now, with its recent past as a provincial outpost well behind it, the city is charging into the future with more creativity and raw energy than ever.

Barcelona's present boom began on October 17, 1987, when Juan Antonio Samaranch, president of the International Olympic Committee, announced that his native city had been chosen to host the 1992 Olympics. This single masterstroke allowed Spain's so-called "second city" to throw off the shadow of Madrid and its 40-year "internal exile" under the Franco regime and resume its rightful place as one of Europe's most dynamic destinations. Not only did the Catalan administration lavish untold millions in subsidies from the Spanish government for the Olympics, they then used the games as a platform to broadcast the news about Catalonia's cultural and national identity from one end of the planet to the other. Madrid who? Calling Barcelona a second city of anyplace is playing with fire; modern Spain has always had two urban focal points, even though official figures dubiously counted Madrid's suburbs, but not Barcelona's, to feed the illusion that the Catalan capital was a provincial port.

More Mediterranean than Spanish, historically closer and more akin to Marseille or Milan than to Madrid, Barcelona has always been ambitious, decidedly modern (even in the 2nd century), and quick to accept the most recent innovations. Its democratic form of government is rooted in the so-called Usatges Laws instituted by Ramon Berenguer I in the 11th century, which amounted to a constitution. This code of privileges represented one of the earliest known examples of democratic rule, while Barcelona's Consell de Cent (Council of 100), constituted in 1274, was Europe's first parliament and is the true cradle of Western democracy. More recently, the city's electric light system, public gas system, and telephone exchange were among the first in the world. The center of an important seafaring commercial empire with colonies spread around the Mediterranean as far away as Athens when Madrid was still a Moorish outpost marooned on the arid Castilian steppe, Barcelona traditionally absorbed new ideas and styles first. Whether it was the Moors who brought navigational tools, philosophers and revolutionaries from nearby France spreading the ideals of the French Revolution, or artists like Picasso and Dalí who bloomed in the city's air of freedom and individualism, Barcelona has always been a law unto itself.

In the end, Barcelona is a banquet for all the senses, though perhaps mainly for sight. Not far behind are the pleasures of the palate. The air temperature is almost always about right, more and more streets are pedestrianized, and tavern after tavern burrows elegantly into medieval walls. Every now and then the fragrance of the sea in the port or in Barceloneta reminds you that this is, after all, a giant seaport and beach city, with an ancient Mediterranean tradition that is, at the outset of its third millennium, flourishing—and bewitching visitors as it has for centuries.

Catalan First, Spanish Second

Throughout a history of political ups and downs, prosperity rarely abandoned Barcelona, as the city continued to generate energy and creativity no matter who imposed authority from afar: Romans, Visigoths, Franks, Moors, Aragonese, French, or Castilians. Catalonia's early history hinges on five key dates: the 801 Frankish conquest by Charlemagne that wrested Catalonia away from the encroaching Moors; the 988 independence from the Franks; the 1137 alliance through marriage with Aragón; the 1474 unification (through the marriage of Fernando of Aragón and Isabella of Castile) of Aragón with the Castilian realms of León and Castile; and the 1714 defeat by Felipe V, who abolished Catalan rights and privileges.

The Roman Empire annexed the city built by the Iberian tribe known as the Laietans and established, in 133 BC, a colony called Colonia Favencia Julia Augusta Paterna Barcino (Favored Colony Barcino of Father Julius Augustus). After Rome's 4th-century decline, Barcelona enjoyed an early golden age as the Visigothic capital under the rule of Ataulf and the Roman empress of the West, Galla Placidia (388–450), daughter of Theodosius I and one of the most influential and fascinating women of early European history. Ataulf, assassinated in Barcelona in 415, was succeeded by Visigothic rulers who moved their capital to Toledo, leaving Barcelona to a secondary role through the 6th and 7th centuries. The Moors invaded in the 8th century; and in 801, in what was to be a decisive moment in Catalonia's history, the Franks under Charlemagne captured the city and made it a buffer zone at the edge of Al-Andalus, the Moors'

empire on the Iberian Peninsula. Moorish rule extended to the Garraf Massif just south of Barcelona, while Catalonia became the Marca Hispánica (Spanish March or, really, "edge") of the Frankish empire.

Over the next two centuries the Catalonian counties, ruled by counts appointed by the Franks, gained increasing autonomy. In 985 the Franks failed to reinforce their allies against a Moorish attack, and as of 988 Catalonia declared itself an independent federation of counties with Barcelona as its capital. The marriage in 1137 of Sovereign Count Ramon Berenguer IV to Petronella, daughter of King Ramiro II of Aragón, united Catalonia with Aragón. The crown of Aragón, with Barcelona as its commercial and naval center, controlled the Mediterranean until the 15th century. The 1474 marriage of Ferdinand II of Aragón and Isabella of Castile and León brought Aragón and Catalonia into a united Spain. As the main city of Aragón's Mediterranean empire, Barcelona had grown in importance between the 12th and the 14th centuries, and only began to falter when maritime emphasis shifted to the Atlantic after 1492.

Despite the establishment of Madrid as the seat of Spain's royal court in 1562, Catalonia continued to enjoy autonomous rights and privileges until 1714, when, in reprisal for having backed the Austrian Habsburg pretender to the Spanish throne during the War of the Spanish Succession (1700–14), all institutions and expressions of Catalan identity were suppressed by the triumphant Felipe V of the French Bourbon dynasty. Not until the mid-19th century would Barcelona's industrial growth bring about a *renaixença* (renaissance) of nationalism and a cultural flowering that recalled Catalonia's former opulence.

Barcelona's power and prosperity continued to grow in the early 20th century. After the abdication of Alfonso XIII and the establishment of the Second Spanish Republic in 1931, Catalonia enjoyed a high degree of autonomy and cultural freedom. Once again backing a losing cause, Barcelona was a Republican stronghold during the Spanish civil war. When the war ended, Catalan language and identity were once again brutally suppressed by such means as book burning, the renaming of streets and towns, and the banning of the Catalan language in schools and in the media. This repression, or "internal exile," lasted until Franco's death in 1975, when it became evident that the Catalans had once again, more stubbornly than ever, managed to keep their language and culture alive. Catalonian home rule was granted after Franco's death in 1975, and Catalonia's parliament, the ancient Generalitat, was reinstated in 1980. Catalan is now Barcelona's co-official language, along with Castilian Spanish. Street names are signposted in Catalan, and newspapers, radio stations, and a TV channel publish and broadcast in Catalan. The culmination of this rebirth was the staging of the Olympics in 1992—ring roads were constructed, new harborside promenades were created, and Catalonia announced its existence and national identity to the world. The urban renewal for the Olympics under Mayor Pasqual Maragall (later president of the Generalitat) was just the beginning. Mayor Joan Clos, with the 2004 Fòrum Universal de les Cultures,

engineered the new Diagonal-Mar development, stretching from Plaça de les Glòries to the mouth of the Besòs River and populated with Jean Nouvel, Oscar Tusquets, and Herzog & de Meuron buildings that keep architecture students on a perennial field trip.

Catalonia's controversial new Autonomy Statute, approved in 2006 under the Socialist government of José Luis Rodríguez Zapatero, placed still more power in local hands. Although there are now varying degrees of Catalonian nationalism in play ranging from radical pro-independence militants to conservative Spain-firsters, most Catalans today think of themselves as Catalans first and Spanish citizens second.

■ TIP→ Learning a few Catalan phrases will give you a much warmer reception than the usual Spanish. A friendly "bon dia" (good day) goes a long way.

THE RAMBLA: THE HEART OF BARCELONA

Sightseeing
★★★★★
Nightlife
★★★★☆
Dining
★★★☆☆
Lodging
★★★★☆
Shopping
★★★☆☆

The Rambla was originally a watercourse, a sandy arroyo called *rmel*. Today seasonal runoff has been replaced by a flood of humanity. No wonder Federico García Lorca called this the only street in the world he wished would never end: the show of humanity rages relentlessly—mimes, acrobats, jugglers, musicians, puppeteers, portraitists, break-dancers, rappers, and rockers stretched out beneath the canopy of plane trees. A pedestrian runway between two traffic lanes, the Rambla remains an essential Barcelona event.

The crowds seethe and dawdle. Couples sit at café tables no bigger than tea trays while nimble-footed waiters dodge traffic, bringing trays from kitchens. Peddlers, kiosk owners, parrots, and parakeets along the Rambla dels Ocells (Rambla of the Birds) create a cacophony of birdsong and catcalls that clamors over the din of taxis and motorbikes. Here, in busy Barcelona, the Rambla is permanently filled with squads of revelers, often more animated at 3 AM than at 3 PM.

The Rambla's original riverbed flowed down from the Collserola hills along the ramparts that encircled the Gothic Quarter. When in the late 13th century the walls were demolished, the open space outside was left as a mid-city promenade. For nearly a thousand years the Rambla has been a forum for peddlers, workers in search of jobs, and farmers selling produce or livestock. These days, visitors from all over the world have joined them.

From the rendezvous point at the head of the Rambla at Café Zurich to the Boqueria produce market, the Liceu opera house, or the Rambla's lower reaches, there is always something for everyone along this vertebral column of Barcelona street life.

MAIN ATTRACTIONS

Fodor's Choice **Boqueria.** Barcelona's most spectacular food market, also known as the
★ Mercat de Sant Josep, is an explosion of life and color sprinkled with
delicious little bar-restaurants. A solid polychrome wall of fruits, herbs,
wild mushrooms, vegetables, nuts, candied fruits, cheeses, hams, fish,
poultry, and provender of every imaginable genus and strain greets
you as you turn in from La Rambla, the air alive with the aromas of
fresh produce and reverberating with the din of commerce. Within this
steel hangar the market occupies a neoclassical square built in 1840 by
architect Francesc Daniel Molina. The Doric columns visible around
the edges of the market were part of the mid-19th-century neoclassical
square constructed here after the Sant Josep convent was torn down.
The columns were uncovered in 2001 after more than a century of being
buried in the busy market. Highlights include the sunny greengrocer's
market outside (to the right if you've come in from the Rambla), along
with **Pinotxo** *(Pinocchio)*, just inside to the right, which has won international acclaim as a food sanctuary. Owner Juanito Bayén and his family
serve some of the best food in Barcelona. (The secret? "Fresh, fast, hot,
salty, and garlicky.") Pinotxo—marked with a ceramic portrait of the
wooden-nosed prevaricator himself—is typically overbooked. But take
heart; the **Kiosko Universal,** over toward the port side of the market, or
Quim de la Boqueria offer delicious alternatives. Don't miss herb- and
wild-mushroom expert Llorenç Petràs at the back of the Boqueria (ask
anyone for the location), with his display of *fruits del bosc* (fruits of
the forest): wild mushrooms, herbs, nuts, and berries. ⊠ *Rambla 91,
Rambla* ⊕ *www.boqueria.info* ☉ *Mon.–Sat. 8–8* Ⓜ *Liceu.*

★ **Gran Teatre del Liceu.** Barcelona's opera house has long been considered
one of the most beautiful in Europe, in the same category as Milan's La
Scala. First built in 1848, this cherished cultural landmark was torched
in 1861, then later bombed by anarchists in 1893, and once again gutted
by a blaze of mysterious origin in early 1994. During that most recent
fire, Barcelona's soprano Montserrat Caballé stood on the Rambla in
tears as her beloved venue was consumed. Five years later a restored
Liceu, equipped for modern productions, opened anew. Even if you
don't see an opera, don't miss a tour of the building; some of the Liceu's
most spectacular halls and rooms (including the glittering foyer known
as the Saló dels Miralls, or Room of Mirrors) were untouched by the
fire of 1994, as were those of Spain's oldest social club, El Círculo del
Liceu. The Espai Liceu downstairs provides the city with daily cultural
and commercial operatic interaction. With a cafeteria; a shop specializing in opera-related gifts, books, and recordings; a small, 50-person-
capacity theater running videos of opera fragments and the history of
the opera house; and a Mediateca (media library) featuring recordings
and filmings of past opera productions, Espai Liceu is the final step in
the Barcelona opera's phoenixlike resurrection. ⊠ *La Rambla 51–59,
Rambla* ☎ *93/485–9913* ⊕ *www.liceubarcelona.com* ✉ *Guided tours
€8.70* ☉ *Tours daily at 10 AM in English (the 75-min visit includes El
Círculo del Liceu, with the extraordinary Ramon Casas collection of
paintings). Unguided express tours at 11 AM, noon, 12:30, and 1 PM are
shorter (20 mins) and less comprehensive; cost is €4.50* Ⓜ *Liceu.*

GETTING ORIENTED

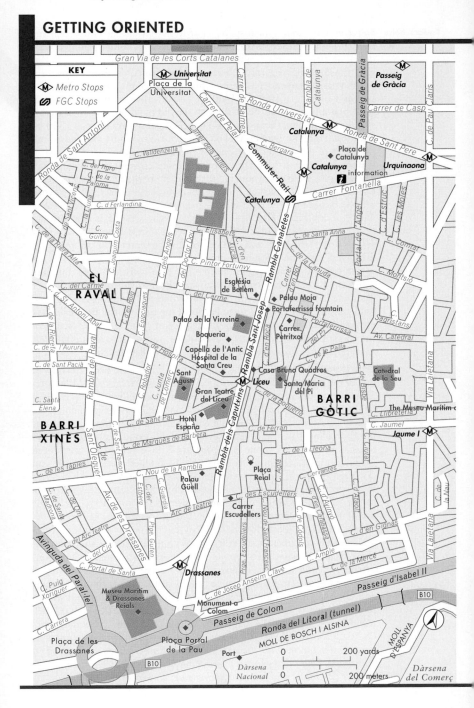

KEY

Ⓜ Metro Stops

Ⓕ FGC Stops

Gran Via de les Corts Catalanes

Ⓜ **Universitat**
Plaça de la Universitat

Passeig de Gràcia

Ⓜ **Passeig de Gràcia**

Carrer de Casp

Ronda Universitat

Ⓜ **Catalunya**

Ronda de Sant Pere

Ⓜ **Urquinaona**

Plaça de Catalunya

Ⓜ **Catalunya** information

Ⓕ **Catalunya**

Carrer Fontanella

Rambla Canaletes

EL RAVAL

Església de Betlem

Palau Moja

Portaferrissa fountain

Palau de la Virreina

Boqueria

Carrer Petritxol

Capella de l'Antic Hospital de la Santa Creu

Sant Agustí

Casa Bruno Quadros

Ⓜ **Liceu**

Santa Maria del Pi

Catedral de la Seu

Gran Teatre del Liceu

BARRI GÒTIC

The Museu Marítim

BARRI XINÈS

Hotel España

Ⓜ **Jaume I**

Plaça Reial

Palau Güell

Carrer Escudellers

Ⓜ **Drassanes**

Museu Marítim & Drassanes Reials

Monument a Colom

Passeig d'Isabel II

B10

Plaça de les Drassanes

Plaça Portal de la Pau

Passeig de Colom

Ronda del Litoral (tunnel)

MOLL DE BOSCH I ALSINA

MOLL D'ESPANYA

Port

Dàrsena Nacional

Dàrsena del Comerç

B10

| 0 | 200 yards |
| 0 | 200 meters |

Timing

Allow three to four hours, including stops, for exploring the Rambla. The best times to find things open and the Rambla rollicking are 9 AM–2 PM and 4 PM–8 PM, although this populous runway has a life of its own 24 hours a day. Some museums remain open through the lunch hour but others close—check hours. Most church hours are 9 AM–1:30 PM and 4:30 PM–8 PM; there is usually a midday closing.

Getting Here

The Plaça Catalunya metro stop will put you at the head of the Rambla in front of Café Zurich, Barcelona's most famous rendezvous point. From here it's just a few steps down to the Canaletes fountain on the right side of the Rambla.

Quick Bites

Café de l'Opera (✉ *La Rambla 74, Rambla* ☎ *93/317-7585* Ⓜ *Liceu*), across from the Liceu opera house, is a favorite Barcelona hangout and a good place to people-watch and bump into someone you might not have expected to encounter—always a mixed blessing. The Thonet chairs and etched mirrors lend historic charm.

Top Attractions

Boqueria

Gran Teatre del Liceu

Museu Marítim

Palau Güell

Top Experiences

Browsing through the Boqueria market

Exploring Palau Güell

Strolling the Rambla

Touring the Liceu opera house

Visiting Drassanes and the Maritime Museum

Where to Eat (⇨ Ch. 3)

Café Viena

Can Culleretes

El Irati

La Taxidermista

La Xina

Happening Nightlife (⇨ Ch. 5)

Bar Pastis

Glaciar

Jamboree-Jazz & Dance-Club

Los Tarantos

Area Shops (⇨ Ch. 7)

Art Escudellers

Bagués Masriera

Custo Barcelona

Ganiveteria Roca

Fodor's Choice
★
☺

Museu Marítim. The superb Maritime Museum is housed in the 13th-century **Drassanes Reials** (Royal Shipyards), at the foot of the Rambla adjacent to the harbor front. This vast covered complex begun in 1378 built and launched the ships of Catalonia's powerful Mediterranean fleet directly from its yards into the port (the water once reached the level of the eastern facade of the building). Today these are the world's largest and best-preserved medieval shipyards; centuries ago, at a time (1377–88) when Greece was a province of the House of Aragón, they were of crucial importance to the sea power of Catalonia (then the heavyweight in an alliance with Aragón). On the Avinguda del Paral.lel side of Drassanes is a completely intact section of the 14th- to 15th-century walls—Barcelona's third and final ramparts—that encircled the Raval along the Paral.lel and the Rondas de Sant Pau, Sant Antoni, and Universitat. (*Ronda* was originally used to specify streets or circumvolutions running around the outside of the city walls.) The earliest part of Drassanes is the section farthest from the sea along Carrer de Portal de Santa Madrona. Subsequent naves were added in the 17th and 18th centuries.

Though the shipyards seem more like a cathedral than a naval construction site, the Maritime Museum is filled with vessels, including a spectacular collection of ship models. The life-size reconstruction of the galley of Juan de Austria, commander of the Spanish fleet in the Battle of Lepanto, is perhaps the most impressive display in the museum. Figureheads, nautical gear, early navigational charts, and medieval nautical lore enhance the experience, and headphones and infrared pointers provide a first-rate self-guided tour. Concerts, often featuring early-music master and viola de gamba virtuoso Jordi Savall, are occasionally held in this acoustical gem. The cafeteria is Barcelona's hands-down winner for dining in the midst of medieval elegance. Don't miss the small bronze reproduction of a sailing ship, commemorating the 1571 Battle of Lepanto, out on the Rambla corner nearest the port. ⊠ *Av. de les Drassanes s/n, Rambla* ☎ *93/342–9920* ⊕ *www. museumaritimbarcelona.org* ⬚ *€6.50; free 1st Sat. of month 3–7* ☉ *Daily 10–7* Ⓜ *Drassanes.*

★

Palau Güell. Partly closed for restoration through 2010, Palau Güell presently admits visitors to the basement stables free of charge from 10 AM to 2:30 PM Tuesday–Saturday. With a Pau Casals recording of Bach's cello suites playing and a video presentation of the rest of the house to watch, this regime rivals the full visit and is highly recommended. Gaudí built this mansion in 1886–89 for textile baron Count Eusebi de Güell Bacigalupi, his main patron and promoter. Gaudí's principal obsession in this project was to find a way to illuminate this seven-story house tightly surrounded by other buildings in the cramped quarters of the Raval. The prominent *quatre barras* (four bars) of the Catalan *senyera* (banner) on the facade between the parabolic (looping) entrance arches attest to the nationalist fervor that Gaudí shared with Güell. The dark facade is a dramatic foil for the treasure housed inside, where spear-shape Art Nouveau columns frame the windows and prop up a series of detailed and elaborately carved wood ceilings.

A shipshape collection of nautical wonders are on display at the Museu Marítim.

The basement stables are famous for the "fungiform" (fungus- or mushroom-like) columns supporting the whole building. Note Gaudí's signature parabolic arches between the columns and the way the arches meet overhead, forming an oasis-like canopy of palm fronds, probably little consolation for political prisoners held here during the 1936–39 Spanish civil war, when the space was used as a *cheka* (the Russian word used for Republican secret-police dungeons). The patio where the horses were groomed receives light through a skylight, one of many Gaudí devices and tricks used to create, or seem to create, more light: mirrors, skylights, even frosted-glass windows over artificial lighting, giving the impression of exterior light. Don't miss the faithful hounds in the grooming room with rings for hitching horses, or the wooden bricks used as cobblestones in the upstairs entryway and on the ramp down to the basement grooming area to deaden the sound of horses' hooves. The chutes on the Carrer Nou de la Rambla side of the basement were for loading feed straight in from street level overhead, while the catwalk and spiral staircase were for the servants to walk back up into the main entry.

Upstairs are three successive receiving rooms, the wooden ceilings progressing from merely spectacular to complex to byzantine in their richly molded floral and leaf motifs. The third receiving room, the one farthest in with the most elaborate ceiling ornamentation, has a jalousie in the balcony over the room, a double grate through which Güell was able to inspect and, almost literally, eavesdrop on his arriving guests. The main hall, with the three-story-tall tower reaching up above the roof, was the room for parties, dances, and receptions. Musicians played from the balcony, and the overhead balcony window was for the main vocalist. A chapel of hammered copper with retractable kneeling pads and a small bench for two built into the right side of the altar is enclosed behind a double door. Around the corner is a small organ, the flutes in rectangular tubes climbing the mansion's central shaft.

The dining room is dominated by a beautiful mahogany banquet table seating 10, an Art Nouveau fireplace in the shape of a deeply curving horseshoe arch, and walls with floral and animal motifs. Note the Star of David in the woodwork over the window and the Asian religious themes in the vases on the mantelpiece. From the outside rear terrace, the polished Garraf marble of the main part of the house is exposed and visible, while the brick servants' quarters rise up on the left. The passageway built toward the Rambla was all that came of a plan to buy an intervening property and connect three houses into a major structure, a scheme that never materialized.

Gaudí is most himself on the roof, where his playful, polychrome ceramic chimneys seem right at home with later works such as Park Güell and La Pedrera. Look for the flying-bat weather vane over the main chimney, symbol of Jaume I el Conqueridor (James I, the Conqueror), who brought the house of Aragón to its 13th-century imperial apogee in the Mediterranean. Jaume I's affinity for bats is said to have stemmed from his Majorca campaign, when, according to one version, he was awakened by the fluttering *rat penat* (literally, "condemned mouse") in time to stave off a Moorish night attack. Another version attributes the presence of the bat in Jaume I's coat of arms to his gratitude to the Sufi sect that helped him successfully invade Majorca, using the bat as a signal indicating when and where to attack. See if you can find the hologram of COBI, Javier Mariscal's 1992 Olympic mascot, on a restored ceramic chimney (hint: the all-white one at the Rambla end of the roof terrace). ⊠ *Nou de la Rambla 3–5, Rambla* ☎ *93/317–3974* ⊕ *www.palauguell.cat* ☜ *€7.50* ◷ *Daily 9–8* Ⓜ *Drassanes, Liceu.*

Plaça Reial. Nobel Prize–winning novelist Gabriel García Márquez, architect and urban planner Oriol Bohigas, and Pasqual Maragall, former president of the Catalonian Generalitat, are among the many famous people said to have acquired apartments overlooking this potentially elegant square, a chiaroscuro masterpiece in which neoclassical symmetry clashes with big-city street squalor. Plaça Reial is bordered by stately ocher facades with balconies overlooking the wrought-iron **Fountain of the Three Graces** and treelike, snake-infested lampposts designed by Gaudí in 1879. Third-rate cafés and restaurants line the square, but the buskers, thieves, and homeless who occupy the benches on sunny days make hanging out here uncomfortable. Plaça Reial is most colorful on Sunday morning, when crowds gather to trade stamps and coins; after dark it's a center of downtown nightlife for the jazz-minded, the young, and the adventurous (it's best to be streetwise touring this area in the late hours). Bar Glaciar, on the uphill corner toward the Rambla, is a booming beer station for young international travelers. La Taxidermista, across the way, is the only good restaurant in the plaza; Tarantos has top flamenco performances; and Jamboree offers world-class jazz. ⊠ *Plaça Reial, Rambla* Ⓜ *Catalunya, Liceu.*

Barcelona's Lovers' Day

Barcelona's best day? Easy. April 23—St. George's Day, La Diada de Sant Jordi, Barcelona's Valentine's day—a day when kissometer readings go off the charts, a day so sweet and playful, so goofy and romantic, that 6 million Catalans go giddy from dawn to dusk.

Patron saint of Catalonia, international knight-errant St. George allegedly slew a dragon about to devour a beautiful princess south of Barcelona. From the dragon's blood sprouted a rosebush, from which the hero plucked the prettiest blossom for the princess. Hence, the traditional Rose Festival celebrated in Barcelona since the Middle Ages to honor chivalry and romantic love, a day for men and mice alike to give their true loves roses. In 1923 the lovers' fest merged with International Book Day to mark the anniversary of the all-but-simultaneous April 23, 1616, deaths of Miguel de Cervantes and William Shakespeare.

More than 4 million roses and half a million books are sold in Catalonia on Sant Jordi's Day, men giving their inamoratas roses and the ladies giving books in return. Bookstalls run the length of the Rambla, and although it's an official workday, nearly all of Barcelona manages to play hooky and wander. In the city Saint George is everywhere, beginning on the facade of the Catalonian seat of government, the Generalitat. Art Nouveau master Eusebi Arnau sculpted Sant Jordi skewering the unlucky dragon on the facade of the Casa Amatller, as well as on the corner of Els Quatre Gats café, while Gaudí dedicated an entire house, Casa Batlló, to the Sant Jordi theme with the saint's cross implanted in the scaly roof and the skulls and bones of the dragon's victims framing the windows.

A Roman soldier martyred for his Christian beliefs in the 4th century, Saint George is one of the most venerated of all saints, patron of England, Greece, and Romania, among other places. Associated with springtime and fertility, Sant Jordi roses include a spike of wheat and a little red and yellow "senyera," the Catalonian flag. And the books? There's the Shakespeare and Cervantes anniversary, and Barcelona's importance as a publishing capital. Language and love have, in any case, always been closely associated.

In Barcelona and all of Catalonia, Sant Jordi's Day erupts joyfully. There is a 24-hour reading of *Don Quixote*. Authors come to bookstalls to sign books. In Sarrià a floral artisan displays 45 kinds of roses representing 45 different kinds of love, from impossible to unrequited to filial and maternal. The *sardana* is reverently performed in Plaça Sant Jaume, while the Generalitat, its patio filled with roses, opens its doors to the public. Choral groups sing love songs in the Gothic Quarter as jazz combos play in Plaça del Pi. The Rambla is solid humanity from the Diagonal to the Mediterranean, 3 km (2 mi) of barcelonins basking in the warmth of spring and romance. Rare is the roseless woman on the streets of Barcelona.

By midnight the Rambla, once a watercourse, is again awash with flower water and covered with rose clippings and tiny red-and-yellow-striped ribbons spelling "Sant Jordi," "Diada de la Rosa" (Day of the Rose), and "t'estimo" (I love you).

2

Portaferrissa fountain. Both the fountain and the ceramic representation of Barcelona's second set of walls and the early Rambla are worth studying carefully. If you can imagine pulling out the left side of the ceramic scene and looking broadside at the amber yellow 13th-century walls that ran down this side of the Rambla, you will see a clear picture of what this spot looked like in medieval times. The sandy Rambla ran along outside the walls, while the portal looked down through the ramparts into the city. As the inscription on the fountain explains, the Porta Ferrica, or Iron Door, was named for the iron measuring stick attached to the wood and used in the 13th and 14th centuries to establish a unified standard for measuring goods. ⊠ *Rambla and Carrer Portaferrissa, Rambla* Ⓜ *Liceu.*

Sant Agustí. This unfinished church is one of Barcelona's most unusual structures, with jagged stone sections projecting down the left side, and the upper part of the front entrance on Plaça Sant Agustí waiting to be covered with a facade. Begun in 1728 and abandoned 20 years later, the projected facade, designed by Pere Costa, was to be baroque in style, but funding stopped and so did the construction. Sant Agustí comes alive on May 22, feast day of Santa Rita, patron saint of *"los imposibles"*—that is, lost causes. Unhappily married women, unrequited lovers, and all-but-hopeless sufferers of every stripe and spot form long lines through the square and down Carrer Hospital. Each carries a rose that will be blessed at the chapel of Santa Rita on the right side of the altar. ⊠ *Pl. Sant Agustí, Raval* ☎ *93/318–6231* Ⓜ *Liceu.*

Santa Maria del Pi. Sister church to Santa Maria del Mar and to Santa Maria de Pedralbes, this early Catalan Gothic structure is perhaps the most fortresslike of all three: hulking, dark, and massive, and perforated only by the main entryway and the mammoth rose window, said to be the world's largest. Try to see the window from inside in the late afternoon to get the best view of the colors. The church was named for the lone *pi* (pine tree) that stood in what was a marshy lowland outside the 4th-century Roman walls. An early church dating back to the 10th century preceded the present Santa Maria del Pi, begun in 1322 and finally consecrated in 1453. Like Santa Maria del Mar, the church of Santa Maria del Pi is one of Barcelona's many examples of Mediterranean Gothic architecture, though the aesthetic distance between the two is substantial. The church's interior is disappointingly cluttered compared with the clean and lofty lightness of Santa Maria del Mar, but the creaky choir loft and the Ramón Amadeu painting La Mare de Deu dels Desamparats (Our Lady of the Helpless), for which the artist reportedly used his wife and children as models for the Virgin and children, are interesting. The lateral facade of the church, around to the left in Plaça Sant Josep Oriol, bears a plaque dedicated to the April 6, 1806, fall of the portly parish priest José Mestres, who slipped off the narrow catwalk circling the outside of the apse. He survived the fall unhurt, and the event was considered a minor miracle commemorated with the plaque.

The adjoining squares, **Plaça del Pi** and **Plaça de Sant Josep Oriol,** are two of the liveliest and most appealing spaces in the Old Quarter, filled with much-frequented outdoor cafés and used as a venue for markets selling natural products or paintings or as an impromptu concert hall for musicians. The handsome entryway and courtyard at No. 4 Plaça de Sant Josep Oriol across from the lateral facade of Santa Maria del Pi is the **Palau Fivaller,** now seat of the Agricultural Institute, an interesting patio to have a look through. From Placeta del Pi, tucked in behind the church, you can see the bell tower and the sunny facades of the apartment buildings on the north side of Plaça Sant Josep Oriol. Placeta del Pi was once the cemetery for the blind, hence the name of the little street leading in: Carrer Cecs de la Boqueria (Blind of the Boqueria). This little space with its outdoor tables is a quiet and cozy place for a coffee or excellent tapas at El Taller de Tapas. ✉ *Pl. del Pi s/n, Rambla* ☎ *93/318–4743* ☾ *Daily 9–1:30 and 4:30–8* Ⓜ *Liceu.*

WORTH NOTING

Carrer Escudellers. Named for the *terrissaires* (earthenware potters) who worked here making *escudellas* (bowls or stew pots), this colorful loop is an interesting sub-trip off the Rambla. Go left at Plaça del Teatre and you'll pass the landmark **Grill Room** at No. 8, an Art Nouveau saloon with graceful wooden decor and mediocre cuisine (still, it's a fine stop for a beverage at the ornate oaken bar). Next is **La Fonda Escudellers,** another lovely, glass- and stone-encased dining emporium best admired from afar but avoided. (The vacuum-packed, nuked risottos leave a lot to be desired.) At Nos. 23–25 is Barcelona's most comprehensive ceramics display, at **Art Escudellers,** with a branch across the street at No. 14. Next door, with chickens roasting over the corner, is **Los Caracoles,** once a not-to-be-missed Barcelona restaurant (now somewhat touristy and dated). Even now, the wooden bar and the walk-through kitchen on the way in are picturesque, as are the dining rooms and tiny stairways within. Unfortunately, the cuisine is mediocre and expensive, and the clientele is almost entirely composed of tourists. Another hundred yards down Carrer Escudellers is **Plaça George Orwell,** named for the author of *Homage to Catalonia,* a space created to bring light and air into this traditionally squalid neighborhood. The little flea market that hums along on Saturday is a great place to browse.

Take a right on Carrer de la Carabassa and walk down this cobbled alley with graceful bridges between several houses and their former gardens. At the end of the street, looming atop her own basilica, is **Nostra Senyora de la Mercè** (Our Lady of Mercy). This giant representation of Barcelona's patron saint is a 20th-century (1940) addition to the roof of the 18th-century Església de la Mercè; the view of La Mercè gleaming in the sunlight, babe in arms, is one of the Barcelona waterfront's most impressive sights. As you arrive at Carrer Ample, note the **15th-century door** with a winged Sant Miquel Archangel delivering a squash backhand to a scaly Lucifer; it's from the Sant Miquel church, formerly part of City Hall, torn down in the early 19th century. From the Mercè, a walk out Carrer Ample (to the right) leads back to the Rambla. Don't miss the grocery store on the corner of Carrer de la Carabassa—**La Lionesa,** at Carrer Ample 21, one of Barcelona's best-preserved 19th-century shops. At No. 7 is the **Solé** shoe store, with handmade shoes from all over the world. You might recognize Plaça Medinaceli, next on the left, from Pedro Almodovar's film *Todo Sobre Mi Madre* (*All*

Barcelona: An Architectural Toy Box

The city's independent outlook has been spectacularly reflected in its anthology of architecture, which covers 2,000 years of history from classical Roman, Romanesque, Gothic, Renaissance, and baroque, neoclassical, and Moderniste to the rationalist, minimalist, and postmodern solutions of Richard Meier, Santiago Calatrava, Rafael Moneo, Norman Foster, Ricardo Bofill, and Jean Nouvel.

If Madrid is about paintings, Barcelona's forte is architecture, notably the work of Antoni Gaudí (1852–1926), whose buildings are the most startling manifestations of Modernisme—the Spanish, and mainly Catalan, chapter of the late-19th-century Art Nouveau movement. Other leading Moderniste architects include Lluís Domènech i Montaner and Josep Puig i Cadafalch.

The richest Art Nouveau area is L'Eixample (the Expansion). Barcelona's Eixample claimed as its own the artistic movement called Art Nouveau in France, Modern Style in England, Sezessionstil in Austria, Jugendstil in Germany, Liberty or Floreale in Italy, Modernisme in Catalonia, and Modernismo in Spain. Scanning these terms provides a good overview of what Art Nouveau is all about: new, modern (in the late 19th century), playful, flowery, revolutionary, and free. Art Nouveau was a reaction to the misery and uniformity brought about by technology and the Industrial Revolution. It is what most characterizes the city: only Barcelona has 50 cataloged Moderniste buildings, as well as more than 250 private houses with Art Nouveau facades, interiors, or other elements.

Barcelona's Roman, Romanesque, and Gothic legacy is equally interesting. The famous Rambla separates the Gothic Quarter and its Roman core from the Raval, where the medieval hospital, the shipyards, and Sant Pau del Camp, Barcelona's oldest church, are the main attractions, along with Richard Meier's rationalist MACBA (Museu d'Art Contemporani de Barcelona) and the CCCB (Centre de Cultura Contemporània de Barcelona) next door.

The medieval intimacy of the Gothic Quarter balances the grace and distinction of the wide boulevards in the Moderniste Eixample, while Roman walls and columns provide counterpoint to sleek new 21st-century structures in the Raval or the Olympic Port. A visit to Gaudí's Sagrada Família followed by a quick hop over to the Mediterranean Gothic Santa Maria del Mar will leave your senses reeling with the gap between Catalan Art Nouveau ornamentation and the early Catalan Gothic's classical economy. Even more dramatically, proceed from Domènech i Montaner's Moderniste showstopper the Palau de la Música Catalana, to Mies van der Rohe's minimalist masterpiece, the Barcelona Pavilion. For a look at contemporary Barcelona architecture, take a tram ride east from Ciutadella–Vil.la Olímpica into the Diagonal Mar district past Ricardo Bofill's Teatre Nacional de Catalunya, Rafael Moneo's Auditori, Jean Nouvel's rocket ship–like Torre Agbar, and ending at the Fòrum building by Herzog & de Meuron. Meanwhile, Ricardo Bofill's W Hotel Barcelona, in the form of a giant sail on the Barceloneta waterfront, is the toast of the town since opening to fanfare in October 2009.

About My Mother); from the scene featuring the heroine's dog and her aging father. Ⓜ *Drassanes.*

Carrer Petritxol. Just in from the Rambla and one of Barcelona's most popular streets, lined with art galleries, *xocolaterías* (hot-chocolate shops), and bookstores, this narrow passageway dates back to the 15th century, when it was used as a shortcut through the backyard of an eponymous property owner. Working up Petritxol from Plaça del Pi, stop to admire the late-17th-century *sgraffiti* (mural ornamentation made by scratching away a plaster surface) some of the city's best, on the facade over the **Ganiveteria Roca** knife store, *the* place for cutlery in Barcelona. Next on the right at Petritxol 2 is the 200-year-old **Dulcinea** hot-chocolate refuge, with a portrait of the great Catalan playwright Àngel Guimerà (1847–1924) over the fireplace and plenty of cozy nooks for conversation and the house specialty, the *suizo* (literally, "Swiss": hot chocolate and whipped cream). Also at Petritxol 2 is the **Llibreria Quera,** one of the city's best hiking and mountaineering bookstores.

Note the plaque to Àngel Guimerà over No. 4 and the **Art Box** gallery at Nos. 1–3 across the street. At No. 5 is **Sala Parès,** founded in 1840, the dean of Barcelona's art galleries and the site for many important art shows, featuring artists like Isidre Nonell, Santiago Russinyol, and Picasso. Farther up are the gallery **Trama** at No. 8 and the **Galeria Petritxol** at No. 10. **Xocoa** at No. 9 is another popular chocolate spot. Look carefully at the "curtains" carved into the wooden door at No. 11 and the floral ornamentation around the edges of the ceiling inside. **Granja la Pallaresa,** yet another enclave of chocolate and *ensaimada* (a light-looking but deathly sweet Majorcan roll in the shape of a snail, with confectioner's sugar dusted on top). Finally on the left at No. 17 is the **Rigol** fine-arts supply store. Ⓜ *Liceu.*

Casa Bruno Quadros. Like something out of an amusement park, this former umbrella shop was whimsically designed (assembled is more like it) by Josep Vilaseca in 1885. A Chinese dragon with a parasol, Egyptian balconies and galleries, and a Peking lantern all bring exotic touches that were very much in vogue at the time of the Universal Exposition of 1888. Now housing the Caixa de Sabadell bank, this prankster of a building is theoretically in keeping with Art Nouveau's eclectic playfulness, though it has never been taken very seriously as an expression of Modernisme and, consequently, is generally omitted from most studies of Art Nouveau architecture. ✉ *La Rambla 82*, *Rambla* Ⓜ *Liceu.*

Església de Betlem. The Church of Bethlehem is one of Barcelona's few baroque buildings, and hulks stodgily on the Rambla just above the Rambla de les Flors. Burned out completely at the start of the Spanish civil war in 1936, the church lacks opulence once inside, whereas the outside, spruced up, is made of what looks like quilted stone. If you find this one of the world's more unsightly churches, don't feel bad: you're in the company of all of Barcelona with the possible exception of Betlem's parishioners. This was where Viceroy Amat claimed the hand of the young virreina (wife)-to-be when in 1780 she was left in the lurch by the viceroy's nephew. In a sense, Betlem has compensated the city with the half-century of good works the young widow was

Summer days bring strollers to Barcelona's main thoroughfare, the Rambla.

able to accomplish with her husband's fortune. The Nativity scenes on display down the stairs at the side entrance on the Rambla at Christmastime are an old tradition here, allegedly begun by St. Francis of Assisi, who assembled the world's first in Barcelona in the early 13th century. ⊠ *Xuclà 2, Rambla* ☎ *93/318–3823* Ⓜ *Catalunya.*

Hotel España. A cut alongside the jagged edge of the Sant Agustí church leads straight to the Hotel España, remodeled in 1904 by Lluís Domènech i Montaner, architect of the Moderniste flagship Palau de la Música Catalana. The interior is notable for its Art Nouveau decor. The hotel is recommendable only for aesthetes who prefer art over life (or, in any case, comfort), as the rooms are less than perfect. The sculpted marble Eusebi Arnau mantelpiece in the breakfast room and the Ramon Casas murals (with mermaids who have legs down to their flippers) in the dining room are, along with the lushly ornate dining room, the hotel's star artistic features. ⊠ *Carrer Sant Pau 9–11, Raval* ☎ *93/318–1758* ⊕ *www.hotelespanya.com* Ⓜ *Liceu.*

Monument a Colom *(Columbus Monument).* This Barcelona landmark to Christopher Columbus sits grandly at the foot of the Rambla along the wide harbor-front promenade of the Passeig de Colom, not far from the very shipyards (**Drassanes Reials**) that constructed two of the ships of his tiny but immortal fleet. Standing atop the 150-foot-high iron column—the base of which is aswirl with gesticulating angels—Columbus seems to be looking out at "that far-distant shore," which he was able to discover thanks to the patronage of Ferdinand and Isabella. In truth, he is pointing—with his 18-inch-long finger—in the general direction of Sicily. The monument was erected for the 1888 Universal Exposition to commemorate the "Discoverer's" commissioning, in Barcelona, by the monarchs in 1491. Since the royal court was at that time (and, until 1561, remained) itinerant, Barcelona's role in the discovery of the New World is, at best, circumstantial. In fact, Barcelona was consequently excluded from trade with the Americas by Isabella, so Catalonia and Columbus have never really seen eye to eye. For a bird's-eye view over the Rambla and the port, take the elevator to the small viewing area at the top of the column. (The entrance is on the harbor side.) ⊠ *Portal de la Pau s/n, Rambla* ☎ *93/302–5224* ⚏ *€3* ☉ *Daily 10–6:30* Ⓜ *Drassanes*.

Palau de la Virreina. The neoclassical Virreina Palace, built by a viceroy to Peru in 1778, is now a major

GEOMETRICAL BARCELONA

Barcelona's three geometrically named communications arteries, Avinguda Diagonal, Avinguda Meridiana, and Avinguda del Paral.lel were devised by Ildefons Cerdà, the urban planner who designed the post-1860 Eixample (Expansion), as high-speed urban thoroughfares that would break and drain the checkerboard symmetry of his vast urban grid. The Paral.lel is so named because it parallels the equator. The Meridiana is perpendicular to the Paral.lel and parallels the Greenwich Meridian. And Diagonal runs at an oblique angle across the Eixample.

center for changing exhibitions of paintings, photography, and historical items. The building also houses a bookstore and a municipal tourist office. Beautiful accents on the exterior include the portal doorway and pediments carved with elaborate floral designs. ⊠ *Rambla de les Flors 99, Rambla* ☎ *93/301–7775* ⊕ *www.bcn.es/virreinaexposicions* ⚏ *Free; €3 charge for some exhibits* ☉ *Mon.–Sat. 11–8, Sun. 11–3* Ⓜ *Liceu*.

Palau Moja. The first palace to occupy this corner on the Rambla was built in 1702 and inhabited by the Marquès de Moja. The present austere palace was completed in 1790 and, with the Betlem church across the street, forms a small baroque-era bottleneck along the Rambla. If there are temporary exhibitions in the Palau Moja, getting inside will also give you a look at the handsome mural and ceiling paintings by Francesc Pla, known as El Vigatà (meaning from Vic, a town 66 km north of Barcelona). In the late 19th century the Palau Moja was bought by Antonio López y López, Marquès de Comillas, and it was here that Jacint Verdaguer, Catalonia's national poet and chaplain of the marquess's multimillion-dollar Compañia Transatlántica shipping company, wrote his famous patriotic epic poem "L'Atlàntida." ⊠ *Portaferrissa 1, Rambla* ☎ *93/316–2740* ☉ *Open on rare occasions for temporary exhibits* Ⓜ *Catalunya*.

Plaça de Catalunya. Barcelona's main transport hub, Plaça de Catalunya, is the frontier between the Old City and the post-1860 Eixample. Comparable in size to Paris's Place de l'Étoile or to Rome's St. Peter's Square, Plaça de Catalunya is generally an unavoidable place to scurry across at high speed on your way to somewhere quieter, shadier, and generally gentler on the senses. The only relief in sight is **Café Zurich**, at the head of the Rambla and the mouth of the metro, which remains the classic Barcelona rendezvous point. The block behind the Zurich, known as

El Triangle, houses a strip of mega-stores, including FNAC and Habitat, among others. Corte Inglés, the monstrous ocean liner–esque department store on the northeast side of the square, offers Spanish goods at standard prices and in good quality.

The underground **tourist office** on the northeast corner is the place to pick up free maps of the city and check on walking tours, some in English, that originate there. The most interesting features in this large but mostly uncharming square are the sensual and exuberant sculptures. Starting from the corner nearest the head of the Rambla, have a close look at, first, the blocky Subirachs monument to Francesc Macià, president of the Generalitat (autonomous Catalan

> ## LA MERCÈ VS. SANTA EULÀLIA
>
> Barcelona's patron saint, Our Lady of Mercy, known as La Mercè, took over as the city's chief protector in 1714. Until then, La Mercè had been co-patroness with Santa Eulàlia, the beautiful daughter of a Sarrià merchant martyred for her Christian faith in the 4th century. Legend has it that the rains that fall on every late-September Mercè Festa Major are the tears of Santa Eulàlia shed in a jealous fury over her loss of municipal status. February's Santa Eulàlia fiesta is, for many faithful *eulalistes*, the true celebration of Barcelona's earliest patron saint.

government) from 1934 to 1936. In the center of the reflecting pool is Clarà's stunning *Déesse* (*Goddess*), kneeling gracefully in the surface film. At the northwest corner is Gargallo's heroic bronze of men, women, and oxen hauling in the grape harvest, and at the northeast corner across from the Corte Inglés is the Federic Marès bronze of a buxom maiden on horseback holding a model of Columbus's ship used to "discover" the New World. Ⓜ *Catalunya*.

Port. Beyond the Columbus monument—behind the ornate Duana (now headquarters for the Barcelona Port Authority)—is the **Rambla de Mar**, a boardwalk with a drawbridge designed to allow boats into and out of the inner harbor. The Rambla de Mar extends out to the **Moll d'Espanya,** with its Maremagnum shopping center, IMAX theater, and the excellent aquarium. Next to the Duana you can board a Golondrina boat for a tour of the port and the waterfront or, from the Moll de Barcelona on the right, take a cable car to Montjuïc or Barceloneta. Trasmediterránea and the fleeter Buquebus passenger ferries leave for Italy and the Balearic Islands from the Moll de Barcelona, while at the end of the quay is Barcelona's World Trade Center and the Eurostars Grand Marina Hotel. Ⓜ *Drassanes*.

2

THE BARRI GÒTIC: MEDIEVAL SPLENDOR

Sightseeing
★★★★★
Nightlife
★★☆☆☆
Dining
★★★★☆
Lodging
★★★☆☆
Shopping
★★★★☆

No other city in Spain displays an ancient quarter that rivals Barcelona's Barri Gòtic in either historic atmosphere or sheer wealth of monumental buildings. It's a stroller's delight, where you can expect to hear reverberations of a flute or a classical guitar playing Bach from around the next corner. At times this area can be eerily quiet, a stone oasis of silence at the eye of the storm.

A jumble of medieval buildings, squares, and streets, the Gothic Quarter is the name given to the area around the Catedral de la Seu, still packed with Roman ruins and the Gothic structures of the late Middle Ages that marked the zenith of Barcelona's power in the 15th century. On certain corners you feel as if you're making a genuine excursion back in time, and, for a brief flash, suddenly the 21st century, not the 15th, seems like a figment of your imagination.

The Gothic Quarter rests squarely atop the first ancient Roman settlement. Sometimes referred to as the *rovell d'ou* (the yolk of the egg), this high ground the Romans called Mons Taber coincides almost exactly with the early-1st-century to 4th-century Roman Barcino. Plaça del Rei (considered one of Barcelona's best plazas), the Roman underground beneath the City History Museum, Plaça Sant Jaume and the area around the onetime Roman Forum, the medieval Jewish Quarter, or Call, and the ancient Plaça Sant Just complete this tour. All in all, this nearly entirely pedestrianized area contains Roman, Gothic, and even Moderniste treasures.

MAIN ATTRACTIONS

Baixada de Santa Eulàlia *(Slope of Santa Eulàlia).* Straight out from the side door of the cathedral cloister down Carrer Sant Sever past the Església de Sant Sever is the tiny overhead niche dedicated to Santa

GETTING ORIENTED

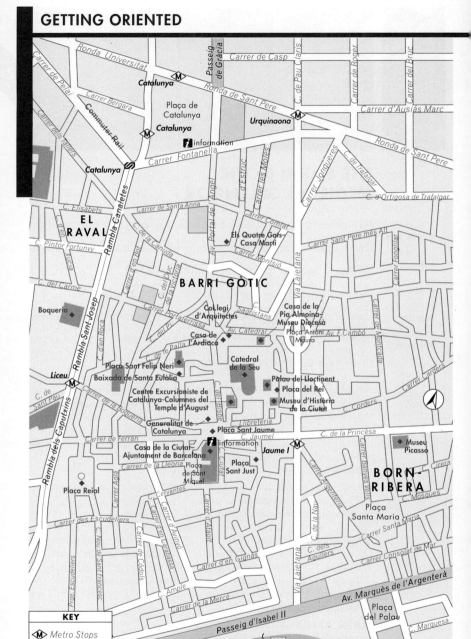

KEY

Ⓜ *Metro Stops*

🜨 *FGC Stops*

Timing

Exploring the Gothic Quarter should take about three hours, depending on stops. Allow another hour or two for the City History Museum. Plan to visit before 1:30 or after 4:30, or you'll miss a lot of street life; some churches are closed, too.

Getting Here

The best way to get to the Gothic Quarter and the cathedral is to start down the Rambla from the Plaça Catalunya metro stop. Take your first left on Carrer Canuda and walk past Barcelona's Ateneu Barcelonès at No. 6, through Plaça Villa de Madrid and its Roman tombstones, and then through Passatge and Carrer Duc de la Victoria and out Carrer Boters (named for early boot makers) to Plaça Nova.

Quick Bites

If you feel inclined to take a breather in a Pakistani restaurant, where you can get a table between two 4th-century Roman watchtowers, seek out **El Gallo Quirico** (⊠ *Carrer d'Avinyó 19, Barri Gòtic* ☎ *93/301–0280*), just a block west of Plaça Sant Jaume, for either lunch or a beverage. **Café de l'Acadèmia** (⊠ *Carrer Lledó 18, Barri Gòtic* ☎ *93/319–8253*) fills with government workers at lunchtime. If a coffee is all you need, look for the **Mesón del Café** (⊠ *Carrer Llibreteria 16, Barri Gòtic* ☎ *93/315–0754*), where a deep breath is nearly as bracing as a cappuccino.

Top Attractions

Catedral de la Seu

Els Quatre Gats–Casa Martí

Museu d'Història de la Ciutat

Plaça Sant Felip Neri

Plaça Sant Jaume

Roman columns of Temple d'August

Top Experiences

Examining Casa de l'Ardiaca's 4th-century Roman walls

Exploring the Jewish Quarter

Gallery browsing along Carrer de la Palla

Sipping a coffee at the historic Els Quatre Gats–Casa Martí

Watching sardanas in Plaça de la Catedral

Where to Eat (⇨ Ch. 3)

Café de l'Acadèmia

Cometacinc

Nonell

Shunka

Happening Nightlife (⇨ Ch. 5)

Harlem Jazz Club

Jamboree-Jazz & Dance-Club

La Vinateria del Call

Area Shops (⇨ Ch. 7)

Antigüedades Fernández

Custo Barcelona

Tascón

Eulàlia, the city's most honored martyr. You look up at this shrine, which is in a kind of alcove. Down this hill, or *baixada* (descent), Eulàlia was rolled in a barrel filled with—as the Jacint Verdaguer verse in ceramic tile on the wall reads—*glavis i ganivets de dos talls* (swords and double-edged knives), the final of the 13 tortures to which the 4th-century martyr was subjected before her crucifixion at Plaça del Pedró. ⊠ *Carrer Sant Sever, past Carrer Sant Domènec del Call, Barri Gòtic* Ⓜ *Catalunya, Liceu, Jaume I.*

Casa de l'Ardiaca *(Archdeacon's House).* The interior of this building, home of the municipal archives (upstairs), has superb views of the inside of the 4th-century Roman watchtowers and walls. Look at the Montjuïc sandstone carefully, and you will see blocks taken from other buildings, carved and beveled into decorative shapes, proof of the haste of the Romans as the Visigoths approached from the north at the end of the Pax Romana. The marble letter box by the front entrance was designed in 1895 by Lluís Domènech i Montaner for the Lawyer's Professional Association and, as the story goes, is meant to symbolize, in the images of the doves, the lofty flight to the heights of justice and, in the images of the turtles, the plodding pace of administrative procedures. The lovely courtyard here, across from the Santa Llúcia chapel, is centered around a fountain, and on the day of Corpus Christi in June the fountain impressively supports *l'ou com balla,* or "the dancing egg," a Barcelona tradition. Eggs are placed atop numerous jets of water as part of the celebration. ⊠ *Carrer de Santa Llúcia 1, Barri Gòtic* 🕾 *93/318–1342* ⊕ *www.bcn.es* ☉ *Mon.–Sat. 10–2 and 4–8, Sun. 10–2* Ⓜ *Catalunya, Liceu, Jaume I.*

Casa de la Ciutat–Ajuntament de Barcelona. The 15th-century city hall on Plaça Sant Jaume faces the Palau de la Generalitat, with its mid-18th-century neoclassical facade, across what was once the Roman Forum. Any opportunity to spend time inside the city hall should be taken, as it is a rich repository for sensual sculptures, paintings, and historic sites. Around the corner to the left is a surprise: the early-15th-century Flamboyant Gothic facade with part of an arch superglued to the abutting neoclassical part (look carefully in the right corner). Inside is the famous Saló de Cent, from which the proto-democratic Council of 100 governed Barcelona between 1249 and 1714. The Saló de les Croniques is filled with Josep Maria Sert's immense black-and-burnished-gold mural (1928) depicting the early-14th-century Catalan campaign in Byzantium and Greece under the command of Roger de Flor. Check out Sert's changing perspective technique that makes his paintings seem to follow you around the room. Adorned with art and sculptures by the great Catalan masters from Marès to Gargallo to Clarà to Subirachs, the interior of the city hall is open to visitors on Sunday and for occasional concerts or events held in the Saló de Cent. ⊠ *Pl. Sant Jaume 1, Barri Gòtic* 🕾 *93/402–7000* ⊕ *www.bcn.es* ☉ *Sun. 10–1* Ⓜ *Catalunya, Liceu.*

★ **Catedral de la Seu.** Barcelona's cathedral (named for La Seu, or See, the seat of the bishopric) is impressively filled with many centuries of city history and legend, even if it does fall short as a memorable work of architecture. This imposing Gothic monument was built between 1298

CLOSE UP

El Call: The Jewish Quarter

Its name derived from the Hebrew word qahal ("meeting place," or "place to be together"), Barcelona's Jewish Quarter is just to the Rambla side of the Palau de la Generalitat. Carrer del Call, Carrer de Sant Domènec del Call, Carrer Marlet, and Arc de Sant Ramón del Call mark the heart of the 7th- to 14th-century quarter. Enclosed in this area at the end of the 7th century, Barcelona's Jews were the private financial resource of Catalonia's sovereign counts (only Jews could legally lend money). One reason the streets in Calls or Aljamas were so narrow was that their inhabitants could only build into the streets for more space. The Jewish community produced many leading physicians, economists, and scholars in medieval Barcelona, largely because practicing the Jewish faith required Bible study, thus ensuring a high degree of literacy. The reproduction of a plaque bearing Hebrew text on the corner of Carrer Marlet and Arc de Sant Ramón del Call was the only physical reminder of the Jewish presence here until the medieval synagogue reopened in 2003.

The **Sinagoga Major de Barcelona** (✉ *Carrer Marlet 2 08002* ⊕ *www.calldebarcelona.org* ▤ *€2* ☉ *Tues.–Sat. 11–2, Sun. 4–7*), the restored original synagogue at the corner of Marlet and Sant Domènec del Call, is the principal remaining evidence of the Jewish presence in Catalonia. Tours are given in English, Hebrew, and Spanish, and a booklet in English (€5) explains the history of the community. The saga of Barcelona's Jewish community came to its culminating moment in August 1391, when during a time of famine and pestilence a nationwide outbreak of anti-Semitic violence reached Barcelona with catastrophic results: nearly the entire Jewish population was murdered or forced to convert to Christianity.

and 1450, with the spire and neo-Gothic facade added in 1892—and even these not completed until 1913. Historians are not sure about the cathedral architect—one name much bandied about is Jaume Fabre, a native of Majorca. The plan of the church is cruciform, with transepts standing in as bases for the great tower—a design also seen in England's Exeter Cathedral. Floodlighted in striking yellow beams at night with the stained-glass windows backlighted from inside and ghostly seagulls soaring over the spiky Gothic spires, Barcelona's main religious building is only a bronze medalist behind the Mediterranean Gothic Santa Maria del Mar and Gaudí's Moderniste La Sagrada Família.

This is reputedly the darkest of all the world's great cathedrals—even at high noon the nave is enveloped by shadows, which give it magically much larger dimensions than it actually has—so it takes a while for eyes to adjust to the rich, velvety pitch of the cathedral. Among the many sights worth seeking out are the beautifully carved choir stalls of the Knights of the Golden Fleece; the intricately and elaborately sculpted organ loft over the door out to Plaça Sant Iu (complete with a celebrated Saracen's Head sculpture); the series of 60-odd wood sculptures of men and women along the exterior lateral walls of the choir in a nearly ani-

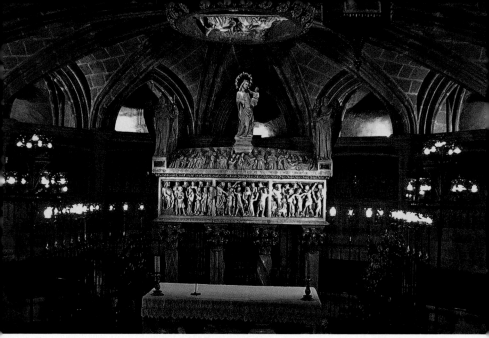

The ornate Gothic interior of the Catedral de la Seu is always enclosed in shadows, even at high noon.

mated succession of evangelistic poses; the famous cloister; and, in the crypt, Santa Eulàlia's tomb.

St. Eulàlia, originally interred at Santa Maria del Mar—then known as Santa Maria de les Arenes (St. Mary of the Sands)—was moved to the cathedral in 1339, and is the undisputed heroine and patron of the Barcelona cathedral. *Eulalistas* (St. Eulàlia devotees, as opposed to followers of La Mercé, or Our Lady of Mercy, Barcelona's official patron) celebrate the fiesta of *La Laia* (the nickname for Eulàlia) February 9–15, and they would prefer that the cathedral be named for their favorite martyr. For the moment, the cathedral remains a virtual no-name cathedral, known universally as La Catedral and more rarely as La Seu.

Appropriately, once you enter the front door (there are also lateral entrances through the cloister and from Carrer Comtes down the left side of the apse), the first thing you see are the high-relief sculptures of the **story of St. Eulàlia,** on the near side of the choir stalls. The first scene, on the left, shows St. Eulàlia in front of Roman Consul Decius with her left hand on her heart and her outstretched right hand pointing at a cross in the distance. In the next scene to the right, Eulàlia is tied to a column and being whipped by Decius-directed thugs. To the right of the door into the choir the unconscious Eulàlia is being hauled away, and in the final scene on the right she is being lashed to the X-shape cross upon which she was crucified in mid-February in the year 303. To the right of this high relief is a sculpture of St. Eulàlia, standing with her emblematic X-shape cross, resurrected as a living saint.

Among the two-dozen ornate and gilded chapels dedicated to all the relevant saints of Barcelona and beyond, one chapel to seek out is the **Capilla de Lepanto,** in the far right corner as you enter through the front door. The main attraction here is the Santo Cristo de Lepanto. This 15th-century polychrome wood sculpture of a somewhat battle-scarred, dark-skinned Christ, visible on the altar of this 100-seat chapel behind a black-clad Mare de Deu dels Dolors (Our Lady of Sorrow), was, according to oral legend, the bowsprit of the commanding Spanish galley at the battle fought between Christian and Ottoman fleets on October 7, 1571.

Note that the explanatory plaque next to the alms box at the right front of the chapel states that, though John of Austria was the

> ### BARCELONA'S DANCING EGG
>
> Barcelona's early June Corpus Christi celebration is a favorite day to visit the city's finest patios to see fountains adorned with the *ou com balla* (dancing egg) balancing miraculously atop the jet of water. The egg, in Christian ritual a symbol of fertility, represents the rebirth of life after Easter's tragic events. In the Mediterranean's megalithic religions that preceded Christianity, the dancing egg augured a successful growing season as spring turned to summer.

commander-in-chief of the Holy League's fleet, the fleet captain and main battle commander was Lluís de Requesens (1528–76), a local Catalan aristocrat and prominent Spanish general during the reign of Felipe II.

Outside the main nave of the cathedral to the right you'll find the leafy, palm tree–shaded **cloister** surrounding a tropical garden and pool filled with 13 snow-white geese, one for each of the tortures inflicted upon St. Eulàlia in an effort to break her faith. Legend has it that they are descendants of the flock of geese from Rome's Capitoline Hill, whose honking alarms roused the city to ward off invaders during the ancient days of the Roman Republic. Don't miss the fountain with the bronze sculpture of an equestrian St. George hacking away at his perennial sidekick, the dragon, on the eastern corner of the cloister. On the day of Corpus Christi this fountain is one of the more spectacular floral displays, featuring *l'ou com balla* (the dancing egg). The intimate **Santa Llúcia chapel** is at the front right corner of the block (reached by a separate entrance or from the cloister). Another Decius victim (although in this version he merely wanted her body), St. Llúcia allegedly plucked out her eyes to dampen the Roman consul's ardor, whereupon new ones were miraculously generated. Patron saint of seamstresses, of the blind, and of the light of human understanding, St. Lucía is portrayed over the altar in the act of presenting her plucked-out eyes, sunny-side-up on a plate, to an impassive Decius.

In front of the cathedral is the grand square of the **Plaça de la Seu,** where on Saturday from 6 PM to 8 PM, Sunday morning, and occasional evenings, Barcelona folk gather to dance the *sardana,* the somewhat dainty and understated circular dance, a great symbol of Catalan identity. Watch carefully: mixed in with heroic septuagenarians bouncing demurely are some young *esbarts* (dance troupes) with very serious coaches working on every aspect of their performance, from posture to the angle of arms to the smooth, cat's paw–like footwork. The rings of dancers deep in concentration repeat the surprisingly athletic movements and steps that represent a thousand years of tradition. Also check out the listings for the annual series of evening organ concerts held inside the cathedral. ⊠ *Pl. de la Seu, Barri Gòtic* ☎ *93/315–1554* ⊕ *www. catedralbcn.org* ⊴ *€4 for special visit* ⊘ *Daily 7:45 AM–7:45 PM; during a special visit, 1–5 PM, visitors can see entire cathedral, museum, bell tower, and rooftop* Ⓜ *Catalunya, Liceu, Jaume I.*

Centre Excursioniste de Catalunya (CEC)–Columnes del Temple d'August *(Outing Center of Catalonia–Columns of the Temple of Augustus).* The highest point in Roman Barcelona is marked with a circular millstone at the entrance to the Centre Excursioniste de Catalunya, a club dedicated to exploring the mountains and highlands of Catalonia on foot and on skis. Inside this entryway on the right are some of the best-preserved 1st- and 2nd-century Corinthian Roman columns in Europe. Massive, fluted, and crowned with the typical Corinthian acanthus leaves in two distinct rows under eight fluted sheaths, these columns remain only because Barcelona's early Christians elected, atypically, not to build their cathedral over the site of the previous temple. The Temple of Augustus, dedicated to the Roman emperor, occupied the northwest corner of the Roman Forum, which coincided approximately with today's Plaça Sant Jaume. ⊠ *Carrer Paradís 10, Barri Gòtic* ☎ *93/315–2311* ⊘ *Mon.–Sat. 10–2 and 5–8, Sun. 11–2* Ⓜ *Catalunya, Liceu.*

★ **Els Quatre Gats–Casa Martí.** Built by Josep Puig i Cadafalch in 1896 for the Martí family, this Art Nouveau house just three minutes' walk from the cathedral holds the Quatre Gats café and restaurant, a good place for a coffee or even a meal, and the legendary hangout of Moderniste minds. The exterior is richly decorated with Eusebi Arnau sculptures, featuring the scene of St. George and the dragon that no Puig i Cadafalch project ever failed to include. Arnau (1864–1934) was the sculptural darling of the Moderniste movement. The interior is spectacularly hung with reproductions of some famous Ramon Casas paintings, such as the scene of the Toulouse Lautrec–ish Casas and the rangy Pere Romeu comedically teamed up on a tandem bicycle—one of Barcelona's most iconic images. The restored (in 2000) Joseph Llimona sculpture of St. Joseph and the Infant Jesus gleaming whitely over St. George and the dragon was torn down in the anticlerical violence of July 1936. Picasso had his first opening here on February 1, 1900, and Antoni Gaudí hung out with Moderniste painters from Casas to Russinyol to the likes of Nonell and Anglada Camarasa, so the creative reverberations ought to be strong. *Quatre Gats* means "four cats" in Catalan, a euphemism for "hardly anybody," but the original four—Casas, Russinyol, and Utrillo, hosted by Pere Romeu—were all definitely somebodies. ⊠ *Carrer Montsió 3 bis, Barri Gòtic* ☎ *93/302–4140* ⊕ *www.4gats.com* ⊘ *Mid-Aug.– July, daily 9 AM–2 AM* Ⓜ *Catalunya, Liceu.*

Generalitat de Catalunya. Housed in the Palau de la Generalitat, opposite city hall, this is the seat of the autonomous Catalan government. Through the front windows of this ornate 15th-century palace the gilded ceiling of the Saló de Sant Jordi (St. George's Hall), named for Catalonia's dragon-slaying patron saint, gives an idea of the lavish decor within. The Generalitat opens to the public only on the Día de

Sant Jordi (St. George's Day), April 23, during the Fiesta de la Mercé in late September, and on various other city or Catalonian holidays. The Generalitat hosts carillon concerts on Sunday at noon, another opportunity to see the inside of the building. ✉ *Pl. de Sant Jaume 4, Barri Gòtic* ☎ *93/402–4600* ⊕ *www.gencat.net* ☯ *On special occasions only; to visit, check with protocol office calling through main telephone number* Ⓜ *Catalunya, Liceu.*

Fodor's Choice ★ **Museu d'Història de la Ciutat** *(City History Museum).* This fascinating museum just off the Plaça del Rei traces Barcelona's evolution from its first Iberian settlement to its founding by the Carthaginian Hamilcar Barca in about 230 BC to Roman and Visigothic times and beyond. Antiquity is the focus here: Romans took the city during the Punic Wars, and the striking underground remains of their *Colonia Favencia Julia Augusta Paterna Barcino* (Favored Colony of the Father Julius Augustus Barcino), through which you can roam on metal walkways, are the museum's main treasure. Archaeological finds include parts of walls and fluted columns as well as recovered busts and vases. Around **Plaça del Rei** are the **Palau Reial Major,** the splendid **Saló del Tinell,** the chapel of **Santa Àgata,** and the **Torre del Rei Martí,** a lookout tower with views over the Barri Gòtic. ✉ *Palau Padellàs, Carrer del Veguer 2, Barri Gòtic* ☎ *93/315–1111* ⊕ *www.museuhistoria.bcn.es* 🗠 *€6 (also covers admission to Monestir de Pedralbes, Center for the Interpretation and Welcome to Park Güell, Museu Verdaguer–Vil.la Joana, and Museu Diocesà). Free 1st Sat. of month 4–8* ☯ *Tues.–Sat. 10–8, Sun. 10–3* Ⓜ *Catalunya, Liceu, Jaume I.*

Plaça del Rei. This plaza is widely considered to be the oldest and most beautiful space in the Gothic Quarter. Long held to be the scene of Columbus's triumphal return from his first voyage to the New World—the precise spot where Ferdinand and Isabella received him is purportedly on the stairs fanning out from the corner of the square (though evidence indicates that the Catholic monarchs were at a summer residence in the Empordá)—the **Palau Reial Major** was the official royal residence in Barcelona. The main room is the **Saló del Tinell,** a magnificent banquet hall built in 1362. Other elements around the square are, to the left, the **Palau del Lloctinent** (Lieutenant's Palace); towering overhead in the corner is the dark 15th-century **Torre Mirador del Rei Martí** (King Martin's Watchtower). The 14th-century **Capilla Reial de Santa Àgueda** (Royal Chapel of St. Agatha) is on the right side of the stairway, and behind and to the right as you face the stairs is the **Palau Clariana-Padellàs,** moved to this spot stone by stone from Carrer Mercaders in the early 20th century and now the entrance to the **Museu d'Història de la Ciutat.** Ⓜ *Catalunya, Liceu, Jaume I.*

Plaça Sant Felip Neri. A tiny square just behind **Plaça de Garriga Bachs** off the side of the cloister of the Catedral de la Seu, this space was once the cemetery for Barcelona's executed heroes and villains, before all church graveyards were moved to the south side of Montjuïc where the municipal cemetery now resides. A favorite spot for early-music concerts, the square is centered on a fountain, whose trickling—a constant E-flat—fills the square with its own water music. A bomb explosion during the

Spanish civil war caused the pock-marks on the walls of the San Felip Neri church. Ⓜ *Catalunya, Liceu.*

Plaça Sant Jaume. This central hub a couple of blocks east of the cathedral is the site of Catalonia's government building, the **Generalitat de Catalunya** in the Palau de La Generalitat, and Barcelona's, the **Casa de la Ciutat–Ajuntament de Barcelona.** This was the site of the Roman Forum 2,000 years ago, though subsequent construction filled the space with buildings. The square was cleared in the 1840s, but the two imposing (and often opposing) government buildings facing each other across it are much older. Ⓜ *Catalunya, Liceu, Jaume I.*

> ### BATS IN THE BELFRY
>
> Spain, like the US, chose the eagle as its national bird, but Catalunya's national bird is, somewhat oddly, the bat; allegedly because King Jaume I was a fan, ever since bats alerted his troops to repel a dawn attack during the Balearic campaign. Barcelona bats hang from the chandeliers in the Town Hall's Saló de Cent, are sculpted into the Triumphal Arch on Passeig Lluís Companys, and preside over the main Carrer Hospital entrance to the medieval hospital.

WORTH NOTING

Casa de la Pia Almoina–Museu Diocesà *(Diocesan Museum).* This 11th-century Gothic almshouse, now a museum, once served soup to 100 of the city's poor, hence its popular name, Pia Almoina (pious alms). Along with temporary art exhibits, the museum houses a permanent collection of religious sculptures and a potpourri of liturgical paraphernalia, from monstrances to chalices to the 12th-century paintings from the apse of the Sant Salvador de Polinyà chapel. Anyone beginning a tour of the Roman walls should take a look at the excellent relief map/scale model of Roman Barcelona (map and model are sold in the nearby Museu d'Història de la Ciutat, the city history museum) in the vestibule. Inside, Roman stones are clearly visible in this much-restored structure, the only octagonal tower of the 82 that ringed the 4th-century Barcino. Look for the Romanesque *Mares de Deu* (Mothers of God) wood sculptures, such as the one from Sant Pau del Camp church in Barcelona's Raval. The museum is behind the massive floral iron grate in the octagonal Roman watchtower to the left of the stairs of the Catedral de la Seu. ✉ *Av. de la Catedral 4, Barri Gòtic* ☎ *93/315–2213* 💲€6 ☉ *Tues.–Sat. 10–2 and 5–8, Sun. 11–2* Ⓜ *Catalunya, Liceu, Jaume I.*

Col.legi d'Arquitectes. Barcelona's architects' college, constructed in 1961 by Xavier Busquets, houses three important gems: a superb library (across the street), where for a small fee the college's bibliographical resources are placed at your disposal for architectural research purposes; a bookstore specializing in architecture, design, and drafting supplies; and a nonpareil restaurant (one of the city's great secrets). And let's not forget the Picasso friezes just above the college's windows, designed by the artist in 1960. Inside the building are two more Picasso friezes, one a vision of Barcelona and the other a poem dedicated to the *sardana,* Catalonia's national dance. ✉ *Pl. Nova 5, Barri Gòtic* ☎ *93/306–7801* ⊕ *www.coac.net* ☉ *Mon.–Sat. 10–8* Ⓜ *Catalunya, Liceu.*

DID YOU KNOW?

The Gothic Quarter actually sits on top of the first Roman settlement. In some parts of the city you can still see Roman ruins.

Palau del Lloctinent *(Lieutenant's Palace)*. The three facades of this fine building face the Carrer dels Comtes de Barcelona on the cathedral side, the Baixada de Santa Clara, and the Plaça del Rei. Typical of late Gothic–early Renaissance Catalan design, it was constructed by Antoni Carbonell in 1557, and remains one of the Gothic Quarter's most graceful buildings. The heavy stone arches over the entry, the central patio, and the intricately coffered wooden roof over the stairs are all good examples of noble 16th-century architecture. The door on the stairway, which replaced an equestrian Sant Jordi sculpture identical to the one over the main entrance of the Generalitat, is a 1975 Antoni Subirachs work portraying scenes from the life of Sant Jordi. The Palau del Lloctinent was inhabited by the king's official emissary or viceroy to Barcelona during the 16th and 17th centuries, and now offers an excellent exhibit on the life and times of Jaume I, one Catalonia's most important founding fathers. The patio also occasionally hosts early music concerts, and during the Corpus Christi celebration is one of the main venues for the *ou com balla,* when an egg "dances" on the fountain amid an elaborate floral display. ⊠ *Carrer dels Comtes de Barcelona s/n, Barri Gòtic* ☎ *93/485–4285* Ⓜ *Catalunya, Liceu.*

Plaça Sant Just. Off to the left side of city hall down Carrer Hèrcules (named for the mythical founder of Barcelona) are this square and the site of the Església de Sant Just i Pastor, one of the city's oldest Christian churches, dating from the 4th century. Christian catacombs are reported to have been found beneath Plaça Sant Just. The Gothic fountain was built in 1367 by famed Barcelona councilman Joan Fiveller. Fiveller had discovered a spring in the Collserola hills, and had the water piped straight to Barcelona. The fountain bears an image of St. Just and city and sovereign count-kings' coats of arms, along with a pair of falcons. The excellent entryway and courtyard to the left of Carrer Bisbe Caçador is the Palau Moixó, the town house of an important early Barcelona family, while down Carrer Bisbe Caçador is the Acadèmia de Bones Lletres, the Catalan Arts and Letters Academy. The church is dedicated to the boy martyrs Just and Pastor; the Latin inscription over the door translates into English almost in reverse syntax as "Our pious patron is the black and beautiful Virgin, together with the sainted children Just and Pastore." Ⓜ *Catalunya, Liceu.*

THE RAVAL: WEST OF THE RAMBLA

Sightseeing
★★★★☆

Nightlife
★★★☆☆

Dining
★★★☆☆

Lodging
★★☆☆☆

Shopping
★★★☆☆

El Raval (from *arrabal,* meaning "suburb" or "slum") is the area to the west of the Rambla, on the right as you walk toward the port. Originally a rough outskirt stuck outside the second set of city walls that ran down the left side of the Rambla, the Raval used to be notorious for its Barri Xinès (or Barrio Chino) red-light district, the lurid attractions of which are known to have fascinated the young Pablo Picasso.

Gypsies, acrobats, prostitutes, and *saltimbanques* (clowns and circus performers) who made this area their home soon found immortality in the many canvases Picasso painted of them during his Blue Period. It was the ladies of the night on Carrer Avinyó, not far from the Barri Xinès, who inspired one of the 20th-century's most famous paintings, Picasso's *Les Demoiselles d'Avignon,* an important milestone on the road to Cubism. Not bad for a city slum.

The Raval, though still rough and ready, has been gentrified and much improved since 1980, largely as a result of the construction of the Museu d'Art Contemporani de Barcelona (MACBA) and the other cultural institutions nearby, such as the Centre de Cultura Contemporània (CCCB) and the Convent dels Àngels. The Rambla del Raval has been opened up between Carrer de l'Hospital and Drassanes, and light and air are pouring into the streets of the Raval for the first time in a thousand years. The medieval Hospital de la Santa Creu, Plaça del Pedró, the Mercat de Sant Antoni, and Sant Pau del Camp are highlights of this helter-skelter, rough-and-tumble part of Barcelona. The only area to consider avoiding is the lower part between Carrer de Sant Pau and the back of the Drassanes Reials shipyards on Carrer del Portal Santa Madrona.

MAIN ATTRACTIONS

Fodor's Choice
★

Antic Hospital de la Santa Creu i Sant Pau. Founded in the 10th century, this is one of Europe's earliest medical complexes, and contains some of Barcelona's most stunningly graceful Gothic architecture, built mostly

GETTING ORIENTED

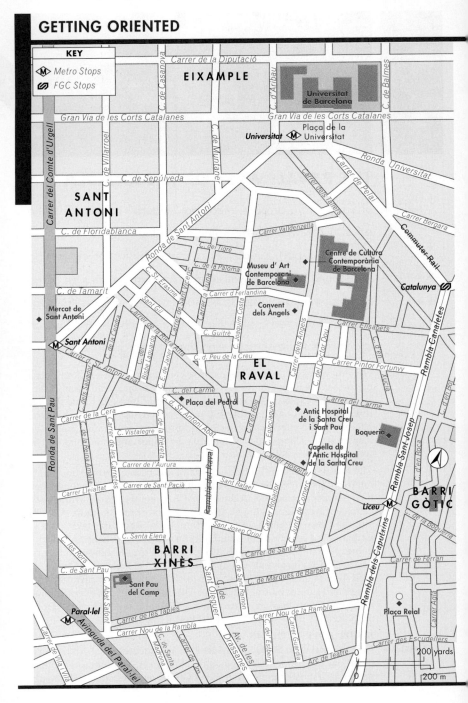

KEY

Ⓜ *Metro Stops*

🌀 *FGC Stops*

EIXAMPLE

Universitat de Barcelona

Carrer de la Diputació

C. de Casanova

C. d'Aribau

C. de Balmes

Gran Via de les Corts Catalanes

Gran Via de les Corts Catalanes

Carrer del Comte d'Urgell

C. de Villarroel

C. de Muntaner

Carrer de Pelai

Ronda Universitat

Carrer Bergara

Commuter-Rail

Universitat Ⓜ Plaça de la Universitat

SANT ANTONI

C. de Sepúlveda

Carrer dels Tallers

Carrer Valldonzelle

Ronda de Sant Antoni

C. de Floridablanca

C. del Tigre

C. de la Paloma

St. Erasme

Sant Vicenç

Carrer d Ferlandina

Museu d' Art Contemporani de Barcelona

Centre de Cultura Contemporània de Barcelona

Catalunya 🌀

C. de Tamarit

Sant Gil

Convent dels Àngels

Mercat de Sant Antoni

C. Joaquim Costa

Carrer de la Riera Alta

C. Guitrè

Carrer dels Àngels

Carrer Elisabets

Rambla Canaletes

Ⓜ *Sant Antoni*

C. d. Peu de la Creu

EL RAVAL

Carrer del Doctor Dou

Carrer Pintor Fortunyv

C. del Carme

Carrer del Carme

C. del Carme

Plaça del Pedró

C. d. St. Antoni Abat

Antic Hospital de la Santa Creu i Sant Pau

Boqueria

Ronda de Sant Pau

Carrer de la Cera

C. Vistalegre

C. de la Riereta

C. d. Roig

Carrer Espciaques

Capella de l'Antic Hospital de la Santa Creu

Rambla Sant Josep

C. d'en Roca

Carrer de l'Aurora

Carrer Hospital

Carrer de Sant Pacià

Sant Rafael

Carrer Robador

Carrer de la Junta de Comerç

Liceu Ⓜ

BARRI GÒTIC

Carrer Lleialtat

Sant Josep Oriol

C. Santa Elena

BARRI XINÈS

Carrer de Sant Pau

C. de les Roïs

C. de Sant Pau

C. Abat Safont

Sant Pau del Camp

C. d. Sant Ramon

Sant Oleguer

C. de Marqués de Barbera

Carrer de Sant Pau

Rambla dels Caputxins

Carrer de Ferran

Plaça Reial

Paral·lel Ⓜ

Avinguda del Paral·lel

Carrer de les Tàpies

Carrer Nou de la Rambla

Av. de les Drassanes

Carrer Nou de la Rambla

Carrer de Vila Vilà

C. de Santa Madrona

Carrer Om

C. del Esborg

Carrer Guardia

Arc de Teatre

Carrer des Escudellers

Carrer Aqla

0   200 yards

0   200 m

Timing

The Raval covers a lot of ground. Plan on a four-hour walk or break your exploration into two two-hour hikes. The cloister of Sant Pau del Camp, a not-to-be-missed visit, is closed mornings on Monday, afternoons on Saturday, and all day Sunday except for mass.

Getting Here

Begin this Raval exploration at Plaça Catalunya, with its convenient metro stop. Walk down the Rambla and take your first right into Carrer Tallers, working your way through to the MACBA.

Quick Bites

Buenas Migas (⊠ *Pl. Bonsuccés 8, Raval* ☎ *93/318-3708* Ⓜ *Catalunya, Liceu*) is a leafy terrace a block in from the Rambla serving good sandwiches (*migas* means crumbs and the expression *buenas migas* refers to new friends hitting it off). **El Jardí** (⊠ *Hospital 56, Raval* ☎ *93/329-1550* Ⓜ *Catalunya, Liceu*) serves tapas and salads in a corner of the medieval hospital courtyard. **Bar Castells** (⊠ *Pl. Bonsuccés 1, Raval* ☎ *93/302-1054* Ⓜ *Catalunya, Liceu*) has a lovely outside marble counter and a gorgeous wood-framed mirror behind the bar.

Top Attractions

Antic Hospital de la Santa Creu i Sant Pau

Museu d'Art Contemporani de Barcelona

Sant Pau del Camp

Top Experiences

Exploring the medieval Hospital de la Santa Creu

Finding the hidden Sant Llàtzer chapel

Inhaling the fragrances of Sant Ponç on Carrer Hospital

Listening to the fountain in the Sant Pau del Camp cloister

Stroking Botero's bronze cat on Rambla del Raval

Watching skateboarders in front of the MACBA

Where to Eat (⇨ Ch. 3)

Ca l'Estevet

Ca l'Isidre

Casa Leopoldo

Tapioles 53

Happening Nightlife (⇨ Ch. 5)

Apolo

London Bar

Marsella

Area Shops (⇨ Ch. 7)

Camper

Espai Vidre

Ras Gallery

in the 15th and 16th centuries. Approached through either the Casa de la Convalescència entry on Carrer del Carme or through the main door on Carrer Hospital, the cluster of medieval architecture surrounds a garden courtyard and a midtown orange grove. The first stone was laid by King Martí el Humà (Martin the Humane) in 1401. As you approach from Carrer del Carme, the first door on the left is the **Reial Acadèmia de Cirurgia i Medecina** (Royal Academy of Surgery and Medicine), a neoclassical 18th-century building of carved stone. On the right is the 17th-century Casa de la Convalescència, and straight ahead is the simple 15th-century Gothic facade of the hospital itself, with the light of the inner cloisters gleaming through the arched portal. The Royal Academy of Surgery and Medicine—open for visits until 2 PM on weekdays—contains an amphitheater originally used for the observation of dissections. Across the way is the door into the patio of the **Casa de la Convalescència** (Convalescence House), with its Renaissance columns and its brightly decorated scenes of the life of St. Paul in the vestibule. The primarily blue and yellow *azulejos* (ceramic tiles) start with the image to the left of the door into the inner courtyard portraying the moment of the saint's conversion: SAVLE, SAVLE, QUID ME PERSEGUERIS (Saul, Saul, why do you persecute me?). The ceramicist, Llorenç Passolas, was also the creator of the late-17th-century tiles around the inner patio. The image of St. Paul in the center of the courtyard over what was once a well is an homage to the building's initial benefactor, Pau Ferran. Look for the horseshoes, two of them around the keyholes, on the double wooden doors in the entryway, wishing good luck to the convalescent and, again, in reference to benefactor Ferran, from *ferro* (iron), as in *ferradura* (horseshoe).

Past the door to the Biblioteca Infantil, the children's library, on both sides of the courtyard, is the 1.5-million-volume **Biblioteca de Catalunya** (✉ *Carrer Hospital 56 or Carrer del Carme 45, Raval* ☎ *93/270–2300* ⊕ *www.bnc.cat* ☉ *Weekdays 9–8, Sat. 9–2*), Catalonia's national library and Spain's second in scope after Madrid's Biblioteca Nacional. The hospital patio, centered on a baroque cross, is filled with orange trees and usually also with students from the Escola Massana art school at the far end on the right. The stairway under the arch on the right leading to the main entrance of the Biblioteca de Catalunya was built in the 16th century, while the Gothic well to the left of the arch is from the 15th century, as is the little Romeo-and-Juliet balcony in the corner to the left of the Escola Massana entry. Inside the library, the wide Gothic arches and vaulting of what was once the hospital's main nave were designed in the 15th century by the architect of Santa Maria del Pi church, Guillem Abiell, who was seeking light and a sense of space. This was the hospital where Antoni Gaudí was taken after he was struck by a trolley on June 7, 1926. Among the library's collections are archives recording Gaudí's admittance and photographs of the infirmary and the private room where he died. The library's staggering resources range from silver medieval book covers to illuminated manuscripts from the *Llibre Vermell* (Red Book), the Catalonian songbook. Guided tours can be arranged at the main desk. Leaving through the heavy wooden door out to Carrer Hospital, from the far sidewalk you can see the oldest section of the medieval hospital, part of the old Hospital de Colom founded by the canon Guillem Colom in 1219 to the left of the door. The facade itself is from the 16th century. ⊠ *Carrer Hospital 56 (or Carrer del Carme 45), Raval* ☎ *93/270–2300* Ⓜ *Catalunya, Liceu.*

Centre de Cultura Contemporània de Barcelona *(CCCB).* No matter what's on the schedule, this multidisciplinary gallery, lecture hall, and concert and exhibition space is worth checking out. Housed in the restored and renovated Casa de la Caritat, a former medieval convent and hospital, the CCCB is, like the Palau de la Música Catalana, one of Barcelona's best combinations of contemporary and traditional architecture and design. A smoked-glass wall on the right side of the patio, designed by architects Albert Villaplana and Helio Piñón, reflects out over the rooftops of the Raval to Montjuïc and the Mediterranean beyond. ⊠ *Montalegre 5, Raval* ☎ *93/306–4100* ⊕ *www.cccb.org* 🎫 *€6; free entry to patio and bookstore* ⊘ *Tues., Thurs., and Fri. 11–2 and 4–8, Wed. and Sat. 11–8, Sun. 11–7* Ⓜ *Catalunya.*

Fodor's Choice
★ **Museu d'Art Contemporani de Barcelona** *(Barcelona Museum of Contemporary Art; MACBA).* Designed by American architect Richard Meier in 1992, this gleaming explosion of light and geometry in the darkest corner of Raval houses a permanent collection of contemporary art as well as traveling exhibits. With barely a nod to Gaudí (via the amorphous tower in front of the main facade), Meier's exercise in minimalism (resembling, to some degree, a bathroom turned inside-out) has been much debated in Barcelona. Basque sculptor Jorge Oteiza's massive bronze *La Ola (The Wave)* on the MACBA's front porch is popular with skateboarders, while the late Eduardo Chillida's *Barcelona* climbs the wall to the left of the main entrance in the sculptor's signature primitive blocky black geometrical patterns. The MACBA's 20th-century art collection (Calder, Rauschenberg, Oteiza, Chillida, Tàpies) is excellent, as is the guided tour carefully introducing the philosophical bases of contemporary art as well as the pieces themselves. ⊠ *Pl. dels Àngels s/n, Raval* ☎ *93/412–0810* ⊕ *www.macba.es* 🎫 *€7 (€3 Wed.); temporary exhibits €4 additional* ⊘ *Mon. and Wed.–Fri. 11–7:30, Sat. 10–8, Sun. 10–3; free guided tours daily at 6, Sun. at noon* Ⓜ *Catalunya.*

Fodor's Choice
★ **Sant Pau del Camp.** Barcelona's oldest church was originally outside the city walls (*del camp* means "in the fields") and was a Roman cemetery as far back as the 2nd century, according to archaeological evidence. A Visigothic belt buckle found in the 20th century confirmed that Visigoths used the site as a cemetery between the 2nd and 7th centuries. What you see now was built in 1127, and is the earliest Romanesque structure in Barcelona, redolent of the pre-Romanesque Asturian churches or of the pre-Romanesque Sant Michel de Cuxà in Prades, Catalunya Nord (Catalonia North, aka southern France). Elements of the church—the classical marble capitals atop the columns in the main entry—are thought to be from the 6th and 7th centuries. The hulking mastodonic shape of the church is a reminder of the church's defensive posture in the face of intermittent Roman persecution and, later, Moorish invasions and sackings. Check carefully for musical performances here, as the church is an acoustical gem. (Rebecca Ryan's Mercyhurst Madrigal Singers sang American composer Horatio Parker's "Lord We

The Fragrances of Sant Ponç

The Raval's big day is May 11, when Carrer Hospital celebrates the Fira de Sant Ponç, a beloved Barcelona holiday. The feast day of Sant Ponç, patron saint of herbalists and bee-keepers, brings Catalonia's *pagesos* (country folk) to Barcelona laden with every natural product they can haul. Everything from bees in glass cases working at their honeycombs to chamomile, rosemary, thyme, lavender, basil, pollens, mint, honeys of every kind, candied fruits, snake oil, headache remedies, and aphrodisiacs, and every imaginable condiment and savory from fennel to saffron to coriander to tarragon, takes over the city's streets and, more important, the air. The mere mention of Sant Ponç to any barcelonin is guaranteed to elicit a backward inclination of the head, closing (even fluttering) of the eyelids, and a deep and luxuriant inhalation.

Everyone seems to find time, especially if the weather is good, to take a walk from the Rambla out to Carrer Hospital to the Rambla del Raval to browse through artisanal sausage, goat cheese, wild mushrooms, cakes, jams, herbal olive oils, homemade wines, pies, cheesecakes, fig bread, hand-carved wooden spoons, knives and forks, teas, coffees, and a thousand medicinal herbal potions and lotions. In medieval times, as farmers cleared their larders for the harvest to come, medicinal herbalists and the sorceress fringe promptly hijacked this tradition and set up stalls along the walls of the 15th-century hospital (where, presumably, there was a heightened interest in their products). Today Sant Ponç is the official start of the Catalonian summer, and one of Barcelona's sweetest days.

Beseech Thee" here in 2009.) The tiny stained-glass window high on the facade facing Carrer Sant Pau may be Europe's smallest, a bookend to Santa Maria del Pi's largest. The tiny cloister is Sant Pau del Camp's best feature, and one of Barcelona's semisecret treasures. Sculpted capitals portraying biblical scenes support tri-lobed Mudéjar arches; birdlike sirens tempt monks from prayer on the southwestern corner capital. This penumbral sanctuary barely a block from the frantic Avinguda del Paral.lel is a gift from time. ⊠ *Sant Pau 101, Raval* ☎ *93/441–0001* 🖾 *€3* ⏱ *Cloister Mon. 5–8, Tues.–Fri. 10–1:30, 5–8, Sat. 10–1:30; Sun. mass at 10:30, 12:30, and 8 PM* Ⓜ *Catalunya, Liceu, Paral.lel.*

WORTH NOTING

Convent dels Àngels. This former Augustinian convent directly across from the main entrance to the MACBA, built by Bartolomeu Roig in the middle of the 16th century, has been converted into a general cultural center with an exhibition hall (El Fòrum dels Àngels), a bookstore, a 150-seat auditorium, and a restaurant and bar. The Foment dels Arts Decoratives (FAD) now operates this handsome Raval resource. The Fòrum dels Àngels is an impressive space, with beautifully carved and restored sculptures of angels in the corners and at the top of the walls. ⊠ *Pl. dels Àngels, Raval* ☎ *93/443–7520* ⊕ *www.fadweb.org* ⏱ *Mon.– Sat. 9–9, Sun. 10–2* Ⓜ *Catalunya.*

One of the earliest medical complexes in Europe is the Antic Hospital de la Santa Creu i Sant Pau.

Mercat de Sant Antoni. An interesting spot for browsing—both for its artistic value and for its jumble of produce on sale—the Sant Antoni market is one of Barcelona's lesser-known gems. This mammoth steel hangar at the junction of Ronda de Sant Antoni and Comte d'Urgell was designed in 1882 by Antoni Rovira i Trias, the winner of the competition for the planning of Barcelona's Eixample. Considered the city's greatest masterpiece of ironwork architecture, the Greek cross–shape market covers an entire block on the edge of the Eixample. A combination food, clothing, and flea market, it becomes a book, comics, stamp, and coin fest on Sunday. Though many of the produce stalls inside remain closed, there are a few excellent bars and restaurants and some of the finest Moderniste stall facades in Barcelona. The hushed environment is reminiscent of the Boqueria market before it became Europe's most celebrated food fair. For market cuisine and good value well off the beaten tourist track, this lofty space merits a look. ⊠ *Carrer Comte d'Urgell s/n, Raval* ☎ *93/443–7520* ✆ *Mon.–Sat. 9–9, Sun. 10–2* Ⓜ *Catalunya, Sant Antoni.*

Plaça del Pedró. This landmark in medieval Barcelona was the dividing point where ecclesiastical and secular paths parted. The high road, Carrer del Carme, leads to the cathedral and the seat of the bishopric, whereas the low road, Carrer de l'Hospital, heads down to the medieval hospital and the Boqueria market, a clear choice between body and soul. Named for a stone pillar, or *pedró* (large stone), marking the fork in the road, the square became a cherished landmark for Barcelona Christians after Santa Eulàlia, co-patron of Barcelona, was crucified there in the 4th century on her distinctive X-shape cross after

Skateboarders enjoy practicing in front of the Museu d'Art Contemporani de Barcelona.

suffering the legendary 13 ordeals designed to persuade her to recant, which she, of course, heroically refused to do. As the story goes, an overnight snowfall chastely covered her nakedness with virgin snow. The present version of Eulàlia and her cross was sculpted by Barcelona artist Frederic Marès and erected in 1951. The bell tower and vacant alcove at the base of the triangular square are the **Sant Llàtzer** church, originally built in the open fields in the mid-12th century and used as a leper hospital and place of worship after the 15th century when Sant Llàtzer (Saint Lazarus) was officially named patron saint of lepers. Presently in the process of being rescued from the surrounding buildings that once completely obscured the church, the Sant Llàtzer chapel has a tiny antique patio and apse visible from the short Carrer de Sant Llàtzer, which cuts behind the church between Carrer del Carme and Carrer Hospital. Ⓜ *Catalunya, Liceu.*

SANT PERE AND LA RIBERA: THE MEDIEVAL TEXTILE AND WATERFRONT DISTRICTS

Sightseeing
★★★★★
Nightlife
★★★★★
Dining
★★★★★
Lodging
★★★★☆
Shopping
★★★★★

The textile and waterfront neighborhoods are studded with some of the city's most iconic buildings, ranging from the Gothic 14th-century basilica of Santa Maria del Mar to the over-the-top Moderniste Palau de la Música Catalana. Over at the Museu Picasso, works of the 20th-century master are displayed in five adjoining Renaissance palaces.

Sant Pere, Barcelona's old textile neighborhood, is centered on the church of Sant Pere. A half-mile closer to the port, the Barri de la Ribera and the former market of El Born, now known as the Born-Ribera district, formed the headquarters for Catalonia's great maritime and economic expansion of the 13th and 14th centuries. Surrounding the basilica of Santa Maria del Mar, the Born-Ribera area includes Carrer Montcada, lined with 14th- to 18th-century Renaissance palaces; Passeig del Born, where medieval jousts were held; Carrer Flassaders and the area around the early mint; the shop- and restaurant-rich Carrer Banys Vells; Plaça de les Olles; and Pla del Palau, where La Llotja, Barcelona's early maritime exchange, housed the fine-arts school where Picasso, Gaudí, Domènech i Montaner, and all of Barcelona's artists and architects studied.

La Ribera began a revival in the 1980s, and with its intimate bars, cafés, taverns, and shops, it continues to gain ground as one of city's hottest spots. El Born, the onetime central market of Barcelona, now offers a fascinating view of pre-1714 Barcelona, dismantled by the victorious troops of Felipe V at the end of the War of the Spanish Succession. The Passeig del Born, considered the Rambla of medieval Barcelona has once again taken its place as one the city's hubs.

GETTING ORIENTED

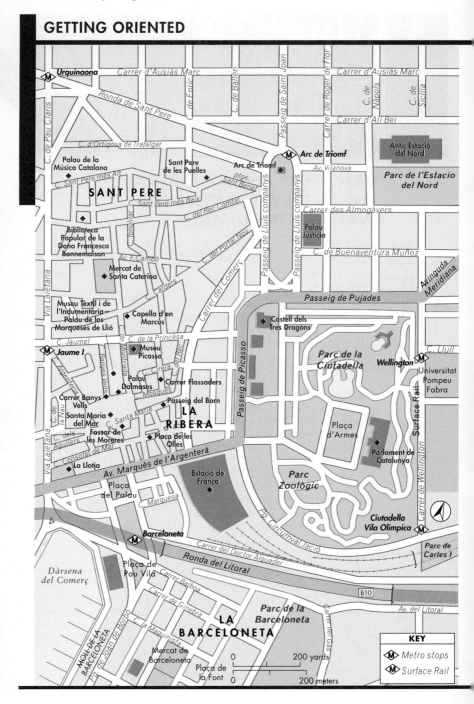

Urquinaona

Carrer d'Ausiàs Marc

Ronda de Sant Pere

C. de Pau Claris

C. de Enric

C. de Bailèn

C. de Roger de Flor

Passeig de Sant Joan

Carrer d'Ausiàs Marc

C. de Nápols

C. de Sicília

Carrer d'Ali Bei

C. d'Ortigosa de Trafalgar

Palau de la Música Catalana

Sant Pere de les Puelles

Arc de Triomf

Arc de Triomf

Av. Vilanova

Antic Estació del Nord

Parc de l'Estacio del Nord

C. Sant Pere mès Alt

SANT PERE

C. Sant Pere mès Baix

ptge. Sant Benet

Carrer de Lluís companys

Passeig de Lluís companys

C. del Rec Comtal

Carrer des Almogàvers

Palau Justicia

Biblioteca Popular de la Dona Francesca Bonnemaison

C. del Portal Nou

Av. F.Cambó

Mercat de Santa Caterina

C. de Buenaventura Muñoz

Avinguda Meridiana

Via Laietana

C. Carders

Carrer del Comerç

Passeig de Pujades

Museu Textil i de l'Indumentària Paldu de los Marqueses de Lió

Capella d'en Marcús

C. de la Princesa

Carrer de Picasso

Castell dels Tres Dragóns

C. Jaume I

Jaume I

Museu Picasso

Parc de la Ciutadella

Wellington

C. Llull

Universitat Pompeu Fabra

Banys Vells

C. de Montcada

Palau Dalmases

Carrer Flassaders

Passeig del Born

Passeig de Picasso

Surface Rall

Carrer Banys Vells

C. Mosques

C. de la Nau

Santa Maria del Mar

Santa Maria

LA RIBERA

Plaça d'Armes

Via Laietana

C. dels Aguilers

Fossar de les Moreres

Plaça de les Olles

Parlament de Catalunya

Carrer de Wellington

C. Consolat de Mar

La Llotja

Av. Marquès de l'Argenterà

Estació de França

Parc Zoològic

Plaça del Palau

C. Marquesa

Barceloneta

Ciutadella Vila Olimpica

Parc de Carles I

Plaça de Pau Vila

Carrer del Doctor Aiguader

Ronda del Litoral

Carrer Balboa

Dàrsena del Comerç

B10

Av. del Litoral

Carrer de Gipebra

LA BARCELONETA

Parc de la Barceloneta

Carrer de Gas

MOLL DE LA BARCELONETA

Pg. de Joan de Borbó

C. La Maquinista

Mercat de Barceloneta

Plaça de la Font

0   200 yards

0   200 meters

KEY
Ⓜ Metro stops
Ⓜ Surface Rail

Timing

Depending on the number of museum visits and stops, exploring these neighborhoods can take a full day. Count on at least four hours of actual walking time. Catching Santa Maria del Mar open is key (it's closed 1:30–4:30). If you make it to Cal Pep for tapas before 1:30, you might get a place at the bar; if you don't, waiting's well worth it. The Picasso Museum is at least a two-hour visit.

Getting Here

From the central Plaça Catalunya metro hub, it's just a 10-minute walk over to the Palau de la Música Catalana for the beginning of this tour. The yellow line's Jaume I metro stop is closer to Santa Maria del Mar, but between the hassle of underground train changing and the pleasures of strolling the city streets, Plaça Catalunya is close enough.

Quick Bites

The patio of **El Café Tèxtil** (✉ *Carrer Montcada 12, Born-Ribera* ☎ *93/268–2598*) is one of the city's best, and an ideal spot for anything from a tea to a light meal. In winter the sun manages to find its way into this quiet space; in summer you can find shade unless you happen to be there at high noon. The patio of **La Vinya del Senyor** (✉ *Pl. de Santa Maria 1, Born-Ribera* ☎ *93/310–3379*) serves top wines from around the world by the glass, along with light tapas, led by the Ibérico ham.

Top Attractions

Museu Picasso

Palau de la Música Catalana

Santa Maria del Mar

Top Experiences

Devouring counter food at Cal Pep

Feasting your eyes at the Mercat de Santa Caterina

Going to a concert in the Palau de la Musica

Inhaling the fragrances of the Casa Gispert store

Listening to music in Santa Maria del Mar basilica

Where to Eat (⇨ Ch. 3)

Cal Pep

Comerç 24

El Passadís d'en Pep

La Báscula

Mundial Bar

Sagardi

Happening Nightlife (⇨ Ch. 5)

La Vinya del Senyor

Nao Colón/Club Bamboo

Ommsession Club

Area Shops (⇨ Ch. 7)

Baraka

Custo Barcelona

Tüsetú

MUSEU PICASSO

✉ Carrer Montcada 15–19, Born-Ribera
☎ 93/319–6310
⊕ www.museupicasso.bcn.es
💳 Permanent collection €9, temporary exhibits €5.80; free 1st Sun. of month
🕐 Tues.–Sat. 10–8, Sun. 10–3
Ⓜ Catalunya, Liceu, Jaume I.

Tips

■ Admission is free the first Sunday of the month, an excellent opportunity if you arrive early enough.

■ *Diumenges al Picasso* (Sundays at the Picasso Museum) offers Sunday morning performances in the museum ranging from classical music to clowns.

■ For a light Mediterranean meal, the terrace café and restaurant provides a good resting point and breaks up your visit into manageable portions.

The Picasso Museum is housed in five adjoining palaces on Carrer Montcada, a street known for Barcelona's most elegant medieval palaces. Picasso spent his key formative years in Barcelona (1895–1904), and this collection, while it does not include a significant number of the artist's best paintings, is particularly strong on his early work. The museum was begun in 1962 on the suggestion of Picasso's crony Jaume Sabartés, and the initial donation was from the Sabartés collection. Later Picasso donated his early works, and in 1981 his widow, Jaqueline Roque, added 141 pieces.

HIGHLIGHTS

Displays include childhood sketches, works from Picasso's Rose and Blue periods, and the famous 1950s Cubist variations on Velázquez's *Las Meninas* (in Rooms 22–26). The lower-floor sketches, oils, and schoolboy caricatures and drawings from Picasso's early years in La Coruña are perhaps the most fascinating part of the whole museum, showing the facility the artist seemed to possess almost from the cradle. His *La Primera Communión (First Communion)*, painted at the age of 16, gives an idea of his early accomplishment. On the second floor you meet the beginnings of the mature Picasso and his Blue Period in Paris, a time of loneliness, cold, and hunger for the artist.

SANTA MARIA DEL MAR BASILICA

⊠ Pl. de Santa Maria, Born-
Ribera
☎ 93/310–2390
🎫 free
🕓 Daily 9–1:30 and 4:30–8
Ⓜ Catalunya, Jaume I

2

Tips

■ Leave at least a half hour
to see Santa Maria del Mar.

■ Check carefully for concerts
in Santa Maria del Mar and
either arrive early to get seats
in the front rows or sit on the
stone steps in the side chapels
near the front of the basilica
to avoid getting lost in the six-
second acoustic delay.

Details

The paintings in the keystones
overhead represent, from the
front, the Coronation of the
Virgin, the Nativity, the Annunciation, the equestrian figure
of the father of Pedro IV, King
Alfons, and the Barcelona coat
of arms.

The 34 lateral chapels are
dedicated to different saints
and images. The first chapel
to the left of the altar (No. 20)
is the Capella del Santo Cristo
(Chapel of the Holy Christ),
its stained-glass window an
allegory of Barcelona's 1992
Olympic Games.

An engraved stone riser to
the left of the side door onto
Carrer Sombrerers commemorates the spot where San
Ignacio de Loyola, founder of
the Jesuit Order, begged for
alms in 1524 and 1525.

The most beautiful example of early Catalan Gothic
architecture, Santa Maria del Mar is extraordinary for
its unbroken lines and elegance. The lightness of the
interior is especially surprising considering the blocky
exterior. The site, originally outside the 1st- to 4th-
century Roman walls at what was then the water's edge,
was home to a Christian cult from the late 3rd century. Built by a mere stonemason who chose, fitted, and
carved each stone hauled down from the same Montjuïc
quarry that provided the sandstone for the 4th-century
Roman walls, Santa Maria del Mar is breathtakingly,
nearly hypnotically, symmetrical. The medieval numero-
logical symbol for the Virgin Mary, the number eight
(or multiples thereof) runs through every element of
the basilica: The 16 octagonal pillars are 6.5 feet in
diameter and spread out into rib vaulting arches at a
height of 52 feet. The painted keystones at the apex of
the arches are 105 feet from the floor. Furthermore, the
central nave is twice as wide as the lateral naves (26
feet each), whose width equals the difference (26 feet)
between their height and that of the main nave. The
result of all this proportional balance and harmony is a
sense of uplift that, especially in baroque and Moderniste Barcelona, is both exhilarating and soothing.

Ironically, the church owes its present form to the anticlerical fury of anarchists who on July 18, 1936 burned
nearly all of Barcelona's churches as a reprisal against
the alliance of army, church, and oligarchy during the
military rebellion. The basilica, filled with ornate side
chapels and choir stalls, burned for 11 days, and nearly
crumbled as a result of the heat. Restored after the end
of the Spanish civil war by a series of Bauhaus-trained
architects, Santa Maria del Mar has become one of the
city's most universally admired architectural gems.

MAIN ATTRACTIONS

Fossar de les Moreres *(Cemetery of the Mulberry Trees)*. This low marble monument runs across the eastern side of the church of Santa Maria del Mar. It honors defenders of Barcelona who gave their lives in the 1714 siege that ended the War of the Spanish Succession. The inscription (in English: "in the cemetery of the mulberry trees no traitor lies") refers to the graveyard keeper's story. He refused to bury those on the invading side, even when one was his son. This is the gathering place for the most radical elements of Catalonia's nationalist (separatist) movement, and the Catalonian national holiday.

From the cemetery, look back at Santa Maria del Mar. The lighter-colored stone on the lateral facade was left by the 17th-century Pont del Palau (Palace Bridge), erected to connect the Royal Palace in the nearby Pla del Palau with the Tribuna Real (Royal Box) over the right side of the Santa Maria del Mar altar, so that nobles could get to mass without walking in the streets. The bridge, regarded as a symbol of imperialist oppression, was finally dismantled in 1987. The controversial steel arch was erected in 2002. ⊠ *Pl. de Santa Maria, Born-Ribera* Ⓜ *Catalunya, Jaume I.*

La Llotja *(Maritime Exchange)*. Barcelona's Llotja, or trade center was designed to be the city's finest example of civic architecture. Originally little more than a roof, Barcelona's present llotja was constructed in the Catalan Gothic style between 1380 and 1392. At the end of the 18th century the facades were (tragically) covered in the neoclassical uniformity of the time, but the interior, the great Saló Gòtic (Gothic Hall), remained unaltered, and was a grand venue for balls and celebrations throughout the 19th century. The Gothic Hall was used as the Barcelona stock exchange until 1975, and until late 2001 as the grain exchange. The hall has now been brilliantly restored, and though public visits have not been formally established, any chance to see the inside of this historic hall will reveal Gothic arches and columns and a marble floor made of light Carrara and dark Genovese marble. ■ **TIP→ To slip into the hall, after touring the Fine Arts Museum head to the Saló Gòtic by walking down the stairs to the second floor, and then descend the marble staircase and turn right.**

The Escola de Belles Arts (Fine Arts School) occupied the southwestern corner of the Llotja from 1849 until 1960. Many illustrious Barcelona artists studied here, including Gaudí, Miró, and Picasso. The **Reial Acadèmia Catalana de Belles Arts de Sant Jordi** (Royal Catalan Academy of Fine Arts of St. George) still has its seat in the Llotja, and its museum is one of Barcelona's semi-secret collections of art. ⊠ *Passeig d'Isabel II, 7, Born-Ribera* ☎ *93/319–2432 museum* ⊕ *www.racba.org* ▧ *Museum free* ⊙ *Museum weekdays 10–2* Ⓜ *Catalunya, Jaume I.*

Mercat de Santa Caterina. This marketplace, a splendid carnival of colors with a roller-coaster rooftop, was restored by the late Enric Miralles. Undulating wood and colored ceramic mosaic ceilings cover a glass floor showing sections of the original building, a 13th-century church and convent. ⊠ *Av. Francesc Cambó s/n, Born-Ribera* ☎ *93/319–5740* ⊕ *www.mercatsbcn.com* Ⓜ *Catalunya.*

A wooden door leads to Barcelona's best 17th-century patio in the Palau Dalmases.

Palau Dalmases. Barcelona's best 17th-century Renaissance patio is show-cased here, built into a 15th-century palace. Note the heavy wooden doors leading into the patio; then take a careful look at the evocation of the Rape of Europa represented in high relief running up the baroque facade of the elegant stairway cutting across the end of the patio. Neptune's chariot, cherubic putti, naiads, dancers, tritons, and myriad musicians accompany Europa's mythological abduction by Zeus, who, in the form of a bull, carries her up the stairs and off to Crete. On either side of the door leading up the stairs, look for the minuscule representations of either putti or maidens covering their nakedness with their arms. These, along with the 15th-century Gothic chapel, with its reliefs of musical angels, and the vaulting in the reception area and in the main salon, are the only remnants of the 15th-century palace originally built here. The building is now the seat of the Omnium Cultural, a center for the diffusion of Catalan culture. Lectures, book presentations, and multiple events are open to the public. The Espai Barroc, on the ground floor, is a café with baroque-era flourishes, period furniture, and occasional musical performances. ⊠ *Carrer Montcada 20, Born-Ribera* 🖾 *Free* ☉ *Palace daily 9–2 and 4:30–7. Café Tues.–Sun. 7 PM–1 AM* Ⓜ *Catalunya, Jaume I.*

★ **Palau de la Música Catalana.** One of the world's most extraordinary music halls, with facades that are a riot of color and form, the Palau de la Música (Music Palace) is a landmark of Carrer Amadeus Vives, set just across Via Laietana, a five-minute walk from Plaça de Catalunya. From its polychrome ceramic ticket windows on the Carrer de Sant Pere Més Alt side to its overhead busts of (from left to right) Palestrina,

Bach, Beethoven, and (around the corner on Carrer Amadeus Vives) Wagner, the Palau is a flamboyant tour de force designed in 1908 by Lluís Domènech i Montaner. It is today considered the flagship of Barcelona's Moderniste architecture. Originally conceived by the Orfeó Català musical society as a vindication of the importance of music at a popular level—as opposed to the Liceu opera house's identification with the Catalan (often Castilian-speaking and monarchist) aristocracy—the Palau and the Liceu were for many decades opposing crosstown forces in Barcelona's musical as well as philosophical discourse.

The exterior is remarkable in itself. The Miquel Blay sculptural group over the corner of Amadeu Vives and Sant Pere Més Alt is Catalonia's popular music come to life, with everyone included from St. George the dragon slayer (at the top) to women and children, fishermen with oars over their shoulders, and every strain and strata of popular life and music, the faces of the past fading into the background. The glass facade over the present ticket window entrance is one of the city's best examples of nonintrusive modern construction over traditional structures.

The Palau's interior is, well, a permanent uproar before the first note of music is ever heard. Wagnerian cavalry explodes from the right side of the stage over a heavy-browed bust of Beethoven; Catalonia's popular music is represented by the flowing maidens of Lluís Millet's song *Flors de Maig* (*Flowers of May*) on the left. Overhead, an inverted stained-glass cupola seems to offer the divine manna of music straight from heaven; painted rosettes and giant peacock feathers explode from the tops of the walls; and even the stage is populated with muselike Art Nouveau musicians all across the back wall. The visuals alone make music sound different here, and at any important concert the excitement is palpably thick. *Ticket office* ✉ *Palau de la Musica 4–6 (just off Via Laietana, around corner from hall), Sant Pere* ☎ *93/295–7200* ⊕ *www.palaumusica.org* ⛱ *Tour €12* ✆ *Tours daily 10–3:30 (10–7 July and Aug.)* Ⓜ *Catalunya.*

Passeig del Born. Once the site of medieval jousts and Inquisitional autos-da-fé, the passeig, at the end of Carrer Montcada behind the church of Santa Maria del Mar, was early Barcelona's most important square. Late-night cocktail bars and miniature restaurants with tiny spiral stairways now line the narrow, elongated plaza. The numbered cannonballs under the public benches are the work of the "poet of space"—a 20th-century specialist in combinations of letters, words, and sculpture—the late Joan Brossa. The cannonballs evoke the 1714 siege of Barcelona that concluded the 14-year War of the Spanish Succession, when Felipe V's conquering Castilian and French troops attacked the city ramparts at their lowest, flattest flank. After their victory, the Bourbon forces obliged residents of the Barri de la Ribera (Waterfront District) to tear down nearly a thousand of their own houses, some 20% of Barcelona at that time, to create fields of fire so that the occupying army of Felipe V could better train its batteries of cannon on the conquered populace in order to repress nationalist uprisings. Walk down to the Born itself—a great iron hangar, once a produce market designed by Josep Fontseré. The initial stages of the construction of a public library

CLOSE UP

Picasso's Barcelona

The city's claim to Pablo Picasso (1881–1973) has been contested by Málaga (the painter's birthplace), as well as by Madrid, where La Guernica hangs, and by the town of Gernika, victim of the 1937 Luftwaffe saturation bombing that inspired the famous canvas. Picasso, an anti-Franco opponent after the war, refused to return to Franco's Spain. In turn, the regime allowed no public display of Picasso's work until 1961, when the artist's Sardana frieze at Barcelona's Architects' Guild was unveiled. Picasso never set foot on Spanish soil for his last 39 years.

Picasso spent a sporadic but formative period of his youth in Barcelona between 1895 and 1904, when he moved to Paris. His father was an art professor at the Reial Acadèmia de les Belles Arts in La Llotja. Picasso, a precocious draftsman, began advanced classes there at 15. The 19-year-old

Picasso first exhibited at Els Quatre Gats, a tavern still thriving on Carrer Montsió. His early Cubist painting Les Demoiselles d'Avignon was inspired not by the French town but by the Barcelona street Carrer d'Avinyó, then known for its brothel. After moving to Paris, Picasso returned occasionally to Barcelona until his last visit in 1934. Considering the artist's off-and-on tenure, it is remarkable that the city and Picasso should be so intertwined in the world's perception. The Picasso Museum, while an excellent visit, is perhaps fourth on any art connoisseur's list of Barcelona galleries.

Iconoserveis Culturals (✉ Carrer Muntaner 185, Eixample ☎ 93/410–1405 ⊕ www.iconoserveis.com) gives walking tours through the key spots in Picasso's Barcelona life, covering studios, galleries, family apartments, and the painter's favorite haunts and hangouts.

in the Born uncovered the perfectly preserved lost city of 1714, complete with blackened fireplaces, taverns, wells, and the canal that brought water into the city. The Museu d'Història de la Ciutat offers free visits overlooking the ruins of the 14th- to 18th-century Barri de la Ribera on weekends 10–3. ✉ Born-Ribera Ⓜ Jaume I.

WORTH NOTING

Biblioteca Popular de la Dona Francesca Bonnemaison (Women's Public Library). Barcelona's (and probably the world's) first library originally established exclusively for women, this lovely spot was founded in 1909 as a female sanctuary, evidence of the city's early-20th-century progressive attitudes and tendencies. Over the opulently coffered main reading room, the stained-glass skylight reads TOTA DONA VAL MES QUAN LETRA APREN (Any woman's worth more when she learns how to read), the first line of a ballad by the 13th-century Catalan troubadour Severí de Girona. Once Franco's Spain composed of church, army, and oligarchy had restored law and order after the Spanish civil war, the center was taken over by Spain's one legal political party, the Falange, and women's activities were reoriented toward more domestic pursuits such as sewing and cooking. Today the library complex includes a small theater and offers a lively program of theatrical and cultural events. ✉ Sant Pere

Més Baix 7, Sant Pere ☎ *93/268–0107* ⊕ *www.bonnemaison-ccd.org* ☺ *Tues., Wed., and Fri. 4–9, Thurs. 10–10, Sat. 11–2* Ⓜ *Catalunya.*

Capella d'en Marcús *(Marcús Chapel).* This Romanesque hermitage looks as if it had been left behind by some remote order of hermit-monks who meant to take it on a picnic in the Pyrenees. The tiny chapel, possibly—along with Sant Llàtzer—Barcelona's smallest religious structure, was originally built in the 12th century on the main Roman road into Barcelona, the one that would become Cardo Maximo just a few hundred yards away as it passed through the walls at Portal de l'Àngel. Bernat Marcús, a wealthy merchant concerned with public welfare and social issues, built a hospital for the poor. The chapel today known by his name was built as the hospital chapel and dedicated to the Mare de Déu de la Guia (Our Lady of the Guide). As a result of its affiliation, combined with its location on the edge of town, the chapel became linked with the Confraria del Correus a Cavall (Pony Express Guild), also known as the *troters* (trotters), and for two centuries (13th and 14th) made Barcelona the key link in overland mail between the Iberian Peninsula and Europe. ✉ *Carrer Carders 2 (Placeta d'en Marcús), Born-Ribera* ☺ *Open for mass only* Ⓜ *Catalunya, Jaume I.*

Carrer Banys Vells. This little pedestrian-only alleyway paralleling Carrer Montcada just gets better and better. Exploring Banys Vells is a delight, from the beautifully appointed and supplied Teresa Ferri restaurant **El Pebre Blau** all the way down the street to the **Taranná** design and bric-a-brac shop all on the corner at No. 4 Carrer Barra de Ferro. Banys Vells means "old baths," referring to the site of the early public baths. Later baths were on the street Banys Nous (New Baths) in the Gothic Quarter near the cathedral.. ✉ *Born-Ribera* Ⓜ *Catalunya, Jaume I.*

Carrer Flassaders. The Carrer Flassaders (named for blanket makers) loop begins on Carrer Montcada opposite La Xampanyet, one of La Ribera's most popular bars (specializing in a sticky sparkling wine best avoided—but otherwise an excellent place for tapas and ambience). Duck into the short, dark Carrer Arc de Sant Vicenç. At the end you'll find yourself face to face with **La Seca,** the Barcelona mint, where money was manufactured until the mid-19th century. Coins bearing the inscription, in Castilian, PRINCIPADO DE CATALUÑA (Principality of Catalonia) were minted here as late as 1836. The interior of La Seca (most of which is not open to the public) is an exquisitely restored split-level maze of wooden beams and pillars. Directly ahead in La Seca is the studio and showroom of internationally famed sculptor Manel Alvarez; look for announcements of openings on the door across from the end of Arc de Sant Vicenç.

Moving left to Carrer de la Cirera, look up overhead to the left for the niche with the image of **Santa Maria de Cervelló,** one of the patron saints of the Catalan fleet, on the back side of the Palau Cervelló on Carrer Montcada. Moving down to the right on Carrer de la Cirera past the Otman shop and tearoom, you arrive at the corner of **Carrer dels Flassaders;** walk left past several shops—**Re-Born** at Flassaders 23; the cozy **La Báscula** café in the former candy factory at No. 30; the restaurant and design store **Café de la Princesa** at the corner of Carrer

Sabateret; and the gourmet Montiel restaurant at No. 19. Then turn back down Flassaders through a gauntlet of elegant little clothing, furnishings, and jewelry design stores past the main entry to La Seca at No. 40, with the gigantic royal Bourbon coat of arms over the imposing archway. At No. 42 is the clothing and curio store **Loisaida,** Spanglish for the Lower East Side in New York City, occupying part of La Seca. The stylish Cortana clothing store is across the street. Look up to your right at the corner of the gated Carrer de les Mosques, famous as Barcelona's narrowest street. The mustachioed countenance peering down at you was once a medieval advertisement for a brothel. **Hofmann,** at No. 44, is the excellent pastry store of famous Barcelona chef Mey Hofmann, whose cooking school is over on nearby Carrer Argenteria. A right on Passeig del Born will take you back to Santa Maria del Mar. ⊠ *Born-Ribera* Ⓜ *Jaume I.*

Museu Tèxtil i de l'Indumentària–Palau de los Marqueses de Lliò. With one of Carrer Montcada's two best courtyards (the other is the Palau Dalmases at No. 20), this peaceful spot has a handy café where you can admire the 14th- to 16th-century loggia, stairway, and windows. The textile museum's displays include every imaginable piece of clothing worn from prehistoric times through the late-19th-century Art Nouveau frenzy of decorative excess. The museum store offers interesting books and artifacts, all related to the textile industry that made medieval Barcelona prosper. ⊠ *Carrer Montcada 12–14, Born-Ribera* ☎ *93/319–7603* ⊕ *www.museutextil.bcn.es* ✎ *€4.20; free 1st Sun. of month 3–8* ⊙ *Tues.–Sat. 10–8, Sun. 10–3* Ⓜ *Catalunya, Jaume I.*

Plaça de les Olles. This pretty little square named for the makers of *olles,* or pots, has been known to host everything from topless sunbathers to elegant Viennese waltzers to tapa grazers stacked three ranks deep at Cal Pep. The balconies at No. 6 over the Café de la Ribera are, somewhat oddly, decorated with colorful blue and yellow tile on the second and top floors. The house with the turret over the street on the right at the corner leading out to Pla del Palau (at No. 2 Plaça de les Olles) is another of Enric Sagnier i Villavecchia's retro-Moderniste works. ⊠ *Born-Ribera* Ⓜ *Jaume I.*

2

LA CIUTADELLA AND BARCELONETA: NEAR THE PORT

Sightseeing
★★★★★
Nightlife
★★★☆☆
Dining
★★★★★
Lodging
★★★☆☆
Shopping
☆☆☆☆☆

Now Barcelona's central downtown park, La Ciutadella was originally the site of a fortress built by the conquering troops of the Bourbon monarch Felipe V after the fall of Barcelona in the 1700–14 War of the Spanish Succession. Barceloneta is the traditional fishermen's quarter, a saltier (and sometimes seedier) Mediterranean getaway from the city.

Barceloneta and La Ciutadella fit together historically and urbanistically, as some 1,000 houses in the Barrio de la Ribera, then the waterfront neighborhood around Plaça del Born, were ordered dismantled by their owners to create fields of fire for La Ciutadella's cannon keeping watch over the rebellious Catalans. Barceloneta, then a marshy wetland, was filled in and developed almost four decades later, in 1753, to compensate families who had lost homes in La Ribera.

Barceloneta has always been a beloved escape from the formality of cosmopolitan Barcelona life, an urban fishing village barcelonins sought for Sunday paella on the beach and a stroll through what feels like a freer, more bohemian ambience. With its tiny original houses, its abundant laundry flapping brightly over the streets, and its history of seafarers and gypsies, Barceloneta remains an enclave of romance with a more spontaneous, carefree flavor.

Open water in Roman times and gradually silted in only after the 15th-century construction of the Barcelona port, Barceloneta is Barcelona's traditional fishing and stevedores' quarter. Originally composed of 15 longitudinal and 3 cross streets and 329 two-story houses, Barceloneta was Europe's earliest planned urban development, built by the military engineer Juan Martin Cermeño under the command of El Marquès de la Mina, Juan Miguel de Guzmán Dávalos Spinola (1690–1767).

GETTING ORIENTED

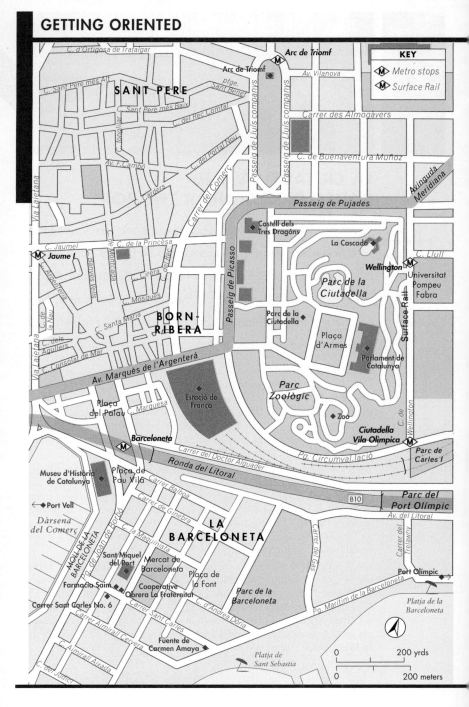

KEY

Ⓜ️ *Metro stops*

◈ *Surface Rail*

Top Attractions

Carrer Sant Carles No. 6

Estació de França

Museu d'Història de Catalunya

Sant Miquel del Port church

Top Experiences

Dining at the edge of the sand

Joining Sunday drumming fests in Ciutadella Park

Renting a windsurfer and sailing

Walking the beachfront from W Hotel Barcelona to the Hotel Arts

Where to Eat (⇨ Ch. 3)

Agua

Barceloneta

Can Majó

Can Manel la Puda

El Lobito

Suquet de l'Almirall

Happening Nightlife (⇨ Ch. 5)

CDLC

Shôko

Timing

Exploring Ciutadella Park and Barceloneta can take from three to four hours. Add another hour if you're stopping for a paella. Try to time your arrival in Barceloneta so you catch the local market in full activity at midday (until 3) and get a chance to graze through the neighborhood on your way to a beachside table for paella. Can Manel la Puda serves paella until 4 in the afternoon.

Getting Here

The Barceloneta stop on the metro's yellow line (Line 4) is the closest subway stop, though a walk through the Gothic Quarter from Plaça de Catalunya is the best way of reaching Barceloneta. For La Ciutadella, the Arc de Triomf stop on the red line (Line 1) is closest.

Quick Bites

Friendly **El Vaso de Oro** (⊠ *Balboa 6, Barceloneta* ☎ *93/319-3098* Ⓜ *Barceloneta*) is a famous tapas specialist, always full and raging. The welcoming **Els Fogons de La Barceloneta** (⊠ *PL de la Font s/n, Barceloneta* ☎ *93/224-2624* Ⓜ *Barceloneta*) serves traditional Barceloneta tapas next to the market.

Rebecca Horn's sculpture on Barceloneta's beach is reminiscent of the little shacks restaurants that once crowded this sandy spot.

MAIN ATTRACTIONS

Carrer Sant Carles No. 6. The last Barceloneta house left standing in its original 1755 two-story entirety, this low, boxlike structure was planned as a single-family dwelling with shop and storage space on the ground floor and the living space above. Overcrowding soon produced split houses and even quartered houses, with workers and their families living in tiny spaces. After nearly a century of living under Madrid-based military jurisdiction, Barceloneta homeowners were given permission to expand vertically, and houses of as many as five stories began to tower over the lowly original dwellings. The house is not open to the public. ⊠ *Carrer Sant Carles 6, Barceloneta* Ⓜ *Barceloneta.*

OFF THE BEATEN PATH **Dipòsit de les Aigües–Universitat Pompeu Fabra.** The Ciutadella campus of Barcelona's private Universitat Pompeu Fabra contains a contemporary architectural gem worth seeking out. It's just two blocks up from the Ciutadella–Vil.la Olímpica metro stop where the tramline out to the Fòrum begins. Once the hydraulic cistern for the Ciutadella waterfall built in 1880 by Josep Fontseré, the Dipòsit de les Aigües was converted to a library in 1999 by contemporary architects Lluís Clotet and Ignacio Paricio. The massive, 3-foot-thick walls, perforated and crowned with arches, are striking, while the trompe-l'oeil connecting corridor between the reading rooms is through-the-looking-glass perplexing. ⊠ *Ramon Trias Fargas 25–27, La Ciutadella* ☎ *93/542–1709* 🎟 *Free* ⊘ *Weekdays 8–1:30 AM, weekends 10–9* Ⓜ *Ciutadella–Vil.la Olímpica.*

Estació de França. The elegantly restored Estació de França, Barcelona's main railroad station until about 1980 and still the stopping point for some trains to and from France and points along the Mediterranean, is outside the west gate of the Ciutadella. No longer very active, this mid-19th-century building is a pleasant place to get a sense of the romance of Europe's traditional railroads. The station has a café that is a good place for an espresso and a croissant or a beer (though not much else), along with the sounds and aromas of an authentic European train station. ⊠ *Marquès de l'Argentera s/n, Born-Ribera* ☎ *93/496–3464* Ⓜ *Barceloneta.*

Museu d'Història de Catalunya. Built into what used to be a port warehouse, this state-of-the-art interactive museum makes you part of Catalonian history from prehistoric times through more than 3,000 years and into the contemporary democratic era. After centuries of "official" Catalan history dictated from Madrid (from 1714 until the mid-19th century Renaixença, and from 1939 to 1975), this is an opportunity to revisit Catalonia's autobiography. Explanations of the exhibits appear in Catalan, Castilian, and English. Guided tours are available on Sunday at noon and 1 PM. The rooftop cafeteria has excellent views over the harbor and is open to the public (whether or not you visit the museum itself) during museum hours. ⊠ *Pl. Pau Vila 1, Barceloneta* ☎ *93/225–4700* ⊕ *www.mhcat.net* ☐ *€4; free 1st Sun. of month* ☉ *Tues. and Thurs.–Sat. 10–7, Wed. 10–8, Sun. 10–2:30* Ⓜ *Barceloneta.*

WORTH NOTING

Arc del Triomf. This imposing, exposed-redbrick arch was built by Josep Vilaseca as the grand entrance for the 1888 Universal Exhibition. Similar in size and sense to the traditional triumphal arches of ancient Rome, this one refers to no specific military triumph anyone can recall. In fact, Catalunya's last military triumph of note may have been Jaume I el Conqueridor's 1229 conquest of the Moors in Mallorca—as suggested by the bats (always part of Jaume I's coat of arms) on either side of the arch itself. The Josep Reynés sculptures adorning the structure represent Barcelona hosting visitors to the Exhibition on the west (front) side, while the Josep Llimona sculptures on the east side depict the prizes being given to its outstanding contributors. ⊠ *Passeig de Sant Joan, La Ciutadella* Ⓜ *Arc de Triomf.*

Castell dels Tres Dragóns *(Castle of the Three Dragons).* Built by Domènech i Montaner as the café and restaurant for the 1888 Universal Exposition, the building was named in honor of a popular mid-19th-century comedy written by the father of Catalan theater, Serafí Pitarra. An arresting building that greets you on the right entering the Ciutadella from Passeig Lluís Companys, it has exposed brickwork and visible iron supports, both radical innovations at the time. Domènech i Muntaner's building later became an arts-and-crafts workshop where Moderniste architects met to experiment with traditional crafts and to exchange ideas. It now holds Barcelona's **Museu de Ciències Naturals/Museu de Zoologia** (Zoology Museum). ⊠ *Passeig Picasso 5, La Ciutadella* ☎ *93/256–2200* ⊕ *www.bcn.cat/museuciencies* ☐ *€5.30* ☉ *Tues., Wed., Fri., and weekends 10–2:30, Thurs. 10–6:30* Ⓜ *Arc de Triomf.*

El Transbordador Aeri del Port. This hair-raising cable-car ride over the Barcelona harbor from Barceloneta to Montjuïc (with a midway stop in the port) is spectacular, though it is not always clear whether the great views are the result of the vantage point or the rush of mortality. The cable car leaving from the tower at the end of Passeig Joan de Borbó connects the Torre de San Sebastián on the Moll de Barceloneta, the tower of Jaume I in the port boat terminal, and the Torre de Miramar on Montjuïc. Critics maintain, not without reason, that the ride is expensive, not very cool, and actually pretty scary. On the positive side, this is undoubtedly the slickest way to connect Barceloneta and Montjuïc, and the Torre de Altamar restaurant in the tower at the Barceloneta end serves excellent food and wine along with nonpareil views. ⊠ *Passeig Joan de Borbó s/n, Barceloneta* ☎ *93/225–2718* 💲 *€12.50 round-trip, €9 one-way* ☉ *Daily 10:45–7* Ⓜ *Barceloneta.*

Farmacia Saim. This ornate house with floral trim around the upper balconies, griffins over the door, and the pharmacist's insignia (the serpent and amphora symbolic of the curative properties of snake oils mixed in the apothecary vial) is the still-operating successor of Barceloneta's first pharmacy. It originally stood across the street; the present house was built in 1902. One of the sturdiest houses in Barceloneta, Farmacia Saim was used as a bomb shelter during the 1936–39 Spanish civil war, when Franco's bombers, in an attempt to paralyze the Barcelona port to slow down Republican resupply, frequently dumped misdirected bombs on Barceloneta. ⊠ *Carrer Sant Carles 7, Barceloneta* ☎ *93/221–7670* Ⓜ *Barceloneta.*

Fuente de Carmen Amaya *(Carmen Amaya Fountain).* Down at the eastern end of Carrer Sant Carles, where Barceloneta joins the beach, is the monument to the famous Gypsy flamenco dancer Carmen Amaya (1913–63), born in the Gypsy settlement known as Somorrostro, part of Barceloneta until 1920, when development sent the gypsies farther east to what is now the Fòrum grounds (from which they were again displaced in 2003). Amaya achieved universal fame at the age of 16, in 1929, when she performed at Barcelona's International Exposition. Amaya made triumphal tours of the Americas and starred in films such as *La hija de Juan Simón* (1934) and *Los Tarantos* (1962). The fountain, and its high-relief representations of cherubic children in the throes of flamenco, has been poorly maintained since it was placed here in 1959, but it remains an important reminder of Barceloneta's roots as a rough-and-tumble, romantic enclave of free-living sailors, stevedores, Gypsies, and fishermen. This Gypsy ambience all but disappeared when the last of the *chiringuitos* (ramshackle beach restaurants specializing in fish and rice dishes) fell to the wreckers' ball shortly after the 1992 Olympics. ⊠ *Carrer Sant Carles, Barceloneta* Ⓜ *Barceloneta.*

La Cascada. The sights and sounds of Barcelona seem far away when you stand near this monumental, slightly overdramatized creation by Josep Fontseré, presented as part of the 1888 Universal Exhibition. The waterfall's rocks were the work of a young architecture student named Antoni Gaudí—his first public works, appropriately natural and organic, and certainly a hint of things to come. ⊠ *La Ciutadella* Ⓜ *Arc de Triomf, Ciutadella.*

🦢 **Parc de la Ciutadella** *(Citadel Park).* Once a fortress designed to consolidate Madrid's military occupation of Barcelona, the Ciutadella is

A massive cascading fountain is a focal point for Barcelona's main downtown park, the Parc de la Ciutadella.

now the city's main downtown park. The clearing dates from shortly after the War of the Spanish Succession in the early 18th century, when Felipe V demolished some 1,000 houses in what was then the Barri de la Ribera to build a fortress and barracks for his soldiers and a glacis or open space used a buffer zone or no-man's-land to put space between rebellious Barcelona and his artillery positions. The fortress walls were pulled down in 1868 and replaced by gardens laid out by Josep Fontseré. Within the park are a cluster of museums, the Catalan parliament, and the city zoo. ⊠ *La Ciutadella* Ⓜ *Arc de Triomf, Ciutadella.*

Parlament de Catalunya. Once the arsenal for the Ciutadella—as evidenced by the thickness of the building's walls—this is the only surviving remnant of Felipe V's fortress, and now houses the Catalan Parliament. ⊠ *Pl. d'Armes, La Ciutadella* ☎ *93/319–5728* 💶 *€4* 🕙 *Tues.–Sat. 10–7, Sun. 10–2* Ⓜ *Arc de Triomf, Ciutadella.*

Port Olímpic. Choked with yachts, restaurants, tapas bars, and mega-restaurants serving reasonably decent fare continuously 1 PM–1 AM, the Olympic Port is 2 km (1 mi) up the beach, marked by the mammoth shimmering goldfish sculpture by Frank Gehry of Bilbao Guggenheim fame (Bilbao got a leviathan; Barcelona got a goldfish). In the shadow of Barcelona's first real skyscraper, the Hotel Arts, the Olympic Port rages on Friday and Saturday nights, especially in summer, with hundreds of young people of all nationalities contributing to a scene characterized by go-go girls (and boys), fast-food chains, ice-cream parlors, and a buzz redolent of spring break in Cancún. Ⓜ *Ciutadella, Vila Olímpica.*

Port Vell. From Pla del Palau, cross to the edge of the port, where the Moll d'Espanya, the Moll de la Fusta, and the Moll de Barceloneta meet.

(*Moll* means docks.) Just beyond the colorful Roy Lichtenstein sculpture in front of the post office, the modern Port Vell complex—an IMAX theater, aquarium, and Maremagnum shopping mall—looms seaward on the Moll d'Espanya. The Palau de Mar, with its five somewhat pricey and impersonal quayside terrace restaurants, stretches down along the Moll de Barceloneta (try Llevataps or the Merendero de la Mari; even better is El Magatzem, by the entrance to the Museu de Història de Catalunya in the Palau de Mar). Key points in the Maremagnum complex are the grassy hillside (for lovers, especially, on April 23, Sant Jordi's Day, Barcelona's variant of Valentine's Day); and the *Ictineo II* replica of the submarine created by Narcis Monturiol (1819–85)—the world's first, launched in the Barcelona port in 1862. Ⓜ *Barceloneta.*

Sant Miquel del Port. Have a close look at this baroque church with its modern (1992), pseudo-bodybuilder version of the winged archangel Michael himself, complete with sword and chain, in the alcove on the facade. One of the first buildings to be completed in Barceloneta, Sant Miquel del Port was begun in 1753 and finished by 1755 under the direction of architect Damià Ribes. Due to strict orders to keep Barceloneta low enough to fire La Ciutadella's cannon over, Sant Miquel del Port had no bell tower and only a small cupola until Elies Rogent added a new one in 1853. Along with the image of Sant Miquel, Sant Elm, and Santa Maria de Cervelló, patrons of the Catalan fleet, also appeared on the baroque facade. All three images were destroyed at the outbreak of the Spanish civil war in 1936. Interesting to note are the metopes, palm-size, gilt bas-relief sculptures around the interior cornice and repeated outside at the top of the facade. These 74 Latin-inscribed allegories each allude to different attributes of St. Michael: for example, the image of a boat and the Latin inscription "iam in tuto" (finally safe), alluding to the protection of St. Michael against the perils of the sea. To the right of Sant Miquel del Port at No. 41 Carrer de Sant Miquel is a house decorated by seven strips of floral sgraffiti and a plaque commemorating Fernando de Lesseps, the engineer who built the Suez Canal, who had lived in the house when serving as French consul to Barcelona. In the square by the church, take a close look at the fountain, with its Barcelona coat of arms, and Can Ganassa, on the east side, a worthy tapas bar. ⊠ *Pl. de la Barceloneta, Barceloneta* Ⓜ *Barceloneta.*

Ⓒ **Zoo.** Barcelona's excellent zoo occupies the whole bottom section of the Parc de la Ciutadella. There's a superb reptile house and a full complement of African animals. The dolphin show usually plays to a packed house. ⊠ *La Ciutadella* ☎ *93/225–6780* ⊕ *www.zoobarcelona. com* ✆ *€16* ⊘ *Daily 10–7* Ⓜ *Arc de Triomf, Ciutadella.*

THE EIXAMPLE: MODERNISTE BARCELONA

Sightseeing
★★★★★
Nightlife
★★★★★
Dining
★★★★★
Lodging
★★★★★
Shopping
★★★★★

Barcelona's most famous neighborhood, this late-19th-century urban development is known for its dizzying unnumbered grid and dazzling Art Nouveau architecture. Named "Expansion" in Catalan, the district appears on the map as a checkerboard above Plaça de Catalunya. Shopping, art-gallery hopping, exploring Moderniste town houses, and sampling the city's finest cuisine is an ongoing pastime for visitors and barcelonins alike.

Somewhat wide, bright, and noisy, the Eixample (ay-shompla), is an open-air Moderniste museum. With its hard-line street grid the Eixample is oddly labyrinthine for a Cartesian network (the planners forgot to number it). Many Barcelona residents find it possible to get lost on these unnumbered and unalphabetized streets, maybe because it's so entertaining. Divided into the well-to-do Dreta to the right of Rambla Catalunya looking inland, and the more working-class Ezquerra to the left of Rambla Catalunya, Eixample locations are also either *mar* (sea side of the street) or *muntanya* (mountain side).

The Eixample was created when the Ciutat Vella's city walls fell in 1860, and Barcelona embarked upon a vast expansion fueled by the return of rich colonials from the Americas, aristocrats who had sold their country estates, and the city's industrial power. The street grid was the work of urban planner Ildefons Cerdà, and much of the building was done at the height of Modernisme by a who's who of Art Nouveau architects, starring Gaudí, Domènech i Montaner, and Puig i Cadafalch. In this architectural feast the main course is Gaudí's Sagrada Família church. The Eixample's principal thoroughfares are Rambla de Catalunya and Passeig de Gràcia, where the city's most elegant shops vie for space among its best Moderniste buildings.

GETTING ORIENTED

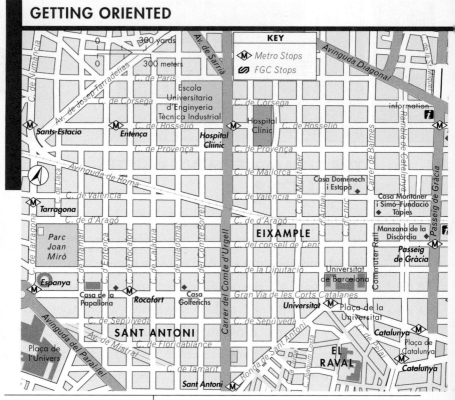

KEY

Ⓜ Metro Stops

🅖 FGC Stops

Timing	Getting Here and Around
Exploring the Eixample can take days, but three hours will cover the main events. Add another two or three hours to explore the Sagrada Família. Look for the *passatges* (passageways) through some of the Eixample blocks; Passatge Permanyer, Passatge de la Concepció, and Passatge Mendez Vigo are three of the best. Beware of the tapas emporiums lining Passeig de Gràcia; almost all of them microwave previously prepared tapas, and are not the best.	The metro stops at Plaça de Catalunya and Provença nicely bracket this quintessential Barcelona neighborhood, while the Diagonal and Passeig de Gràcia stops right in the center.
	Barcelona's unnumbered Eixample (Expansion), the post-1860 grid, is a perfect place to get lost, but fear not: the Eixample is vertebrate. Carrer Balmes divides the Eixample's working-class *Esquerra* (left, looking uphill) from its bourgeois *Dreta* (right). Even the blocks are divided into *davant* (front) or *darrera* (behind) apartments. The sides of the streets are either *mar* (sea) or *muntanya* (mountain).

GRACIA

Hospital de
Sant Pau

C. de Sant Antoni Maria

C. de Corsega

Casa Asia–Palau Baró
de Quadras

Casa de
les Punxes

Diagonal
Casa Milà

Verdaguer

C. de Provença

C. de Mallorca

C. de València

C. del Rosselló

Sagrada
Família

Casa
Macaia

Plaça de la
Sagrada
Família

La Sagrada
Família

Avinguda Diagonal

C. de d'Aragó

C. del consell de Cent

Passatge
Permanyer

C. de la Diputació

Monumental

Plaça de
Toros

Gran Via de les Corts Catalanes

Passeig de Gràcia

Plaça de
Tetuán

Gran Via de les Corts

Tetuán

C. de Caspe

Casa Calvet

Urquinaona

C. d'Ausiàs Marc

Ronda de Sant Pere

C. d'Ali Bei

Arc de Triomf

C. de Marina

Top Attractions

Casa Milà

Casa Montaner i Simó–
Fundació Tàpies

Manzana de la Discòrdia

Temple Expiatori de la
Sagrada Família

Top Experiences

Art Gallery hopping on Consell
de Cent

Exploring the Sagrada Família
ornamental facades

Shopping the hyperchic flagship stores and small quirky
boutiques alike

Strolling down the leafy tunnel
of Rambla de Catalunya

Walking the rooftop of Casa
Milà

Where to Eat (⇨ Ch. 3)

Drolma

Inòpia Clàssic Bar

Petit Comité

Tapaç 24

Discount Tickets

The Ruta del Modernisme (Moderniste Route) ticket offers
coupon booklets, including discounted visits, to more than
100 Moderniste buildings in and around Barcelona. For
€18, a manual published in various languages allows you
to self-guide through the city's Art Nouveau architecture.
Inquire at your hotel or the tourist office, or purchase tickets directly at the **Modernisme Centre** (✉ Pl. Catalunya
17, Eixample ☎ 93/317-7652 ⊕ www.rutadelmodernisme.
com ☉ Mon.–Sat. 10-7, Sun. 10-2 Ⓜ Catalunya), which is
part of the Barcelona Tourist Information Center. You can
also purchase tickets at the Pavellons de la Finca Güell
(Av. de Pedralbes 7) or at the Hospital de la Santa Creu i
de Sant Pau (Sant Antoni Maria Claret 167).

MAIN ATTRACTIONS

Casa Àsia–Palau Baró de Quadras. The neo-Gothic and plateresque (intricately carved in silversmith-like detail) facade of this house built in 1904 for Baron Quadras has one of the most spectacular collections of Eusebi Arnau sculptures in town (other Arnau sites include the Palau de la Música Catalana, Quatre Gats–Casa Martí, Casa Amatller, and Casa Lleó Morera). Look for the theme of St. George slaying the dragon once again, this one in a spectacularly vertiginous rush of movement down the facade. Don't miss the intimate-looking row of alpine chalet–like windows across the top floor. Casa Àsia, an excellent and comprehensive resource for cultural and business-related research, opened here in 2003. ⊠ *Av. Diagonal 373, Eixample* ☎ *93/238–7337* ⊕ *www.casaasia. es* ⊒ *Free* ☉ *Tues.–Sat. 10–8, Sun. 10–2* Ⓜ *Diagonal.*

★ **Casa Milà.** Usually referred to as **La Pedrera** (The Stone Quarry), with a wavy, curving stone facade that undulates around the corner of the block, Casa Milà is one of Gaudí's most celebrated yet initially reviled designs. Topped by chimneys so eerie they were nicknamed *espantabruxes* (witch-scarers), the building was unveiled in 1910 to the horror of local residents. The sudden appearance of these cavelike balconies on their most fashionable street led to the immediate coining of descriptions such as "the Stone Quarry"—or, better yet, "Rockpile"—along with references to the Gypsy cave dwellings in Granada's Sacromonte. Other observers were undone by the facade, complaining, as one critic put it, that the rippling, undressed stone made you feel "as though you are on board a ship in an angry sea." Seemingly defying the laws of gravity, the exterior has no straight lines, and is adorned with winding balconies covered with wrought-iron seaweedlike foliage sculpted by Josep Maria Jujol.

The building was originally meant to be dedicated to the Mother of God and crowned with a sculpture of the Virgin Mary. The initial design was altered by owner Pere Milà i Camps, who, after the anticlerical violence of the Setmana Tràgica (Tragic Week) of 1909, decided that the religious theme would be an invitation for a new outbreak of mayhem. Gaudí's rooftop chimney park, alternately interpreted as veiled Saharan women or helmeted warriors, is as spectacular as anything in Barcelona, especially in late afternoon, when the sunlight slants over the city into the Mediterranean. Inside, the handsome **Espai Gaudí** (Gaudí Space) in the attic has excellent critical displays of Gaudí's works from all over Spain, as well as explanations of theories and techniques, including an upside-down model (a reproduction of the original in the Sagrada Família museum) of the Güell family crypt at Santa Coloma made of weighted hanging strings. This hanging model is based on the theory of the reversion of the catenary, which says that a chain suspended from two points will spontaneously hang in the exact shape of the inverted arch required to convert the stress to compression, thus structural support. The **Pis de la Pedrera** apartment is an interesting look into the life of a family that lived in La Pedrera in the early 20th century. Everything from the bathroom to the kitchen is filled with reminders of how comprehensively life has changed in the last century. People still live in the other apartments. ⊠ *Passeig de Gràcia 92, Eixample* ☎ *93/484–5995*

€9.50 *(for Espai Gaudí and Pis de la Pedrera)* ⊙ *Daily 10–8; guided tours weekdays at 6. Espai Gaudí roof terrace open for drinks evenings June–Sept.* Ⓜ *Diagonal, Provença.*

Hospital de Sant Pau. Certainly one of the most beautiful hospital complexes in the world, the Hospital de Sant Pau is notable for its Mudejar motifs and sylvan plantings. The hospital wards are set among gardens under exposed brick facades intensely decorated with mosaics and polychrome ceramic tile. Begun in 1900, this monumental production won Lluís Domènech i Montaner his third Barcelona "Best Building" award, in 1912. (His previous two prizes were for the Palau de la Música Catalana and Casa Lleó Morera.) The Moderniste enthusiasm for nature is apparent here; the architect believed patients were more apt to recover surrounded by trees and flowers than in sterile hospital wards. Domènech i Montaner also believed in the therapeutic properties of form and color, and decorated the hospital with Pau Gargallo sculptures and colorful mosaics. ⊠ *Carrer Sant Antoni Maria Claret 167, Eixample* ☎ *902/076–621 for daily tours in English at 10:15 and 12:15; 93/256–2504 for guided tours by appointment* ⊕ *www.santpau. es* ⊠ €5 ⊙ *Daily 9–8* Ⓜ *Hospital de Sant Pau.*

Fodor's Choice
★ **Manzana de la Discòrdia.** The name is a pun on the Spanish word *manzana*, which means both apple and city block, alluding to the three-way architectural counterpoint on this block and to the classical myth of the Apple of Discord (which played a part in that legendary tale about the Judgment of Paris). The houses here are spectacular, and encompass three monuments of Modernisme—Casa Lleó Morera, Casa Amatller, and Casa Batlló. Of the three competing buildings (four if you count Sagnier i Villavecchia's comparatively tame 1910 Casa Mulleras at No. 37), Casa Batlló is clearly the star attraction, and the only one of the three offering visits to the interior.

The ornate **Casa Lleó Morera** (⊠ *Passeig de Gracia 35, Eixample* Ⓜ *Passeig de Gracia*) was extensively rebuilt (1902–06) by Palau de la Música Catalana architect Domènech i Montaner and is a treasure house of Catalan Modernisme. The facade is covered with ornamentation and sculptures depicting female figures using the modern inventions of the age: the telephone, the telegraph, the photographic camera, and the Victrola. The inside, presently closed to the public, is even more astounding, another anthology of Art Nouveau techniques assembled by the same team of glaziers, sculptors, and mosaicists Domènech i Montaner directed in the construction of the Palau de la Música Catalana. The Eusebi Arnau sculptures around the top of the walls on the main floor are based on the Catalan lullaby "La Dida de l'Infant del Rei" (The Nurse of the King's Baby), while the stained-glass scenes in the old dining room of Lleó Morera family picnics resemble Moderniste versions of Impressionist paintings. (Though Casa Lleó Morera is not open to the public at this writing, check the current status with the Modernisme Centre (☎ 93/317–7652) and ask how to arrange a visit.)

The neo-Gothic, pseudo-Flemish **Casa Amatller** (⊠ *Passeig de Gràcia 41, Eixample* ☎ 93/487-7217 ⊕ *www.amatller.org* Ⓜ *Passeig de Gràcia*) was built by Josep Puig i Cadafalch in 1900, when the architect was 33 years old. Eighteen years younger than Domènech i Montaner and 15 years younger than Gaudí, Puig i Cadafalch was one of the leading statesmen of his generation, mayor of Barcelona and, in 1917, president of Catalonia's first home-rule government since 1714, the Mancomunitat de Catalunya. Puig i Cadafalch's architectural historicism sought to recover Catalonia's proud past, in combination with eclectic elements from Flemish or Netherlandish architectural motifs. The Eusebi Arnau sculptures range from St. George and the dragon to the figures of a handless drummer with his dancing bear. The flowing-haired "Princesa" is thought to be Amatller's daughter, while the animals up above are pouring chocolate, a reference to the source of the Amatller family fortune. Casa Amatller is generally closed to the public, although the Fundació Institut Amatller d'Art Hispànic holds occasional cultural events and visits. The boutique and small gallery inside the entryway sells Art Nouveau objects and organizes exhibits related to Modernisme.

Gaudí at his most spectacular, the colorful and bizarre **Casa Batlló** (⊠ *Passeig de Gràcia 43, Eixample* ☎ *93/216–0306* ⊕ *www.casabatllo. es* ⊠ *€17* ⊙ *Daily 9–8* Ⓜ *Passeig de Gràcia*), with its mottled facade resembling anything from an abstract pointillist painting to a rainbow of colored sprinkles on an ice-cream cone, is usually easily identifiable by the crowd of tourists snapping photographs on the sidewalk. Nationalist symbolism is at work here: the scaly roof line represents the Dragon of Evil impaled on St. George's cross, and the skulls and bones on the balconies are the dragon's victims. These motifs are allusions to Catalonia's Middle Ages, its codes of chivalry, and religious fervor. Gaudí is said to have directed the chromatic composition of the facade from the middle of Passeig de Gràcia, calling instructions to workmen on scaffolding equipped with baskets of multicolored fragments of ceramic tiling. The interior design follows a gently swirling maritime motif in stark contrast to the terrestrial strife represented on the facade.

WORTH NOTING

Casa Calvet. This exquisite but more conventional town house (for Gaudí, anyway) was the architect's first commission in the Eixample (the second was the dragonlike Casa Batlló, and the third, and last— he was never asked to do another—was the stone quarry–esque Casa Milà). Peaked with baroque scroll gables over the unadorned (no ceramics, no color, no sculpted ripples) Montjuïc sandstone facade, Casa Calvet compensates for its structural conservatism with its Art Nouveau details, from the door handles to the benches, chairs, vestibule, and spectacular glass-and-wood elevator. Built in 1900 for the textile baron Pere Calvet, the house includes symbolic elements on the facade, ranging from the owner's stylized letter "C" over the door to the cypress, symbol of hospitality, above. The wild mushrooms on the main (second) floor reflect Pere Calvet's (and perhaps Gaudí's) passion for mycology, while the busts at the top of the facade represent St. Peter, the owner's patron saint; and St. Genis of Arles and St. Genis of Rome, patron saints of Vilassar, the Calvet family's hometown in the coastal Maresme north of Barcelona. For an even more sensorial taste of Gaudí, dine in the same building's next-door **Casa Calvet restaurant,** elaborately

DID YOU KNOW?

Casa de les Punxes (AKA House of the Spikes) is one of the only freestanding buildings in the Moderniste Eixample neighborhood visible from 360 degrees.

decorated in Moderniste ornamentation. ✉ *Carrer Casp 48, Eixample* Ⓜ *Catalunya, Urquinaona.*

Casa de la Papallona. This extraordinary apartment house crowned with an enormous yellow butterfly (*papallona*) made of *trencadis* (broken ceramic chips used by the Modernistes to add color to curved surfaces) was built in 1912 by Josep Graner i Prat. Next to Plaça de Espanya, directly overlooking the Arenes de Barcelona bullring, the building displays lines of a routine, late-19th-century design—that is, until you reach the top of the facade. ✉ *Llançà 20, Eixample* Ⓜ *Plaça Espanya.*

Casa de les Punxes *(House of the Spikes).* Also known as Casa Terrades for the family that owned the house and commissioned Puig i Cadafalch to build it, this extraordinary cluster of six conical towers ending in impossibly sharp needles is another of Puig i Cadafalch's northern European inspirations, this one rooted in the Gothic architecture of Nordic countries. One of the few freestanding Eixample buildings, visible from 360 degrees, this ersatz-Bavarian or Danish castle in downtown Barcelona is composed entirely of private apartments. Some of them are built into the conical towers themselves and consist of three circular levels connected by spiral stairways, about right for a couple or a very small family. Interestingly, Puig i Cadafalch also designed the Terrades family mausoleum, albeit in a much more sober and respectful style. ✉ *Av. Diagonal 416–420, Eixample* Ⓜ *Diagonal.*

Casa Domènech i Estapà. This less radical example of Eixample Art Nouveau architecture is interesting for its balconies and curved lines on the facade, for its handsome doors and vestibule, and for the lovely etched designs on the glass of the entryway. Built by and for the architect Domènech i Estapà in 1908–09, eight years before his death, this building represents a more conservative interpretation of the aesthetic canons of the epoch, revealing the architect's hostility to the Art Nouveau movement. Domènech i Estapà built more civil projects than any other architect of his time (Reial Acadèmia de Cièncias y Artes, Palacio de Justicia, Sociedad Catalana de Gas y Electricidad, Hospital Clínico, Observatorio Fabra) and was the creator of the Carcel Modelo (Model Prison), considered a state-of-the-art example of penitentiary design when it was built in 1913. ✉ *Valencia 241, Eixample* Ⓜ *Passeig de Gràcia.*

Casa Golferichs. Gaudí disciple Joan Rubió i Bellver built this extraordinary house, known as El Xalet (The Chalet) for the Golferichs family when he was not yet 30. The rambling wooden eaves and gables of the exterior enclose a cozy and comfortable dark-wood-lined interior with a pronounced verticality. The top floor, with its rich wood beams and cerulean walls, is often used for intimate concerts; the ground floor exhibits paintings and photographs. ✉ *Gran Via 491, Eixample* ☎ *93/323–7790* ⊕ *www.golferichs.org* ☉ *Weekdays 9–2 and 4–8, Sat. 9–2* Ⓜ *Urgell, Rocafort.*

Casa Macaia. This graceful Puig i Cadafalch building constructed in 1901 was the former seat of the ubiquitous Centre Cultural Fundació "La Caixa," a deep-pocketed, far-reaching cultural entity funded by the Caixa Catalana (Catalan Savings Bank). Look for the Eusebi Arnau sculptures over the door depicting, somewhat cryptically, a

Continued on page 111

TEMPLE EXPIATORI DE LA
SAGRADA FAMÍLIA

Antoni Gaudí's striking and surreal masterpiece was conceived as nothing short of a Bible in stone, an arresting representation of the history of Christianity. Today this Roman Catholic church is Barcelona's most emblematic architectural icon. Looming over Barcelona like a mid-city massif of grottoes and peaks, the Sagrada Família strains skyward in piles of stalagmites. Construction is ongoing and continues to stretch toward the heavens.

CONSTRUCTION, PAST AND PRESENT

"My client is not in a hurry," was Gaudí's reply to anyone curious about his project's timetable . . . good thing, too, because the Sagrada Família was begun in 1882 under architect Francesc Villar, passed on in 1891 to Gaudí, and is still thought to be 10 to 20 years from completion. Gaudí added Art Nouveau touches to the crypt and in 1893 started the Nativity facade. Conceived as a symbolic construct encompassing the complete story and scope of the Christian faith, the church was intended by Gaudí to impact the viewer with the full sweep and force of the Gospel. At the time of his death in 1926 only one tower of the Nativity facade had been completed.

By 2026, the 100th anniversary of Gaudí's death, after 144 years of construction in the tradition of the great medieval and Renaissance cathedrals of Europe, the Sagrada Família may well be complete enough to call finished. Architect Jordi Bonet continues in the footsteps of his father, architect Lluís Bonet, to make Gaudí's vision complete as he has since the 1980s.

(left) Twilight at the Sagrada Família, still under construction today. (top) Shepherds gather to witness the birth of Christ in the Nativity facade.

PART OF GOD'S PLAN

THE EXTERIOR

Gaudí's plans called for three immense facades; the **Nativity facade** facing northeast and the **Passion facade** facing southwest are presently visible. The even larger **Glory facade**, designed as the building's main entry is in the preliminary stages of construction. In its finished state, the church will feature a staggering **eighteen towers**: The four **bell towers** over each facade (12 in total) would represent the 12 apostles. Four **larger towers** will represent the evangelists Mark, Matthew, John, and Luke. Between the central tower and the reredos at the northwestern end of the nave, the **second-highest tower** will rise in honor of the Virgin Mary. Finally in the center, surrounded by the evangelists, the **Torre del Salvador** (Tower of the Savior), representing Christ, will be crowned by an illuminated cross and soar to a final height of 564 feet.

THE INTERIOR

Inside, the floorplan for the church forms a **Latin cross** with five naves intersected by three. The **naves** are not supported by buttresses but by treelike helicoidal (spiraling) columns. The **apse**, covered but still incomplete, will have space for 15,000 people, a choir loft for 1,500, and occupy an area large enough to encompass the entire Santa Maria del Mar basilica, Barcelona's giant Gothic church.

WHAT YOU CAN SEE TODAY

At present, two of the facades are complete: the **Nativity facade** and the **Passion facade**. Their **eight bell towers** (four each) crown each entrance. The **apse** at the east end of the church is also near completion and contains seven chapels. The **Glory facade** has little to show at the moment, but recently the door for this main entrance was revealed.

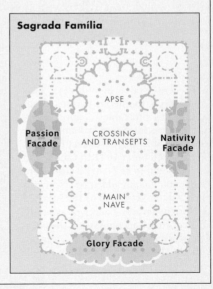

Sagrada Família

APSE

Passion Facade

CROSSING AND TRANSEPTS

Nativity Facade

MAIN NAVE

Glory Facade

BIBLE STUDIES IN STONE: THE FACADES

Gaudí intended the Sagrada Família to depict the great stories of the bible, but reading the facades is a challenge, even for scholars.

THE NATIVITY FACADE

Built during Gaudí's lifetime, this facade displays his original vision. It is divided into three sections of doors: **Charity** in the center, **Faith** on the right, and **Hope** on the left.

The **Portal of Charity** in the center shows the birth of Christ; above that, the Annunciation is under a grotto of ice. Overhead is the Christmas sky at Bethlehem, with two babies, representing Gemini, and the horns of a bull, for Taurus. The cypress tree above symbolizes eternity; the white doves are souls seeking life everlasting.

The **Portal of Faith** on the right shows Christ preaching as a youth and Zacharias prophetically writing the name of John. Higher up are the Eucharistic symbols of grapes and wheat, and a hand and eye, symbols of divine providence.

(facing page, top left) An illustration of the finished Sagrada Família. (facing page, top right) The treelike columns. (above, left) The ornamental Nativity facade. (above, top right) A figure in the Portal of Faith. (above, center right) The spiraling staircase. (above, bottom right) A decorative cross.

The focal point in the Nativity facade: Joseph and Mary presenting the infant Jesus.

The **Portal of Hope** on the left shows the slaughter of the innocents, the flight into Egypt, Joseph gazing at his son surrounded by his carpenter's tools, and the marriage of Joseph and Mary with Mary's parents, Joaquin and Anna. Above is a boat, representing the Church, piloted by Joseph and the Holy Spirit represented as a dove, under a stalagmite from Montserrat.

This facade is crowned by **four bell towers**. Gaudí planned his slender towers for carillons capable of more complex music than traditional bell-ringing changes. The apostles Barnabas, Jude, Simon, and Matthew are seated on the bell towers.

THE PASSION FACADE

On the **Passion facade** over Carrer Sardenya, Gaudí planned to dramatize the abyss between the birth of a child and the death of a man. In 1986, Josep Maria Subirachs, an artist with a hard-edged sculptural style, was commissioned to finish the Passion facade. The contrast is sharp between this facade and the more classical Nativity facade.

Framed by tibia-like bones the Passion facade illustrates the last days of Christ and his resurrection. The scenes are laid out chronologically in an S-shaped path begin left-to-right on the lowest level, then right-to-left on the second tier, and back left-to-right on the third tier.

On the bottom left, the story begins with the **Last Supper**, the faces of the disciples contorted in confusion. Judas is especially anguished, clutching his bag of money behind his back over a reclining hound, the symbol of fidelity, in contrast with the disciple's perfidy. To the right is the Garden of Gethsemane and Peter awakening, followed by the **Kiss of Judas**. The numerical cryptogram behind contains 16 numbers offering 310 combinations adding up to 33, the age of Christ. To the right of the door depicts **Peter's Denial** with a rooster showing Peter at his third denial of Christ "ere the cock crows." Farther to the right are **Pontius Pilate and Jesus** with the crown of thorns. The far right is **Jesus' Trial**.

Above on the second tier is the **Three Marys** with Simon helping Jesus carry

Judas kissing Jesus while a cryptogram behind contains a numerical combination adding up to 33, Christ's age at death.

The stark, geometric Passion facade.

the cross. Over the center, **Jesus carries the cross**. He consoles the women of Jerusalem (cf., Book of Revelation): "Don't cry for me; cry for your children . . .", while Veronica displays the veil with which she wiped the face of Jesus. To the left, Gaudí himself is portrayed, pencil in hand, while farther left a **mounted centurion** pierces the side of the church with his spear, the church representing the body of Christ.

At the top left, **soldiers gamble for Christ's clothing**. At the top center is **Christ's crucifixion**; the moon to the right of the cross referring to the darkness at the moment of Christ's death and to the full moon of Easter. Finally to the right of that, Peter and Mary grieve at **Christ's entombment**, an egg overhead symbolizing rebirth and the resurrection.

At a height of 148 feet are the four Apostles on their bell towers. Bartholomew, on the left, looks upward toward the 26-foot gold risen Christ between the four bell towers at a height of 198 feet.

THE GLORY FACADE

At this time, there is little to see in the Glory facade, in its preliminary stages of construction, but one new element revealed is a massive bronze gateway, the work of Subirachs, which will be the main doorway of the future facade. The doors are inscribed with the Lord's Prayer in fifty different languages. In the center standing in relief is the Lord's Prayer in Catalan.

The sculptures on the Glory facade, still in production, will present man within the overall order of creation.

A new element in the Sagrada Família: the bronze doorway of the Glory facade.

DETAILS TO DISCOVER

Gaudí in the Passion facade

GAUDÍ IN THE PASSION FACADE

Subirachs pays double homage to the great Moderniste master in the Passion facade: Gaudí himself appears over the left side of the main entry making notes or drawings, the evangelist in stone, while the Roman soldiers are modeled on Gaudí's helmeted, Star Wars–like warriors from the roof of La Pedrera.

TOWER TOPS

Break out the binoculars and have a close look at the pinnacles and peaks of the Sagrada Familia's towers. Sculpted by Japanese artist Etsuro Sotoo, these clusters of grapes and different kids of fruit are symbols of fertility, of rebirth, and of the Resurrection of Christ.

Sotoo's ornamental fruit

SUBIRACHS IN THE PASSION FACADE

At Christ's feet in the entombment sculpture is a blocky figure with a furrowed brow, thought to be a portrayal of the agnostic's anguished search for certainty. This figure is generally taken as a self-portrait of Subirachs, characterized by the sculptor's giant hand and an "S" on his massive right arm.

DONKEY ON THE NATIVITY FACADE

On the left side of the Nativity facade over the Portal of Hope is a *burro*, a small donkey, known to have been modeled from a donkey that Gaudí saw near the work site. The *ruc català* (Catalan donkey) is a beloved and iconic symbol of Catalonia, often displayed on Catalonian bumpers as a response to the Spanish fighting bull.

The donkey in the Nativity facade

THE ROSE TREE DOOR

The richly sculpted Rose Tree Door, between the Nativity facade and the cloisters, portrays Our Lady of the Rose Tree with the infant Jesus in her arms, St Dominic and St Catherine of Siena in prayer, with three angels dancing overhead. The sculptural group on the wall known as "The Death of the Just" portrays the Virgin and child comforting a moribund old man, the Spanish prayer "Jesús, José, y María, asistidme en mi última agonía" (Jesus, Joseph, and María, help me in my final agony). The accompanying inscriptions in English, "Pray for us sinners now and at the hour of our death, Amen." are the final words of the Ave María prayer.

The heavily embelished Rose door

COLUMN FROM THE PORTAL OF CHARITY
The column, dead center in the Portal of Charity, is covered with the genealogy of Christ going back through the House of David to Abraham. At the bottom of the column is the snake of evil, complete with the apple of temptation in his mouth, closed in behind an iron grate, symbolic of Christianity's mission of neutralizing the sin of selfishness.

The column in the Portal of Charity

FACELESS ST. VERONICA
Because her story is considered legendary, not historical fact, St. Veronica appears faceless in the Passion facade. Also shown is the veil she gave Christ to wipe his face with on the way to Calvary that was said to be miraculously imprinted with his likeness. The veil is torn in two overhead and covers a mosaic that Subirachs allegedly disliked and elected to conceal.

St. Veronica with the veil

STAINED GLASS WINDOWS
The stained-glass windows of the Sagrada Família are work of Joan Vila-Grau. The windows in the west central part of the nave represent the light of Jesus and a bubbling fountain in a bright chromatic patchwork of shades of blue with green and yellow reflections. The main window on the Passion facade represents the Resurrection. Gaudí left express instructions that the windows of the central nave have no color so as not to alter the colors of the tiles and trencadis (mosaics of broken tile) in green and gold representing palm leaves. These windows will be clear or translucent, as a symbol of purity and to admit as much light as possible.

Stained-glass windows

TORTOISES AND TURTLES
The sea tortoise on the Mediterranean side of the Portal of Hope and the land turtle on the inland Portal of Faith are said to symbolize the slow and steady stability of the cosmos and of the church. Gaudí, a nature devotee, attempted to include all elements of the natural world in his stone bible.

SAINT THOMAS IN THE BELL TOWER
Above the Passion facade, St Thomas demanding proof of Christ's resurrection (thus the expression "doubting Thomas") and perched on the bell tower is pointing to the palm of his hand asking to inspect Christ's wounds.

St. Thomas pointing to his palm

MAKING THE MOST OF YOUR TRIP

The Nativity facade

WHEN TO VISIT

To avoid crowds, come first thing in the morning. While visiting the facades, you'll spend a significant amount of time outside, so save your trip for a sunny day if possible.

WHAT TO WEAR AND BRING

Keep in mind that you're visiting a church, even if it is a top tourist destination. Leave the shorts and beach clothes at the hotel and cover bare shoulders. Bring an umbrella at any chance of rain, since you'll be outside to study the facades. It's a good idea to bring binoculars to absorb details all the way up.

TIMING

If you're just walking around the exterior, an hour or two should cover it. If you'd like to go inside to the crypt, visit the museum, and take the elevator up the towers and walk down the spiraling stairway, you'll need three to four hours.

FOR FREE

If you're looking to visit Sagrada Família on the cheap, remember this: the entire exterior, which packs the most visual punch, can be explored without spending a single Euro.

HIGHLIGHTS

The Passion facade, the Nativity facade, the Portal of Faith, the Portal of Hope, and the stained-glass windows.

BONUS FEATURES

The **museum** displays Gaudí's scale models and shows photographs of the construction. The **crypt,** which has its own entrance through the Sagrada Família's parish church on Carrer Provença, holds Gaudí's remains. For a €2 additional charge (and a 45-minute wait in line), you can take an elevator skyward to the top of the **bell towers** for spectacular city views. Walking up the towers is no longer permitted. Walking down the towers is recommended (on the Nativity facade this is the only way down), especially on the Passion facade where you can get very close to the sculpted figures.

TOURS

English-language tours of the Sagrada Família are given daily at 11 AM, 1 PM, 3 PM, and 5 PM and cost €4.

VISITOR INFORMATION

✉ Pl. de la Sagrada Família, Eixample ☎ 93/207–3031 ⊕ www.sagradafamilia.org 🎫 €11, bell tower elevator €2, audio guides €4 ⊙ Oct.–Mar., daily 9–6; Apr.–Sept., daily 9–8 Ⓜ Sagrada Família.

Above the Passion facade, a gilded Christ sits resurrected

man mounted on a donkey and another on a bicycle, reminiscent of the similar Arnau sculptures on the facade of Puig i Cadafalch's Casa Amatller on Passeig de Gràcia. ⊠ *Passeig de Sant Joan 108, Eixample* Ⓜ *Verdaguer.*

Casa Montaner i Simó–Fundació Tàpies. This former publishing house—and the city's first building to incorporate iron supports, built in 1880—has been handsomely converted to hold the work of preeminent contemporary Catalan painter Antoni Tàpies, as well as temporary exhibits. Tàpies is an abstract painter, although influenced by Surrealism, which may account for the sculpture atop the structure—a tangle of metal entitled *Núvol i cadira* (*Cloud and Chair*). The modern, airy split-level gallery also has a bookstore that's strong on Tàpies, Asian art, and Barcelona art and architecture. ⊠ *Carrer Aragó 255, Eixample* ☎ *93/487–0315* ⊕ *www.fundaciotapies.org* ⌨ *€7* ⊙ *Tues.–Sun. 10–8* Ⓜ *Passeig de Gràcia.*

OFF THE BEATEN PATH

Museu Egipci de Barcelona. Even though you came to Barcelona to study, presumably, Catalonia, not ancient Egypt, you might be making a mistake by skipping this major collection of art and artifacts. Housing what is probably Spain's most comprehensive exhibition on Egypt, this excellent museum takes advantage of state-of-the-art museological techniques that are nearly as interesting as the subject matter, which ranges from Egyptian mummies to exhibits on Cleopatra. ⊠ *Fundació Arqueòlogica Clos, Valencia 284, Eixample* ☎ *93/488–0188* ⊕ *www. fundclos.com* ⌨ *€11* ⊙ *Mon.–Sat. 10–8, Sun. 10–2; guided tour with Egyptologists Sat. at noon and 2; night visits with actors and theatrical scenes Fri. and Sat. 9:30–11 PM by reservation; tours in English Fri. at 5 or by previous reservation* Ⓜ *Passeig de Gràcia.*

Passatge Permanyer. Cutting through the middle of the block bordered by Pau Claris, Roger de Llúria, Consell de Cent, and Diputació, this charming, leafy mid-Eixample sanctuary is one of 46 *passatges* (alleys or passageways) that cut through the blocks of this gridlike area. Inspired by John Nash's neoclassical Regent's Park terraces in London (with their formal and separate town houses), Ildefons Cerdà originally envisioned many more of these utopian mid-block gardens, but Barcelona never endorsed his vision. Once an aristocratic enclave and hideaway for pianist Carles Vidiella and poet, musician, and illustrator Apel.les Mestre, Passatge Permanyer is, along with the nearby Passatge Méndez Vigo, the best of these through-the-looking-glass downtown Barcelona alleyways. ⊠ *Enter near Carrer Pau Claris 118, Eixample* Ⓜ *Passeig de Gràcia.*

GRÀCIA: RADICAL CHIC

Sightseeing
★★★☆☆
Nightlife
★★★★☆
Dining
★★★★☆
Lodging
★★☆☆☆
Shopping
★★☆☆☆

Gràcia is a state of mind. More than a neighborhood, it is a village republic that has periodically risen in armed rebellion against city, state, and country, whose jumble of streets have names (Llibertat, Fraternitat, Progrès, Venus) that suggest the ideological history of this fierce little nucleus of working-class citizens and progress. Today Gràcia has a young, hip vibe, a rolling street party well endowed with cinema, terrace cafés, and restaurants.

The site of Barcelona's first collectivized manufacturing operations (i.e., factories) provided a dangerous precedent as workers organized and developed into radical groups ranging from anarchists to feminists to Esperantists. Once an outlying town that joined the municipality of Barcelona only under duress, Gràcia attempted to secede from the Spanish state in 1856, 1870, 1873, and 1909.

Lying above the Diagonal from Carrer de Còrsega all the way up to Park Güell, Gràcia's lateral borders run along Via Augusta and Balmes to the west and Carrer de l'Escorial and Passeig de Sant Joan to the east. Today the area is filled with appealing bars and restaurants, movie theaters, and outdoor cafés—always alive and usually thronged by young couples in the throes of romantic ecstasy or agony of one kind or another. Mercé Rodoreda's famous novel *La Plaça del Diamant* (translated by the late David Rosenthal as *The Time of the Doves*) begins and ends in Gràcia's square of the same name during the August Festa Major, a festival that fills the streets with the rank-and-file residents of this always lively yet intimate little pocket of general resistance to Organized Life.

MAIN ATTRACTIONS

★ **Casa Vicens.** Antoni Gaudí's first important commission as a young architect was begun in 1883 and finished in 1885. For this house Gaudí had still not succeeded in throwing away his architect's tools, particularly the T square. The historical eclecticism (that is, borrowing freely from past architectural styles around the world) of the early Art Nouveau movement is evident in the Orientalist themes and Mudejar motifs lavished throughout the facade. The fact that the house was commissioned by a ceramics merchant may explain the use of the green ceramic tiles that turn the facade into a striking checkerboard. Casa Vicens was the first polychromatic facade to appear in Barcelona. The chemaro palm leaves decorating the gate and surrounding fence are thought to be the work of Gaudí's assistant Francesc Berenguer, while the comic iron lizards and bats oozing off the facade are Gaudí's playful version of the Gothic gargoyle. The interior (in the rare event that the owners open the house to the public) is even more surprising than the outside, with its trompe-l'oeil birds painted on the walls of the salon and the intricately Mocarabe, or Moorish-style, carved ceiling in the smoking room. Gaudi's second commission, built in 1885, was in the little town of Comillas in Santander, for the Marquès de Comillas, Antonio López y López, a shipping magnate and the most powerful man of his time. Not surprisingly, the two houses bear a striking resemblance to each other. ⊠ *Carrer de les Carolines 24–26, Gràcia* ☎ *93/488–0139* Ⓜ *Gràcia, Fontana.*

★ **Gran de Gràcia.** This central artery up through Gràcia would be a lovely stroll if the car and (worse) motorcycle din weren't so overpowering. (A tunnel would do the trick nicely.) However, many of the buildings along Gran de Gràcia are of great artistic and architectural interest, beginning with **Can Fuster,** at the bottom of Gran de Gràcia 2–4. Built between 1908 and 1911 by Palau de la Música Catalana architect Lluís Domènech i Montaner in collaboration with his son Pere Domènech i Roure, the building shows a clear move away from the chromatically effusive heights of Art Nouveau. More powerful, and somehow less superficial, than much of that style of architecture, it uses the winged supports under the balconies and the floral base under the corner tower as important structural elements instead of as pure ornamentation, as Domènech i Montaner the elder might have. As you move up Gran de Gràcia, probable Francesc Berenguer buildings can be identified at No. 15; No. 23, with its scrolled cornice; and Nos. 35, 49, 51, 61, and 77. Officially attributed to a series of architects—since Berenguer lacked a formal degree (having left architecture school to become Gaudí's "right hand")—these Moderniste masterworks have long inspired debate over Berenguer's role. Ⓜ *Fontana, Gràcia.*

★ **Mercat de la Llibertat.** This uptown version of the Rambla's Boqueria market is one of Gràcia's coziest spaces, a food market big enough to roam in and small enough to make you feel at home. Built by Francesc Berenguer between 1888 and 1893, the Llibertat market reflects, in its name alone, the revolutionary and democratic sentiment strong in Gràcia's traditionally blue-collar residents. Look for Berenguer's decorative swans swimming along the roofline and the snails surrounding Gràcia's coat of arms. ⊠ *Pl. Llibertat 27, Gràcia* ☎ *93/217–0995* ⊕ *www.bcn. es/mercatsmunicipals* ☉ *Daily 7–3* Ⓜ *Gràcia.*

Mercat de la Revolució. Officially the Abaceria Central, the market got its early name from the nearby Plaça de la Revolució de Setembre de

GETTING ORIENTED

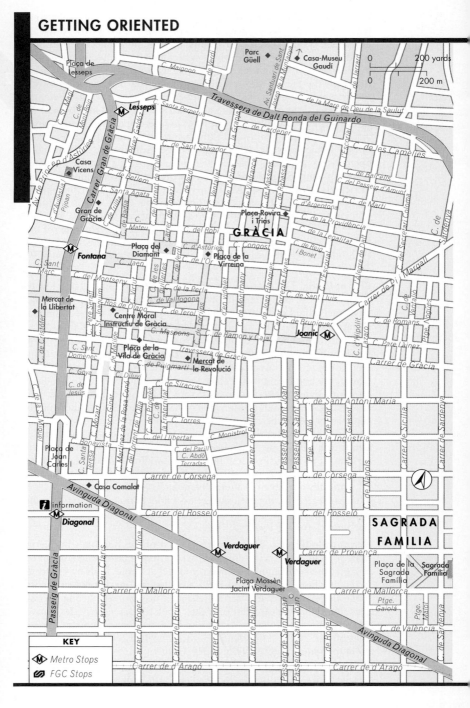

Parc Güell

Casa-Museu Gaudí

Plaça de Lesseps

0   200 yards

0   200 m

Travessera de Dalt   Ronda del Guinardó

Lesseps

C. de les Camèlies

Casa Vicens

Gran de Gràcia

Plaça Rovira i Trias

GRÀCIA

Fontana

Plaça del Diamant

Plaça de la Virreina

Mercat de la Llibertat

Centre Moral Instructiu de Gràcia

Joanic

Plaça de la Vila de Gràcia

Mercat de la Revolució

Carrer de Gràcia

Plaça de Joan Carles I

Casa Comalat

information

Diagonal

Avinguda Diagonal

Carrer del Rosselló

C. del Rosselló

SAGRADA FAMILIA

Verdaguer

Verdaguer

Plaça Mossèn Jacint Verdaguer

Carrer de Provença

Plaça de la Sagrada Família

Sagrada Família

Carrer de Mallorca

Avinguda Diagonal

Carrer de d'Aragó

Carrer de d'Aragó

KEY

Ⓜ Metro Stops

Ⓖ FGC Stops

Timing

Exploring Gràcia is a three- to four-hour outing that could take five with lunch included or an entire day to really get the full feel of the neighnborhood. Evening sessions at the popular Verdi cinema (v.o.—showing films in their original language) usually get out just in time for a late-night supper in any of a number of bars and restaurants, including Botafumeiro, which closes at 1 AM. Güell Park is best in the afternoon, when the sun spotlights the view east over the Mediterranean. Exploring Gràcia with the Llibertat and Revolució markets closed is a major loss, so plan to reach the markets before 2 PM.

Getting Here

By metro, the Gràcia stop on the FGC (Ferrocarril de la Generalitat de Catalunya) trains that connect Sarrià, Sabadell, Terrassa, and Sant Cugat with Plaça Catalunya is your best option. The metro's green line (Line 3) stops at Fontana and Lesseps drop you in the heart of Gràcia and near Park Güell, respectively. The yellow line (Line 4) stop at Joanic is a short walk from Gràcia's northeast side.

Quick Bites

The **Bar Candanchú** (⊠ *Pl. de la Vila de Gràcia 9, Gràcia* ☎ *93/237-7362* Ⓜ *Gràcia*), a refreshing stop, runs tables until early morning. For an upscale treat, **Botafumeiro** (⊠ *Gran de Gràcia 81, Gràcia* ☎ *93/218-4230* Ⓜ *Gràcia*) never disappoints; the counter is the place to be for icy Albariño white wine and *pop a feira* (octopus on potato slices with smoked paprika), a Galician favorite.

Top Attractions

Casa Vicens

Gran de Gràcia

Mercat de la Llibertat

Park Güell

Plaça de la Vila de Gràcia

Top Experiences

Browsing the Mercat de la Llibertat

Doing the classic "dinner and a movie" Barcelona-style, with the movie first and a late supper after

Exploring the Moderniste buildings on Gran de Gràcia

Sitting at an outdoor café terrace in Plaça del Sol

Walking down through Gràcia from Park Güell

Where to Eat (⇨ Ch. 3)

Bilbao

Botafumeiro

Folquer

Ipar-Txoko

Roig Robí

Happening Nightlife (⇨ Ch. 5)

Otto Zutz

Rat King Retro Lounge

Salsabor

Area Shops (⇨ Ch. 7)

Bateau Lune

BBB

Herbolari del Cel

1868 just a block away up Carrer dels Desamparats. Browse your way through, and consider having something delicious such as a plate of wild mushrooms or a *tortilla de patatas* (potato omelet) at the very good bar and restaurant at the far corner on the lower east side. ✉ *Travessera de Gràcia 186, Gràcia* ☏ *93/213–6286* ⊕ *www.bcn.es/ mercatsmunicipals (look under the official name, "Abaceria Central")* ☉ *Daily 7–3* Ⓜ *Joanic, Gràcia.*

Fodor's Choice   **Park Güell.** Güell Park is one of Gaudí's, and Barcelona's, most pleasant
★   and stimulating places to spend a few hours. Whereas Gaudí's landmark Sagrada Família can be exhaustingly bright and hot in its massive energy and complexity, Park Güell is invariably light and playful, uplifting and restorative. Alternately shady, green, floral, or sunny, the park always has a delicious corner for whatever one needs. Named for and commissioned by Gaudí's main patron, Count Eusebi Güell, it was originally intended as a hillside garden community based on the English Garden City model, centered, amazingly enough, on an open-air theater built over a covered marketplace. Only two of the houses were ever built (one of which, designed by Gaudí assistant Francesc Berenguer, became Gaudí's home from 1906 to 1926 and now houses the park's Gaudí museum). Ultimately, as Barcelona's bourgeoisie seemed happier living closer to "town," the Güell family turned the area over to the city as a public park.

An Art Nouveau extravaganza with gingerbread gatehouses topped with, respectively, the hallucinogenic red-and-white fly ammanite wild mushroom (rumored to have been a Gaudí favorite) on the right and the *phallus impudicus* (no translation necessary) on the left, Park Güell is a perfect visit for a sunny afternoon when the blue of the Mediterranean is best illuminated by the western sun. The gatehouse on the right holds the Center for the Interpretation and Welcome to Park Güell. The center has plans, scale models, photos, and suggested routes analyzing the park in detail. Other Gaudí highlights include the **Casa-Museu Gaudí** (a house in which Gaudí lived), the Room of a Hundred Columns—a covered market supported by tilted Doric-style columns and mosaic-encrusted buttresses, and guarded by a patchwork lizard— and the fabulous serpentine, polychrome bench that snakes along the main square. The bench is one of Gaudí assistant Josep Maria Jujol's most memorable creations, and one of Barcelona's best examples of the *trencadis* technique of making colorful mosaics with broken bits of tile. ✉ *Carrer d'Olot s/n; take Metro to Lesseps; then walk 10 mins uphill or catch Bus 24 to park entrance, Gràcia* ☉ *Oct.–Mar., daily 10–6; Apr.–June, daily 10–7; July–Sept., daily 10–9* Ⓜ *Lesseps.*

★   **Plaça de la Vila de Gràcia.** Originally named (until 2009) for the memorable Gràcia mayor Francesc Rius i Taulet, this is the town's most emblematic and historic square, marked by the handsome clock tower in its center. The tower, built in 1862, is just over 110 feet tall. It has public water fountains around its base, royal Bourbon crests over the fountains, and an iron balustrade atop the octagonal brick shaft stretching up to the clock and belfry. The symbol of Gràcia, the clock tower was bombarded by federal troops when Gràcia attempted to secede from the Spanish state during the 1870s. Always a workers' neighborhood

DID YOU KNOW?

Park Güell was originally built to be a private garden community. One of the houses built here became Gaudí's residence from 1906 to 1926.

and prone to social solidarity, Gràcia was mobilized by mothers who refused to send their sons off as conscripts to fight for the crumbling Spanish Imperial forces during the late 19th century, thus requiring a full-scale assault by Spanish troops to reestablish law and order. Today sidewalk cafés prosper under the leafy canopy here. The Gràcia Casa de la Vila (town hall) at the lower end of the square is yet another Francesc Berenguer opus. Ⓜ *Gràcia.*

WORTH NOTING

Casa Comalat. At the bottom of Gràcia between the Diagonal and Carrer Còrsega, this often overlooked Moderniste house (not open to the public) built in 1911 is a good one to add to your collection. For a look at the best side of this lower Gràcia Art Nouveau gem, cut down past Casa Fuster at the bottom of Gran de Gràcia, take a left on Bonavista, then a right on Santa Teresa down to Casa Comalat just across Carrer Còrsega. This Salvador Valeri i Pupurull creation is one of Barcelona's most interesting Moderniste houses, especially this side of it, with its bulging polychrome ceramic balconies and its melted wax–like underpinnings. Look for the curious wooden galleries, and check out the designer bar, SiSiSi, around on the less interesting facade at Diagonal 442. ✉ *Carrer de Còrsega 316, Gràcia* Ⓜ *Diagonal.*

Casa-Museu Gaudí. Within **Park Güell,** the museum occupies a pink, Alice-in-Wonderland house in which Gaudí lived with his niece from 1906 to 1926. Exhibits in this house museum include Gaudí-designed furniture and decorations, drawings, and portraits and busts of the architect. ✉ *Park Güell, up hill to right of main entrance, Gràcia* ☎ *93/219–3811* 💶 *€5* 🕐 *May–Sept., daily 10–8; Oct.–Feb., daily 10–6; Mar. and Apr., daily 10–7* Ⓜ *Lesseps.*

Centre Moral Instructiu de Gràcia. Another creation by Gaudí's assistant Francesc Berenguer (Gràcia is Berenguer country), this building is one of the few in Barcelona with an exposed-brick Mudejar facade. The Centre Moral Instructiu was built in 1904 and still functions as a YMCA-like cultural institution; Berenguer was its president at one time. ✉ *Carrer Ros de Olano 9, Gràcia* Ⓜ *Gràcia.*

Plaça de la Virreina. The much-punished and oft-restored church of Sant Joan de Gràcia in this square stands where the Palau de la Virreina once stood, the mansion of the same virreina (wife, in this case widow, of a viceroy) whose 18th-century palace on the Rambla (Palau de la Virreina) is now a prominent municipal museum and art gallery. The story of La Virreina, a young noblewoman widowed at an early age by the elderly viceroy of Peru, is symbolized in the bronze sculpture in the center of the square portraying Ruth (of the Old Testament), represented carrying the sheaves of wheat she was gathering when she learned of the death of her husband, Boaz. Ruth is the Old Testament paradigm of wifely faith to her husband's clan, a parallel to La Virreina's lifelong performance of good deeds with her husband's fortune.

The rectorial residence at the back of the church is the work of Gaudí's perennial assistant and right-hand man Francesc Berenguer. Just across the street, the house at Carrer de l'Or 44 was built in 1909, also by Berenguer. Giddily vertical and tightly packed into its narrow slot, it

BERENGUER: GAUDÍ'S RIGHT HAND

Francesc Berenguer's role in Gaudí's work and the Moderniste movement, despite his leaving architecture school prematurely to work for Gaudí, was significant (if not decisive), and has been much debated by architects and Art Nouveau scholars. If Barcelona was Gaudí's sandbox, Gràcia was Berenguer's. Although unlicensed to legally sign his projects, Berenguer is known to have designed nearly every major building in Gràcia, including the Mercat de la Llibertat. The house at Carrer de l'Or 44 remains one of his greatest achievements, a vertical exercise with pinnacles at the stress lines over rich stacks of wrought-iron balconies. The Gràcia Town Hall in Plaça Rius i Taulet and the Centre Moral Instructiu de Gràcia at No. 9 Carrer Ros de Olano are confirmed Berenguer houses, while the buildings on Carrer Gran de Gràcia at Nos. 15, 23, 35, 49, 51, 61, 77, and 81 are all either confirmed or suspected Berenguer designs. Even Gaudí's first house, Casa Vicens, owes its chemaro-palm-leaf iron fence to Berenguer. After Berenguer's premature death at the age of 47 in 1914, Gaudí said he had "lost his right hand." Indeed, in his last 12 years, Gaudí built nothing but the Sagrada Família and, in fact, progressed little there.

demonstrates one of his best tricks: building town houses sharing walls with adjacent construction. Ⓜ *Fontana.*

Plaça del Diamant. This little square is of enormous sentimental importance in Barcelona as the site of the opening and closing scenes of 20th-century Catalan writer Mercé Rodoreda's famous 1962 novel *La Plaça del Diamant.* Translated by the late American poet David Rosenthal as *The Time of the Doves,* it is the most widely translated and published Catalan novel of all time: a tender yet brutal story of a young woman devoured by the Spanish civil war and, in a larger sense, by life itself. A bronze statue in the square portrays Colometa, the novel's protagonist, caught in the middle of her climactic scream. The bronze birds represent the pigeons that Colometa spent her life obsessively breeding; the male figure on the left pierced by bolts of steel is Quimet, her first love and husband, whom she met at a dance in this square and later lost in the war. Ⓜ *Fontana.*

Plaça Rovira i Trias. This charming little square and the story of Antoni Rovira i Trias shed much light on the true nature of Barcelona's eternal struggle with Madrid and Spanish central authority. Take a careful look at the map of Barcelona positioned at the feet of the bronze effigy of the architect and urban planners near the center of the square and you will see a vision of what the city might have looked like if Madrid's (and the Spanish army's) candidate for the design of the Eixample in 1860, Ildefons Cerdà, had not been imposed over the plan devised by Rovira i Trias, initial and legitimate winner of the open competition for the commission. Rovira i Trias's plan shows an astral design radiating out from a central Eixample square that military minds saw as avenues of approach; Cerdà's design, on the other hand, made the Diagonal into a natural barrier. Ⓜ *Lesseps.*

UPPER BARCELONA: SARRIÀ AND PEDRALBES

Sightseeing
★★★☆☆
Nightlife
★★☆☆☆
Dining
★★★★☆
Lodging
★★★☆☆
Shopping
★★★☆☆

Sarrià was originally a medieval country village overlooking Barcelona from the foothills of the Collserola. Gradually swallowed up over the centuries by the westward-encroaching city, Sarrià has become a haven for petit-bourgeois merchants, writers, and artists, as well as a home for many Barcelona schools occupying what were once summer mansions for the city's commercial leaders.

St. Eulàlia, Barcelona's co-patroness, is always described as "the beautiful daughter of a wealthy Sarrià merchant," a reminder of Sarrià's perennially well-off citizenry. J. V. Foix, the famous Catalan poet, is an honored citizen here, his descendants the proprietors of Sarrià's two famous Foix pastry shops. Now largely a pedestrian sanctuary, Sarrià still retains much of its village atmosphere, although it is just 15 minutes by the Generalitat train from the Rambla. The miniature original town houses sprinkled through Sarrià are a reminder of the not-so-distant past, when this enclave was an even more bougainvillea-festooned eddy at the edge of Barcelona's roaring urban torrent.

Pedralbes clings to the beginnings of the Collserola hills above Sarrià, a neighborhood of mansions scattered around the 14th-century Monestir de Pedralbes (Pedralbes Monastery). Peripheral points of interest include some of Gaudí's most memorable works, including the Pavellons de la Finca Güell on Avinguda de Pedralbes, Torre Bellesguard above Plaça de Sant Gervasi, and the Teresianas convent and school. The Palau Reial de Pedralbes is a 20-minute walk downhill on the Diagonal (just behind the Finca Güell gate and the Càtedra Gaudí), while the Futbol Club Barcelona's monstrous, 98,000-seat Nou Camp sports complex and museum are another 20 minutes' walk down below the Hotel Princesa Sofia on the Diagonal.

2

MAIN ATTRACTIONS

Camp Nou. If you're in Barcelona between September and June, a chance to witness the celebrated FC Barcelona play soccer (preferably against Real Madrid, if you can get in) at Barcelona's gigantic stadium, Camp Nou, is a seminal Barcelona experience. Just the walk down to the field from the Diagonal with another hundred thousand fans walking fast and hushed in electric anticipation is unforgettable. Games are played Saturday night at 9 or Sunday afternoon at 5, though there may be international Champion's League games on Tuesday or Wednesday evenings as well. A worthwhile alternative to seeing a game is the guided tour of the FC Barcelona museum and facilities. ⊠ *Arístides Maillol, Les Corts* ☎ *93/496–3608* ⊕ *www.fcbarcelona.com* ⊠ *Museum €6; combined ticket including tour of museum, field, and sports complex €10* ☺ *Museum Mon.–Sat. 10–6:30, Sun. 10–2* Ⓜ *Collblanc, Palau Reial.*

OFF THE
BEATEN
PATH ☺

CosmoCaixa–Museu de la Ciència Fundació "La Caixa." Young scientific minds work overtime in this interactive science museum, just below Tibidabo. Among the many displays designed for children seven and up are the Geological Wall, a history of rocks and rock formations; and the Underwater Forest, showcasing a slice of the Amazonian rain forest in a large greenhouse. ⊠ *Teodor Roviralta 55, Sant Gervasi* ☎ *93/212–6050* ⊕ *www.cosmocaixa.com* ⊠ *€3.50 (€2 per interactive activity inside)* ☺ *Tues.–Sun. 10–8* Ⓜ *Avinguda de Tibidabo and Tramvia Blau at stop halfway up to Tibidabo.*

Fodor's Choice ★ **Monestir de Pedralbes.** This marvel of a monastery, named for its whitish stones (*pedres albes*), is really a convent for the Franciscan order of Poor Clares founded in 1326 by Reina Elisenda (Queen Elisenda). The three-story Gothic cloister, one of the finest in Europe, surrounds a lush garden. The day cells, where the nuns spent their mornings praying, sewing, and studying, circle the arcaded courtyard. Reina Elisenda's cell, the Capella de Sant Miquel, just to the right of the entrance, has murals painted in 1346 by Catalan master Ferrer Bassa. Look for the letters spelling out "Joan no m'oblides" (John do not forget me) scratched between the figures of St. Francis and St. Clare (with book and quill), written by a brokenhearted novice. Farther along, inscriptions over the tombs of nuns who died here can be seen through the paving grates. The nuns' upstairs dormitory contains the convent's treasures: paintings, liturgical objects, and seven centuries of artistic and cultural patrimony. Temporary exhibits are displayed in this space. The refectory where the Poor Clares dined in silence has a pulpit used for readings, while wall inscriptions exhort "Silentium" (Silence), "Audi tacens" (Listening makes you wise), and "Considera morientem" (Consider we are dying). Don't miss the fading mural in the corner or the paving tiles broken by heavy cannon during the 1809 Napoleonic occupation. ⊠ *Baixada Monestir 9, Pedralbes* ☎ *93/203–9282* ⊠ *€5.50; free 1st Sun. of month* ☺ *Oct.–May, Tues.–Sun. 10–2; June–Sept., Tues.–Sun. 10–5* Ⓜ *Reina Elisenda.*

Pavellons de la Finca Güell–Càtedra Gaudí. The former stables of the Güell family contain the Càtedra Gaudí, a Gaudí library and study center (open to all). This structure was crucial to Gaudí's architectural career as one of the three Ruta del Modernisme centers (along with Hospital de

GETTING ORIENTED

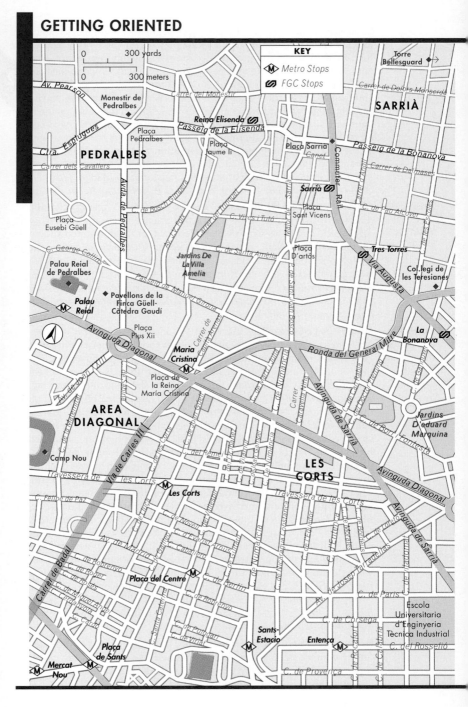

KEY

Ⓜ Metro Stops
🐚 FGC Stops

Timing

An exploration of Sarrià and Pedralbes is a three-to-four hour jaunt, including at least an hour in the monastery. Count four or five with lunch included. The Monestir de Pedralbes closes at 2 PM, so go in the morning. Bar Tomás serves its famous potatoes with *allioli* 1–4 and 7–10, another key timing consideration, while the Foix de Sarrià pastry emporium is open until 9.

Getting Here

Sarrià is best reached on the FGC (Ferrocarril de la Generalitat de Catalunya) train line, which is part of the city metro system, though a cut above. These trains leave Plaça Catalunya every few minutes, and will drop you at the Reina Elisenda or Sarrià stops in 15 minutes. Bus 64 also runs the length and width of Barcelona, from Barceloneta to Plaça Sarrià and Pedralbes.

Quick Bites

Bar Tomàs (✉ *Major de Sarrià 49, Sarrià* ☎ *93/203–1077* Ⓜ *Sarrià*), on the corner of Jaume Piquet, is a Barcelona institution, home of the finest potatoes in town. Order the famous *doble mixta* of potatoes with *allioli* and hot sauce. Draft beer (ask for a *caña*) is the de rigueur beverage.

Top Attractions

Foix pastry store

Monestir de Pedralbes

Plaça de Sarrià

Torre Bellesguard

Top Experiences

Browsing through the Sarrià market

Hiking up to the Torre de Bellesguard

Sitting in the cloister of the Pedralbes Monastery

Tucking into patatas allioli at Bar Tomás

Wandering the leafy village streets

Where to Eat (⇨ Ch. 3)

Bar Tomás

El Mató de Pedralbes

Gouthier

Tram-Tram

Vivanda

Happening Nightlife (⇨ Ch. 5)

Elephant

La Cave

Sala B

Area Shops (⇨ Ch. 7)

Foix de Sarrià

Julie Sohn

Neoceramica

Pepa Paper

Zapata Joyero

Sant Pau, and the Plaça Catalunya Tourist Office). The fierce wrought-iron dragon crafted by Gaudí is a reference to national poet Jacint Verdaguer's epic poem *L'Atlàntida,* published in 1877. To get here from Sarrià, walk through the park at the Casal de Sarrià at the western end of Vives i Tutó and the Jardins de la Vil.la Amèlia and then through Carrer Claudi Güell to Passeig Manuel de Girona to Avinguda de Pedralbes. A walk through the side entrance into the gardens of the Palau Reial de Pedralbes next door will complete a 3-km (2-mi) sylvan excursion through upper Barcelona's leafiest reaches, and leave you just a block or two from Jean-Louis Neichel's excellent and eponymous gourmet restaurant. ⊠ *Av. Pedralbes 7, Pedralbes* ☎ *93/204–5250* ◷ *Daily 9–8* Ⓜ *Sarrià, Palau Reial.*

Plaça Sarrià. The village of Sarrià was originally a cluster of farms and country houses overlooking Barcelona from the hills. Once dismissively described as "Sarrià: winds, brooks, and convents," this quiet enclave is now a haven at the upper edge of the roaring metropolis. Start an exploration at the square, which hosts an antiques and crafts market on Tuesday morning, *sardana* dances on Sunday morning, and Christmas fairs in season. The Romanesque church tower, lighted a glowing ocher at night, looms overhead. Across Passeig Reina Elisenda from the church (50 yards to the left), wander through the brick-and-steel hangar **produce market** and the tiny, flower- and bougainvillea-choked **Plaça Sant Gaietà** just behind it. For a quick tour of upper Sarrià, walk behind the market along the cobbled Carrer Pare Miquel de Sarrià to Major de Sarrià, turn uphill to the left and then right into Carrer Graus. A left on Carrer Avió Plus Ultra will take you past Sarrià's most wisteria- and ivy-covered house (on the right) and past the studio of floral artisan Flora Miserachs in the ancient village house at No. 21. Loop around to the left back into Major de Sarrià and walk back down past the tiny old village houses at Nos. 188 and 126 (the latter with the year 1694 engraved in the stone over the door) to return to Plaça Sarrià.

Cut through the Placeta del Roser to the left of the church to the elegant **town hall** in the Plaça de la Vila; note the buxom bronze sculpture of **Pomona,** goddess of fruit, by famed Sarrià sculptor Josep Clarà (1878–1958). At the corner of Major de Sarrià, go back to the Pomona bronze and turn left into tiny Carrer dels Paletes. The saint displayed in the niche is Sant Antoni, patron saint of bricklayers (*paletes*). You'll come out on Major de Sarrià. Continue down this pedestrian-only street and turn left into bougainvillea- and honeysuckle-clad **Carrer Canet,** with its diminutive, cottagelike artisans' quarters. The tiny houses at Nos. 15, 21, and 23 are some of the few remaining original village houses in Sarrià. Turn right at the first corner on Carrer Cornet i Mas and walk two blocks down to Carrer Jaume Piquet.

On the left is No. 30, Barcelona's most perfect small-format **Moderniste house,** thought to be the work of architect Domènech i Montaner, complete with faux-medieval upper windows, wrought-iron grillwork, floral and fruited ornamentation, and organically curved and carved wooden doors either by or inspired by Gaudí himself. The next stop down Cornet i Mas is Sarrià's prettiest square, **Plaça Sant Vicens,** a leafy space ringed by old Sarrià houses and centered on a statue of Sarrià's

A quiet space for reflection: the courtyard of the Monestir de Pedralbes.

patron, St. Vincent, portrayed, as always, beside the millstone used to sink him to the bottom of the Mediterranean after he was martyred in Valencia in 302. Can Pau, the café on the lower corner with Carrer Mañé i Flaquer, is the local hangout, a good place for coffee and once a haven for authors Gabriel García Marquez and Mario Vargas Llosa, who lived in Sarrià in the late 1960s and early 1970s.

Other Sarrià landmarks to look for include the two **Foix** pastry stores, one at Plaça Sarrià 9–10 and the other at Major de Sarrià 57, above Bar Tomás. Both have excellent pastries, breads, and cold *cava* (Catalan sparkling wine). The late J. V. Foix (1893–1987), son of the store's founders, was one of the great Catalan poets of the 20th century, a key player in keeping the Catalan language alive during the 40-year Franco regime. The Plaça Sarrià Foix, a good spot for homemade ice cream, has a bronze bust of the poet, whereas the Major de Sarrià location has a bronze plaque identifying the house as the poet's birthplace and inscribed with one of his most memorable verses, translated as, "Every love is latent in the other love/every language is part of a common tongue/every country touches the fatherland of all/every faith will be the essence of a higher faith." ✉ *Pl. Sarrià (take Bus 22 from the bottom of Av. de Tibidabo, or the U-6 train on the FGC subway to Reina Elisenda), Sarrià* Ⓜ *Reina Elisenda.*

Torre Bellesguard. For Gaudí to the last drop, climb up above Plaça de la Bonanova to this private residence built between 1900 and 1909 over the ruins of the summer palace of the last of the sovereign count-kings of the Catalan-Aragonese realm, Martí I l'Humà (Martin I the Humane), whose reign ended in 1410. This homage to the king has a bell arch, tower, gargoyles, and crenellated battlements that are all Gaudí winks to Gothic architecture; the catenary arches and the puzzles of *trencadis* (broken bits of stone) of colored slate on the facade and over the windows are pure Gaudí. Built of rough slate from the Collserola hills up behind the site, Torre Bellesguard blends into the background in what seems an early example of low-impact environmental design. Look for the stained-glass red and gold markings of the Catalan *senyera* (banner) on the tower, which is topped by the typical four-armed Greek cross favored by Gaudí. Over the front door is the inscription sens pecat fou concebuda (without sin was she conceived) referring to the Immaculate Conception of the Virgin Mary, while above on the facade appears a colorful Bell Esguard (beautiful view). On either side of the front door are benches with trencadis mosaics of playful fish bearing the crimson *quatre barres* (four bars) of the Catalan flag as well as the Corona d'Aragó (Crown of Aragón). Alas, the surprisingly colorful and ornate interior of the residence is rarely viewable. ⊠ *Bellesguard 16–20, Sant Gervasi* ◎ *For visits consult the Ruta del Modernisme* ☎ *93/317–7652* Ⓜ *Sarrià.*

Vallvidrera. This perched village is a quiet respite from Barcelona's headlong race. Oddly, there's nothing exclusive or upmarket—for now—about Vallvidrera, as most well-off barcelonins prefer to be closer to the center. From **Plaça Pep Ventura,** in front of the Moderniste funicular station, there are superb views over the Vallvidrera houses and the Montserrat. Vallvidrera can be reached from the Peu Funicular train stop and the Vallvidrera funicular, by road, or on foot from Tibidabo or Vil.la Joana. The cozy Can Trampa at the center of town in Plaça de Vallvidrera, and Can Martí down below are fine spots for a meal. Ⓜ *Peu Funicular.*

OFF THE BEATEN PATH ★

WORTH NOTING

Col.legi de les Teresianes. Built in 1889 for the Reverend Mothers of St. Theresa, when Gaudí was still occasionally using straight lines, this building, still a school, showcases upper floors reminiscent of those in Berenguer's apartment house at Carrer de l'Or 44, with its steep peaks and verticality. Hired to finish a job begun by another architect, Gaudí found his freedom of movement somewhat limited in this project. The dominant theme here is the architect's use of steep, narrow catenary arches and Mudejar exposed-brick pillars. The most striking effects are on the second floor, where two rows of a dozen catenary arches run the width of the building, each of them unique because, as Gaudí explained, no two things in nature are identical. The brick columns are crowned with T-shape brick capitals (for St. Theresa). Look down at the marble doorstep for the inscription by mystic writer and poet Santa Teresa de Avila (1515–82), the much-quoted TODO SE PASA (all things pass). For visits, cónsult the **Ruta del Modernisme** (☎ *93/317–7652, 902/076621 within Spain* ⊕ *www.rutadelmodernisme.com*). ⊠ *Ganduxer 85, Sant Gervasi* ☎ *93/254–1670* Ⓜ *Les Tres Torres, Sarrià.*

Palau Reial de Pedralbes *(Royal Palace of Pedralbes).* Built in the 1920s as the palatial estate of Count Eusebi Güell—one of Gaudí's most important patrons—this mansion was transformed into a royal palace by architect Eusebi Bona i Puig and completed in 1929. King Alfonso

XIII, grandfather of Spanish king Juan Carlos I, visited the palace in the mid-1920s before its completion. In 1931, during the Second Spanish Republic, the palace became the property of the municipal government, and it was converted to a decorative arts museum in 1932. In 1936 the rambling, elegant country-manor-house palace was used as the official residence of Manuel Azaña, last president of the Spanish Republic. Today the palace houses the **Museu Tèxtil i d'Indumentària** (which maintains its Carrer Montcada site for temporary exhibits), the **Museu de Ceràmica,** and the **Disseny Hub** (Design Hub), previously known as the Museu de les Arts Decoratives. ✉ *Av. Diagonal 686, Pedralbes* ☎ *93/280–5024 decorative arts museum, 93/280–1621 ceramic museum* ⊕ *www.dhub-bcn.cat* ⌦ *€5 includes both museums; free 1st Sun. of month* ⊙ *Tues.–Sat. 10–6, Sun. 10–3* Ⓜ *Palau Reial.*

OFF THE
BEATEN
PATH

Tibidabo. One of Barcelona's two promontories this hill bears a particularly distinctive name, generally translated as "To Thee I Will Give" and referring to the Catalan legend that this was the spot from which Satan tempted Christ with all the riches of the earth below (namely, Barcelona). When the wind blows the smog out to sea, the views from this 1,789-foot peak are legendary. Tibidabo's skyline is marked by a commercialized neo-Gothic church built by Enric Sagnier in 1902, a radio mast that used to seem tall, and—looking like something out of the 25th century—the 854-foot communications tower, the **Torre de Collserola,** designed by Sir Norman Foster. There's not much to see here except the vista, particularly from the tower. Clear days are few and far between in 21st-century Barcelona, but if you hit one, this two-hour excursion is worth considering. The restaurant **La Venta** (✉ *Pl. Doctor Andreu s/n, Vallvidrera* ☎ *93/212–6455*) at the base of the funicular is excellent, and a fine place to sit in the sun in cool weather (straw sun hats are provided). **El Mirador de la Venta** (✉ *Pl. Doctor Andreu s/n, Vallvidrera* ☎ *93/212–6455*) has great views and contemporary cuisine to match. The bar **Mirablau** (✉ *Pl. Doctor Andreu s/n* ☎ *93/418–5879*), overlooking the city lights, is a popular late-night hangout. ✉ *Take Tibidabo train (U-7) from Pl. de Catalunya; Buses 24 and 22 to Pl. Kennedy; or a taxi. At Av. Tibidabo, catch Tramvía Blau (Blue Trolley), which connects with the funicular to the summit* Ⓜ *Tibidabo.*

OFF THE
BEATEN
PATH

Torre de Collserola. The Collserola Tower was designed by Norman Foster for the 1992 Olympics, amid controversy over defacement of the traditional skyline. A vertigo-inducing elevator ride takes you to the observation deck. Take the funicular up to Tibidabo; from Plaza Tibidabo there is free transport to the tower. ✉ *Av. de Vallvidrera, Vallvidrera* ☎ *93/211–7942* ⌦ *€6* ⊙ *Wed.–Sun. 11–6* Ⓜ *Tibidabo.*

MONTJUÏC

Sightseeing
★★★★★
Nightlife
★★★☆☆
Dining
★★★☆☆
Lodging
☆☆☆☆☆
Shopping
★★★☆☆

This hill overlooking the south side of the port is said to have originally been named Mont Juif for the Jewish cemetery once on its slopes, though a 3rd-century Roman document referring to the construction of a road between Mons Taber (around the cathedral) and Mons Jovis (Mount of Jove) suggests that in fact the name may derive from the Roman deity Jove, or Jupiter. Regardless, Montjuïc is now Barcelona's art enclave, with nearly every painting in town hanging in the colossal Palau Nacional or the Miró Foundation.

Compared to the booming street life, the human warmth, hustle, and bustle of Barcelona, Montjuïc may feel remote, but the art and architecture concentrated around this lush promontory more than justify spending a day or two of exploring. The Miró Foundation, the Museu Nacional d'Art de Catalunya, the minimalist Mies van der Rohe Pavilion, the lush Jardins de Mossèn Cinto Verdaguer, and the gallery and auditorium CaixaFòrum (Casaramona) are all undoubtedly among Barcelona's must-see sights. The Museu Nacional d'Art de Catalunya contains what is considered the world's best collection of Romanesque murals and frescoes removed for restoration from Pyrenean chapels in the 1930's. In addition, the MNAC is the home of the Art Modern collection of impressionist and Moderniste painters, as well as an impressive Gothic collection. Other Montjuïc attractions—the fortress, the Olympic stadium, Palau Sant Jordi, and the Poble Espanyol—are interesting enough, though second-tier visits compared to options such as Park Güell and the Monestir de Pedralbes.

MAIN ATTRACTIONS

★ **CaixaFòrum.** This redbrick, neo-Mudejar Art Nouveau fortress, built to house a factory in 1911 by Josep Puig i Cadafalch (architect of Casa de les Punxes, Casa Amatller, Casa Martí, and Casa Quadras),

Architect Arata Isozaki designed the futuristic Palau Sant Jordi Sports Palace.

is a center for art exhibits, concerts, lectures, and cultural events. Well worth keeping an eye on in daily listings, Casaramona, now Caixa-Fòrum, has come back to life as one of Barcelona's hottest art venues. The restoration work is one more example of the fusion of ultramodern design techniques with traditional (even Art Nouveau) architecture. ⊠ *Av. Marquès de Comillas 6–8, Montjuïc* ☎ *93/476–8600* ⊕ *www. fundacio.lacaixa.es* ✉ *Free; charge for evening concerts* ☉ *Tues.–Sun. 10–8; later for concerts.*

Fodor's Choice
★ **Fundació Miró.** The Miró Foundation, a gift from the artist Joan Miró to his native city, is one of Barcelona's most exciting showcases of contemporary art. The airy, white building, with panoramic views north over Barcelona, was designed by Josep Lluís Sert and opened in 1975; an extension was added by Sert's pupil Jaume Freixa in 1988. Miró's playful and colorful style, filled with Mediterranean light and humor, seems a perfect match for its surroundings, and the exhibits and retrospectives that open here tend to be progressive and provocative. Look for Alexander Calder's fountain of moving mercury. Miró himself rests in the cemetery on Montjuïc's southern slopes. During the Franco regime, which he strongly opposed, Miró first lived in self-imposed exile in Paris, then moved to Majorca in 1956. When he died in 1983, the Catalans gave him a send-off amounting to a state funeral. ⊠ *Av. Miramar 71, Montjuïc* ☎ *93/443–9470* ⊕ *www.bcn.fjmiro.es* ✉ *€8* ☉ *Tues., Wed., Fri., and Sat. 10–7, Thurs. 10–9:30, Sun. 10–2:30.*

★ **Mies van der Rohe Pavilion.** One of the architectural masterpieces of the Bauhaus School, the legendary Pavelló Mies van der Rohe—the German contribution to the 1929 International Exhibition, reassembled

GETTING ORIENTED

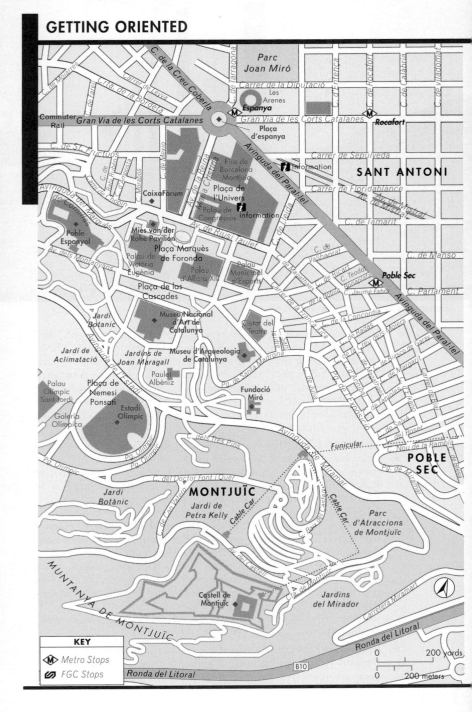

Parc Joan Miró

C. de la Creu Coberta

Carrer de la Diputació

Les Arenes

Espanya

Gran Via de les Corts Catalanes

Commuter Rail

Gran Via de les Corts Catalanes

Rocafort

Plaça d'espanya

C. de St. Fructuós

Carrer de Sepúlveda

Information

SANT ANTONI

Fira de Barcelona Montjuïc

Carrer de Floridablanca

CaixaForum

Plaça de l'Univers

Palau de Congressos

information

C. de Tamarit

Mies van der Rohe Pavilion

Poble Espanyol

Plaça Marquès de Foronda

Palau de Victoria Eugènia

C. de Vallhonrat

C. de Manso

Plaça de las Cascades

Palau d'Alfons XII

Palau Municipal d'Esports

Poble Sec

C. Parlament

Jardí Botànic

Museu Nacional d'Art de Catalunya

Ciutat del Teatre

Jardí de Aclimatació

Jardins de Joan Maragall

Museu d'Arqueologia de Catalunya

Paulet Albèniz

Palau Olímpic Sant Jordi

Plaça de Nemesi Ponsati

Fundació Miró

Galería Olímpica

Estadi Olímpic

C. dels Tres Pins

Funicular

POBLE SEC

MONTJUÏC

Jardí Botànic

Jardí de Petra Kelly

Cable Car

Cable Car

Parc d'Atraccions de Montjuïc

C. del Doctor Font I Quer

Pg. Olímpic

Pg. Olímpic

MUNTANYA DE MONTJUÏC

Castell de Montjuïc

Jardins del Mirador

Ronda del Litoral

Ronda del Litoral

B10

KEY	
M	*Metro Stops*
⊘	*FGC Stops*

0   200 yards

0   200 meters

Top Attractions

CaixaFòrum

Fundació Miró

Mies van der Rohe Pavilion

Museu Nacional d'Art de Catalunya

Timing

With unhurried visits to the Miró Foundation and any or all of the Museu Nacional d'Art de Catalunya collections in the Palau Nacional, this is a four- to five-hour excursion, if not a full day. Have lunch afterward in the Poble Espanyol just up from Mies van der Rohe's Barcelona Pavilion or in the excellent restaurant at the Fundació Miró. Even better, find your way down into the Poble Sec neighborhood east of Montjuïc and graze your way back to the Rambla.

Getting Here

The most dramatic approach to Montjuïc is the cross-harbor cable car (Transbordador Aeri) from Barceloneta or from the mid-station in the port; Montjuïc is accessed by taxi or Bus 61 (or on foot) from Plaça Espanya, or by the funicular that operates from the Paral.lel (Paral.lel metro stop, Line 3). The Telefèric de Montjuïc up from the funicular stop to the Castell de Montjuïc is the final leg to the top.

Word of Mouth

"For a change of pace, [check out] Montjuïc with the Fundació Miró and the 1992 Olympic venues, including the pools, which are public and 9 euro per day." —rbartizek

Top Experiences

Browsing through paintings at the MNAC

Cleansing your esthetic palate at the Mies van der Rohe Pavilion

Listening to Concerts in CaixaFòrum

Sampling Spain's best architecture in Poble Espanyol

Visiting the Calder mobile in the Fundació Miró

Watching the sunset from the top of the MNAC stairs

Where to Eat (⇨ Ch. 3)

Fundació Miró Café

Oleum (in MNAC)

Happening Nightlife (⇨ Ch. 5)

El Tablao de Carmen

Area Shops (⇨ Ch. 7)

CaixaFòrum gift shop

Fundació Miró gift shop

Mies van der Rohe Pavilion shop

MNAC gift shop

Poble Espanyol studios and shops

between 1983 and 1986—remains a stunning "less is more" study in interlocking planes of white marble, green onyx, and glass. In effect, it is Barcelona's aesthetic antonym (possibly in company with Richard Meier's Museu d'Art Contemporani de Barcelona, Rafael Moneo's Auditori, and the Mediterranean Gothic Santa Maria del Mar) to the hyper–Art Nouveau Palau de la Música and the city's myriad Gaudí spectaculars. Don't fail to note the matching patterns in the green onyx panels or the mirror play of the black carpet inside the pavilion with the reflecting pool outside, or the iconic Barcelona chair designed by Ludwig Mies van der Rohe (1886–1969); reproductions of the chair have graced modern interiors around the world for decades. ☒ *Av. Marquès de Comillas s/n, Montjuïc* ☎ *93/423–4016* ⊕ *www.miesbcn.com* ☒ *€4.50* ☉ *Daily 10–8.*

Fodor'sChoice
★ **Museu Nacional d'Art de Catalunya** *(MNAC; Catalonian National Museum of Art).* Housed in the imposingly domed, towered, frescoed, and columned **Palau Nacional,** built in 1929 as the centerpiece of the International Exposition, this superb museum was renovated in 1995 by Gae Aulenti, architect of the Musée d'Orsay in Paris. In 2004 the museum's three collections—Romanesque, Gothic, and the Cambó Collection, an eclectic trove, including a Goya, donated by Francesc Cambó—were joined by the 19th- and 20th-century collection of Catalan impressionist and Moderniste painters. Also now on display is the Thyssen-Bornemisza collection of early masters, with works by Zurbarán, Rubens, Tintoretto, Velázquez, and others. With this influx of artistic treasure, the MNAC becomes Catalonia's grand central museum. Pride of place goes to the Romanesque exhibition, the world's finest collection of Romanesque frescoes, altarpieces, and wood carvings, most of them rescued from chapels in the Pyrenees during the 1920s to save them from deterioration, theft, and art dealers. Many, such as the famous *Cristo de Taüll* fresco (from the church of Sant Climent de Taüll in Taüll), have been reproduced and replaced in their original settings. ☒ *Mirador del Palau 6, Montjuïc* ☎ *93/622–0360* ⊕ *www.mnac.es* ☒ *€9* ☉ *Tues.–Sat. 10–7, Sun. 10–2:30.*

WORTH NOTING

Castell de Montjuïc. Built in 1640 by rebels against Felipe IV, the castle has had a dark history as a symbol of Barcelona's military domination by foreign powers, usually the Spanish army. The fortress was stormed several times, most famously in 1705 by Lord Peterborough for Archduke Carlos of Austria. In 1808, during the Peninsular War, it was seized by the French under General Dufresne. Later, during an 1842 civil disturbance, Barcelona was bombed from its heights by a Spanish artillery battery. After the 1936–39 Spanish civil war, the castle was used as a dungeon for political prisoners. Lluís Companys, President of the Generalitat de Catalunya during the civil war, was executed by firing squad here on October 14, 1940. In 2007 the fortress was formally ceded back to Barcelona. The future uses of the space include a Interpretation Center for Peace, a Space for Historical Memory, and a Montjuïc Interpretation Center, along with cultural and educational events and activities. A popular weekend park and picnic area, the moat contains attractive gardens, with one side given over to an archery

range, and the various terraces have panoramic views over the city and out to sea. ⊠ *Ctra. de Montjuïc 66, Montjuïc* ☎ *93/329–8613* ⊕ *www. bcn.cat/castelldemontjuic* ⊠ *Free* ⊙ *Tues.–Sun. 10–8.*

★ **Estadi Olímpic.** The Olympic Stadium was originally built for the International Exhibition of 1929, with the idea that Barcelona would then host the 1936 Olympics (ultimately staged in Hitler's Berlin). After failing twice to win the nomination, the city celebrated the attainment of its long-cherished goal by renovating the semiderelict stadium in time for 1992, providing seating for 70,000. The **Galeria Olímpica,** a museum about the Olympic movement in Barcelona, displays objects and shows audiovisual replays from the 1992 Olympics. An information center traces the history of the modern Olympics from Athens in 1896 to the present. Next door and just downhill stands the futuristic **Palau Sant Jordi Sports Palace,** designed by the noted Japanese architect Arata Isozaki. The Isozaki structure has no pillars or beams to obstruct the view, and was built from the roof down—the roof was built first, then hydraulically lifted into place. ⊠ *Passeig Olímpic 17–19, Montjuïc* ☎ *93/426–2089* ⊕ *www.fundaciobarcelonaolimpica.es* ⊠ *Gallery €5* ⊙ *Tues.–Sat. 10–2 and 4–7.*

Museu d'Arqueologia de Catalunya. Just downhill to the right of the Palau Nacional, the Museum of Archaeology holds important finds from the Greek ruins at Empúries, on the Costa Brava. These are shown alongside fascinating objects from, and explanations of, megalithic Spain. ⊠ *Passeig Santa Madrona 39–41, Montjuïc* ☎ *93/424–6577* ⊕ *www. mac.es* ⊠ *€3* ⊙ *Tues.–Sat. 9:30–7, Sun. 10–2:30.*

Plaça de Espanya. This busy circle is a good place to avoid, but sooner or later you'll probably need to cross it to go to the convention center or to the Palau Nacional. It's dominated by the so-called Venetian Towers (they're actually Tuscan) built in 1927 as the grand entrance to the 1929 International Exposition. The fountain in the center is the work of Josep Maria Jujol, the Gaudí collaborator who designed the curvy and colorful benches in Park Güell. The sculptures are by Miquel Blay, one of the master artists and craftsmen who put together the Palau de la Música. The neo-Mudejar bullring, Les Arenes, is now used for theater and political rallies. On the corner of Carrer Llançà, just down to the right looking at the bullring, you can just get a glimpse of the kaleidoscopic lepidopteran atop the Art Nouveau Casa de la Papallona (House of the Butterfly). From the plaza, you can take the metro or Bus 38 back to the Plaça de Catalunya.

☉ **Poble Espanyol.** Created for the 1929 International Exhibition as a sort of artificial Spain-in-a-bottle, with faithful reproductions of Spain's various architectural styles punctuated with boutiques, workshops, and studios, the Spanish Village takes you from the walls of Ávila to the wine cellars of Jerez de la Frontera. The liveliest time to come is at night, and a reservation at one of the half-dozen restaurants gets you in for free, as does the purchase of a ticket for the two discos or the Tablao del Carmen flamenco club. ⊠ *Av. Marquès de Comillas s/n, Montjuïc* ☎ *93/508–6300* ⊕ *www.poble-espanyol.com* ⊠ *€7.50* ⊙ *Mon. 9–8, Tues.–Thurs. 9–2, Sat. 9–4, Sun. 9–noon.*

Where to Eat

WORD OF MOUTH

"I'm not sure this counts as 'off the beaten path,' but our favorite meal in Barcelona was at a tapas spot called Cal Pep. Lots of locals, very small. Not unusual to stand in line for a little while to get in."

—pacman57

By George
Semler

Barcelona's restaurant scene is an ongoing adventure. Between avant-garde culinary innovation and the more rustic dishes of traditional Catalan fare, there is a fleet of brilliant classical chefs producing some of Europe's finest Mediterranean cuisine.

Catalans are legendary lovers of fish, vegetables, rabbit, duck, lamb, game, and natural ingredients from the Pyrenees or the Mediterranean. The *mar i muntanya* (literally, "sea and mountain"—that is, surf and turf) is a standard. Rabbit and prawns, cuttlefish and meatballs, chickpeas and clams are just a few examples. Combining salty and sweet tastes—a Moorish legacy—is another common theme, as in duck with pears, rabbit with figs, or lamb with olives.

The Mediterranean diet, based on olive oil, seafood, fibrous vegetables, onions, garlic, and red wine, is at home in Barcelona, embellished by Catalonia's four basic sauces—*allioli* (whipped garlic and olive oil), *romescu* (almonds, hazelnuts, tomato, garlic, and olive oil), *sofregit* (fried onion, tomato, and garlic), and *samfaina* (a ratatouille-like vegetable mixture).

Typical entrées include *habas a la catalana* (a spicy broad-bean stew), *bullabesa* (fish soup-stew), and *espinacas a la catalana* (spinach cooked with oil, garlic, pine nuts, raisins, and bits of bacon). Toasted bread is often doused with olive oil and spread with squeezed tomato to make *pa amb tomaquet,* delicious on its own or as a side order.

Barcelona may have more bars and cafés per capita than any other place in the world. Cafés serve an important function: outdoor living room, meeting place, and giant cocktail party to which everyone is invited. Be advised: the sidewalk cafés along the Rambla are noisy, dusty, overpriced, and overexposed to thieves and pickpockets. Bars and cafés close at varying hours, though most of the hot spots in and around the Born are good until about 2:30 AM.

■**TIP→** Menús del día (menus of the day), served only at lunchtime, are good values.

WHERE TO EAT PLANNER

Eating Out Strategy

The selection here represents the best this city has to offer—from tapas bars to haute cuisine. Search "Best Bets" for top recommendations by price, cuisine, and experience. Or find a review quickly in the alphabetical listings by neighborhood.

Using the Maps

Throughout the chapter, you'll see mapping symbols and coordinates (✛ F2) at the end of the reviews that correspond to the atlas the end of this chapter. The letter and number after the ✛ symbol indicates the property's coordinates on the map grid.

Hours

Barcelona dines late. Lunch is served 2–4 and dinner 9–11. If you arrive a half-hour early, you may score a table but miss the life and fun of the place. Restaurants serving continuously 1 PM–1 AM are rarely the best ones. (Botafumeiro is an exception.) Hunger attacks between meals are easily resolved in the city's numerous cafés and tapas bars.

Tipping and Taxes

Tipping, though common, is not required; the gratuity is included in the check. If you do tip as an extra courtesy, anywhere from 5% to 10% is perfectly acceptable. No one seems to care much about tipping, though all parties seem to end up happier if a small gratuity is left.

The 7% Value Added Tax (IVA) will not appear on the menu, but is tacked onto the final tally on your check.

Reservations

Nearly all of Barcelona's best restaurants require reservations. As the city has grown in popularity, more and more receptionists are perfectly able to take your reservations in English. Your hotel concierge will also be happy to call and reserve you a table. Beware of taxi drivers and hotel receptionists who try to send you to other restaurants they claim are better.

Prices

Barcelona is no longer a bargain. Whereas fixed lunch menus can be found for as little as €10, most good restaurants cost closer to €30 to €40 ordering à la carte. For serious evening dining, plan on spending €45–€75 per person, the most expensive places costing upward of €80. For a better deal, Barcelona restaurants, even many of the pricey establishments, offer a daily lunchtime menu (*menú del día*) consisting of two courses plus wine, coffee, or dessert.

WHAT IT COSTS IN EUROS				
¢	$	$$	$$$	$$$$
Under €10	€10–€14	€15–€22	€23–€29	Over €29

Prices are per person for a median main course or equivalent combination of smaller dishes at dinner.

A Primer on Barcelona's Cuisine

Menus in Catalan are as musical as they are aromatic, with rare ingredients such as *salicornia* (seawort, or sea asparagus) with *bacalao* (cod) or fragrant wild mushrooms such as *rossinyols* (chanterelles) and *moixernons* (field agaric) accompanying dishes such as *mandonguilles amb sepia* (meatballs with cuttlefish).

Four sauces grace the Catalan table: *sofregit* (fried onion, tomato, and garlic—a base for nearly everything); *samfaina* (a ratatouille-like sofregit with eggplant and sweet red peppers); *picada* (garlic, almonds, bread crumbs, olive oil, pine nuts, parsley, saffron, or chocolate); and *allioli* (pounded garlic and virgin olive oil).

The three *e*'s deserve a place in any Catalan culinary anthology: *escalivada* (roasted red peppers, eggplants, and tomatoes served in garlic and olive oil); *esqueixada* (shredded salt-cod salad served raw with onions, peppers, olives, beans, olive oil, and vinegar); and *escudella* (a winter stew of meats and vegetables with noodles and beans).

Universal specialties are *pa amb tomaquet* (toasted bread with squeezed tomato and olive oil), *espinaques a la catalana* (spinach cooked with raisins, garlic, and pine nuts), and *botifarra amb mongetes* (pork sausage with white beans). The *mar i muntanya* (Catalan surf and turf) has been a standard since Roman times. Rice dishes are simply called *arròs*, and range from standard seafood paella to the *arròs a banda* (paella with shelled prawns, shrimp, and mussels), to *arròs negre* (paella cooked in cuttlefish ink), to *fideuà* (paella made of vermicelli noodles) or *arròs caldoso* (a brothy risotto-like dish made with lobster).

Fresh fish such as *llobarro* (sea bass, *lubina* in Spanish) or *dorada* (gilthead bream) cooked *a la sal* (in a shell of salt) are standards, as are grilled *llenguado* (sole) and *rodaballo* (turbot). Duck, goose, chicken, and rabbit frequent Catalan menus, as do *cabrit* (kid or baby goat), *xai* (lamb), *llom* (pork), and *bou* (beef). Finally, come the two Catalan classic desserts, *mel i mató* (honey and fresh cream cheese) and *crema catalana* (a crème brûlée, custard with a caramelized glaze).

A typical session *à table* in Barcelona might begin with *pica-pica* (hors d'oeuvres), a variety of delicacies such as *jamón ibérico de bellota* (acorn-fed ham), *xipirones* (baby squid), *pimientos de Padrón* (green peppers, some piquante), or *bunyols de bacallà* (cod fritters or croquettes), and *pa amb tomaquet* (bread with tomato). From here you can order a starter such as *canelones* (cannelloni) or you can go straight to your main course.

In This Chapter

3

Wines to Watch for

Wines from Catalonia's 10 DO (denominación de origen) wine-growing zones begin at the Penedès region just west of Barcelona, famous for *cava*, the local *méthode champenoise* sparkling wine. Bottles to look for include reds such as Gran Caus, Coronas, Gran Coronas, Raimat, Oliver Conti, Can Feixes, and all of the Priorats; whites such as Costers del Segre, Raimat Chardonnay, Abadal Picapoll, Gran Viña Sol, and Marques de Alella; or cavas including bruts and brut naturs from Agustí Torelló, Gramona, and Juvé & Camps Reserva de la Familia.

BEST BETS
FOR BARCELONA DINING

Need a cheat sheet for Barcelona's thousands of restaurants? Our Fodor's writer has selected some of his favorites by price, cuisine, and experience in the lists shown here. You can also search by neighborhood or find specific details about a restaurant in our full reviews—just peruse the following pages. Happy dining in Catalonia's capital by the sea. ¡Bon profit!

Fodor'sChoice ★

Àbac, $$$$, p. 175
Botafumeiro, $$$$, p. 171
Ca l'Isidre, $$$, p. 151
Cal Pep, ¢, p. 148
Can Fabes, $$$, p. 176
Can Majó, $$, p. 154
Casa Leopoldo, $$$, p. 151
Cinc Sentits, $$, p. 158
Comerç 24, $$$, p. 148
Drolma, $$$$, p. 159
Manairó, $$$, p. 161
Neichel, $$$$, p. 174
Sant Pau, $$$$, p. 176
Silvestre, $, p. 174
Tapioles 53, $$, p. 152
Tram-Tram, $$$, p. 175

By Price

¢

Ca l'Estevet, p. 151
Cal Pep, p. 148

$

Agut, p. 144
Can Manel la Puda, p. 154
El Mató de Pedralbes, p. 173
Folquer, p. 171
Silvestre, p. 174

$$

Café de l'Acadèmia, p. 144
Can Majó, p. 154
Cinc Sentits, p. 158
Cometacinc, p. 144
La Taxidermista, p. 151
Suquet de l'Almirall, p. 156
Tapioles 53, p. 152
Vivanda, p. 175

$$$

Ca l'Isidre, p. 151
Can Fabes, p. 176
Casa Leopoldo, p. 151
Comerç 24, p. 148
Manairó, p. 161
Tram-Tram, p. 175

$$$$

Àbac, p. 175
Botafumiero, p. 171
Can Gaig, p. 157
Drolma, p. 159
Neichel, p. 174
Sant Pau, p. 176

By Cuisine

BASQUE

Ipar-Txoko, p. 172
Taktika Berri, p. 162

CAFÉS

Café de la Princesa, p. 147
Café Paris, p. 156
Café Viena, p. 150
Dole Café, p. 173
Els Quatre Gats, p. 145
La Cerería, p. 145
Schilling, p. 146
Venus, p. 147

CONTEMPORARY CATALAN

Àbac, p. 175
Andaira, p. 153
L'Olivé, p. 160
Sant Pau, p. 176

LA NUEVA COCINA/ EXPERIMENTAL CUISINE

Alkimia, p. 156
Cinc Sentits, p. 158
Comerç 24, p. 148
Manairó, p. 161
Tapioles 53, p. 152

MEDITERRANEAN

Neichel, p. 174
Can Gaig, p. 157
Ca l'Isidre, p. 151
Sant Pau, p. 176
Cinc Sentits, p. 158

PAELLA

Barceloneta, p. 153
Can Majó, p. 154
Suquet de l'Almirall, p. 156

SEAFOOD

Antiga Casa Solé, p. 153
Botafumeiro, p. 171
El Lobito, p. 154
Fishhh!, p. 173

STEAK HOUSE

El Asador de Aranda, p. 175
Gorría, p. 159

TAPAS

Cal Pep, p. 148
Casa Lucio, p. 157
El Vaso de Oro, p. 154
Inòpia Clàssic Bar, p. 159
Mantequeria Can Ravell, p. 161
Sagardi, p. 162
Tapaç 24, p. 162

TRADITIONAL CATALAN

Antiga Casa Solé, p. 153
Ca l'Isidre, p. 151
Can Gaig, p. 157
Casa Leopoldo, p. 151
Drolma, p. 159
Hispania, p. 176
Neichel, p. 174
Tram-Tram, p. 175

TRADITIONAL SPANISH

El Asador de Aranda, p. 175

By Experience

BEST BANG FOR YOUR BUCK

Barceloneta, p. 153
Cal Pep, p. 148
Silvestre, p. 174
Vivanda, p. 175

CHILD-FRIENDLY

Can Majó, p. 154
Can Manel, p. 154

GOOD FOR GROUPS

Cometacinc, p. 144
Can Majó, p. 154
Can Manel, p. 154

GREAT VIEW

Torre d'Altamar, p. 156
Can Majó, p. 154
Dos Cielos, p. 158

HISTORIC INTEREST

Ca l'Isidre, p. 151
Café de l'Opera, p. 150
Can Culleretes, p. 151
Casa Calvet, p. 157
Els Quatre Gats, p. 145
Espai Barroc, p. 149
La Cerería, p. 145
La Palma, p. 146
Sagardi, p. 150

HOTEL DINING

Drolma, p. 159
Can Gaig, p. 157
Lasarte, p. 160

LATE-NIGHT DINING

Agua, p. 153
Botafumeiro, p. 171
Ciudad Condal, p. 158
Petit Comité, p. 162
Tragaluz, p. 162

QUAINT AND COZY

Agut, p. 144
Antiga Casa Solé, p. 153
Ca l'Estevet, p. 151
Casa Lucio, p. 157

SUMMER DINING

Can Majó, p. 154
Tram-Tram, p. 175
Vivanda, p. 175

SPECIAL OCCASION

Àbac, p. 175
Ca l'Isidre, p. 151
Can Fabes, p. 176
Can Gaig, p. 157
Comerç 24, p. 148
Drolma, p. 159
Manairó, p. 161
Tram-Tram, p. 175

YOUNG AND HAPPENING

Cinc Sentits, p. 158
Comerç 24, p. 148
Manairó, p. 161
Nonell, p. 146

3

TAPAS, PINCHOS, MONTADITOS, AND OTHER BITE-SIZED FOOD

Barcelona arrived late on the tapas scene, which originated in Andalusia and flourished in the Basque Country, but once Catalans figured out that there was gold in those little morsels, they were embraced with abandon.

Tapas themselves, a small morsel or hors d'oeuvre, derived their moniker from the verb *tapar*, meaning "to cover." These little bites do cover a wide range of dining, from individual bites on toothpicks to steaming earthenware pots of stick-to-your-ribs creations served in small portions to be shared among friends. An evening weaving from one tapas bar to the next is a dining adventure in Barcelona, and it needn't preclude a late dinner.

A BRIEF HISTORY

Tapas owe much to the Moorish presence on the Iberian Peninsula. The Moorish taste for small and varied delicacies has become Spain's best-known culinary innovation. The term *tapa* itself is said to have come from pieces of ham or cheese laid across glasses of wine to keep flies out and stage-coach drivers sober.

Spanish king Alfonso X (1221–1284) took small morsels with wine on doctor's advice and so enjoyed the cure that he made it a regular practice in his court. Miguel de Cervantes, in his universal classic, *Don Quixote,* refers to tapas as *llamativos* (attention getters), for their stimulating properties.

TAPAS 101

Just belly up to the bar, order a beverage, and dig in. Usually, you will receive a plate for staging your tapas and collecting your toothpicks, which is how the bartender will tally up your bill. It's a good idea to wait to see what comes out of the kitchen piping hot. Avoid bready or puddinglike offerings put upon the bar.

The term *tapas* covers various forms of small-scale nibbling. *Tentempiés* are "keep you on your feet" snacks. *Pinchos* are bite-size offerings impaled on toothpicks; *banderillas* are similar, wrapped in colorful paper resembling the batons used in bullfights. *Montaditos* are canapés, delicacies "mounted" on toast; *raciones* (rations, or servings) are hot tapas served in small earthenware casseroles.

A few delicious tapas to try: *calamares* (fried cuttlefish, often mistaken for onion rings), *pulpo a feira* (octopus on slices of potato), *chistorra* (fried spicy sausage), *champiñones* (mushrooms), *gambas al ajillo* (shrimp cooked in parsley, oil, and garlic), *langostinos* (jumbo shrimp or prawns), *pimientos de Padrón* (peppers from the Galician town of Padrón).

TAPAS AROUND TOWN

3 QUICK BITES
Relax and refuel at one of these neighborhood haunts.

Café Viena (✉ *Rambla 115*, ☎ *93/317–1492*) serves a memorable *flauta de jamón ibérico* (a thin loaf of fresh-made bread with acorn-fed Ibérico ham) and a *caña* (draft beer) that never fails to be cold and refreshing.

Sagardi (✉ *Argenteria 62*, ☎ *93/319–9993*) is a cider house with colorful Basque *pintxos* (pinchos) on toothpicks arranged along the long bar. The cider is too sweet for more than a glass, but the Txakoli is tart and ideally bracing in any weather.

Bar Tomàs (✉ *Major de Sarrià 49*, ☎ *93/203–1077*) serves the best patatas bravas with alioli in Barcelona (and, in all certainty, the world). The draft beer is light, freezing, and perfect.

3

BARCELONA, TAPAS, AND $$

Catalonia was always too busy making and marketing things to have any time for tapas or the leisurely lifestyle that comes with wandering from bar to bar grazing on small portions—that is until the tourist industry made it clear that tapas were profitable. Curiously, what began as a lagniappe provided gratis with drinks only made sense in Catalonia when attached to a price tag. Barcelona, once nearly barren of quality tapas opportunities, presently boasts some of Spain's finest and most creative miniature cuisine.

WORD OF MOUTH
"Tapas bars/taverns in Barcelona are a constantly evolving creature and somewhat different from what you will find in Madrid and in the Basque country, where tapas are called pintxos. And no, they are not like 'appetizers.' Most are like haute cuisine."

—Robert2533

RESTAURANT REVIEWS

Listed alphabetically within neighborhoods

CIUTAT VELLA (OLD CITY)

BARRI GÒTIC

$–$$
CATALAN
✕ **Agut.** Wainscoting and 1950s canvases are the background for the mostly Catalan crowd in this homey restaurant in the lower reaches of the Gothic Quarter. Agut was founded in 1924, and its popularity has never waned—after all, hearty Catalan fare at a fantastic value is always in demand. In season (September–May), try the *pato silvestre agridulce* (sweet-and-sour wild duck). There's a good selection of wine, but no frills such as coffee or liqueur. ⊠ *Gignàs 16, Barri Gòtic* ☎ *93/315–1709* ▤ *AE, MC, V* ⊗ *Closed Mon. and July. No dinner Sun.* Ⓜ *Jaume I* ✛ *I:13.*

$–$$
CATALAN
✕ **Ateneu Restaurant.** Specializing in country cuisine from northern Catalonia's volcanic Garrotxa region, this clean-lined dining room stressing glass and wood in the entryway to Barcelona's Ateneu (the cultural and literary club) is a find. Near the top of the Rambla and overlooking Plaça Vila de Madrid, favorites here include traditional recipes based on duck, goose, rabbit, and lamb. ⊠ *Canuda 6, Barri Gòtic* ☎ *93/318–5238* ▤ *AE, DC, MC, V* ⊗ *Closed Sun.* Ⓜ *Catalunya* ✛ *H:12.*

$$
CATALAN
✕ **Café de l'Acadèmia.** With wicker chairs, stone walls, and background classical music, this place is sophisticated-rustic, and the excellent contemporary Mediterranean cuisine specialties such as *timbal d'escalibada amb formatge de cabra* (roast vegetable salad with goat cheese) or *crema de pastanaga amb gambes i virutes de parmesá* (cream of carrot soup with shrimp and Parmesan cheese shavings) make it more than a mere café. Politicians and functionaries from the nearby Generalitat frequent this dining room, which is always boiling with life. Be sure to reserve at lunchtime. ⊠ *Lledó 1, Barri Gòtic* ☎ *93/319–8253* ▤ *AE, DC, MC, V* Ⓜ *Jaume I* ✛ *I:13.*

$$
CATALAN
✕ **Cometacinc.** This stylish place in the Barri Gòtic, an increasingly chic neighborhood of artisans and antiquers, is a fine example of Barcelona's new-over-old architecture and interior design panache. Although the 30-foot floor-to-ceiling wooden shutters are already a visual feast, the carefully prepared interpretations of old standards such as the *carpaccio de toro de lidia* (carpaccio of fighting bull) with basil sauce and pine nuts, awaken the palate brilliantly. The separate dining room, for anywhere from a dozen to two dozen diners, is a perfect place for a private party. ⊠ *Carrer Cometa 5, Barri Gòtic* ☎ *93/310–1558* ▤ *AE, DC, MC, V* ⊗ *Closed Tues.* Ⓜ *Jaume I* ✛ *I:13.*

$$–$$$
ECLECTIC
✕ **Cuines Santa Caterina.** A lovingly restored market designed by the late Enric Miralles and completed by his widow Benedetta Tagliabue provides a spectacular setting for one of the city's most original dining operations. Under the undulating wooden superstructure of the market, the breakfast and tapas bar, open from dawn to midnight, offers a variety of culinary specialties cross-referenced by cultures (Mediterranean, Asian) and products (pasta, rice, fish, meat), all served on sleek counters and long wooden tables. ⊠ *Av. Francesc Cambó, Barri*

Gòtic ☎ 93/268–9918 ⊟ *AE, DC, MC, V* Ⓜ *Catalunya, Liceu, Jaume I* ✛ *J:12.*

$$ ✕ **Dos Palillos.** After ten years as the chief cook and favored disciple
ASIAN of the pioneer chef Ferran Adrià, Albert Raurich has opened an Asian
fusion restaurant with a Spanish-Mediterranean touch. Past the typi-
cal Spanish bar in the front room, the designer space inside stresses
rich black surfaces around the kitchen, where an international staff of
Japanese, Chinese, Colombian, and Scottish cooks do show-cooking
performances of Raurich's eclectic assortment of tastes and textures.
Fetge de rap al vapor (vapor-cooked hake liver), dumplings, *dim sum,
and ventresca de tonyina* (tuna belly) vie for space on the €45 and €60
tasting menus. ⊠ *Elisabets 9, Eixample* ☎ 93/304–0513 ⊟ *AE, DC,
MC, V* ☺ *Closed Sun., no dinner Mon.* Ⓜ *Catalunya, Liceu* ✛ *H:11.*

¢–$ ✕ **El Bitxo.** An original wine list and ever-rotating choices of interesting
TAPAS cava selections accompany creative tapas and small dishes from foie
(duck or goose liver) to Ibérico hams and cheeses, all in a rustic wooden
setting 50 yards from the Palau de la Música, close enough for inter-
missions. ⊠ *Verdaguer i Callis 9, Sant Pere* ☎ 93/268–1708 ☺ *Daily
7 PM–12 PM* Ⓜ *Catalunya* ✛ *I:12.*

¢–$ ✕ **El Irati.** There's only one drawback to this lively Basque bar between
TAPAS Plaça del Pi and the Rambla: it's narrow at the street end and harder to
squeeze into than the Barcelona metro at rush hour. Try coming on the
early side at 1 PM or 7:30 PM. The tapas—skip the ones on the bar and
opt for the plates brought out piping hot from the kitchen—should be
accompanied by a freezing and refreshing txakolí. The dozen tables in
the back are surprisingly relaxed and crowd-free, and serve excellent
Basque cuisine. ⊠ *Cardenal Casañas 17, Barri Gòtic* ☎ 93/302–3084
☺ *Tues.–Sat. noon–midnight, Sun. noon–4* Ⓜ *Liceu* ✛ *H:12.*

¢–$ ✕ **Els Quatre Gats.** A mythical artists' café, this is where Picasso had his
CAFÉ first exhibition in 1899. Surrounded by colorful Toulouse Lautrec–like
paintings by Russinyol and Casas, the café offers variations of *pa tor-
rat* (slabs of country bread with tomato, olive oil, and anything from
anchovies to cheese to cured ham or omelets), while the restaurant
serves the full gamut of fish and meat dishes. The building itself, Casa
Martí (1896), by Moderniste master Josep Puig i Cadafalch with sculp-
tural detail by Eusebi Arnau, is the best treat of all. ⊠ *Montsió 3, Barri
Gòtic* ☎ 93/302–4140 ☺ *Daily 8 AM–1 AM* Ⓜ *Catalunya* ✛ *I:12.*

$$ ✕ **Koy Shunka.** Two blocks away from their mothership Shunka, part-
JAPANESE ners Hideki Matsuhisa and Xu Changchao have done it again. This
time, with more space to work with, the Japanese-Chinese team of
master chefs has organized a tribute to Asian fusion cooking based on
products from the Catalan larder. *Berberechos en salsa de sake* (cockles
in sake sauce), *cerdo ibérico con ciruela* (Ibñerico pork with plums), and
ventresca de atun (tuna belly with grated tomato and lemon) are several
of the infinite variations on the Asia meets Catalonia theme in this sleek,
contemporary setting. ⊠ *Copons 7, Barri Gòtic* ☎ 93/412–7939 ⊟ *AE,
DC, MC, V* Ⓜ *Liceu* ✛ *I:12.*

¢–$ ✕ **La Cerería.** At the corner of Baixada de Sant Miquel and Passatge de
CAFÉ Crèdit, this ramshackle little terrace and café has a charm all its own.
The tables in the Passatge itself are shady and breezy in summer, and

cuisine is light and Mediterranean; look for the plaque at No. 4 commemorating the birth there of Catalan painter Joan Miró (1893–1983). ⊠ *Baixada de Sant Miquel 3–5, Barri Gòtic* ☎ *93/301–8510* ⊙ *Daily 10* AM*–1* AM Ⓜ *Liceu* ✢ *H:13.*

¢–$ ✗ **La Palma.** Behind the Plaça Sant Jaume's *ajuntament* (city hall), toward
TAPAS the post office, sits this cozy and ancient café with marble tables, wine barrels, sausages hanging from the ceiling, and newspapers to linger over. An old favorite of early-20th-century artists ranging from Salvador Dalí to Pablo Picasso, this rustic space staunchly retains its antique charm while the rest of the city relentlessly redesigns itself. ⊠ *Palma Sant Just 7, Barri Gòtic* ☎ *93/315–0656* ⊙ *Daily 8* AM*–3* PM *and 7–10* PM Ⓜ *Jaume I* ✢ *I:13.*

$$ ✗ **La Xina.** The Catalanized spelling says it all: Mediterranean-Chinese
ASIAN fusion is what this attractive designer space on the Rambla is all about. That said, the black silk–clad staffers are fast and smart, and while the dim sum might not please a Cantonese purist, the wonton soup, the lacquered pork chops, and the garlic rice wrapped in a banana leaf are all delicious. Open every day of the year, la Xina offers a 15-euro lunch menu that is a top value in an iconic location on the Rambla in the corner of the Hotel 1898. ⊠ *Pintor Fortuny 3, Rambla* ☎ *93/342–9628* ▭ *AE, DC, MC, V* Ⓜ *Catalunya* ✢ *H:12.*

$$–$$$ ✗ **Nonell.** With cosmopolitan cuisine and the polished and polyglot ser-
ECLECTIC vice to go with it, this relatively recent addition to the city's gastronomic scene is succeeding well. Dishes range from classic Mediterranean to Castilian roast suckling pig to Middle Eastern creams and sauces. The wine list is largely original, featuring labels you may never have heard of but will be glad to get to know; service is impeccable—and often delivered in perfect English. ⊠ *Pl. Isidre Nonell, Barri Gòtic* ☎ *93/301–1378* ▭ *AE, DC, MC, V* Ⓜ *Catalunya, Liceu* ✢ *I:12.*

$–$$ ✗ **Pla.** Filled with young couples night after night, this combination
CATALAN music, drinking, and dining place is candlelit and sleekly designed in glass over ancient stone, brick, and wood. The cuisine is light and contemporary, featuring inventive salads and fresh seafood. Open until 3 AM (kitchen open until 1) on Friday and Saturday, Pla is a good postconcert option. ⊠ *Carrer Bellafila 5, Barri Gòtic* ☎ *93/412–6552* ▭ *AE, DC, MC, V* ⊙ *Closed Tues. No lunch* Ⓜ *Jaume I* ✢ *I:13.*

¢–$ ✗ **Schilling.** Near Plaça Reial, Schilling always seems to be packed to the
CAFÉ point where you might have some difficulty getting a table. Home to an international set of merry visitors and cruising barcelonins winding up for the club scene that officially begins after 1 AM, this is a good place for coffee by day, drinks and tapas by night. ⊠ *Ferran 23, Barri Gòtic* ☎ *93/317–6787* ⊙ *Daily 10* AM*–2* AM Ⓜ *Liceu* ✢ *H:13.*

$$ ✗ **Shunka.** Widely regarded as Barcelona's finest Japanese restaurant,
JAPANESE this cozy hideaway behind the Hotel Colón serves straight across the counter from the burners to the diners. Mediterranean and Japanese cuisines have much in common (such as raw fish dishes); at Shunka the Asian-European fusion creations are peerlessly crafted and wholly delectable. ⊠ *Sagristans 5, Barri Gòtic* ☎ *93/412–4991* ⌦ *Reservations essential* ▭ *AE, DC, MC, V* Ⓜ *Liceu* ✢ *I:12.*

Picasso's first exhibition was in the artists' café Els Quatre Gats.

¢–$ ✕ **Taberne Les Tapes.** Proprietors and chefs Barbara and Santi offer a spe-
TAPAS cial 10-selection tapas anthology at this narrow, cozy, cheery place, just
behind the town hall and just seaward of Plaça Sant Jaume. Barbara,
originally from Worcestershire, England, takes especially good care of
visitors from abroad. ✉ *Pl. Regomir 4, Barri Gòtic* ☎ *93/302–4840*
☉ *Mon.–Sat. 9 AM–midnight; closed Aug.* Ⓜ *Jaume I* ✢ *I:14.*

¢–$ ✕ **Taller de Tapas.** Next to Plaça del Pi, facing the eastern side of Santa
TAPAS Maria del Pi, this tapas specialist has it all: cheery young staff, tradi-
tional Catalan dishes in single-bite format, and service from midday
to midnight. Another branch of Taller de Tapas at Argenteria 51 near
Santa Maria del Mar is equally good. ✉ *Pl. de Sant Josep Oriol 9, Barri
Gòtic* ☎ *93/302–6243* ☉ *Daily noon–midnight* Ⓜ *Liceu* ✢ *J:13.*

¢–$ ✕ **Venus.** Pivotally placed on the corner of Comtessa de Sobradiel, Escu-
CAFÉ dellers, and Avinyó in the Barri Gòtic, this cozy delicatessen, restaurant,
and café has an ideal location. The window overlooking Comtessa de
Sobradiel seems perfectly designed for reading, writing, and people-
watching in the best tradition of sidewalk cafés. ✉ *Avinyó 25, Barri
Gòtic* ☎ *93/301–1585* ☉ *Daily 9 AM–2 AM* Ⓜ *Liceu* ✢ *I:13.*

BORN-RIBERA

¢–$ ✕ **Café de la Princesa.** One street in behind Carrer Montcada and the
CAFÉ Picasso Museum, this little boutique, restaurant, and café is a unique
space dedicated to design, crafts, books, and wine and food tastings. The
ancient exposed-brick walls and cozy nooks in this lovely spot merit a
visit. ✉ *Flassaders 21, Born-Ribera* ☎ *93/268–2181* ☉ *Daily 9 AM–2 PM
and 4:30 PM–8 PM* Ⓜ *Jaume I* ✢ *J:13.*

¢–$ ✗ **Cal Pep.** Cal Pep is in permanent feeding frenzy and has been this way
TAPAS   for 30 years. Two minutes' walk east from Santa Maria del Mar, Pep's
Fodor'sChoice has Barcelona's best selection of tapas, cooked and served hot over the
★   counter. For budget reasons, avoid ordering a fish dish (unless you are
willing to part with an extra €35–€50), and stick with green peppers,
fried artichokes, garbanzos and spinach, baby shrimp, the "trifasic"
(mixed tiny fish fry), the nonpareil *tortilla de patatas* (potato omelette),
and *botifarra trufada en reducción de Oporto* (truffled sausage in Port
wine reduction sauce). The house wines are good, but the Torre la
Moreira Albariño white perfectly complements Pep's offerings. ⊠ *Pl.
de les Olles 8, Born-Ribera* ☎ *93/319–6183* ☉ *Tues.–Sat. 1 PM–4 PM
and 8–11 PM, Mon. 8 PM–11 PM* Ⓜ *Jaume I ✢ J:13.*

$$$–$$$$ ✗ **Comerç 24.** Artist, aesthete, and chef Carles Abellán playfully reinter-
CATALAN   prets traditional Catalan favorites at this minimalist treasure. Try the
Fodor'sChoice *arròs a banda* (paella with peeled mollusks and crustaceans), *tortilla de
★   patatas* (potato omelet), and, for dessert, a postmodern version of the
traditional after-school snack of chocolate, olive oil, salt, and bread.
The menu is pretty far out, yet it always hits the mark. ⊠ *Carrer Com-
erç 24, Born-Ribera* ☎ *93/319–2102* ⩗ *Reservations essential* ▭ *AE,
DC, MC, V* ☉ *Closed Sun.* Ⓜ *Jaume I ✢ J:12.*

$–$$ ✗ **El Foro.** This hot spot near the Born is always full to the rafters with
ECLECTIC   lively young and not-so-young people. Painting and photographic exhib-
its line the walls, and the menu is dominated by meat cooked over coals,
pizzas, and salads. Flamenco and jazz performances downstairs are a
good post-dinner diversion. ⊠ *Princesa 53, Born-Ribera* ☎ *93/310–
1020* ▭ *AE, DC, MC, V* ☉ *Closed Mon.* Ⓜ *Jaume I ✢ J:13.*

$$$$ ✗ **El Passadís d'en Pep.** Squirreled away through a tiny passageway off
SEAFOOD   the Pla del Palau near the Santa Maria del Mar church, this lively bistro serves a rapid-fire succession of delicious seafood tapas and wine
as soon as you appear. Sometime later in the proceedings you may be
asked to make a decision about your main course, usually fish of one
kind or another. Feel free to stop at this point. And avoid *bogavante*
(lobster) unless you're on an expense account. ⊠ *Pla del Palau 2, Born-
Ribera* ☎ *93/310–1021* ▭ *AE, DC, MC, V* ☉ *Closed Sun. and last 2
wks of Aug.* Ⓜ *Jaume I ✢ J:13.*

$–$$ ✗ **El Pebre Blau.** This handsome space, surrounded by centuries-old
MEDITERRANEAN   wooden doors and shutters, offers an ever-changing selection of dishes
collected from all over the Mediterranean. The choices here range from
down-home Catalan cooking to Greek salads or Lebanese tabbouli.
A sybaritic bonanza on the site of the early baths (*banys vells*) of the
waterfront district, this is a soothing setting for contemporary dining
at reasonable prices. ⊠ *Bany Vells 21, Born-Ribera* ☎ *93/319–1308*
▭ *AE, DC, MC, V* ☉ *No lunch* Ⓜ *Jaume I ✢ J:13.*

¢–$ ✗ **El Xampanyet.** Just down the street from the Picasso Museum, hanging
TAPAS   *botas* (leather wineskins) announce one of Barcelona's liveliest and prettiest *xampanyerias* (champagne bars), usually stuffed to the gills with a
rollicking mob of local and out-of-town celebrants. Avoid the oversweet
house sparkling wine (pick draft beer or wine), but do indulge in *pa amb
tomaquet* (toasted bread with squeezed tomato and olive oil) served
on marble-top tables near walls decorated with azulejos (glazed tiles).

⊠ *Montcada 22, Born-Ribera* ☎ *93/319–7003* ☉ *Tues.–Sat. noon–4 PM and 6:30 PM–midnight; Sun. noon–4* Ⓜ *Jaume I ✛ J:13.*

¢–$ ✕ **Espai Barroc.** This unusual baroque *espai* (space) is in Carrer Mont-
CAFÉ   cada's most beautiful patio, the 15th-century Palau Dalmases (one of
the many houses built by powerful Barcelona families between the 13th
and 18th century). The stairway, decorated with a bas-relief of the rape
of Europa and Neptune's chariot, leads up to the Omnium Cultural, a
key center for the study and dissemination of Catalonian history and
culture. The patio merits a look even if you find the café too lugubrious.
⊠ *Carrer Montcada 20, Born-Ribera* ☎ *93/310–0673* ☉ *Tues.–Sun.
8 PM–2 AM* Ⓜ *Jaume I ✛ J:13.*

¢–$ ✕ **Euskal Etxea.** This elbow-shape, pine-paneled space is one of the better
TAPAS   Basque bars around the Gothic Quarter, with a colorful array of tapas
and canapés on the bar ranging from the olive-pepper-anchovy on a
toothpick to chunks of tortilla or *pimientos de piquillo* (red piquillo
peppers) stuffed with codfish paste. An excellent and usually completely
booked restaurant and a Basque cultural circle and art gallery round out
this social and gastronomical oasis. ⊠ *Placeta de Montcada 13, Born-
Ribera* ☎ *93/310–2185* ☉ *Mon.–Sat. 9 AM–1 AM, Sun. 9 AM–4:30 PM*
Ⓜ *Jaume I ✛ J:13.*

¢–$ ✕ **La Báscula.** This cozy café is on one of the Born area's most pictur-
CAFÉ   esque streets. Curiously, the building, the next over from the medieval
mint (La Seca) at Carrer Flassaders 42, was the main candy factory in
19th- and early-20th-century Barcelona. Look up outside this artistic café and study the sign still engraved into the concrete: FÁBRICA
DE DULCES—CARAMELOS–CONSERVAS–TURRONES–CHOCOLATES–GRAGEAS–
PELADILLAS: the entire gamut of Barcelona bonbons. Sandwiches, cakes,
pies, coffee, tea, and juices are served in this gracefully decorated, peaceful spot on the street behind Carrer Montcada and the Picasso Museum.
⊠ *Flassaders 30 bis, Born-Ribera* ☎ *93/319–9866* ☉ *Mon.–Sat. 9:30
AM–11:30 PM* Ⓜ *Jaume I ✛ J:13.*

$–$$ ✕ **La Habana Vieja.** If you have an itch for a taste of Old Havana—*ropa
CARIBBEAN vieja* (shredded beef) or *moros y cristianos* (black beans and rice) with
mojitos (a cocktail of rum, mint, and sugar), or a round of *plátanos
a puñetazos* (punched plantains)—this is your Barcelona refuge. The
upstairs tables overlooking the bar are cozy little crow's nests, and the
neighborhood is filled with quirky dives and saloons for pre- and post-
dinner carousing. ⊠ *Bany Vells 2, Born-Ribera* ☎ *93/268–2504* ▭ *AE,
DC, MC, V* ☉ *Closed Sun.* Ⓜ *Jaume I ✛ J:13.*

$–$$ ✕ **Mundial Bar.** For a taste of traditional Barcelona, unchanged and
CATALAN unspoiled by sleek interior design, this regular old everyday bar—one
of the last of its kind—serves delicious tapas and small portions of
traditional morsels, from pimientos de Padrón (green peppers from
Padrón, Galicia) to xipirones (baby squid). Whether at the bar or at the
little tables in the front and extending into the cavernous back rooms,
you can enjoy the kitchen's consistently tasty fare. Try the thin-sliced
aubergines with goat cheese or the *solomillo con salteado de setas y
reducción de Módena y trufa* (filet mignon with sautéed wild mushrooms, reduction of Módena, and truffles). ⊠ *Plaça Sant Agustí Vell*

1, Born-Ribera ☎ *93/319–9056* ▭ *AE, DC, MC, V* ◷ *Closed Mon.* Ⓜ *Jaume I* ✛ *J:12.*

¢–$ ✕ **Sagardi.** This attractive wood-and-stone cider-house replica comes
TAPAS close to re-creating its Basque prototype with its ersatz cider barrel
shooting frothy blasts into wide-mouthed glasses. A full and groaning
counter offers a hundred varieties of tapas, usually over-breaded creations from the suburban tapas factory that turns out these mediocre
morsels. Stick with the better hot tapas straight from the kitchen. The
restaurant in the back also cooks first-rate *txuletas de buey* (beefsteaks)
over coals. ✉ *Carrer Argenteria 62, Born-Ribera* ☎ *93/319–9993*
◷ *Daily 1:30* PM*–3:30* PM *and 8* PM*–midnight* Ⓜ *Jaume I* ✛ *I:13.*

¢–$ ✕ **Santa Maria.** A combination of cutting-edge industrial design with
TAPAS medieval stone walls and innovative tapa creations keeps Santa Maria
thriving. The kitchen's inventions have even lured in Barcelona's leading
chefs to dine on anything from *espardenyes* (sea cucumber) to *escamar-*
lans amb salicornia (prawns with saltwort). ✉ *Comerç 17, Born-Ribera*
☎ *93/315–1227* ◷ *Tues.–Sat. 1:30* PM*–3:30* PM *and 8:30* PM*–12:30;*
closed last 2 wks of Aug. Ⓜ *Jaume I* ✛ *J:12.*

¢–$ ✕ **Taverna del Born.** All manner of tapas and cazuelitas, with everything
TAPAS from stewed lentils to *pulpo a feira* (slices of octopus on potatoes), are
served at this terrace, bar, and restaurant overlooking the Born market.
The tables outside manage to be breezy in summer and sunny in winter,
and the intersection is one of the Born area's liveliest. ✉ *Passeig de Born*
27–29, Born-Ribera ☎ *93/315–0964* ◷ *Tues.–Sat. 11* AM*–12:30* AM,
Sun. 11 AM*–5* PM Ⓜ *Jaume I* ✛ *J:13.*

RAMBLA

¢–$ ✕ **Café de l'Opera.** Directly across from the Liceu opera house, this high-
CAFÉ ceilinged Art Nouveau interior has welcomed operagoers and performers for more than 100 years. It's a central point on the Rambla traffic
pattern, and de rigueur; locals know that just about any Barcelona
resident passes through this much-frequented haunt. ✉ *Rambla 74,*
Rambla ☎ *93/317–7585* ◷ *Daily 9:30* AM*–2:15* AM Ⓜ *Liceu* ✛ *H:12.*

¢–$ ✕ **Café Viena.** The rectangular perimeter of this little classic is always
CAFÉ packed with local and international travelers enjoying what Mark Bitt-
man of *the New York Times* has consecrated as "the best sandwich
in the world." The *flautas de jamón ibérico* (thin bread "flutes" of
Ibérico ham anointed with tomato squeezings) may not be made with
the absolute top level of acorn-fed ham, but they're close enough for a
high pass and, at under €7, a great value accompanied by an icy *caña*
(draft beer). The pianist in the balcony, when present, lends a honky-
tonk café touch. ✉ *Rambla dels Estudis 115, Rambla* ☎ *93/317–1492*
◷ *Daily 9* AM*–2* AM Ⓜ *Catalunya* ✛ *H:11.*

¢–$ ✕ **Café Zurich.** Of key importance to all of Barcelona's rank-and-file
CAFÉ society, this traditional café overlooking the top of the Rambla and
directly astride the main Metro and transport hub remains the city's
prime meeting point. The outdoor tables offer peerless people-watching;
the interior is high-ceilinged and elegant. For a beer or a coffee in the eye
of the hurricane, there is no better terrace in town. ✉ *Pl. Catalunya 1,*
Rambla ☎ *93/317–9153* ◷ *Daily 9* AM*–2* AM Ⓜ *Catalunya* ✛ *H:11.*

$$–$$$ ✗ **Can Culleretes.** Just off the Rambla in the Gothic Quarter, this fam-
CATALAN ily-run restaurant founded in 1786 breathes tradition in both decor
and culinary offerings. As Barcelona's oldest restaurant (listed in the
Guinness Book of Records), generations of the Manubens and Agut
families have kept this unpretentious spot at the forefront of the city's
dining options for over two centuries. Wooden beams overhead and
bright paintings of sea- and landscapes on the walls surround a jumble
of tables. Traditional Catalan specialties such as spinach cannelloni
with cod, wild boar stew, or the classic white beans with botifarra
sausage are impeccably prepared by a fleet of skilled family chefs.
✉ *Carrer Quintana 5, Rambla/Barri Gòtic* ☎ *93/317–6485* ▭ *AE,
DC, MC, V* ☾ *Closed Mon. and July. No dinner Sun.* Ⓜ *Catalunya,
Liceu* ✛ *H:13.*

$$–$$$ ✗ **La Taxidermista.** Don't worry: you won't dine surrounded by stuffed
MEDITERRANEAN squirrels. A former natural-science museum and taxidermy shop (Dalí
once purchased 200,000 ants and a stuffed rhinoceros here), this is
the only recommendable restaurant in the sunny Plaça Reial. Decora-
tor Beth Gali designed the interior around original beams and steel
columns. Delicacies such as *bonito con escalibada y queso de cabra*
(white tuna with braised aubergines, peppers, and goat cheese) are
served at outside tables best enjoyed in the winter sun. ✉ *Pl. Reial 8,
Rambla* ☎ *93/412–4536* ▭ *AE, DC, MC, V* ☾ *Closed Mon.* Ⓜ *Liceu*
✛ *H:13.*

RAVAL

¢–$ ✗ **Ca l'Estevet.** Journalists, students, and artists haunt this romantic little
CATALAN spot near the MACBA (contemporary art museum), across the street
from Barcelona's journalism school, and around the block from Barcelona's *La Vanguardia* daily newspaper. Estevet and family are charming,
and the carefully elaborated Catalan cuisine sings, especially at these
prices. Try the asparagus cooked over coals, the *chopitos gaditanos*
(deep-fried baby octopus), or the *magret de pato* (duck breast). The
house wine is inexpensive, light, and perfectly drinkable. ✉ *Valdoncella 46, Raval* ☎ *93/302–4186* ▭ *AE, DC, MC, V* ☾ *Closed Sun.*
Ⓜ *Catalunya* ✛ *G:11.*

$$$–$$$$ ✗ **Ca l'Isidre.** A favorite with Barcelona's art mob, this place is shellacked
CATALAN with pictures and engravings, some original, by Dalí and other art stars.
Fodor's Choice Just inside the Raval from Avinguda del Paral.lel, the restaurant relies
★ on fresh produce from the nearby Boqueria for its traditional Catalan
cooking. Isidre's wines are invariably novelties from all over the Iberian
Peninsula; ask for his advice and you will get a great wine as well as an
enology, geography, and history course delivered with charm, brevity,
and wit. The slight French accent in cuisine is evident in superb home-
made foie gras. Come and go by cab at night; it's not easy to find and
the streets here can be shady. ✉ *Les Flors 12, Raval* ☎ *93/441–1139*
☙ *Reservations essential* ▭ *AE, MC, V* ☾ *Closed Sun., Easter wk, and
mid-July–mid-Aug.* Ⓜ *Paral.lel* ✛ *F:13.*

$$$–$$$$ ✗ **Casa Leopoldo.** Hidden in a dark Raval pocket west of the Rambla,
CATALAN this restaurant owned by the Gil family serves fine seafood and Catalan
Fodor's Choice fare. To get here, approach along Carrer Hospital, take a left through
★ the Passatge Bernardí Martorell, and go 50 feet right on Sant Rafael

Café Zurich has been a popular meeting spot for locals since the 1920s.

to the Gil front door. Try the *revuelto de ajos tiernos y gambas* (eggs scrambled with young garlic and shrimp) or the famous *cap-i-pota* (stewed head and hoof of pork). Albariños and Priorats are among Rosa Gil's favorite wines. ⊠ *Sant Rafael 24, Raval* ☎ *93/441–3014* ▤ *AE, DC, MC, V* ⊘ *Closed Mon. No dinner Sun.* Ⓜ *Liceu* ✥ *G:12.*

$$–$$$
MEDITERRANEAN

✕ **El Cafetí.** Candlelit and romantic, this little hideaway at the end of the passageway in from Carrer Hospital is an intimate bistro with a menu encompassing various ingredients from foie gras to cod to game in season. Try the *ensalada tibia de queso de cabra* (warm goat-cheese salad) or the *solomillo de corzo al foie* (roebuck filet mignon with foie gras). ⊠ *Hospital 99 (at end of Passatge Bernardí Martorell), Raval* ☎ *93/329–2419* ▤ *AE, DC, MC, V* ⊘ *Closed Mon. No dinner Sun.* Ⓜ *Liceu* ✥ *G:12.*

¢–$$
TAPAS

✕ **Quimet-Quimet.** A foodie haunt, this tiny place lined with wine and whiskey bottles is stuffed with products and people. If you come too late, you might not be able to get in. Come before 1:30 PM and 7:30 PM and you will generally find a stand-up table. Chef-owner Quimet improvises ingenious canapés. All you have to do is orient him toward cheese, anchovies, or whatever it is you might crave, and Quimet masterfully does the rest, *and* recommends the wine to go with it. ⊠ *Poeta Cabanyés 25, Poble Sec* ☎ *93/442–3142* ⊘ *Weekdays noon–4 and 7–10:30, Sat. noon–4* Ⓜ *Paral.lel* ✥ *E:13.*

$$–$$$
ECLECTIC
Fodor'sChoice
★

✕ **Tapioles 53.** A onetime umbrella-maker's shop beyond the Raval on the hillside descending from Montjuïc, this little gem of a restaurant in a ground floor loft has become a big favorite of English-speaking visitors and local food buffs alike. Aussie Sarah Stothart's three-course menu for less then €40 and a five-course set taster's menu at under €60 are original and delicious. Everything here fascinates, from the spinach gnocchi made with goat cheese from Ronda (described by Stothart as "like eating clouds") to the *dhoa*, an Egyptian speciality made of ground almonds, coriander, cumin, cinnamon, and other ingredients that vary according to the season. The lunch menu offers salads, sandwiches, and soups. ⊠ *Carrer Tapioles 53, Poble Sec* ☎ *93/329–2238* ▭ *AE, DC, MC, V* ☺ *Open for lunch weekdays 10–8. Open for dinner Tues.–Sat. 9 PM–1 AM. Closed Sun. No dinner Mon. No lunch Sat.* Ⓜ *Paral.lel-Poble Sec* ✛ *E:13.*

3

BARCELONETA AND THE PORT OLÍMPIC

$$$–$$$$ ✕ **Agua.** With views through gnarled and ancient olive trees over the
MEDITERRANEAN   beach into the Mediterranean, this sleek slot hidden "under the board-walk" near Frank Gehry's gleaming goldfish may not be classical Barce-loneta in decor or cuisine, but it's an exciting place to dine, whether on the terrace on warm summer nights or sunny winter days, or inside the immense bay windows. Seafood is the main draw and value on the menu here, but risottos, steaks, and lamb are also equally available. Expect action, bustle, streamlined design surroundings, beautiful people, and acceptable-if-not-spectacular fare at this very popular tourist favorite. Be sure to reserve in advance. ⊠ *Passeig Marítim de la Barceloneta 30 (Marina Village), Port Olímpic* ☎ *93/225–1272* ▭ *AE, DC, MC, V* Ⓜ *Ciutadella–Vila Olímpica, Barceloneta* ✛ *L:15.*

$$$–$$$$ ✕ **Andaira.** New flavors and innovative, contemporary cooking distin-
SEAFOOD   guish this restaurant from the standard Barceloneta dining panorama. It's not that Andaira doesn't do the traditional waterfront rice and fish dishes, but that they do them with a sleek, modern flair, all within sight of the Mediterranean from a contemporary streamlined second-floor dining room surrounded by picture windows. ⊠ *Vila Joiosa 52–54, Bar-celoneta* ☎ *93/221–1616* ▭ *AE, DC, MC, V* Ⓜ *Barceloneta* ✛ *J:16.*

$$$–$$$$ ✕ **Antiga Casa Solé.** Just two blocks from Barceloneta's prettiest square,
SEAFOOD   the charming Plaça de Sant Miquel, this traditional midday Sunday pilgrimage site occupies a typical waterfront house and serves fresh, well-prepared seafood. Whether it's *llenguado a la plancha* (grilled sole) or the exquisite *arròs negre amb sepia en su tinta* (black rice with squid in its ink), everything here comes loaded with taste. In winter try to get close to the open kitchen for the aromas, sights, sounds, and warmth. ⊠ *Sant Carles 4, Barceloneta* ☎ *93/221–5012* ▭ *AE, DC, MC, V* ☺ *Closed Mon. and last 2 wks of Aug. No dinner Sun.* Ⓜ *Bar-celoneta* ✛ *J:15.*

$$–$$$ ✕ **Barceloneta.** This enormous riverboat-like building at the end of the
SEAFOOD   yacht marina in Barceloneta is hardly an intimate space where the chef greets every patron. On the other hand, the food is delicious, the service impeccable, the hundreds of fellow diners make the place feel like a cheerful New Year's Eve celebration, and, all in all, a bad time has never been had here. Rice and fish dishes are the house specialty, and the salads are excellent. ⊠ *L'Escar 22, Barceloneta* ☎ *93/221–2111* ▭ *AE, MC, V* Ⓜ *Barceloneta* ✛ *I:15.*

$$-$$$
SEAFOOD
Fodor's Choice
★

✕ **Can Majó.** At the edge of the beach in Barceloneta, this is one of Barcelona's premier seafood restaurants. House specialties are *caldero de bogavante* (a cross between paella and lobster bouillabaisse) and *suquet* (fish stewed in its own juices), but whatever you choose will be excellent. In summer the terrace overlooking the Mediterranean is the closest you can now come to the Barceloneta *chiringuitos* (shanty restaurants) that used to line the beach here. ⊠ *Almirall Aixada 23, Barceloneta* ☎ *93/221–5455* ☰ *AE, DC, MC, V* ☉ *Closed Mon. No dinner Sun.* Ⓜ *Barceloneta* ✛ *J:16.*

$-$$
MEDITERRANEAN

✕ **Can Manel la Puda.** The first choice for paella in the sun, year-round, Can Manel is near the end of the main road out to the Barceloneta beach. Any time before 4 o'clock will do; it then reopens at 7 PM. *Arròs a banda* (rice with peeled shellfish) and paella *marinera* (with seafood) or *fideuá* (with noodles) are all delicious. The paella, prepared for a minimum of two diners, will easily feed three (or even four if you're planning to dine a few more times that day). ⊠ *Passeig Joan de Borbó 60, Barceloneta* ☎ *93/221–5013* ☰ *AE, DC, MC, V* ☉ *Closed Mon.* Ⓜ *Barceloneta* ✛ *I:16.*

$$$-$$$$
ECLECTIC

✕ **CDLC.** Carpe Diem Lounge Club is a combination restaurant, chill crash pad, and nightclub, with spectacular views over the beach and a continuously open kitchen from noon until 1 AM every day of the year. The cuisine is Asian fusion, with everything from the 120-piece sushi selection to Kobe beef from Japan to fiery Indian curry. A plate of *jamón iberico de bellota* (acorn-fed Ibérico ham) is also within easy grasp here, as are fresh Mediterranean and Atlantic fish from *llenguado a la plancha* (grilled sole) to *lubina a sal* (sea bass baked in a carapace of salt). ⊠ *Passeig Marítim del Port Olímpic 32, Barceloneta* ☎ *93/224–0470* ☰ *AE, DC, MC, V* ☉ *Barceloneta–Port Olímpic* ✛ *L:15.*

$$-$$$
SEAFOOD

✕ **El Lobito.** Although it can get filled to the gills with diners in full feeding frenzy spilling out onto a terrace in summer, the only thing really wrong with this place is that they serve you too much. Pure fish and seafood flows out of this kitchen, and the uproar tells you everyone's here to have fun. The wine list meets the standards of the savvy seafood. ⊠ *Ginebra 9, Barceloneta* ☎ *93/319–9164* ☰ *AE, DC, MC, V* ☉ *Closed Mon.* Ⓜ *Barceloneta* ✛ *J:15.*

¢-$$
TAPAS

✕ **El Vaso de Oro.** A favorite with food lovers from Barcelona and beyond, this often overcrowded little counter serves some of the best beer and tapas in town. The artisanal draught beer, specially brewed for this classic bar, is drawn and served with loving care, with just the right amount of foam and always at the correct temperature. The high rate of consumption ensures you will never encounter a stale keg. To eat, the *solomillo con foie y cebolla* (beef filet mignon with duck liver and onions) is an overwhelming favorite, but the fresh fish prepared *a la plancha* (on the grill) is also excellent. If you avoid peak local lunch and dinner hours (2–4 PM and 9–11 PM) you will have better luck finding space at the bar. ⊠ *Balboa 6, Barceloneta* ☎ *93/319–3098* ☉ *Daily 9 AM–midnight* Ⓜ *Barceloneta* ✛ *J:14.*

$$-$$$
SEAFOOD
☾

✕ **Els Pescadors.** A kilometer northeast of the Olympic Port in the interesting Sant Martí neighborhood, this handsome late-19th-century bistro-style dining room has a lovely terrace on a little square shaded by immense ficus trees. Kids can range freely in the traffic-free square while their parents concentrate on well-prepared seafood specialties such as paella, fresh fish, or *fideuá* (paella made with noodles). ✉ *Pl. de Prim 1, Sant Martí* ☎ *93/225–2018* 🖃 *AE, MC, V* ☯ *Closed Mon.* Ⓜ *Poblenou* ✛ *L:15.*

$–$$
SEAFOOD

✗ **La Mar Salada.** A handy alternative next door to the sometimes crowded Can Manel la Puda, this little seafood and rice restaurant has a sunny restaurant and whips up excellent paella, black rice, *fideuá* (paella made of vermicelli noodles), bouillabaisse, and fresh fish. Order an Albariño white wine from Galicia's Rias Baixas and a mixed salad—you can't do much better for value and quality in Barceloneta. ✉ *Passeig Joan de Borbó 58, Barceloneta* ☎ *93/221–2127* 🖃 *AE, MC, V* ☯ *Closed Tues.* Ⓜ *Barceloneta* ✛ *J:16.*

LA BARCELONETA, LAND OF PAELLA

Sunday paella in La Barceloneta is a classic Barcelona family outing. Paella or, in Catalan, *arròs* (rice), comes in various forms. Paella *marinera* is a seafood rice boiled in fish stock, made with arroz bomba (especially absorbent rice ideal for paella) and seasoned with clams, mussels, prawns, and jumbo shrimp. *Arròs negre* (black rice) is rice cooked in squid ink. *Arròs a banda* presents the ingredients without shells. *Fideuá* is made with vermicelli noodles mixed with the standard ingredients. Paella is for a minimum of two diners, and is usually enough for three.

$$$–$$$$
CATALAN

✗ **Lluçanès.** The newly renovated Barceloneta market was fertile ground for chefs Àngel Pascual and Francesc Miralles when they moved their legendary restaurant from the country town of Prat de Lluçanès to the big city. Upstairs is the grand gourmet option, Lluçanès: it's contemporary and creative, serving such refined interpretations as scallop tartare with white summer truffles. The downstairs **Els Fogons de la Barceloneta** serves typical Barceloneta tapas and seafood; think *bombas* (potato croquettes) and the standard *calamares a la plancha* (grilled cuttlefish), impeccably prepared. ✉ *Plaça de la Font 1, Barceloneta* ☎ *93/224–2525* 🖃 *AE, DC, MC, V* ☯ *Closed Mon. No dinner Sun.* Ⓜ *Barceloneta* ✛ *J:15.*

$$$–$$$$
MEDITERRANEAN

✗ **Mondo.** Just off Barceloneta in the port's Maremagnum complex on the upper level of the IMAX theater, Mondo has gained fame for fine seafood in a contemporary design setting overlooking Barcelona's yachting marina and, not coincidentally, the afternoon fish auction by the clock tower over on the Moll dels Pescadors. Original creations such as *foie con albaricoque y pétalos de tomate seco* (duck liver with apricot and julienned sun-dried tomatoes) join seafood classics such as *caldoso de bogavante* (lobster bouillabaisse) on an inventive and original menu. Mondo morphs into a fashionable dance club and disco after the dinner hours. ✉ *Moll d'Espanya s/n (IMAX bldg.), Maremagnum, Barceloneta* ☎ *93/221–3911* 🖃 *AE, DC, MC, V* Ⓜ *Drassanes, Barceloneta* ✛ *I:15.*

$$–$$$
SEAFOOD

✗ **Reial Club Marítim.** For harbor views at sunset, excellent maritime fare, and a sense of escape from urban chaos, hit Barcelona's yacht club, El Marítim, just around the harbor through Barceloneta. Highlights are *paella marinera* (seafood paella), *rodaballo* (turbot), *lubina* (sea bass), and *dorada* (sea bream). Or just ask for the freshest fish and you won't be disappointed. ⊠ *Moll d'Espanya, Barceloneta* ☎ *93/221–7143* ▭ *AE, DC, MC, V* ☻ *No dinner Sun.* Ⓜ *Barceloneta* ✢ *H:15.*

\$\$–\$\$\$ ✕ **Suquet de l'Almirall.** With a handy terrace for alfresco dining in sum-
SEAFOOD   mer, "The Admiral's Fish Stew" indeed serves fare fit for the admiralty. Specialists in rice dishes and *caldoso de bogavante*, an abundantly brothy rice dish with lobster, this is one of Barceloneta's best. ⊠ *Passeig Joan de Borbó 65, Barceloneta* ☎ *93/221–6233* ▭ *AE, DC, MC, V* ☻ *Closed Mon. No dinner Sun.* Ⓜ *Barceloneta* ✢ *I:16.*

\$\$\$–\$\$\$\$ ✕ **Torre d'Altamar.** Seafood of every stripe, spot, fin, and carapace ema-
MEDITERRANEAN   nates from the kitchen here, but the filet mignon under a colossal slab of foie is a tour de force. Housed inside the cable-car tower over the far side of the port, this restaurant has spectacular views of Barcelona as well as far out into the Mediterranean. ⊠ *Passeig Joan de Borbó 88–Torre de San Sebastián, Barceloneta* ☎ *93/221–0007* ▭ *AE, DC, MC, V* ☻ *Closed Sun. No lunch Mon.* Ⓜ *Barceloneta* ✢ *H:16.*

EIXAMPLE

\$\$\$–\$\$\$\$ ✕ **Alkimia.** Chef Jordi Vilà is making news here with his inventive cre-
CATALAN   ations and tasting menus at €44 and €58 that pass for a bargain at the top end of Barcelona culinary culture. It's usually packed, but the alcoves are intimate and the stark decor is parceled out among them. Vilà's deconstructed *pa amb tomaquet* (in classical usage, toasted bread with olive oil and squeezed tomato) in a shot glass give a witty culinary wink (as it were) before things get deadly serious with raw tuna strips, baby squid, or turbot. A dark-meat course, venison or beef, brings the taste progression to a close before dessert provides more comic relief. Alkimia, as its name suggests, is pure magic. ⊠ *Indústria 79, Eixample* ☎ *93/207–6115* ▭ *AE, DC, MC, V* ☻ *Closed Sat. lunch, Sun., Easter wk, and Aug. 1–21* Ⓜ *Sagrada Família* ✢ *L:7.*

\$\$–\$\$\$ ✕ **Bar Mut.** This elegant retro space just above Diagonal serves first-
CATALAN   rate products ranging from wild sea bass to the best Ibérico hams. Crowded, expensive, noisy, chaotic, delicious: it's everything a great tapas bar or restaurant should be. The name is a play on the word vermut (vermouth), which, not so long ago, was about as close to tapas as Barcelona was apt to get. The wine selections and range of dishes proposed on the chalkboard behind the bar are creative and traditional. Don't let the friendly and casual feel of the place lull you into thinking that la cuenta (the check) will be anything but deadly serious. ⊠ *Pau Claris 192, Eixample* ☎ *93/217–4338* ▭ *AE, DC, MC, V* ☻ *Provença, Diagonal* ✢ *I:8.*

¢–\$ ✕ **Café Paris.** Always a popular place to kill some time, the lively Café
CAFÉ   Paris has hosted everyone from Prince Felipe, heir to the Spanish throne, to poets and pundits of all spots and stripes. The tapas are excellent, the beer is cold, and this old-fashioned bar de toda la vida (everyday bar) with its long counter and jumble of tables is open 365 days a year. ⊠ *Carrer Aribau 184, at Carrer Paris, Eixample* ☎ *93/209–8530* ☻ *Daily 6* AM*–2* AM Ⓜ *Provença* ✢ *G:7.*

Casa Calvet restaurant offers the chance to dine inside a Moderniste masterpiece.

$$$$
CATALAN
✗ **Can Gaig.** This Barcelona favorite is justly famous for combining superb interior design with carefully prepared cuisine. Market-fresh ingredients and original combinations are solidly rooted in traditional recipes from Catalan home cooking, while the menu balances seafood and upland specialties, game, and domestic raw materials. Try the *perdiz asada con jamón ibérico* (roast partridge with Iberian ham), or, if it's available, *becada* (woodcock), in which Carles Gaig is a recognized master. ⊠ *Carrer d'Aragó 214, Eixample* ☎ *93/429–1017* ⚑ *Reservations essential* ▤ *AE, DC, MC, V* ⊘ *Closed Mon., Easter wk, and Aug.* Ⓜ *Passeig de Gràcia* ✛ *G:9.*

$$$–$$$$
MEDITERRANEAN
✗ **Casa Calvet.** It's hard to pass up the opportunity to break bread in one of the great Moderniste's creations. Designed by Antoni Gaudí from 1898 to 1900, the Art Nouveau Casa Calvet includes this graceful dining room decorated in Moderniste ornamentation from looping parabolic door handles to polychrome stained glass, etched glass, and wood carved in floral and organic motifs. The Catalan and Mediterranean fare is light and contemporary, though refreshingly innocent of *nueva cocina* influence. ⊠ *Casp 48, Eixample* ☎ *93/412–4012* ▤ *AE, DC, MC, V* ⊘ *Closed Sun. and last 2 wks of Aug.* Ⓜ *Urquinaona* ✛ *J:10.*

$–$$$
TAPAS
✗ **Casa Lucio.** With preserved and fresh ingredients and original dishes flowing from the kitchen, this miniaturesque and handsome (though expensive) dazzler just two blocks south of the Mercat de Sant Antoni is well worth tracking down. Lucio's wife, chef Maribel, is relentlessly inventive. Try the *tastum albarole* (cured sheep cheese from Umbria) or the *pochas negras con morcilla* (black beans with black sausage). ⊠ *Viladomat 59, Eixample* ☎ *93/424–4401* ⊘ *Mon.–Sat. 1–4 and 8–11* Ⓜ *Sant Antoni* ✛ *E:11.*

$$-$$$ ✗ **Cinc Sentits.** The engaging Artal family—maître d' and owner Rosa,
CATALAN   server and eloquent food narrator Amy, and chef Jordi—a Catalan fam-
Fodor's Choice   ily with a couple of decades in Canada and the United States, offers a
★   unique Barcelona experience: cutting-edge contemporary *cuina d'autor* in
a minimalist setting, and explained in detail in native English. Three fixed
menus—light, tasting, and *omakase* (a "trust the chef" surprise menu,
including wine pairings of the chef's choice)—provide a wide range of
tastes and textures. At the end of the meal a special printout reprises the
nine mini-courses and seven wines that have just crossed your palate. This
is foodie nirvana. ✉ *Aribau 58, Eixample* ☎ *93/323–9490* ▭ *AE, DC,
MC, V* ⊘ *Closed Sun. No dinner Mon.* Ⓜ *Provença* ✛ *G:9.*

¢-$$ ✗ **Ciudad Condal.** At the bottom of Ramba Catalunya, this long wooden
TAPAS   bar covered with an anthology of tapas is always filled with a throng of
hungry, mostly international, clients. The *solomillo* (miniature beef filet)
is a winner here, as is the *brocheta d'escamarlans* (brochette of jumbo
shrimp). A good late-night or post-concert solution, there is usually
room to squeeze in at the bar, though reservations à table provide more
seclusion and space. ✉ *Rambla de Catalunya 18, Eixample* ☎ *93/318–
1997* ⊘ *Daily 7:30 AM–1:30 AM* Ⓜ *Passeig de Gràcia* ✛ *H:10.*

$$-$$$ ✗ **Colibrí.** Known for fresh market cuisine prepared in innovative—
MEDITERRANEAN   though never radical or self-conscious ways—Colibrí (hummingbird
in Catalan) has managed to hum happily along, largely under the inter-
national radar. The kitchen offers everything from artichoke hearts
stuffed with duck liver in French onion and tarragon sauce, to sea
bream with eggplant and chestnuts. The soothing, minimalist decor in
creams and beiges gives center stage to the tastes and textures of the
food. The wine list contains exciting surprises, such as the gentle but
authoritative Taberner Syrah from Cádiz. ✉ *Casanova 212, Eixample*
☎ *93/443–2306* ⌂ *Reservations essential* ▭ *AE, DC, MC, V* ⊘ *Closed
Mon. No dinner Sun.* Ⓜ *Diagonal, Provença* ✛ *G:7.*

$$ ✗ **Dolso.** Known primarily for inventive sweets and desserts such its
ECLECTIC   famous gintonic, a clear jelly that tastes uncannily like the drink for
which it is named, this creative pudding-café just off Rambla Catalunya
also serves excellent fish and meat dishes as well as superb salads. The
€12 lunch menu is one of the best bargains in Barcelona. ✉ *València
227, Eixample* ☎ *93/487–5964* ▭ *AE, DC, MC, V* ⊘ *Closed Sun., No
dinner Mon.* Ⓜ *Passeig de Gràcia, Provença* ✛ *H:9.*

$$$-$$$$ ✗ **Dos Cielos.** Twins Javier and Sergio Torres have leapt to the tops of
MEDITERRANEAN   Barcelona's culinary charts as well as to the top tower of the Hotel
ME. Combining Brazilian, French, and Valencian touches reflecting
the twins' accumulated culinary experiences around the world, it only
seems fitting that the Torres brothers should be working in a tower,
and that their restaurant be named Dos Cielos, *cielo* being Spanish
for sweetheart (the boys *are* cute). Contemporary innovation wed to
profound respect for traditional palates produces an interesting cuisine
based on fresh local produce, some of it grown in the hotel's own roof
garden. The views over the Mediterranean are spectacular. ✉ *Pere IV
272–286, Eixample* ☎ *93/367–2070* ▭ *AE, DC, MC, V* ⊘ *Closed Sun.,
Mon.* Ⓜ *Poble Nou* ✛ *L:12.*

$$$$
MEDITERRANEAN
Fodor's Choice
★

✗ Drolma. Named (in Sanskrit) for Buddha's female side, chef Fermin Puig's intimate perch in the Hotel Majestic was an instant success. The *menú de degustació* (tasting menu) might have pheasant cannelloni in foie-gras sauce with fresh black truffles or giant prawn tails with *trompettes de la mort* (black wild mushrooms) with *sôt-l'y-laisse* (free-range chicken nuggets). Fermin's foie gras *a la ceniza amb ceps* (cooked over wood coals with wild mushrooms)—a recipe rescued from his boyhood farmhouse feasts—is typical of Drolma's signature blend of tradition and inspiration. ☒ *Passeig de Gràcia 70, Eixample* ☎ *93/496–7710* ⌂ *Reservations essential* ⊟ *AE, DC, MC, V* ⊘ *Closed Sun. and Aug.* Ⓜ *Provença, Passeig de Gràcia* ✛ *I:9.*

$$
CATALAN

✗ Embat. An embat is a puff of wind in Catalan (also a crashing wave), and this relatively new (November 2008) restaurant is indeed a breath of fresh air in the swashbuckling and hyper-commercial Eixample. The market cuisine by a brace of partner chefs, Santi Rebés and Fidel Puig, is always impeccably fresh and freshly conceived, starring thoughtful combinations such as the *cazuelita de alcachofas con huevo poché y papada* (casserole of artichokes and poached egg with pork dewlap) or the *pichón con bizcocho de cacao y cebolla confitada* (wood pigeon with cacao biscuit and onion confit). ☒ *Mallorca 304, Eixample* ☎ *93/458–0885* ⊟ *AE, DC, MC, V* ⊘ *Closed Sun., Mon. No dinner Tues., Wed.* Ⓜ *Diagonal* ✛ *J:8.*

$–$$
CATALAN

✗ Fonda Gaig. A rustic interpretation of the traditional cuisine that has made the Gaig family synonymous with top Barcelona dining since 1869, this new enterprise is making a place for itself in Barcelona's relentlessly evolving culinary world. With some of the steam leaking out of the radically innovative and experimental cookery movement led by Ferran Adrià and El Bulli, Carles Gaig and a growing number of top chefs are going back to simpler and more affordable food. Look for standards such as *botifarra amb mongetes de ganxet* (sausage with white beans) or *canelons de l'Avia* (Grandmother's cannelloni) or *pollastre de gratapallers a la casssola* (stewed free-range chicken). The ample dining room is, in contrast to the cuisine, stylishly contemporary, with comfortable armchairs à table. ☒ *Còrsega 200, Eixample* ☎ *93/453–2020* ⊟ *AE, DC, MC, V* ⊘ *Closed Sun., Mon. No dinner Sun.* Ⓜ *Hospital Clínic, Provença* ✛ *G:8.*

$$$–$$$$
BASQUE

✗ Gorría. Named for founder Fermín Gorría, this quite simply the best straightforward Basque-Navarran cooking in Barcelona. Everything from the stewed *pochas* (white beans) to the heroic *chuletón* (steak) is as clean, clear, and pure as the Navarran Pyrenees. The Castillo de Sajazarra reserva '95, a semisecret brick-red Rioja, provides the perfect accompaniment at this delicious pocket of Navarra in the Catalan capital. ☒ *Diputació 421, Eixample* ☎ *93/245–1164* ⊟ *AE, DC, MC, V* ⊘ *Closed Sun.* Ⓜ *Monumental* ✛ *L:10.*

¢–$$
TAPAS

✗ Inòpia Clàssic Bar. Albert Adrià, younger brother of El Bulli's überfamous chef Ferran Adrià, has opened his own tapas bar just a few blocks west of the Mercat de Sant Antoni. Products and preparations are uniformly fascinating, from the soupy and aromatic Torta del Casar Extremaduran sheep cheese served in individual mini-crates to the eclectic Iberian olive sampler presented in a ceramic flute. The table for 16 can be partly or entirely reserved in advance; otherwise you take your chances with bar or stand-up table space. (Caveat: lines form on Fridays and Saturdays). ⊠ *Tamarit 104, Eixample* ☎ *93/424–5231* ⊘ *Tues.– Sat. 7:30 PM–11 PM, Sun. 1–4* Ⓜ *Rocafort, Poble Sec* ✛ *E:11.*

$$$–$$$$

MEDITERRANEAN

✗ **Jaume de Provença.** Locals come here because they want to discover more of famed chef Jaume Bargués's haute-cuisine repertoire. Winning dishes include *lenguado relleno de setas* (sole stuffed with mushrooms) and the *lubina* (sea bass) soufflé. The traditionally designed restaurant, complete with a bar and a spacious yet intimate dining room, is in the Hospital Clinic part of the Eixample. ⊠ *Provença 88, Eixample* ☎ *93/430–0029* ⚱ *Reservations essential* ▭ *AE, DC, MC, V* ⊘ *Closed Mon., Aug., Easter wk, and Dec. 25 and 26. No dinner Sun.* Ⓜ *Entença* ✛ *E:6.*

¢–$

CAFÉ

✗ **La Bodegueta.** If you can find this dive (literally: it's a short drop below sidewalk level), you'll find a warm and cluttered space with a dozen small tables, a few spots at the marble counter, and lots of happy couples drinking coffee or beer, usually accompanied by the establishment's excellent *pa amb tomaquet* (toasted bread with squeezed tomato and olive oil) and either Manchego cheese, Iberian cured ham, or *tortilla de patatas* (potato-and-onion omelet). ⊠ *Rambla de Catalunya 100, Eixample* ☎ *93/215–4894* ⊘ *Daily 8 AM–2 AM* Ⓜ *Provença* ✛ *I:8.*

¢–$

TAPAS

✗ **La Flauta.** The name of this boisterous restaurant refers to the staple flutelike sandwiches that are the house specialty, but there is also an infinite number of tapas and small portions of everything from wild mushrooms in season to wild asparagus or *xipirones* (baby octopuses) served in this vast counter space flanked with dozens of tables. Try a *sobrassada* (pork paste with paprika from Majorca) *flauta* (thin, flutelike sandwich). A second, equally excellent location is in Eixample at Carrer Aribau 23. ⊠ *Carrer Balmes 171, Eixample* ☎ *93/415–5186* ⊘ *Mon.–Sat. 1–4 and 8–midnight* Ⓜ *Provença* ✛ *H:7.*

¢–$

CAFÉ

✗ **Laie Librería Café.** Much than a mere bookstore, the café and restaurant serves dinner until 1 AM. Readings, concerts, and book presentations round out an ample program of events. ⊠ *Pau Claris 85, Eixample* ☎ *93/302–7310* ⊘ *Mon.–Sat. 9 AM–1 AM* Ⓜ *Urquinaona* ✛ *I:10.*

$$$–$$$$

BASQUE

✗ **Lasarte.** Martin Berasategui, one of San Sebastián's fleet of master chefs, opened his Barcelona restaurant in early 2006 and triumphed from day one. Berasategui has placed his kitchen in the capable hands of Alex Garés, who trained with the best (Pellicer of Àbac and Manolo de la Osa in Cuenca's Las Rejas) and serves an eclectic selection of Basque, Mediterranean, market, and personal interpretations and creations. Expect whimsical aperitifs and surprising and serious combinations such as foie and smoked eel or simple wood pigeon cooked to perfection. (For a lighter, more economical Berasategui-directed experience, try Loidi, across the street in the Hotel Condes de Barcelona annex. ⊠ *Mallorca 259, Eixample* ☎ *93/445–0000* ▭ *AE, DC, MC, V* ⊘ *Closed weekends* Ⓜ *Provença* ✛ *I:9.*

$$$–$$$$

CATALAN

✗ **L'Olivé.** Comforting Catalan home cooking means this busy and attractive spot is always packed with trendy diners having a great time. Excellent hearty food, smart service, and some of the best *pa amb tomaquet* (toasted bread with olive oil and squeezed tomato) in town leaves you wanting to squeeze in, too. ⊠ *Balmes 47, Eixample* ☎ *93/452–1990* ▤ *AE, DC, MC,* ¥ ⊗ *No dinner Sun.* Ⓜ *Provença* ✢ *H:9.*

$$$–$$$$ ✗ **Manairó.** A *manairó* is a mysterious Pyrenean elf who helps make
CATALAN things happen, and Jordi Herrera may be a culinary one. A demon with
Fodor's Choice everything from blowtorch-fried eggs to meat cooked *al clavo ardiente*
★ (à la burning nail)—fillets warmed from within by red-hot spikes pro-
ducing meat both rare and warm and never undercooked—Jordi also
cooks cod under a lightbulb at 220°F (*bacalao iluminado,* or illumi-
nated codfish) and serves a palate-cleansing gin and tonic with liquid
nitrogen, gin, and lime. The intimate though postmodern, edgy design
of the dining room is a perfect reflection of the cuisine. ⊠ *Diputació
424, Eixample* ☎ *93/231–0057* ⚐ *Reservations essential* ▤ *AE, DC,
MC,* V ⊗ *Closed Sun., Mon., and last 3 wks of Aug.* Ⓜ *Monumental*
✢ *L:10.*

¢–$$ ✗ **Mantequeria Can Ravell.** Lovers of exquisite wines, hams, cheeses, oils,
TAPAS whiskies, cigars, caviars, baby eels, anchovies, and any other delicacy
you can think of, this is your spot. The backroom table open from mid-
morning to early evening is first come, first served; complete strangers
share tales, tastes, and textures at this foodie forum. The upstairs dining room serving lunch (and dinners Thursday and Friday), through
the kitchen and up a spiral staircase, has a clandestine, *Through the
Looking-Glass* vibe. ⊠ *Carrer Aragó 313, Eixample* ☎ *93/457–5114*
⊗ *Mon. 10–7, Tues., Wed. 10–9, Thurs.–Fri. 10–10, Sat. 10–6.* Ⓜ *Passeig de Gràcia* ✢ *J:9.*

¢–$$ ✗ **Moncho's Barcelona.** One of José Ramón Neira's (nicknamed Moncho)
TAPAS many establishments (including the upscale Botafumeiro), this rangy bar
and café serves very respectable *cazuelitas* (small earthenware dishes),
offering minitastes of Gallego and Catalan classics such as *alubias* (kid-
ney beans) and *calamares en su tinto* (squid stewed in its own ink).
⊠ *Travessera de Gràcia 44–46, Eixample* ☎ *93/414–6622* ⊗ *Daily
noon–1:30 AM* Ⓜ *Gràcia* ✢ *G:6.*

$$$–$$$$ ✗ **Murmuri.** The restaurant attached to the boutique hotel of the same
ASIAN name lured Ian Chalermkittichai from his semi-eponymous New York
restaurant (Kittichai) to bring his unique interpretation of Asian *cuisine
d'auteur* (original recipes) to Barcelona. With preparations based on
Thai and pan-Asian traditions and Mediterranean influences, appetiz-
ers might include monkfish and sesame wrapped in pandan leaf, or
crispy rock shrimp with Japanese eggplant and tamarind sauce. Main
courses range from Vietnamese crispy fish with pickled daikon and
chili to clay-pot-cooked chicken with butternut squash in lemongrass
sauce. ⊠ *Rambla de Catalunya 104, Eixample* ☎ *93/550–0600* ⚐ *Res-
ervations essential* ▤ *AE, DC, MC,* V ⊗ *Closed Mon. No dinner Sun.*
Ⓜ *Diagonal* ✢ *I:8.*

$$–$$$ ✗ **Ot.** Streamlined and original contemporary recipes make Ot (Otto,
CATALAN in Catalan), just two blocks up from Gaudí's Sagrada Família, a good
choice for hungry and foot-weary diners. An eight-course tasting menu
(€58 at this writing) composed of two appetizers, two starters, fish,
meat, and two desserts is the standard Ot formula. The abbreviated
tasting menu (€45) isn't much less expensive, but you get a lot less to
eat (one of everything and a choice of fish or meat). The menu changes

frequently and includes zingers such as cauliflower soup with herring eggs. ⊠ *Carrer Còrsega 537, Eixample* ☎ *93/435–8048* ▭ *AE, DC, MC, V* ☉ *No lunch Mon.* Ⓜ *Sagrada Família* ✢ *L:7.*

¢–$$
TAPAS

✘ **Paco Meralgo.** The name, a pun on *para comer algo* (to eat something), may be only marginally amusing, but the tapas here are no joke, from the classical *calamares fritos* (fried cuttlefish rings) to the *pimientos de Padrón* (green peppers, some fiery, from the Galician town of Padrón.) Whether à table, at the counter, or in the private dining room upstairs, this glittery space always rocks. ⊠ *Carrer Muntaner 171, Eixample* ☎ *93/430–9027* ☉ *Mon.–Sat. 1–4 and 8–midnight* Ⓜ *Provença* ✢ *G:8.*

$$–$$$
CATALAN

✘ **Petit Comité.** Fermin Puig of the famous Drolma at the Hotel Majestic, created Petit Comité as a more rustic country cousin of his sleek high-end dining room across the street. Traditional Catalan cooking is the theme in this contemporary design space with a square counter in the middle for bar fare. Serving around the clock from midday to midnight (1 PM–1 AM) makes reservations essential only at peak hours. Traditional favorites include *trinxat* (chopped cabbage with potato and bacon) or *caneloni amb béchamel de tòfona* (canelonni with truffled béchamel) to the traditional dessert of *mel i mató* (fresh cheese and honey). ⊠ *Passatge de la Concepció 13, Eixample* ☎ *93/550–0620* ⌨ *Reservations essential* ▭ *AE, DC, MC, V* ☉ *Open daily 1 PM–1 AM* Ⓜ *Diagonal* ✢ *I:8.*

$$–$$$
BASQUE

✘ **Sagardi Muntaner.** Basque favorites from *alubias de Tolosa* (diminutive but potent black beans from Tolosa) to *pimientos de piquillo* (sweet red bell peppers) to *txuletón de buey* (ox steak) are on the menu at this mid-Eixample address open from noon to midnight every day of the week. The bar displays the full range of typical Basque tapas and serves freezing *txakolí* (a young white wine from the Basque Country) for openers. ⊠ *Muntaner 70–72, Eixample* ☎ *93/902–520–522* ▭ *AE, DC, MC, V* Ⓜ *Universitat, Provença* ✢ *G:9.*

$$$–$$$$
BASQUE

✘ **Taktika Berri.** Specializing in San Sebastián's favorite dishes, the only drawback for this Basque restaurant is that a table is hard to score unless you call weeks in advance (an idea to consider before you hit the airport). The tapas served over the first come, first served bar, however, are of such a high quality that you can barely do better à table. The charming family that owns and runs this semisecret gem is the definition of hospitality. ⊠ *Valencia 169, Eixample* ☎ *93/453–4759* ⌨ *Reservations essential* ▭ *AE, DC, MC, V* ☉ *Closed Sun. No dinner Sat.* Ⓜ *Provença* ✢ *G:9.*

¢–$$
TAPAS

✘ **Tapaç 24.** Carles Abellán has done it again. His irrepressibly creative Comerç 24 has been a hit since the day it opened, and his new tapas emporium is headed in the same direction. Here Abellán shows us how much he admires traditional Catalan and Spanish bar food, from *patatas bravas* (potatoes in hot sauce) to *croquetas de jamón ibérico* (croquettes made of Iberian ham). ⊠ *Carrer Diputació 269, Eixample* ☎ *93/488–0977* ☉ *Mon.–Sat. 8 AM–midnight* Ⓜ *Passeig de Gràcia* ✢ *I:10.*

$$–$$$
MEDITERRANEAN

✘ **Tragaluz.** *Tragaluz* means skylight—literally, "light-swallower"—and this is an excellent choice if you're still on a design high from Vinçon

Continued on page 170

Vineyard in Rioja.

THE WINES OF SPAIN

After years of being in the shadows of other European wines, Spanish wines are finally gunning for the spotlight—and what has taken place is nothing short of a revolution. The wines of Spain, like its cuisine, are currently experiencing a firecracker explosion of both quality and variety that has brought a new level of interest, awareness, and recognition throughout the world, propelling them to superstar status. A generation of young, ambitious winemakers has jolted dormant areas awake, rediscovered long-forgotten local grapes, and introduced top international varieties. Even the most established regions have undergone makeovers in order to keep up with these dramatic changes and to compete in the global market.

THE ROAD TO GREAT WINE

Frank Gehry designed the visitor center for the Marqués de Riscal winery in Rioja.

Spain has a long wine history dating back to the time when the Phoenicians introduced viticulture, over 3,000 years ago. Some of the country's wines achieved fame in Roman times, and the Visigoths enacted early wine laws. But in the regions under Muslim rule, winemaking slowed down for centuries. Starting in the 16th century, wine trade expanded along with the Spanish Empire, and by the 18th and 19th centuries the Sherry region *bodegas* (wineries) were already established.

In the middle of the 19th century, seeds of change blossomed throughout the Spanish wine industry. In 1846, the estate that was to become Vega Sicilia, Spain's most revered winery, was set up in Castile. Three years later the famous Tío Pepe brand was established to produce the excellent dry fino wines. Marqués de Murrieta and the Marqués de Riscal wineries opened in the 1860s creating the modern Rioja region and clearing the way for many centenary wineries. *Cava*—Spain's white or pink sparkling wine—was created the following decade in Catalonia.

After this flurry of activity, Spanish wines languished for almost a century. Vines were hit hard by phylloxera, and then a civil war and a long dictatorship left the country stagnant and isolated. Just 30 short years ago, Spain's wines were split between the same dominant trio of Sherry, Rioja, and cava, and loads of cheap, watered-down wines made by local cooperatives with little gumption to improve and even less expertise.

Starting in the 1970s, however, a wave of innovation crashed through Rioja and emergent regions like Ribera del Duero and Penedés. In the 1990s, it turned into a revolution that spread all over the landscape—and is still going strong. Today, Spain is the third largest wine producer in the world and makes enticing wines at all price ranges, in never before seen quality and variety. As a result, in 2006 Spain became the second largest wine exporting country by volume, beating out France and trailing just behind Italy.

SPANISH WINE CATEGORIES BY AGE

A unique feature of Spanish wines is their indication of aging process on wine labels. DO wines (see "A *Vino* Primer" on following page) show this on mandatory back panels. Aging requirements are longer for reds, but also apply to white, rosé, and sparkling wines. For reds, the rules are as follows:

Vino Joven
A young wine that may or may not have spent some time aging in oak barrels before it was bottled. Some winemakers have begun to shun traditional regulations to produce cutting-edge wines in this category. An elevated price distinguishes the ambitious new reds from the easy-drinking *jóvenes*.

Crianza
A wine aged for at least 24 months, six of which are in barrels (12 in Rioja, Ribera del Duero, and Navarra). A great bargain in top vintages from the most reliable wineries and regions.

Reserva
A wine aged for a minimum of 36 months, at least 12 of which are in oak.

Gran Reserva
Traditionally the top of the Spanish wine hierarchy, and the pride of the historic Rioja wineries. A red wine aged for at least 24 months in oak, followed by 36 months in the bottle before release.

Joven or Cosecha	Crianza	Reserva		Gran Reserva
Minimum Aging Period in Months	24	36	48	60

READING LABELS LIKE A PRO

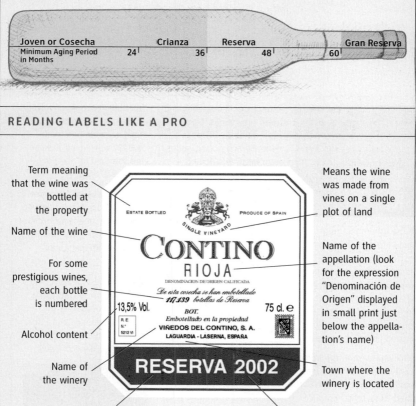

Term meaning that the wine was bottled at the property

Name of the wine

For some prestigious wines, each bottle is numbered

Alcohol content

Name of the winery

Aging category

Means the wine was made from vines on a single plot of land

Name of the appellation (look for the expression "Denominación de Origen" displayed in small print just below the appellation's name)

Town where the winery is located

Vintage year

ESTATE BOTTLED PRODUCE OF SPAIN

SINGLE VINEYARD

CONTINO
RIOJA
DENOMINACION DE ORIGEN CALIFICADA

De esta cosecha se han embotellado
117.139 botellas de Reserva

13,5% Vol.

BOT.
Embotellado en la propiedad
VIÑEDOS DEL CONTINO, S. A.
LAGUARDIA - LASERNA, ESPAÑA

R.E.
N.°
5212 VI

75 cl. ℮

RESERVA 2002

A *VINO* PRIMER

Spain offers a daunting assortment of wine styles, regions, and varietals. But don't worry: a few pointers will help you understand unfamiliar names and terms. Most of Spain's quality wines come from designated regions called *Denominaciones de Origen* (Appellations of Origin), often abbreviated as DO. Spain has more than 60 of these areas, which are tightly regulated to protect the integrity and characteristics of the wines produced there.

Beyond international varieties like Cabernet Sauvignon and Chardonnay, the country is home to several high-quality varietals, both indigenous and imported. Reds include Tempranillo, an early-ripening grape that blends and ages well, and Garnacha (the Spanish name for France's Grenache), a spicy, full-bodied red wine. The most popular white wines are the light, aromatic Albariño, and the full-bodied Malvasia.

Rioja wines

GENTES DE FORASTI
RIOJA

❶ The green and more humid areas of the Northwest deliver crisp, floral white albariños in Galicia's **Rías Biaxas.** In the **Bierzo** DO, the Mencía grape distills the essence of the schist slopes, where it grows into minerally infused red wines.

❷ Moving east, in the iron-rich riverbanks of the Duero, Tempranillo grapes, here called "Tinto Fino," produce complex and age-worthy

Ribera del Duero reds and hefty **Toro** wines. Close by, the **Rueda** DO adds aromatic and grassy whites from local Verdejo and adopted Sauvignon Blanc.

❸ The **Rioja** region is a winemaker's paradise. Here a mild, nearly perfect vine-growing climate marries limestone and clay soils with Tempranillo, Spain's most noble grape, to deliver wines that possess the two main features of every great region: personality and quality. Tempranillo-based Riojas evolve from a young cherry color and aromas of strawberries and red fruits, to a brick hue, infused with scents of tobacco and leather. Whether medium or

full-bodied, tannic or velvety, these reds are some of the most versatile and food-friendly wines, and have set the standard for the country for over a century.

Nearby, **Navarra** and three small DO's in Aragón deliver great wines made with the local Garnacha, Tempranillo, and international grape varieties.

❹ Southwest of Barcelona is the region of **Catalonia,** which encompasses the areas of Penedès and Priorat. Catalonia is best known as the heartland of *cava,*

Chardonnay vines in Navarra.

Grapes harvested for Sherry

the typically dry, sparkling wine made from three indigenous Spanish varietals: Parellada, Xarel-lo, and Macabeo. The climatically varied Penedès—just an hour south of Barcelona—produces full-bodied reds like Garnacha on coastal plains, and cool-climate varietals like Riesling and Sauvignon Blanc in the mountains. Priorat is a region that has emerged into the international spotlight during the past decade, as innovative winemakers have transformed winemaking practices there. Now, traditional grapes like Garnacha and Cariñena are blended with Cabernet Sauvignon and Syrah to produce rich, concentrated reds with powerful tannins.

❺ The region of **Valencia** is south of Catalonia on the Mediterranean coast. The wines of this area have improved markedly in recent years, with red wines from Jumilla and other appellations finding their way onto the international market. Tempranillo and Monastrell (France's Mourvèdre) are the most common reds. A local specialty of the area is Moscatel de Valencia, a highly aromatic sweet white wine.

❻ In the **central plateau south of Madrid**, rapid investment, modernization, and replanting is resulting in medium bodied, easy drinking, and fairly priced wines made with Tempranillo (here called

"Cencíbel"), Cabernet, Syrah, and even Petit Verdot, that are opening the doors to more ambitious endeavors.

❼ In sun-drenched Andalusia, where the white albariza limestone soils reflect the powerful sunlight while trapping the scant humidity, the fortified **Jerez** (Sherry) and **Montilla** emerge. In all their different incarnations, from dry finos, Manzanillas, amontillados, palo cortados, and olorosos, to sweet creams and Pedro Ximénez, they are the most original wines of Spain.

JUST OFF THE VINE: NEW WINE DEVELOPMENTS

Beyond Tempranillo: The current wine revolution has recovered many native varieties. Albariño, Godello, and Verdejo among the whites, and Callet, Cariñena, Garnacha, Graciano, Mandó, Manto Negro, Mencía, and Monastrell among the reds, are gaining momentum and will likely become more recognized.

Vinos de Pagos:
Pago, a word meaning plot or vineyard, is the new legal term chosen to create Spain's equivalent of a *Grand Cru* hierarchy, by protecting quality oriented wine producers that make wine from their own estates.

Petit Verdot: Winemakers in Spain are discovering that Petit Verdot, the "little green" grape of Bordeaux, ripens much easier in warmer climates than in its birthplace. This is contributing to the rise of Petit Verdot in red blends, and even to the production of single varietal wines.

Andalusia's New Wines: For centuries, scorching southern Andalusia has offered world-class Sherry and Montilla wines. Now trailblazing winemakers are making serious inroads in the production of quality white, red, and new dessert wines, something deemed impossible a few years back.

Cult Wines: For most of the past century, Vega Sicilia Unico was the only true cult wine from Spain. The current explosion has greatly expanded the roster: L'Ermita, Pingus, Clos Erasmus, Artadi, Cirsion, Terreus, and Termanthia are the leading names in a list that grows every year.

V.O.S. and V.O.R.S: Sherry's most dramatic change in over a century is the creation of the "Very Old Sherry" designation for wines over 20 years of age, and the addition of "Rare" for those over 30, to easier distinguish the best, oldest, and most complex wines.

Innovative New Blends:
A few wine regions have strict regulations concerning the varieties used in their wines, but most allow for experimentation. All over the country, *bodegas* are crafting wines with creative blends that involve local varieties, Tempranillo, and famous international grapes.

Island Wines: In both the Balearic and Canary Islands the strong tourist industry helped to revive local winemaking. Although hard to find, the best Callet and Manto Negro based red wines of Majorca, and the sweet *malvasías* of Lanzarote will reward the adventurous drinker.

SPAIN'S SUPERSTAR WINEMAKERS

Mariano García   Peter Sisseck   Alvaro Palacios   Josep Lluís Pérez

The current wine revolution has made superstars out of a group of dynamic, innovative, and visionary winemakers. Here are some of the top names:

Mariano García. His 30 years as winemaker of Vega Sicilia made him a legend. Now García displays his deft touch in the Ribera del Duero and Bierzo through his four wineries: Aalto, Mauro, San Román, and Paixar.

Peter Sisseck. A Dane educated in Bordeaux, Sisseck found his calling in the old Ribera del Duero vineyards, where he crafted Pingus, Spain's most coveted cult wine.

Alvaro Palacios. In Priorat, Palacios created L'Ermita, a Garnacha wine that is one of Spain's most remarkable bottlings. Palacios also is a champion of the Bierzo region, where he produces wines from the ancient Mencía varietal, known for their vibrant berry flavors and stony minerality.

Josep Lluís Pérez. From his base in Priorat and through his work as a winemaker, researcher, teacher, and consultant, Pérez (along with his daughter Sara Pérez) has become the main driving force in shaping the modern Mediterranean wines of Spain.

MATCHMAKING KNOW-HOW

A pairing of wine with *jamón* and Spanish olives.

Spain has a great array of regional products and cuisines, and its avant-garde chefs are culinary world leaders. As a general rule, you should match local food with local wines—but Spanish wines can be matched very well with some of the most unexpected dishes.

Albariños and the white wines of Galicia are ideal partners for seafood and fish. Dry sherries complement Serrano and Iberico hams, *lomo, chorizo,* and *salchichón* (white dry saugage), as well as olives and nuts. Pale, light, and dry finos and Manzanillas are the perfect aperitif wines, and the ideal companion for fried fish. Fuller bodied amontillados, palo cortados, and olorosos go well with hearty soups. Ribera del Duero reds are the perfect match for the outstanding local lamb. Try Priorat and other Mediterranean reds with strong cheeses and barbecue meats. Traditional Rioja harmonizes well with fowl and game. But also take an adventure off the beaten path: manzanilla and fino are great with sushi and sashimi; Rioja *reserva* fit tuna steaks; and cream sherry will not be out of place with chocolate. *¡Salud!*

In good weather, the restaurant Tragaluz opens its sliding roof so you can dine under the stars.

or Gaudí's Pedrera. The sliding roof opens to the stars in good weather, while the chairs, lamps, and fittings by Javier Mariscal (creator of 1992 Olympic mascot Cobi) reflect Barcelona's passion for whimsy and playful design. The Mediterranean cuisine remains light and innovative. ⊠ *Passatge de la Concepció 5, Eixample* ☎ *93/487–0196* ▭ *AE, DC, MC, V* ☉ *Closed Jan. 5. No lunch Mon.* Ⓜ *Diagonal* ⊹ *I:8.*

$$
ECLECTIC

✗ **Ya Ya Amelia.** Just two blocks uphill from Gaudí's Sagrada Família church, this kitchen serves lovingly prepared and clued-in dishes ranging from warm goat-cheese salad to foie (duck or goose liver) to *chuleton de buey a la sal* (beef cooked in salt). The "Ya Ya" (an affectionate term for grandmother in Spanish) was apparently of Basque origin, as the cuisine here is a pleasantly schizoid medley of Basque and Catalan. Serving from noon to 5 PM and from 8 PM to midnight, the Ya Ya is a welcome relief for the ravenous and weary fresh from touring the nearby Sagrada Família. ⊠ *Sardenya 364, Eixample* ☎ *93/456–4573* ▭ *AE, DC, MC, V* ☉ *Closed Mon.* Ⓜ *Sagrada Família* ⊹ *L:7.*

GRÀCIA

¢–$
TAPAS

✗ **Adarra.** In Gràcia not far from the Plaça del Diamant, this wood-paneled Basque tavern is handy for the Verdi movie theaters as well as the Teatre Lliure. A good selection of *pintxos* (single tapas on toothpicks) and *cazuelitas* (little earthenware casseroles) is well accompanied by cider, txakolí, Rioja wines, and draft beer. ⊠ *Torrent de l'Olla 148, Gràcia* ☎ *93/218–9237* ☉ *Daily 6 PM–1 AM* Ⓜ *Fontana* ⊹ *J:6.*

¢–$
MEDITERRANEAN

✗ **Amrit.** The delicious Syrian cuisine here is usually a "double feature" combined with catching a flick at the Verdi movie theater a couple of

CLOSE UP

With Children?

Barceloneta's beachfront paella specialists are great favorites for Sunday lunches, with children free to get up and run, skate, cycle, or generally race up and down the boardwalk while their parents linger over brandies and coffee. **Els Pescadors,** a seafood restaurant, has a lovely terrace opening onto a little square that is very handy for children letting off steam.

Serving coffee and light meals, **Aula Zero** is a popular upper Barcelona spot with outdoor tables. Parents peruse the newspapers while children race around the gardens and play on the jungle gyms and slides.

For sandwiches on the go, served in fresh, warm bread, an inexpensive and very respectable snack, try the **Pans & Company** stores all over town. Children will always gobble the Catalan staple *pa amb tomaquet* (toasted bread with olive oil and squeezed tomato), and most cafés, bars, and terraces can whip up a plate on short notice. And for dessert, Barcelona's ubiquitous ice-cream parlors and vendors are another favorite.

Aula Zero (✉ *Carrer del Desert s/n, Jardines de Can Sentmenat* ☎ *93/597–1313* Ⓜ *Reina Elisenda*).
Els Pescadors (✉ *Pl. de Prim 1, Port Olímpic* ☎ *93/225–2018* ☉ *Closed Mon.* Ⓜ *Poblenou*).

3

---

doors up the street. *Hummus, baba ghanouge* (baba ghanoush), *bulgar* (minced meat with bulgar wheat), and *shawarma* (mutton with flat Syrian bread) are all tasty post-cinema dinner options. ✉ *Verdi 18, Gràcia* ☎ *93/217–6550* ⊟ *AE, DC, MC, V* ☉ *Closed Sun.* Ⓜ *Fontana* ⊹ *J:6.*

¢–$
MEDITERRANEAN

✗ **Bilbao.** A cheery bistro near the bottom of Gràcia, this place is always packed with hungry epicureans having a festive time. Unpretentious, straightforward Mediterranean market cuisine is well prepared and sold at reasonable prices here, but the best feature is the generally gleeful din—a good sign. Try the fried egg with black truffles and look for the Montsant red wines, always great values. ✉ *Perill 33, Gràcia* ☎ *93/458–9624* ⊟ *AE, DC, MC, V* ☉ *Closed Sun.* Ⓜ *Diagonal, Joanic* ⊹ *J:7.*

$$$$
SPANISH
Fodor's Choice
★

✗ **Botafumeiro.** On Gràcia's main thoroughfare, Barcelona's finest Galician restaurant has maritime motifs, snowy tablecloths, wood paneling, and fleets of waiters in spotless white outfits all moving at the speed of light. The bank-breaking *Mariscada Botafumeiro* is a seafood medley from shellfish to fin fish to cuttlefish to caviar. An assortment of *media ración* (half-ration) selections is available at the bar, where *pulpo a feira* (squid on slices of potato), *jamón ibérico de bellota* (acorn-fed Iberian ham), and *pan con tomate* (toasted bread topped with olive oil and tomato) make peerless late-night snacks. ✉ *Gran de Gràcia 81, Gràcia* ☎ *93/218–4230* ⊟ *AE, DC, MC, V* Ⓜ *Gràcia* ⊹ *I:6.*

$–$$
CATALAN

✗ **Folquer.** With one of the best-value taster's menus in Barcelona, this artsy little hideaway at the bottom of Gràcia serves creatively prepared traditional Catalan specialties. Chef Juanjo Carrillo, who has worked with Andoni Aduriz at the famous Mugaritz near San Sebastián, produces surprising combinations such as *tartin de poma amb escalope de*

Ground Rules for Coffee

Coffee culture in Barcelona has certain linguistic peculiarities. A normal espresso, black coffee, is simply *un café*. Try saying *café solo*, Madrid-style, and observe the looks you get. A *tallat*, from the verb, in Catalan, *tallar* (to cut) is coffee with just a little milk (*café cortado* in the rest of Spain). For the very best-tasting coffee, nearly rivaling the aroma of fresh-ground coffee beans, order the *café corto*, a true espresso with less liquid and more taste. *Café amb llet* is Catalan for *café con leche* or coffee with milk.

If you really want to see the waiter's eyes glaze over, order a *café descafeinado de maquina con leche desnatada natural* (decaffeinated coffee made in the espresso machine with skimmed milk applied at room temperature).

And a word of warning for those who prefer their java on the run: coffee is still, for the most part, a sit-down or belly-up-to-the-bar affair. So take time to stop and smell the fresh roast.

foie y salsa lima (apple tart with breaded duck liver in a lime sauce) or *bacallà amb mongetes vermellas i pil-pil de pernil* (codfish cooked at low temperature with red beans and Ibérico ham gelatin). The two tasting-menu options (€13 and €17) are among Barcelona's top values. ⊠ *Torrent de l'Olla 3, Gràcia* ☎ *93/217–4395* ▭ *AE, DC, MC, V* ⊗ *Closed Sun. and last 2 wks of Aug. No lunch Sat.* Ⓜ *Diagonal* ✛ *J:7.*

$$$–$$$$
MEDITERRANEAN

✗ **Hofmann.** German-born, Catalonia-trained Mey Hofmann's new locale, uptown just below Travessera de Gràcia, is a graceful designer space with a glassed-in kitchen as center stage. After two decades in the shadow of Santa Maria del Mar on Carrer Argenteria, Hofmann's creative Mediterranean and international cuisine proved that, in this case, "location-location-location" has little to do with unrelenting quality. Sardine tartare, foie gras in puff pastry, prawn risotto, and lovingly prepared baby vegetables are among the best choices at this carefully managed culinary tour de force. ⊠ *La Granada del Penedes 14-16, Gràcia* ☎ *93/218–7165* ⚐ *Reservations essential* ▭ *AE, MC, V* ⊗ *Closed Sat., Sun., Easter wk, and Aug.* Ⓜ *Gràcia* ✛ *H:6.*

$$–$$$
BASQUE

✗ **Ipar-Txoko.** This excellent little Basque enclave has managed to stay largely under the radar, and for that reason, among others, the cuisine is authentic, the prices are fair, and the service is personal and warm. A balanced menu offers San Sebastián specialties such as *txuleta de buey* (beef steak) or *besugo* (sea bream), flawlessly prepared, while the wine list offers classic Riojas and freezing txakolí from Txomin Etxaniz. ⊠ *Carrer Mozart 22, Gràcia* ☎ *93/218–1954* ⚐ *Reservations essential* ▭ *AE, DC, MC, V* ⊗ *Closed Sun., Mon., and last 3 wks of Aug.* Ⓜ *Gràcia, Diagonal* ✛ *I:7.*

$$$–$$$$
CATALAN

✗ **Roig Robí.** Rattan chairs and a garden terrace characterize this simple-yet-polished dining spot in the bottom corner of Gràcia just above the Diagonal (near Via Augusta). Rustic and relaxed, Roig Robí (ruby red in Catalan, as in the color of certain wines) maintains a high level of culinary excellence, serving market cuisine with original personal touches directed by chef Mercé Navarro. Try the *arròs amb espardenyes i carxofes* (rice with sea cucumbers and artichokes). ⊠ *Seneca 20, Gràcia* ☎ *93/218–9222* ⌂ *Reservations essential* ⊟ *AE, DC, MC, V* ☉ *Closed Sun. and 3 wks in Aug. No lunch Sat.* Ⓜ *Gràcia, Diagonal* ⊕ *I:7.*

SARRIÀ, PEDRALBES, AND SANT GERVASI

$$–$$$ ✘ **Acontraluz.** A stylish covered terrace in the leafy upper-Barcelona
CATALAN   neighborhood of Tres Torres, Acontraluz, so named for its translucent ceiling, has a strenuously varied menu ranging from game in season, such as *rable de liebre* (stewed hare) with chutney, to the more northern *pochas con almejas* (beans with clams). All dishes are prepared with care and talent, and the lunch menu is a bargain. ⊠ *Milanesat 19, Tres Torres* ☎ *93/203–0658* ⊟ *AE, DC, MC, V* ☉ *Closed middle 2 wks of Aug.* Ⓜ *Tres Torres* ⊕ *E:3.*

¢   ✘ **Bar Tomás.** Famous for its *patatas bravas amb allioli* (potatoes with
TAPAS   fiery hot sauce and allioli, an emulsion of crushed garlic, and olive oil), accompanied by freezing mugs of San Miguel beer, this old-fashioned Sarrià classic is worth seeking out. On Wednesday, when Bar Tomás is closed, its eager patrons crowd into Iborra (just behind it on Carrer d'Ivorra), which serves the same legendary fare. ⊠ *Major de Sarrià 49, Sarrià* ☎ *93/203–1077* ☉ *Thurs.–Tues. 1–4, 6 –10* Ⓜ *Sarrià* ⊕ *D:2.*

¢–$ ✘ **Dole Café.** Little more than a slender slot on the corner of Capità
CAFÉ   Arenas and Manuel de Falla, this famous upper Barcelona café is absolutely vital to the Sarrià and Capità Arenas neighborhoods. Along with extraordinarily good coffee, sandwiches and pastries here are uncannily well made and tasty. A star attraction is the Popeye ("paw-pay-yay") a spinach, goat cheese and Ibérico ham sandwich not to be missed. ⊠ *Manuel de Falla 16–18, Sarrià* ☎ *93/204–1120* ☉ *Weekdays 6–6, Sat. 6 AM–1:30 PM* Ⓜ *Sarrià, Maria Cristina* ⊕ *C:3.*

$–$$ ✘ **El Mató de Pedralbes.** Named for the *mató* (cottage cheese) tradition-
CATALAN   ally prepared by the Clarist nuns across the street in the Monestir de Pedralbes, this is a fine choice for a lunch stop after exploring the monastery. It also has one of the most authentically Catalan menus around at a great value. Look for *sopa de ceba gratinée* (onion soup), *trinxat* (chopped cabbage with bacon bits), or *truite de patata i ceba* (potato and onion omelet). ⊠ *Bisbe Català 10, Pedralbes* ☎ *93/204–7962* ⊟ *AE, DC, MC, V* ☉ *Closed Sun.* Ⓜ *Reina Elisenda* ⊕ *B:2.*

$$–$$$ ✘ **Fishhh!** Everyone needs to go to a shopping mall sooner or later, and
MEDITERRANEAN   at L'Illa Diagonal, a mile west of Plaça Francesc Macià, you can shop *and* dine on some of Barcelona's best seafood at Lluís Genaro's first-rate fish emporium. Long a major seafood supplier of Barcelona's top restaurants (his seafood-central command post off the back left corner of the Boqueria market, with massive Doric columns framing a world of fish, is worth a look), Genaro and his staff have put together a lively and popular dining space that exudes Boqueria market-style excitement in the midst of a busy shopping venue. ⊠ *Av. Diagonal 557, Sant Gervasi, Les Corts* ☎ *93/444–1139* ⊟ *AE, DC, MC, V* ☉ *Closed Sun.* Ⓜ *Les Corts* ⊕ *D:5.*

$$$-$$$$
CATALAN

✕ **Freixa Tradició.** When wunderkind molecular gastronomist Ramón Freixa turned the family restaurant back over to his father, Josep Maria Freixa, there was some speculation about the menu's headlong rush into the past. Now that the results are in, Barcelona food cognoscenti are coming in droves for the authentic Catalan fare that made El Racó d'en Freixa great before experimental cuisine took over the culinary landscape. Creamy rice with cuttlefish, monkfish with fried garlic, pig trotters with prunes and pine nuts and robust selection of local specialties are making the new-old Freixa better than ever. ⊠ *San Elies 22, Sant Gervasi* ☎ *93/209–7559* ▤ *AE, MC, V* ☻ *Closed Sun. Easter wk, and Aug.* Ⓜ *Sant Gervasi-Muntaner* ✛ *H:5.*

$-$$
FRENCH

✕ **Gouthier.** Thierry Airaud's attractive, minimalist dining space at the bottom of Plaça Sant Vicenç de Sarrià specializes in oysters, caviars, foies (duck and goose livers), and cavas and Champagnes to go with these exquisite products. Fortunately, the tasting portions allow you to indulge your wildest food fantasies without sustaining massive financial damage. Ask for advice on oysters and compare different tastes and textures. ⊠ *Carrer Mañé i Flaquer 8, Sarrià* ☎ *93/205–9969* ▤ *AE, DC, MC, V* ☻ *Closed Sun. and Mon.* Ⓜ *Sarrià* ✛ *D:2.*

$$$-$$$$
JAPANESE

✕ **Icho.** Asian cuisine expert Ana Saura's much respected restaurant just behind L'Illa Diagonal shopping emporium is widely regarded as offering the best Japanese food in Barcelona. Chef Maestro Tan prepares sushi and sashimi of impeccable quality and purity, often working only three feet away from diners at the polished oak bar, with the best views into the glass-walled kitchen. Cockles steamed in sake, miso soup, prawns in tempura, or sauteed yakisoba noodles with vegetables are excellent starters. Steak tartare made with Wagyu Kobe beef is a specialty of the house, as are the tuna tartare with cream of tofu and wasabi and the scallop tartare. ⊠ *Déu i Mata 69, Les Corts* ☎ *93/444–3370* ▤ *AE, DC, MC, V* ☻ *Closed Sun. Les Corts* ✛ *D:6.*

$$$-$$$$
ITALIAN

✕ **Le Quattro Stagioni.** For excellent, streamlined Italian fare far from your stereotypical red-sauce joint (think urban postmodern cuisine), this chic spot just down the street from the Tres Torres metro stop is a winner. It's always filled with intriguing-looking bon vivants evenly balanced between hip locals and clued-in tourists, and the garden is cool and fragrant on summer nights. ⊠ *Dr. Roux 37, Sant Gervasi* ☎ *93/205–2279* ▤ *AE, DC, MC, V* Ⓜ *Tres Torres* ✛ *E:4.*

$$$$
MEDITERRANEAN
Fodor's Choice
★

✕ **Neichel.** Originally from Alsace, chef Jean-Louis Neichel skillfully manages a vast variety of exquisite ingredients such as foie gras, truffles, wild mushrooms, herbs, and the best seasonal vegetables. His flawless Mediterranean delicacies include *ensalada de gambas de Palamós al sésamo con puerros* (shrimp from Palamós with sesame-seed and leeks) and *espardenyes amb salicornia* (sea cucumbers with saltwort) on sundried tomato paste. The dining room is contemporary decor muffled by thick carpets and heavy drapes. ⊠ *Carrer Bertran i Rózpide 1 (off Av. Pedralbes), Pedralbes* ☎ *93/203–8408* ⌂ *Reservations essential* ▤ *AE, DC, MC, V* ☻ *Closed Sun., Mon., and Aug.* Ⓜ *Maria Cristina* ✛ *B:4.*

$-$$
MEDITERRANEAN
Fodor's Choice
★

✕ **Silvestre.** This graceful and easygoing young constellation in Barcelona's culinary galaxy serves modern cuisine to some of the city's most discerning and distinguished diners. Just below Via Augusta, a series of intimate dining rooms and cozy corners are carefully tended by chef Guillermo (Willy) Casañé and his charming wife Marta Cabot, a fluent English–speaking maître d' and partner. Look for fresh market produce lovingly prepared in dishes such as tuna tartare, noodles and shrimp, or wood pigeon with duck liver. Willy's semi-secret list of house wines is always surprising for its quality and value. ⊠ *Santaló 101, Sant Gervasi* ☎ *93/241–4031* ⊟ *AE, DC, MC, V* ⊙ *Closed Sun., middle 2 wks of Aug., and Easter wk. No lunch Sat.* Ⓜ *Muntaner* ⊹ *G:5.*

$$$–$$$$
CATALAN
Fodor's Choice
★

✕ **Tram-Tram.** At the end of the old tram line above the village of Sarrià, Isidre Soler and his wife Reyes have put together one of Barcelona's finest culinary offerings. Try the *menú de degustació* and you might be lucky enough to get marinated tuna salad, cod medallions, and venison filet mignon, among other tasty creations. Perfectly sized portions and a streamlined reinterpretation of space within this traditional Sarrià house—especially in the garden out back—make this a memorable dining experience. ⊠ *Major de Sarrià 121, Sarrià* ☎ *93/204–8518* ⊟ *AE, DC, MC, V* ⊙ *Closed Sun. and late Dec.–early Jan. No lunch Sat.* Ⓜ *Reina Elisenda* ⊹ *D:1.*

$$–$$$
MEDITERRANEAN

✕ **Vivanda.** Just above Plaça de Sarrià, this leafy garden is especially wonderful between May and mid-October, when outside dining is a delight. The new menu designed by Alkimia's Jordi Vilà has traditional Catalan miniatures *"para picar"* (small morsels), *platillos* (little dishes), and half-rations of meat and fish listed as *platillos de pescado* and *platillos de carne.* The *coca de pa de vidre con tomate* (a delicate shell of bread with tomato and olive oil) and the venisonlike *presa de Ibérico* (fillet of Ibérico pig) are both exquisite. ⊠ *Major de Sarrià 134, Sarrià* ☎ *93/203–1918* ⊟ *AE, DC, MC, V* ⊙ *Closed Sun.* Ⓜ *Reina Elisenda* ⊹ *D:1.*

TIBIDABO

$$$$
NUEVA COCINA
Fodor's Choice
★

✕ **Àbac.** In the tradition of Catalonia's finest restaurants, Xavier Pellicer leaves no detail to chance here, preparing carefully selected ingredients in innovative recipes based on culinary canons learned from Europe's top chefs. The taster's menu is the only reasonable choice here: trust Xavi (any attempt at economy here is roughly analogous to quibbling about deck chairs on the Titanic). Located until October 2007 on Carrer del Rec in the Ribera-Born neighborhood, Àbac's new digs are in an uptown boutique hotel. ⊠ *Av. del Tibidabo 1–7, Tibidabo* ☎ *93/319–6600* ⊟ *AE, DC, MC, V* ⊙ *Closed Sun. and Aug. No lunch Mon.* Ⓜ *Tibidabo* ⊹ *H:2.*

$$$–$$$$
SPANISH

✕ **El Asador de Aranda.** This immense palace a few minutes walk above the Avenida Tibidabo metro station is a hike—but worth it if you're in upper Barcelona. The kitchen specializes in Castilian cooking, with *cordero lechal* (roast suckling lamb), *morcilla* (black sausage), and *pimientos de piquillo* (sweet red peppers) as star players. The dining room has a terra-cotta floor and a full complement of Art Nouveau ornamentation, from carved-wood trim to stained-glass partitions, acid-engraved glass, and Moorish archways. ⊠ *Av. del Tibidabo 31, Tibidabo* ☎ *93/417–0115* ⊟ *AE, DC, MC, V* ⊙ *Closed Easter wk and Sun. in Aug. No dinner Sun.* Ⓜ *Tibidabo* ⊹ *H:1.*

OUTSKIRTS OF BARCELONA

With the many fine in-town dining options available in Barcelona, any out-of-town recommendations must logically rank somewhere in the uppermost stratosphere of gastronomic excellence. These three, all rated among the top five or six establishments below the Pyrenees (one at the foot of Montseny, the other on the coast) undoubtedly do.

$$$–$$$$
CATALAN
Fodor'sChoice
★

✕ **Can Fabes.** Santi Santamaria's master class in Mediterranean cuisine merits the 45-minute train ride (or 30-minute drive) north of Barcelona to Sant Celoni. One of the five top-rated restaurants in Spain (along with El Bulli in Roses, Sant Pau in nearby Sant Pol de Mar, and Arzak, Akelaré, and Berasategui in San Sebastián), this is a must for anyone interested in fine dining. Every detail, from the six flavors of freshly baked bread to the cheese selection, is superb. The taster's menu is the wisest solution. The RENFE stations are at Passeig de Gràcia or Sants (the last train back is at 10:24 PM, so this is a lunchtime-only transport solution). Fortunately, there are five guest rooms available just a few steps from your last glass of wine. ⊠ *Carrer Sant Joan 6, Sant Celoni* ☎ *93/867–2851* ▭ *AE, DC, MC, V* ☉ *Closed Mon., 1st 2 wks of Feb., and late June–early July. No dinner Sun.* ✛ *M:5.*

$$$–$$$$
CATALAN

✕ **Hispania.** This famous pilgrimage—one of the best restaurants in Catalonia for the last 50 years—is just 39 km (24 mi) up the beach north of Barcelona, easily reached by the Calella train from the RENFE station in Plaça Catalunya. Sisters Francisca and Dolores Reixach continue to turn out the same line of classical Catalan cuisine that, despite the name Hispania, has characterized this graceful dining room from the start. *Faves amb botifarra negre* (fava beans with black sausage) ranks high on the list of signature dishes here, but the fresh fish and seafood from the Arenys de Mar fish auction are invariably excellent. ⊠ *Carrer Real 54 (Ctra. N II, 2 km south of Arenys de Mar), Arenys de Mar* ☎ *93/791–0457* ▭ *AE, DC, MC, V* ☉ *Closed Tues., Easter wk, and Oct. No dinner Sun.* ✛ *L:15.*

$$$$
CATALAN
Fodor'sChoice
★

✕ **Sant Pau.** Carme Ruscalleda's Sant Pol de Mar treasure, one of the six top restaurants below the Pyrenees, is a scenic 40-minute train ride along the beach from Plaça Catalunya's RENFE station: the Calella train stops at the door. Inside are clean, spare lines and a garden overlooking the Mediterranean. Dishes change with the seasons, but picture *vieiras* (scallops) with crisped artichoke flakes on roast potato, or *lubina* (sea bass) on baby leeks and chard in *garnatxa* (sweet Catalan wine) sauce. If you're there for Sant Jordi, Barcelona's Lovers' Day on April 23rd, you might score a *misiva de amor* (love letter), a pastry envelope containing julienned berries and peaches. ⊠ *Carrer Nou 10, Sant Pol de Mar* ☎ *93/760–0662* ▭ *AE, DC, MC, V* ☉ *Closed Mon., 2 wks in Mar., and 2 wks in Nov. No dinner Sun.* ✛ *L:15.*

Dining and Lodging Atlas

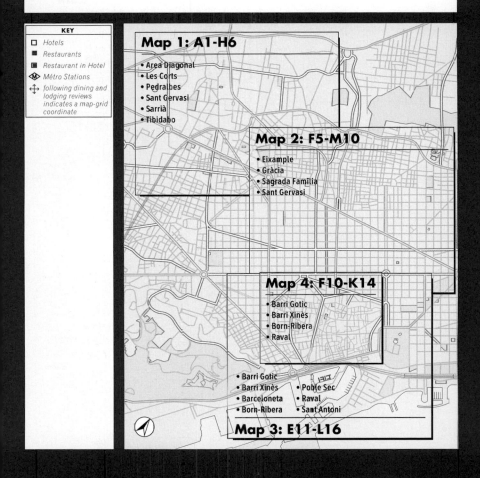

KEY

- □ Hotels
- ■ Restaurants
- ▣ Restaurant in Hotel
- ◆ Métro Stations
- ✛ following dining and lodging reviews indicates a map-grid coordinate

Map 1: A1-H6

- Àrea Diagonal
- Les Corts
- Pedralbes
- Sant Gervasi
- Sarrià
- Tibidabo

Map 2: F5-M10

- Eixample
- Gràcia
- Sagrada Família
- Sant Gervasi

Map 4: F10-K14

- Barri Gotic
- Barri Xinès
- Born-Ribera
- Raval

- Barri Gotic
- Barri Xinès
- Barceloneta
- Born-Ribera
- Poble Sec
- Raval
- Sant Antoni

Map 3: E11-L16

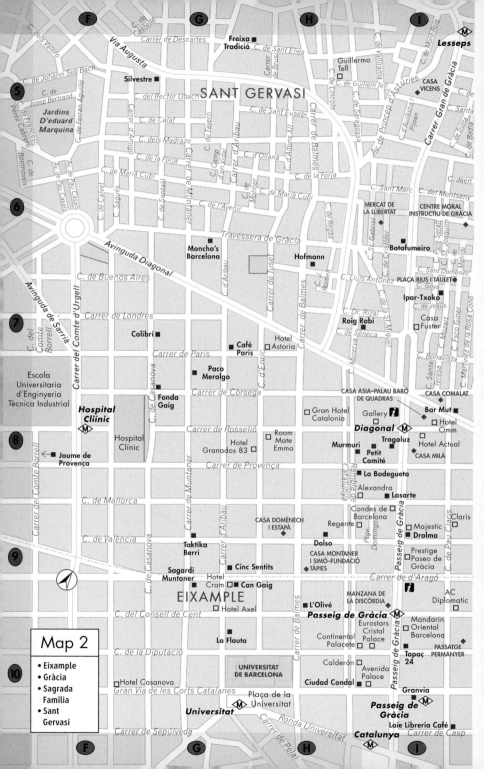

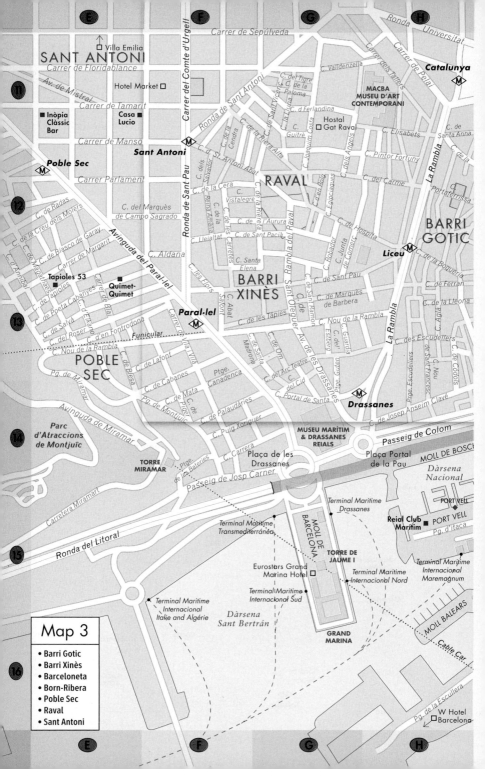

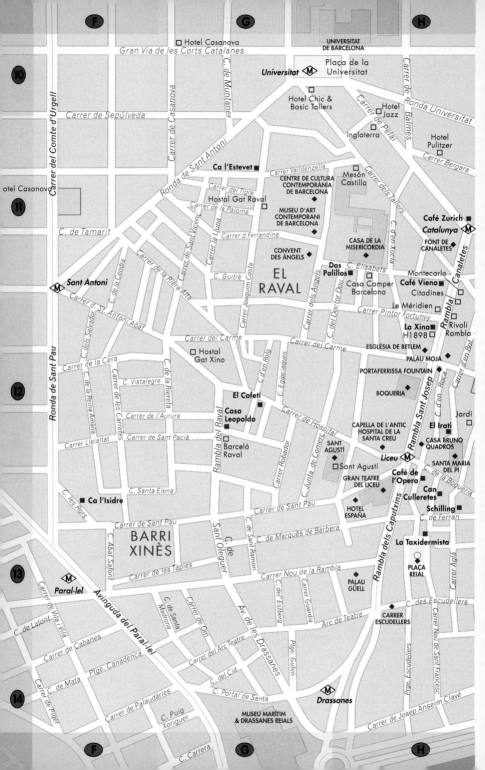

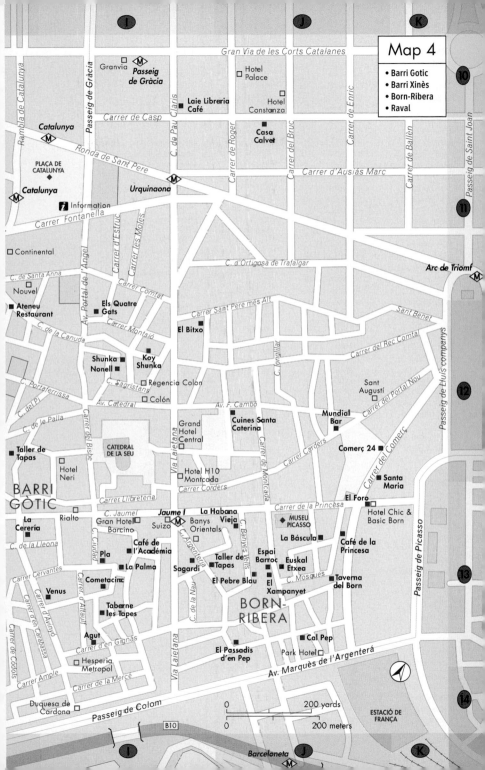

Restaurants

Hotels

4

Where to Stay

WORD OF MOUTH

"[Hotel Granados 83] has a 4 star superior rating and while the rooms themselves are small, they are so well organized and so attractive that you don't even notice . . . The staff is very helpful— and hip . . . I would stay there again and again, especially when the great low season prices are in effect."

—JulieVikmanis

By George
Semler

The hotel trade may seem centuries removed from Miguel de Cervantes's 17th-century description of Barcelona as "repository of courtesy, travelers' shelter" but, as the author of *Don Quijote* discerned over 400 years ago, the city has a weakness for pampering and impressing visitors to its leafy streets and boulevards.

Barcelona's pre-Olympics hotel surge in the early 1990s was matched only by its post-Olympics hotel surge in the early 2000s. New hotels now spring forth all over town while old standards frantically renovate and redesign in an effort to keep up. Architects Ricardo Bofill and Rafael Moneo are busy creating new and surprising skyscrapers, facades, atriums, and halls, while hotel restaurants have become increasingly important, with the Majestic's Drolma, the Arts's Arola, the Condes de Barcelona's Lasarte, the ME's Dos Cielos, and the Hotel Omm's Moo, all at the pinnacle of the city's gastronomy.

Hotels in the Gothic Quarter and along the Rambla no longer lag in luxury behind the newer lodgings in the Eixample or west along the Diagonal, with waterfront monoliths such as the Arts, W Hotel Barcelona, and the Eurostars Grand Marina leading the way. Many Eixample hotels are set in restored and streamlined late-19th- or early-20th-century town houses and offer midtown excitement and easy access to all of Barcelona. The Claris, the Majestic, the Condes de Barcelona, the Neri, and the Colón probably best combine style and luxury with a sense of where you are, while sybaritic modern palaces such as the Arts, the Omm, the H1898, and the new W Hotel offer design excitement and state-of-the-art technology and comfort. The Hotel Omm, in the Eixample, caused a sensation with its Zen-inspired design and culinary excellence.

Smaller hotels in the Ciutat Vella, such as the Sant Agustí, Hotel Market, or Hotel Chic & Basic Born are less than half as expensive and more a part of city life, though they tend to be noisier and less luxurious. Overlooking Barcelona is the Gran Hotel La Florida for those who want to be up and out of the fray.

WHERE SHOULD I STAY?

	Neighborhood Vibe	Pros	Cons
Rambla	A solid stream of humanity around the clock, the Rambla is always alive and palpitating. A promenade that is chock-full of every type of street life, this is where you can feel the city's pulse.	The Rambla is the city's most iconic runway and always an exciting strip. The Boqueria market, the flower stalls, the opera house, and Plaça Reial are all quintessential Barcelona.	The incessant crush of humanity can be overwhelming, especially if FC Barcelona wins a championship and the entire city descends upon the Rambla.
Gothic Quarter & Ribera-Born	With 19th-century gaslight-type lamps glowing in the corners of Roman and Gothic areas, this is a romantic part of town. The Picasso Museum and Santa Maria del Mar basilica sit nearby.	The architecture of the Gothic Quarter is tangible evidence of the city's past. Plaça Sant Jaume, the cathedral, Plaça del Rei, and the Born-Ribera district are the main reasons to visit the city.	Echoes reverberate around this ancient sound chamber. And while there is little serious noise, what there is goes a long way.
Raval	The Raval has always been a rough-and-tumble part of town. But the nightlife is exciting and the diversity of the neighborhood is exemplary. Bonus: living behind the Boqueria market.	For the closest thing to Marrakesh in Barcelona, the Raval has a buzz all its own. A contemporary art museum, the medieval hospital, and the Mercat de Sant Antoni offer plenty to explore.	The Raval can seem dangerous, whether it is or not. Certain corners teem with prostitutes, drug dealers, and Barcelona's seamiest elements.
Eixample	Some of Gaudí's best buildings line the sidewalks, and many of the city's finest hotels and restaurants are right around the corner. And then there's the shopping…	Eixample remains the world's only Art Nouveau neighborhood, constantly rewarding to the eye. Gaudí's unfinished masterpiece La Sagrada Família is within walking distance.	A bewildering grid without numbers or alphabetization, the Eixample can seem hard-edged compared to the older, quirkier, parts of Barcelona.
Barceloneta & Port Olímpic	The onetime fisherman's quarter, Barceloneta retains its informal and working-class ambience, with laundry flapping over the streets and sidewalk restaurants lining Passeig Joan de Borbó.	Near the beach, this part of town has a laid-back feel. The Port Olímpic is a world apart, but Barceloneta is brimming with the best seafood dining spots in town.	Barceloneta offers few hotel opportunities, while the Port Olímpic's principal offering, the monolithic Hotel Arts, can feel like a tourist colony away from the rest of town.
Pedralbes, Sarrià & Upper Barcelona	Upper Barcelona is leafy and residential, and the air is always a few degrees cooler. Pedralbes holds Barcelona's finest mansions; Sarrià is a rustic village suspended in the urban sprawl.	Getting above the madding fray and into better air has distinct advantages, and the upper reaches of Barcelona offers them. A 15-minute train ride connects Sarrià with the Rambla.	The only drawback to staying in upper Barcelona is the 15-minute commute to the most important monuments and attractions. After midnight on weeknights this will require a taxi.

4

BARCELONA LODGING PLANNER

Lodging Strategy

Scan the "Best Bets" following this page for top recommendations by price and experience. Or find a review quickly in the listings. Search by neighborhood, then alphabetically.

In This Chapter

Meal Plans

If breakfast is included in the rate, we've noted it at the end of each review with abbreviations: the European Plan (EP, with no meals), the Breakfast Plan (BP, with a full breakfast), or Continental Plan (CP, with a continental breakfast).

Facilities

Hotel entrances are marked with a plaque bearing the letter H and the number of stars. The letter R (standing for *residencia*) after the letter H indicates an establishment with no meal service. The designations *fonda* (F), *pensión* (P), *hostal* (Hs), and *casa de huéspedes* (CH) indicate budget accommodations.

Hotel ratings used by the Turisme de Barcelona are based on stars, with five stars as the highest rating. Two stars and above are dependable ratings, while one-star ratings should be considered budget options with a high likelihood of flaws. You should specify when reserving whether you prefer two beds or one double bed. Although single rooms (*habitación sencilla*) are usually available, they are often on the small side, and you might prefer to pay a bit extra for single occupancy in a double room (*habitación doble uso individual*).

Using the Maps

Throughout the chapter, you'll see mapping symbols and coordinates (✛ F2) at the end of the reviews that correspond to the atlas the end of the Where to Eat chapter. The letter and number after the ✛ symbol indicates the property's coordinates on the map grid.

Prices

Budget travelers, backpackers, and students will all find affordable options throughout the Ciutat Vella; just look up, and you will see *pensiones* and *hostales*. But for the discerning traveler, Barcelona's finer hotels are, alas, as expensive as those of any other major city.

Most prices include a V.A.T. (Value Added Tax) of 8%.

WHAT IT COSTS IN EUROS					
	¢	$	$$	$$$	$$$$
Hotels	Under €75	€75–€124	€125–€174	€175–€225	Over €225

Prices are for two people in a standard double room in high season.

BEST BETS
FOR BARCELONA LODGING

Fodor's offers a selective listing of quality lodging experiences in every price range, from the city's best budget choice to its most sophisticated luxury hotel. Here we've compiled our top recommendations by price and experience. The very best properties—in other words, those that provide a particularly remarkable experience in their price range—are designated in the listings with the Fodor's Choice logo.

Fodor's Choice

Casa Fuster, $$$, p. 214

Claris, $$$, p. 206

Colón, $$, p. 192

Condes de Barcelona, $$$, p. 207

Duquesa de Cardona, $$$, p. 198

Hostal Gat Raval, $, p. 196

Hotel Granados 83, $$$, p. 210

Hotel Neri, $$$$, p. 193

Hotel Omm, $$$$, p. 211

Jardí, $, p. 193

Majestic, $$$, p. 212

Sant Agustí, $$, p. 197

Turó de Vilana, $$$, p. 218

W Hotel Barcelona, $$$$, p. 203

By Price

$

Jardí, p. 193

Hostal Gat Raval, p. 196

Hotel Chic & Basic Born, p. 194

$$

Colón, p. 192

Continental Palacete, p. 207

Sant Agustí, p. 197

$$$

Casa Fuster, p. 214

Claris, p. 206

Condes de Barcelona, p. 207

Duquesa de Cardona, p. 198

Gran Hotel la Florida, p. 218

Hotel Granados 83, p. 210

Majestic, p. 212

Turó de Vilana, p. 218

$$$$

Hotel Arts, p. 202

Hotel Neri, p. 193

Hotel Palace, p. 211

Hotel Omm, p. 211

W Hotel Barcelona, p. 203

By Experience

BEST CONCIERGE

Majestic, p. 212

BEST HIPSTER HOTELS

Hotel Casanova, p. 210

Hotel Chic & Basic Born, p. 194

Hotel Granados 83, p. 210

BEST FOR HISTORY BUFFS

Colón, p. 192

Continental Palacete, p. 207

BEST HOTEL RESTAURANT

Majestic (Drolma), p. 212

Hotel Cram (Can Gaig), p. 210

ME Barcelona (Dos Cielos), p. 212

Condes de Barcelona (Lasarte), p. 207

BEST LOBBY

W Hotel Barcelona, p. 203

Claris, p. 206

Hotel Arts, p. 202

BEST VIEWS

Hotel Arts, p. 202

W Hotel Barcelona, p. 203

CHILD-FRIENDLY

Casa Camper Barcelona, p. 195

Gran Hotel la Florida, p. 218

Villa Emilia, p. 214

GOOD FOR GROUPS

Gran Derby, p. 208

ME Barcelona, p. 212

MOST ROMANTIC

Gran Hotel la Florida, p. 218

Hotel Neri, p. 193

HOTEL REVIEWS

Listed alphabetically within neighborhoods

CIUTAT VELLA (OLD CITY)

The Ciutat Vella includes the Rambla, Barri Gòtic, Born-Ribera, and Raval districts between Plaça de Catalunya and the port.

BARRI GÒTIC

$$–$$$

Fodor's Choice

★

▣ **Colón.** There's something clubby about this elegant Barcelona standby, surprisingly intimate and charming for such a sizable operation. The location is ideal—directly across the plaza from the cathedral, overlooking weekend *sardana* dancing, Thursday antiques markets, and, of course, the floodlit cathedral by night. Rooms are comfortable and furnished with traditional pieces, some of them antiques; try to get one with a view of the cathedral. The Colón was a favorite of the artist Joan Miró. **Pros:** walking distance from all of central Barcelona; views of cathedral; friendly staff. **Cons:** slightly old-fashioned; undistinguished dining. ⊠ *Av. Catedral 7, Barri Gòtic* ☎ *93/301–1404* ⊕ *www.hotelcolon.es* ⇨ *140 rooms, 5 suites* ⌂ *In-room: Wi-Fi, safe, refrigerator. In-hotel: restaurant, bar* ▤ *AE, DC, MC, V* ⦿| *EP* Ⓜ *Catalunya* ✛ *I:12.*

$$$

▣ **Gran Hotel Barcino.** Appropriately named for the ancient Roman settlement of Barcelona that once surrounded this hotel (the site was once part of the Roman Forum), the Barcino offers nearly unparalleled ease for exploring the Gothic Quarter and Born-Ribera. Rooms are small but well planned, and sparsely filled with modern furniture in gray tones and marble bathrooms, while the reception area enclosed by an immense pane of glass feels like part of the Gothic Quarter. The concierge will advise you about not-to-miss events in either the nearby City Hall or the Catalan seat of government, the Generalitat. **Pros:** central location; bright contemporary design; friendly staff. **Cons:** small rooms; on a busy street in the dead center of town; not a lot of amenities; no room service. ⊠ *Jaume I 6, Barri Gòtic* ☎ *93/302–2012* ⊕ *www.hotelbarcino.com* ⇨ *53 rooms* ⌂ *In-room: Wi-Fi, safe.* ⌂ *In-hotel: bar, Wi-Fi hotspot* ▤ *AE, DC, MC, V* ⦿| *EP* Ⓜ *Jaume I* ✛ *I:13.*

$$$$

▣ **Grand Hotel Central.** At the edge of the Gothic Quarter, very near the Barcelona cathedral, this fashionable midtown hideaway is becoming a magnet for the hip and hot-to-trot. Rooms are flawlessly furnished with stark furniture and equipped with high-tech design features, from flat-screen TVs to DSL hookups. The restaurant, supervised by internationally acclaimed chef Ramón Freixa, is bound for glory, and the roof terrace and top-floor pool offer a unique perch over the city's 2,000-year-old Roman and Gothic central nucleus. The higher the better is the rule here, as street level can be noisy, soundproofing or not. **Pros:** excellent location between the Gothic Quarter and the Born; attentive service; full gamut of high-tech amenities. **Cons:** the street outside is noisy and fast. ⊠ *Via Laietana 30, Barri Gòtic* ☎ *93/295–7900* ⊕ *www.grandhotelcentral.com* ⇨ *141 rooms, 6 suites* ⌂ *In-room: Wi-Fi. In-hotel: restaurant, bar, Internet terminal, Wi-Fi hotspot, pool, gym, parking (paid)* ▤ *AE, DC, MC, V* ⦿| *EP* Ⓜ *Catalunya, Jaume I* ✛ *I:12.*

$-$$ ⬚ **Hesperia Metropol.** A block in from the port and midway between the Rambla and Via Laietana, this modestly priced hotel has a central location on a classic Gothic Quarter thoroughfare, and cheerful guest rooms decorated in primary colors and modern simplicity. Equidistant from the beach and the cathedral, this handy and unassuming hotel maintains an under-the-radar chic. A bright, upbeat lobby and sliding-glass entryway display the sweeping lines of a 19th-century town house converted to a contemporary hotel. **Pros:** central location; the beach a 15-minute walk away; friendly staff. **Cons:** not the most elegant part of town; motorbikes blasting down Carrer Ample. ⊠ *Ample 31, Barri Gòtic* ☎ *93/310–5100* ⊕ *www.hesperia-metropol.com* ⤥ *71 rooms* ⚬ *In-room: Wi-Fi, safe. In-hotel: bar, parking (paid)* ⊟ *AE, DC, MC, V* ⑩ *EP* Ⓜ *Drassanes, Jaume I* ✢ *I:13.*

$$$$ ⬚ **Hotel Neri.** Built into a 17th-century palace over one of the Gothic
Fodor's Choice   Quarter's smallest and most charming squares, Plaça Sant Felip Neri,
★   the Neri is a singular counterpoint of ancient and avant-garde design. The facade and location are early Barcelona, but the cavernous interior spaces are unfailingly contemporary and edgy. Rooms stress straight lines, sheer and angular precision, and expanses of wood and stone with Rothko-like artwork. **Pros:** central location; design; roof terrace for cocktails and breakfast. **Cons:** noise from the echo-chamber square can be a problem on summer nights (and winter morning school days); impractical design details such as the hanging bed lights. ⊠ *St. Sever 5, Barri Gòtic* ☎ *93/304–0655* ⊕ *www.hotelneri.com* ⤥ *22 rooms* ⚬ *In-room: Wi-Fi, refrigerator. In-hotel: Internet terminal, Wi-Fi hotspot, restaurant, bar* ⊟ *AE, DC, MC, V* ⑩ *EP* Ⓜ *Liceu, Catalunya* ✢ *I:12.*

$ ⬚ **Jardí.** Perched over the traffic-free and charming Plaça del Pi and
Fodor's Choice   Plaça Sant Josep Oriol, this chic budget hotel has rooms with views
★   of the Gothic church of Santa Maria del Pi and outfitted with simple pine furniture. The in-house breakfast (€6) is excellent, and the alfresco tables at the Bar del Pi, downstairs, are ideal in summer. There are five floors—the higher, the quieter—and an elevator. It's not the Ritz, and it can be noisy in summer, but all in all the Jardí is great value. **Pros:** central location; good value; impeccable bathrooms. **Cons:** flimsy beds and furnishings; scarce amenities, including no room service. ⊠ *Pl. Sant Josep Oriol 1, Barri Gòtic* ☎ *93/301–5900* ⊕ *www.hoteljardi-barcelona. com* ⤥ *40 rooms* ⚬ *In-room: Wi-Fi. In-hotel: Internet terminal, Wi-Fi hotspot* ⊟ *AE, DC, MC, V* ⑩ *EP* Ⓜ *Liceu, Catalunya* ✢ *H:12.*

$-$$ ⬚ **Regencia Colon.** Behind the Colón hotel, and with just about all the same conveniences (minus the cathedral view) at half the price, the Regencia Colon is a solid option to consider. It may even be a little quieter back here, where you're not listening to street minstrels on the main drag. Rooms are unexceptional but serviceable, with standard wood furnishings. Note that the restaurant does not serve dinner. **Pros:** central location near cathedral; near excellent restaurants. **Cons:** small lobby; no bar; lacks its own scene. ⊠ *Sagristans 13, Barri Gòtic* ☎ *93/318–9858* ⊕ *www.hotelregenciacolon.com* ⤥ *51 rooms* ⚬ *In-room: Wi-Fi, safe. In-hotel: Wi-Fi hotspot* ⊟ *AE, DC, MC, V* ⑩ *EP* Ⓜ *Catalunya* ✢ *I:12.*

$–$$ ⛑ **Rialto.** With its glass-walled reception area on the corner of Pas de l'Ensenyança and Carrer Ferran, this bright, spotless, well-lighted place gives way to subdued rooms with wooden floorboards, white walls, patterned gray drapes and bedspreads, and solid walnut doors. Passatge del Crèdit, on the other side of the hotel, was where iconic Catalan painter Joan Miró was born. Miró's birth room is now the Rialto's suite 330 (€225), a perfect spot for dreams filled with the painter's signature shooting red and blue stars. **Pros:** central location; friendly staff. **Cons:** one of the busiest streets in the city; no room service. ⊠ *Ferran 42, Barri Gòtic* ☎ *93/318–5212* ⊕ *www.hotel-rialto.com* ⇆ *199 rooms, 1 suite* ⟁ *In-room: Wi-Fi, safe. In-hotel: restaurant, bar, Wi-Fi hotspot, laundry service* ▭ *AE, DC, MC, V* ⏀⊚*EP* Ⓜ *Liceu, Catalunya* ⊕ *I:13.*

$–$$ ⛑ **Suizo.** The lobby and public rooms in this Barcelona classic have sweeping spaces around a curving reception desk, modern furniture, and good views over the busy square just east of Plaça del Rei. Guest rooms have gleaming whitewashed walls set off by mustard- and coffee-colored drapes, bedspreads, and wood: colorful but soothing and sober. The location places you in the middle of most of Ciutat Vella's most important attractions: the Picasso Museum, Santa Maria del Mar, and the bustling Born-Ribera neighborhood are all a two-minute walk away, and the City History Museum is across the street. **Pros:** central location over a subway stop; cheerful and sunny new rooms; friendly staff. **Cons:** a maelstrom of tourists and pedestrians passes the door; subway rumblings begin very early for rooms on lower floors. ⊠ *Pl. del Àngel 12, Barri Gòtic* ☎ *93/310–6108* ⊕ *www.hotelsuizo.com* ⇆ *60 rooms* ⟁ *In-room: Wi-Fi, safe. In-hotel: bar, Wi-Fi hotspot, laundry service* ▭ *AE, DC, MC, V* ⏀⊚*EP* Ⓜ *Jaume I* ⊕ *I:13.*

BORN-RIBERA

$ ⛑ **Banys Orientals.** This contemporary-design hotel presents innovative lighting and imaginative touches, such as four-poster beds and Gaudí-esque chairs. (Despite its name, the "Oriental Baths" has, for the moment, no spa.) With the popular Senyor Parellada restaurant downstairs, rooms overlooking the street can be noisy, not from traffic but from the flow of humanity moving up and down Carrer Argenteria, one of the city's liveliest arteries. Two steps from Santa Maria del Mar and the Born area, this is a good base camp for most of early Barcelona's finest treasures. **Pros:** central location; interesting design; recent technology. **Cons:** noisy nightlife thoroughfare; mediocre restaurant. ⊠ *Argenteria 37, Born-Ribera* ☎ *93/268–8460* ⊕ *www.hotelbanysorientals.com* ⇆ *56 rooms* ⟁ *In-room: Wi-Fi. In-hotel: restaurant, bar, Internet terminal, Wi-Fi hotspot* ▭ *AE, DC, MC, V* ⏀⊚*EP* Ⓜ *Jaume I* ⊕ *I:13.*

$$–$$$ ⛑ **Hotel Chic & Basic Born.** A revolutionary concept best illustrated by the middle-of-your-room glass shower stalls, the Chic & Basic is a hit with young hipsters looking for a Barcelona combo package of splashy design, surprise, and originality at less-than wallet-rocking prices. The restaurant, called the White Bar for its completely albino decor, serves excellent Mediterranean cooking. Designer Xavier Claramunt has come up with a winner here. **Pros:** perfectly situated for Barcelona's hot Born-Ribera scene; clean-lined sleek and impeccable design. **Cons:** tumultuous nightlife around the hotel requires closed windows on

weekends; rooms and spaces are small. ✉ *Carrer Princesa 50, Born-Ribera* ☎ *93/295–4652* ⊕ *www.chicandbasic.com* ➟ *31 rooms* � *In-room: Wi-Fi. In-hotel: restaurant, bar, Internet terminal, Wi-Fi hotspot* ⊟ *AE, DC, MC, V* |◯| *EP* Ⓜ *Jaume I* ✛ *J:13.*

$$-$$$ ⊡ **Hotel H10 Montcada.** Übermodern, this high-tech hotel at the edge of the Gothic Quarter (part of the sleek H10 chain popping up all over Spain) is a sure bet for contemporary design and comfort—though the minimalist decor can seem a little anemic compared to the rest of Barcelona's eye candy. A five-minute walk from some of the city's most medieval corners, the rooms, though small, are efficient and offer every state-of-the-art commodity you could ask for. The sun terrace on the roof overlooks the port and much of the Gothic Quarter's medieval architecture. **Pros:** central location; high-tech amenities. **Cons:** no restaurant or bar;no scene of its own; no room service. ✉ *Via Laietana 24, Born-Ribera* ☎ *93/268–8570* ⊕ *www.h10.es* ➟ *87 rooms* ⚫ *In room: Wi-Fi, safe, refrigerator. In-hotel: bar, gym* ⊟ *AE, DC, MC, V* |◯| *EP* Ⓜ *Jaume I* ✛ *I:12.*

$$-$$$ ⊡ **Park Hotel.** Backing into some of Barcelona's prime art, architecture, and wine and tapas territory, this semi-budget hotel offers sleek new rooms with espresso-colored wood details situated across the street from the elegant old Estació de França train station. The hotel is modest and unassuming but efficient, full of modern conveniences and staffed with cheerful and hardworking young professionals. **Pros:** central location; good value; friendly staff. **Cons:** small rooms; no glamour; no room service. ✉ *Av. Marquès de l'Argentera 11, Born-Ribera* ☎ *93/319–6000* ⊕ *www.parkhotelbarcelona.com* ➟ *91 rooms* ⚫ *In room: Wi-Fi, refrigerator. In-hotel: bar* ⊟ *AE, DC, MC, V* |◯| *EP* Ⓜ *Barceloneta* ✛ *J:13.*

EL RAVAL

$$-$$$ ⊡ **Barceló Raval.** This cylindrical black rocket ship looming over the Raval offers designer surroundings and, from the roof terrace, 360-degree vistas of all of Barcelona. The upper floors on the Mediterranean side of the hotel have sea views. Rooms are equipped with everything from espresso machines to iPod docks, while the bathrooms are bright and open to the room. For a contemporary design-lodging environment at moderate rates over one of Barcelona's most tumultuous neighborhoods, this is one of the city's recent revelations. **Pros:** central location five minutes from the Rambla; panoramic views over city; hip young clientele. **Cons:** space-age design features not to everyone's liking; the Raval might too wild for some customers. ✉ *Rambla del Raval 17–21, Raval* ☎ *93/320–1490* ⊕ *www.barcelo-raval.com* ➟ *186 rooms* ⚫ *In-room: Wi-Fi, refrigerator, safe. In-hotel: restaurant, Wi-Fi hotspot, bar, pool, parking (paid)* ⊟ *AE, DC, MC, V* |◯| *EP* Ⓜ *Liceu* ✛ *G:12.*

$$$ ⊡ **Casa Camper Barcelona.** The mutual brainchild of the Camper footwear empire and Barcelona's nonpareil Vinçon design store, this 21st-century hotel sits halfway between the Rambla and the MACBA (Museum of Contemporary Art). No smoking, no tips, a free 24-hour snack facility where you can invite your friends, ecologically recycled residual waters, children up to 12 staying free of charge, and the Dos Palillos restaurant next door, serving some of Barcelona's finest Asian-fusion cuisine, all add up to a brave and exciting new world in the formerly

sketchy Raval. **Pros:** handy location in mid-Raval just off the Rambla; ultramodern technology and concept; handy to MACBA and a handful of trendy shops. **Cons:** snacking redundant, as you're two steps from the Boqueria; no way to get a car close to the hotel door. ⊠ *C. Elisabets 11, Raval* ☎ *93/342–6280* ⊕ *www.casacamper.com* ↩ *20 rooms, 5 suites* ⑤ *In-room: Wi-Fi, safe. In-hotel: restaurant, bicycles, laundry service* ⊟ *AE, DC, MC, V* ⑩ *BP* Ⓜ *Catalunya* ⊕ *H:11.*

$ ☷ Hostal Chic & Basic Tallers. Another sleek budget choice in the upper Raval, this even-more-economical version of the Hotel Chic & Basic over in the Born offers three sizes of rooms from medium to extra large, and has a living room called Chill & Basic with Wi-Fi access and free snacks. Other surprising assets include in-room music speakers that allow you to listen to the mix created by the hotel's music director or plug in your own iPod. **Pros:** perfectly designed and situated for an exciting, low-cost Barcelona experience; young and friendly staff. **Cons:** the streets in the Raval can reverberate noisily at night; space is tight in these rooms. ⊠ *Carrer Tallers 82, Raval* ☎ *93/302–5183* ⊕ *www. chicandbasic.com* ↩ *14 rooms* ⑤ *In-room: Wi-Fi. In-hotel: Internet terminal, Wi-Fi hotspot* ⊟ *AE, DC, MC, V* ⑩ *EP* Ⓜ *Catalunya, Universitat* ⊕ *G:10.*

¢–$ ☷ Hostal Gat Raval. This hip little hole-in-the-wall opens into a surpris-
Fodor's Choice   ingly bright and sleekly designed modern space with rooms that come
★   in different shapes, styles, and numbers of beds, all cheerily appointed and impeccably maintained. Just around the corner from the MACBA, the Gat Raval seems to have been influenced by Richard Meier's shining contemporary structure, though you'd never guess it from the street. **Pros:** central location in the deepest Raval; contemporary design; recent technology. **Cons:** noisy street at threshold; somewhat cramped rooms and public spaces; few amenities. ⊠ *Joaquin Costa 44, Raval* ☎ *93/481–6670* ⊕ *www.gataccommodation.com* ↩ *22 rooms* ⑤ *In-room: Wi-Fi. In-hotel: Internet terminal, Wi-Fi hotspot* ⊟ *AE, DC, MC, V* ⑩ *BP* Ⓜ *Universitat* ⊕ *G:11.*

$ ☷ Hostal Gat Xino. A cheery space in what was once the darkest Raval, Gat places the adventurous traveler in the middle of what may seem more like a North African souk than a modern textile and design metropolis. Near the intersection of Carrers Carmen and Hospital, the Gat Xino gives you an up-close look at one of Barcelona's most cosmopolitan and traditionally tumultuous neighborhoods. (*Gat* is Catalan for cat, and xino for *chino* or Chinese, referring to the Raval's infamously seedy "Chinatown.") Rooms are decorated in bright colors, and the value is excellent. In the bargain, you may discover that the Raval and its raucous street life are inhabited by some of Barcelona's friendliest citizens. **Pros:** central location; smart and sassy design; up-to-date technology; hostel-like friendly clients and staff. **Cons:** busy and noisy section of the Raval at your doorstep; small rooms and public spaces. ⊠ *Hospital 155, Raval* ☎ *93/324–8833* ⊕ *www.gataccommodation. com* ↩ *35 rooms* ⑤ *In-room: Wi-Fi. In-hotel: Internet terminal, Wi-Fi hotspot* ⊟ *AE, DC, MC, V* ⑩ *BP* Ⓜ *Sant Antoni* ⊕ *G:12.*

$–$$ ☷ Hotel Market. A wallet-friendly boutique hotel and yet another Barcelona design triumph, the Hotel Market is so named for the Mercat de

Sant Antoni. On a little alleyway a block from the market and walking distance from all of the Raval and Gothic Quarter sites and attractions, this ultramodern, high-tech, designer lodging opportunity is one of Barcelona's best bargains. Rooms are simply but solidly furnished with dark-wood trim and beams setting off bright white bedspreads and lacquered surfaces. The hotel restaurant offers superlative fare and excellent value. Pros: well equipped, designed, and positioned for a low-cost Barcelona visit; young and friendly staff. Cons: rooms are a little cramped. ⊠ *Carrer Comte Borrell 68 (entrance on Passatge Sant Antoni Abat 10), Raval* 🕾 *93/325–1205* ⊕ *www.markethotel.com.es* ⤴ *37 rooms* ⌂ *In-room: Wi-Fi, refrigerator, safe. In-hotel: restaurant, bar, Internet terminal, Wi-Fi hotspot* ⊟ *AE, DC, MC, V* ⦿❘ *EP* Ⓜ *Sant Antoni* ✛ *F:11.*

4

$$$ Ⓣ **Inglaterra.** A welcoming Moderniste stairway in this neoclassical building leads to sleek guest rooms decorated in light-color wood with Japanese motifs. The cafeteria-restaurant-library is an experimental multiuse space designed as a refuge for rest and reflection at the edge of the Ciutat Vella. Pros: central location; modern facilities; near the Raval and the MACBA. Cons: noisy avenue in front of hotel; in the epicenter of Barcelona. ⊠ *Pelai 14, Raval* 🕾 *93/505–1100* ⊕ *www.hotel-inglaterra.com* ⤴ *60 rooms* ⌂ *In-room: Wi-Fi, safe. In-hotel: restaurant, bar, laundry service* ⊟ *AE, DC, MC, V* ⦿❘ *EP* Ⓜ *Catalunya* ✛ *H:11.*

$–$$ Ⓣ **Mesón Castilla.** A few steps up Carrer Tallers from the top of the Rambla, this little hotel is well positioned for exploring medieval Barcelona and the Moderniste Eixample. Just around the corner from the MACBA and the rest of the Raval, rooms here are quiet and, though slightly old-fashioned, a good value for the price. Pros: central location; comfortable public rooms and furnishings. Cons: on a busy street; very mid-city without green spaces. ⊠ *Valdoncella 5, Raval* 🕾 *93/318–2182* ⊕ *www.mesoncastilla.com* ⤴ *56 rooms* ⌂ *In-room: Wi-Fi, safe. In-hotel: bar, Wi-Fi hotspot* ⊟ *AE, DC, MC, V* ⦿❘ *EP* Ⓜ *Catalunya* ✛ *H:11.*

$$
Fodor's Choice
★
Ⓣ **Sant Agustí.** In a leafy square just off the Rambla, the Sant Agustí has long been popular with musicians performing at the Liceu opera house. Rooms are small but graceful and attractively designed, with plenty of bright wood trim and clean lines. Pros: central location near the Boqueria market, the Rambla, and the opera house; cozy, wood-beamed, traditional design. Cons: noisy square usually requiring closed windows; short on amenities and room service. ⊠ *Pl. Sant Agustí 3, Raval* 🕾 *93/318–1658* ⊕ *www.hotelsa.com* ⤴ *77 rooms* ⌂ *In-room: Wi-Fi, safe. In-hotel: bar, Wi-Fi hotspot* ⊟ *AE, DC, MC, V* ⦿❘ *EP* Ⓜ *Liceu* ✛ *J:12.*

THE RAMBLA

$$ Ⓣ **Citadines.** This Rambla hotel is bright, modern, and soundproof. Lodgings range from apartments with sitting rooms to one-room studios with kitchenettes and small dining areas. The rooftop solarium has views of Montjuïc and the Mediterranean. Across the Rambla is the tower over the Poliorama theater, where George Orwell, author of *Homage to Catalonia*, was posted during the Spanish civil war. Ask for a back room over Plaça Villa de Madrid for a quieter spot set over a leafy square with a 3rd-century Roman roadway and tombs. Pros:

central location; facilities and technology perfect. **Cons:** noisy Rambla a constant hubbub; apartments small and motel-like. ⊠ *Rambla 122, Rambla* ☎ *93/270–1111* ⊕ *www.citadines.com* ➔ *115 studios, 16 apartments* & *In-room: Wi-Fi, kitchen. In-hotel: bar* ⊟ *AE, DC, MC, V* ⎮⦿⎮ *EP* Ⓜ *Catalunya* ✛ *H:12.*

$ ⊡ **Continental.** This modest hotel stands at the top of the Rambla, just below Plaça de Catalunya. Space is tight, but the rooms manage to accommodate large, firm beds. It's high enough over the Rambla to escape street noise, so ask for a room overlooking Barcelona's most emblematic street. This is a good place to read *Homage to Catalonia*, as George Orwell stayed here with his wife in 1937 after recovering from a bullet wound. **Pros:** in the heart of the city; historically significant; high enough over Rambla to be quiet, with balconies from which to admire the human flow below. **Cons:** slightly old-fashioned and down at the heel; small rooms. ⊠ *Rambla 138, Rambla* ☎ *93/301–2570* ⊕ *www. hotelcontinental.com* ➔ *35 rooms* & *In-room: Wi-Fi, safe* ⊟ *AE, DC, MC, V* ⎮⦿⎮ *EP* Ⓜ *Catalunya* ✛ *H:11.*

$$$–$$$$ ⊡ **Duquesa de Cardona.** This refurbished 16th-century town house over-
Fodor's Choice looking the port has ultracontemporary facilities with designer touches,
★   all housed in an early-Renaissance structure. The exterior rooms have views of the harbor, the World Trade Center, and the passenger-boat terminals. The hotel is a 10-minute walk from everything in the Gothic Quarter or Barceloneta, and no more than a 30-minute walk from the main Eixample attractions. The miniature rooftop pool, more for a dip than a swim, is cooling in summer. **Pros:** contemporary technology in a traditional palace at a key spot over the port; roof terrace with live music in summer. **Cons:** rooms on the small side; roof terrace tiny; sea views restricted by Maremagnum complex. ⊠ *Passeig de Colom 12, Rambla* ☎ *93/268–9090* ⊕ *www.hduquesadecardona.com* ➔ *44 rooms* & *In-room: Wi-Fi. In-hotel: restaurant, pool* ⊟ *AE, DC, MC, V* ⎮⦿⎮ *EP* Ⓜ *Drassanes* ✛ *I:14.*

$$$–$$$$ ⊡ **H1898.** This elegant hotel overlooking the Rambla occupies a building with an illustrious history as the headquarters of the Compañia de Tabacos de Filipinas. Named for the fateful year when Spain was stripped of its final colonial possessions, the Philippines among them, the hotel's elegance pays homage to bygone imperial days as well as providing a symbol of the city's present opulence. Rooms are superbly equipped with state-of-the-art appliances and decorated in a maritime, South Seas idiom. The upper rooms with terraces on the side away from the Rambla have lovely views of Montjuïc, the Mediterranean, and the Collserola hills behind the city. **Pros:** central location on the Rambla; top-level design and technology. **Cons:** subway rumble discernible in lower rooms on Rambla side. ⊠ *La Rambla 109, Rambla* ☎ *93/552– 9552* ⊕ *www.hotel1898.com* ➔ *166 rooms, 3 suites* & *In-room: Wi-Fi. In-hotel: restaurant, bar, pool, gym, parking (paid)* ⊟ *AE, DC, MC, V* ⎮⦿⎮ *EP* Ⓜ *Catalunya* ✛ *H:12.*

$$$–$$$$ ⊡ **Le Méridien Barcelona.** Le Méridien vies with the Rivoli Ramblas as the premier hotel in the Rambla area. Rooms are sumptuously decorated in bright colors and rich wood trim, complete with plush beds, flat-screen TVs, and marble bathrooms. The top floors also have terrific views over

the city. The hotel is very popular with businesspeople—fax machines and computers for your room are available on request—and celebrities alike. Rooms overlooking the Rambla are completely soundproof. **Pros:** central location; amply endowed with amenities of all kinds; great views over the Rambla from some rooms. **Cons:** if your face hasn't appeared recently on the cover of *Us Weekly*, hotel service can be a little perfunctory and impersonal. ✉ *Rambla 111, Rambla* ☎ *93/318–6200* ⊕ *www.lemeridien.com* ↗ *217 rooms, 16 suites* ♿ *In-room: Wi-Fi, safe. In-hotel: restaurant, bar, gym, parking (paid)* ▬ *AE, DC, MC, V* |◯| *EP* Ⓜ *Catalunya* ✛ *H:12.*

$$$-$$$$ ☷ **Montecarlo.** The ornate, illuminated entrance takes you from the Rambla through an enticing marble hall; upstairs, you enter a sumptuous reception room with a dark-wood Art Nouveau ceiling. Rooms, which vary wildly in size and facilities, are modern and bright; many overlook the Rambla, a debatable bonus depending on your susceptibility to noise. Some of the back rooms overlook the moist and intimate palm-shaded *jardín romántico* (literally, "romantic garden") of the Ateneu Barcelonès, Barcelona's literary club and library, all to the tune of the hotel's waterfall, reminiscent of the Rambla's early days as a spate river. **Pros:** centrally positioned; top-drawer new equipment and furnishings. **Cons:** on the tumultuous Rambla; slightly impersonal in design and service. ✉ *Rambla 124, Rambla* ☎ *93/412–0404* ⊕ *www.montecarlobcn. com* ↗ *50 rooms* ♿ *In-room: Wi-Fi. In-hotel: restaurant, bar, parking (paid)* ▬ *AE, DC, MC, V* |◯| *EP* Ⓜ *Catalunya* ✛ *H:11.*

$$ ☷ **Nouvel.** White marble, etched glass, elaborate plasterwork, and carved, dark woodwork blend into a handsome Art Nouveau interior here. Rooms have marble floors, firm beds, and chic bathrooms. The narrow street, just below Plaça de Catalunya, is pedestrian-only and therefore blissfully quiet. **Pros:** centrally positioned; charming Moderniste details; quiet pedestrianized street. **Cons:** rooms on the small side; not especially high-tech. ✉ *Santa Anna 18–20, Rambla* ☎ *93/301–8274* ⊕ *www.hotelnouvel.com* ↗ *71 rooms* ♿ *In-room: Wi-Fi, safe. In-hotel: restaurant, bar* ▬ *AE, DC, MC, V* |◯| *EP* Ⓜ *Catalunya* ✛ *H:11.*

$$$-$$$$ ☷ **Rivoli Rambla.** Behind this traditional upper-Rambla facade lies a surprisingly original marble-floored interior equipped with state-of-the-art facilities. The rooms are pastel in hue and contemporary in design, with avant-garde details. Guests run the gamut from hip honeymooners to discerning retirees. The roof-terrace bar has panoramic views. **Pros:** good location on the Rambla; all top-notch comfort and facilities present and accounted for. **Cons:** somewhat large and impersonal; noisy and tumultuous Rambla raging at the doorstep. ✉ *Rambla 128, Rambla* ☎ *93/481–7676* ⊕ *www.rivolihotels.com* ↗ *119 rooms, 6 suites* ♿ *In-room: Wi-Fi, safe. In-hotel: restaurant, bar, gym, parking (paid)* ▬ *AE, DC, MC, V* |◯| *EP* Ⓜ *Catalunya* ✛ *H:12.*

BARCELONETA, PORT OLÍMPIC, AND FÒRUM

$$$-$$$$ ☷ **Eurostars Grand Marina Hotel.** An alabaster cylindrical fortress built around a central patio, the Grand Marina offers maximum luxury just two minutes from the Rambla over Barcelona's port. With stunning views of the city or the Mediterranean, this ultracontemporary monolith

CLOSE UP

Lodging Alternatives

APARTMENT RENTALS

If you want a home base that's roomy enough for a family and comes with cooking facilities, consider a furnished rental. These can save you money, especially if you're traveling with a group. Apartment rentals are increasingly popular in Barcelona these days. Aparthotels rents apartments in residences subdivided into small living spaces at prices generally more economical than hotel rates. Rentals by the day or week can be arranged, though prices may rise for short stays. Prices range from €100 to €300 per day depending on the quality of the accommodations, but perfectly acceptable lodging for four can be found for around €150 per night. Apartment accommodations can be arranged through any of the agencies listed below.

LOCAL APARTMENT AGENCIES

Aparthotel Bertran (✉ Bertran 150, Eixample ☎ 93/212–7550 ⊕ www.hotelbertran.com). **Aparthotel Bonanova** (✉ Bisbe Sivilla 7, Eixample ☎ 93/253–1563 ⊕ www.aparthotelbonanova.com). **Aparthotel Nàpols** (✉ Napols 116, Eixample ☎ 93/246–4573 ⊕ www.napols.net). **Apartment Barcelona** (✉ Valencia 286, Eixample ☎ 93/215–7934 ⊕ www.apartmentbarcelona.com). **Apartments Ramblas** (☎ 93/301–7678 ⊕ www.apartmentsramblas.com). **BarcelonaForrent** (☎ 93/457–9329 ⊕ www.barcelonaforrent.com). **Barcelona Rentals/Atlanta-Ads** (☎ 404/849–5827 ⊕ www.atlanta-ads.com). **Barceloneta Suites** (☎ 93/221–4225 ⊕ www.barcelonetasuites.com). **Feel Barcelona** (✉ Balmes 28, ☎ 93/301–9341 ⊕ www.feelbarcelona.com). **Flats By Days** (☎ 93/342–6481 ⊕ www.flatsbydays.com). **Friendly Rentals** (✉ Pasaje Sert 8 Bis, ☎ 93/268–8051 ⊕ www.friendlyrentals.com). **Goben Apartments** (✉ Selva de Mar 202, Eixample ☎ 93/278–1156 ⊕ www.gobcn.com). **Lofts & Apartments** (✉ València 284, Eixample ☎ 93/366–8800 ⊕ www.lofts-apartments.com). **Oh-Barcelona** (✉ Roger de Llúria 50, 1a, Eixample ☎ 93/467–3782 ⊕ www.oh-barcelona.com). **Rent a Flat in Barcelona** (✉ Fontanella 18, Eixample ☎ 93/342–7300 ⊕ www.rentaflatinbarcelona.com)

INTERNATIONAL AGENTS

Hideaways International (✉ 767 Islington St., Portsmouth, NH ☎ 603/430–4433 or 800/843–4433 ⊕ www.hideaways.com); annual membership $185.

HOME EXCHANGES

If you would like to exchange your home for someone else's, join a home-exchange organization, which will send you its updated listings of available exchanges for a year and will include your own listing in at least one of them. It's up to you to make specific arrangements. Home-exchange directories sometimes list rentals as well as exchanges. Exchange Club

HomeLink International (✉ Box 47747, Tampa, FL 33647 ☎ 813/975–9825 or 800/638–3841 ⊕ www.homelink.org); $105 yearly for a listing and online access. Extra fee for catalog.

HOSTELS

No matter how old you are, you can save on lodging costs by staying at hostels (albergue juvenil, and not a hostal, a popular term for a modest hotel without major facilities, signaled by a small "s" next to the "H" on the hotel doorway's blue plaque).

In some 4,500 locations in more than 70 countries around the world, Hostelling International (HI), the umbrella group for a number of national youth-hostel associations, offers single-sex, dorm-style beds and, at many hostels, rooms for couples, and family accommodations. Membership in any HI national hostel association, open to travelers of all ages, allows you to stay in HI-affiliated hostels at member rates; one-year membership is about $28 for adults; hostels charge about $10–$30 per night. Members have priority if the hostel is full.

Turisme Juvenil Catalunya (TUJUCA–La XANASCAT) can help you locate any of 43 youth hostels in Barcelona. Many of these hostels happily take people of all ages, though you may have to pay an extra fee to become a card-carrying member. Many older youth-hostel fans find hostels—where people tend to exchange tips and chat freely—friendlier and more inclusive than hotels. Nearly all Barcelona hostels offer common rooms for television, card games, and general socializing, dining rooms for meals, and sleeping accommodations ranging from double bedrooms to dormitories, the latter arrangement more frequent.

ORGANIZATIONS
Hostelling International—USA
(✉ 8401 Colesville Rd., Suite 600, Silver Spring, MD ☎ 301/495–1240 ⊕ www.hiusa.org). **Turisme Juvenil Catalunya** (TUJUCA-La Xanascat ✉ Calàbria 147, Eixample ☎ 93/483–8363 ⊕ www.tujuca.com or www.xanascat.cat).

HOSTELS
Alberg Abba (✉ Passeig de Colom 9, Barri Gòtic ☎ 93/319–4545 ⊕ www.abbayouthhostel.com). **Alberg Kabul** (✉ Pl. Reial 17, Rambla ☎ 93/318–5190 ⊕ www.kabul.es). **Alberg Palau** (✉ Palau 6, Barri Gòtic ☎ 93/412–5080 ⊕ www.bcnalberg.com). **Alberg-Residencia La Ciutat** (✉ Ca l'Alegre de Dalt 66, Eixample ☎ 93/213–0300).**Center Ramblas** (✉ Hospital 63, Raval ☎ 93/412–4069 ⊕ www.center-ramblas.com). **Gothic Point** (✉ Vigatans 5, Born-Ribera ☎ 93/268–7808 ⊕ www.gothicpoint.com). **Ideal Youth Hostel** (✉ Carrer Unió 12, Raval ☎ 93/342–6177 ⊕ www.idealhostel.com). **Sea Point** (✉ Pl. del Mar 1–4, Barceloneta ☎ 93/224–7075 ⊕ www.seapointhostel.com).

4

is in the middle of, though well above, Barcelona's best sights. Rooms are bright and comfortable, albeit somewhat generic, with dark brown graphic decor, and the public spaces are geometrical expanses of sleek glass and steel. Guests tend to be conventioneers and business travelers. **Pros:** centrally positioned over the port and the Rambla; great views out to sea; excellent restaurant. **Cons:** high-rise impersonal construction; primarily a convention center and business hotel. ⊠ *Moll de Barcelona (World Trade Center), Port Olímpic* ☎ *93/603–9000* ⊕ *www. grandmarinahotel.com* ⇗ *291 rooms* � ⅄ *In-room: safe, Wi-Fi, refrigerator. In-hotel: 3 restaurants, bar, pool, gym, parking (paid)* ⊟ *AE, DC, MC, V* Ⓜ *Drassanes* ⓘⓄⅠ *EP* ✛ *G:15.*

$$–$$$ ⊡ **Hotel 54.** With rooms overlooking the Barceloneta port and just a few minutes' walk from the beach, this modern, minimalist newcomer to the Barcelona hotel scene offers much for travelers seeking location, comfort, and economy. The sleek lines and a blue-curtained facade announce the property's brash and sassy attitude, and the interior lives up to the space-age starkness on the outside. **Pros:** well positioned for the beach and the nearby Born-Ribera neighborhood; latest technology and equipment. **Cons:** buses roar back and forth around the clock on Passeig Joan de Borbó; rooms are minimalist almost to a fault; a little chilly and mechanical. ⊠ *Passeig Joan de Borbó 54, Barceloneta* ☎ *93/225–0054* ⊕ *www.hotel54barceloneta.com* ⇗ *28 rooms* ⅄ *In-room: Wi-Fi, refrigerator. In-hotel: restaurant, bar, Internet terminal, Wi-Fi hotspot* ⊟ *AE, DC, MC, V* ⓘⓄⅠ *EP* Ⓜ *Barceloneta* ✛ *I:15.*

$$$$ ⊡ **Hotel Arts.** This luxurious Ritz-Carlton-owned skyscraper overlooks Barcelona from the Olympic Port, providing stunning views of the Mediterranean, the city, and the mountains behind. The hotel's main drawback is that it's somewhat in a world of its own, a short taxi ride (or a good 20-minute walk) from the center of the city. That said, it an exciting world to be in. True to its name, fine art—from Chillida drawings to Susana Solano sculptures—hangs everywhere. Rooms are decorated in contrasting beige and dark-wood accents and stocked with Acqua di Parma toiletries. Sergi Arola's restaurant is a chic, postmodern culinary playground. **Pros:** excellent views over Barcelona; first-rate, original art all over the halls and rooms; fine restaurants; general comfort and technology. **Cons:** a 20-minute hike from the Born, the nearest point of Barcelona; hotel feels like a colony of (mostly American) tourists set apart from local life. ⊠ *Calle de la Marina 19, Port Olímpic* ☎ *93/221–1000* ⊕ *www.hotelartsbarcelona.es* ⇗ *397 rooms, 59 suites, 27 apartments* ⅄ *In-room: safe, Wi-Fi, refrigerator. In-hotel: 3 restaurants, room service, bar, pool, beachfront, laundry service, parking (paid)* ⊟ *AE, DC, MC, V* ⓘⓄⅠ *EP* Ⓜ *Ciutadella–Vil.la Olímpica* ✛ *L:15.*

$$$$ ⊡ **Hotel Princess.** Designed by architect Óscar Tusquets, this skyscraper towers over the 2004 Fòrum de les Cultures complex at the eastern end of the Diagonal, Barcelona's major crosstown avenue. If this sort of urban jamboree (tall buildings and thousands of people) appeals to you, then don't miss this spectacularly equipped spa-like environment, with a hot tub in every room and endless views out over the 2004 Fòrum site and the Mediterranean. **Pros:** the ultimate high-tech hotel; bubbling in-hotel action for conventioneers. **Cons:** a half-hour taxi ride

from the center of town; chilly geometrical architecture. ⊠ *Av. Diagonal 1, Diagonal Mar* ☎ *93/356–1000* ⊕ *www.princess-hotels.com* ⊳ *364 rooms* ⚘ *In-room: Wi-Fi. In-hotel: restaurant, bar, pool, gym* ⊟ *AE, DC, MC, V* ▯◯▮ *EP* Ⓜ *Maresme–Fòrum* ✢ *L:15.*

¢–$ 🖼 **Marina Folch.** This little hideaway in the pungent fishermen's quarter of Barceloneta is surprisingly clean, crisp, and contemporary. Rooms are small and equipped with somewhat matchstick furnishings, but most have views over the Barcelona harbor. Five minutes from the beach and with an excellent restaurant and a generous, caring family at the helm, it's a budget winner. Pros: great value; five minutes from the beach; surrounded by fine tapas and dining opportunities. Cons: bed frames somewhat light and flimsy; spaces cramped. ⊠ *Carrer Mar 16 entsol., Barceloneta* ☎ *93/310–3709* ⊕ *www.hotelmarinafolchbcn. com* ⊳ *11 rooms* ⚘ *In-room: Wi-Fi. In-hotel: restaurant, bar* ⊟ *AE, DC, MC, V* ▯◯▮ *Barceloneta* ✢ *J:14.*

$$$$ 🖼 **W Hotel Barcelona.** Architect Ricardo Bofill's W Barcelona, locally
Fodor's Choice known as Hotel Vela ("Hotel Sail"), finally opened in late 2009. The
★ towering sail-shaped monolith's golden glow now joins the Hotel Arts as the dominant and most iconic shape on the Barcelona waterfront. With top in-room and in-hotel technology joining features such as the WET pool, the Bliss spa, the Living Room/Lobby, and the Whatever/ Whenever Service, the W has set its sights on uncontested leadership of the city's hotel scene, with master chef Carles Abellán at the helm of his own eponymous restaurant. Pros: unrivalled views and general design excitement and glamour; excellent restaurants; rooms are bright, clean-lined, and have nonpareil views in all directions. Cons: the high-rise icon could seem garish to some; a good hike from the Gothic Quarter. ⊠ *Plaça Rosa dels Vents 1, Barceloneta* ☎ *93/295–2800* ⊕ *www. starwoodhotels.com* ⊳ *473 rooms, 67 suites* ⚘ *In-room: safe, Wi-Fi, refrigerator. In-hotel: 3 restaurants, bar, pool, gym, parking (paid)* ⊟ *AE, DC, MC, V* Ⓜ *Barceloneta* ▯◯▮ *EP* ✢ *H:16.*

EIXAMPLE

$$–$$$$ 🖼 **AC Diplomatic.** On the corner of Consell de Cent and just a block from Barcelona's busiest explosion of Moderniste architecture, the Manzana de la Discòrdia on Passeig de Gràcia, this hotel is also midway between the Eixample's two best mid-block passageways, Mendez Vigo and Passatge Permanyer. Decorated in pastel tones and sweeping economical lines, the Diplomatic offers good value and comfort for a central Eixample address. Rooms are well lighted, decorated with contemporary furnishings and heavy drapes. Pros: bright contemporary lobby; friendly staff; high-tech equipment; well soundproofed. Cons: rooms on the Pau Claris side of the hotel are exposed to street noise. ⊠ *Pau Claris 122, Eixample* ☎ *93/272–3810* ⊕ *www.ac-hotels.com* ⊳ *209 rooms, 2 suites* ⚘ *In-room: Wi-Fi. In-hotel: restaurant, bar, pool, gym, parking (paid)* ⊟ *AE, DC, MC, V* ▯◯▮ *EP* Ⓜ *Diagonal* ✢ *I:9.*

$$$$ 🖼 **Alexandra.** Behind a reconstructed Eixample facade, everything here is slick and contemporary. The rooms are spacious and attractively furnished with dark-wood chairs, and those that face inward have thatch screens on the balconies for privacy. From the airy marble hall

Fodor's Choice ★

Duquesa de Cardona

Claris

Condes de Barcelona

HOTEL SANT AGUSTI

Sant Agusti

W Hotel Barcelona

Casa Fuster

Hotel Omm

Majestic

on up, the Alexandra is a dependable mid-Eixample lodging option. **Pros:** central to the Eixample and a 20-minute walk from the port; light and upbeat contemporary. **Cons:** rooms seem constricted after all the space in the lobby. ⊠ *Mallorca 251, Eixample* ☎ *93/467–7166* ⊕ *www.hotel-alexandra.com* ⤳ *95 rooms, 5 suites* ⚥ *In-room: Wi-Fi. In-hotel: restaurant, bar, laundry service, parking (paid)* ⊟ *AE, DC, MC, V* ⵠⵔ *EP* Ⓜ *Provença* ✢ *I:8.*

$$$$ ⛱ **Avenida Palace.** At the bottom of the Eixample, between the Rambla de Catalunya and Passeig de Gràcia, this hotel conveys elegance and antiquated style, despite dating from only 1952. The lobby is wonderfully ornate, with curving staircases spinning off in many directions. Everything is patterned, from the carpets to the plasterwork, a style largely echoed in the bedrooms. (Read: if you want contemporary minimalism, stay elsewhere.) **Pros:** prime location; facilities and technology perfect. **Cons:** old-fashioned and overly ornate; no trace of cutting-edge, contemporary-design-happy Barcelona here. ⊠ *Gran Via 605–607, Eixample* ☎ *93/301–9600* ⊕ *www.avenidapalace.com* ⤳ *146 rooms, 14 suites* ⚥ *In-room: Wi-Fi. In-hotel: restaurant, bar* ⊟ *AE, DC, MC, V* ⵠⵔ *EP* Ⓜ *Passeig de Gràcia* ✢ *I:10.*

$$–$$$ ⛱ **Calderón.** On the chic and leafy Rambla de Catalunya, this modern high-rise has facilities normally found in hotels farther out of town. Public rooms are huge, with cool, white-marble floors, and the bedrooms follow suit. Aim high: the views from sea to mountains and over the city on top floors are stunning. **Pros:** upbeat, bright, contemporary design; ample public spaces; friendly service. **Cons:** the antiseptic, glass-and-steel tower can seem impersonal and generic. ⊠ *Rambla de Catalunya 26, Eixample* ☎ *93/301–0000* ⊕ *www.nh-hoteles.es* ⤳ *224 rooms, 29 suites* ⚥ *In-room: Wi-Fi. In-hotel: restaurant, bar, pools, gym, parking (paid)* ⊟ *AE, DC, MC, V* ⵠⵔ *EP* Ⓜ *Passeig de Gràcia* ✢ *H:10.*

$$$–$$$$
Fodor's Choice
★
⛱ **Claris.** Universally acclaimed as one of Barcelona's best hotels, the Claris is a fascinating mélange of design and tradition. From the street, a late-20th-century glass and steel upper annex seems to have sprouted from the stone and concrete 19th-century town house below. Rooms come in 60 different modern layouts, some with restored 18th-century English furniture and some with contemporary furnishings from Barcelona's playful legion of designers. Lavishly endowed with wood and marble, the hotel also has a Japanese water garden, a rooftop cocktail terrace and pool, and two first-rate restaurants, including East 47, which has become one of the most admired dining spots in Barcelona. **Pros:** elegant service and furnishings; central location for shopping and Moderniste architecture; facilities and technology perfect. **Cons:** noisy corner; bathrooms are designer chic but impractical. ⊠ *Carrer Pau Claris 150, Eixample* ☎ *93/487–6262* ⊕ *www.derbyhotels.es* ⤳ *80 rooms, 40 suites* ⚥ *In-room: Wi-Fi. In-hotel: 2 restaurants, bar, pool, gym, laundry service, parking (paid)* ⊟ *AE, DC, MC, V* ⵠⵔ *EP* Ⓜ *Passeig de Gràcia* ✢ *I:9.*

$ ⛱ **Colors.** This friendly little hotel in Horta, formerly an outlying village like Gràcia and Sarrià near Eixample, is an intimate residence with simple but well-cared-for rooms dotted with punchy pop-art hues. It's a good budget choice, named for its Crayola-color range of decors on different floors of the hotel. **Pros:** small enough for intimacy and personalized, friendly service; bright and modern design. **Cons:** a long way (20 minutes by subway) from the Gothic Quarter and the Eixample; spaces small and economy-minded. ✉ *Campoamor 79, Horta* ☏ *93/274–9920* ⊕ *www.hotelcolors.com* ⇗ *25 rooms* ☖ *In-room: safe* ▭ *AE, DC, MC, V* ⏐⏐ *EP* Ⓜ *Valldaura* ✛ *H:1.*

$$–$$$$ ☷ **Condes de Barcelona.** One of Barcelona's most popular hotels, the
Fodor's Choice Condes de Barcelona retains a grand charm with a marble-floored pen-
★ tagonal lobby and the original columns and courtyard dating from the 1891 building. Rooms are decorated in contemporary neutrals. The newest rooms have hot tubs and terraces overlooking interior gardens. An affiliated fitness club around the corner offers golf, squash, and swimming. Chef Martín Berasategui's two restaurants, Lasarte and Loidi, are among Barcelona's most sought-after dining spots. Reserve rooms well in advance—demand is high, and early reservations score bargain rates. **Pros:** elegant Moderniste building with chic contemporary furnishings; prime spot in the middle of the Eixample. **Cons:** too large for much of a personal touch; staff somewhat overextended; restaurant Lasarte difficult to book. ✉ *Passeig de Gràcia 75, Eixample* ☏ *93/467–4780* ⊕ *www.condesdebarcelona.com* ⇗ *181 rooms, 2 suites* ☖ *In-room: safe, Wi-Fi. In-hotel: restaurant, bar, pools, gym, parking (paid)* ▭ *AE, DC, MC, V* ⏐⏐ *EP* Ⓜ *Passeig de Gràcia* ✛ *I:9.*

$$–$$$ ☷ **Continental Palacete.** This former in-town mansion, or *palacete*, provides a splendid drawing room, a location nearly dead center for Barcelona's main attractions, views over the leafy tree-lined tunnel of Rambla Catalunya, and a 24-hour free buffet. Ask specifically for one of the exterior rooms; the interior rooms on the elevator shaft can be noisy. **Pros:** elegant town house with abundant ornamentation; around-the-clock food and drink at the open buffet; attentive owners and staff; central location. **Cons:** rooms on the elevator shaft can be noisy; suites seem over-draped and under-spacious. ✉ *Rambla de Catalunya 30, Eixample* ☏ *93/445–7657* ⊕ *www.hotelcontinental.com* ⇗ *17 rooms, 2 suites* ☖ *In-room: Wi-Fi. In hotel: Wi-Fi hotspot, parking (paid)* ▭ *AE, DC, MC, V* ⏐⏐ *BP* Ⓜ *Passeig de Gràcia* ✛ *I:10.*

$$$$ ☷ **Eurostars Cristal Palace.** Just off Rambla Catalunya and near the gardens of Barcelona's University, this hotel is in the middle of the art-gallery district and within walking distance of the Rambla, the Ciutat Vella, and the Moderniste architecture of the Eixample. Guest rooms are modern and decorated in wood, marble, and bright colors. **Pros:** well positioned for exploring both the Eixample and the Gothic Quarter on foot; handy for making the university patios your private garden. **Cons:** street side over Carrer Diputació can be noisy. ✉ *Diputació 257, Eixample* ☏ *93/487–8778* ⊕ *www.eurostarshotels.com* ⇗ *147 rooms, 1 suite* ☖ *In-room: Wi-Fi. In-hotel: restaurant, bar, Internet terminal, Wi-Fi hotspot, parking (paid)* ▭ *AE, DC, MC, V* ⏐⏐ *EP* Ⓜ *Passeig de Gràcia* ✛ *I:10.*

$$–$$$ ☷ **Gallery.** In the upper part of the Eixample below the Diagonal, this modern hotel offers impeccable service and a central location for middle and upper Barcelona. (In the other direction, you're only half an hour's walk from the waterfront.) It's named for its proximity to the

city's prime art-gallery district, a few blocks away on Rambla de Catalunya and Consell de Cent. Rooms are comfortable, contemporary in decor, spotless, and without much personality, but perfectly sufficient. **Pros:** well located for Eixample shopping and Moderniste architecture; intimate enough to feel a personal touch. **Cons:** slightly cold and high-tech, minimalist lines and ambience. ⊠ *Roselló 249, Eixample* ☎ *93/415–9911* ⊕ *www.galleryhotel.com* ↴ *108 rooms, 5 suites* ♿ *In-room: Wi-Fi. In-hotel: restaurant, bar, gym, parking (paid)* ▭ *AE, DC, MC, V* ⅋ *EP* Ⓜ *Provença* ✛ *I:8.*

$$$$ 🖫 **Gran Derby.** Contemporary and sleek, this Eixample hotel is ideal for families, since it's composed entirely of suites and duplexes with sitting rooms. Rooms are decorated in crisp tones and lined with lavish leather or faux leather fabrics and zebra patterns, while baths are covered with coffee-colored tiles. Only the location is less than ideal; for sightseeing purposes, it's a bit out of the way, but a 20-minute march down the Diagonal puts you right on Passeig de Gràcia. **Pros:** rooms and suites are spacious and well equipped; on a quiet side street; friendly service. **Cons:** far from the city's main attractions in an undistinguished neighborhood. ⊠ *Loreto 28, Eixample* ☎ *93/322–2062* ⊕ *www.derbyhotels. es* ↴ *29 rooms, 12 suites* ♿ *In-room: Wi-Fi. In-hotel: restaurant, bar, pool, parking (paid)* ▭ *AE, DC, MC, V* ⅋ *EP* Ⓜ *Muntaner, Hospital Clinic* ✛ *E:6.*

$$–$$$ 🖫 **Gran Hotel Catalonia.** A late-19th-century Eixample building filled with contemporary decor just two blocks from Passeig de Gràcia, this hotel has rooms that are soundproofed to combat the roaring, traffic-flooded Balmes, in additional to being ultramodern, bright, and dotted with punchy red touches. The direct garage entrance will instantaneously solve your what-to-do-with-this-rental-car problem. Staff is extremely helpful with suggestions and arrangements. **Pros:** good for exploring the Eixample and the old part of the city. **Cons:** Balmes is the city's main up-and-down artery, and traffic is intense day and night. ⊠ *Balmes 142, Eixample* ☎ *93/415–9090* ⊕ *www.hoteles-catalonia.es* ↴ *84 rooms* ♿ *In-room: Wi-Fi, safe. In-hotel: restaurant, room service, bar, laundry service, Internet terminal, parking (paid)* ▭ *AE, DC, MC, V* ⅋ *EP* Ⓜ *Provença* ✛ *H:8.*

$$$–$$$$ 🖫 **Gran Hotel Havana.** Specializing in both business and pleasure, the Havana may not remind you at all of the Greater Antilles, but the efficient service, the lofty patio with its rooftop skylight, and the bustling, busy feel of the place will help to boost your biorhythms to those of energetic Barcelona. This hotel is about equidistant from everything in the city, and its soundproofed rooms provide the refuge you need from the roaring Gran Via. **Pros:** well positioned; lively lobby filled with savvy clients from all over the world; friendly staff. **Cons:** on a major cross-town artery, where traffic is usually frantic all day; sometimes booked by groups; undistinguished architecture and design. ⊠ *Gran Via 647, Eixample* ☎ *93/412–1115* ⊕ *www.hoteles-silken.com* ↴ *141 rooms, 4 suites* ♿ *In-room: Wi-Fi. In-hotel: restaurant, bar, gym, parking (paid)* ▭ *AE, DC, MC, V* ⅋ *EP* Ⓜ *Passeig de Gràcia* ✛ *J:10.*

$$ 🛏 **Granvia.** A 19th-century town house and Moderniste enclave with a hall-of-mirrors breakfast room and an ornate staircase, the Granvia allows you to experience Barcelona's Art Nouveau even while you're sleeping. (To stay in character, go around the block to Gaudí's Casa Calvet, at No. 48 Carrer de Casp, for lunch or dinner.) Guest rooms have plain alcoved walls, bottle-green carpets, and Regency-style furniture; those overlooking Gran Via itself have better views but are quite noisy. **Pros:** waking up surrounded by Barcelona's famous Moderniste design; only a 15-minute walk from the Gothic Quarter. **Cons:** somewhat antiquated; service a little tourist-weary. ⊠ *Gran Via 642, Eixample* ☎ *93/318–1900* ⊕ *www.nnhotels.es* 🛏 *53 rooms* ♿ *In-room: Wi-Fi. In-hotel: Wi-Fi hotspot, parking (paid)* ⊟ *AE, DC, MC, V* �|◎| *EP* Ⓜ *Passeig de Gràcia* ✛ *I:10.*

$$ 🛏 **Hotel Actual.** This hotel between Passeig de Gràcia and Pau Claris offers good value with contemporary technology, polished design, and a central Eixample location. Small rooms have plenty of light, and are appointed with crisp modern furnishings. The owners are the Gimeno sisters of the nearby Gimeno design store, so it's no wonder the place is sleek and hip. Some rooms have views of Gaudí's La Pedrera rippling around the corner of Passeig de Gràcia. **Pros:** a contemporary design triumph with smart public spaces; helpful and friendly service. **Cons:** rooms are small, and those on the street side can be noisy. ⊠ *Roselló 238, Eixample* ☎ *93/552–0550* ⊕ *www.hotelactual.com* 🛏 *29 rooms* ♿ *In-room: Wi-Fi, refrigerator, safe. In-hotel: bar, lounge, Wi-Fi hotspot, parking (paid)* ⊟ *AE, DC, MC, V* ⌊◎⌋ *EP* Ⓜ *Diagonal* ✛ *I:8.*

$–$$ 🛏 **Hotel Astoria.** Three blocks west of Rambla Catalunya, near the upper middle of the Eixample, this streamlined, fresh fresh-feeling space has been recently renovated into one of Barcelona's most esthetically pleasing and economical lodging options. The public spaces are relaxing and chic, while guest rooms are bright and stylish. Warm wood accents and inset lighting add tasteful touches. A rooftop pool and terrace bar provide a combination nightclub/country club, while the minimalist dining room offers an economical fixed-price lunch menu. **Pros:** prime location at the eye of the urban hurricane; clean-lined and cutting-edge design and equipment; soothing refuge. **Cons:** busy mid-Eixample thoroughfare at the door; rooms on the street side can be noisy. ⊠ *Carrer Paris 203, Eixample* ☎ *93/209--8311* ⊕ *www.derbyhotels.com* 🛏 *114 rooms* ♿ *In-room: safe, refrigerator, Wi-Fi. In-hotel: restaurant, bar, Internet terminal, Wi-Fi hotspot, gym, pool, spa, Internet terminal* ⊟ *AE, DC, MC, V* ⌊◎⌋ *EP* Ⓜ *Hospital Clínic* ✛ *H:7.*

$$–$$$ 🛏 **Hotel Axel.** This hotel catering primarily (but by no means exclusively) to gays has spacious and spotless rooms with every possible comfort, a mid-Eixample location in what has come to be known as the "Gayxample." Rooms are soundproof and luminous, decked out in white-on-white decor punctuated by primary colors. Free bottled water is available in every corridor. The hotel restaurant is excellent, and the rooftop Skybar has wonderful views over the city. **Pros:** exciting minimalist contemporary design; graceful public spaces and lighting; friendly service. **Cons:** erotic in-room art could be outside some guests' comfort zone. ⊠ *Aribau 33, Eixample* ☎ *93/323–9393* ⊕ *www.*

hotelaxel.com ⤴ *66 rooms* ⏃ *In-room: Wi-Fi. In-hotel: restaurant, bar, gym, spa, pool, Internet terminal, Wi-Fi hotspot, parking (paid)* ▤ *AE, DC, MC, V* ▯◯▯ *EP* Ⓜ *Universitat* ⊕ *G:9.*

$$$ ▦ **Hotel Casanova.** A sleek part of Barcelona's top-end lodging options, this carefully produced operation is nearly perfect, just a 15-minute walk from the top of the Rambla. Rooms are decorated in dusty charcoal tones, some with private balconies. Fine Mediterranean-Mexican fusion cuisine is served in the restaurant Mexiterranée. Spa treatments are available at the Stone Spa therapy center; and the mint or strawberry water at the reception desk is just icing on the cake. The bar at street level, thoroughly soundproofed, offers bustling street life and people-watching while you sip your tequila. **Pros:** maximum comfort in a hip and happening environment; good location. **Cons:** this is 21st-century, post-contemporary Barcelona: no trace of classical Europe. ⊠ *Gran Via de les Corts 559, Eixample* ☎ *93/396–4800* ⊕ *www.casanovabcnhotel. com* ⤴ *118 rooms, 6 suites* ⏃ *In-room: Wi-Fi. In-hotel: restaurant, bar, spa, pool, gym, parking (paid)* ▤ *AE, DC, MC, V* Ⓜ *Universitat* ⊕ *G:10.*

$–$$ ▦ **Hotel Constanza.** This contemporary boutique hotel offers top value along with cool white surfaces accented with the occasional slash of fire-engine-red sofas and chairs. Burgundy hallways and rooms furnished in woods and leathers, along with well-equipped and designed bathrooms, complete the sense of postmodern chic. **Pros:** well positioned for walking the Eixample or the Gothic Quarter; contemporary design worthy of Barcelona's design legacy; friendly service. **Cons:** rooms on the Carrer Bruc side can be noisy; interior soundproofing not good; somewhat lax attitude toward customer service. ⊠ *Bruc 33, Eixample* ☎ *93/270–1910* ⊕ *www.hotelconstanza.com* ⤴ *29 rooms* ⏃ *In-room: Wi-Fi, safe. In-hotel: gym, laundry service* ▤ *AE, DC, MC, V* ▯◯▯ *EP* Ⓜ *Urquinaona* ⊕ *J:10.*

$$–$$$$ ▦ **Hotel Cram.** A sparkling cast of famous interior decorators had a hand in assembling this Eixample design hotel. The result is a warm avant-garde aesthetic with luxurious details such as high-pressure shower heads. Just a block behind the leafy, orange tree–filled patio of the University of Barcelona's philology and letters school, a short walk from the central Eixample and the Rambla, home of Carles Gaig's famous restaurant (Can Gaig), the Cram is good place to keep in mind for impeccable accommodations in midtown Barcelona. **Pros:** dazzlingly designed; well positioned for the Eixample and Rambla; smart and friendly staff. **Cons:** Aribau is a major uptown artery and traffic careens through at all hours; rooms are not spacious. ⊠ *Carrer Aribau 54, Eixample* ☎ *93/216–7700* ⊕ *www.hotelcram.com* ⤴ *67 rooms* ⏃ *In-room: Wi-Fi, refrigerator. In-hotel: restaurant, bar, Internet terminal, Wi-Fi hotspot* ▤ *AE, DC, MC, V* ▯◯▯ *EP* Ⓜ *Universitat* ⊕ *G:9.*

$$$–$$$$

Fodor's Choice

★

▦ **Hotel Granados 83.** Constructed with an exposed brick, steel, and glass factory motif with Buddhist and Hindu art giving the hotel a Zen tranquillity, this relative newcomer to the local hotel panorama has established itself as one of Barcelona's best design hotels. A few steps below the Diagonal and well situated for exploring the Eixample and the rest of the city, the hotel, named for Barcelona's famous composer and pianist Enric Granados, is an interesting compendium of materials and taste. Rooms have a certain masculine aesthetic, with leather, chrome, and dark bedding. The first-rate Mediterranean restaurant and the rooftop pool and solarium provide the cherry on top of this sundae. **Pros:** quiet semi-pedestrianized street; elegant building with chic design in wood, marble, and glass; polished service. **Cons:** room prices here vary wildly according to availability and season. ⊠ *Carrer Enric Granados 83, Eixample* ☎ *93/492–9670* ⊕ *www.derbyhotels.es* ⊅ *70 rooms, 7 suites* ⚹ *In-room: safe, Wi-Fi, refrigerator. In-hotel: restaurant, bar, pools, spa, gym, parking (paid)* ⊟ *AE, DC, MC, V* †⊙†*EP* Ⓜ *Provença* ✛ *H:8.*

$$–$$$ 📺 **Hotel Jazz.** Bright wood and plenty of glass give this mid-city newcomer a contemporary, hip feel—and the young party animals from around the world walking through the lobby do nothing to dispel the notion that something very clued-in must be going on here. Rooms are pristine, if a little sterile, with state-of-the-art bathrooms and light, sleek furnishings. A step from the Rambla at the lower edge of the Eixample, the location is dead center in the heart of Barcelona. **Pros:** exciting and sleek lobby; design-focused hipsters clientele; smart and friendly staff. **Cons:** in the point of a triangle too close to the raging Carrer Pelai; inner-city brouhaha only a few feet away. ⊠ *Pelai 3, Eixample* ☎ *93/552–9696* ⊕ *www.hoteljazz.com* ⊅ *108 rooms* ⚹ *In-room: Wi-Fi, safe. In-hotel: restaurant, bar, pool* ⊟ *AE, DC, MC, V* †⊙†*EP* Ⓜ *Catalunya* ✛ *H:11.*

$$$$ 📺 **Hotel Omm.** Another on Barcelona's lengthening list of design hotels,
Fodor's Choice this postmodern architectural tour de force was conceived by a team
★ of designers who sought to create, in a playful way, a mystic sense of peace mirroring its mantra. Minimalist rooms, a soothing reception area, and even the pool all contribute to this aura. The upper rooms overlook the roof terrace of Gaudí's Casa Milà. The restaurant, Moo, serves modern cuisine orchestrated by the Roca brothers—Joan, Josep, and Jordi—who achieved international prestige with their Celler de Can Roca near Girona. **Pros:** a perfect location for the upper Eixample; a design triumph; a sense of being at the epicenter of style; great nightlife scene around the bar on weekends. **Cons:** slightly pretentious staff; the restaurant, Moo, is pricey and a little precious. ⊠ *Roselló 265, Eixample* ☎ *93/445–4000* ⊕ *www.hotelomm.es* ⊅ *87 rooms, 4 suites* ⚹ *In-room: Wi-Fi. In-hotel: restaurant, bar, pool, parking (paid)* ⊟ *AE, DC, MC, V* †⊙†*EP* Ⓜ *Diagonal, Provença* ✛ *I:8.*

$$$$ 📺 **Hotel Palace.** Founded in 1919 by Caesar Ritz, this is the original Ritz, the grande dame of Barcelona hotels, renamed in 2005. The imperial lobby is at once loose and elegant; guest rooms contain Regency furniture, and some have Roman-style mosaics in the baths. The restaurant, Caelis, serves first-rate French cuisine. **Pros:** equidistant from Gothic Quarter and central Eixample; elegant and excellent service; consummate old-world luxury in rooms. **Cons:** a little stuffy; painfully pricey. ⊠ *Gran Via 668, Eixample* ☎ *93/318–5200* ⊕ *www.hotelpalacebarcelona.com* ⊅ *122 rooms* ⚹ *In-room: Wi-Fi. In-hotel: restaurant, bar, gym* ⊟ *AE, DC, MC, V* †⊙†*EP* Ⓜ *Passeig de Gràcia* ✛ *J:10.*

4

$$–$$$ ⊡ **Hotel Pulitzer.** Built squarely over the metro's central hub and within walking distance of everything in town, this elegant new hotel could not be better situated to take advantage of Barcelona's many attractions. With ultramodern, high-tech equipment of every stripe and spot—from DSL Internet and Wi-Fi hookups to hot tubs—the Pulitzer combines smart service with chic decor at moderate prices. **Pros:** surprisingly quiet and collected sanctuary considering the central location; well-equipped bar and public Internet rooms; breakfast room bright and cheery. **Cons:** too large and busy for intimacy or much personal attention from staff. ⊠ *Vergara 8, Eixample* 🕾 *93/481–6767* ⊕ *www.hotelpulitzer.es* ⇗ *91 rooms* ⚫ *In-room: safe, Wi-Fi. In-hotel: restaurant, bar, Internet terminal, Wi-Fi hotspot* ▤ *AE, DC, MC, V* ⫟〇⫠ *EP* Ⓜ *Catalunya* ✢ *H:11.*

$$$–$$$$ ⊡ **Majestic.** With an unbeatable location on Barcelona's most stylish
Fodor's Choice boulevard, surrounded by fashion emporiums of every denomination,
★ the Majestic is a near-perfect place to stay. The building is part Eixample town house and part modern extension, but pastels and Mediterranean hues warm each room. The superb restaurant, Drolma, is a destination in itself. **Pros:** perfectly placed in the center of the Eixample; good balance between technology and charm; one of Barcelona's best restaurants. **Cons:** facing one of the city's widest, brightest, noisiest, most commercial thoroughfares. ⊠ *Passeig de Gràcia 68, Eixample* 🕾 *93/488–1717* ⊕ *www.hotelmajestic.es* ⇗ *271 rooms, 32 suites* ⚫ *In-room: Wi-Fi. In-hotel: 2 restaurants, bar, pool, gym, parking (paid)* ▤ *AE, DC, MC, V* ⫟〇⫠ *EP* Ⓜ *Passeig de Gràcia* ✢ *I:9.*

$$$–$$$$ ⊡ **Mandarin Oriental Barcelona.** Since opening with a rush of excitement in November of 2009, this ultracontemporary art-deco palace by Oviedo-born designer Patricia Urquiola has quickly become a Barcelona mainstay at the very hub of the city's elegant Eixample. With views of Gaudí's Casa Batlló, this sleek new lodging option offers rooms overlooking a lush interior landscaped garden or over Passeig de Gràcia just a few blocks down from La Pedrera. Built into a renovated mid-20th-century townhouse, rooms are light and airy in off-white tones with a hint of oriental minimalism. The hotel's gourmet restaurant Moments is managed by one of Catalonia's top chefs, Carme Ruscalleda, with her son Raúl Balam at the burners, while four other restaurants offer different dining environments. **Pros:** gorgeous high-tech equipment and design; central position for shopping and sightseeing. **Cons:** on a busy thoroughfare; slightly over-modern and antiseptic. ⊠ *Passeig de Gràcia 38-40, Eixample* 🕾 *93/151–8888* ⊕ *www. mandarinoriental.com* ⇗ *98 rooms* ⚫ *In-room: Wi-Fi, refrigerator, safe. In-hotel: 5 restaurants, bar, Wi-Fi hotspot, pool, spa, parking (paid)* ▤ *AE, DC, MC, V* ⫟〇⫠ *EP* Ⓜ *Passeig de Gràcia, Diagonal, Provença* ✢ *I:10.*

$$$$ ⊡ **ME Barcelona.** With the new ME hotel east of Plaça de les Glòries, the Meliá hotel group has taken a serious run at the heights of Barcelona's hotel scene. Everything from the Dos Cielos restaurant with star chefs the Torres twins at the burners to the Angels & Kings pool and restaurant flamboyantly parades the hippest design. Showers with natural rain showerheads, thread counts in the gazillions, feather pillows provided by Elysian geese, an organic herb garden for the restaurant: the ME has haute details to spare. **Pros:** well placed for a look at the Barcelona of the 21st century; handy to the Sagrada Familia, the beach, and the torrid Poble Nou nightlife scene. **Cons:** a long taxi or subway ride from the Gothic Quarter; surrounded by new, high-rise architecture. ✉ *Pere IV 272–286, Eixample* ☎ *93/488–1717* ⊕ *www.me-barcelona.com* ⤴ *259 rooms* ⟳ *In-room: Wi-Fi. In-hotel: 2 restaurants, bar, pool, gym, parking (paid)* ▭ *AE, DC, MC, V* ⦿⎮*EP* Ⓜ *Poblenou* ⟐ *L:12.*

$$–$$$ 📺 **Meliá Barcelona.** The lobby here has a waterfall with a hydraulic rush that dominates the reception and the piano bar (aptly christened Drinking in the Rain). Dark-wood shelves and dressers line amply sized rooms equipped with top-of-the-line technology, from flat-screen TV to high-speed Internet and Wi-Fi. Although the hotel is hardly convenient to the sights you come to Barcelona to see, its famous brunches are gigantic feasts, an unnecessary extra with all the city's dining options, but for serious breakfast lovers, this may be Barcelona's best. **Pros:** relaxed and restful lobby, with ample and abundant spaces; friendly and helpful staff. **Cons:** far from most of Barcelona's main attractions; on a roaring avenue generally clogged with traffic. ✉ *Av. de Sarrià 50, Eixample* ☎ *93/410–6060* ⊕ *www.solmelia.es* ⤴ *333 rooms, 21 suites* ⟳ *In-room: Wi-Fi. In-hotel: restaurant, room service, bar, gym* ▭ *AE, DC, MC, V* ⦿⎮*EP* Ⓜ *Hospital Clinic, Muntaner* ⟐ *E:6.*

$–$$ 📺 **Onix.** This hotel is next to the Barcelona convention center and other Montjuïc attractions such as the Miró Foundation and the Romanesque collection; Sants train terminal is within a 15-minute walk; it overlooks Barcelona's onetime-bullring-now-concert-venue Les Arenes as well as the Parc Joan Miró. Three buildings away is the Casa de la Papallona (House of the Butterfly), one of Barcelona's most spectacular Art Nouveau facades. Add to this the hotel's multilingual staff and fresh rooms, and the result is an impressive small-though-inexpensive hotel. **Pros:** near some of Barcelona's best art venues on Montjuïc; bright and contemporary design; cheerful service. **Cons:** far from the city's main attractions in the Gothic Quarter and the central Eixample; beds and furnishings modern but flimsy. ✉ *Llançà 30, Eixample* ☎ *93/426–0087* ⊕ *www.hotelsonix.com* ⤴ *80 rooms* ⟳ *In-room: Wi-Fi.* ⟳ *In-hotel: bar, pool, parking (paid)* ▭ *AE, DC, MC, V* ⦿⎮*EP* Ⓜ *Espanya* ⟐ *D:6.*

$$–$$$ 📺 **Prestige Paseo de Gràcia.** A triumph of design built around a (mostly original) 1930s staircase, this hotel offers purity of line and sleek minimalism as the reigning aesthetic principles, especially inside the rooms with their stark monochromatic palette. The roof terrace is a tour de force, the different sections divided by contrasting colors and textures. **Pros:** ideally positioned in the middle of the Eixample, superbly balanced minimalist design; elegant service. **Cons:** opens onto a wide, bustling, bright, loud boulevard; understaffed, thus poor service; small rooms. ✉ *Passeig de Gràcia 62, Eixample* ☎ *93/272–4180* ⊕ *www. prestige-paseo-de-gracia.com* ⤴ *45 rooms* ⟳ *In-room: Wi-Fi. In-hotel: 2 restaurants, bar, pool, gym, Internet terminal, Wi-Fi hotspot, parking (paid)* ▭ *AE, DC, MC, V* ⦿⎮*EP* Ⓜ *Passeig de Gràcia* ⟐ *I:9.*

$$–$$$ 📺 **Regente.** Moderniste style and copious stained glass lend glamour and appeal to this smallish hotel. The cozy hotel bar is a colorful bonanza of stained glass, while guest rooms are more elegantly restrained, with contemporary furnishings in soothing cream and beige tones. A verdant roof terrace (with a small pool) and a prime position on the Rambla de Catalunya seal the positive verdict. **Pros:** intimate hotel with traditional Moderniste furnishings; leafy Rambla Catalunya is a quiet but lively promenade. **Cons:** small public rooms; small rooms; tiny swimming pool. ⊠ *Rambla de Catalunya 76, Eixample* ☎ *93/487–5989* ⊕ *www. hcchotels.com* ⤵ *79 rooms* ♿ *In-room: Wi-Fi, safe. In-hotel: restaurant, bar, pool* ⊟ *AE, DC, MC, V* ⌶⊙⌶ *EP* Ⓜ *Passeig de Gràcia* ✢ *I:9.*

$-$$ ⊡ **Room Mate Emma.** This 2009 addition to Barcelona's hotel fleet operates under the motto "daring, cheerful, creative," and seems to consistently fill the bill. Along with minimalist lines and design details, Emma's pivotal location allows easy walking to everything in Barcelona (with the exception of Montjuïc and its art treasures). Following the less-is-more leads of architects Mies van der Rohe and, more recently, Rafael Moneo, the contemporary Barcelona aesthetic is sharp and simple, a welcome respite from Modernisme's opulence. The rooms have a certain space-age look, with white-on-white details and a few contrasting doses of purple, while the lobby and public rooms are futuristic and functional in patterned etched glass. **Pros:** perfectly positioned in the center of the Eixample; quintessential minimalist chic; smart, hip staff. **Cons:** on a busy street; lower rooms can be noisy. ⊠ *Carrer Rosselló 205, Eixample* ☎ *93/238–5606* ⊕ *www.room-matehotels.com* ⤵ *56 rooms* ♿ *In-room: safe, refrigerator, Wi-Fi. In-hotel: restaurant, bar, Internet terminal, Wi-Fi hotspot* ⊟ *AE, DC, MC, V* ⌶⊙⌶ *EP Diagonal* ✢ *H:8.*

$$-$$$$ ⊡ **Villa Emilia.** This sleek design hotel offers fine lodging at prices that are generally affordable, except at moments of peak demand, halfway between Sants station and the convention center. Rooms on the 6th floor have more light and less noise, while rooms ending in 2 or 8 (68, 62, 58, 52, etc.) are larger and have superior views. If you pick a room over the street, you'll have views of Montjuïc paired with quiet interiors. All rooms are fully equipped with of-the-moment technology, from Wi-Fi connections to plasma TVs. The 7th-floor roof terrace is a popular spot for breakfast and drinks. **Pros:** popular terrace for drinks and socializing; top technology and gadgetry; easy on the budget. **Cons:** not the most picturesque part of the Eixample; noisy streets. ⊠ *Calàbria 115–117, Eixample* ☎ *93/252–5285* ⊕ *www.hotelvillaemilia.com* ⤵ *53 rooms* ♿ *In-room: safe, Wi-Fi. In-hotel: bar, Internet terminal, Wi-Fi hotspot* ⊟ *AE, DC, MC, V* ⌶⊙⌶ *EP* Ⓜ *Rocafort* ✢ *E:11.*

GRÀCIA

$$$-$$$$
Fodor's Choice
★

⊡ **Casa Fuster.** Casa Fuster is your only chance to stay in an Art Nouveau building designed by Lluís Domènech i Montaner, architect of the retina-rattling Palau de la Música Catalana. His last project, built in 1911, this elegant hotel at the bottom of the village of Gràcia shows a tendency toward the more classical Noucentisme that followed the decorative delirium of the Moderniste movement. The rooms and public spaces reinforce the Moderniste theme with Gaudí-designed chairs, *trencadis* (broken tile) floors and door handles, and Art Nouveau–inspired lamps and fixtures. The hotel restaurant serves fine Mediterranean cuisine, while the sumptuously decorated Café Vienés was a historic meeting place for Barcelona's movers and shakers of the early 20th century. **Pros:** well placed for exploring Gràcia as well as the Eixample, equidistant from the port and upper Barcelona's Tibidabo. **Cons:** the design can feel a little heavy and mournful; some in-room facilities look better than they work (such as the showers that require you to spray cold water on yourself to turn on). ⊠ *Passeig de Gràcia 132, Gràcia* ☎ *93/255-3000* ⊕ *www. hotelcasafuster.com* ⤳ *66 rooms, 39 suites* ♿ *In-hotel: restaurant, room service, Wi-Fi hotspot, bar, pool, gym, laundry service, parking (paid)* ☰ *AE, DC, MC, V* ⏆*EP* Ⓜ *Diagonal* ✥ *I:7.*

$-$$ 🏨 **Guillermo Tell.** Stashed away between Via Augusta and the village of Gràcia, this is about as close to

sleeping in Gaudí's first house, Casa Vicens, as you can get. Rooms are amply sized, if a little plain, while the bathrooms are lavishly outfitted in marble. **Pros:** on a quiet street; not far from the village of Gràcia; small enough for friendly and personalized service. **Cons:** a short subway ride to Plaça Catalunya; building of scant architectural interest or value. ⊠ *Guillem Tell 49, Gràcia* ☎ *93/415-4000* ⊕ *www. hotelguillermotell.com* ⤳ *61 rooms* ♿ *In-room: Wi-Fi, safe. In-hotel: bar, Wi-Fi hotspot, parking (paid)* ☰ *AE, DC, MC, V* ⏆*EP* Ⓜ *Sant Gervasi, Gràcia* ✥ *H:5.*

SARRIÀ, SANT GERVASI, PUTXET, AND PEDRALBES

¢ 🏨 **Alberg Mare de Deu de Montserrat.** This youth hostel accepts guests over 25 with youth hostel cards (€3.50 per night for first six nights, available at check-in desk). The lobby, a Moderniste exhibition featuring Moorish horseshoe arches and polychrome marquetry right out of the Arabian Nights, has been featured in Barcelona art books. This is one of the city's great bargains—shared rooms and bathrooms notwithstanding—overlooking the city near Gaudí's Güell Park. Bus 28 from the Rambla and the green line's Vallcarca metro station get you home. Doors close at midnight, but open every 30 minutes for late arrivals, i.e., everyone. **Pros:** excellent budget choice; takes all ages; friendly service; lavish Art Nouveau design. **Cons:** accommodations vary from dormitory-like multiple-bed rooms to smaller rooms for two to four; front door opens only at intervals after midnight; far from downtown Barcelona and popular landmarks. ⊠ *Passeig de la Mare de Déu del Coll 41–51, Vallcarca,* ☎ *93/210-5151* ⊕ *www.xanascat.cat* ⤳ *209 beds in rooms for 2, 3, 4, 6, 8, and 12* ♿ *In-room: no TV. In-hotel: restaurant, bar, parking (paid)* ☰ *AE, DC, MC, V* ⏆*EP* Ⓜ *Vallcarca* ✥ *H:1.*

$-$$ ⚏ **Bonanova Park.** In upper Barcelona near Sarrià, this somewhat bare-bones hotel provides a break from the downtown crush at a moderate cost. Several good restaurants are within walking distance in Sarrià, as are the metro stops of Sarrià and the Green Line's Maria Cristina, each five minutes walk away. The rooms are bright and breezy, and the predominantly residential neighborhood is quiet. Children enjoy the Quinta Amelia Park a block west of the hotel. **Pros:** a good budget choice; small enough for personalized service. **Cons:** a long way from the center of town; rooms are small and lackluster; amenities few and far between. ✉ *Capità Arenas 51, Sarrià* ☎ *93/204–0900* ⊕ *www.hotelbonanovapark. com* ⟿ *60 rooms* ♿ *In-room:Wi-Fi. In-hotel: bar, Wi-Fi hotspot* ▭ *AE, DC, MC, V* ⟦◯⟧ *EP* Ⓜ *Sarrià, Maria Cristina* ✛ *C:3.*

$$ ⚏ **Castellnou.** A miniscule and semi-secret uptown residence, the Castellnou is just two steps from the FGC train that whisks you to the middle of town in 10 minutes. It's also near the freeway to the Pyrenees and handy to upper Barcelona's attractions in Sarrià, Pedralbes, and Sant Gervasi. The restaurant (closed in August) is small and intimate, but there are also a dozen good places to dine within easy walking distance. Rooms are contemporary, with sleek new furnishings, and service is warm and friendly. **Pros:** a refuge from the city; small enough for personalized service; modern design. **Cons:** a long way from the Gothic Quarter and the Eixample; rooms and public spaces cramped. ✉ *Castellnou 61, Tres Torres* ☎ *93/203–0550* ⊕ *www.hoteles-catalonia. es* ⟿ *49 rooms* ♿ *In-hotel: restaurant, room service* ▭ *AE, DC, MC, V* ⟦◯⟧ *EP* Ⓜ *Tres Torres* ✛ *D:3.*

$$ ⚏ **Catalonia Park Putxet.** Next to lush and junglelike parks and private enclaves, this hideaway in upper Barcelona has the advantage of being far enough from the Rambla to provide a sense of refuge. Park Putxet offers adequate comforts and particularly elegant bathrooms at reasonable prices. Walking distance from Gràcia and just a few minutes by train or taxi from the center of town, this is a good choice if you like to stroll. **Pros:** next to a leafy park and not far from Park Güell; well connected with the center of town by subway. **Cons:** far from most of the city's main attractions; rooms and public lack space and personality. ✉ *Putxet 68, Sant Gervasi* ☎ *93/212–5158* ⊕ *www.hoteles-catalonia.es* ⟿ *152 rooms* ♿ *In-room: Wi-Fi. In-hotel: restaurant, laundry service, Wi-Fi hotspot, parking (paid)* ▭ *AE, DC, MC, V* ⟦◯⟧ *EP* Ⓜ *El Putxet* ✛ *H:3.*

$ ⚏ **Catalonia Rubens.** A little out of the way above Plaça Lesseps, this hotel has easy access to Güell Park—a few minutes' walk away—and to downtown Barcelona by taxi or public transportation. Rooms are streamlined, with attractive wooden furniture. **Pros:** good value; better and cooler air above the hue and cry of the city; friendly service. **Cons:** far from the center of town; plainly decorated. ✉ *Passeig de la Mare de Déu del Coll 10, Sant Gervasi* ☎ *93/219–1204* ⊕ *www. hoteles-catalonia.es* ⟿ *139 rooms* ♿ *In-room: Wi-Fi. In-hotel: restaurant, laundry service, Wi-Fi hotspot, parking (paid)* ▭ *AE, DC, MC, V* ⟦◯⟧ *EP* Ⓜ *Vallcarca* ✛ *H:1.*

$$$ ⚏ **Hesperia Sarrià.** Well connected to downtown Barcelona by the Sarrià train, this is a modern hotel set on a leafy street just a block up from

Via Augusta. The rooms are medium to small in size but well designed. Service is swift and friendly, and the general demeanor of the place is smart and efficient. **Pros:** on a quiet street in a quiet neighborhood; walking distance from the village of Sarrià and its fleet of excellent restaurants. **Cons:** 20 minutes by subway from the Gothic Quarter and the Eixample; small rooms and public spaces. ⊠ *Vergós 20, Sarrià* ☎ *93/204–5551* ⊕ *www.hesperia-sarria.es* ⇨ *134 rooms* ⚷ *In-room: Wi-Fi, safe. In-hotel: restaurant, bar, Wi-Fi hotspot, parking (paid)* ⊟ *AE, DC, MC, V* ⏣⎮*EP* Ⓜ *Tres Torres* ✛ *E:3.*

\$–\$\$ 🏨 **Husa Pedralbes.** The two best things about this simple little hotel are its location on the edge of leafy Sarrià (a 20-minute walk from the Monestir de Pedralbes, 15 minutes from the FC Barcelona soccer stadium, and 5 minutes from the Sarrià train stop) and its intimate, personal atmosphere. Rooms are modern and elegant, though somewhat cramped. **Pros:** intimate and friendly service; bright and modern design. **Cons:** a long way (though just 15 minutes by subway) from the Gothic Quarter; rooms and public spaces small. ⊠ *Fontcoberta 4, Sarrià* ☎ *93/203–7112* ⊕ *www.husa.es* ⇨ *30 rooms* ⚷ *In-room: Wi-Fi. In-hotel: restaurant, Wi-Fi hotspot, parking (paid)* ⊟ *AE, DC, MC, V* ⏣⎮*EP* Ⓜ *Sarrià, Maria Cristina* ✛ *C:3.*

\$\$\$–\$\$\$\$ 🏨 **Rey Juan Carlos I.** This skyscraper is an exciting commercial complex as well as a luxury hotel, with sleek, contemporary rooms. Glass elevators whip up and down the spaceship-like atrium. Jewelry, furs, art, flowers, caviar, and even limousines are all for sale here. The lush garden, which includes a pond with swans, has an Olympic-size swimming pool, and the green expanses of Barcelona's finest in-town country club, El Polo. There are two restaurants: Chez Vous serves French cuisine, and Café Polo has a sumptuous buffet as well as an American bar. **Pros:** 10 minutes from the airport; supremely comfortable and complete; various restaurants and everything you might need without ever leaving the hotel; polished and attentive service. **Cons:** well removed (at least 20 minutes by taxi) from all of Barcelona's main sites. ⊠ *Av. Diagonal 661–671, Diagonal* ☎ *93/364–4040* ⊕ *www.hrjuancarlos.com* ⇨ *395 rooms, 38 suites* ⚷ *In-room: Wi-Fi, safe, refrigerator. In-hotel: 2 restaurants, bars, tennis court, pool, gym, spa, Wi-Fi hotspot, parking (paid)* ⊟ *AE, DC, MC, V* ⏣⎮*EP* Ⓜ *Zona Universitàri* ✛ *A:4.*

\$\$–\$\$\$ 🏨 **Sansi Pedralbes.** A contemporary polished-marble and black-glass box overlooking the gardens of the Monestir de Pedralbes, this hotel may seem out of place, but the views up into the Collserola hills and over Barcelona are splendid. Rooms are impeccable in equipment and design, with blond wood and plasma-screen TVs. It's only a 15-minute climb to the Carretera de les Aigües, Barcelona's best running track, across the side of the mountain behind the city, and the air in this part of town can be a welcome relief. **Pros:** small and intimate; excellent and friendly service; ultramodern design. **Cons:** the nearest subway, the Reina Elisenda FGC train, is a 20-minute hike away, so plan on plenty of taxi time. ⊠ *Av. Pearson 1–3, Pedralbes* ☎ *93/206–3880* ⊕ *www. sansihotels.com* ⇨ *70 rooms* ⚷ *In-room: Wi-Fi. In-hotel: restaurant, bar, pool, Wi-Fi hotspot, parking (paid)* ⊟ *AE, DC, MC, V* ⏣⎮*EP* Ⓜ *Reina Elisenda* ✛ *A:1.*

4

$$–$$$$
Fodor'sChoice
★
⊡ **Turó de Vilana.** Surrounded by bougainvillea-festooned villas above Barcelona's Passeig de la Bonanova, this shiny place has a hot tub in every room, gleaming halls, and public areas of stone, steel, and glass run by a pleasant staff. Rooms are polished with state-of-the equipment and contemporary designer furnishings. In summer, upper Barcelona is noticeably cooler, not to mention quieter at night. The Turó de Vilana is a 10-minute walk from the Sarrià train that connects you with the city center in a quarter of an hour. **Pros:** new furnishings and latest technology in rooms; bright and cheery service and design; verdant and refreshing surroundings. **Cons:** in upper Sarrià and a long way (30 minutes in all) from the center of town. ⊠ *Vilana 7, Sant Gervasi* ☎ *93/434–0363* ⊕ *www.turodevilana.com* ↝ *20 rooms In-room: Wi-Fi.* ⅄ *In-hotel: restaurant, room service (until 10 pm), Wi-Fi hotspot, parking (paid)* ▭ *AE, DC, MC, V* ⍥*EP* Ⓜ *Sarrià* ✛*F:2.*

TIBIDABO

$$$–$$$$
⊡ **Gran Hotel la Florida.** With nonpareil views over Barcelona, water sculptures everywhere but in your bed, a superb restaurant (L'Orangerie), and designer suites that are difficult to leave behind, it's easy to forgive the 20-minute (and €20) taxi drive from the port to reach this gem. The L-shaped horizon pool is a delight, as are the spas and exercise facilities. Originally opened in 1925, this design hotel has roared back to the forefront of Barcelona's most stylish lodging. **Pros:** cool air and panoramic views; artistic design; horizon pool; friendly and attentive service. **Cons:** a long taxi ride from the center of town. ⊠ *Ctra. Vallvidrera al Tibidabo 83–93, Tibidabo* ☎ *93/259–3000* ⊕ *www.hotellaflorida.com* ↝ *74 rooms, 22 suites* ⅄ *In-room: safe, Wi-Fi. In-hotel: restaurant, bar, Internet terminal, Wi-Fi hotspot, pool, gym, spa, parking (paid)* ▭ *AE, DC, MC, V* ⍥*EP* Ⓜ *Tibidabo* ✛*H:1.*

Nightlife and the Arts

WORD OF MOUTH

"The Catalans know how to celebrate like nobody else in the world. If you go for La Merce in late September, you will have the thrill of the energy in the city when Catalans are in a celebratory mood. You will probably see some parades with gegants (giants) and the castellers (human towers . . . absolutely amazing . . .)."

—debiness

NIGHTLIFE AND THE ARTS PLANNER

Where to Get Information

To find out what's on, check "*agenda*" listings in Barcelona's leading daily newspapers *El País, La Vanguardia,* and *El Periódico de Catalunya* or the weekly *Guía del Ocio,* available at newsstands all over town. *Activitats* is a monthly list of cultural events, published by the *Ajuntament* (Town Hall) and available from its information office in Palau de la Virreina (Rambla 99). *Metropolitan* magazine, published monthly in English, is given away free in English-language bookstores and hotel lobbies.

Hours

Daily events in the arts scene race headlong from 7 o'clock lectures and book presentations, *inauguraciones* and *vernissages* (art show openings), to 9 o'clock concerts, theater, and dance performances. And then, sometime after 1 or 2 in the morning, the *real* nightlife kicks in.

Top Five Nightlife Experiences

Concerts in the Palau de la Música Catalana followed by tapas at the Botafumeiro bar (FCh. 2).

Red-hot salsa at Antilla BCN Latin Club or Salsabor.

Movies at the Verdi multi-cine and nomadic dinners in Gràcia.

Dinner and dancing until the wee hours above the beach at Shôko.

The sun rising out of the Mediterranean from bar Mirablau on Tibidabo.

What to Wear

Dress codes in Barcelona are eclectic, elastic, and casual, but never sloppy. While there are rarely hard and fast rules at elegant restaurants or concert venues, tourists in shorts, tank tops, and baseball caps will feel out of place. Discos are another kettle of fish: often autocratic bouncers inspect aspiring clients carefully. (Read: the better you dress the better chance you have of getting in.) The Liceu Opera House often has black-tie gala evenings, and while tourists are not expected to go out and rent tuxedos, a coat with lapels (necktie optional) blends better. The Palau de la Música Catalana and the Auditori are less formal than the Liceu, but a modicum of care with one's appearance is expected.

Scoring Tickets

Tickets for performances are available either at the theater or via Tel-Entrada (www.telentrada.com) and Servicaixa (www.servicaixa.com) both online or by telephone at 902/101212. After ordering your seats and giving credit card information, you pick up tickets at the door of the venue.

By George
Semler

Barcelona's nocturnal roll call, from art openings and concerts to tapas bars, music bars, and clubbing, offers a wild mix of options. From the early-evening browsing and tapas-grazing through the area around the Born to stand-up howling and drinking at the Universal or the Hotel Omm's Ommsession to late live and recorded music at Bikini, Shôko, CDLC, or Luz de Gas, Barcelona offers a thousand and one ways to make it through the night without resorting to slumber.

NIGHTLIFE

Barcelona nights are long and as wild as you want, filling all of the hours of darkness and often rolling until dawn. Most of the best clubs don't even open until well after midnight, but cafés and music bars serve as recruiting venues for the night's mission. The typical progression begins with drinks (wine or beer), tapas and dinner, a jazz or flamenco concert around 11 PM, then a pub or a music bar or two, and then, if the body can keep up with the spirit, dancing. Busting a move can be done in a variety of locales, from clubs to ballroom dance halls, and is apt to continue until the sun comes up. Late-night bars and early-morning cafés provide an all-important break to refresh and refuel before doing another lap around the dance floor.

New wine bars, cafés, music bars, and tiny live-music clubs are constantly scraping plaster from 500-year-old brick walls to expose medieval structural elements that offer striking backdrops for postmodern people and conversations. The most common closing time for 90% of Barcelona's nocturnal bars is 3 AM, though this may vary according to clientele flow and increasingly strict civic regulations.

BARS

TAVERNS, PUBS, AND BARS

Bar Almirall. The twisted wooden fronds framing the bar's mirror and Art Nouveau touches from curvy door handles to organic-shape table lamps to floral chair design make this one of the prettiest bars in Barcelona, and also the second-oldest, dating from 1860. (The oldest is the Marsella, another Raval favorite.) It's good spot for drinks after hitting the nearby the MACBA (Museu d'Art Contemporani de Barcelona). ⊠ *Joaquín Costa 33, Raval* ☎ *93/412–1535* Ⓜ *Universitat.*

Bar Muy Buenas. This Art Nouveau gem just behind the medieval hospital has curvaceous wooden framing and a balcony overlooking the bar that mark this historic saloon as one of the city's finest Moderniste bars. The codfish basins at the edge of the counter are the original soaking and cleaning sinks once used here when the place was a fish market. ⊠ *Carme 63, Raval* ☎ *93/442–5053* Ⓜ *Catalunya, Universitat.*

★ **Bar Pastis.** Near the bottom of the Rambla, just above the Santa Mònica art center, this tiny hole-in-the-wall has live performances Sunday (French singers), Tuesday (tango), and Wednesday (singer-songwriters). When singers are not on stage, clients are treated to an encyclopedic tour of every Edith Piaf song ever recorded. There is no cover charge. ⊠ *Santa Mònica 4, Rambla* ☎ *93/318–7980* Ⓜ *Drassanes.*

George & Dragon. Named for Barcelona's ubiquitous symbols of good and evil, the city's virtual yin and yang, this is a rollicking English pub just off Passeig de Gràcia with live music on Saturday night (no cover charge) and a full offering of international rugby, soccer, and NFL games. The menu combines standard English pub fare with Spanish tapas specialties. ⊠ *Diputació 269, Eixample* ☎ *93/488–1765* Ⓜ *Passeig de Gràcia.*

★ **Glaciar.** This simple, old-fashioned bar in the southwest corner of Plaça Reial is *the* spot for young travelers, especially in summer. The crowd spills out into the square's smoke-free air, making a rolling block party under the palm trees and the stars beyond. ⊠ *Pl. Reial 13, Rambla* ☎ *93/302–1163* Ⓜ *Liceu.*

La Sede. A simple saloon in the Marià Cubí–Aribau area, this is a music bar with no extravagant design on display, just good cheer and eclectic music at an endurable decibel level. Like nearby The End, La Sede serves as a respite from the crush of the madding crowd over on Marià Cubí. ⊠ *Laforja 140, Eixample* ☎ *93/319–2314* Ⓜ *Muntaner.*

Les Gens que J'aime. A Bohemian fantasy from a late-19th-century novel is reproduced in this time-warp salon. Neatly tucked under the sidewalk, this bar is saturated in the yellow glow of lighting and the deep reds and ochers of the sofas and armchairs, all suggesting a luxury smoking car on the *Orient Express:* perfect for an intimate tête-à-tête. ⊠ *Carrer València 286, Eixample* ☎ *93/215–6879* Ⓜ *Passeig de Gràcia.*

London Bar. The trapeze (often in use) suspended above the bar adds even more flair to this Art Nouveau circus haunt in the Barrio Chino. Stop in at least for a look, as this is one of the Raval's old standards, which, despite the wholly unbreathable air, has entertained generations of Barcelona visitors and locals. ⊠ *Nou de la Rambla 34, Raval* ☎ *93/302–3102* Ⓜ *Liceu.*

L'Ovella Negra. With heavy wooden tables, stone floors, and some cozy nooks and crannies to drink in, the Black Sheep is the city's top student tavern, especially for the barely legal. Aromas of brews gone by never completely abandon the air in this cavernous hangout, and the troglodytic behavior is usually a good match for the surroundings. ⊠ *Sitges 5, Raval* ☎ *93/317–1087* Ⓜ *Catalunya.*

Marsella. French poet and playwright Jean Genet was known to have been a regular here while "researching" and writing *La Marge*, his novel set in Barcelona's steamily picturesque Raval. A cross between a speakeasy and a Euro-bohemian café and beer hall, the Marsella serves cold beer that goes down exceptionally well. ⊠ *Sant Pau 65, Raval* ☎ *93/442–7263* Ⓜ *Liceu.*

Michael Collins Irish Pub. This congenial Irish pub near Gaudí's unfinished masterpiece has a strong international following, predominantly English-speakers. International sporting events with everything from steeplechase to yacht racing find their way onto one of the multiple screens. Live Irish music takes the stage Thursday–Sunday. A traditional Irish lunch is the star attraction on Sunday at 1 PM. ⊠ *Plaza Sagrada Família 4, Eixample* ☎ *93/459–1964* Ⓜ *Sagrada Família.*

Mirablau. This bar is a popular hangout for evening drinks, but it's even more frequented as a romantic late-night and dawn vantage point for watching the city lights down below and, eventually, the sunrise gathering over the Mediterranean horizon to the east. Take the Tibidabo train (U-7) from Pl. de Catalunya or Buses 24 and 22 to Plaça Kennedy. At Avinguda Tibidabo, catch the Tramvía Blau (Blue Trolley), which connects with the funicular to the summit. ⊠ *Plaça del Doctor Andreu s/n, Tibidabo* ☎ *93/418–5879* Ⓜ *Tibidabo.*

Nick Havanna. Open Thursday–Saturday only, this mid-Eixample uproar is a favorite with university students primed to boogie until dawn. With a consistently hot program of recorded music ranging from rock to pop to house, nonstop action is guaranteed here, as well as Barcelona's only looking-glass urinals. ⊠ *Rosselló 208, Eixample* ☎ *93/215–6591* Ⓜ *Provença.*

Opiniao. In the upper reaches of Barcelona's Sant Gervasi district, this taste of Brazil above Via Augusta offers a low-key, quiet, and intimate sanctuary filled with booths and tables tucked into corners with occasional live performances for graduates and postgraduates still actively on the hunt. ⊠ *Ciutat de Balaguer 67, Bonanova* ☎ *93/418–3399* Ⓜ *Tibidabo.*

Salero. This café-restaurant-bar always packs in rows and ranks of gorgeous young models of both sexes and the accompanying pilot fish that bask in their reflected light. The menu is light and inventive Mediterranean fare, and the charged energy is generally that of a feeding frenzy. ⊠ *Carrer del Rec 60, Eixample* ☎ *93/318–4399* Ⓜ *Jaume I.*

Sherlock Holmes. Above Via Augusta sits a corner of Barcelona that will forever be England, with live musical performances (no cover charge) and darkly intimate nooks. As with most English and Irish pubs in Barcelona, sports broadcasts from all over the world are a staple. ⊠ *Copernic 42–44, Eixample* ☎ *93/414–2184* Ⓜ *Diagonal.*

NIGHTS OF WINE AND REVELRY

Wine-tasting (with Cava-sipping on the side) has proliferated in Barcelona over the last decade. With light tapas for accompaniment, nomadic tippling is an unbeatable way to begin an evening.

A typical night out in Barcelona has several stages. Discos and music bars don't jump to life until well after midnight, so the early part of the evening is a culinary and oenological prologue. The city is well equipped with opportunities to take advantage of this warm-up time; wine bars, specializing in light fare and new and interesting vintages, have become a popular part of Barcelona's nocturnal routine. Whether in Sarrià, the Eixample, or the Ciutat Vella, there is a plethora of taverns to choose from. Wine served by the glass is usually chalked up on a blackboard and selections change frequently. Walking between stops is important for the longevity of your nightlife plans; covering a couple of miles with short hops between copas is essential and will keep you clearheaded enough to last through the wee hours.

A GOOD WINE BAR CRAWL

Starting at **Terrabacus** (✉ *Muntaner 185* ☎ *93/410–8633*), ask one of the fleet of sommeliers for suggestion. Next head to **La Bodegueta Provença** (✉ *Provença 245* ☎ *93/487–5221*) where an interesting selection of wines is detailed on the chalkboard. Nearby is the original **La Bodegueta** (✉ *Rambla de Catalunya 100* ☎ *93/215–4894*), a charming dive—literally. Ten minutes west is **Cata 1.81** (✉ *Valencia 181* ☎ *93/323–6818*) a wine-tasting (*cata*) bar with creative fare. **La Barcelonina de Vins i Esperits** (✉ *Valencia 304* ☎ *93/215–7083*) is a vast cava and wine emporium.

SIPS TO SAMPLE

When you're eyeballing the wine list, keep a look out for these *copas*.

TORRE LA MOREIRA

This full-bodied and acidic Albariño wine from northwestern Spain's Rias Baixas winegrowing region is a refreshing and fully satisfying accompaniment for seafood tapas at Cal Pep, Botafumeiro, or nearly any tavern with a good Albariño selection.

JUVÉ I CAMPS RESERVA DE LA FAMILIA

A Barcelona favorite, this mid-range cava made with the standard Penedès grape varietals of Macabeu (40%), Parellada (40%), and Xarel.lo (20%) grapes is a tawny gold hue with feisty bubbles and a tart apple and citrus flavor. Crisp and fresh on the palate, the finish is balanced and clean as a whistle.

GRANS MURALLES

This Torres single-vineyard red wine will cost you well over a $100 a bottle, so this is one to look for sold by the glass at La Vinya del Senyor, Vinoteca Torres, or Cata 1.81. Made with ancient, pre-Phylloxera grapes (Monastrell, Garnacha Tinto, Carró, Samsó, and Cariñena), some of which are now extinct, this vineyard tucked in under the medieval walls of the Cistercian monastery of Poblet is a taste of history: dense, complex, peppery, tannic, and fruity.

KRIPTA GRAN RESERVA

Agustí Torrelló, one of the fathers of Catalonia's cava, created this excellent Gran Reserva in homage to the Mediterranean winemaking tradition. The bottle is shaped like an amphora, requiring the use of an ice bucket *à table*. Made from old vines and aged for five years, the wine is a straw-colored gold, intensely bubbly, and superbly crisp and refreshing. Complex on the palate, tastes range from chocolate to butter, with a solid mineral base.

PAIR THAT WITH . . .

Start light with a few of Catalonia's own Arbequina olives. *Boquerones* (small, fresh, pickled, white anchovies) are another excellent and refreshing morsel to pair with an Albariño wine or a flute of *cava*. A *ración* (portion) of regular anchovies wouldn't be a bad idea either. Beyond those preliminaries, *pimientos de Padrón*, lovely deep green peppers from Galicia's village of Padrón, are always welcome additions at this point, as are *croquetas* (croquettes) small breaded fritters with minced meat filling of ham or chicken. La Barceloneta has its own mega-croquetas called *bombas*, round slightly-larger-than-golf-ball-sized fritters filled with mashed potato and ham. *Chopitos* (baby octopi), cooked to a dry crisp, are delicious with white wines and *cavas*, while, as wines turn darker, a plate of *jamón ibérico de bellota* might be the perfect closer, unless a *ración de albóndigas* (meatballs) or a sizzling *chistorra* (spicy sausage) proves irresistible.

5

The End. This bar is one of the most popular in the area, with a cool, breezy terrace for summer evenings. After a tour through the more populous and jam-packed saloons along Marià Cubí, The End is a relatively quiet refuge for conversations and carousing alike. ⊠ *Santaló 34, Eixample* ☎ *93/200–3942* Ⓜ *Muntaner.*

Universal. From early evening to late night, the Universal has been the hottest music bar in town for 30 years running. Dim lighting and music played at a level where you can still converse make this a perfect meet-up spot for late nocturnal activities ahead. ⊠ *Marià Cubí 182–184, Eixample* ☎ *93/200–7470* Ⓜ *Muntaner.*

COCTELERÍAS (COCKTAIL BARS)

Boadas. A small, rather formal saloon near the top of the Rambla, Boadas is emblematic of the Barcelona *coctelería* concept, which usually entails an air of decorum, expensive mixed drinks, wood and leather surroundings, and an impenetrable curtain of cigar smoke. ⊠ *Tallers 1, Rambla* ☎ *93/318–9592* Ⓜ *Catalunya.*

Dry Martini Bar. The namesake drink of this stately and discreet establishment is the best bet here, if only to partake of the ritual. This is a popular hangout for mature romantics: husbands and wives (though not necessarily each other's) in an environment of genteel wickedness. ⊠ *Aribau 162, Eixample* ☎ *93/217–5072* Ⓜ *Provença.*

El Born. This former codfish emporium is now an intimate haven for drinks, raclettes, and fondues. The marble cod basins in the entry and the spiral staircase to the second floor are the quirkiest details, but everything seems devised to charm the eye. ⊠ *Passeig del Born 26, La Ribera* ☎ *93/319–5333* Ⓜ *Jaume I.*

El Copetín. Right on Barcelona's best-known cocktail avenue, this bar catering to young professionals in the thirty- to forty-year-old range has good cocktails and Irish coffee. It's dimly lighted and romantic, with South Seas motifs. ⊠ *Passeig del Born 19, La Ribera* ☎ *93/319–4496* Ⓜ *Jaume I.*

Harry's. This is Barcelona's version of the Parisian "sank roo-doe-noo" (5, rue Daunou) favorite that intoxicated generations of American literati, faux and otherwise, in Paris. While the formal art of mixology remains somewhat alien to the Barcelona scene, those in need of a serious drink will find it here at Harry's. ⊠ *Aribau 143, Eixample* ☎ *93/430–3423* Ⓜ *Provença.*

Miramelindo. Famed for caipirinhas and a Brazil–meets–South Pacific stylistic confusion designed to liberate the Catalan yuppie from his mercantile moorings, this venerable bar has survived for three decades and appears to be moving forward without missing a bossa nova beat. The musical buzz ranges from Latin jazz to samba. ⊠ *Passeig del Born 15, La Ribera* ☎ *93/310–3727* Ⓜ *Jaume I.*

WINE BARS

Ateneu Gastronòmic. Across the parking lot from the Town Hall in what was once the site of the Roman baths, this restaurant-*enoteca* (wine library) with an outdoor terrace in summer offers a wide selection of wines and fine meals to go with them. ⊠ *Pl. de Sant Miquel 2 bis, Barri Gòtic* ☎ *93/302–1198* ☉ *Tues.–Sat. 1:30 PM–3:30 PM and 8:30 PM–12:30 AM* Ⓜ *Liceu.*

★ **Cata 1.81.** Wine tasting (la cata) in this contemporary design space comes with plenty of friendly advice about enology and some of the world's most exciting new vintages. Small delicacies such as truffle omelets and foie gras make this streamlined sliver of a bar a gourmet haven as well. ⊠ Valencia 181, Eixample ☎ 93/323–6818 ☼ Mon.–Sat. 6 PM–1 AM Ⓜ Provença.

La Barcelonina de Vins i Esperits. This vast room surrounded by several hundred bottles of wine and cava (Catalan méthode champenoise sparkling wine) on the shelves overhead is an excellent choice for evening wine tastings accompanied by light tapas. ⊠ Carrer Valencia 304, Eixample ☎ 93/215–7083 ☼ Weekdays 6 PM–2 AM, Sat. 7:30 PM–2 AM, Sun. 8 PM–2 AM Ⓜ Provença.

La Cave. With 450 wines from around the world arranged by color and cost spectrums around a cool barrel-like wine cellar, this enoteca (wine library) is an oenophile's paradise. Selected small offerings from magret de pato (duck breast) to French cheeses ranging from Reblochon to Cabecou to Pont l'Éveque make this an ideal wine cellar for tastings and a light dinner. ⊠ Av. Josep Vicenç Foix 80, Sarrià ☎ 93/206–3846 ☼ Mon.–Sat. 1:30–5 PM and 8 PM–midnight Ⓜ Sarrià.

La Taverna del Palau. Behind a glass facade facing the Palau de la Música, this sleek little tavern is perfect for a hit of cava during intermission or a beer and a flauta (thin, flutelike sandwich) of cured ham. ⊠ Sant Pere més Alt 8, Sant Pere ☎ 93/268–8481 ☼ Mon.–Sat. 8AM–midnight Ⓜ Catalunya.

La Tinaja. Part wine bar, part tapas emporium, this handsome cavern just around the corner from that other tapas favorite, Cal Pep, offers a good selection of wines from all over Spain and fine acorn-fed Iberian ham to go with it. The salads are excellent, and the tone of La Tinaja is refined and romantic. ⊠ L'Esparteria 9, Born-Ribera ☎ 93/310–2250 ☼ Tues.–Sat. noon–4 PM and 6:30 PM–midnight Ⓜ Jaume I.

La Vinateria del Call. Just a block and a half from the cathedral cloister in the heart of the Call, Barcelona's medieval Jewish Quarter, this dark and candlelit spot serves a wide variety of well-thought-out wines, tapas, and full meals. ⊠ Sant Domènec del Call 9, Barri Gòtic ☎ 93/302–6092 ☼ Mon.–Sat. 6 PM–1 AM Ⓜ Liceu.

Fodor's Choice **La Vinoteca Torres.** Miguel Torres of the Torres wine dynasty has finally
★ given Passeig Gràcia a respectable address for tapas and wine, with more than 50 selections from Torres wineries around the world. The menu runs from selected Spanish olives to Ramón Peña seafood from the Rías de Galicia to stick-to-your-ribs lentejas estofadas (stewed lentils) or diced chunks of Galician beef with peppers from Gernika. ⊠ Passeig de Gràcia 78, Eixample ☎ 93/272–6625 Ⓜ Passeig de Gràcia.

La Vinya del Senyor. Ambitiously named "The Lord's Vineyard," this excellent wine bar directly across from the entrance to the lovely church of Santa Maria del Mar changes its list of international wines every week. ⊠ Pl. de Santa Maria 5, Born-Ribera ☎ 93/310–3379 ☼ Tues.–Sun. noon–1 AM Ⓜ Jaume I.

Fodor's Choice **Monvínic.** "Wineworld" in Catalan, this sleek designer space offers
★ 3,500 wines ranging in price from €10 to €500. Eggs with black truffles and creative riffs on classical Catalan cuisine complement your vino.

Care to Order a Beer?

The standard local beers made by the venerable Damm company are basically two: Estrella Dorada and Voll Damm. The darker Voll Damm bock beer is a potent, highly alcoholic brew. The lighter Estrella Dorada (translatable as "Golden Star"), normally ordered as simply "una Estrella," is a cleansing lager with some bite to it (as opposed to the watery San Miguel, another less-common option). "Una mediana" is a middle-size bottled beer, as opposed to "un quinto," which is a small bottle, a fifth of a liter, or "una litrona," a full liter. "Una caña" is a draft beer drawn from the caña (cane, or tap). The standard choice for most Barcelona beer drinkers is "una caña," but ask for "una caña pequeña" (a small draft) or you might get a stein of the stuff, known as "una jarra." Some places serve "zurritos" (literally, a little slap, a hit)—shallow glasses with a couple of inches of beer splashed in the bottom. Watch out for an insidious new invention: a caña or tap with a small sign on it saying LIMÓN, meaning lemon beer, a disappointingly sweet premixed shandy. If you want a shandy, a mix of beer and lemon-flavored fizzy water, order a "clara" and mix it yourself. This brew is sometimes served in a glass porrón, a jar with a slender spout designed to be poured from overhead at full arm's length and passed around. This is best attempted while wearing clothes you don't mind soaking with a little Bacchian overflow.

✉ *Diputació 249, Eixample* ☎ *93/272–6187* ◷ *Tues.–Sun. noon–1* AM Ⓜ *Passeig de Gràcia*

Terrabacuş 24. A sleek new tapas idea: combine an extensive wine list offering 250 different wines (50 served by the glass) with a wide variety of tapas from Catalonia, Spain, and beyond. Through the advice of a sommelier, various different wines are recommended for specific tapas, be they seafood, sashimi, or ibérico ham. The result is an exciting and different tapas and wine-tasting emporium with a happening young buzz. ✉ *Carrer Muntaner 185, Eixample* ☎ *93/410–8633* ◷ *Mon.–Sat. 1:30–4 and 9–midnight* Ⓜ *Provença.*

Xampú Xampany. One of Barcelona's few authentic xampanyerias, specializing in cava, the Catalan version of the renowned sparkling wine from France's Champagne region, this bar and delicatessen also offers fine Iberian hams, foies, and charcuterie. ✉ *Gran Via 702, Eixample* ☎ *93/265–0483* ◷ *Mon.–Sat. 8* PM–1:30 AM Ⓜ *Tetuan.*

CASINOS

Gran Casino de Barcelona. Open daily 1 PM–5 AM, this casino under the Hotel Arts has everything from slot machines to roulette, a dance club, floor shows, ballroom dancing, tango, line dancing, and a restaurant. ✉ *Calle de la Marina, Port Olímpic* ☎ *93/225–7878* Ⓜ *Ciutadella–Vil. la Olímpica.*

Singer-songwriters take the stage at Bar Pastis on Wednesdays.

CLUBS AND DJ VENUES

Some clubs have a discretionary cover charge that ranges €3–€15, depending on the live music offering or merely on the law of supply and demand. Bouncers like to inflict this cover charge on unsuspecting foreigners, so dress up and be prepared to talk your way in. Any story can work: for example, you own a chain of nightclubs and are on a world research tour. The party won't really get started until 1:30 or 2 AM. For a guide to Barcelona's after-dark activities, check out ⊕ *www. bcn-nightlife.com.*

Agua de Luna. Open Wednesday–Sunday, this seriously hip club with top DJs and everything from salsa to hip-hop entertains until dawn on the western side of the Eixample. The Sunday session begins at 8 PM, whereas on Friday and Saturday the dancing doesn't start until 11 PM or so, though you'll probably have the place to yourself if you show up before 1 AM. ⊠ *Viladomat 211, Eixample* ☎ *93/410–0440* ⊕ *www. aguadeluna.com* Ⓜ *Urgell.*

Antilla BCN Latin Club. This exuberantly Caribbean spot sizzles with salsa, son cubano, and merengue from opening time at 11 PM until dawn. Dance instructors "teach you the secrets of the hips" during the first opening hours. The self-proclaimed "Caribbean cultural center" cranks out every variation of salsa ever invented, as well as its own magazine, *Antilla News,* to keep you abreast of the latest happenings in the world of Latin moves and grooves in the Mediterranean. ⊠ *C. Aragó 141, Eixample* ☎ *93/451–2151* ⊕ *www.antillasalsa.com* Ⓜ *Urgell.*

Apolo. Live music reigns supreme at this hot and happening refuge for hard-partying reprobates of all ages. Since it is down at the western end of Nou de la Rambla, just walking over there from the Rambla through the Barrio Chino will be enough to get your adrenalin pumping (but no worries, danger is minimal despite the extensive display of illegal activities going down in the street). ⊠ *C. Nou de la Rambla 111, Raval-Poble Sec* ☎ *93/441–4001* ⊕ *www.sala-apolo.com* Ⓜ *Urgell.*

Barcelona City Hall. Wednesday-night Pigs & Diamonds parties starring electro house music and red-hot guest DJs from neighboring clubs guarantee dancing till you drop at this raging mid-city favorite. Deep, tech, groove, and microfunk are just some of the musical specialties you will experience in this party powder keg. ⊠ *Rambla Catalunya 2–4, Eixample* ☎ *93/238–0722* ⊕ *www.cityhall-bcn.com* Ⓜ *Catalunya.*

Bikini. This haven for postgraduates offers three ecosystems: Espai BKN with music from the '80s and '90s along with funk, dance-pop, and house; Espai Arutanga with salsa and Latin fusion; and Dry Bikini, which serves cocktails, sandwiches, and, of course, *bikinis* (Spanish for grilled-cheese sandwiches). Bikini opens at midnight and charges a cover of €11 with your *second* drink included. ⊠ *Deu i Mata 105, at Entença, Eixample* ☎ *93/322–0005* ⊕ *www.bikinibcn.com* Ⓜ *Les Corts.*

Búcaro. This straight-up disco rocks till dawn, especially on weekends, when it remains open until 5 AM. The floor-to-ceiling mirrors seem to elongate the human form marvelously, encouraging a narcissistic rush that can lead to gyrating mayhem. Just be aware, the very young can pass for grown-ups here in the cacophony of music and inventive lighting. The DJs embrace everything: house, ska, electropop, hip-hop, and funk. ⊠ *Aribau 195, Eixample* ☎ *93/209–6562* ⊕ *www.grupocostaeste. com* Ⓜ *Gràcia.*

Buda Barcelona. The hottest nightspot in the Eixample, Buda Barcelona is a magnet for Spanish and international celebrities. Local guests have included flamenco dancer Joaquín Cortés and actress Penelope Cruz. Even Hollywood casting legend Gretchen (Grudles) Rennell has been spotted on the prowl for new talent. Unabashedly claiming to be Barcelona's beautiful-people hangout, Buda Barcelona packs in a glamorous crowd that, when not basking in the gold wallpaper, is prone to dancing on the bar. ⊠ *Pau Claris 92, Eixample* ☎ *93/318–4252* ⊕ *www. budarestaurante.com* Ⓜ *Catalunya.*

Caravan. The Raval's hottest disco and DJ scene is in the new Barceló Raval hotel, and specializes in bringing DJs from the Canary Islands every other year and merely playing hot music during their regular gigs. For an exciting and safe perch over the rowdy Raval, this is an interesting nightlife alternative to the Rambla and Raval areas. ⊠ *Rambla del Raval 17–21, Raval* ☎ *93/320–1490* ⊕ *www.caravan.com* Ⓜ *Liceu.*

CDLC. The Carpe Diem Lounge Club—in case you are marooned out near the Olympic Port, staying at the Hotel Arts, or looking for post-cinema action—is the best and glitziest of the clubs out this way, complete with conveniently compartmentalized *sofa-camas* (sofa beds of a sort) encouraging horizontal time. ⊠ *Passeig Maritim 32, Port Olímpic* ☎ *93/224–0470* ⊕ *www.cdlcbarcelona.com* Ⓜ *Ciutadella–Vil.la Olímpica.*

Costa Breve. Open Thursday–Saturday midnight to dawn, this hip and happening disco just above the Diagonal has DJs that spin pop, funk, and dance music until 6 AM. Though popular with the young college crowd, postgraduates still manage to find some dance-floor turf. ⊠ *Aribau 230, Eixample* ☎ *93/414–2778* ⊕ *www.grupocostabreve.com* Ⓜ *Provença.*

Elephant. It could be a catwalk, with models showing off the latest fashions and strutting their stuff at Elephant's Lust & Luxury Nights, all in a graceful Pedralbes terrace and chalet. The June 23 Sant Joan midsummer eve party is not to be missed. (If you come dressed all in white you get in free.) ⊠ *Passeig dels Til.lers 1, Pedralbes* ☎ *93/334–0258* ⊕ *www. elephantbcn.com* Ⓜ *Maria Cristina.*

La Paloma. Wonderfully peculiar and kitschy 1950s furnishings fill this old-fashioned *sala de baile* (dance hall) that dates to 1903. The balcony is a great place for viewing both the dance floor and the frescoed ceiling. A live orchestra plays big-band tango, mambo, bolero, cha-cha, and different genres of ballroom music until 1 or 2 AM on weekends. Later a DJ takes over until 5 AM. La Paloma is open Thursday–Sunday. ⊠ *Tigre 27, Raval* ☎ *93/301–6897* ⊕ *www.lapaloma-bcn.com* Ⓜ *Universitat.*

Loft. An offshoot of Sala Razzmatazz, this funky space dedicated to house and electronic music draws an edgy crowd of twenty- and thirtysomethings. The club opens at 1 AM on Friday and Saturday, and the energy generated between then and dawn could provide electricity for the entire city if someone could figure out how to harness the stuff. ⊠ *Pamplona 88, Poble Nou* ☎ *93/272–0910* ⊕ *www.salarazzmatazz. com* Ⓜ *Marina, Bogatell.*

Luz de Gas. This always-wired hub of musical and general nightlife activity has something going on every night, from live performances to wild late-night dancing. Though the weekly schedule may vary with the arrival of famous international names, you can generally plan for Monday blues; Tuesday jazz; Wednesday, Saturday, and Sunday cover bands; Thursday soul; and rock on Friday. ⊠ *Muntaner 246, Eixample* ☎ *93/209–7711* ⊕ *www.luzdegas.com* Ⓜ *Muntaner, Provença.*

Luz de Luna. This torrid Latin specialist puts out compelling Caribbean rhythms for a crowd that knows exactly what to do with them. Like snooty ski instructors, the professional *salseros,* straight in from "the pearl of the Antilles" (aka Cuba), offer their skills to beginners and experts alike for tours of an endless repertory of moves and maneuvers straight from Havana. ⊠ *Comerç 21, Born-Ribera* ☎ *93/310–7542* ⊕ *www.salsapower.com* Ⓜ *Jaume I.*

Ommsession Club. The Hotel Omm attracts an army of the thirty-five to fortysomething crowd looking for excitement on Friday and Saturday nights. DJs and occasional live performances keep this well-groomed mob of young and not-so-young professionals clustered around the lobby bar with frequent dives down into the torrid dance floor downstairs. ⊠ *Rosselló 265, Born-Ribera* ☎ *93/445–400* ⊕ *www. ommsession.es* Ⓜ *Diagonal.*

Otto Zutz. Just off Via Augusta, above the Diagonal, this nightclub and disco is a perennial Barcelona favorite that keeps attracting a glitzy mix of Barcelona movers and shakers, models, ex-models, wannabe models, and the hoping-to-get-lucky mob that predictably follows this sort of pulchritude. Music is usually recorded, with occasional live performers.

A live orchestra encourages dancers to cut a rug at La Paloma.

✉ *Lincoln 15, Eixample* ☏ *93/238–0722* ⊕ *www.ottozutz.com* Ⓜ *Sant Gervasi, Plaça Molina.*

Pachá. First famous in Ibiza as the wildest club in Europe, Pachá has hit the ground running in Barcelona. Half a dozen bars, two VIP areas, a chill-out room, and a breezy terrace all equipped with supersonic sound gear and the latest in avant-garde decor entertain a heterogeneous crowd checking each other out with gleeful prurience. Open Friday, Saturday, and nights before holidays, Pachá's keeps the music hot with DJs, and groups from around the world spice up the live entertainment. ✉ *Av. Gregorio Maranon 17, Les Corts* ☏ *93/334–3233* ⊕ *www. clubpachabcn.com* Ⓜ *Zona Universitària.*

Rat King Retro Lounge. Wired with rockabilly and swing music and oozing bourbon on the rocks, this is an irresistible upper Eixample dive with live music on Thursday nights, when well-known guitarist Ignasi Corominas organizes a jam session after 10 PM with the help of a stand-up base and vibraphone. ✉ *Passatge de Marimon 17, Eixample* ☏ *93/414–2456* ⊕ *www.theratkinglounge.es* Ⓜ *Gràcia.*

Sala B. Music described as "humana" (suggesting no teeth-rattling techno) keeps Sala B filled with the mid-twenties and thirtysomething set until 5 in the morning on Fridays and Saturdays. Just above the Diagonal near Luz de Gas, this veteran night spot is an offshoot of the parent club as evidenced by the shared Web site. Concerts and DJ music for dancing alternate at this comfortable club designed for semi-civilized nightlife. ✉ *Muntaner 244, Sarrià-Sant Gervasi* ☏ *93/209–7711* ⊕ *www.luzdegas.com* Ⓜ *Provença.*

Sala Razzmatazz. Razzmatazz stages weeknight concerts featuring international draws from James Taylor to Moriarty. The small-format environment is extraordinarily intimate, and beats out sports stadiums or the immense Palau Sant Jordi as a top venue for concerts. It shares its Friday and Saturday club madness with neighboring sister venture the Loft around the corner. ⊠ *Almogavers 122, Poble Nou* ☎ *93/320–8200* ⊕ *www.salarazzmatazz.com* Ⓜ *Marina, Bogatell.*

Salsabor. Popular with Barcelona's Latin Kings and Queens Cultural Association and their president Erika Jaramillo, this Latin American disco and salsa school cranks out salsa, merengue, and bachata (among other Latin dance sensations) for a young crowd that knows exactly how to groove to these incandescent rhythms. Simply joining the ranks of awed spectators to watch world-class salsa athletically performed is worth the price of admission, which, incidentally, is free on Thursday, and otherwise €10 with a drink included. ⊠ *Carrer Moiá 1, Eixample* ☎ *676/694477* ⊕ *www.salsabor.es* Ⓜ *Gràcia, Provença.*

Salsitas. Both restaurant and Latin dance club, this red-hot joint just off the Rambla and practically smack across from Gaudí's Palau Güell packs in a happy crowd of hard partyers. Models and the generally babelicious come here decked out in sleek and chic designer kit to shake to house music laid on by star DJs. Alabaster pillars are disguised as date palms, and a range of exotic touches goes for the extreme opposite of rustic. ⊠ *Nou de la Rambla 22, Raval* ☎ *93/318–0840* Ⓜ *Liceu.*

Shôko. The hottest of the glitzerati spots below the Hotel Arts and the Frank Gehry fish, this is the place to see and be seen in Barcelona these days. The excellent restaurant morphs into a disco around midnight and continues until the wee hours of the morning, with all manner of local and international celebrities perfectly liable to make an appearance at one time or another. ⊠ *Passeig Marítim de la Barceloneta 36, Port Olímpic-Barceloneta* ☎ *93/225–9200* ⊕ *www.shoko.biz* Ⓜ *Ciutadella– Vila Olímpica.*

Up and Down. Locally pronounced "Pen-*dow*," this has been a classic for well-heeled party animals for more than 30 years, and it's still kicking out the jams. The club is so named for its two separate spaces, one downstairs for younger carousers and one upstairs for more mature and accomplished night owls. The FC Barcelona soccer team is apt to let off steam here after great triumphs, while upper-Barcelona's beautiful people make this their downhill base camp for nocturnal pursuits. ⊠ *Numancia 179, Les Corts–Diagonal* ☎ *93/280–2922* Ⓜ *Maria Cristina.*

THE GAY SCENE

The Guía del Ocio (⊕ *www.guiadelociobcn.com*), in its *"Tarde y Noche"* (evening–night) section devotes a full page (following the nightclub section under the heading "Ambiente") to listings for gay establishments.

Arena Madre. Though frequented by gay and straight customers alike, this mid-Eixample club seems to be a safe hub and haven for gay women from all over Barcelona, Europe, and the world at large. ⊠ *Balmes 32, Eixample* ☎ *93/487–8342* ⊕ *www.areanadisco.com* Ⓜ *Passeig de Gràcia.*

Boyberry. This gay hub combines a wide range of resources, from films and darkrooms to Internet connections, and a lounge. Information, parties, maps of the Gaixample: everything you need to get tuned into the city's gay scene is available here. ⊠ *Calàbria 96, Eixample* ☎ *93/451–7707* ⊕ *www.boyberry.com* Ⓜ *Rocafort.*

El Dulce Deseo de Lorenzo. A gay *chiringuito* (beach shack) on a nudist beach at the eastern end of the Barceloneta beaches, "Lorenzo's Sweet Desire" puts on catwalk shows, projects films, provides information about the city's gay scene, and welcomes all, with or without bathing suits. ⊠ *Platja de la Mar Bella s/n, Poble Nou* ☎ *93/415–7123* ⊕ *www. chiringuitogay.com* Ⓜ *Poble Nou.*

Metro Disco. Two dance floors offer a choice of disco history or Latin rhythms for a somewhat older set of men here, though all ages are represented. Porn on the tiny screens over the urinals and a solid party vibe keep this place filled to the gills and rocking. ⊠ *Sepúlveda 185, Eixample* ☎ *93/323–5227* ⊕ *www.metrodisco.com* Ⓜ *Urgell, Universitat.*

New Chaps. This off-Gaixample jeans and leather bar has steer horns mounted on the walls, plenty of racy videos, and a labyrinthine dark room downstairs for a more mature gay crowd. ⊠ *Av. Diagonal 365, Eixample* ☎ *93/215–5365* Ⓜ *Diagonal, Verdaguer.*

Space Barcelona. Touted as the most daring club in Barcelona's gay scene, this is the place to go on Sunday when much of the competition is closed. Between Plaça Espanya and Sants train station, Space Barcelona is known for superb music, top DJs, and its superior sound system. Four different bars surround the giant stage, which is usually heavily populated with dancers and vocalists. ⊠ *Carrer Tarragona 141–147, Sants-Plaça Espanya* ☎ *93/426–8444* Ⓜ *Plaça Espanya.*

Punto BCN. A musical bar with billiards tables, this mid-Eixample hub is a clearing house for all persuasions and tastes, with women often outnumbering the men, pool tables or not. ⊠ *Carrer Muntaner 63–65, Eixample* ☎ *93/453–6123* Ⓜ *Universitat.*

JAZZ AND BLUES

Barcelona's jazz festival convenes top artists from around the world. The Palau de la Música Catalana hosts an **international jazz festival** (☎ *93/481–7040*) in November.

Harlem Jazz Club. Good jazz and country singers perform at this small but exciting music venue just a five-minute walk from Plaça Reial. Cece Gianotti and Joan Vinyals are regular country guitarists and vocalists here. ⊠ *Comtessa de Sobradiel 8, Barri Gòtic* ☎ *93/310–0755* Ⓜ *Jaume I, Liceu.*

Jamboree-Jazz & Dance-Club. This pivotal nightspot, another happy fiefdom of the imperial Mas siblings, is a center for jazz, rock, and flamenco in the evening's early stages (11 PM) and turns into a wild and woolly dance club after performances. Jazz greats Joe Smith, Jordi Rossy, Billy McHenry, Gorka Benítez, and Llibert Fortuny all perform here regularly, while in Los Tarantos, the upstairs space, some of Barcelona's finest flamenco can be heard. ⊠ *Pl. Reial 17, Rambla* ☎ *93/301–7564* Ⓜ *Liceu.*

Jazz Sí Club. Run by the Barcelona contemporary music school next door, this workshop and (during the day) café is a forum for musicians, teachers, and fans to listen and debate their art. There is jazz on Monday; pop, blues, and rock jam sessions on Tuesday; jazzmen jamming on Wednesday; Cuban salsa and son on Thursday; flamenco on Friday; and rock and pop on weekends. If the entrance isn't free, the small cover charge includes a drink. ⊠ *Requesens 2, Raval* ☎ *93/329–0020* ⊕ *www.tallerdemusics.com* Ⓜ *Sant Antoni.*

La Cova del Drac-Jazzroom. An emblematic jazz venue dating back to Barcelona's very first jazz performances, La Cova de Drac (The Dragon's Cave) was revived in this new location by the ubiquitous Mas family of Mas i Mas fame. Jordi Rossy, Llibert Fortuny, Joe Smith, Billy McHenry, Ben Waltzer, and a long list of jazz greats perform here over the course of the year. The upper Barcelona address makes La Cova an easy stroll for Sarrià and Sant Gervasi jazz aficionados, though downtown connections on the FCG train or by taxi are also quick and painless. ⊠ *Carrer Vallmajor 33, Sant Gervasi* ☎ *93/245–7396* ⊕ *www. masimas.com* Ⓜ *Muntaner, Pàdua.*

Nao Colón/Club Bamboo. Across from the Estació de França, this hot spot serves contemporary Mediterranean cuisine and presents concerts Tuesday–Thursday at 10 PM. Anything from jazz and blues to flamenco fusion might take the stage here, but at midnight Nao Colón turns into a pumpkin and Club Bamboo materializes with sounds from Latin house and funk to Brazilian and Cuban Afro rhythms. ⊠ *Av. Marquès de l'Argentera 19, Born-Ribera* ☎ *93/268–7633* Ⓜ *Jaume I.*

Zacarías. Folk, rock, blues, and a wide variety of musical attractions keep Zacarías on the cutting edge of Barcelona's live-music scene. Well positioned near the center of the Diagonal, this veteran nightlife hub has entertained barcelonins for several generations. Upcoming attractions include stars ranging from Sam Lardner's country-flamenco fusion group Barcelona to flamenco master Enrique Morente and his daughter Estrella Morente. ⊠ *Av. Diagonal 477, Eixample* ☎ *93/207–5643* ⊕ *www.zac-club.com* Ⓜ *Provença.*

BARCELONA JAZZ

Barcelona has loved jazz ever since Sam Wooding and his Chocolate Kiddies triumphed here in 1929. Jack Hilton's visits in the early '30s paved the way for Benny Carter and the Hot Club of Barcelona in 1935 and 1936. In the early years of the post–Spanish civil war Franco dictatorship, jazz was viewed as a dangerous influence from beyond, but by 1969 Duke Ellington's Sacred Concerts smuggled jazz into town under the protective umbrella of the same Catholic Church whose conservative elements cautioned the Franco regime against the perils of this "degenerate music."

THE ARTS

A glance through the daily agenda page of *La Vanguardia* or *El País* will remind you, every day, that it would be physically impossible to make it to all the art-exhibit openings, concerts, book presentations by famous authors, lectures, free films, or theatrical events that you would like to attend in Barcelona that day. Gallery openings and book presentations alone, many of which serve drinks and canapés, could probably eliminate any need for a food or party budget in Barcelona's boiling cultural scene. The comprehensive *Guía del Ocio* (⊕ *www.guiadelociobcn.com*), which includes a brief but well-researched and well-written English section, comes out Thursday for the following week, costs €1, and includes all musical listings, restaurants, bars, nightclubs, and novelties of the week.

FESTIVALS

The **Barcelona Guitar Festival** (☎ *93/301–7775* ⊕ *www.theproject.es*), held between late March and early June, features concerts in the Palau de la Música Catalana and other venues by master guitarists of all musical genres and styles. Folk, jazz, classical, and flamenco starring Spain's national instrument includes performances by guitar legends from Paco de Lucía to flamenco singer Niña Pastori.

El Grec (*Festival del Grec* ☎ *93/301–7775* ⊕ *www.bcn.es/grec*), Barcelona's annual summer arts festival, runs from late June to the end of July. Many of the concerts and theater and dance performances take place outdoors in such historic places as Plaça del Rei and the Teatre Grec, as well as in the Mercat de les Flors.

The **Festival de Música Antiga** (*Early Music Festival* ☎ *93/404–6000* ⊕ *www.kadmusarts.com*) brings the best early-music groups from all over Europe to town from late April to mid-May. Concerts are held all over town, though most lectures and performances are at the **Caixa-Fòrum** (⊠ *Av. Marquès de Comillas 6–8, Eixample* Ⓜ *Espanya*).

The **Festival Internacional de Poesia** (☎ *93/301–7775* ⊕ *www.bcn.es/icub*), sponsored by the Institut de Cultura in May, is one of the city's most extraordinary and exciting events, with poets from places as disparate as Ethiopia, China, Poland, Ireland, and Canada joining local Catalan, Basque, Gallego, and Spanish poets reciting their work, always in the original languages. The Palau de la Música is sold out for the final recital, after a week of events in Barcelona's finest architectural gems. The festival is directly descended from Barcelona's *Jocs Florals* (Floral Games) first held in 1393, so it's no wonder that emotions run high.

The **International Music Festival** (☎ *93/301–7775*), in late September, forms part of the feast of Nostra Senyora de la Mercè (Our Lady of Mercy), Barcelona's patron saint. The main venues are Palau de la Música, Mercat de les Flors, and Plaça del Rei.

ART GALLERIES

For art-gallery shopping, see Chapter 7.

CaixaFòrum. The building itself, a restored textile factory, is well worth exploring (and is directly across from the Mies van der Rohe Pavillion on Montjuïc at the bottom of the steps up to the Palau Nacional). Temporary exhibits show the work of major artists from around the world, while the Músics del Món (Musicians of the World) series stages everyone from Renaissance lutenist Hopkinson Smith to sitar master Ravi

Shankar in the intimate auditorium. ⊠ *Av. Marquès de Comillas 6–8, Montjuïc* 🕾 *902/223040* ⊕ *www.fundacio.lacaixa.es* Ⓜ *Espanya.*

Centre Cultural Metropolità Tecla Sala. Some of the most avant-garde exhibits and installations that come through Barcelona find their way to this cultural powerhouse, a 15-minute metro ride away in the suburb of Hospitalet de Llobregat. (Note that the Josep Tarradellas address is not the in-town Barcelona street that runs between Estació de Sants and Plaça Francesc Macià). ⊠ *Av. Josep Tarradellas 44, Hospitalet* 🕾 *93/338–5771* ⊕ *www.teclasala.net* Ⓜ *La Torrasa.*

Col.legi Oficial d'Arquitectes de Catalunya. Architectural exhibits here are always interesting, as is the excellent restaurant just down the stairs. The Picasso frieze around the facade was the first Picasso work allowed in Spain after the 1936–39 Spanish civil war. ⊠ *Plaza Nova 5, Barri Gòtic* 🕾 *93/301–5000* ⊕ *www.coac.net* Ⓜ *Liceu, Catalunya.*

Fundació La Caixa. La Caixa's various galleries are all important for seeing local contemporary art or for the excellent touring art shows, from Córdoba's Julio Romero de Torres to the Flemish Brueghels, that come through Barcelona regularly. ⊠ *La PedreraProvença 261–265, Eixample* 🕾 *93/484–5979* ⊕ *www.fundacio.lacaixa.es* Ⓜ *Provença Sala Montcada* ⊠ *Carrer Montcada 14, Born-Ribera* 🕾 *93/310–0699* Ⓜ *Diagonal* ⊕ *www.caixacatalunya.es.*

La Capella de l'Antic Hospital de la Santa Creu. In this chapel, as in many Barcelona art galleries, the space itself is half the show. The choir loft, the inside of the cupola, and the vaulting in the side chapels are all lovely, while the exhibits and installations are invariably young artists showing experimental works. ⊠ *Hospital 56, Raval* 🕾 *93/442–7171* ⊕ *www.bcn.cat/capella* Ⓜ *Liceu.*

Palau de la Virreina. With the Espai Xavier Miserachs showing photography and two other spaces and the patio available for other temporary exhibits, this is an important Barcelona art resource in a convenient location next to the Boqueria market. ⊠ *La Rambla 99, Rambla* 🕾 *93/316–1000* ⊕ *www.bcn.cat/cultura* Ⓜ *Catalunya, Liceu.*

CONCERTS

For details on concerts throughout the year, check the *"agenda"* page in either *La Vanguardia* or *El País*, buy the handy *Guia del Ocio* (published every Thursday), or call the tourist information office's English line (🕾 010) and ask for information. **Cultural information** (🕾 906/427017) is another way to find out if and when events are taking place, along with the city Web site at www.bcn.es. For tickets to many events, call **Servicaixa** (🕾 902/101212) to order in Spanish with a credit card, or stop by the tourist office in Plaça de Catalunya.

Fodor'sChoice ★ **Auditori de Barcelona.** Minimal, like the inside of a guitar, the Auditori schedules a full program of classical music with occasional jazz or pop concerts near Plaça de les Glòries. Orchestras that perform here include the Orquestra Simfònica de Barcelona i Nacional de Catalunya (OBC) and the Orquestra Nacional de Cambra de Andorra. ⊠ *Lepant 150, Eixample* 🕾 *93/317–1096* ⊕ *www.auditori.com* Ⓜ *Glòries.*

Auditori Winterthur. Behind the L'Illa Diagonal shopping mall, this intimate, 650-seat venue places you close to major artists such as Austrian mezzo-soprano Angelika Kirschlager and Yo-Yo Ma. ⊠ *Av. Diagonal 547, Eixample* ☎ *93/290–1090* ⊕ *www.winterthur.es* Ⓜ *Les Corts.*

Fodor's Choice
★ **CaixaFòrum.** A beautifully restored and converted former textile mill, this neo-Mudéjar Puig i Cadalfalch structure is one of the city's newest venues for cultural events from concerts to art openings to lectures. Concerts here range from the Musics del Mon series with European early music to master baroque lutenist Hopkinson Smith or India's legendary santoor (hammer dulcimer) player Shiv Kumar. ⊠ *Av. Marquès de Comillas 6–8, Montjuïc* ☎ *93/476–8600* ⊕ *www.fundacio.lacaixa. es* Ⓜ *Espanya.*

Gran Teatre del Liceu. Barcelona's famous opera house on the Rambla runs a full season from September through June, combining the Liceu's own chorus, orchestra, and players with first-tier invited soloists from June Anderson to Plácido Domingo or Barcelona's own Montserrat Caballé. In addition, touring dance companies—ballet, flamenco, and modern dance—appear here. The downstairs foyer holds early-evening recitals, puppet shows for children on weekends, and occasional analytical discussions. The Espai Liceu café under the opera house includes (along with excellent light fare) a store filled with music-related gifts, instruments, and knickknacks, and a tiny 50-seat theater projecting fragments of operas and a video of the history of the Liceu opera house. Seats can be expensive and hard to get (reserve well in advance), but occasionally a cheap seat or two may become available. ⊠ *La Rambla 51–59, Rambla* ☎ *93/485–9913* ⊕ *www.liceubarcelona.com* Ⓜ *Liceu.*

Fodor's Choice
★ **Palau de la Música Catalana.** Barcelona's most spectacular concert hall is a Moderniste masterpiece in the Ciutat Vella, off the Barri Gòtic. Performances run September–June, with Sunday-morning concerts at 11 AM a popular tradition. The calendar here is packed—everyone from Sir Neville Marriner, directing the Academy of Saint Martin's in the Field, to flamenco singer Estrella Morente has performed here, while the house troupe, the Orfeó Català, holds choral concerts several times a year. Tickets are €6–€90, and are best purchased well in advance. The ticket office is open weekdays 11–1 and 5–8, Saturday 5–8 only. ⊠ *Palau de la Música 4-6, Sant Pere* ☎ *93/295–7200* ⊕ *www.palaumusica.org* Ⓜ *Catalunya.*

Palau Sant Jordi. Arata Isozaki's huge venue hosts massively attended pop concerts for stars like Bruce Springsteen or Paul McCartney, though occasional operas and other musical events are also presented here. ⊠ *Palau Sant Jordi, Passeig Olímpic 5–7, Montjuïc* ☎ *93/426–2089* Ⓜ *Espanya.*

Saló de Cent. Check for occasional free ceremonies and performances that allow you to visit this incomparable setting, the first protodemocratic municipal parliament (dating from 1274) in Europe. ⊠ *Pl. Sant Jaume s/n, Barri Gòtic* ☎ *93/402–7000* ⊕ *www.bcn.es* Ⓜ *Jaume I.*

DANCE

L'Espai de Dansa i Música de la Generalitat de Catalunya. Generally listed as L'Espai, or "The Space," this is one of the city's prime venues for ballet and modern dance, as well as occasional musical offerings. ⊠ *Travessera de Gràcia 63, Eixample* ☎ *93/241–6810* Ⓜ *Gràcia.*

The Gran Teatre del Liceu hosts operas and concerts in an appropriately opulent setting.

Mercat de les Flors. Near Plaça de Espanya, this theater makes a traditional setting for modern dance as well as theater. ⊠ *Lleida 59, Eixample* ☎ *93/426–1875* ⊕ *www.mercatflors.com* Ⓜ *Poble Sec.*

Teatre Apolo. This historic player in Barcelona's theater scene stages opera and dance spectacles ranging from flamenco to ballet to contemporary. ⊠ *Av. del Paral.lel 59, Raval* ☎ *93/441–9007* ⊕ *www.teatreapolo.com* Ⓜ *Paral.lel.*

Teatre Tívoli. One of the city's most beloved traditional theater and dance venues, the Tívoli has staged everything from the Ballet Nacional de Cuba to flamenco. It's just above Plaça de Catalunya. ⊠ *Casp 10, Eixample* ☎ *93/412–2063* ⊕ *www.grupbalana.com* Ⓜ *Catalunya.*

FLAMENCO

The **Festival de Flamenco de Ciutat Vella** (☎ *93/443–4346* ⊕ *www.tallerdemusics.com*), organized by the Taller de Músics (Musicians' Workshop) and based in and around the Raval's CCCB (Centre de Cultura Contemporani de Barcelona), offers a chance to hear the real thing and skip the often disappointing tourist fare available at most of the formal flamenco dinner-and-show venues around town

Los Tarantos. This standby spotlights some of Andalusia's best flamenco, and has been staging serious artists in a largely un-touristy environment for the last quarter century. The flamenco shows upstairs give way to disco action downstairs at the Jamboree Dance Club by 1 AM or so. ⊠ *Pl. Reial 17, Barri Gòtic* ☎ *93/318–3067* Ⓜ *Liceu.*

Palacio del Flamenco. This Eixample address showcases some of the city's best flamenco at hefty prices starting from 30 for a drink and the show up to 40–60 for dinner and a show. ⊠ *Balmes 139, Eix-*

Double the fun: the Palau de la Música Catalan offers a great performance in a great Moderniste setting.

ample ☎ 93/218–7237 ⊕ *www.palaciodelflamenco.com* Ⓜ *Provença, Diagonal.*

Pisamorena. Serving dinner and *copas* (wine by the glass), this little restaurant and club is known for its flamenco performances and genuine flamenco character. ✉ *Consolat de Mar 37–41, Born-Ribera* ☎ *93/268–0904* Ⓜ *Jaume I.*

Soniquete. A minuscule flamenco purists' haven tucked between the post office and Plaça Reial, Soniquete resonates with stamping feet Thursday–Sunday 9 PM–3 AM. ✉ *Milans 5, Barri Gòtic* ☎ *93/351–8757* Ⓜ *Jaume I.*

TiriTiTran. This *colmado flamenco* (an antique term for a place where flamenco was sung and danced, with trade taking place as well) offers sherries and hams while improvised flamenco may erupt at any moment. Keep a discreet profile here if you want to see any action; the catch-22 of flamenco for foreigners is that if potential performers feel that tourists are prominently present, they won't perform. ✉ *Buenos Aires 28, Eixample* ☎ *93/363–0591* ⊕ *www.tirititran.com* Ⓜ *Provença, Hospital Clínic.*

FILM

Though some foreign films are dubbed, Barcelona has a full assortment of original-language cinema; look for listings marked VOS (*Versión original subtitulada*). Yelmo Cineplex Icària near the Vil.la Olímpica is the main movie mill, with 30 films, all in VOS playing daily. Films in VOS are shown at the following theaters.

Alexandra. Conveniently placed on Rambla Catalunya, the Alexandra runs recent releases in their original language. ⊠ *Rambla de Catalunya 90, Eixample* ☎ *93/215–0503* ⊕ *www.laurenfilms.es* Ⓜ *Provença.*

Boliche. In the upper Eixample, not far from a good selection of post-flick restaurants, four intimate theaters show original language versions of hot new mainstream releases of all kinds. ⊠ *Diagonal 508–510, Eixample* ☎ *93/218–1788* ⊕ *Provença, Diagonal.*

Casablanca-Kaplan. A satisfyingly quirky movie house, the Casablanca plays art-house flicks in their original language. ⊠ *Passeig de Gràcia 115, Eixample* ☎ *93/218–4345* Ⓜ *Diagonal.*

Filmoteca de Catalunya. This Generalitat cultural resource has VOS films and specializes in international documentaries and films made by and about women. ⊠ *Av. Sarrià 33, Eixample* ☎ *93/410–7590* ⊕ *www. cultura.gencat.net/filmo* Ⓜ *Hospital Clinic.*

Icària Yelmo. This complex near the Carles I metro stop has the city's largest selection of English-language films. ⊠ *Salvador Espriu 61, Port Olímpic* ☎ *93/221–7912* ⊕ *www.yelmocineplex.com* Ⓜ *Carles I.*

Renoir-Les Corts. Convenient to Sarrià and Sant Gervasi dwellers, this cinema behind Diagonal's El Corte Inglés is a good choice for recently released English-language features of all kinds. ⊠ *Eugeni d'Ors 12, Diagonal/Les Corts* ☎ *93/490–5510* ⊕ *www.cinesrenoir.com* Ⓜ *Maria Cristina.*

Verdi. Gràcia's movie center and a great favorite for the pre- and post-show action, the Verdi unfailingly screens recent releases in their original-language versions. ⊠ *Carrer Verdi 32, Gràcia* ☎ *93/238–7990* ⊕ *www.cines-verdi.com* Ⓜ *Gràcia, Fontana.*

CATALAN FLAMENCO

Considered—like bullfighting—a foreign import from Andalusia, Catalonia and flamenco may sound incongruous, but Barcelona has a burgeoning and erudite flamenco audience. For the best flamenco available in Barcelona, consult listings and hotel concierges. Estrella Morente and her father Enrique, Chano Domínguez, Farruquito, Sara Baras, Paco de Lucía, and local *cantaora* Mayte Martín have had big successes in Barcelona.

OPERA

Fodor's Choice ★ **Gran Teatre del Liceu.** Myriad events from October through mid-July—including 10 operas, four dance productions, five concerts, and 10–15 recitals—take place in this opulent setting. It was brilliantly restored following the 1994 fire that gutted the original building. Tickets range €10–€150. In addition, a series of small concerts in the foyer promotes and enhances comprehension of the operas performing during the season. The *Sesiones Golfas* (after-hour sessions) are late-night (10 PM) entertainment events. Tickets are hard to get; reserve well in advance for all events. ⊠ *Rambla 51–59, Rambla* ☎ *93/485–9913 box office, 902/332211 for tickets through Servicaixa* ⊕ *www.liceubarcelona. com* Ⓜ *Liceu.*

THEATER

Most plays are performed in Catalan, though some are performed in Spanish.

☺ **La Puntual Putxinel.lis de Barcelona.** The city's dedicated puppet (in Catalan, *putxinel.li*) theater is in the off-Born area just off Carrer del Comerç. Weekend matinee performances are major kid magnets. ☒ *Allada-Vermell s/n, Born-Ribera* ☎ *639/305353* ⊕ *www.lapuntual. info* Ⓜ *Jaume I.*

Mercat de les Flors. Near Plaça de Espanya, this is one of the city's most traditional dance and theater venues. ☒ *Lleida 59, Montjuïc* ☎ *93/426– 1875* ⊕ *www.mercatflors.org* Ⓜ *Poble Sec.*

Sala Beckett. Tucked away in upper Gràcia two blocks east of Plaça Rovira i Trias, this intimate space stages some of Barcelona's most interesting and thoughtful theater events. ☒ *Alegre de Dalt 55 bis, Gràcia* ☎ *93/284–5312* ⊕ *www.salabeckett.com* Ⓜ *Joanic.*

Sala Muntaner. Next to the central university in the bottom of the Eixample, this little theater venue has been a Barcelona mainstay for decades. ☒ *Muntaner 4, Eixample* ☎ *93/451–5752* ⊕ *www.salamuntaner.com* Ⓜ *Universitat.*

Teatre Grec. *(Greek Theater)* The open-air summer festival in July and August takes place here; plays, music, and dance are also presented in Plaça del Rei and Mercat de les Flors. ☒ *Santa Madrona 36, Montjuïc* ☎ *93/316–1000* ⊕ *www.bcn.es/grec* Ⓜ *Espanya.*

Fodor's Choice **Teatre Nacional de Catalunya.** Near Plaça de les Glòries, at the eastern end
★ of the Diagonal, this glass-enclosed classical temple was designed by Ricardo Bofill, architect of Barcelona's airport. Programs cover everything from Shakespeare to ballet to avant-garde theater. ☒ *Pl. de les Arts 1, Eixample* ☎ *93/306–5700* ⊕ *www.tnc.cat* Ⓜ *Glòries.*

Teatre Poliorama. Just below Plaça de Catalunya, this famous and traditional theater nearly always has a hot-ticket show. ☒ *Rambla 15, Rambla* ☎ *93/317-7599* ⊕ *www.teatrepoliorama.com* Ⓜ *Catalunya.*

Teatre Romea. Behind the Boqueria market just off Plaça Sant Agustí, the Romea has been entertaining barcelonins for a century, with everything from avant-garde Els Joglars to Shakespeare in Catalan. ☒ *Hospital 51, Raval* ☎ *93/301–5504* ⊕ *www.teatreromea.com* Ⓜ *Liceu.*

Victòria. This venerable theater in the heart of Barcelona's show district is a historic venue for musicals, reviews, and dance productions. ☒ *Av. del Paral.lel 67–69, Raval* ☎ *93/443–2929* ⊕ *www.teatrevictoria.com* Ⓜ *Paral.lel.*

Sports and the Outdoors

WORD OF MOUTH

"A chance to see FC Barcelona's 2009 trifecta team, winners of the League, the Cup, and the European Champions title in Camp Nou is not to be missed. The 90,000 spectators follow the team's movements as if it were a ballet choreography, applauding an elegant fake here or an intricate passing combination there."

—luciahay

By George
Semler

Any talk of sport in Barcelona is inevitably going to revolve around Futbol Club Barcelona (Barça), the local soccer team that, during the Franco regime, was not only one of Spain's two greatest soccer teams but the only legal means of expressing Catalan nationalism.

In 2009 Barça won the all-but-impossible triumvirate of the Spanish League, the Spanish King's Cup, and European Champions League. Even the British press wrote that this might have been the greatest soccer team of all time. Passion for Barça is so powerful that the emcee of the 2007 Barcelona poetry festival found it necessary to publicly thank the Barcelona soccer team for not reaching the European Cup finals that year, thus assuring the festival's closing ceremony an audience.

In case Barça is playing away, R.C.D. (Reial Club Deportiu) Espanyol is also a first-division soccer team, and plays in their new suburban stadium in Cornellà. Barcelona's Conde de Godó tennis tournament brings the world's best rackets here every April, while the Spanish Grand Prix at Mont Meló draws the top Formula One racing teams. As for keeping active yourself, there are diving, windsurfing, surfing, sailing, and watersports activities in Barceloneta and all along the coast north and south of Barcelona. Tennis and squash courts are available in various public and semiprivate clubs around town, and Barcelona now has nearly two dozen golf courses less than an hour away from town. Bicycle tracks run the length of the Diagonal, and bike-rental agencies are popping up everywhere.

BEACHES

See the illustrated feature for details on Barcelona's beaches.

BICYCLES AND IN-LINE SKATES

Barcelona Bici. Barcelona's tourist office rents bicycles at various points around the edges of Ciutat Vella: the sea end of the Rambla, the top of the Rambla at Plaça Catalunya, and in Barceloneta. ⊠ *Pl. Portal de la Pau 1,*

Rambla ☎ *93/285–3832* ✉ *Pl. Catalunya 9, Eixample* ☎ *93/285–3832* Ⓜ *Catalunya* ✉ *Passeig Joan de Borbó 45, Barceloneta* ☎ *93/285–3832* ⊕ *www.barcelonaturisme.com* Ⓜ *Barceloneta.*

Bike Tours Barcelona. This company offers a three-hour bike tour (in English) for €22, with a drink included. Just look for the guide with a bike and red flag at the northeast corner of the Town Hall in Plaça Sant Jaume, outside the Tourist Information Office at 11 AM daily or 4:30 PM (Monday, Wednesday, Friday) or 5:30 PM (Tuesday, Thursday, Saturday). ✉ *Carrer Esparteria 3, Barri Gòtic* ☎ *93/268–2105* ⊕ *www.biketoursbarcelona.com.*

TOP OUTDOOR ACTIVITIES

■ Watching European Champion Futbol Club Barcelona play in Camp Nou.

■ Playing the PGA Catalunya golf course in the Empordà.

■ Scuba diving in the Isles Medes off the Costa Brava.

■ Jogging the Carretera de les Aigües over Barcelona.

■ Watching Rafa Nadal win his next Conde de Godó championship.

Bikes de Cool. Just across from the Estació de França, this shop rents bikes and skates on weekends only. ✉ *Passeig Picasso 44, Born-Ribera* ☎ *636/401997 mobile phone.*

Classic Bikes. Just off pivotal Plaça Catalunya, bicycles are available for rent here every day of the week from 9:30 AM to 8 PM. The 24-hour rate is €20; half-day costs €13; 2 hours cost €8. ✉ *Tallers 45, Raval* ☎ *93/317–1970.*

Un Cotxe Menys. "One Car Less" in Catalan—meaning one less automobile on the streets of Barcelona—organizes various kinds of guided tours (including some in English) and bicycle outings. ✉ *Esparteria 3, Born-Ribera* ☎ *93/268–2105.*

GOLF

Club de Golf de Sant Cugat. This hilly 18-hole course, par 68, costs €65 Monday–Thursday and €150 Friday–Sunday. ✉ *Sant Cugat del Vallès* ☎ *93/674–3958.*

Club de Golf Terramar. On this breezy seaside 18-hole course—par 72—you'll pay weekday greens fees of €70, and €110 on weekends and holidays. ✉ *Sitges* ☎ *93/894–0580.*

Club de Golf Vallromanes. Thirty kilometers (19 mi) north of Barcelona, between Masnou and Granollers, this challenging 18-hole, par-72 course requires a handicap of 28 or less to play. The club is closed Tuesday. Greens fees are €80 weekdays and €132 weekends. ✉ *Vallromanes* ☎ *93/572–9064.*

Reial Club de Golf El Prat. In its new location near Terrassa, 30 km (19 mi) north of Barcelona, Reial Club de Golf El Prat is a lovely but extremely difficult 18-hole, par-72 course. It's open to nonmembers only on non-holiday weekdays for €100. ✉ *Terrassa* ☎ *93/728–1000.*

BARCELONA'S BEST BEACHES

It's an unusual combination in Europe: a major metropolis fully integrated with the sea. Barcelona's 4.2 km (2.5 mi.) of beaches allow for its yin/yang of urban energy and laid back beach vibe. When you're ready for a slower pace, seek out a sandy refuge.

Over the last decade, Barcelona's *platjas* (beaches) have improved and multiplied in number. Barceloneta's southwestern end is the Platja de Sant Sebastià, followed northward by the platjas de Sant Miquel, Barceloneta, Passeig Marítim, Port Olímpic, Nova Icària, Bogatell, Mar Bella (the last football-field length of which is a nudist enclave), La Nova Mar Bella, and Llevant. The Barceloneta beach is the most popular stretch, easily accessible by several bus lines, notably the No. 64 bus and by the L4 metro stop at Barceloneta or at Ciutadella–Vil.la Olímpica. The best surfing stretch is at the northeastern end of the Barceloneta beach, while the boardwalk itself offers miles of runway for walkers, bicyclers, and joggers. Topless bathing is common on all beaches in and around Barcelona.

WORD OF MOUTH

"Any beach recommendations in Barcelona?"
—robinlb

"The beaches between Port Olimpic and Barceloneta…near Barceloneta [it's] a bit more popular because you have small supermarkets a stone's throw away from the beach in case you need some food or drinks. Or [you can try] the beachfront restaurants and bars…take the metro to Barceloneta station and walk down Pg J.Borbo on the nice promenade along the old harbor. Several bus lines go down to the beach from many parts of the city. I'd try to avoid Sundays because it gets really busy, and the beach bars (almost) double their prices." —Cowboy 1968

PLATJA DE LA BARCELONETA

Just to the left at the end of Passeig Joan de Borbó, this is the easiest beach to get to, hence the most crowded and the most fun from a people-watching standpoint. Along with swimming, there are windsurfing and kite surfing rentals to be found just up behind the beach at the edge of La Barceloneta. Rebecca Horn's sculpture L'Estel Ferit, a rusting stack of cubes, expresses nostalgia for the beach shack restaurants that lined the beach here until 1992. Surfers trying to catch a wave wait just off the breakwater in front of the excellent beachfront Agua restaurant.

PLATJA DE LA MAR BELLA

Closest to the Poblenou metro stop near the eastern end of the beaches, this is a thriving gay enclave and the unofficial nudist beach of Barcelona (but clothed bathers are welcome, too). The water sports center Base Nàutica de la Mar Bella rents equipment for sailing, surfing, and windsurfing. Outfitted with showers, safe drinking fountains, and a children's play area, La Mar Bella also has lifeguards who warn against swimming near the breakwater. The excellent Els Pescadors restaurant is just inland on Plaça Prim.

PLATJA DE LA NOVA ICÀRIA

One of Barcelona's most popular beaches, this strand is just east of the Olympic Port with the full range of

entertainment, restaurant, and refreshment venues close at hand. (Mango and El Chiringuito de Moncho are two of the most popular restaurants.) The beach is directly across from the neighborhood built as the residential Olympic Village for Barcelona's 1992 Olympic Games, an interesting housing project that has now become a popular residential neighborhood.

PLATJA DE SANT SEBASTIÀ

Barceloneta's most southwestern beach (to the right at the end of Passeig Joan de Borbó) now stretches out in the shadow of the W Hotel, somewhat compromising its role as the oldest and most historic of the city beaches. But it was here 19th-century barcelonins cavorted in bloomers and bathing costumes. The right end of the beach is the home of the Club Natació de Barcelona and there is a semi-private feel that the beaches farther east seem to lack.

PLATJA DE GAVÀ-CASTELLDEFELS

A 15-minute train ride south of Barcelona near the Gavà stop is a wider and wilder beach, with better water quality and a windswept strand that feels light years removed from the urban sprawl and somewhat dusty beaches of Barcelona. Alighting at Gavà and returning from Castelldefels allows a hike down the beach to Can Patricio or any of the other beach restaurants dishing out delicacies like calçots or paella.

6

GYMS AND SPAS

DiR. The DiR network has 12 branches all over Barcelona. The minimum one-week membership costs €35 and includes fitness classes and the use of the sauna, steam room, swimming pool, and squash courts. Day passes cost from €15.20 in the morning to €20.25 in the early evening. Those working out with the equipment can pump in time to the videos playing on MTV or watch CNN or BBC news in English. ☎ *901/304030 for general information* ✉ *DiR Main branch Ganduxer 25–27, Sant Gervasi* ☎ *93/202–2202* ⊕ *www.dir.es.*

Seven7SportsClub. Off Passeig de Gràcia near the hotel Condes de Barcelona, this winner has a gym, sauna, pool (summer only), squash courts, and paddle tennis. Day membership here costs €25 for 24 hours (so it can work for two days if you time it right), with a small supplement for the squash and paddle-tennis courts. ✉ *Passatge Domingo 7, Eixample* ☎ *93/215–2755* ⊕ *www.sevensportsclub.com.*

02 Centro Wellness. A minimalist-design triumph created by Alonso Balaguer in lower Sarrià, this streamlined glass-and-steel hydrotherapy spa cures whatever might be ailing you. ✉ *Passeig Manuel Girona 23, Sarrià, Sant Gervasi* ☎ *93/206–3988* ⊕ *www.o2centrowellness.com.*

HIKING

The Collserola hills behind the city offer well-marked trails, fresh air, and lovely views. Take the San Cugat, Sabadell, or Terrassa FFCC train from Plaça de Catalunya and get off at Baixador de Vallvidrera; the information center, 10 minutes uphill next to Vil.la Joana (now the Jacint Verdaguer Museum), has maps of this mountain woodland just 20 minutes from downtown. The walk back into town can take from two to five hours depending on your speed and the trails you choose. For longer treks, try the 15-km (9-mi) Sant Cugat–to–Barcelona hike, or take the train south to Sitges and make the three-day walk to Montserrat.

Associació Excursionista, Etnogràfica i Folklorica advises on and organizes outings of all kinds. ✉ *Avinyó 19, Barri Gòtic* ☎ *93/302–2730.*

Club Excursionista de Catalunya has information on hiking far afield, including in the Pyrenees. ✉ *Paradis 10, Barri Gòtic* ☎ *93/315–2311.*

SCUBA DIVING

The Costa Brava's Illes Medes underwater nature preserve offers some of the Mediterranean's finest diving adventures. Seven tiny islands off the coastal town of L'Estartit are the home of some 1,400 species of flora and fauna and an underwater wonderland of tunnels and caves. Colorful fish, crabs, squid, and diverse plant life are observable before wetting a toe (for nonswimmers or those reluctant to dive), and deeper there are lobsters, gilthead bream, grouper, and a dazzling range of fish and marine life of all kinds. Dives of over 150 feet may let you see rays. Other diving options are available at the Illes Formigues off the coast of Palamós and Els Ullastres off Llafranc.

Aquàtica – Centro de Buceo teaches diving, rents equipment, and organizes outings to the Illes Medes. With top safety-code requirements in place and certified instructors and biologists directing the programs in English, French, Catalan, or Spanish, this is one of Estartit's best diving opportunities. ⊠ *Camping Rifort,* ☎ *972/75–06–56* ⊕ *www. aquatica-sub.com.*

SAILING AND WINDSURFING

Proa 7. Part of the Barceloviatjes agency, Proa 7 charters riverboats, catamarans, power yachts, and canal tours, and arranges all manner of fluvial boating opportunities. ⊠ *Consell de Cent 344, Eixample* ☎ *93/487–0920.*

Reial Club Marítim de Barcelona. Barcelona's most exclusive and prestigious yacht club can advise visitors on matters maritime, from where to charter yachts and sailboats to how to sign up for sailing programs. ⊠ *Moll d'Espanya 1, Port Vell* ☎ *93/221–4859* ⊕ *www.maritimbarcelona.org.*

Ronáutica. Rent a sailboat, power craft, or windsurfing equipment here. ⊠ *Moll de la Marina 11, Port Olímpic* ☎ *93/221–0380.*

SOCCER

Futbol Club Barcelona. Founded in 1899, the Futbol Club Barcelona attained its greatest glory in May of 2009, when their victory over Manchester United in Rome sealed the club's third European Championship and Spain's first-ever *triplete* (triple), taking home all of the silverware: League, Cup, and European titles. Even more impressive, to friend and foe alike, was the way they did it, playing a wide-open razzle-dazzle style of soccer rarely seen in age of cynical defensive lockdowns and muscular British-style play. Barça, as the club is affectionately known, is Real Madrid's perennial nemesis (and vice-versa) as well as a sociological and historical phenomenon of deep significance in Catalonia. Supported by more than 150,000 season-ticket holders, the team was the only legal outlet for Catalan nationalist sentiment during the 40-year Franco regime. Despite giant budgets and the world's best players, Barcelona's results never seemed to live up to full potential, an anomaly Catalans were quick to blame on Madrid and the influence and manipulation, real or imagined, of the Franco regime. This all changed after 1975, with

EL BARÇA: MORE THAN A CLUB

El Barça: més qu'un club is the motto for this soccer superpower out to win every championship. Basketball, roller-skate hockey, and team handball have all won national and European titles, while the club's star-studded soccer team has conquered dozens of Spanish Leagues and European championships in 1992 and 2006. "More than a club" refers to FC Barcelona's key role in Catalonian nationalism. With teams at all levels, el Barça is financed by 500,000 season-ticket holders, generating an annual operating capital of more than 100 million euros.

6

Barcelona winning four consecutive league titles and 10 of the last 27. Nevertheless, Madrid's nine European cups (to Barcelona's mere three) are still a sore point for long-suffering Barcelona soccer fans. Ticket windows at Access 14 to the stadium are open Monday–Saturday and game-day Sundays 10–2 and 5–8; you can also buy tickets at Servicaixa, an ATM at Caixa de Catalunya bank entrances, and elsewhere. ⊠ *Camp Nou, Arístides Maillol, Les Corts* ☎ *93/496–3600* ⊕ *www.fcbarcelona.com.*

RCD Espanyol. Another local first-division team, RCD Espanyol attracts somewhat less attention, although their new stadium, opened in August 2009, is a state-of-the-art gem seating 40,500 spectators. Tickets are best purchased at Servicaixa machines. Take the T1 tramway from Plaça Francesc Macià. ⊠ *Nou Estadi, Av. Baix Llobregat 100, Cornellà de Llobregat* ☎ *93/292–7700* ⊕ *www.rcdespanyol.com.*

The **Spain Ticket Bureau,** not far from the Columbus monument, can score seats for home FC Barcelona games as well as any other event in Spain. ⊠ *Rambla 31, Rambla* ☎ *902/903912* ⊕ *www.spainticketbureau. com* Ⓜ *Liceu.*

SWIMMING

All fees are €8–€10 per day.

Club Natació de Barceloneta. Also known as Complex Esportiu Municipal Banys Sant Sebastià, this club has an indoor pool that overlooks the beach. It's open daily 7 AM–11 PM. ⊠ *Passeig Joan de Borbó, Barceloneta* ☎ *93/221–0010* ⊕ *www.cnb.es.*

Piscines Bernat Picornell. The daily fee at this swimming center with indoor and outdoor pools includes use of a sauna, gymnasium, and fitness equipment. It's open daily 7 AM–midnight. ⊠ *Av. del Estadi 30–40, Montjuïc* ☎ *93/423–4041* ⊕ *www.picornell.com.*

TENNIS

Trofeo Godó – Open Seat. Barcelona's main tennis tournament, held in late April, is a clay-court event long considered a French Open warm-up. For tickets to this event, consult with the Real Club de Tenis de Barcelona or the tournament Web site listed below beginning in late February. Tickets may also be obtained at *www.servicaixa.com.* ⊠ *Carrer de Bosch i Gimpera 21, Pedralbes* ☎ *902/332211* ⊕ *www.barcelonaopenbancosbadell.com.*

Complex Esportiu Municipal Nou Can Caralleu. A 30-minute walk uphill from the Reina Elisenda subway stop (FFCC de la Generalitat), this center offers hard courts and clean air. It's open daily 8 AM–11 PM and costs €12 per hour by day, €15 at night. ⊠ *Carrer Esports 2–8, Pedralbes* ☎ *93/203–7874* ⊕ *www.claror.org.*

7

Shopping

BARCELONA SHOPPING PLANNER

Hours

Most stores are open Monday–Saturday 9–1:30 and 5–8. Virtually all stores close Sunday except during the Christmas season. Many top-end stores in the Eixample and in the malls such as L'Illa Diagonal stay open through the lunch hour. The big department stores such as Corte Inglés and FNAC are open nonstop from 9 AM to 9 PM. Designated pharmacies are open all night.

Taxes

While food and basic necessities are taxed at the lowest rate, most consumer goods are taxed at 16%. Non-EU citizens can request a Tax-Free Cheque on purchases of €90.15 and over in shops displaying the Tax-Free Shopping sticker. This check must be stamped at the customs office to the right of the arrivals exit in Barcelona's Airport's Terminal A. After that's done, present it to one of the Caixa or Banco de España offices. The bank issues a certified check or credits the amount to your credit card.

Best Got-It-in-Spain Purchases

Saffron: the lightest, most aromatic, and best-value buy left in all of Spain.

Rope-soled espadrilles from La Manual Alpargatera.

Avarca sandals (also called Menorquinas) from Menorca.

Custo Barcelona's ever-original tops.

Ceramics from all over Spain at Art Escudellers.

Shopping Guides and Transportation

Barcelona's tourist offices in the airport and in Plaça de Catalunya give away a free shopping guide booklet (updated annually) with an accompanying map and complete instructions and advice on everything from how to get your value-added tax refund at the airport to how to use the special BSL (Barcelona Shopping Line) bus (aka TOMBUS) that covers the length of the city's 5-km (3-mi) shopping circuit. With an all-day T-Shopping Card ticket (€10.50), you can hop and off the shuttle and its leather seats until it (and you) are done (weekday service 7:30 AM–9:45 PM, Saturday 9 AM–9:20 PM). Stops are served about every seven minutes.

Word of Mouth

"In Barcelona, we saw the cutest shoes we've ever seen. If you live in the US, try to find out your European shoe size before you leave home. It's on lots of boxes of shoes we buy here. Also, if you're doing serious shoe shopping, try to go in the mornings, before the stores get too crowded. We didn't find any 'self service' shoe stores." —missypie

SARRIÀ
antiques stores, designer boutiques, pastry emporiums and wine shops

GRÀCIA
galleries and crafts studios alongside boutiques and jewelry shops

EIXAMPLE
flagship stores, a dizzying array of fashion designers, and smaller hip boutiques

EL RAVAL
museum-worthy jewelry, art, and design shops; bookstores and gift shops

BARRI GÒTIC
antiques, art galleries, shoe shops, and eclectic boutiques

BORN-RIBERA
cool design shops with jewelry and knickknacks of all kinds

Colegio de les Teresianas
Ronda del Gen. Mitre
Casa Vicens
Plaça de Lesseps
Trav. de Dalt
C. de Sant Salvador
C. de les Camèlies
C. de la Providència
Via Augusta
Pl. de Francesc Macià
C. Gran de Gràcia
Plaça Rius i Taulet
Avda. de Josep Tarradellas
Av. Diagonal
C. de Casanova
Passeig de Gràcia
Plaça de Joan Carles I
C. de Roger de Flor
C. de Nàpols
C. de Sicília
C. de Sardenya
C. de Viladomat
C. del Comte Borrell
C. del Comte d'Urgell
C. de Villarroel
C. de Provença
C. de Mallorca
C. de València
Avda. de Roma
C. d'Aragó
C. d'Aragó
Rambla de Catalunya
C. de Pau Claris
C. de Roger de Llúria
C. del Bruc
C. de Girona
C. de Bailèn
Passeig de S. Joan
Av. Diagonal
C. Consell de Cent
C. de la Diputació
Gran Via de les Corts Catalanes
C. de Sepúlveda
C. de Floridablanca
Plaça de Catalunya
Plaça Tetuan
C. de Casp
C. d'Ausias Marc
Ronda S. Pere
Pelai
La Rambla
Del Hospital
C. de Sant Pau
C. Nou de la Rambla
Santa Mònica
Ronda de Sant Antoni
Riera Alta
C. de Tànger
C. dels Almogàvers
Pg. de Picasso
C. Lluis Companys
C. de Wellington
Av. Meridiana
Pg. de Carles I
Parc de la Ciutadella
LA RAMBLA
Pg. de Colom
Plaça Portal de la Pau
Moll d'Espanya
BARCELONETA
Pg. de Colom
Moll de Sant Bertran
Moll d'Espanya

0   450 yards
0   450 meters

THE BOQUERIA MARKET

La Boqueria market, a daily fiesta stuffed with color and life, is the stomach, sensorial nerve center, and heart of the city, conveniently located on the Rambla near the crossroads of the Ciutat Vella.

Just as people tend to be most themselves in the kitchen, Barcelona is most itself in its food markets, and no European city has more covered, open-air markets than the Catalan capital, with a staggering total of 40. Paris lost its mid-city produce market, Les Halles, in 1971, but Barcelona has managed to maintain its most famous central market, La Boqueria, along with 39 other steel hangar-covered neighborhood food emporiums spread all over town. Although similar in their brightly illuminated and colorful displays of fruits, vegetables, wild mushrooms, meats, cheeses, and hundreds of species of fish and seafood, each of these markets has its own distinctive neighborhood flavor and architectural personality, but none of them surpasses the Boqueria's rich color and vitality.

THE BOQUERIA'S HISTORY

Europe's oldest mid-city food market, the Boqueria market, officially Mercat de Sant Josep, was designed in 1840 as a neoclassical square by Francesc Daniel i Molina. The square was hijacked by the meat market that operated in Pla de la Boqueria just down the Rambla. La Boqueria grew from the late 19th century until 2001, when a remodeling project revealed the original columns.

#359 Morilla:
spices, wild mushrooms,
and nuts

Information

#466 Pinotxo:
show-shopping tapas

#886 Tocinerias
Marcos:
Ibérico hams
and sausages

#579 Jesús i Carme:
an explosion of peppers

#945 Formatgeria
Pach Font:
artisanal cheeses
from Spain

#691 Kiosko Universal:
tapas in the sun

KEY		
🛈 Information	🟦 Pork Products	🟦 Dried Fish
🛉🛉 Restrooms	🟦 Poultry, Egg	🟦 Specialties
🟦 Bars, Restaurants	🟦 Fish	🟦 Others
🟦 Fruit, Vegetables	🟦 Seafood	

BOQUERIA'S TOP BUYS

Cheeses, dried wild mushrooms and peppers, herbs, spices including saffron, sausage, and *jamón ibérico de bellota* (acorn-fed Ibérico ham) are the prime products available at the Boqueria for visitors to the city who, unless they have a kitchen in a rented apartment, are probably not in the market for fresh fish, lamb, or beef. As the Boqueria has developed into a major attraction, more and more fruits stands sell handy little boxes with assortments of melon, grapes, and berries for healthy and economical nibbling and noshing on the march.

A VISUAL FEAST

The Moderniste stained-glass trim at the top of the Rambla entrance to the market and the neoclassical Doric columns around the edges are the architectural gems of the market. The Vidal Pons and Soley vegetable, fruit, and wild mushroom displays on the left at the entrance are the most colorful stands, while Pinotxo, the Boqueria's world-famous counter is to the right. The fish and seafood amphitheater at the heart of the market is a mid-city breath of salt sea freshness. To the left is one of the Boqueria's prettiest corners. Past the Verdures Ramona stand and the excellent El Quim de la Boqueria restaurant, across from the Genaro seafood counter, is Jesús i Carme (stall #579-81), a Van Gogh painting of peppers, nuts, vegetables, new potatoes, and tiny onions. In the eastern corner is the popular Kiosko Universal restaurant counter with terrace tables under the massive columns, while Avinova (#703-07) displays red leg partridge, pheasant, and hare.

7

By George Semler

Characterized by originality and relative affordability, shopping in Barcelona has developed into a jubilant fashion, design, craft, and gourmet-food fair. The fact that different parts of town provide distinct contexts for shopping makes exploring the city and browsing boutiques inclusive activities.

The Ciutat Vella, especially the Born-Ribera area, is rich in small-crafts shops, young designers, and an endless potpourri of artisans and merchants operating in restored medieval spaces that are often as dazzling as the wares on sale. Even the pharmacies and grocery stores of Barcelona are often sumptuous aesthetic feasts, filled with charming details.

Shopping for design objects and chic fashion in the Eixample is like buying art supplies at the Louvre: it's an Art Nouveau architecture theme park spinning off into dozens of sideshows—textiles, furnishings, curios, and knickknacks of every kind. Any specific shop or boutique will inevitably lead you past a dozen emporiums that you didn't know were there. Original and surprising, yet wearable clothing items—what one shopper described as "elegant funk"—are Barcelona's signature contribution to fashion. Rather than copying the runways, Barcelona designers are relentlessly daring and innovative, combining fine materials with masterful workmanship.

Browsing through shops in this originality-obsessed metropolis feels more like museum hopping than a shopping spree, although it can, of course, be both. Design shops like Vinçon and BD Ediciones de Diseño delight the eye and stimulate the imagination, while the Passeig del Born is attracting hip young designers from all over the globe. Passeig de Gràcia has joined the ranks of Paris's Champs Elysées and Rome's Via Condotti as one of the great shopping avenues in the world, with the planet's fashion houses amply represented, from Armani to Zara. Exploring Barcelona's antiques district along Carrer Banys Nous and Carrer de la Palla is always an adventure. The shops opening daily around Santa Maria del Mar in the Born-Ribera district range from Catalan and international design retailers to shoe and leather-handbag designers, to T-shirt decorators, to dealers in nuts and spices or coffee emporiums. The megastores in Plaça de Catalunya, along the Diagonal, and in L'Illa Diagonal farther west are commercial cornucopias selling fashions, furniture, furs, books, music, and everything else under the sun. The villagelike environment of both Sarrià and Gràcia lends an intimate warmth to antiques or clothes shopping, with friendly boutique owners adding a personal touch often lost in mainstream commerce.

BOUTIQUES AND SPECIALTY STORES

ANTIQUES

Antiques shopping is centered in the Barri Gòtic, where Carrer de la Palla, Carrer Banys Nous, and the Baixada de Santa Eulàlia are lined with shops full of prints, maps, books, ceramic tiles, paintings, and furniture. An antiques market is held in front of the cathedral every Thursday 10–8. The Bulevard dels Antiquaris at Passeig de Gràcia 55 concentrates 73 antiques shops, while the end of the Rambla and Port Vell have outdoor markets on Sunday. In upper Barcelona, the village of Sarrià is becoming an antiquer's destination, with shops along Cornet i Mas, Pedró de la Creu, and Major de Sarrià.

Acanto. This shop, in the pivotal Bulevard dels Antiquaris, is a major clearinghouse for buying and selling a wide range of items from paintings, furniture, silver, sculpture, and bronzes to wood carvings, marble, clocks, watches, tapestries, porcelain, and ceramics. ⊠ *Passeig de Gràcia 55–57, Eixample* ☎ *93/215–3297* Ⓜ *Passeig de Gràcia.*

Antigüedades Erika Niedermeier-Àlex Talese. Near the Carrer Banys Nous end of Carrer de la Palla, Erika Niedermeier trades in collectors' items or objects dating from the 14th to the 18th century. Ceramics, painted copper, silver, ivory, stained glass, wrought iron, and tooled leather from the Middle Ages and from the Renaissance (much of it crafted by Islamic or Jewish artisans) find their way through this hands-on history book of a store. ⊠ *Carrer de la Palla 11, Barri Gòtic* ☎ *93/412–7924* Ⓜ *Liceu.*

Antigüedades Fernández. Bric-a-brac is piled high in this workshop near the middle of this slender artery in the medieval Jewish Quarter. This master craftsman restores and sells antique furniture of all kinds. Stop by and stick your head in for the fragrance of the shellacs and wood shavings and a look at one of the last simple carpentry and woodworking shops you'll encounter in contemporary, design-mad, early-21st-century Barcelona. ⊠ *Carrer Sant Domènec del Call 9, Barri Gòtic* ☎ *93/301–0045* Ⓜ *Liceu.*

Centre d'Antiquaris. Look carefully for the little stairway leading into this 73-store mother ship of all antiques arcades off Passeig de Gràcia. You never know what you might find here in this eclectic serendipity: dolls, icons, Roman or Visigothic objects, paintings, furniture, cricket kits, fly rods, or toys from a century ago. ⊠ *Passeig de Gràcia 55, Eixample* ☎ *93/215–4499* Ⓜ *Passeig de Gràcia.*

Gothsland. Art Nouveau furniture, art objects, and decorative paraphernalia share space here with sculpted terra-cotta figures, vases, mirrors, and furniture, nearly all in Barcelona's signature Moderniste style. Paintings by Art Nouveau stars from Santiago Rusiñol to Ramón

7

Casas might turn up here, along with lamps, clocks, and curios of all kinds. ⊠ *Consell de Cent 331, Eixample* ☎ *93/488–1922* Ⓜ *Passeig de Gràcia.*

Fodor's Choice **L'Arca de L'Àvia.** As the name of the place ("grandmother's trunk") suggests, this is a miscellaneous potpourri of ancient goods of all kinds, especially period clothing from shoes to gloves to hats and hairpins. Despite the found-object attitude and sense of the place, they're not giving away these vintage baubles, so don't be surprised at the costumes' cost. ⊠ *Banys Nous 20, Barri Gòtic* ☎ *93/302–1598* ⊕ *www. larcadelavia.com* Ⓜ *Liceu.*

Novecento. A standout primarily for being so out of place among all the design emporiums and fashion denizens on this great white way of high commerce, Novecento is an antique-jewelry store with abundant items from all epochs and movements from Victorian to Art Nouveau to Belle Époque. ⊠ *Passeig de Gràcia 75, Eixample* ☎ *93/215–1183* Ⓜ *Passeig de Gràcia.*

ART GALLERIES

For art-gallery nightlife, see the Nightlife and the Arts chapter.

Art openings and gallery browsing are a way of life in Barcelona. Any time you see wine being consumed in an art gallery, assume that you are invited and have a look around. A key cluster of art galleries is lined up on Carrer Consell de Cent between Passeig de Gràcia and Carrer Balmes and around the corner on Rambla de Catalunya. In the Gothic Quarter, Carrer Petritxol, Carrer de la Palla, and Carrer Banys Nous have several interesting galleries. The Born-Ribera quarter is another art destination, with Carrer Montcada and the parallel Carrer Banys Vells the top streets to prowl.

Antonio de Barnola. Installations with an architectural bent are the regulars here, with work by Catalan conceptualist Margarita Andreu and Basques such as Itziar Okariz and José Ramón Amondarain among the regular artists. ⊠ *C/Palau 4, Barri Gòtic* ☎ *93/412–2214* Ⓜ *Jaume I, Liceu.*

Artur Ramón—Espai Colleccionisme. Artur Ramon shows paintings, sculptures, and drawings such as those by 18th-century engraver and architect Giovanni Battista Piranesi. In addition, antiques, glass, and ceramics find their way to this very seriously orchestrated collector's haven. ⊠ *Carrer de la Palla 23 and 25, Barri Gòtic* ☎ *93/302–5970* Ⓜ *Liceu.*

Artur Ramón—Espai Contemporani. An eclectic selection of young artists from Catalonia, Spain, France, Germany, and beyond usually hovers near the edge of the latest vanguards. Notable shows here have exhibited the fascinating Spanish-Argentinian abstractionist Esteban Lisa, the realist paintings of the Santilari brothers from Barcelona, and the colorist work of German artist Anke Blaue. ⊠ *Carrer de la Palla 10, Barri Gòtic* ☎ *93/302–5970* Ⓜ *Liceu.*

Base Elements Urban Art Gallery. Robert Burt, originally of California, founded this gallery in 2003 to provide a space where young street artists and graffiti-meisters could display their talents without risking jail time. Burt himself is a talented painter and restorer of found objects.

Browsing is perfectly acceptable at the Galeria Carles Taché.

The gallery is a workshop and hangout for young artists. ⊠ *Baixada de Viladecols 2, Barri Gòtic* ☎ *93/268–8312* Ⓜ *Jaume I.*

Galeria Aunkan. Located near the MACBA, Barcelona's contemporary art museum, Galeria Aunkan showcases contemporary and avant-garde installations from artists ranging from Jesus Vilallonga to Tom Carr and Joan Pere Viladecans. ⊠ *Ferlandina 32-D, Raval* ☎ *93/301–3027* Ⓜ *Catalunya.*

Galeria Carles Taché. An always-busy exhibition space with shows ranging from Alexis de Villar's African prints to Lawrence Carroll's colorful creations, Carles Taché displays painting and photography by established artists ⊠ *Consell de Cent 290, Eixample* ☎ *93/487–8836* ⊕ *www.carlestache.com* Ⓜ *Passeig de Gràcia.*

Galeria Claramunt. Another gallery that seems to have sprung up in the reflected light of the Richard Meier–designed Museu d'Art Contemporani de Barcelona serves as a good postscript to an exploration of the museum's treasures. ⊠ *Ferlandina 27, Raval* ☎ *93/442–1847* Ⓜ *Catalunya.*

Galeria Joan Prats. "La Prats" has been one of the city's top galleries since the 1920s, showing international painters and sculptors from Henry Moore to Antoni Tàpies. Barcelona painter Joan Miró was a prime force in the founding of the gallery when he became friends with Joan Prats. The motifs of bonnets and derbies on the gallery's facade attest to the trade of Prats's father. José Maria Sicilia and Juan Ugalde have shown here, while Perejaume and Eulàlia Valldosera are regulars. ⊠ *Rambla de Catalunya 54, Eixample* ☎ *93/216–0284* Ⓜ *Passeig de Gràcia.*

Galeria Maeght. The Paris-based Maeght gallery is not as prestigious in Barcelona, but the Renaissance palace it inhabits is spectacular. The list of superstar artists who have hung work here ranges from Antoni Tàpies to the late Pablo Palazuelo to the late Eduardo Chillida. It's usually a good idea to drop in during any Born-Ribera browsing and grazing tour to have a look at the permanent works downstairs or the current exhibit up on the first floor. ⊠ *Montcada 25, Born-Ribera* 🕾 *93/310–4245* ⊕ *www.maeght. com* Ⓜ *Jaume I.*

Galeria Maria Villalba. In the Eixample's Dreta (right side, looking away from the sea), this gallery is a Barcelona mainstay and well worth seeking out if you're in the neighborhood. A contemporary painting and sculpture specialist, Maria Villalba has shown abstract sculptures by Lilia Luján and Marisa Ordóñez and paintings by Sophie Dumont, Eloisa Ibarra, and Francisco Castillo Real. ⊠ *Bailèn 110, Eixample* 🕾 *93/457–5177* ⊕ *www.galeriamariavillalba.com* Ⓜ *Verdaguer, Girona.*

Galeria Sargadelos. A Galician porcelain store with an exhibition space dedicated to showing ceramicists and young artists from Spain's northwestern region of Galicia, Sargadelos is an interesting and unusual point of reference in the upper Eixample. ⊠ *Provença 276, Eixample* 🕾 *93/215–0368* ⊕ *www.sargadelos.com* Ⓜ *Provença.*

Galeria Toni Tàpies. The son of Barcelona's most esteemed living painter Antoni Tàpies, Toni Tàpies shows young artists from Catalonia, visiting painters from as far away as Canada, and even his father's recent work. ⊠ *Consell de Cent 282, Eixample* 🕾 *93/487–6402* ⊕ *www.tonitapies. com* Ⓜ *Catalunya.*

Joan Gaspar. One of Barcelona's most prestigious galleries, Joan Gaspart and his father before him brought Picasso and Miró back to Catalunya during the '50s and '60s, along with other artists considered politically taboo during the Franco regime. These days you'll find leading contemporary lights such as Joan Pere Viladecans, Rafols Casamada, or Susana Solano here. ⊠ *Pl. Letamendi 1, Eixample* 🕾 *93/323–0748* Ⓜ *Passeig de Gràcia.*

Marlborough. This international giant occupies an important position in Barcelona's art-gallery galaxy with exhibits of major contemporary artists from around the world, as well as local stars. Recent shows featured Jacques Lipchitz and primitive art followed by a retrospective on the graphic work of Spain's leading daily newspaper *El Pais.* ⊠ *València 284, Eixample* 🕾 *93/216–0480* ⊕ *www.galeriamarlborough.com* Ⓜ *Passeig de Gràcia.*

> **FASHION MEETS INTERIOR DESIGN**
>
> As if attempting to compete with Barcelona's landmarks, many of the best boutiques here have had leading contemporary interior decorators and merit visits whether purchases materialize or not. Emporiums such as Vinçon, BD (Barcelona Design), Habitat, and stores such as Arkitektura or Ras Gallery display furnishings and interior-design objects in designer settings. And Sita Murt, the bookshop Central del Raval, Le Boudoir, La Carte des Vins, Xocoa, and Julie Sohn are as much about the space's interior design as the merchandise on sale.

Metrònom. Radical performance and installation art, erotic photography, and video work inevitably make their way to this gallery at the uptown end of the Born. ⊠ *Carrer Fusina 4, Born-Ribera* ☏ *93/268–4298* Ⓜ *Jaume I.*

Sala Dalmau. Part of the always-boiling Consell de Cent scene, Sala Dalmau shows an interesting and heterodox range of Catalan and international artists. ⊠ *Consell de Cent 347, Eixample* ☏ *93/215–4592* Ⓜ *Passeig de Gràcia.*

Sala Parés. The dean of Barcelona's art galleries, Sala Parés has shown every Barcelona artist of note since it opened in 1840. Picasso and Miró showed here, as did Casas and Rossinyol before them. ⊠ *Petritxol 5, Barri Gòtic* ☏ *93/318–7008* Ⓜ *Liceu, Catalunya.*

Sala Rovira. Both established and up-and-coming artists, including local stars Tom Carr and Blanca Vernis, have shown their work at this upper Rambla de Catalunya gallery. ⊠ *Rambla de Catalunya 62, Eixample* ☏ *93/215–2092* Ⓜ *Provença.*

Trama. Another Petritxol favorite, Trama, with occasional exceptions, tends to hang paintings that look as if they might be happier in low-price hostelry establishments, but the gallery merits a look if you find yourself on this picturesque little passageway. ⊠ *Petritxol 8, Barri Gòtic* ☏ *93/317–4877* Ⓜ *Liceu, Catalunya.*

BOOKS

Bookstore browsing in Barcelona is always quiet and curiosity-provoking. Besides the stores listed below, El Corte Inglés department stores stock a limited selection of English guidebooks and novels. FNAC, in L'Illa Diagonal, also has English titles available.

Altair. Barcelona's premier travel and adventure bookstore stocks many titles in English. Book presentations and events scheduled here feature a wide range of interesting authors from Alpinists to Africanists. ⊠ *Gran Via 616, Eixample* ☏ *93/342–7171* Ⓜ *Catalunya.*

BCN Books. This midtown Eixample bookstore is a prime address for books in English. ⊠ *Roger de Llúria 118, Eixample* ☏ *93/476–3343* Ⓜ *Passeig de Gràcia.*

Casa del Llibre. On Barcelona's most important shopping street, Casa del Llibre is a major book feast with a wide variety of English titles. ⊠ *Passeig de Gràcia 62, Eixample* ☏ *93/272–3480* Ⓜ *Passeig de Gràcia.*

FNAC. For musical recordings and the latest book publications, this is one of Barcelona's most dependable and happening addresses. Regular concerts, presentations of new recordings, and art exhibits take place in FNAC. Much more than a bookstore, it's an important cultural resource. ⊠ *Centre Comercial L'Illa, Av. Diagonal 555–559, Eixample* ☏ *93/444–5900* ⊕ *www.fnac.es* Ⓜ *Maria Cristina, Les Corts* ⊠ *Pl. Catalunya 4, Eixample* ☏ *93/344–1800* Ⓜ *Catalunya.*

Fodor's Choice ★ **La Central.** Hands-down, Barcelona's best bookstore for years, La Central has creaky, literary wooden floors and piles of recent publications with many interesting titles in English. ⊠ *Carrer Mallorca 237, Eixample* ☏ *93/487–5018* Ⓜ *Provença.*

La Central del Raval. This luscious bookstore in the former chapel of the Casa de la Misericòrdia sells books amid stunning architecture and offers an excellent restaurant as well. ⊠ *Carrer Elisabets 6, Raval* ☎ *93/317–0293* Ⓜ *Catalunya.*

Laie. A café, restaurant, jazz-performance, and cultural-events space, Laie is rimmed with stacks of books, creating the perfect sanctuary. ⊠ *Pau Claris 85, Eixample* ☎ *93/318–1357* Ⓜ *Catalunya.*

Palau de la Virreina. The bookstore in this cultural center and art gallery stocks good titles (some in English) on art, design, and Barcelona in general. ⊠ *Rambla 99, Rambla* ☎ *93/301–7775* Ⓜ *Liceu.*

Quera. This is the bookstore to seek out if you're interested in the Pyrenees or in exploring any part of the Catalonian hinterlands. Maps, charts, and books detailing everything from Pyrenean ponds and lakes to Romanesque chapels are available in this diminutive giant of a resource. ⊠ *Petritxol 2, Barri Gòtic* ☎ *93/318–0743* Ⓜ *Liceu.*

Ras Gallery. Specialized in books and magazines on art, architecture, design, and photography, with a store design by Jaime Salazar, Ras neatly connects with the gallery's main theme. ⊠ *Carrer Doctor Dou 10, Raval* ☎ *93/412–7199* Ⓜ *Catalunya, Liceu.*

CERAMICS

Although perusing the smaller establishments is always worthwhile, Barcelona's big department stores, including El Corte Inglés, FNAC, and Habitat, are good bets for ceramics shoppers.

Fodor's Choice **Art Escudellers.** Ceramic pieces from all over Spain converge here at both
★ of these stores across the street from the restaurant Los Caracoles; more than 140 different artisans are represented, with maps showing what part of Spain the work is from. There are wine, cheese, and ham tastings downstairs, and you can even throw a pot yourself in the display workshop. ⊠ *Carrer Escudellers 23–25, Barri Gòtic* ☎ *93/412–6801* Ⓜ *Liceu, Drassanes.*

Baraka. Barcelona's prime purveyor of Moroccan goods, ceramics chief among them, Baraka is the city's general cultural commissar for matters relating to Spain's neighbor to the south. The pre-haggled goods here are generally cheaper (and the quality better) than you could bring back from Morocco. ⊠ *Canvis Vells 2, Born-Ribera* ☎ *93/268–4220* ⊕ *www. barakaweb.com* Ⓜ *Jaume I.*

Caixa de Fang. Glazed tiles, glass objects, and colorful sets of cups and saucers are on sale at this little shop just off Plaça Sant Jaume. Translatable as "Box of Mud" in Catalan, Caixa de Fang shows handmade earthenware cooking vessels from all over Spain, as well as boxwood and olive-wood kitchen utensils. ⊠ *Freneria 1, Barri Gòtic* ☎ *93/315– 1704* Ⓜ *Jaume I.*

Espai Vidre. Glass is the thing here. This gallery allows you to admire, study, research, and buy a wide range of this ancient yet innovative material. ⊠ *Carrer dels Àngels 8, Raval* ☎ *93/318–9833* Ⓜ *Catalunya.*

Itaca. Everything from Lladró porcelain to standard ceramic plates, bowls, and inspired objects of all kinds, including pottery from Talavera de la Reina and La Bisbal, finds its way to the surface here. ⊠ *Carrer Ferrán 26, Barri Gòtic* ☎ *93/301–3044* Ⓜ *Liceu, Catalunya.*

Lladró. This Valencia company is famed worldwide for the beauty and quality of its figures. Barcelona's only Lladró factory store, this location has exclusive pieces of work, custom-designed luxury items of gold and porcelain, classic and original works, and a video explaining the Lladró production process in their Valencia factory. Fans of this idiosyncratic porcelain can even organize factory visits. The store guarantees all of its products for a full year after purchase. ⊠ *Passeig de Gràcia 11, Eixample* ☎ *93/270–1253* ⊕ *www.lladro.com* Ⓜ *Catalunya.*

Molsa—Nou i Vell. An address you will almost certainly pass, at the beginning of Carrer del Pi next to the Santa Maria del Pi church, this is a long-standing Barcelona ceramics institution, with, as the name suggests, both old pieces and new. Lladró, ceramics, tiles, and pottery are all colorfully stacked in this attractive space. ⊠ *Pl. Sant Josep Oriol 1, Barri Gòtic* ☎ *93/302–3103* Ⓜ *Liceu.*

Neoceramica. This is the store to visit if you need an order of handsome tiles for your kitchen back home. With some truly striking patterns and the shipping system to get them to you in one piece (each tile, that is), you can trust the Vidal-Quadras clan for care and quality. ⊠ *Mandri 43, Sarrià* ☎ *93/211–8958* Ⓜ *Sarrià, El Putxet.*

Reflexió. Arts and crafts with a North African flavor fill this tiny corner on the charming Baixada de Viladecols tucked in behind Plaça de Sant Just. Serving dishes, brightly colored conical tagines (stewing and serving dishes from Morocco), and a potpourri of goods ranging from rugs to ruanas are on display here in the souk-like chaos of color and form. ⊠ *Baixada de Viladecols 2, Barri Gòtic* ☎ *93/511–3986* ⊕ *www.aaa-bcn.es* Ⓜ *Jaume I.*

CIGARS

Gimeno 102. Smoking items of every kind along with pipes and cigarettes of all sorts are sold in this tobacco sanctuary, but cigars from Havana are the top draw. ⊠ *Rambla 100, Barri Gòtic* ☎ *93/302–0983* Ⓜ *Liceu.*

L'Estanc de Laietana. Famous for its underground cave and humidor at sea level, this is a shrine to the Cuban cigar unparalleled in Barcelona. Cigarettes and rolling tobacco in an all-but-infinite variety of brands are also staples here. ⊠ *Via Laietana 4, Barri Gòtic* ☎ *93/310–1034* Ⓜ *Catalunya.*

CLOTHING

Barcelona women of all ages have a special knack for throwing themselves together with elegant nonchalance, a talent best termed as "funky grace." Spain's Milan-with-an-attitude, Barcelona remains on the cutting edge of a booming national fashion front. Clothing, footwear, leather, and lingerie shops have proliferated in all parts of town, from the Born-Ribera district around Santa Maria del Mar to Passeig de Gràcia and out to the Diagonal in both directions, east and west.

Adolfo Domínguez. One of Barcelona's longtime fashion giants, this is one of Spain's leading clothes designers, with four locations around town. Famed as the creator of the Iberia Airlines uniforms, Adolfo Domínguez has been in the not-too-radical mainstream and forefront of Spanish clothes design for the last quarter century. ⊠ *Passeig de Gràcia 89, Eixample* ☎ *93/272–0492* Ⓜ *Diagonal* ⊠ *Passeig de Gràcia 32, Eixample* ☎ *93/487–4170* Ⓜ *Catalunya* ⊠ *Diagonal 490, Eixample* ☎ *93/215–1339* Ⓜ *Muntaner* ⊠ *Pau Casals 5, Eixample* ☎ *93/414–1177* ⊕ *www.adolfo-dominguez.com* Ⓜ *La Bonanova.*

Ever fashion-forward, the windows at Custo Barcelona.

Ágatha Ruiz de la Prada. An Eixample address not to miss, Ágatha Ruiz de la Prada is a Madrid-born, Barcelona-educated design Vesuvius whose bright-color motifs in men's, women's, and children's clothing as well as furniture, carpets, ceramics, lamps, pens, pencils, towels, sheets—even Band-Aids—are characterized by Miró-like stars, suns, moons, hearts, or bright polka dots. ⊠ *Consell de Cent 314–316, Eixample* ☎ *93/487–1667* Ⓜ *Passeig de Gràcia.*

Anna Povo. This stylish boutique near Plaça de les Olles displays an elegant and innovative selection of designer knits for women. In general, Anna Povo's designs are sleek and minimalist, more influenced by Mies van der Rohe than Gaudí. Colors follow this aesthetic, with cool tones in gray and beige. ⊠ *Carrer Vidrieria 11, Born-Ribera* ☎ *93/319–3561* Ⓜ *Jaume I.*

Antonio Miró. With his Miró jeans label making major inroads with the young and fashionably adventurous, classicist Toni Miró is known for the very upper stratosphere of Catalan haute couture, with clean lines fortified by blacks and dark grays for both men and women. Miró's look is, in fact, so unisex that couples of similar sizes could probably get away with sharing some androgynous looks and saving closet space. ⊠ *Consell de Cent 349, Eixample* ☎ *93/487–0670* Ⓜ *Passeig de Gràcia* ⊠ *Valencia 272, Eixample* ☎ *93/272–2491* Ⓜ *Passeig de Gràcia* ⊠ *Vidrieria 5, Born-Ribera* ☎ *93/268–8203* Ⓜ *Jaume I* ⊠ *Carrer del Pi 11, Barri Gòtic* ☎ *93/342–5875* ⊕ *www.antoniomiro.es* Ⓜ *Liceu.*

Benetton. This international youth favorite and paladin for social freedoms and racial tolerance has three stores in the Eixample showing off their brightly colored basics. ⊠ *Passeig de Gràcia 49, Eixample* ☎ *93/216–0983* Ⓜ *Catalunya* ⊠ *Passeig de Gràcia 69, Eixample*

🕾 *93/505–2560* Ⓜ *Passeig de Gràcia* ⊠ *Rambla de Catalunya 118, Eixample* 🕾 *93/218–4179* ⊕ *www.benetton.com* Ⓜ *Provença.*

Carolina Herrera. Originally from Venezuela but professionally based in New York, Carolina Herrera and her international CH logo have become Barcelona mainstays. (Daughter Carolina Herrera Jr. is a Spain resident and married to former bullfighter Miguel Baez.) Fragrances for men and women and clothes with a simple, elegant line—a white blouse is the CH icon—are the staples here. Herrera's light ruffled dresses and edgy urban footwear add feminine flourishes. ⊠ *Passeig de Gràcia 87, Eixample* 🕾 *93/272–1584* ⊕ *www.carolinaherrera.com* Ⓜ *Diagonal.*

Cintia. International brands for women in an elegant uptown setting include exclusive pieces by designers ranging from Jill Sander and Emilio Pucci to Matthew Williamson and Elie Saab. Cintia tends toward a somber classical palette with an ethereal and mysterious melancholy. ⊠ *Ganduxer 32, Sant Gervasi* 🕾 *93/201–6283* Ⓜ *Bonanova.*

Conti. A favorite men's fashions outlet, Conti stocks top international designers such as Armani, Cerruti, Armand Basi, Tommy Hilfiger, Polo Jeans, and Lacoste, and serves up everything from suits to shorts. ⊠ *Av. Diagonal 512, Eixample* 🕾 *93/416–1211* Ⓜ *Diagonal* ⊠ *Av. Pau Casals 7, Eixample* 🕾 *93/201–1933* Ⓜ *Muntaner* ⊠ *Carrer Tuset 30, Eixample* 🕾 *93/217–4954* Ⓜ *Gràcia.*

★ **Cortana.** A sleek and breezy Balearic-island look for women is what this young designer from Majorca brings to the steamy alleyways of urban Barcelona. The contrast is a refreshing lift in the confines of this narrow street. ⊠ *Flassaders 43, Born-Ribera* 🕾 *93/310–3112* Ⓜ *Jaume I.*

Fodor'sChoice
★ **Custo Barcelona.** Ever since Custido Dalmau and his brother David returned from a round-the-world motorcycle tour with visions of California surfing styles dancing in their heads, Custo Barcelona has been a runaway success doling out clingy cotton tops in bright and cheery hues. Now scattered all over Barcelona and the globe, Custo is scoring even more acclaim by expanding into footwear and denim. ⊠ *Pl. de les Olles 7, Born-Ribera* 🕾 *93/268–7893* Ⓜ *Jaume I* ⊠ *Plaça del Pi 2, Barri Gòtic* 🕾 *93/304–2753* Ⓜ *Liceu* ⊠ *La Rambla 109, Rambla* 🕾 *93/481–3930* Ⓜ *Catalunya* ⊠ *Carrer Ferran 36, Barri Gòtic* 🕾 *93/342–6698* Ⓜ *Liceu* ⊠ *Av. Diagonal 557, Les Corts* 🕾 *93/322–2662* ⊕ *www.custo-barcelona.com* Ⓜ *Maria Cristina.*

Erre de Raso. With no fewer than eight stores scattered all over Barcelona, this fast-growing designer founded in 1983 makes clothes in bright and breezy colors and patterns. With colors ranging from electric fuchsias to bright indigo blues and materials ranging from satin (*raso*) to cottons and silks, the objective is to outfit stylish women in chameleonic outfits that look equally appropriate picking up the kids from school, dropping by an art gallery opening, and hitting a cocktail party in the same sortie. ⊠ *Aribau 69, Eixample* 🕾 *93/452–3754* Ⓜ *Provença* ⊠ *Casp 47, Eixample* 🕾 *93/301–1485* Ⓜ *Catalunya* ⊠ *València 310, Eixample* 🕾 *93/487–9595* Ⓜ *Verdaguer* ⊠ *La Forja 71, Sant Gervasi* 🕾 *93/209–6506* Ⓜ *Muntaner* ⊠ *Via Augusta 25, Gràcia* 🕾 *93/218–9688* ⊕ *www.errederaso.com* Ⓜ *Gràcia.*

Furest. This centenary menswear star, with four stores in town and another at the airport, markets its own designs as well as selections from Armani Jeans, Ralph Lauren, Boss Hugo Boss, Brooksfield, and others. ✉ *Passeig de Gràcia 12–14, Eixample* ☎ *93/301–2000* Ⓜ *Catalunya* ◪ *Av. Diagonal 468, Eixample* ☎ *93/416–0665* Ⓜ *Maria Cristina* ◪ *Av. Diagonal 609–615, Eixample* ☎ *93/419–4006* Ⓜ *Maria Cristina* ◪ *Av. Pau Casals, Eixample* ☎ *93/201–2599* ⊕ *www.furest. com* Ⓜ *Muntaner.*

Giorgio Armani. The 2,000-square-feet floor space here guarantees plenty of privacy while exploring offerings for men and women. Armani's minimalist esthetic is a good chaser for Barcelona's unabashed baroque cocktail. ✉ *Av. Diagonal 620, Eixample* ☎ *93/414–6077* ⊕ *www. giorgioarmani.com* Ⓜ *Maria Cristina.*

Gonzalo Comella. Since 1970 Gonzalo Comella has known how to stock his stores with top men's and women's fashions, from Armani Jeans to Polo Ralph Lauren to Antonio Miró or Ermenegildo Zegna. ✉ *Passeig de Gràcia 6, Eixample* ☎ *93/412–6600* ⊕ *www.gonzalocomella.com* Ⓜ *Passeig de Gràcia.*

Heritage. A compilation of retro clothing matches the handsome antique storefront in this Gothic Quarter classic just a few steps from Plaça del Pi. Balenciaga, Yves Saint Laurent, and the 1950 Spanish Pertegaz label are just a few of the stars of yesteryear back in the limelight here. ✉ *Carrer Banys Nous 14, Barri Gòtic* ☎ *93/317–8515* ⊕ *www.heritage. com* Ⓜ *Passeig de Gràcia.*

Fodor's Choice
★

Julie Sohn. A rehabilitated industrial space with a dropped and vaulted ceiling now holds Julie Sohn's collection of women's clothing and accessories. Korean-born and Barcelona-based Sohn creates clothing that combines elegance and edginess. The store design (by Sohn's husband Conrado Carrasco's firm, CCT Arquitectos) manages to do the same with this handsome space. ✉ *Carrer Diputació 299, Eixample* ☎ *93/487–5796* Ⓜ *Passeig de Gràcia* ◪ *Carrer Joan d'Austria 126, Eixample* ☎ *93/309–0653* Ⓜ *Marina* ◪ *Carrer Mestre Nicolau 8, Sarrià, Sant Gervasi* ☎ *93/446–6957* Ⓜ *Muntaner.*

Kukuxumusu. As with more and more of Barcelona's boutiques, this one comes with a worldview. T-shirts, mugs, hats, pencils, notebooks, handkerchiefs, and just about anything you can apply a design to is decorated with Mikel Urmeneta's zany zoological characters in the throes of love. ✉ *Argenteria 69, Born-Ribera* ☎ *93/310–3647* Ⓜ *Jaume I* ◪ *Arcs 6, Barri Gòtic* ☎ *93/342–5789* Ⓜ *Catalunya* ◪ *Passeig de Gràcia 55–57, Eixample* ☎ *93/487–2238* ⊕ *www.kukuxumusu.com* Ⓜ *Catalunya.*

Le Boudoir. Women's lingerie and intimate garments, erotic cosmetics, toys and books, and all manner of wicked artifacts are sold in this attractive space designed by Mónica Sans, Julie Potter, and Paul Reynolds. The period furniture is as handsome and valuable looking as anything for sale here. ✉ *Carrer Canuda 21, Barri Gòtic* ☎ *93/302–5281* ⊕ *www.leboudoir net* Ⓜ *Catalunya.*

Loewe. Occupying the ground floor of Lluís Domènech i Montaner's Casa Lleó Morera, Loewe is Spain's answer to Hermès, a classical Barcelona clothing and leather emporium for men's and women's fashions and luxurious handbags that whisper status. ✉ *Passeig de Gràcia 35, Eixample* ☎ *93/216–0400* Ⓜ *Passeig de Gràcia* ◪ *Av. Diagonal 570, Eixample* ☎ *93/200–0920* Ⓜ *Maria Cristina* ◪ *Av. Diagonal 606,*

Eixample ☎ *93/240–5104* ⊕ *www. loewe.es* Ⓜ *Muntaner.*

Mango. With 10 stores (and counting) around Barcelona, Mango shares hegemony with the ubiquitous Zara over shoppers young and old, male and female. Smart lines and superior tailoring for pencil skirts, studded shifts, and fitted knits are trademarks at this Barcelona favorite, with red-hot items designed by Penelope Cruz and her sister Mónica. The locations listed here are only four of the ten stores presently open in Barcelona. ✉ *Passeig de Gràcia 65, Eixample* ☎ *93/216–0400* Ⓜ *Passeig de Gràcia* ✉ *Passeig de Gràcia 12–14, Eixample* ☎ *93/240–5104* Ⓜ *Catalunya* ✉ *Carrer Portaferrissa 16, Barri Gòtic* ☎ *93/301–8483* Ⓜ *Catalunya* ✉ *Av. Diagonal 280, Eixample* ☎ *93/486–0310* ⊕ *www.mango. es* Ⓜ *Glòries.*

CUSTO GUSTO

Only Barcelona could come up with Custo, an idiosyncratic fashion line created by a couple of motorcycling brothers. Since their 1980s start, the brothers Dalmau—Custido and David—have parlayed their passion for colorful and original tops into an empire that now includes footwear, denims, handbags, knits, and more. With stores scattered around Barcelona and the world (30 countries and counting), Custo's quirky embroidery and metallic graphic prints have become nearly as iconic as Gaudí's organic stalagmites or Miró's colorful asteroids.

7

Otman. With a branch in Morocco, this shop tucked into a little groove between Carrer Montcada and Carrer Flassaders specializes in light frocks, belts, blouses, and skirts made in North Africa. Sit down for a mint tea in the back of this mysteriously illuminated shop and imagine Arabian nights. ✉ *Carrer Cirera 4, La Ribera* ☎ *93/310–2265* Ⓜ *Jaume I.*

Purificación García. Known as a gifted fabric expert whose creations are invariably based on the qualities and characteristics of her raw materials, Purificación García enjoys solid prestige in Barcelona as one of the city's fashion champions. Understated hues and subtle combinations of colors and shapes place this contemporary designer squarely in the camp of the less-is-more school of a Barcelona aesthetic movement that departs radically from the over-ornamentation of the city's Art Nouveau past. ✉ *Passeig de Gràcia 21, Eixample* ☎ *93/487–7292* Ⓜ *Passeig de Gràcia* ✉ *Av. Pau Casals 4, Eixample* ☎ *93/200–6089* Ⓜ *Muntaner* ✉ *Diagonal 557, Eixample* ☎ *93/444–0253* ⊕ *www.purificaciongarcia. es* Ⓜ *Maria Cristina.*

Rquer. Conxa Jofresa stocks local Spanish and Catalan designers including Sybilla, Sita Murt, Juan Pedro Lopez, David Valls, and Viviana Uribe. The name of the store, a play on the Spanish expression *erre que erre* (stubbornly, pigheadedly) can be taken as a statement of Conxa's fidelity to her founding idea of sticking with home-born designers through thick and thin. ✉ *Carrer del Rec 75, Born-Ribera* ☎ *93/315–2391* Ⓜ *Jaume I.*

Sita Murt. Local Catalan and Spanish clothing designers from Julie Sohn to Rutzü, Paul & Joe, and Anna Pianura to the Sita Murt home label hang in this cavelike space near Plaça Sant Jaume in the center of the

Gothic Quarter. Colorful chiffon dresses and light, gauzy tops characterize the popular young line of clothing. ⊠ *Carrer Avinyó 18, Barri Gòtic* ☎ *93/301–0006* Ⓜ *Liceu.*

Tüsetú. One street east of Santa Maria del Mar, this tiny hole-in-the-wall is a showroom for eclectic yet elegant collections by Zoe and other young innovators in women's fashions. ⊠ *Ases 1, Born-Ribera* ☎ *93/268–3890* Ⓜ *Jaume I.*

Zara. This affordable chain is popular with *barcelonins* and visitors alike for its cool and casual styles for men, women, and children. There are Zara stores throughout the city, but the Passeig de Gràcia store is the most central and generally frequented, for better or for worse. Hot new styles rematerialize here in affordable form. Be prepared for sizes that run small and pants made for legs that go on forever. Zara's recipe for success has won over the world, but items are cheaper on its home turf. Well-executed, affordable copies of catwalk styles appear on the rails in a fashion heartbeat. The women's section is the front-runner, but the men's and kid's sections cover good ground too. The Zara Home department is still only found in Europe. ⊠ *Passeig de Gràcia 16, Raval* ☎ *93/318–7675* Ⓜ *Catalunya* ⊠ *Carrer Pelai 58, Eixample* ☎ *93/301–0978* Ⓜ *Passeig de Gràcia* ⊠ *Rambla de Catalunya 67, Eixample* ☎ *93/216–0868* ⊕ *www.zara.com* Ⓜ *Passeig de Gràcia.*

DESIGN AND INTERIORS

Near the Pedrera on Passeig de Gràcia are Barcelona's two top design sanctuaries: Vinçon and BD. Habitat has stores on Tuset at the Diagonal and in the Plaça de Catalunya Triangle complex behind Bar Zurich at the head of the Rambla. The area around the basilica of Santa Maria del Mar and the Passeig del Born, an artisans' quarter since medieval times, is now chock-full of textile and leather design stores and gift shops with attitude.

Arkitektura. Lighting design and kitchen and bathroom fixtures along with furniture and diverse objects by acclaimed architects and designers are on display here in this clean-lined upper Barcelona shop designed by architects and interior designers Marta Ventós, Carlos Tejada, and Conrado Carrasco. ⊠ *Via Augusta 185, Eixample* ☎ *93/362–4720* ⊕ *www.arkitekturabcn.com* Ⓜ *Muntaner.*

Fodor's Choice
★ **BD Ediciones de Diseño.** The BD stands for "Barcelona design," and this spare, cutting-edge home-furnishings store is inside a Moderniste gem: Lluís Domènech i Montaner's Casa Thomas. BD cofounder Oscar Tusquets, master designer and architect, gives contemporary design star Javier Mariscal plenty of space here, while past giants such as Gaudí with his Casa Calvet chair, or Salvador Dalí and his Gala love seat are also available—if your pockets are deep enough. ⊠ *Carrer Mallorca 291–293, Eixample* ☎ *93/458–6909* ⊕ *www.bdediciones.com* Ⓜ *Diagonal.*

Gimeno. Items from clever suitcases to the latest in furniture or sofas all display an innovative flair here. Household necessities, decorative goods, and gifts ranging from bags to benches share a hallmark of creativity and quality, nearly always with an edge. ⊠ *Passeig de Gràcia 102, Eixample* ☎ *93/237–2078* Ⓜ *Diagonal.*

Vinçon sells a variety of hyper-designed home goods in a space that was once painter Ramón Casas's studio.

Habitat Barcelona. British designer Terence Conran's emporium of beautiful objects, household items, and home furnishings is a hit with the design-appreciative denizens of Barcelona. The Habitat line of goods is produced by Conran's team of designers and is more affordable than those in his higher-end Conran Shop. ⊠ *Av. Diagonal 514, Eixample* ☎ *93/415–2992* Ⓜ *Passeig de Gràcia* ⊠ *Pl. Catalunya, 2–4, Eixample* ☎ *93/301–7484* ⊕ *www.habitat.net* Ⓜ *Diagonal, Catalunya.*

MDM. Reasonably priced household gear and design furnishings make this an interesting store to explore. Stainless steel from Rosle, WMF implements from Germany, Danish brands such as BUM and Eva Solo, and French home goods from Le Creuset are just a few of the prestigious international brand names in wood, stainless steel, and porcelain available here. ⊠ *Av. Diagonal 405 bis, Eixample* ☎ *93/238–6767* Ⓜ *Diagonal.*

Fodor's Choice **Vinçon.** A design giant some 50 years old, Vinçon steadily expanded its
★ chic premises through a rambling Moderniste house that was once the home of Art Nouveau poet-artist Santiago Rusiñol and the studio of the painter Ramón Casas. It stocks everything from Filofaxes to handsome kitchenware. If you can tear your eyes away from all the design, seek out the spectacular Moderniste fireplace designed in wild Art Nouveau exuberance with a gigantic hearth in the form of a stylized face. The back terrace is a cool respite and a breath of fresh air with views up to the next-door rooftop warriors of Gaudí's Casa Milà. ⊠ *Passeig de Gràcia 96, Eixample* ☎ *93/215–6050* Ⓜ *Diagonal.*

FINE FOODS AND WINES

Food items can be some of the best buys in Barcelona, but be sure to check the ever-changing customs before purchasing edibles. Spanish wines from La Rioja are world renowned, but Ribera de Duero, Priorat, and other areas are producing the modern "high expression" wines popularized by American wine critic Robert Parker. Lavinia is an omnipresent wine emporium found in Barcelona and Bilbao, and will help you find a drinkable, affordable modern wine. Spain's wines are matched by its superb cured hams, generically called *jamón serrano,* which simply means "mountain ham." The finest cured ham is *jamón ibérico de bellota* (Iberian free-range, acorn-fed, black pig). Top-notch ham shops in Barcelona sell vacuum-sealed packets of sliced, cured ham that pack easily and make a tasty souvenir, though there is no guarantee that U.S. customs will not kidnap this precious product. Where there are fine wines and hams, cheeses cannot be far behind, with Extremadura's Torta del Casar making international headlines and on sale in specialized shops in Barcelona. Spanish saffron is possibly the last of the great foodstuff bargains available worldwide: light, legal, and cheap, while dried wild mushrooms are another aromatic favorite.

Caelum. At the corner of Carrer de la Palla and Banys Nous, this tearoom and coffee shop sells crafts and foods such as honey and preserves made in convents and monasteries all over Spain. The café and tearoom section extends neatly out into the intersection of Carrer Banys Nous (which means "new baths") and Carrer de la Palla, directly over the site of the medieval Jewish baths. ⊠ *Carrer de la Palla 8, Barri Gòtic* ☎ 93/302–6993 Ⓜ *Liceu, Catalunya.*

Fodor's Choice
★ **Casa Gispert.** On the inland side of Santa Maria del Mar, this is one of the most aromatic and picturesque shops in Barcelona, bursting with teas, coffees, spices, saffron, chocolates, and nuts. The star element in this olfactory and aesthetic feast is an almond-roasting stove in the back of the store dating from 1851, like the store itself. But don't miss the acid engravings on the office windows or the ancient wooden back door. ⊠ *Sombrerers 23, La Ribera* ☎ 93/319–7547 Ⓜ *Jaume I.*

El Magnífico. This coffee emporium just up the street from Santa Maria del Mar is famous for its sacks of coffee beans from all over the globe. A couple of deep breaths here will keep you caffeinated for hours. ⊠ *Carrer Argenteria 64, Born-Ribera* ☎ 93/310–3361 Ⓜ *Jaume I.*

Foix de Sarrià. Pastry and poetry under the same roof merit a stop. The verses of J. V. Foix, a major Catalan poet who managed to survive the Franco regime with his art intact, are engraved in bronze on the outside wall of the Major de Sarrià location, where he was born. Excellent pastries, breads, wines, cheeses, and cavas, all available on Sunday, have made Foix de Sarrià a Barcelona landmark. ⊠ *Pl. Sarrià 9–10, Sarrià* ☎ 93/203–0473 Ⓜ *Reina Elisenda* ⊠ *Major de Sarrià 57, Sarrià* ☎ 93/203–0714 Ⓜ *Sarrià.*

Formatgeria La Seu. Scotswoman Katherine McLaughlin has put together the Gothic Quarter's most delightful cheese-tasting sanctuary on the site of an ancient buttery. (A 19th-century butter churn is visible in the back room.) A dozen artisanal cow, goat, and sheep cheeses from all over Spain, and olive oils can be tasted and taken home. La Seu is named for a combination of La Seu cathedral, as the "seat" of cheeses, and for cheese-rich La Seu d'Urgell in the Pyrenees. Katherine's wrapping paper, imaginatively chosen sheets of newspaper, give a final flourish to purchases. ✉ *Carrer Dagueria 16, Born-Ribera* ☎ *93/412–6548* ⊕ *www. formatgerialaseu.com* Ⓜ *Jaume I.*

Hofmann. Mey Hofmann, a constellation in Barcelona's gourmet galaxy for the last three decades, moved into this Born address in 2009 with her first shop dedicated exclusively to pastry. Everything from the lightest, flakiest croissants to the cakes, tarts, and ice creams are about as good they get in this sweets emporium just off the Passeig del Born on one of Barcelona's quirkiest shopping streets. ✉ *Flassaders 44, Born-Ribera* ☎ *93/268–8221* ⊕ *www.hofmann-bcn.com* Ⓜ *Jaume I.*

Iskia. Good wine advice and a perennially renewing stock of new values to try make Iskia one of upper Barcelona's best wine emporiums. The proprietors speak English and are glad to talk about latest wine trends or explain their products at length. ✉ *Major de Sarrià 132, Sarrià* ☎ *93/205–0070* ⊕ *www.iskiavins.com* Ⓜ *Sarrià.*

Jobal. Long known as the secret saffron outlet around the corner from the Picasso museum, this fragrant spice emporium sells the full range of spices and savory items from cumin to coriander, along with teas from every corner of the globe. ✉ *Carrer Princesa 38, Born-Ribera* ☎ *93/319–7802* Ⓜ *Jaume I.*

La Botifarreria de Santa Maria. This booming pork merchant next to the church of Santa Maria del Mar offers excellent cheeses, hams, pâtés, and homemade *sobrassadas* (pork pâté with paprika). *Botifarra*, Catalan for sausage, is the main item here, with a wide range of varieties including egg sausage for meatless Lent and sausage stuffed with spinach, asparagus, cider, cinnamon, and Cabrales cheese. ✉ *Carrer Santa Maria 4, La Ribera* ☎ *93/319–9784* Ⓜ *Jaume I.*

La Carte des Vins. Enological books and accessories, and a carefully selected list of top international vintages fill this gorgeous wine shop decorated in fresh wood tones, many of them coming from tops of wine crates arranged around the tops of the display racks. Architect Daniel Nassat and interiorist Laurent Godel, authors of this graceful space, seem to have studied nearby Santa Maria del Mar to come up with such pure lines. ✉ *Sombrerers 1, Born-Ribera08003* ☎ *93/268–7043* Ⓜ *Jaume I.*

La Casa del Bacalao. This cult store decorated with cod-fishing memorabilia specializes in salt cod and books of codfish recipes. Slabs of salt and dried cod, used in a wide range of Catalan recipes such as *esqueixada*, in which shredded strips of raw salt cod are served in a marinade of oil and vinegar, can be vacuum-packed for portability. ✉ *Comtal 8, just off Porta de l'Àngel, Barri Gòtic* ☎ *93/301–6539* Ⓜ *Catalunya.*

La Cave. When in Sarrià, have a stop at this original wine cellar and restaurant. With every wine color-coded by taste, price, and geography, you are brilliantly rescued from pandemic wine store bewilderment. La Cave also provides a printout of tasting notes and technical data for every bottle, so that you not only know what you're getting, but what you've had and why. In addition, co-owner and manager Claude Cohen is an English-French-Spanish linguist and can dispense expert advice

7

and plenty of humor as well. ⊠ *Av. J. V. Foix 80, Sarrià* ☎ *93/206–3846* Ⓜ *Sarrià.*

Mantequeria Can Ravell. Arguably Barcelona's best all-around fine-food and wine emporium, Can Ravell is a cult favorite with a superb selection of everything you ever wanted to savor, from the finest anchovies from La Scala to the best cheese from Idiazabal. Through the kitchen and up the tiny spiral staircase, the dining room offers one of Barcelona's best lunch menus. The tasting table downstairs operates on a first come, first served basis and brings together foodies from all over the world to swap tasting tales. It's closed Sunday and Monday. ⊠ *Aragó 313, Eixample* ☎ *93/457–5114* Ⓜ *Passeig de Gràcia, Girona.*

Orígens 99.9%. Restaurant and delicatessen Orígens 99.9% occupies a former glassblowing shop with the original wooden balcony overhead beautifully restored and conserved. Olive oils, wines, and cheeses— all organically grown products from Catalonia—are the specialties in this *espai gastrònomic* (gastronomical space) and restaurant. Over the store's main produce display, don't miss the wood carving of San Antonio de Padua, patron saint of lost objects. ⊠ *Vidrieria 6–8, Born-Ribera* ☎ *93/310–7531* Ⓜ *Jaume I.*

Queviures Murria. Founded in 1890, this historic Moderniste shop, its windows decorated with Ramón Casas paintings and posters, has a superb selection of some 200 cheeses, sausages, wines, and conserves from Spain, Catalunya, and beyond. The ceramic Casas reproductions lining the interior walls are eye candy, as are all the details in this work of art–cum–grocery store (*queviures* means foodstuffs, literally, "things to keep you alive"). ⊠ *Roger de Llúria 85, Eixample* ☎ *93/215–5789* Ⓜ *Diagonal.*

Tea Shop. Earl Grey, black, white, red, green—every kind of tea you've ever heard of and many you probably haven't are available at this encyclopedic tea repository on Gràcia's main drag. The Taller de Cata (Tasting Workshop) held Thursday 5:30–7:30 PM will stimulate your tea culture in the event that you are interested in learning how to distinguish a Pai Mu Tan (white tea) from a Lung Ching (green tea) or how to correctly prepare and serve different varieties of this universal world brew and beverage. ⊠ *Gran de Gràcia 91, Gràcia* ☎ *93/217–4923* Ⓜ *Passeig de Gràcia.*

Tot Formatge. This small but chock-full and bustling shop in the Born-Ribera district manages to fit cheeses from all over Spain and the world onto its shelves. Specializing in local Catalan, French, and Spanish produce, this is the place for a comprehensive cheese tour of the Iberian Peninsula or across the length of the Pyrenees. The staff can provide fascinating explanations of the geographical and social histories behind the methods used by different regions to prepare and produce their respective cheeses. ⊠ *Passeig del Born 13, La Ribera* ☎ *93/319–5357* Ⓜ *Jaume I.*

Tutusaus. With an anthological selection of cheeses, hams, pastries, and delicacies of all kinds, this famous café, restaurant, and delicatessen is a hallowed upper Barcelona hangout just off Turo Park. Whether for coffee, a taste of cheese or foie, or a full meal composed of a selection of delicacies, this little hideaway is superb. ⊠ *Francesc Perez Cabrero 5, Sant Gervasi* ☎ *93/209–8373* Ⓜ *La Bonanova.*

Vilaplana. Just up the street from Tutusaus next to Turo Park, this is a famous address for Barcelona food lovers, known for its pastries, cheeses, hams, pâtés, caviars, and fine deli items. ⊠ *Francesc Perez Cabrero, Eixample* ☎ *93/201–1300* Ⓜ *La Bonanova.*

Fodor'sChoice
★
Vila Viniteca. Near Santa Maria del Mar, this is the best wine treasury in Barcelona, with tastings, courses, and events meriting further investigation. The tiny family grocery store across the street offers exquisite artisanal cheeses ranging from French goat cheese to Extremadura's famous Torta del Casar. ⊠ *Carrer Agullers 7, Born-Ribera* ☎ *93/268–3227* Ⓜ *Jaume I.*

FOOD AND FLEA MARKETS

Besides the Boqueria, other spectacular food markets include two in Gràcia—the Mercat de la Llibertat (near Plaça Gal.la Placidia) and the Mercat de la Revolució (on Travessera de Gràcia)—the Mercat de Sarrià (near Plaça de Sarrià and the Reina Elisenda train stop), the Merca de la Concepció on Carrer Aragó, and the Mercat de Santa Caterina across Via Laietana from the cathedral.

Fodor'sChoice
★
Boqueria. The oldest of its kind in Europe, Barcelona's most colorful and bustling food market appears here on the Rambla between Carrer del Carme and Carrer de Hospital. Open Monday–Saturday, it's most active before 3 PM, though many of the stands remain open all day. Standout stalls include Petràs, the wild mushroom guru in the back of the market on Plaça de la Gardunya, and Juanito Bayen of the world-famous collection of bar stools known as Pinotxo. ⊠ *Rambla 91, Rambla* ۞ *Mon.–Sat. 8–4* ☎ *93/318–2017* Ⓜ *Liceu, Catalunya.*

Els Encants. Barcelona's biggest flea market, an event with distinctly bohemian allure, spreads out at the end of Carrer Dos de Maig. The center of the circular Plaça de les Glòries Catalanes also fills with ill-gotten goods of all kinds. Keep close track of your wallet or you might come across it as an empty item for sale. ⊠ *Carrer Dos de Maig 177, Eixample* ۞ *Wed.–Sat. 9–2* ☎ *93/246–3030* Ⓜ *Glòries.*

Herbolari del Cel. Gràcia's "Herbolarium from Heaven" is widely considered among the best in Barcelona for herbal remedies, teas, spices, oils, natural cures and treatments and cosmetics of all kinds. A mere deep breath of air here will probably cure whatever ails you. ⊠ *Travessera de Gràcia 120, Gràcia* ☎ *93/218–6907* Ⓜ *Gràcia.*

Mercat Gòtic. A browser's bonanza, this market for antique books and art objects occupies the Plaça de la Seu, in front of the cathedral, on Thursday. ⊠ *Pl. de la Catedral s/n, Barri Gòtic* ۞ *Thurs. 9–9* Ⓜ *Catalunya.*

Mercat de Sant Antoni. Just outside the Raval at the end of Ronda Sant Antoni, this steel-hangar colossus is an old-fashioned food and second-hand clothing and books (many in English) market. Sunday morning is the most popular time to browse through the used-book and video game market. ⊠ *Carrer del Comte d'Urgell 1, Raval* ۞ *Sun. 9–2, Tues.–Sat. 8–2.* Ⓜ *Sant Antoni.*

Plaça del Pi. This little square fills with the interesting tastes and aromas of a natural-produce market (honeys, cheeses) on Thursday, while neighboring Plaça Sant Josep Oriol holds a painter's market every Sunday.

7

A cornucopia of produce is available at Barcelona's markets.

✉ *Pl. del Pi s/n, Barri Gòtic* ⊘ *Fri.–Sun. 1st and 2nd weekends of the month and special holidays 8–8* Ⓜ *Catalunya, Liceu.*

Plaça Reial. The nightlife in this area has just barely evaporated off the streets on Sunday morning when a stamp and coin market sets up. Not far away, there's a general crafts and flea market near the Columbus monument at the port end of the Rambla. ✉ *Pl. Reial s/n, Rambla* ⊘ *Sun. 9–2* Ⓜ *Liceu.*

Sarrià. Tuesday antiques markets in Sarrià's town square provide another good reason to explore this charming onetime outlying village in the upper part of the city. The nearby produce market, a mini-Boqueria, is the place for coffee, while Tram-Tram, Vivanda, and Vell Sarrià, just downhill in front of the town hall, are excellent choices for lunch after a hike over to the Monestir de Pedralbes and back. ✉ *Pl. de Sarrià, Sarrià* ⊘ *Tues. 9–3* Ⓜ *Sarrià, Reina Elisenda.*

GIFTS, SOUVENIRS, AND STATIONERY

Alonso. The storefront and interiors of this ancient little glove and accessory shop is well worth the visit. Lovely antique cabinets painstakingly stripped of centuries of paint display gloves, fans, shawls, mantillas, and a miscellany of textile crafts and small gifts. ✉ *Santa Anna 27, Barri Gòtic* ☎ *93/317–6085* Ⓜ *Catalunya.*

🌣 **Bateau Lune.** Crafts, disguises, puzzles, games and a thousand things to make you want to be a kid again are on display in this creative child-oriented gift shop on one of Gràcia's most emblematic squares. ✉ *Pl. de la Virreina 7, Gràcia* ☎ *93/218–6907* Ⓜ *Fontana.*

Cereria Subirà. Known as the city's oldest shop, having remained open since 1761 (though it was not always a candle store), this "waxery" (*cereria*) offers candles in all sizes and shapes, ranging from wild mushrooms to the Montserrat massif, home of the Benedictine abbey dear to the heart of every *barcelonin*. ⊠ *Baixada Llibreteria 7, Barri Gòtic* ☎ 93/315–2606 Ⓜ *Jaume I.*

Fodor's Choice **Ganiveteria Roca.** Directly opposite the giant rose window of the Santa
★ Maria del Pi church, the knife store (*ganivet* is Catalan for knife) beneath this lovely sgraffito-decorated facade takes cutlery culture to a new level. Knives, razors, scissors, hatchets, axes, swords, nail clippers, tweezers, and penknives are all displayed in this comprehensive cutting edge emporium. ⊠ *Pl. del Pi 3, Barri Gòtic* ☎ 93/302–1241 Ⓜ *Liceu.*

Natura. A gracefully decorated store in the Natura chain, this crafts specialist stocks a good selection of global trifles, including pieces from India and North Africa. Incense, clothing, tapestries, candles, furniture, and surprises of all kinds appear in this cross-cultural craft shop. ⊠ *Argenteria 78, Born-Ribera* ☎ 93/268–2525 Ⓜ *Jaume I.*

Papers Coma. On Barcelona's most artistic street, home of the Picasso Museum and the Maeght gallery, Papers Coma offers inventive gadgets and knickknacks from wildly colorful paperclips to Picasso blank notebooks. ⊠ *Montcada 20, La Ribera* ☎ 93/319–7601 Ⓜ *Jaume I.*

Fodor's Choice **Papirum.** Exquisite hand-printed papers, marbleized blank books, and
★ writing implements await you and your muse at this tiny, medieval-tone shop. ⊠ *Baixada de la Llibreteria 2, Barri Gòtic* ☎ 93/310–5242 Ⓜ *Jaume I.*

Fodor's Choice **Pepa Paper.** Barcelona's most famous paper and stationery store, Pepa
★ Paper (Pepa is a nickname for Josefina and Paper, Catalan for—you guessed it—paper) carries a gorgeous selection of cards, paper, and myriad objects and paraphernalia related to correspondence. ⊠ *Carrer Valencia 266, Eixample* ☎ 93/215–9223 Ⓜ *Provença, Passeig de Gràcia* ⊠ *Carrer Paris 167, Eixample* ☎ 93/494–8420 Ⓜ *Provença* ⊠ *Av. Diagonal 557–575, Sarrià, Sant Gervasi* ☎ 93/405–2478 Ⓜ *Maria Cristina.*

JEWELRY

Bagués Masriera. An iconic Barcelona jeweler with its main headquarters on the Rambla at the corner of Carrer del Carmen, Bagués has bejeweled *barcelonins* since 1839. His Lluís Masriera line of Art Nouveau jewels, intricate flying nymphs, and lifelike golden insects are his most recognizable creations. The location in Moderniste architect Puig i Cadafalch's Casa Amatller in the famous Mansana de la Discòrdia on Passeig de Gràcia is worth the visit just to get a closer look at the house. ⊠ *La Rambla 105, Rambla* ☎ 93/481–7050 Ⓜ *Catalunya* ⊠ *Passeig de Gràcia 41, Eixample* ☎ 93/216–0174 ⊕ *www.bagues.es* Ⓜ *Catalunya.*

Forum Ferlandina. A wide gamut of creations by some 50 international designers of jewelry is on display in this slender shop directly across the street from the MACBA. ⊠ *Ferlandina 31, Raval* ☎ 93/441–8018 Ⓜ *Catalunya.*

Galeria Alea/Majoral. Enric Majoral's jewelry design takes inspiration from organic and natural shapes such as pea pods. With gold and pearl creations that seem to have sprouted from the forest floor, this collection makes even the most hard-core urbanite appreciate nature. ⊠ *Carrer Argenteria 66, Born-Ribera* ☎ 93/310–1373 ⊕ *www.sargantana.net*

7

Ⓜ *Jaume I* ✉ *Consell de Cent 308, Eixample* ☎ *93/467–7209* Ⓜ *Passeig de Gràcia.*

Moska. Working from a stunning 18th-century house bordering and named for Barcelona's narrowest street, Carrer de les Mosques (Street of the Flies), this artesan shop specializes in antique jewelry for collectors as well as original avant-garde pieces made on the premises. ✉ *Flassaders 42, Born-Ribera* ☎ *93/310–1701* Ⓜ *Jaume I.*

Puig Doria. This popular jeweler, with two locations in town and another in the airport, designs and sells a full range of personal accessories of great style and taste. Lariat necklaces with ropes of pearls and bangles speckled in colorful geometrical forms are some of the luxurious baubles on sale. ✉ *Av. Diagonal 612, Eixample* ☎ *93/201–2911* ⊕ *www.puigdoria.com* Ⓜ *Diagonal* ✉ *Rambla de Catalunya 88, Eixample* ☎ *93/215–1090* Ⓜ *Passeig de Gràcia.*

Zapata Joyero. The Zapata family, with three stores around town, has been prominent in Barcelona jewelry design and retail for the last half-century. With original designs of their own and a savvy selection of the most important Swiss and international watch designers, this family business is now in its second generation, and makes a point of taking good care of clients with large or small jewelry needs. Their L'Illa store, for example, specializes in jewelry accessible to the budgets of younger clients. ✉ *Av. Diagonal 557, Eixample* ☎ *93/430–6238* Ⓜ *Provença* ✉ *Mandri 20, Sant Gervasi* ☎ *93/211–6774* Ⓜ *Sarrià* ✉ *L'Illa, Diagonal 557 (stores no. 126 and 133), Diagonal* ☎ *93/444–0063* Ⓜ *Maria Cristina.*

SHOES

BBB. Any shoe store that satisfies the legendary three B requirements— *bueno, bonito, and barato* (good, beautiful, and cheap)—is not to be missed. Shoes in many styles from sandals to stilletto heels pack this popular Gràcia shoe emporium. ✉ *Gran de Gràcia 233, Gràcia* ☎ *93/237–3514* Ⓜ *Fontana.*

Camper. Just off Plaça Catalunya and not far from the 25-room boutique hotel of the same name (and company) this internationally famous Spanish shoe emporium offers a comprehensive line of funky boots, heels, and shoes of all kinds. Both men and women's shoes, all in line with the company's rugged outdoor philosophy, are displayed against a rocky mountainous background deisgned by Martí Guixé and the Camper Studio. ✉ *Carrer Pelai 13–37, Raval* ☎ *93/302–4124* Ⓜ *Catalunya.*

Casas International. This is one of the city's best shops for browsing through a wide range of international trendsetting footwear. Sister stores at Porta de l'Àngel 40 and Portaferrissa 25 show surprising and original in-house designs, but this branch on the Rambla is predominantly Italian, with heels high and low, round and stiletto, and square toes and a savvy mix of shoes for men and women. ✉ *Rambla 125, Barri Gòtic* ☎ *93/302–4598* Ⓜ *Liceu.*

Fodor's Choice ★   **Farrutx.** Shoes, including sandals and espadrilles, made in the tradition of the Balearic Islands for the dynamic modern woman are the specialty here. Brilliantly designed, these kicks will set you back plenty, but the quality is undeniable. ✉ *Rosselló 218, Eixample* ☎ *93/215–0685* Ⓜ *Provença* ✉ *Pau Casals 18–20, Sarrià, Sant Gervasi* ☎ *93/200–6920* Ⓜ *Muntaner, La Bonanova.*

Fodor's Choice
★ **La Manual Alpargatera.** If you appreciate old-school craftsmanship in footwear, visit this boutique just off Carrer Ferran. Handmade rope-sole sandals and espadrilles are the specialty, and this shop has sold them to everyone—including the Pope. The beribboned espadrilles model used for dancing the sardana is also available, but these artisans are capable of making any kind of creation you can think of. ⊠ *Avinyó 7, Barri Gòtic* ☎ *93/301–0172* Ⓜ *Liceu.*

THESE BOOTS . . .

If footwear is your fetish, Barcelona can be a dangerous destination. From Camper's funky boots to rope-soled espadrilles, shoe-obsession rages. Portal de l'Àngel is the classic shoe-shopping street. Carrer Muntaner above Diagonal is rife with shoe boutiques, and Rambla Catalunya between Plaça Catalunya and the Diagonal has shoe stores by the dozens. Carrer Elisabets, between the Rambla and the MACBA, is home to Camper, as well as Twiggy's shoes. S'avarca de Menorca is the place for leather sandals from the Balearic Islands, and Carrer Pelai's Noel Barcelona displays and sells the best cowboy boots.

Noel Barcelona. Cowboy boots of every imaginable style and color are on display at this stupendous surprise in midtown Barcelona. High-heel, low-heel, stilletto-toe, round-toe, higher, lower, hand-tooled or plain leather, this is said to be the finest collection of cowboy boots in Europe. Espadrilles and other kinds of shoes are also available. ⊠ *Carrer Pelai 48, Raval* ☎ *93/317–8638* Ⓜ *Catalunya.*

Fodor's Choice
★ **S'avarca de Menorca.** For a range of handmade leather sandals (often referred to as Abarcas) with straps across the heels in an infinity of variations and colors, this is Barcelona's finest store for footwear from the Balearic Isles. Abarcas come with thicker soles for city walking or lighter ones for wearing around the house. ⊠ *Capellans 2, Barri Gòtic* ☎ *93/342–5738* Ⓜ *Catalunya, Jaume I.*

Solé. One of Barcelona's most original shoemakers, this artisan makes footwear by hand, imports handmade shoes from all over Spain, and sells other models from Indonesia and Morocco. With boots, sandals, and a wide range of selections for both men and women, the rugged, rustic look prevails. ⊠ *Carrer Ample 7, Barri Gòtic* ☎ *93/301–6984* Ⓜ *Drassanes.*

Tascón. International footwear designers and domestic shoemakers alike fill these stores with solid urban footwear and brands such as Panama Jack, Timberland, Camper, and Doc Martens. These walking and hiking shoes are for people with miles on their minds. ⊠ *Av. Diagonal 462, Eixample* ☎ *93/415–5616* Ⓜ *Diagonal* ⊠ *Passeig de Gràcia 64, Eixample* ☎ *93/487–4447* Ⓜ *Passeig de Gràcia* ⊠ *Passeig del Born 8, Born-Ribera* ☎ *93/268–7293* Ⓜ *Jaume I.*

DEPARTMENT STORES AND MALLS

Bulevard Rosa. This alleyway off Passeig de Gràcia, as much a social event as a shopping venue, is composed of more than 100 clothing, jewelry, perfume, and footwear shops. Lunch is a major element in the shopping process, and the Jardí del Bulevard restaurant down the stairway under this raging commercial maelstrom is an opportunity to see and be seen and recharge acquisitive batteries. ⊠ *Passeig de Gràcia 53–55, Eixample* ☎ *93/378–9191* Ⓜ *Passeig de Gràcia.*

El Corte Inglés. Otherwise known as ECI, this iconic and ubiquitous Spanish department store has its main Barcelona branch on Plaça Catalunya, with a books and music annex 100 yards away in Porta de l'Àngel. Spain's most powerful and comprehensive clothing and general goods emporium (its name means "The English Cut") can be tedious, but you can find just about anything you're looking for. The encyclopedic range of quality items here can save you hours of questing around town. ⊠ *Pl. de Catalunya 14, Eixample* ☎ *93/306–3800* Ⓜ *Catalunya* ⊠ *Porta de l'Àngel 19–21, Barri Gòtic* ☎ *93/306–3800* Ⓜ *Catalunya* ⊠ *Pl. Francesc Macià, Av. Diagonal 471, Eixample* ☎ *93/419–2020* Ⓜ *La Bonanova* ⊠ *Av. Diagonal 617, Diagonal, Les Corts* ☎ *93/419–2828* Ⓜ *Maria Cristina.*

El Triangle. The Triangle d'Or or Golden Triangle at the top end of the Rambla on Plaça Catalunya is a stylish and popular complex and home for, among other stores, FNAC, where afternoon book presentations and CD launches bring together crowds of literati and music lovers. ⊠ *Pl. Catalunya 4, Rambla* ☎ *93/344–1800* Ⓜ *Catalunya.*

L'Illa Diagonal. This rangy complex buzzes with shoppers swarming through 100 stores ranging from food specialists to decathlon sports gear and Bang & Olufsen sound system purveyors, FNAC, and the Zapata jewelers downstairs. ⊠ *Av. Diagonal 545–57, Eixample* ☎ *93/487–1699* Ⓜ *Maria Cristina.*

Pedralbes Centre. A conglomeration just a few blocks west of L'Illa Diagonal includes a Lavinia wine store and ends with the Diagonal branch of the ubiquitous El Corte Inglés. ⊠ *Av. Diagonal 609–615, Eixample* ☎ *93/410–6821* Ⓜ *Maria Cristina.*

Catalonia Highlights

WORD OF MOUTH

"We still didn't [get enough] Dalí and drove over to Figueres. There is an old theater which was converted into a giant piece of artwork by Salvador Dalí. Do not expect a typical art museum with pictures hanging on the walls. The [Teatre-Museu Dalí] is different, very different."

—traveller1959

WELCOME TO CATALONIA

TOP REASONS TO GO

★ **Cadaqués:** Art and nature in Dalí's "most beautiful place on earth."

★ **Girona's Jewish Quarter:** A medieval past, restored.

★ **Catalan Nouveau:** Serious foodies argue that the fountainhead of creative gastronomy has moved from France to Spain, and in particular, this eastern corner along the Costa Brava.

★ **The Dalí Triangle:** Figueres, Púbol, Port Lligat

1 **The Costa Brava.** Fierce, beautiful, and wild—but never dull—the Costa Brava is one of Spain's most bewitching places. The name means "rugged coast," a description first coined in 1905 by Catalan journalist Ferran Agulló to describe one of Europe's most abrupt and rocky coastlines.

GETTING ORIENTED

In the northeast corner of the Iberian Peninsula, Catalonia spreads out north, south, and west of its capital city of Barcelona over four provinces: Girona, Barcelona, and Tarragona—from north to south along the Mediterranean coast—and, to the west, landlocked Lleida. The provinces are, in turn, subdivided into *comarques*, or counties—for example, the Alt (upper) and Baix (lower) Empordà, in the upper northeast part of the province of Girona, both famed for their landscape and cuisine, are two comarques. Moving north to Girona province, you'll find both the Costa Brava—Spain's rocky response to the Côte d'Azur and the Amalfi Coast—and the historic city of Girona. Tarragona Province to the south is famous for its Roman capital city.

8

2 Inland to Girona.

Northern Catalonia contains the soft, green hills of the Empordà (in Spanish, Ampurdan) farm country and the Alberes mountain range, the eastern tip of the Pyrenees. The ancient city of Girona, often ignored by people bound for the Costa Brava, is an easy and interesting day trip from Barcelona. The upland towns of Besalú and Olot are Catalonia at its most authentic.

3 Southern Catalonia.

West of Barcelona, from the Montserrat massif and its legendary monastery through the Penedès wine-growing region and the Cistercian monasteries farther west, southern Catalonia unfolds through coastal treasures such as Sitges and culminates just north of the Ebro Delta in the ancient Roman capital of Tarragona.

CATALONIA PLANNER

When to Go

For sun and swimming in the Mediterranean, late spring to early autumn is prime time. Starting in mid-May the weather gets warm enough to take that first dip, though the water will still be cold. Torrid temperatures arrive in late July and most of August. Unfortunately, it's difficult to find a place to lie down on a beach in August, when all of Europe is on vacation. Late summer and early fall are perfect times to enjoy the pleasures of the Catalan coast without excessive heat or hordes of people. The local bounty of seasonal wild mushrooms and game is at its best from mid-October to mid-January. Winters are usually brisk but stimulating, a good time for hiking and visiting cultural sights.

Planning Your Time

If you're out to explore Catalonia, who can resist waking up in Barcelona and heading first to the Costa Brava? From the metropolis you can drive to just about anywhere in Catalonia in two hours (even to the higher reaches of the Pyrenees), but to get a good impression of the countryside, a trip of several days is advisable. In three days you can head north from Barcelona to see a good slice of Catalonia and get a real taste of the country. In 10 days you can contemplate seeing most of Catalonia's highlights, from beaches to mountains to monasteries.

If You Have 3 Days

Starting from Barcelona, make your first stop in the central Costa Brava at **Tossa de Mar,** with its walled medieval town perched next to the sea. On Day 2, drive inland and explore **Girona,** with its Gothic cathedral and Jewish Quarter, which still preserves an ancient heritage. On Day 3, drive north to **Figueres** and visit the Teatre-Museu Gala-Salvador Dalí. Have lunch at one of the town's many choice restaurants, and in the evening you can return to Barcelona in under two hours down the A7 highway.

If You Have 5 Days

On the first day, drive two hours to the Iberian Peninsula's easternmost point, Cap de Creus, just north of **Cadaqués,** and see Dalí's house at Port Lligat. On Day 2, start working back toward Barcelona and points south. Stop in **Figueres** to visit the Dalí museum, then continue south to the history-rich city of **Girona.** On Day 3, have lunch at the medieval village of **Peratallada** and see the Iberian ruins of **Ullastret** before driving south and west past Barcelona to the monastery at **Santa Maria de Poblet.** Spend the night there after exploring the medieval town of Montblanc and the Cistercian triangle of monasteries completed by Santes Creus and Vallbona de les Monges. On Day 4, head for **Tarragona** for a browse through the ruins of what was the Roman Empire's capital of Hispania Citerior. On the last of this five-day tour, relax at the seaside resort of **Sitges,** where the sun setting into the Mediterranean is an unforgettable sight.

About the Restaurants

Catalonia's restaurants are increasingly and deservedly famous. From el Bulli (Cala Montjoi, near Roses) to the Celler de Can Roca (Girona), to Mas de Torrent (La Bisbal) and a host of other first-rate establishments, fine dining in Catalonia, which began in the hinterlands at the legendary Hotel Empordà, seems to have remained and proliferated in the country. But don't get the idea that you need to go to an internationally acclaimed restaurant to dine well. It's well known that El Bulli's star chef Ferran Adrià dines regularly at no-frills dives in Roses, where straight-up fresh fish is the day-in, day-out attraction. Northern Catalonia's Empordà region is known not only for seafood, but also for a rich assortment of inland and upland products. Beef from Girona's verdant pastureland is prized throughout Catalonia, while wild mushrooms from the Pyrenees and game from the Alberes range offer seasonal depth and breadth to menus across the region. From a simple beachside paella or *llobarro* (sea bass) at a *chiringuito* (shack) with tables on the sand, to the splendor of a meal at Celler de Can Roca or Mas de Torrent, playing culinary hopscotch through Catalonia is a good way to organize a tour.

Getting Here

Girona is the closest airport to the northern end of this area, and a good option if you're flying here from another part of Spain or the United Kingdom.

Barcelona's RENFE train system is an efficient and cheap way of discovering Catalonia. From Plaça Catalunya and Sants Station, RENFE accesses all the major towns, although you need to pay attention to take local trains where necessary, and along the Costa Brava, you may need to connect to your destination with a car. Catalonia also has excellent roads, although you'll encounter some high tolls on the *autopistas* (highways). ⇨ *For more information, see Planning.*

About the Hotels

Lodgings on the Costa Brava range from the finest, most sophisticated hotels to spartan *pensions* that are no more than a place to sleep and change clothes between beach, bar, restaurant, and disco outings. The better accommodations are usually well situated and have splendid views of the seascape. Many simple, comfortable hotels provide a perfectly adequate stopover and decent dining. If you plan to visit during the high season (July and August), be sure to book reservations well in advance at almost any hotel in this area, especially the Costa Brava, which remains one of the most popular summer resort areas in Spain. Many Costa Brava hotels close down in the winter season, between November and March.

DINING & LODGING PRICE CATEGORIES (IN EUROS)

	¢	$	$$	$$$	$$$$
Restaurants	Under €10	€10–€15	€16–€20	€21–€25	over €25
Hotels	under €85	€85–€120	€121–€150	€151–€175	over €175

Restaurant prices are per person for a main course at dinner. Hotel prices are for a standard double room for two people, excluding service and tax.

8

By James C. Townsend Updated by George Semler

Touring Catalonia—the nation within a nation (officially, an Autonomous Community) occupying the northeastern corner of Spain—is simplified by the fact that nearly all roads lead to or from Barcelona. But although Barcelona is the capital of Catalonia, the city is too cosmopolitan to be its authentic soul. To find the real Catalonia, remember that all roads also lead from Barcelona into the hinterlands.

It is widely known that Barcelona is a city of second sons who—the *hereu* (the heir and firstborn) having inherited the family lands—had to leave their country roots to seek their fortunes in the metropolis. Today even the city's hippest artists and busiest entrepreneurs still flee the capital every summer to return to the timeless inland villages and picturesque coastal hamlets of Catalonia.

In fact, the sea and the sierra are the two primal forces that define the spirit of Catalonia. The Mediterranean borders one side of the region and the Pyrenees the other, and legend ascribes the birth of Catalonia's very heart to the love of a shepherd for a mermaid (the region known as the Empordà). The result, so to speak, scattered Catalonia's landscape with memorable sights and places. The Costa Brava, a celebrated resort area, extends along nearly a hundred miles of coast from Blanes, at the mouth of the Tordera River some 65 km (40 mi) north of Barcelona, up to Portbou on the French border. It contains Catalonia's most idyllic *platjes* (beaches), often separated by rocky salients indented by innumerable *calas* (coves). Crowded with fig trees and vineyards, cacti and mimosa, eucalyptus trees, pines, birches, and its famous cork oak trees; and perfumed by the scents of lavender, thyme, and rosemary, this coast has both hidden, unspoiled villages, like Calella de Palafrugell, and resorts like Lloret de Mar, overrun with tourists. The glory of the Costa Brava Catalana—to use its full name—remains in those villages and hamlets where the outside walls of houses glow like mother-of-pearl in the sun. Such towns are a source of infinite pleasure to anyone with an eye for beauty, so it's little wonder that the surrealist master Salvador Dalí embraced Cadaqués as home, or that Marc Chagall found his "blue paradise" at Tossa de Mar. In unspoiled spots along this coast traditional and iconic scenes remain: fishing boats painted green and blue—the favorite color of Catalonia—drawn up on the sandy beach, women mending nets, wine being sipped in small bars and taverns.

Inland, Girona and Figueres are rich in art and architecture, while west of Barcelona the Montserrat sanctuary and the Cistercian monasteries at Poblet and Santes Creus are ancient pockets of spirituality just west of the Penedès winegrowing region. Tarragona, the Roman capital of the region, has the finest Roman ruins in Catalonia.

Those in search of more historical glamour will want to head inland to Girona, the biggest city of Northern Catalonia (population 92,186) and an amalgam of many ages and styles, symbolized by its cathedral, first built in splendid Romanesque and then transformed in willowy Gothic and overlaid in florid Catalan baroque. Arab, Christian, and Jewish communities all lived side by side in Girona, so you can wander down arcaded alleyways and along the Onyar River to discover not only the cathedral complex but the Banys Arabs (Arab Baths) and El Call, the most fully preserved historic Jewish neighborhood in Spain. All three are remnants of Girona's medieval golden age. A university town, Girona also has fashionable cafés, fine bookstores, and a full cultural calendar. Not far to its north lies another cultural must-do: Figueres and its spectacular Teatre-Museu Dalí, the leading shrine to the region's most famous native son.

Heading inland, you can see some of Catalonia's most extraordinary landscapes in the pillowy hills of Montseny or the eerie, volcanic Garrotxa region. Northwest of Barcelona is the most revered pilgrimage spot in Catalonia, the "sawtooth mountain" shrine of Montserrat—monastery of La Moreneta ("The Black Virgin") and legendarily the site where Parsifal found the Holy Grail.

8

PLANNING

GETTING HERE AND AROUND
AIR TRAVEL

AIRPORTS Girona's airport, alternately referred to as Girona–Costa Brava, Barcelona–Girona, or, simply Girona Airport, about 13 km (8 mi) south of the city, has become Catalonia's low-cost flight hub. Ryanair and other carriers fly regularly from this handy terminal an hour north of Barcelona. There is bus transportation between the airport and both Girona and Barcelona. **Barcelonabus** (✉ *Passeig de Sant Joan 52 Girona* ☎ *902/130014*) buses take an average of 75 minutes and cost €12 one-way, €21 round-trip. **Sagales** (☎ *902/130014*, ⊕ *www.sagales. com*) runs buses to various points along the coast from Girona–Costa Brava Airport.

Airport Information Girona–Costa Brava Airport (✉ *Afores s/n, Vilobí d'Onyar* ☎ *972/186600* ⊕ *www.girona-airport.net*). **Reus–Barcelona Airport** (✉ *Ctra. N240 [Km 4], Reus* ☎ *977/772204* ⊕ *www.reus-airport.es*).

CARRIERS   Besides the major Spanish carrier Iberia, Girona Airport serves a large number of charter and low-cost airlines, many of which are centralized under a single telephone number with the name Service Air.

Airlines and Contacts Air Europa (✉ *Afores s/n, Vilobí d'Onyar* ☎ *972/474014* ⊕ *www.aireuropa.com*). **Iberia** (✉ *Pl. Marqués de Camps 8 Girona* ☎ *972/474192*). **Monarch** (✉ *Afores s/n, Vilobí d'Onyar* ☎ *972/474017* ⊕ *www.monarch.com*). **Ryanair** (✉ *Afores s/n, Vilobí d'Onyar* ☎ *902/361550 or 807/220220* ⊕ *www.ryanair.com*). **Service Air** (☎ *972/186697* ⊕ *www.serviceair. com*). **Spanair** (✉ *Afores s/n, Vilobí d'Onyar* ☎ *902/131415* ⊕ *www.spanair.com*).

CAR RENTALS AT GIRONA– COSTA BRAVA AIRPORT   **Agencies Avis** (✉ *Girona–Costa Brava Airport Vilobí d'Onyar* ☎ *972/474333*). **Europcar** (✉ *Girona–Costa Brava Airport Vilobí d'Onyar* ☎ *972/209946*). **Hertz** (✉ *Girona–Costa Brava Airport Vilobí d'Onyar* ☎ *972/186619*).

BIKE TRAVEL

Most Spanish biking is done on road bikes. Watch out for the lack of a shoulder on many Spanish roads. Cars travel very fast, and though drivers are used to encountering bikers, they do not go out of their way to make you feel safe and cared for. Spain's numerous nature areas are perfect for mountain biking; many have specially marked trails.

Catalonia's alternating lush and rugged terrain has become more accessible to mountain bikers with the advent of *Centres BTT* ("BTT" stands for *bicicleta tot terreny,* Catalan for "mountain bike"; in Castilian, it's *bicicleta todo terreno*). BTT Centers are natural areas where a minimum of 100 km (62 mi) of biking trails have been—and continue to be—created. The bike circuits are signposted and marked according to difficulty, so families with kids and pros alike can access the trails. Overseen by the Federació Catalana de Ciclisme (Catalan Cycling Federation), these biking areas have information centers where you can pick up maps and tourist information; bicycle services, from rentals to repair; and showers and bathrooms. There are presently 14 BTT Centers all over Catalonia. A map pinpointing these centers and including contact information is available at the Generalitat de Catalunya BTT Web site (www.gencat.es).

It is better to rent a bike locally, rather than facing the logistics and complications of bringing your own bike with you. Bikes are usually not allowed on trains; they have to be packed and checked as luggage. Most Spanish nature areas have at least one agency offering mountain bikes for rent and, in many cases, guided biking tours. Check with park visitor centers for details. In addition, hotels in rural areas often have bikes available for guests, either for rent or for free.

Information Centres BTT/FCC Catalunya (✉ *Passeig de la Generalitat 21 Banyoles* ☎ *972/580639* ⊕ *www.gencat.es*).

BIKE RENTALS   **Alberg de Joventut Cerverí** (✉ *Carrer Ciutadans 9 Girona* ☎ *972/218003*). **Cicles Empordà** (✉ *Av. Gola Estany 33 Roses* ☎ *972/152478*). **Trafalch Bikes** (✉ *Carrer Major 14 Salt (2 km [1 mi] from Girona center)* ☎ *972/234943*). **The World Rent a Bike** (✉ *Camprodon i Artesa 14 Lloret de Mar* ☎ *636/302112*).

BOAT AND FERRY TRAVEL

Many short-cruise lines along the coast give you a chance to get a view of the Costa Brava from the sea. Visit the port areas in the main towns listed below and you will quickly spot several tourist cruise lines. Plan on spending around €15–€25, depending on the length of the cruise. The glass-keeled Nautilus boats for observation of the Islas Medes underwater park cost €15 and run on weekends only between October and March.

Boat and Ferry Information Creuers Badia de Roses (✉ *Passeig Marítim s/n, Roses* ☎ *972/255499*). **Marina Princess** (✉ *Passeig Marítim 34 L'Estartit* ☎ *972/750643* ⊕ *www.marinaprincess.com*). **Nautilus** (✉ *Passeig Marítim 23 L'Estartit* ☎ *972/751489* ⊕ *www.nautilus.es*). **Roses Serveis Marítims** (✉ *Passeig Marítim s/n, Roses* ☎ *972/152426*). **Viajes Marítimos** (✉ *Passeig Sant Pere 5 Lloret de Mar* ☎ *972/369095* ⊕ *www.viajesmaritimos.com*). **Viatges Marítims Costa Brava** (✉ *Aquarium, L'Estartit* ☎ *972/750880*).

BUS TRAVEL

Sarfa operates buses to Lloret, Sant Feliu de Guíxols, S'Agaró, Platja d'Aro, Palamós, Begur, Roses, Cadaqués, and other destinations on the Costa Brava. The bus line Barna Bus overlaps and complements some of these services; buses leave from the same Estació del Nord in Barcelona as Sarfa buses. Buses can also be caught at the Estació del Nord if you're heading south to destinations like Sitges or Tarragona. Teisa handles buses inland from Girona city and is next to the Girona train station. Other bus transportation hubs are Lloret de Mar and Figueres.

FARES AND SCHEDULES Only Girona and Tarragona have major municipal bus transportation services. The Old Quarter of Girona does not have bus service through its narrow streets. City TMG (Transporte Municipal Girona) buses in Girona run daily 7 AM–10 PM. The fare is €1.20 for multiple journeys; you can purchase a ticket for 10 rides for €8.70. Route maps are displayed at bus stops. In Tarragona, which is more spread out, city buses run daily from about 7 AM until after 10 PM. Extra lines in summer take people to the beaches. The fare is €1.20 for multiple journeys; you can purchase a ticket for 10 rides for €8.70.

Bus Information Barna Bus (☎ *93/232–0459*). **Figueres** (✉ *Pl. de l'Estació s/n* ☎ *972/673354*). **Girona Buses** (✉ *Pl. d'Espanya s/n* ☎ *972/212319*). **Lloret de Mar** (✉ *Ctra. Hostalric a Tossa s/n* ☎ *972/365788*). **Sarfa** (✉ *Estació del Nord, Alí Bei 80 Eixample, Barcelona* ☎ *93/265–1158 or 902/302025* Ⓜ *Arc de Triomf*). **Tarragona Buses** (✉ *C/Pere Martell s/n, Tarragona* ☎ *977/229126* ⊕ *www.autobuses-tarragona.es*). **Teisa** (✉ *Estació d'Autobusos, Pl. d'Espanya s/n, Girona* ☎ *972/200275* ⊕ *www.teisa-bus.com*).

CAR TRAVEL

The proximity of the towns and villages of northeastern Catalonia and good modern roads make for easy access to the many sights and points of interest. From Barcelona, the fastest way to the Costa Brava is to start up the inland AP7 *autopista* tollway toward Girona, and then take Sortida (Exit) 10 for Blanes, Lloret de Mar, Tossa de Mar, Sant Feliu de Guíxols, S'Agaró, Platja d'Aro, Palamós, Calella de Palafrugell, and Palafrugell. From Palafrugell, you can head inland for La Bisbal, and from there on to the city of Girona. From Girona you can easily

8

travel to the inland towns of Banyoles, Besalú, and Olot. To head to the middle section of the Costa Brava, get off at Sortida 6, the first exit after Girona; this will point you directly to the Iberian ruins of Ullastret. To reach the northern part of the Costa Brava, get off the AP7 before Figueres at Sortida 4 to get to L'Estartit, L'Escala, Empúries, Castelló d'Empúries, Aïguamolls de l'Empordà, Roses, Cadaqués, Sant Pere de Rodes, and Portbou. Sortida 4 will also take you directly to Figueres, Peralada, and the Alberes range. The old national route, NII, is slow, heavily traveled, and more dangerous, especially in summer.

To reach Sitges from Barcelona, take the autopista C32 south along the coast; the AP7–E15 highway also runs south inland to Tarragona. To head west toward Lleida and the monasteries of Santes Creus and Santa Maria de Poblet and the medieval town of Montblanc, and on to Madrid, take the AP7 south from Barcelona and turn west onto the AP2–E90 at L'Arboç. To get to Montserrat, take highway A18 off the AP7 from Barcelona.

ROAD CONDITIONS Catalonia is a geographically undulating country, with a few interspersed mountain ranges such as the Montseny, just north of Barcelona; only the Pyrenees mountains are especially rugged. Here roads twist and turn, and to get anywhere takes considerable time. All the towns on the Costa Brava are interconnected by a road network that is very congested in summer; traffic can be slow and frustrating.

CAR RENTAL **Agencies Atesa** (✉ *Plaça d'Espanya s/n Girona* ☎ *972/221364 or 902/100101*). **Avis** (✉ *Plaça d'Espanya Girona* ☎ *972/224664* ✉ *Enric Granados 24 Lloret de Mar* ☎ *972/373023* ✉ *España 24 Sitges* ☎ *93/894–0287*). **Europcar** (✉ *Carrer del Freu s/n, L'Estartit* ☎ *972/751731* ✉ *Pl. de l'Estació s/n, Figueres* ☎ *972/ 673434* ✉ *Ctra. Blanes a Tossa s/n, Lloret de Mar* ☎ *972/363366*). **Hertz** (✉ *Pl. de l'Estació s/n, Girona* ☎ *972/210108* ✉ *Pl. de l'Estació s/n, Figueres* ☎ *972/672801* ✉ *Artur Carbonell 27 Sitges* ☎ *93/894–8986*).

TRAIN TRAVEL
Most of the Costa Brava is *not* served directly by railroad. A local line heads up the coast from Barcelona, but takes you only to Blanes; from there it turns inland and connects at Maçanet-Massanes with the main line up to France. Direct trains only stop at major towns, such as Girona, Flaçà, and Figueres. If you want to get off at a small town, be sure to take a local train; or you can take a fast direct train to, let's say, Girona, and get off and wait for a local to go by (the words for local, express, and direct are basically the same in Spanish as in English). The stop on the main line for the middle section of the Costa Brava is Flaçà, where you can take a bus or taxi to your final destination. Girona and Figueres are two other towns with major bus stations that feed out to the towns of the Costa Brava. The train does serve the last three towns on the north end of the Costa Brava, Llançà, Colera, and Portbou. In the southern direction, Sitges and Tarragona are also served directly by train. A short railroad line serves Montserrat, and takes you to Monistrol, where you can catch the funicular to the monastery.

The Estació de França near the port, Barcelona's original train terminal, handles only certain local trains, since Sants-Estació became the main station in the late 1980s.

With its picturesque rivers, Girona is often called the Spanish Venice.

Train Information Estació de França (✉ *Marquès de l'Argentera s/n, Born-Ribera, Barcelona* ☎ *93/496-3464*). **Passeig de Gràcia** (✉ *At Aragó, Eixample, Barcelona* ☎ *902/240202*). **Sants-Estació** (✉ *Pl. dels Països Catalans s/n, Eixample, Barcelona* ☎ *902/240202* ⊕ *www.renfe.es*).

TOURS

For tours to Montserrat, contact Julià Tours or Pullmantur.

Fees and Schedules Julià Tours (✉ *Ronda Universitat 5 Eixample, Barcelona* ☎ *93/317-6454* ⊕ *www.juliatravel.com*). **Pullmantur** (✉ *Gran Via de les Corts Catalanes 645 Eixample, Barcelona* ☎ *93/317-1297* ⊕ *www.pullmantur-spain.com*).

TRAVEL AGENCIES

Local Agents Alfa Tours (✉ *Pl. de Francesc Calvet i Rubalcaba 5 Girona* ☎ *972/220381*). **Crom Raid & Adventure** (✉ *Av. de les Alegries 12 Lloret de Mar* ☎ *972/365412*). **Viatges Berga** (✉ *Carrer Sant Agustí 11 Tarragona* ☎ *977/252610*).

VISITOR INFORMATION

The tourist offices throughout this area are very helpful and well informed. Don't hesitate to go to one if you have any problem or question about any place you will be visiting. The Patronat de Turisme Costa Brava Girona, a consortium that deals with all tourist activities in northeastern Catalonia, has a useful Web site.

Tourist Information Patronat de Turisme Costa Brava Girona (☎ *972/208401* ⊕ *www.costabrava.org*). **Blanes** (✉ *Pl. de Catalunya s/n* ☎ *972/330348*). **Cadaqués** (✉ *Cotxe 2-A* ☎ *972/258315*). **Figueres** (✉ *Pl. del Sol s/n* ☎ *972/503155*). **Girona** (✉ *Rambla de la Llibertat 1* ☎ *972/226575*).

Lloret de Mar (✉ *Pl. de la Vila s/n* ☎ *972/364735*). **Palafrugell** (✉ *Pl. de la Església s/n* ☎ *972/611820*). **Palamós** (✉ *Passeig de Mar s/n* ☎ *972/600550*). **Platja d'Aro** (✉ *Mossèn Jacint Verdaguer 4* ☎ *972/817179*). **Roses** (✉ *Av. de Rhode 101* ☎ *972/257331*). **Sant Feliu de Guíxols** (✉ *Pl. Monestir s/n* ☎ *972/820051*). **Sitges** (✉ *Carrer Sínia Morera 1* ☎ *93/894–4251*). **Tarragona** (✉ *Carrer Major 39* ☎ *977/250795*). **Tossa de Mar** (✉ *Av. de Pelegrí 25* ☎ *972/340108*).

THE COSTA BRAVA

The Costa Brava is a nearly unbroken series of sheer rock cliffs dropping down to crystalline waters, capriciously punctuated with innumerable coves and tiny beaches on narrow inlets, each of which is called a *cala*. Hundreds of bays and peninsulas calm the waters before they hit land, allowing fishermen to make a living and also, in centuries gone by, pirates to gain plunder. When pirates plied the Mediterranean in the 16th and 17th centuries and threatened the Catalan coast, towns were built inland away from danger and the coastline was all but deserted. Miguel de Cervantes, the author of *Don Quixote,* was captured by Barbary pirates in 1575 and held for five years in Algiers (recent scholarship has concluded that he was captured on the Costa Brava's Bay of Roses). Today the only plundering is done by hotel owners, who make fortunes every summer from the busloads of tour groups that swamp the Costa in high season.

This Costa Brava is a comparatively recent discovery. The first tourists arrived at the beginning of the 20th century: well-to-do families from Barcelona, who came to escape the ovenlike temperatures of the big city by bathing along the shore. They were trailed, in turn, by artists and bohemians. Picasso, Marc Chagall, Santiago Rusiñol, and Salvador Dalí all came and were swiftly conquered as much by the coast's natural charms as by the physical beauty of its inhabitants (Tossa de Mar's Greek-profiled villagers once attracted a large colony of artists). Today different styles of tourism have developed along the Costa Brava: one aimed at mass tourism, at resorts like Lloret de Mar and Roses, another found at more selective, family-oriented ports of call like Cadaqués and Tossa de Mar.

Ascending the coast of Northern Catalonia's Girona province—ranging from Blanes (north of Barcelona) to Portbou near the border with France—the Costa Brava is a succession of inlets, bays, and coves. A landscape of lush deep-green mountains serves as a backdrop to the rocky shore and aquamarine foreground of the coast and sandy beaches, many dotted by modern tourist developments. Inland there is more tranquillity, with small towns and villages that remain relatively untouched. The landscape is one of carefully tended fields and orchards, vineyards and olive groves, and tree-covered hills. Here and there small fortified towns recall the turbulent history of these places dating back to the Middle Ages or earlier. You will quickly see why Catalonia acquired its name from the ancient Latin word *castellum,* meaning "fortified settlement."

BLANES

60 km (37 mi) northeast of Barcelona, 45 km (28 mi) south of Girona.

The southernmost outpost of the Costa Brava, Blanes was first settled by Iberian tribes, followed by the Romans in the 1st century BC. The town's castle of Sant Joan, on a mountain overlooking the town, goes back to the 11th century. The watchtower along the coastline was built in the 16th century to protect against Barbary pirates. Blanes was flourishing even before the tourism boom of the late 1950s, with light industry (especially textiles) and a large fishing fleet. But its long beaches—the southernmost strands in Girona Province—and adjacent coves were too perfect to be passed up by northern Europeans flocking to Spain in search of sun and low prices. Today many travelers skip the working port of Blanes, but it's a must-do for green-thumbers, thanks to the area's celebrated botanical gardens.

The Costa Brava begins here with five different beaches, running from Punta Santa Anna on the far side of the port—a tiny cove with a pebbly beach at the bottom of a chasm encircled by towering cliffs, fragrant pines, and deep blue-green waters—to the 2½-km-long (1½-mi-long) S'Abanell beach, which draws the crowds.

EXPLORING

★ **Jardí Botànic Marimurtra.** Terrace upon terrace of exotic plants grip the steeply slanting hillside above the sea at this garden created by the German Karl Faust in 1928. It holds more than 7,000 species, the collection of cacti from the arid regions of South Africa and Central America being especially notable. Poisonous, medicinal, and aromatic plants, ferns, cork, kermes (scarlet oak), and conifers flourish in lush variety. ⊠ *Passeig Karl Faust 1017300* ☎ *972/330826* ⊕ *www.jbotanicmarimurtra. org* 🏷 *€6* ⊘ *Apr.–Oct., daily 9–6; Nov.–Mar., weekdays 10–5, weekends 10–2.*

★ **Jardí Botànic Pinya de Rosa.** An impressive 4,000 plant species are contained here. Created in 1945 by industrial engineer Dr. Fernando Riviere de Caralt, the botanical garden is noted for its collection of cacti (some as tall as 50 feet), aloe, century, and yucca plants. American botanists consider its collection of more than 600 species of *Opuntia* (prickly pear) one of the finest in the world. ⊠ *Platja de Santa Cristina* ☎ *972/355290* 🏷 *€5* ⊘ *Daily 9–6.*

NIGHTLIFE AND THE ARTS

☾ The summer event in Blanes that everyone waits for is the **fireworks competition,** held every night at 10:30 July 21–27; it coincides with the town's yearly festival. The fireworks are launched over the water from a rocky outcropping in the middle of the seaside promenade known as Sa Palomera, while people watch from the beach and surrounding area as more gunpowder is burned in half an hour than at the battle of Trafalgar.

8

SPORTS AND THE OUTDOORS

Launches from **Dofijets Boats** (☎ 609/356301) and **Viajes Marítims** (☎ 616/909100) on the harbor front can take you up the coast to neighboring towns and beaches from May through September.

WHERE TO STAY

¢–$ 🖫 **Horitzó.** Overlooking the main Blanes beach, this is the town's best hotel. Though far from luxurious, rooms are adequate and the balconies overlooking the Mediterranean give the place its main charm. Thirty minutes from Barcelona by car and an hour via a panoramic railroad along the edge of the beach, this is an economical and viable alternative for visiting the Costa Brava and Barcelona as well. **Pros:** handy to Barcelona by train, a peaceful beach hideaway. **Cons:** Blanes can be over-touristed in summer, not really far enough from Barcelona to get a sense of what the Costa Brava is really all about. ✉ *Passeig Marítim S'Abanell 11* ☎ *972/330400* ⊕ *www.hotelhoritzo.com* 💭 *110 rooms* ⚒ *In-room: Wi-Fi. In-hotel: restaurant* ☰ *AE, DC, MC, V* ⊗ *Closed Nov.–Mar.* ❑ *EP.*

LLORET DE MAR

10 km (6 mi) north of Blanes, 67 km (42 mi) northeast of Barcelona, 43 km (27 mi) south of Girona.

The Costa Brava officially begins at Lloret de Mar, but one look at it and you might be tempted to head back to Barcelona. The many concrete-tower hotels fill up with thousands of young people on a tight budget out to drink, dance, and work on a tan. Of course, if you're looking for that spring-break atmosphere—this is the place. Swamped by faux English pubs and German beer gardens, the town also offers quiet pedestrian zones and some gorgeous architecture to admire. The town's cultural opportunities range from concerts and art openings to the Iberian ruins at Turó Rodó and the medieval castle of Sant Joan.

If you want nothing between you and the sun, head to the *cala* (cove) near Lloret de Mar called Boadella and reserved for nudists. Given the heavy tourist buildup, the beach that stretches along the promenade is Lloret de Mar's main attraction, but it's usually packed, and you'll probably have to put up with your neighbor's boom box. At the northern end of this strand is Sa Caleta, a cove that offers more sheltered swimming. On the twisting scenic road between Lloret and Tossa de Mar is the small pristine Cala Morisca (Moorish Cove).

EXPLORING

Jardins de Santa Clotilde. These neo-Renaissance gardens designed in 1919 by architect Nicolau Maria Rubió i Tudurí and based on Florence's Boboli Gardens, are characterized by an emphasis on plants and shrubbery—flower lovers should look elsewhere. ✉ *Ctra. de Blanes, Km 652* ☎ *972/364735* 💶 *€6* ⊗ *June–Oct., Tues. 4–7, Wed.–Sun. 10:30–1 and 4–7.*

Santa Cristina. Three kilometers (2 mi) south of Lloret is this sheltered sandy cove with an 18th-century chapel amid soaring pine and eucalyptus trees that grow to the shore. The allegorical mural painting by

Joaquín Sorolla entitled *Catalunya* on view at the Hispanic Society of America in New York City was purportedly modeled in part on this landscape. Every July there is a pilgrimage by boat to the chapel. You can take a break for lunch to enjoy a succulent fish paella at one of the beach's three *chiringuitos* (makeshift beach restaurants under awnings). ⊠ *Signposted off Ctra. de Blanes*

WHERE TO STAY

$–$$ **⊡ Roger de Flor Palace.** This dignified villa stands in stark contrast to the cookie-cutter concrete columns of Lloret. On the eastern edge of town, it has the finest panoramic views of any lodging in the vicinity. The gardens, with a saltwater pool and geraniums, bougainvillea, and palms, add an elegant touch. High-ceilinged rooms with somewhat threadbare furnishings are simple yet comfortable. L'Estelat restaurant ($–$$) is a prime spot for gazing at the Mediterranean—and dining on local fare such as *ensalada de bacalao con habas* (cod salad with broad beans). Pros: unbeatable views and traditional surroundings. Cons: surrounding town excessively tourist-ridden; restaurant often serves large groups. ⊠ *Turó de l'Estelat s/n* ☎ *972/364800* ⊕ *www.hotelrogerdeflor.com* ⌁ *87 rooms* ⚿ *In-room: Wi-Fi. In-hotel: Internet terminal, restaurant, tennis court, pool* ☐ *AE, DC, MC, V* ☉ *Closed Nov.–Mar.* ⦿⊦*EP.*

NIGHTLIFE

Notorious as the Costa Brava's hottest nightlife destination, Lloret de Mar explodes after dark. Foreigners and locals of all ages rage until dawn at the happening **Moby's** (⊠ *Av. Just Marlès 49* ☎ *972/364214*). Around the corner from the manic nightlife beacon Moby's is **Tropics** (⊠ *Carrer Ferran Agulló 47* ☎ *972/364214*), an electronically laser-lighted and audio-powered brawl with two dance floors and five bars. **Bumper's** (⊠ *Pl. del Carme 4* ☎ *972/362071*) is another hot Lloret de Mar music bar and disco. **Hollywood Disco** (⊠ *Ctra. de Tossa 5* ☎ *972/643693*) may be the wildest scene of all on the Costa Brava, with go-go dancers and strippers.

TOSSA DE MAR

11 km (7 mi) north of Lloret de Mar, 80 km (50 mi) northeast of Barcelona, 41 km (25 mi) south of Girona.

Set around a blue buckle of a bay, Tossa de Mar is a symphony in two parts: the Vila Vella, or the Old Town—a knotted warren of steep, narrow, cobblestone streets with many restored buildings (some dating back to the 14th century)—and the Vila Nova, or the New Town. The former is encased in medieval walls and towers, but the New Town is open to the sea and is itself a lovely district threaded by 18th-century lanes. Girdling the Old Town, on the Cap de Tossa promontory that juts out into the sea, the 12th-century walls and towers at water's edge are a local pride and joy, considered the only example of a fortified medieval town on the entire Catalan coast.

Artist Marc Chagall vacationed in Tossa de Mar for four decades, and called it his "blue paradise." Ava Gardner filmed the 1951 Hollywood extravaganza *Pandora and the Flying Dutchman* here (a statue dedicated to her stands on a terrace on the medieval walls); today the film is compelling for its location scenes of an untouched Costa Brava. Things may have changed since those days, but all in all this beautiful village retains much of the magic of the unspoiled Costa Brava. The primary beach at Tossa de Mar is the Platja Gran (Big Beach) in front of the town beneath the walls, and just next to it is Mar Menuda (Little Sea). Small, fat, colorfully painted fishing boats—maybe the same ones that caught your dinner—are pulled up onto the beach, heightening the charm.

The main bus station (the local tourist office is here) is on Plaça de les Nacions Sense Estat. Take Avinguda Ferran and Avinguda Costa Brava to head down the slope to the waterfront and the Old Town, which is entered by the Torre de les Hores, and head to the Vila Vella's heart, the Gothic church of Sant Vicenç. Then just saunter around and take a dip in the Middle Ages.

EXPLORING

Museu Municipal de Tossa de Mar. Housed in the Palau Batlle, this 12th-century palace named for the Batlle family displays ancient Roman objects and mosaics from the Vila Romana. It also has paintings by 19th-century Catalan painters and by Marc Chagall, Foujita, Masson, and others. ⊠ *Pl. del Pintor Roig i Soler 117320* ☏ *972/340709* ☜ *€3* ⊙ *Mid-June–mid-Sept., daily 10–8; mid-Sept.–mid-June, Tues.–Sun. 11–1 and 3–5.*

Vila Romana. The Romans knew a good place when they saw it, as Turissa's (the name they gave Tossa de Mar) famous ancient villa, uncovered in 1914, proves. At *Els Ametllers* (the Almond Trees), near the back of the town and bounded on one side by Avinguda Pelegrí, are the ruins of this villa, which include an oil press, warehouses, and several rooms with magnificent mosaic pavements (one of which bears the owner's name: Salve Vitale). Additional discoveries revealed a sunken swimming pool, a hot-air heating system, and a monumental fountain—all indications this family lived in imperial luxury. The villa is not open to public view, but you can see many of the excavated finds in the Museu Municipal de Tossa de Mar.

WHERE TO EAT

$$–$$$ ✗ **La Cuina de Can Simon.** Elegantly rustic, this restaurant right beside the
CATALAN town's medieval walls serves a combination of classical cuisine with very up-to-date touches. The *caldereta de gambas con verduras y rebanadas de pan con ajo* (shrimp bouillabaisse with vegetables and garlic bread) is a great winter dish. The service is top-shelf, from the welcoming tapa with a glass of *cava* (sparkling wine) to the little pastries accompanying coffee. ⊠ *Portal 2417320* ☏ *972/341269* ⊕ *www.lacuinadecansimo.es* ⊟ *AE, DC, MC, V* ⊙ *Closed last 2 wks of Nov.; last 2 wks of Jan.; and Mon. and Tues. Oct.–May. No dinner Sun.*

$–$$ ✗ **Las Tapas de Can Sisó.** Tucked in under Tossa's defensive walls, this
CATALAN usually booming place has a good-sized terrace and a cozy countrified dining room where tapas, *raciones* (small portions), and full meals are served with elegance and style. Try the *croquetas de espinacas* (spinach croquettes), the *brandada* (purée of cod), or the *cim i tomba* (a Catalan

fish and potato stew). ⊠ *Pl. de las Armas 117320* ☎ *972/340708* ▤ *AE, DC, MC, V* ☺ *Closed Nov. 10–Dec. 10 and Mon. Oct.–May.*

WHERE TO STAY

$$$–$$$$ ⊞ **Gran Hotel Reymar.** Built in the unornamented rationalist style in the
★ 1960s on a spectacular rocky promontory at the edge of the sea, this hotel has graceful modern lines that contrast with the jagged rocks around it—and it's just a 10-minute walk from the historic walls of the Old Town. Reymar has fairly dazzling restaurants and bars. Rooms have satellite TV, marble-covered bathrooms, fine modern furniture, and seafront balconies. **Pros:** long on comforts and technology. **Cons:** short on charm and architectural grace. ⊠ *Platja de Mar Menuda s/n,* ☎ *972/340312* ⊕ *www.ghreymar.com* ⌇ *148 rooms, 18 suites* ⚥ *In-room: Wi-Fi. In-hotel: 4 restaurants, bars, tennis court, pools, some pets allowed* ▤ *AE, DC, MC, V* ☺ *Closed Nov.– Apr. 15* ⧦*EP.*

¢–$ ⊞ **Hotel Capri.** Maria Eugènia Serrat, a native Tossan, displays local hospitality at her small family hotel. Set on the beach with the medieval walls looming behind it, the hotel has a super location. Rooms are individually decorated in different styles and colors. **Pros:** very warm and personal hostessing; good combination of medieval surroundings and modern technology. **Cons:** tight quarters in general; rooms a little small. ⊠ *Passeig del Mar 17* ☎ *972/340358* ⊕ *www.hotelcapritossa. com* ⌇ *22 rooms* ⚥ *In-room: Wi-Fi. In-hotel: Wi-Fi hotspot, some pets allowed* ▤ *MC, V* ☺ *Closed Nov.–Mar.* ⧦*BP.*

$–$$ ⊞ **Hotel Diana.** Built by the Moderniste architect Antoni Falguera, this Art Nouveau gem is one of the finest places on the Costa Brava to cozy up with a glass of sherry and while away the early evening. Overlooking a beach, the Diana also contains an enticing inner courtyard— a lush garden with palm trees, flowers, and fountains, and inside, a stunning Art Nouveau fireplace that incorporates a bust by Frederic Marés of Falguera's wife. Guest rooms have contemporary furnishings. **Pros:** first-rate art and architecture; verdant surroundings. **Cons:** somewhat lacking in amenities; no Internet terminal. ⊠ *Pl. de Espanya 6* ☎ *972/341886* ⊕ *www.diana-hotel.com* ⌇ *20 rooms, 1 suite* ⚥ *In-room: Wi-Fi. In-hotel: bar, some pets allowed* ▤ *AE, DC, MC, V* ☺ *Closed Nov.–Easter* ⧦*BP.*

¢ ⊞ **Hotel Sant March.** This family hotel in the center of town, run by Francesc Zucchitello, is just two minutes from the beach. His wife and mother-in-law care for an interior garden that is the envy of many. All rooms open onto the garden—making for much-appreciated tranquility in a sometimes hectic town. **Pros:** intimate, family-run hotel with a warm personal touch. **Cons:** though the rooms are largely shielded from the midtown din, the location is at the very eye of the storm. ⊠ *Av. del Pelegrí 2* ☎ *972/340078* ⊕ *www.hotelsantmarch.en.eresmas. com* ⌇ *29 rooms* ⚥ *In-hotel: Wi-Fi hotspot, bar* ▤ *AE, DC, MC, V* ☺ *Closed Oct.–Mar.* ⧦*BP.*

8

SANT FELIU DE GUÍXOLS

23 km (14 mi) north of Tossa de Mar, 100 km (62 mi) northeast of Barcelona, 37 km (23 mi) southeast of Girona.

In this fishing and shipping town set in a small bay, handsome Moderniste mansions line the seafront promenade, recalling the town's former wealth from the cork industry. In front of that, an arching beach of fine white sand leads around to the fishing harbor at its north end. Behind the promenade, a well-preserved old quarter of narrow streets and squares leads to a 10th-century gateway with horseshoe arches (all that remains of a pre-Romanesque monastery); nearby, a church still stands that combines Romanesque, Gothic, and baroque styles.

Indeed, the next time you open a bottle of vintage champagne, you might say a little prayer for this venerable town. Surrounded by dark-green cork forests (as is much of northeastern Catalonia), it first found its place in the sun during the 17th century, when French abbot Dom Pérignon, on a trip to the Benedictine monastery of Sant Pere de Rodes, 64 km (40 mi) north of here, discovered that the properties of cork allow it to contain the high pressure that builds up inside a champagne bottle. Before long, the cork forests of this town became famous, with the stripped bark of the cork oak (*quercus suber*) used to make cork stoppers (and other products such as insulation). Before the Dom's discovery, hemp plugs soaked in oil or wooden bungs had been used. At first corks were made by hand, each one cut to shape by a craftsman. It was a good job, and cork makers, paid by the piece, enjoyed a certain social standing. Eventually, of course, power-driven blades and punches took over, but not before many Sant Feliu de Guíxols residents made their fortunes.

EXPLORING

Museu d'Història de la Ciutat. Interesting exhibits about the town's cork and fishing trades are housed in this museum. It also displays local archaeological finds. ⊠ *Carrer Abadia s/n* ☎ *972/821575* 🎟 *Free* ⊙ *July–Sept., Tues.–Sat. 11–2 and 5–8, Sun. 11–2; Oct.–June, Tues.–Sat. 11–2 and 4–7, Sun. 11–2.*

WHERE TO EAT AND STAY

$$–$$$
CATALAN
★

✕ **El Dorado Mar.** Around the southern end of the beach, perched over the entrance to the harbor, this superb family restaurant offers fine fare at unbeatable prices. Whether straight seafood such as *lubina* (sea bass) or *dorada* (gilthead bream) or *revuelto de setas* (eggs scrambled with wild mushrooms), everything served here is fresh and flavorful. ⊠ *Passeig Irla 15* ☎ *972/326286* ▭ *AE, DC, MC, V* ⊙ *No dinner mid-Oct.–Easter.*

$$
CATALAN
★

✕ **Eldorado.** Lluis Cruanya, who once owned Barcelona's top restaurant and another in Manhattan, has done it again with Eldorado. With his daughter Suita running the dining room and Iván Álvarez as chef, this smartly designed restaurant with contemporary lines a block back from the beach serves tasty morsels from *llom de tonyina a la plancha amb tomàquets agridolços, ceba i chíps d'escarchofa* (grilled tuna with pickled tomato, baby onions, and artichoke chips) to *llobarro rostít amb emulsió de cítrics i espàrrecs trigueros* (roast sea-bass with a citric emulsion and wild asparagus), all cooked to perfection. Try the *patates braves* (new potatoes in *allioli* and hot sauce), as good as any in Catalonia. ⊠ *Rambla Vidal 1917220* ☎ *972/821414* ▭ *AE, DC, MC, V* ⊘ *Closed Tues. Oct.–Easter.*

¢ 🏨 **Can Segura.** Half a block in from the beach, Can Segura is the best deal
★ in town, with home-cooked seafood and upland specialties. The dining room ($-$$) is always full, with customers waiting their turn in the street, but the staff is good at finding spots at the jovially long communal tables. Small but proper rooms are available for overnight sojourns. **Pros:** two minutes from the beach, with great-value dining downstairs. **Cons:** no Wi-Fi or Internet terminal, weak on technology and amenities, a budget choice. ⊠ *Carrer de Sant Pere 11 17220* ☎ *972/321009* ⇱ *11 rooms* ⚹ *In-hotel: restaurant, bar* ▭ *AE, DC, MC, V* ⊘ *Closed Nov.–Easter (except New Year's Eve weekend)* ⦿ *EP.*

S'AGARÓ

★ *3 km (2 mi) north of Sant Feliu, 103 km (64 mi) northeast of Barcelona, 42 km (26 mi) south of Girona.*

S'Agaró is one of the Costa Brava's most elegant clusters of villas and seaside mansions, built up around S'Agaró Vell, a fashionable private development that often hosted the likes of John Wayne and Cole Porter. Set by the sea, S'Agaró itself has a delightful promenade along the seawall from La Gavina—the noted hotel in S'Agaró Vell—to Sa Conca beach.

S'Agaró Vell, by the beach of Sant Pol, is one of the earliest examples in Spain of a tourist resort created specifically as such. It was designed by poet and architect Rafael Masó i Valentí in the fashionable style of the time known as Noucentisme: an alluring post–Art Nouveau return to a more classical style. The promoter was the visionary Josep Ensesa, son of a wealthy Girona industrialist, who in the 1920s created S'Agaró Vell as a luxury residential resort aimed exclusively at the pleasures of summer. Today more than 50 homes have been built—all with the well-proportioned, subdued lines that Noucentisme derived from Greek and Roman classical architecture, each required to adhere to the stylistic specifications originally established by Masó.

WHERE TO EAT AND STAY

$$-$$$ ✗ **Villa Mas.** For excellent dining at nonstratospheric costs in S'Agaró,
CATALAN this Moderniste villa with a lovely turn-of-the-20th-century zinc bar
★ inside works with fresh products recently retrieved from the Mediterranean. The terrace is a popular and shady spot just across the road from the beach, and the clientele is predominantly young and savvy. ⊠ *Platja de Sant Pol 95* ☎ *972/822526* ▭ *AE, DC, MC, V* ⊘ *Closed Mon. Oct.– Mar. and Dec. 12–Jan 12. No dinner weekdays Oct.–Mar.*

$$$$ 🏨 **L'Hostal de la Gavina.** This is the place for the last remnants of Costa
Fodor's Choice Brava chic. Big rollers such as Cole Porter followed upper-class couples
★ from Barcelona who began honeymooning here in the 1930s. In S'Agaró Vell, on the eastern corner of Sant Pol beach, the hotel is an outstanding display of design and cuisine (don't miss the fresh fish and seafood), opened in 1932 by Josep Ensesa. Guest rooms have fine wood furniture

DID YOU KNOW?

The artist Marc Chagall loved to vacation in Tossa de Mar and felt inspired by its vivid blue ocean landscape.

and Oriental rugs. Tennis, golf, and riding are nearby, and on a summer evening the loggia overlooking the sea is sublime. **Pros:** superbly decorated and appointed; wonderful traditional European environment. **Cons:** hard on the budget *and* habit-forming. ⊠ *Pl. de la Rosaleda s/n,* ☎ *972/321100* ⊕ *www.lagavina.com* ⊅ *58 rooms, 16 suites* ⚬ *In-room: Wi-Fi, safe. In-hotel: restaurant, pool, tennis court, gym, some pets allowed* ⊟ *AE, DC, MC, V* ⊗ *Closed Nov.–Easter (except New Year's Eve weekend)* ⧈ *EP.*

PLATJA D'ARO

3 km (2 mi) north of S'Agaró, 108 km (64 mi) northeast of Barcelona, 39 km (24 mi) southeast of Girona.

Platja d'Aro has 3 km (2 mi) of splendid beach to recommend it, though it is heavily built up. Like many other places on the coast, it was a knot of fishing shacks attached to the inland main town of Castell d'Aro, but tourist development changed that.

WHERE TO EAT AND STAY

$–$$

CATALAN

✗ **Aradi.** This typical Costa Brava tavern and restaurant serves fare based on market products bought daily. Try the *esparracat d'ous amb patates i gambes a l'all* (fried eggs with potatoes and garlic shrimp), a star dish. The terrace is the place to be year round when the weather is good. ⊠ *Av. Cavall Bernat 78* ☎ *972/817376* ⊕ *www.restaurantaradi. com* ⊟ *AE, DC, MC, V* ⊗ *Closed Mon. No dinner Sun. Nov.–Mar.*

$$
★

⧓ **Costa Brava.** Built on the rocks over the beach, this family-run hotel and restaurant offers splendid views from comfortable (though not luxurious) rooms facing the sea, as well as from the bar and sitting room. Rooms are bright and airy but indistinguished though contemporary in design and furnishings. The restaurant, Can Polda ($–$$), is a traditional dining space with sea views. **Pros:** right *in* the Mediterranean over the beach; great panoramas. **Cons:** the design of the building itself and the rooms and furnishings is unremarkable. ⊠ *Ctra. de Palamós – Punta d'en Ramis 17250* ☎ *972/817308* ⊕ *www.hotelcostabrava.com* ⊅ *57 rooms* ⚬ *In-hotel: restaurant, bar* ⊟ *AE, DC, MC, V* ⊗ *Restaurant closed Nov. 21–Mar. 4* ⧈ *BP.*

NIGHTLIFE

Come summer, Platja d'Aro is a major party hub on the Costa Brava, overflowing with young foreigners and Spaniards who carouse at the many nightclubs and discos and then crash on the beach or in pensions. One of the most popular—and pulsating—discos in town is **Ithaka** (⊠ *Parc d'Aro* ☎ *972/826537*) in the new Parc d'Aro residential neighborhood and raging in summer. Crowds of people seek out the **Ático** (⊠ *Av. Cavall Bernat 44* ☎ *972/819152*) for dancing and partying. **Carroll's** (⊠ *Av. S'Agaró* ☎ *972/818410*), a standout for its antique-car DJ booth, tends to fill with a young crowd in the early evening. **900 House Club** (⊠ *Carrer Església 54* ☎ *972/814230*) plays—you guessed it—house music for hotties and their hovering entourage until dawn.

PALAMÓS

7 km (4 mi) north of Platja d'Aro, 109 km (68 mi) northeast of Barce-lona, 46 km (29 mi) southeast of Girona.

Facing south, Palamós is a working harbor town sited on a headland that protects it from the prevailing north wind. The town was founded as a royal port in 1277 by the king of Aragón, Peter II, and the Old Quarter is well preserved, although its walls (built in the 16th century as protection against pirates) are no longer standing.

EXPLORING

★ **Castell.** To see what the Costa Brava looked liked before development, visit the beach Castell, north of Palamós and the better-known La Fosca beach. As the road emerges from a thick green Mediterranean forest of evergreen oak, pine, and spiny underbrush, you are greeted by 280 yards of wide, sandy beach. At one end are several fishing shacks, with a couple of tumbledown restaurants, their awnings scattered along the beach. No other buildings, let alone apartments or hotels, block the sight, so it's no wonder Castell has been praised for its scenic beauty. The Catalan government purchased a part of the Castell area and declared it to be a "place of natural interest," with an eye to keeping developers out.

On the southern end of the beach overlooking the cove is **Mas Juny,** the (still privately owned) farmhouse that once belonged to Josep Maria Sert (1874–1945), the Catalan mural painter who was one of the most acclaimed painters of the 1930s and '40s. With the money he received for decorating New York City's Waldorf-Astoria hotel he bought Mas Juny in 1929 for his third wife and transformed this typical Catalan stone farmhouse into an elegant retreat. The Serts' extravagant par-ties drew the likes of Marlene Dietrich and Baron de Rothschild. At the northern end of the beach, atop the rocky promontory of Agulla (Needle) del Castell, are extensive, partially excavated **Iberian ruins.** Unlike other such remains uncovered in urban settings, these ruins are set in the natural habitat where the people lived 2,600 years ago.

Hidden in the woods a 10-minute walk behind the beach is a studio that painter Salvador Dalí designed and had built. It has an irregularly shaped door and is known as **La Barraca de la Porta Torta** (The Shack of the Crooked Door). The studio is open to the public.

To get to Castell, take the road north from the port of Palamós and look for signs to La Fosca; Castell is past La Fosca, on a sand road. This will bring you there in a few minutes. Arrive early; it gets crowded in summer.

Fish Market. Palamós has the second-largest fishing fleet on the Costa Brava, and its bounty is on display at the highly esteemed fish market, including Palamós shrimp, among the most prized in Spain. Sleek sea bass, gargoyle-ish anglerfish, hefty grouper, and colorful rockfish are auctioned, making the market an exciting place to visit when the fish-ing boats begin to come in around six o'clock in the evening. ⊠ *Moll Pesquer s/n* ☏ *No phone*

Museu de la Pesca. The world of fishing on the Costa Brava, from lateen-rigged sailing craft to nets and thousand and one objects and artifacts of the trade are on display at this excellent and edifying museum. ⊠ *Moll Pesquer s/n* ☎ *972/400424* ⊠ *€3* ⊙ *June 15–Sept. 15, daily 11–9; Sept. 16–June 14, Tues.–Sat. 10–1:30 and 3–7, Sun. 10–2 and 4–7.*

CALELLA DE PALAFRUGELL

11 km (7 mi) north of Palamós, 120 km (74 mi) north of Barcelona, 44 km (27 mi) east of Girona.

A pretty fishing village that has managed to retain some of its original charm, Calella de Palafrugell is especially popular for its July *habanera* song festival. With an arcaded seafront—called Les Voltes (The Vaults)—and with fishing boats pulled up onto the beach, this is but the first of a series of one small *cala* (cove) after another with tiny fishing villages offering secluded places to swim. They're all worth a stop, if only to imagine what the Costa Brava was like before the tourist boom. Other coves or inlets include Sa Riera, Aiguablava, Sa Tuna, Tamariu, and Llafranc. The sheer cliffs, transparent waters, and abundant vegetation in this region make this the quintessential Costa Brava.

Evidence of the isolation of this stretch of the coast is its own dialect. Note the feminine article "sa" or masculine "es," as in Sa Riera or Es Pianc, in front of many area place names—a feature of the *salat*, or salty, Catalan variant spoken along this coast. In earlier times locals rarely traveled inland, and this isolation preserved this archaic usage, which locals as far south as Tossa de Mar and as far north as Cadaqués use in their daily speech.

EXPLORING

Cap Roig. From this promontory you'll see panoramic views of the soaring Formigues (Ants) Isles. The islands were the site of a decisive battle in 1285, in which the Catalan fleet, led by the great Catalan admiral Roger de Llúria, destroyed the French fleet sailing to supply Felipe the Bold's siege of Girona. The battle ended, temporarily, French aspirations in the Mediterranean. Cap Roig is less than 2 km (1 mi) south of Calella de Palafrugell, and makes for an pretty half-hour walk from town.

WHERE TO STAY

$$$$ ☲ **El Far de Sant Sebastiá.** A 17th-century hermitage attached to a 15th-
★   century watchtower, this jumble of elegant stairways and terraces overlooking the Mediterranean lavishes visitors with a full complement of sensorial rewards and pleasures. Overlooking the Bay of Llafranc from a rocky aerie leading down to a sandy beach, El Far (lighthouse or watchtower) is an hour and a half from Barcelona at the heart of the Costa Brava. Rooms are high-ceilinged and breezy with sea views, and the restaurant ($–$$$) specializes in local Empordà and Mediterranean cuisine. **Pros:** one of the best combinations of graceful architecture and spectacular views on the Costa Brava. **Cons:** somewhat isolated from Costa Brava village life. ⊠ *Platja de Llafranc, Llafranc–Palafrugell* ☎ *972/301639* ⊕ *www.elfar.net* ↗ *9 rooms* ♿ *In-room: Wi-Fi. In-hotel: restaurant, Wi-Fi hotspot* ☰ *AE, DC, MC, V* ⧖ *BP.*

8

$$$–$$$$ ⊞ **Hotel Aigua Blava.** What began as a small *hostal* in the mid-1920s
★   is now a full-fledged luxury hotel, run by the fourth generation of the
same family. Traditional touches—rocking chairs and wooden furni-
ture in the sitting rooms, black-and-white photos tracing the evolution
of the hotel—blend pleasantly with the breezy pastel decoration of
the rooms and the luscious sea views. The bright, sun-filled restaurant
($–$$) overlooks the water and serves traditional Mediterranean fish
dishes, including *bacalao* (cod) and *merluza* (hake). Hotel Aigua Blava
is about 9 km (6 mi) north of Calella de Palafrugell. **Pros:** personalized, family-run environment; comfortable and traditional design; surrounded by gardens and greenery. **Cons:** equipment and furnishings are
somewhat antique; not a state-of-the-art Jacuzzi-and-spa kind of operation. ⊠ *Platja de Fornells, Begur* ☎ *972/624562* ⊕ *www.aiguablava.
com* ⤴ *85 rooms* ⚑ *In room: Wi-Fi. In-hotel: restaurant, bar, tennis
court, pool, Wi-Fi hotspot* ⊟ *AE, DC, MC, V* ⎮◎⎮ *BP.*

$$–$$$ ⊞ **Parador de Aiguablava.** The vista from this modern, blindingly white
★   parador, 9 km (6 mi) north of Calella de Palafrugell, is the classic post-
card Costa Brava: the rounded Cala d'Aiguablava wraps around the
shimmering blue Mediterranean. On the terrace you can bask in the
sun while waves break at the rocky shore and dissolve into white froth
below. The parador maximizes its cliff-top perch with large windows
everywhere—in the cool-tone rooms, the bright and airy restaurant
($–$$$), and the many comfortable sitting rooms. The restaurant
serves fine Costa Brava favorites, including the much-heralded *anchoas*
(anchovies) from nearby L'Escala. **Pros:** once inside, you see the mag-
nificent surrounding views. **Cons:** the barracks-like alabaster structure
atop the cliffs is something of an eyesore. ⊠ *Platja d'Aiguablava, Begur*
☎ *972/622162* ⊕ *www.parador.es* ⤴ *78 rooms* ⚑ *In-hotel: restaurant,
pool, gym, Internet terminal* ⊟ *AE, DC, MC, V* ⎮◎⎮ *EP.*

NIGHTLIFE AND THE ARTS

A throwback to the romantic 19th century is the lingering presence on
Costa Brava of the *habanera*, a musical lament strummed on a guitar
in a swaying Cuban rhythm and sung mostly in Spanish, though some
songs are in Catalan. Telling of longing for the homeland and the hard
conditions of life in the colonies, these popular songs are performed by
groups at events and clubs throughout the summer.

The Calella de Palafrugell **habanera** (*songfest* ☎ *972/614475 for infor-
mation from tourist office*) takes place on the first Saturday in July. The
festival is held in the cozy *plaça* (plaza) of Port Bo; tickets cost €20.

PALAFRUGELL

*5 km (3 mi) west of Calella de Palafrugell, 123 km (76 mi) north of
Barcelona, 39 km (24 mi) east of Girona.*

This busy inland market town has preserved its Catalan flavor, with old
streets and shops around a 16th-century church. Palafrugell is ineluta-
bly connected with the Catalan writer Josep Pla (1897–1981), a chroni-
cler of daily life in Catalonia, especially that of his home turf. His works
can be considered vast memoirs that cover a half-century of Catalan
life, seen through the eyes—sometimes ironically, sometimes pained—of

a man who laments the collapse of the rural world. Though he sided with the fascist Franco forces during the Spanish civil war (something that was held against him by many Catalan intellectuals), in 1947 he published his books in Catalan rather than Spanish—anathema to the Franco regime. Pla is omnipresent in Palafrugell: bookstores, posters, even Josep Pla menus in restaurants. In an effort to expand the resort image of the Costa Brava, Palafrugell sponsors cultural events and festivals outside the summer season.

EXPLORING

Fundació Josep Pla. Consider this your first stop, it's the best place to get information on local activities; there is also a large library. You can pick up a map (€7) with Josep Pla places of interest for a do-it-yourself tour of the town. Guided Pla walks can be scheduled on Saturday mornings by calling to reserve ahead. The literary walk, including recitations and readings of Pla's prose, costs €5. ⊠ *Carrer Nou 51* ☎ *972/305577* ⊕ *www.fundaciojoseppla.cat* ⊠ *€5* ⊘ *Mid-June–mid-Sept., Tues.–Sat. 10–1 and 5–8:30, Sun. 10–1; mid-Sept.–mid-June, Tues.–Fri. 5–8, Sat. 9:30–1 and 5–8, Sun. 10–1.*

WHERE TO EAT

$–$$

CATALAN

✗ **Pa i Raïm.** "Bread and grapes" in Catalan, this excellent restaurant in Josep Pla's ancestral family home has one rustic dining room as well as another glassed-in, winter garden space. In summer the leafy terrace is the place to be. The menu ranges from traditional country cuisine to more streamlined contemporary fare such as strawberry gazpacho. The *canelón crujiente de verduritas y setas con romescu* (crisped canelloni with young vegetables and wild mushrooms with romesco sauce) and the *vieiras y verduritas salteadas con aceite de sésamo* (scallops and baby vegetables sautéed with sesame-seed oil) are two standouts. ⊠ *Torres i Jonama 56* ☎ *972/304572* ⊕ *www.pairaim.com* ⊟ *AE, DC, MC, V* ⊘ *Closed Dec. 22–Jan. 7, May 11–May 26, and Mon. and Tues. No dinner Sun.*

LA BISBAL

8 km (5 mi) northwest of Palafrugell, 125 km (78 mi) northeast of Barcelona, 28 km (18 mi) east of Girona.

An inland town, La Bisbal has been famous since the 16th century as a pottery-producing center. The land around the town conceals clay deposits from thousands of years of alluvial remains.

WHERE TO STAY

$$$$

Fodor's Choice

★

▥ **Mas de Torrent.** In the tiny village of Torrent, but very close to La Bisbal, lies one of Spain's most refined retreats. A vision of easy elegance and rustic Catalan style, this converted 18th-century *masia* (farmhouse) resembles something from a coffee-table art book. The stylish suites are in the hotel's gardens; the bungalows overlook the gardens. The panache carries over to its restaurant, which serves the best of sea and land from the Baix (Lower) Empordà. For total idleness, tempt yourself with the summer poolside buffet; the more active will utilize the sports facilities—golf, riding, deep-sea fishing, tennis, water sports—nearby. **Pros:** fine cuisine; impeccable design and decor; superior service. **Cons:**

8

isolated from easy access to local life; slightly redolent of a gated tourist community. ⊠ *Afores s/n, Torrent* ☎ *972/303292* ⊕ *www.mastorrent. com* ⟿ *32 rooms, 7 suites* ⚷ *In-room: Wi-Fi. In-hotel: restaurant, pool, gym, tennis court, some pets allowed* ▭ *AE, DC, MC, V* ⍐*EP.*

SHOPPING

Pottery shops line **Carrer de l'Aigüeta,** where you can find everything from kitschy to elegant. In antiques shops you can discover beautiful old Catalan pottery. You can go directly to the pottery makers at several local factories, but the best outlet in town is **Terrisseria Salamó** (⊠ *Carrer del Padró 54* ☎ *972/640255*); for five generations this small crafts center has been producing sets from the most traditional to the latest marbled designs.

PERATALLADA

5 km (3 mi) east of La Bisbal, 11 km (7 mi) north of Palafrugell, 128 km (80 mi) northeast of Barcelona, 31 km (19 mi) east of Girona.

Medieval and miniature Peratallada (population 411) is an enchanting town that seems quite happily stuck in the Middle Ages. Beautifully preserved ancient buildings, narrow cobbled streets, arched walkways, and tiny hidden squares invite you to lose yourself in another century. A spectacular moat carved entirely out of rock encircles the town—hence its name, which means "carved rock."

WHERE TO EAT AND STAY

$-$$ ✗**Can Nau.** Overlooking the Plaça Esquiladors in the heart of town, SPANISH this restaurant in a snug *casa de pagès* (country house) exudes warmth and rustic charm, from its sturdy wooden tables to the bright paintings of the local landscape. The menu stars simple, time-honored Catalan comfort food such as *conill amb salsa d'ametlles* (rabbit in almond sauce) and *botifarra dolç amb compota de poma* (sweet country sausage with stewed apples). ⊠ *Pl. Esquiladors 2* ☎ *972/634035* ⊕ *www. cannau.iespana.es* ▭ *MC, V* ⊗ *Closed Wed., mid-June–mid-July, and Dec. 18–27. No dinner Sun. (except in Aug.)*

¢ ⬚**Ca L'Aliu.** Antique furniture and comfortable beds with thick quilts
★ and plump pillows fill the fresh-smelling rooms of this soothing, small country house. The owners, a friendly family, can fill you in on what's going on around town, and will even lend you a bicycle for a tour of the nearby countryside. **Pros:** rustic, medieval furnishings and structure fit perfectly with the town's ancient aesthetic. **Cons:** rooms are small; public spaces are tiny. ⊠ *Roca 6* ☎ *972/634061* ⊕ *www.calaliu.com* ⟿ *7 rooms* ⚷ *In-room: no a/c, no phone. In-hotel: bicycles.* ▭ *MC, V* ⍐*BP.*

NIGHTLIFE AND THE ARTS

Peratallada has its share of sprightly festivals, such as the **Festa Medieval** on the first weekend in October. Everyone dresses up in medieval costume and parades through the streets. The **Fira Peratallada,** the last Sunday in April, includes a bustling cheese market and arts-and-crafts stands in the main square.

Continued on page 310

Arzak's seabass with vegetable confetti

El Bulli's small pies of crystal almonds with cherries

Icy carrot and passion fruit truffles at El Bulli

SPAIN'S FOOD REVOLUTION

Every night is a performance in Spain's houses of haute cuisine, with chefs releasing new "collections" of dishes that thrill more than a diner's tastebuds. One rollercoaster meal may span six hours and more than 30 courses of a few bites apiece. You may not recognize what's on your plate, but that's part of the fun. *by Erica Duecy*

Spain is home to the world's most cutting-edge culinary scene. Chefs of *la nueva cocina*—as the avant-garde movement is called—relentlessly explore new techniques, resulting in dishes that defy convention. By playing with the properties of food, they can turn liquid into solids, and solids into powders. Olive oil "caviar," hot ice cream, and Parmesan "glass" are just a few of the alchemic presentations that have emerged.

Early on, the movement seemed to some critics like experimentation for experimentation's sake. Now it has become more refined, showcasing dishes that pleasure the palate as much as the mind. You're still likely to find yourself sipping rum "snow," eating flavored "air," and handling tweezers as eating utensils. If you decide to pull up a chair at the table of *la nueva cocina*, get ready for an unforgettable eating adventure.

FERRAN ADRIÀ — *LA NUEVA COCINA'S* VISIONARY

(clockwise from top left): black sesame sponge cake with miso; sea vegetable salad; hibiscus paper with blackcurrant; caviar of snail consomme; the El Bulli kitchen; the staff prepping tomatoes

Adrià has often been called the world's top chef, but his rise to fame didn't happen overnight. Adrià was an emerging talent in 1987 when he attended a cooking demonstration by French chef Jacques Maximin who spoke about his belief that "creativity means not copying." By Adrià's account, that statement transformed his approach to cooking.

The changeover to conceptual cuisine— where techniques and concepts became the driving force for his creativity— occurred in 1994, when Adrià developed a technique for producing dense foam from various liquids. A handful of new techniques emerged in those early years, but "nowadays, that process is accelerated," he says. "Within one year, I am working with several types of techniques."

Some of Adrià's most famous dishes include spherical olives (olive puree and herbs made to look like intact olives), deconstructed Caprese salad, black sesame sponge cake with miso, suckling pig tails with melon consomme, and "co-co," a giant egg made from coconut milk. These creative concoctions are served at El Bulli in meals of 26 to 35 courses, with each course just one or two bites. A meal for one costs about €250, without wine.

EL BULLI'S FUTURE

At the time of this writing, El Bulli's future remains uncertain. Adrià plans to close the restaurant at the end of 2011, and it's still to be determined if that close will be permanent. But don't fret—the El Bulli name lives on, and Adrià has already mentioned a possible culinary institute in its place. Whatever he decides, it's certain that his fans will follow.

TRICKS OF THE TRADE

Daniel Garcia at El Calima using liquid nitrogen

(clockwise from top left): dry ice changes from a solid directly to a gas without becoming liquid; liquid nitrogen boils in a glass container at room temperature; a nitro-cooled pistachio truffle; a nitro-cooled caipirinha with tarragon essence

Many techniques of *la nueva cocina* are borrowed from the food processing industry, including the use of liquid nitrogen, freeze-drying, and gellifying agents. This technological approach to cooking may seem like a departure from Spain's ingredient-driven cuisine, but avant-garde chefs say their creations are no less rooted in Spanish culture than traditional fare.

One leading chef, Juan Mari Arzak, describes his approach as "Basque evolutionary, investigative cuisine." He says, "We are doing things that haven't been done before." Using the freeze-drying technique *lyophilization*, or *LYO*, Arzak makes powders from items like tomatoes and peanuts. "You use the powder to add flavor to things," he says. "If you dust tuna with peanut powder and salt, it concentrates the underlying flavors to make the tuna taste like a more intense version of tuna."

Additionally, an unprecedented spirit of collaboration has defined the movement. "It is true that in other culinary movements chefs have been reluctant to share their knowledge," Adrià says. "Some people ask us, why do you share everything? Why do you share your secrets? The answer is that that's the way we understand cooking—that it's meant to be shared."

Quick-freezing: Liquid nitrogen can be used to make instant ice cream from any liquid, even olive oil. Just pour olive oil into a bowl of liquid nitrogen, then scoop out the solid that forms.

Spherification: To create a liquidy ball that looks like a raw egg yolk, first mix a puree, say mango puree, with sodium alginate; then ladle it by the spoonful into a bath containing calcium salts. The result is a mango sphere with a liquid center.

Gellification: Liquids like soy sauce can be used to make noodles with this technique. When soy sauce is mixed with methylcellulose, it solidifies and can be extruded through a tube to form soy sauce "noodles."

Freeze-drying: The technique behind instant soup is used to create concentrated powders from items like ham and strawberries. First, the berry is frozen. Then, the pressure is lowered while applying heat so the frozen water in the berry becomes a gas. What remains is a brittle berry that can be crumbled into a powder.

THE SPANISH ARMADA

Among the most recognized contributors to *la nueva cocina* are Juan Mari Arzak, Martín Berasategui, Alberto Chicote, Daniel García, Joan Roca, and Paco Roncero. Here's where to find them:

(top left) lobster in crunchy potato shell; (top right) "Lunar Rocks" of frozen cocoa "rocks" and orange-passionfruit syrup pools; (left) Chef Juan Mari Arzak and his daughter Elena

Juan Mari Arzak is recognized for modernizing and reinvigorating Basque cuisine at Restaurante Arzak in San Sebastián. He now operates it with his daughter Elena, who represents the fourth generation of Arzak restaurateurs. Despite his deep culinary roots and decades-long career, Arzak says he works to maintain a fresh perspective. "It's important to look at the world through a cook's eyes, but to think like a little kid," he says. "Because when you are a boy, you have the capacity to be amazed and surprised." **Restaurante Arzak** ⊠ Avda. Alcalde Jose Elosegui, 273 / San Sebastián ☎ 943/278465 ⊕ www.arzak.info

At his eponymous fine-dining restaurant in Lasarte, **Martín Berasategui** is known for his dedication to local products and fresh flavors. Notable dishes have included foie gras, smoked eel, apple terrine, and *percebes* (barnacles) served with fresh peas in vegetable broth. **Restaurante Martín Berasategui** ⊠ Calle Loidi, 1 / Lasarte-Oria ☎ 943/366471 ⊕ www.martinberasategui.com

The cuisine at **Alberto Chicote's** Nodo fuses Spanish and Japanese ingredients and techniques. His version of tuna tataki, for example, features seared tuna macerated in soy sauce and rice vinegar, then chopped and served with chilled garlic cream, and garnished with drops of olive oil and black olive powder. **Nodo** ⊠ Calle Velázquez, 150 / Madrid ☎ 915/644044 ⊕ www.restaurantenodo.es

In his mid-thirties, **Daniel García** is one of the younger practitioners of *la nueva*

cocina, as well as head chef at El Calima, the restaurant in the Hotel Don Pepe in Marbella. "My cultural inspiration comes from the area where I work, in Andalusia, the south of Spain," he says. Acclaimed dishes include gazpacho with anchovies and *queso fresco* snow, and a passionfruit flan with herb broth and eucalyptus-thyme essence. **Restaurante El Calima** ✉ Ave. José Meliá / Marbella ☎ 952/764252 ⊕ www.restaurantecalima.com

Joan Roca is chef at El Celler de Can Roca in Girona, which he runs with his two brothers, Josep and Jordi. Roca is known for his work exploring the intersection between aroma and flavor, with dishes such as his "Adaptation of the Perfume *Angel* by Thierry Mugler," featuring cream of toffee, chocolate, gelée of violet and bergamot, and red-fruits ice cream with vanilla. Savories include smoked lemon prawn with green peas and licorice, and white and green asparagus with cardamom oil and truffles. **El Celler de Can Roca** ✉ Carretera de Taialá, 40 / Girona ☎ 972/222157 ⊕ www.cellercanroca.com

Chefs in action, demonstrating their creativity in the kitchen: (top) Alberto Chicote with his assistants; (bottom) Martín Berasategui

Paco Roncero is chef at Restaurante La Terraza in Madrid. He is considered one of Ferran Adrià's most outstanding students. "When I started working with Ferran [in 1998], my whole concept of cuisine changed," he says. "I started researching and trying to do new things. Now my cuisine is modern, *vanguardia*, without losing sight of tradition." **Restaurante La Terraza** ✉ Alacalá 15 / Madrid ☎ 915/218700 ⊕ www.casinodemadrid.es

ULLASTRET

4 km (2½ mi) north of Peratallada, 130 km (81 mi) northeast of Barcelona, 35 km (22 mi) east of Girona.

For anyone unaccustomed to seeing massive Iberian stonework other than Greek or Roman ruins, the vast dimensions of Ullastret can be a surprising experience. With a rural setting about 2 km (1 mi) north of the village of Ullastret, in the direction of Torroella de Montgrí, the archaeological site of Ullastret contains the remains of houses, temples, cisterns, grain silos, and burial sites. A sense of calm pervades the carefully tended and landscaped site, while soaring, fragrant cypress trees shade and cool you.

The people who lived at Ullastret were the *Indiketes,* an aboriginal Iberian civilization already long settled here when the first Phoenician traders arrived in about 600 BC. The Greeks landed at nearby Empúries in about 630 BC; the temples built at the highest point of the village display an example of their Hellenizing influence. Start your visit by first following the outside wall; then enter the fortress through the main door. At the top of the rise, the **Museu d'Arqueologia de Catalunya–Ullastret** (archaeological museum) contains a collection of Attic (Athenian) pottery, another example of how the Greeks influenced the Iberians. On the first Sunday of the month from April to September, a young woman called Indiketa, dressed in native Iberian costume, gives guided tours of the site at noon. With a prior reservation you can take this tour in English. ⊠ *Puig de Sant Andreu s/n* ☎ *972/179058* ⊕ *www.mac.es/ullastret* ⊠ *€3.50* ☉ *Oct.–May, Tues.–Sun. 10–2 and 3–6; June–Sept 30 and Easter Week, Tues.–Sun. 10–8.*

WHERE TO EAT

$–$$ ✗ **Restaurant Ibèric.** This excellent pocket of authentic Costa Brava tastes
CATALAN   and aromas serves everything from snails to woodcock in season. Wild mushrooms scrambled with eggs or stewed with hare are specialties here, as are the complex and earthy red wines made by enologist Jordi Oliver of the Oliver Conti vineyard in the Upper Empordà's village of Capmany. ⊠ *Carrer Valls 6* ☎ *972/757108* ▭ *AE, DC, MC, V* ☉ *Closed Mon. No dinner Sun. Nov.–Mar.*

L'ESCALA

10 km (6 mi) north of Ullastret, 135 km (84 mi) northeast of Barcelona, 39 km (24 mi) northeast of Girona.

On the beautiful Bay of Roses, L'Escala faces north and feels the full effects of the *tramuntana,* the blustery northwest wind that affects the Girona and Empordà area of Catalonia and is particularly strong in fall. With that in mind, and with more than a touch of irony, the Catalan writer Josep Pla said of L'Escala's natives, "The inhabitants of this village have, for the mere fact of living in it, a certain merit." Like many others, this fishing village has felt the effects of tourism, tacky souvenir stands and all. But the beach, the Greek ruins of Empúries (best explored from here), and the divine anchovies make a trip to L'Escala worthwhile. Instead of shipping the local anchovies to the market, the fishermen of L'Escala kept these little treasures for themselves at home. In due time, these sublimely salted morsels were discovered by the earliest tourists, and what had been a cottage industry became a small industrial operation. Today five shops selling the anchovies have obtained quality certificates. Be sure to stop at any restaurant in town to try this treat as an appetizer—a slice of crisp toast with anchovies dripping with olive oil, accompanied by a glass of freezing white wine, amounts to nirvana on the Costa Brava.

WHERE TO EAT AND STAY

$–$$ **✕ El Roser 2.** All the tables have views of the spectacular Bay of Roses
SEAFOOD at this edge-of-town restaurant, which serves blissful nouvelle seafood cuisine. Salads include *bogavant amb pernil i salsa de safrà* (lobster with ham and saffron sauce) and *barat amb melmelada de tomàquet* (mackerel with tomato jam). One of the most succulent dishes is *turbot rostit amb favetes a la catalana i espaguetis de calamar* (roasted turbot with stewed *faves*—a lima-bean-like legume—and squid spaghetti). ⊠ *Passeig Lluís Albert 1* ☎ *972/771102* ⊟ *AE, DC, MC, V* ☺ *Closed Feb. and Wed. Sept.–June. No dinner Sun.*

$–$$ **⊞ Nieves–Mar.** This bright, modern family hotel on the seafront is famous for its Ca la Neus restaurant ($-$$), which offers up all the usual suspects: suquet (Catalan fish-and-potato stew), *llamantol al forn* (baked lobster), and paella. They also make a smashing bouillabaisse. The suites and many guest rooms have fine views of the Bay of Roses, and some have balconies. **Pros:** bright, well-lighted place with unforgettable views. **Cons:** when the powerful northwest tramuntana is blowing out of the Pyrenees, expect a mild sandstorm. ⊠ *Passeig Marítim 8* ☎ *972/770300* ⊕ *www.nievesmar.com* ⌨ *65 rooms, 10 suites* ⚹ *In-room: Wi-Fi. In-hotel: tennis court, pool, some pets allowed* ⊟ *AE, DC, MC, V* ☺ *Closed Nov.–Feb.* ⍰ *BP.*

EMPÚRIES

★ *1 km (½ mi north of L'Escala, 135 km (84 mi) northeast of Barcelona, 39 km (24 mi) northeast of Girona.*

Empúries is the only Greek city still in existence on the Iberian Peninsula; the exact location of others has never been established. Back in the days when the *Odyssey* was the first travel guidebook of note, the Greeks settled here from Massalia (modern Marseilles), for trading purposes, in the 6th century BC. Originally hailing from Phocaea in Ionia (today's western coast of Turkey), they set sail as part of the colonial expansion of the Greek city-states. They founded a city whose very name, Emporion or Emporium (which translates to "market"), symbolized prosperity, exports, and commerce, and whose site—on the south shore of the Bay of Roses, near L'Escala—was a promising one. This scenic site backdropped by the sea has more than 30 acres of excavations to explore (including some beautiful mosaic floor remnants) and a fascinating museum.

When Scipio landed in Emporium in 218 BC he found a vigorous Greek settlement, comprising two towns: Paleopolis, the old city, and Neapolis, the new one. Paleopolis was where the modern walled village of

Sant Martí d'Empúries stands today (if you want a quick lunch, head here); once an island, it has been united with the mainland by the sedimentation of the Ter River, which empties into the Bay of Roses. Work on Neapolis, begun by Barcelona archaeologists some 80 years ago, revealed that Emporium was made up of two separate towns housing Greeks and Iberians. Greeks had access to the Iberian ghetto, but not vice-versa, probably due to security considerations. The arrangement— Greeks on the island, Iberians on the mainland with no access to the sea, enabled the Greeks to monopolize trade. The Greeks eventually moved to the mainland, where they founded Neapolis and continued their prosperous trade with the natives, as attested by the abundant finds of Greek pottery in the surrounding area.

In 218 BC the Romans landed at Empúries at the start of the Second Punic War against the Carthaginians (who were led by Hannibal), inaugurating a period of Roman occupation of the Iberian Peninsula that lasted several centuries (and served as the basis of the languages and culture of Spain and Portugal). The Romans added their own town to the place named, in the plural, Emporiae. Empúries eventually declined as other Roman cities, such as Tarragona, gained importance. It was abandoned in the 4th century AD and rediscovered only in the 19th century.

Highlights of the site—many structures have nothing remaining but their foundations—include the defensive walls, the open agora, and the site of the Asklepion, the temple of the Greek god of medicine. In 1909 a statue of Asclepius was uncovered in a cistern in front of this temple, dated to the 4th century BC, and promptly moved to the Archaeological Museum in Barcelona (there are copies on-site). Recent excavations have uncovered the Roman baths of Empúries, but only 10%–15% of the Roman city is excavated. What you see today above ground is mostly the later Roman city, although the street grid is of the Greek settlement; beneath lie many of the Greek ruins, which will probably remain where they are. Enter the excavations from the seafront pedestrian promenade (most people find this by walking along the coast for 15 minutes from L'Escala or hopping the little Carrilet train that departs from L'Escala on the hour) from mid-June to mid-September; at other times, the only access is via a road on the main Figueres route.

Further digging is likely to reveal important new discoveries in addition to the previously excavated goodies, including mosaic floors and phallic icons, that are now on view in the small **Museu d'Arqueologia de Catalunya–Empúries** here. ⊠ *Ctra. del Museu s/n, L'Escala* ☎ *972/ 770208* ⊕ *www.mac.es* ⊠*€6* ☉ *June–Sept. and Easter wk, Tues.–Sun. 10–8; Oct.–May, Tues.–Sun. 10–2 and 3–6.*

CASTELLÓ D'EMPÚRIES

11 km (7 mi) northwest of Empúries, 139 km (86 mi) northeast of Barcelona, 47 km (29 mi) northeast of Girona.

The seignorial silhouette of the cathedral of Santa Maria rises majestically above the Empordà plain, a particularly impressive picture from the fields east of town. Castelló d'Empúries is fundamentally an agricultural town, but has an adjacent, self-contained, and not terribly appealing resort development on the Bay of Roses known as Empuriabrava. Castelló itself is a handsomely historic town with Gothic palaces and an intricate warren of cobbled streets; its heart is the Plaça dels Homes, where a tourist office can provide a town map. Marshes surround the town, which now lies several miles inland, but in the Middle Ages ships (and Viking raiders) sailed up the Muga River from the sea to dock here.

EXPLORING

Cathedral of Santa Maria. Outside the cathedral, dating to the 13th and 14th centuries, pride of place is given to the Romanesque bell tower and the portal sculpted with figures of the apostles and the Epiphany. Inside the spacious building a fine 15th-century alabaster altar has delicate, highly detailed expressive figures. ⊠ *Pl. Mosén Cinto Verdaguer s/n* ☏ *972/158019*

PARC NATURAL DELS AÏGUAMOLLS DE L'EMPORDÀ

Less than 1 km (½ mi) east of Castelló d'Empúries, 139 km (86 mi) north of Barcelona, 47 km (29 mi) northeast of Girona.

It's almost a miracle that this natural refuge has survived. Set beside the modern resort of Empuriabrava—which was carved out of the same terrain in the mid-'60s—this parcel of land was scheduled for development when a conservation movement was founded in 1976 to save it. In 1983 the Catalan parliament declared the area a nature preserve, and it has since become a haven for birds migrating from northern Europe to Africa. Thanks to this sanctuary, the bird population of all the Empordà plain continues to prosper. Hundreds of species flock here, including avocets, black-winged stilts, ringed plovers, common sandpipers, water rails, hoopoes, purple gallinules, rollers, marsh harriers, and Montagu's harrier. In addition, otters, marine cows, Camargue horses, and fallow deer have been reintroduced to this habitat. Fittingly, park administrators like to stress that silence is one of their most valued resources. There's an information center in Castelló d'Empúries. ⊠ *Entrance off Ctra. de Sant Pere Pescador, Castelló d'Empúries* ☏ *972/454222* ⊕ *www.roses.cat/en/turisme/natura/aiguamollsemporda.aspx* ⊠ *Free* ☉ *Daily dawn–dusk.*

ROSES

9 km (5½ mi) northeast of Castelló de Empúries, 153 km (95 mi) northeast of Barcelona, 56 km (35 mi) northeast of Girona.

The opening lines of C.S. Forester's Horatio Hornblower novel *Flying Colors* read, "Captain Hornblower was walking up and down along the sector of the ramparts of Rosas . . . Overhead shone the bright autumn sun of the Mediterranean, hanging in a blue Mediterranean sky, and shining on the Mediterranean blue of Rosas Bay—the blue water fringed with white where the little waves broke against the shore of golden sand and grey-green cliff." It's not surprising that Forester raised the curtain here, as the Golf de Roses has often been called the most splendid gulf

8

on the Costa Brava. Today you can still visit those ramparts—which surround the remains of the old Greek, Roman, and medieval cities of Roses—and take in the view of the town, sitting at the head of the bay. Roses may not excel in scenic beauty any longer—many modern hotels, discos, and modern boats have intruded—but it's loaded with history.

Roses began as a Greek colony from the island of Rhodes (hence, its name) and was a branch of the big Empúries settlement down the coast. The Roman writer Cato states that the Greeks settled here in 776 BC, although archaeological excavations have not found any evidence earlier than 600 BC. But the Greeks were simply the first in a long line of settlers.

Unfortunately, the little that remains of old Roses is swamped in summer, when the native population of 13,500 booms to over 120,000. To serve these teeming numbers, the town has countless restaurants, discotheques, and amusement parks for the young. Almost everyone's main activity is going to the immense beaches that line the Bay of Roses. If you head out along the coast between Roses and the next village to the north, Cadaqués, you'll discover an enchanting continuum of steep and bare rocky mountains covered with spiny underbrush. Although the Mediterranean sun beats down mercilessly in summer, coves ringed by towering red pines dip into sheltered sandy beaches, allowing all to sunbathe, swim, and play. The last two coves before Cadaqués, Cala Montjoi and Cala Jònculs, are relatively free of development, with only a couple of hotels and restaurants (one of them the famous El Bulli). Between these two inlets, the jagged cliffs of the Norfeu headlands tumble into the unruly sea. Motorboats and sailboats cruise this coast, anchoring in the shelter of coves and inlets to spend the day on the water before heading back to Roses and its ongoing fiesta.

EXPLORING

Ciutadella. The concentration of civilizations inside Roses's *citadel* is unlike any other in Spain. Within these walls settlements of Greeks, Romans, and Visigoths followed each other in turn, with a residential quarter here up to the late 19th century. Inside the citadel is the Romanesque Benedictine **monastery and cloister of Santa Maria,** a pentagonal structure begun in 1543. Walls were important back then: much of Roses's strategic importance lay in the fact that its site offered ships a safe haven from the coast's blustery *tramuntana* wind. An archaeologist gives free guided visits inside the citadel on Sunday and Wednesday mornings at 11 AM in winter and 10 AM in summer; it's open to the public from 9 AM until dark. The Museu Històric i Arqueològic, opened in 2004, and the Sala de Exposiciones, with temporary exhibits, complete the offerings available here. ⊠ *Av. de Rhodes s/n* ☎ *972/151466* ⊕ *www. rosesfhn.org* ⬛ *€3* ☉ *Apr.–Sept., daily 10–8; Oct.–Mar., daily 10–6.*

WHERE TO EAT AND STAY

$$$$
LA NUEVA
COCINA
Fodor's Choice
★

✕ **el Bulli.** A gastronomic Disney World, this seaside hideaway has become a sacrosanct foodie pilgrimage—just don't show up without reservations. And scoring one is pretty much a catch-22: the restaurant gets booked for a full calendar year, and according to recent press, 2011 could be the last year El Bulli remains open. If you do manage to get to the top of the waiting list, be prepared for a bizarre and wonderful culinary spectacle. Chef Ferran Adrià makes your palate his playground with a 35-course taster's menu that has been known in the past to feature concoctions such as *espuma de humo* (foam of smoke), rosewater bubbles, and *aire de zanahoria con coco amargo* (air of carrot with bitter coconut), faux caviar made of congealed melon drops, or rabbit ear chips. Don't come here planning on having anything resembling a feast or a big meal; this is just a joyride for the senses. But do plan on spending at least €200 per person. ✉ *Cala Montjoi, Roses, Girona* ☎ *972/150457* ⊕ *www.elbulli.com* ⚑ *Reservations essential, consult the Web site* ▭ *AE, DC, MC, V* ⊘ *Closed Dec. 21–June 15.*

$$$-$$$$

SPANISH

★

✗ **Rafa's.** One of the best places for fresh fish in the area, this relaxed and rustic spot decorated with unpretentious furnishings and seafaring items is a big favorite among discerning foodies from around the world and certain hyper-creative local chefs longing for a simple and satisfying meal of traditional Mediterranean seafood. ✉ *Carrer Sant Sebastià 56* ☎ *972/254003* ⚑ *Reservations essential* ▭ *AE, DC, MC, V* ⊘ *Closed Sun., Mon.*

$$$-$$$$

★

▭ **Almadraba Park Hotel.** This stunning hotel run by Jaume Subirós, proprietor of the Hotel Empordà in Figueres, sits on a bluff overlooking the horseshoe-shape Cala Almadraba—a cove about a half-mile wide, 4 km (2½ mi) from Roses—with access to a white-sand beach. The Figueres hotel is considered the cradle of modern Catalan cuisine, and the kitchen here offers the same level of sophisticated cooking, so try one of the fine rice-dish specialties on the terrace with an incomparable view of the entire Bay of Roses. The hotel's look and style throughout are modern, clean-lined, and angular. **Pros:** polished, highly professionalized service, excellent views and sense of getting away to a secluded refuge. **Cons:** somewhat isolated from anything else, Roses is a long, winding (though scenic) 5-km (3-mi) drive away. ✉ *Platja de l'Almadraba s/n, 17480* ☎ *972/256550* ⊕ *www.almadrabapark.com* ⌁ *60 rooms, 6 suites* ⚭ *In-room: Wi-Fi, safe. In-hotel: restaurant, bar, Wi-Fi hotspot, tennis court, pool* ▭ *AE, DC, MC, V* ⊘ *Closed mid-Oct.–mid-Mar.* ⦿ *BP.*

$$-$$$

▭ **Terraza.** Lovely views straight out to sea and a swimming pool overlooking the beach make this semi-secluded address on the way into Roses a natural stopping place. The accomplished restaurant staff ensures a high gastronomical level at this traditional yet modernized Roses hotel, one of the deans of Empordà hospitality. **Pros:** a 15-minute walk down the beach from the town of Roses, with its lively bars, shops, restaurants, and nightlife. **Cons:** just off the main drag into town, the hotel lacks the remote refuge feel of other Roses lodging options. ✉ *Av. Rhode 32 17480* ☎ *972/256154* ⊕ *www.hotelterraza.com* ⌁ *87 rooms, 3 suites* ⚭ *In-room: Wi-Fi. In-hotel: restaurant, pool, Wi-Fi hotspot* ▭ *AE, DC, MC, V* ⊘ *Closed Jan. 1–Mar. 7* ⦿ *BP.*

$$$-$$$$

▭ **Vistabella.** Small and elegant, this quiet hotel is placed high up on a cliff overlooking the cove of Canyelles Petites, 2½ km (1½ mi) up the coast from Roses. It has excellent service and there are opportunities to pursue a variety of water sports. The kitchen serves international cuisine. **Pros:** self-sufficient complex offering everything you need from sailboats to supper; nonpareil Mediterranean panoramas. **Cons:** almost

8

too peaceful; somewhat removed from the lively vibe of a Costa Brava village resort. ⊠ *Av. Díaz Pacheco 26 17480* ☎ *972/256200* ⊕ *www. vistabellahotel.com* ⤴ *21 rooms, 8 suites* ♿ *In-room: Wi-Fi. In-hotel: 2 restaurants, pool, gym, beachfront, some pets allowed* ⊟ *AE, DC, MC, V* ⊘ *Closed mid-Oct.–mid-Mar.* ⅏ *BP.*

NIGHTLIFE

Roses and the area ringing the Golf de Roses have a multitude of booming nightspots, especially in summer—but keep in mind that until 1 AM or so these places are empty. For a quiet start, everyone's favorite bar is **La Sirena** (⊠ *Pl. Sant Pere 7* ☎ *972/257294*). All of the Plaça Sant Pere terrace bars and cafés are, in fact, an ongoing street party. Kick things off at **Barbarossa** (⊠ *Carrer Sant Isidre 3* ☎ *972/255507*), a music bar that fills with potential miscreants as the sunset dies. **Si Us Plau** (⊠ *Av. de Rhode 58* ☎ *972/254264*) is a small villa near the beach that rocks during summer evenings. From smaller bars people head out to the big discos in Empuriabrava, starting with **Danzatoria** (⊠ *Ctra. Figueres–Roses, Km 38.5* ☎ *972/452121*). **Pasarela** (⊠ *Passeig Marítim s/n* ☎ *972/452097*) is another of Roses' action-packed nightclubs.

CADAQUÉS

★ *17 km (11 mi) northeast of Roses, 167 km (104 mi) northeast of Barcelona, 70 km (43 mi) northeast of Girona.*

Cadaqués (pronounced cada-*kess*) has been called the most beautiful village on the Costa Brava. Its jumble of white houses roofed with red tiles, massed upon each other, and capped by the church of Santa Maria—which seems suspended in the air—has been immortalized by hundreds of artists. A full list of the writers, musicians, and artists who stayed here at one time or another would be encyclopedic—Federico García Lorca, Luis Buñuel, Marcel Duchamp, Salvador Dalí, John Cage, and Pablo Picasso are just a few of the greatest names. Dalí—the founder of Spanish Surrealism and the man who created the *Persistence of Memory* (housed in New York City's Museum of Modern Art) and those melting watches—spent many childhood summers here, and Picasso may have been inspired by the boxlike, whitewashed houses of the Costa Brava (and France's nearby Côte Vermeille) to create Cubism.

Today Cadaqués has been discovered: the horse-drawn carts that threaded their way up and down the mountain of El Pení have long ago been traded in for Mercedeses, and there are more expensive art galleries than impoverished artists. Still, the town is off the beaten highway and can only be reached by one snaking road that travels over the Serra de Rodes range. (For years, many couples had wedding pictures taken in Sardinia, as it was easier to sail there than to go to Figueres overland.) Thanks to this seclusion, Cadaqués remains one of the most unspoiled and loveliest towns of the coast.

The village is a labyrinth of steep and narrow pebble-paved streets. Its serpentine waterfront is lined with whitewashed private homes and inlets where small fishing boats have been pulled up onto the black, slate sand. The social center is the *Rambla,* a street promenade crowded with outdoor cafés. When the sun goes down, these fill up with people having

The popular harbor of Cadaqués.

a few drinks before going off to dinner, and they fill up again in the late hours with people as eager to talk the night away as to catch the sea breezes. At the Bar Melitón on this waterfront a plaque commemorates the many hours Marcel Duchamp spent here playing chess.

EXPLORING

Museu Municipal d'Art. If you don't want to gallery-hop, head for the town's small museum, which entices with its temporary collections of landscape and seascape paintings inspired by the scenery of the Costa Brava. In summer the museum showcases art by Dalí. ✉ *Carrer Narcís Monturiol 15* ☎ *972/258877* ✆€6 ⊙ *Easter–mid-Nov., daily 10:30–1:30 and 3–8; mid-Nov.–Easter, Mon.–Sat. 10:30–1:30 and 4–8.*

Port Lligat. One cove up the coast from Cadaqués—just a 15-minute walk away—is this port where Salvador Dalí (1904–89) built his famous house in the 1930s, which became a love nest for him and his adored wife and model Gala (who left famed Surrealist poet Paul Éluard to become Madame Dalí).

★ **Casa Museu Salvador Dalí.** Tours in English, French, and Catalan escort you through the artist's abode and his many "wonders": the stuffed polar bear hung with turquoise jewels, the dismembered mannequins, the dressing area filled with photos of the artist and celebrities, the bedroom with the panoramic view over Cap de Creus, the easternmost point on the Spanish peninsula (Dalí liked to boast that he was the first man in Spain to see the sun every morning), and the swimming pool designed to look like either a phallus or the floor plan of the Alhambra, Granada's iconic Moorish palace (depending on who was asking the question). The view from the garden—which is full of amazing egg-shape sculptures—will be familiar, as it was a frequent backdrop in Dalí's paintings. Note that the tour takes 40 minutes and must be booked in advance. ⊠ *Port Lligat* ☎ *972/251015*   ⊕ *www.salvador-dali.org* ⊠ *€10* ⊗ *By appointment Mar. 15–June 14 and Sept. 16–Jan. 6, Tues.–Sun. 10:30–5:10; June 15–Sept. 15, daily 9:30–8:10.*

★ **Cap de Creus.** Dalí called this headland to the north of Port Lligat "a grandiose geological delirium"— a fairly apropos description, since the rocky mineral formations of this cape twist and curl in the most extraordinary way, as if the earth had been convulsed, then wrung out and dropped into the sea and battered by surging waves. The area was declared a maritime and terrestrial natural park in 1998. To continue the Dalí theme, opt for a cruise out to Cap de Creus on the *Gala*, now helmed by Senyor Caminada, the son of a longtime Dalí employee; the boat is moored at Port Lligat's shore, and 55-minute excursions are offered daily to the cape and back for €12 per person.

NEED A BREAK?   Gaze down at heart-knocking views of the craggy coast and crashing waves with a warm mug of coffee in hand or fine fare on the table at **Bar Restaurant Cap de Creus** (⊠ *Ctra. Cap de Creus* ☎ *972/199005*), which sits on a rocky crag above the Cap de Creus.

WHERE TO EAT

$–$$
SEAFOOD
✗ **Can Pelayo.** This family-run button of a place, hidden behind Plaça Port Alguer a five-minute walk south of town, serves excellent seafood. Straight-up fresh fish is the best bet here: *llobarro* (sea bass), *dorada* (gilt-head bream), or *llenguado* (sole) cooked over coals and accompanied by a green salad and a freezing bottle of a local white wine such as the prize-winning Oliver-Conti Gewürztraminer–sauvignon blanc from nearby Capmany make for an excellent meal. ⊠ *Carrer Nou 11* ☎ *972/258356* ⊟ *AE, DC, MC, V* ⊗ *Closed weekdays Oct.–May.*

¢–$
SPANISH
Fodor's Choice
★
✗ **Casa Anita.** Simple, fresh, and generous cuisine is the draw at this tiny place on the street that leads to Port Lligat and Dalí's house. The crowd's *couleur locale* includes hippies, drifters, beachcombers, and other loafers on a budget. Try the salads and the sardine, mussel, and sea bass dishes, and get there early. ⊠ *Carrer Miquel Rosset 16* ☎ *972/258471* ⊟ *AE, DC, MC, V* ⊗ *Closed Mon. Sept.–May; last 2 wks of Nov.; and mid-Jan.–mid-Feb.*

$$
SEAFOOD
★
✗ **Es Trull.** Some people consider this cedar-shingled cafeteria on the harbor side street in the center of town the best kitchen in town. An ancient

olive press in the interior gave Es Trull its name. It specializes in fish dishes such as *escórpora* (scorpion fish) and rice dishes, such as the star player, *arròs de calamar i gambes* (rice with squid and shrimp), or *arròs negre amb calamar i sèpia* (rice in ink of squid and cuttlefish). ☒ *Port Ditxós s/n* ☎ *972/258196* ═ *AE, MC, V* ☯ *Closed Nov.–Easter.*

WHERE TO STAY

$–$$ ⚏ **Llané Petit.** An intimate, typically Mediterranean bayside hotel, Llané Petit caters to people who want to make the most of their stay in the village and don't want to spend too much time in their hotel rooms. Rooms are simple and serene—as is the cuisine, which uses lots of grilled meats and fish. **Pros:** the semi-private beach next to the hotel is less crowded that the main Cadaqués beach. **Cons:** rooms on the small side; somewhat lightweight beds and furnishings. ☒ *Carrer Dr. Bartomeus 37* ☎ *972/251020* ⊕ *www.llanepetit.com* ⤳ *37 rooms* ⚄ *In-room: Wi-Fi. In-hotel: restaurant, Internet terminal, Wi-Fi hotspot* ═ *AE, MC, V* ☯ *Closed 2 wks in Dec.* ⊚ *EP.*

$$–$$$ ⚏ **Playa Sol.** Open for more than 40 years, this hotel has the experience that comes with age. The rooms are done tastefully in red and ocher; some overlook the sea. The Playa Sol is in the cove of Es Pianc on the left side of the bay of Cadaqués as you face the sea, a five-minute walk from the village center. Boaters will love this place—all types of craft tie up here, as master Costa Brava chronicler Josep Pla spread its fame as the best place to drop anchor in Cadaqués. **Pros:** powerful historic vibrations and a cozy, refuge-in-the-eye-of-the-maelstrom feel. **Cons:** rooms on the small side; public spaces constricted. ☒ *Platja Es Pianc 3* ☎ *972/258100* ⊕ *www.playasol.com* ⤳ *49 rooms* ⚄ *In-room: Wi-Fi. In-hotel: restaurant, bar, Wi-Fi hotspot, pool* ═ *AE, DC, MC, V* ☯ *Closed mid-Nov.–mid-Feb.* ⊚ *EP.*

SHOPPING

Cadaqués is all about art, and there are quite a few galleries—most active June–September, December, and around Easter—worth visiting. **Galeria de la Riba** (☒ *Riba Pianc s/n* ☎ *972/159273*) handles well-known Spanish, Catalan, and international artists. The village social center, **L'Amistat** (☒ *Dr. Trèmols 1* ☎ *972/258800*), is a good place to start; in addition to being the place where villagers bide their time playing cards, it regularly holds art exhibitions of local and international artists with homes in Cadaqués. **L'Ateneu** (☒ *Av. Caritat Serinyana 8* ☎ *972/159209*), a nonprofit organization, regularly exhibits Catalan, Spanish, and international artists; once a year it holds a three-day collective fund-raiser exhibition at Cap de Creus. **Port Doguer** (☒ *Guillem Bruguera 10* ☎ *972/258910*) has managed such established artists as the Moscardó brothers, Japanese painter Shigeyoshi Koyama, Sabala, Vilallonga, and Roca-Sastre, with exhibitions in a wonderful space— an old olive press. **Taller Fort** (☒ *Hort d'en Sanés* ☎ *972/258549*) deals in international small-format art and also sponsors an annual painting competition. **Galeria Carlos Lozano** (☒ *Riba Pianc 2* ☎ *972/159209*), founded by a Dalí crony and pivotal force in the Cadaqués art scene until his death in 2000, remains a key gallery, showing, among other prestigious artists, the work of Miguel Condé.

8

NIGHTLIFE

On Carrer Miquel Roset, the town's main night-crawling street, the dark, wood-paneled **Bar Anita Nit** (⊠ *Miquel Roset 6* ☏ *972/258471*) is a *whiskeria* with an excellent selection of old whiskeys. **Bar Habana** (⊠ *Dr. Bartomeus 2* ☏ *972/159438*) is a favorite night hub with live music in summer. The cavernous **L'Hostal** (⊠ *Passeig 8* ☏ *972/258000*) is an institution and a draw for Dalí fans. The great man used to hang out here, and lent a hand in redesigning it in 1975. As you walk in, look down: Dalí designed the "eye"-tiled floor. The original German-born owner Marci played host to everyone from Mick Jagger to Gabriel García Márquez, who left a pen-and-ink sailboat drawing inscribed PARA MARCI, CON UN BARCO—GABRIEL (To Marci, With a Boat—Gabriel) on display in the bar.

SANT PERE DE RODES

Fodor's Choice ★ *18 km (11 mi) west of Cadaqués, 170 km (105 mi) northeast of Barcelona, 67 km (42 mi) northeast of Girona.*

Once commanding territory and power on both sides of the Pyrenees, the Benedictine monastery of Sant Pere de Rodes rises majestically on a steep mountainside overlooking Cap de Creus. The dignity of its architecture and the beauty of its view—which overlooks the Creus Peninsula and the waters of the Mediterranean—make it a must-visit. First built in 878 and reformed and expanded between the 9th and 12th centuries, it is one of the finest examples of Romanesque architecture in Spain, with exceptional examples of masonry laid in the *opus spicatum* (herringbone) pattern. Particularly notable are the church, with its two-tiered ambulatory, 12th-century bell tower, and defense tower. On the left-hand side of the church's altar as you enter, a winding stairway barely wide enough for one person leads to the second level. Also note the nave's 11th-century columns, decorated with wolf's and dog's heads.

Repeatedly sacked over the centuries, Sant Pere de Rodes lost most of its influence in the 18th century. The monastery contains a study center for the Cap de Creus nature preserve. Sant Pere de Rodes can be reached from the village of Vilajuïga or from Port de la Selva. The road winding up from Vilajuïga passes several groups of prehistoric dolmens, all signposted. Megaliths are very common in this area, more than 130 of them having been counted to date in the *comarca* (county) of the Alt Empordà alone. ⊠ *Port de la Selva* ☏ *972/387559, 972/193192 for study center* ⊙ *€4.50 Oct.–May, Tues.–Sun. 10–5:30; June–Sept., daily 10–8. Closed Mon., Dec. 25 and 26, Jan. 1 and 6.*

FIGUERES

23 km (14 mi) southwest of Sant Pere de Rodes, 42 km (26 mi) north of Girona, 150 km (93 mi) northeast of Barcelona.

Figueres is the capital of the *comarca* (county) of the Alt Empordà, the bustling county seat of this predominantly agricultural region. Local

The dramatic seaside Benedictine monastery of San Pere de Rodes.

people come from the surrounding area to shop at its many stores and stock up on farm equipment and supplies. Thursday is market day, and farmers gather at the top of the Rambla to do business and gossip, taking refreshments at cafés and discreetly pulling out and pocketing large rolls of bills, the result of their morning transactions. But among the tractors and mule carts is the main reason tourists come to Figueres: the jaw-dropping Dalí Museum, one of the most-visited museums in Spain.

Painter Salvador Dalí is Figueres's most famous son. With a painter's technique that rivaled that of Jan van Eyck, a flair for publicity so aggressive it would have put P. T. Barnum in the shade, and a penchant for shocking (he loved telling people Barcelona's historic Gothic Quarter should be knocked down), Dalí scaled the ramparts of art history as one of the foremost proponents of Surrealism, the art movement launched in the 1920s by André Breton. His most lasting image may be the melting watches in his iconic 1931 painting *The Persistence of Memory*. The artist, who was born in Figueres (1904) and was to die here (1989), decided to create a museum-monument to himself during the last two decades of his life. Dalí often frequented the Cafeteria Astòria at the top of the Rambla (still the center of social life in Figueres), signing autographs for tourists or just being Dalí: he once walked down the street with a French omelet in his breast pocket instead of a handkerchief.

GETTING HERE AND AROUND
Figueres is one of the stops on the regular train service from Barcelona to the French border. Local buses are also frequent, especially from nearby Cadaqués, with more than eight services daily. The town is sufficiently small to explore on foot.

ESSENTIALS
Visitor Information Figueres (✉ *Pl. del Sol* ☎ *972/503155*).

EXPLORING

Casa-Museu Gala Dalí. The third point of the Dalí triangle is the medieval castle of Púbol, where the artist's wife Gala is buried in the crypt. During the 1970s this was Gala's residence, though Dalí also lived here in the early 1980s. It contains paintings and drawings, Gala's haute-couture dresses, elephant sculptures in the garden, furniture, and other objects chosen by the couple. Púbol, roughly between Girona and Figueres, is near the C255, and is not easy to find. If you are traveling by train, get off at the Flaçà station on the Barcelona-Portbou line of RENFE railways; walk or take a taxi 4 km (2½ mi) to Púbol. By bus, the Sarfa bus company has a stop in Flaçà and on the C255 road, some 2 km (1 mi) from Púbol. ✉ *Púbol* ☎ *972/677500* ⊕ *www.salvador-dali.org* ☜ *€7* ⊙ *Mid-Mar.–mid-June and mid-Sept.–Oct., Tues.–Sun. 10:30–6; mid-June–mid-Sept., daily 10:30–8. Last admission 45 mins before closing.*

Castell de Sant Ferran. An imposing 18th-century fortified castle that is one of the largest in Europe, this structure stands 1 km (½ mi) northwest of town. Only when you start exploring the castle grounds (and walking around its perimeter of roughly 4 km [2½ mi]) can you appreciate how immense it is. The parade grounds extend for acres, and the arcaded stables can hold more than 500 horses. This castle was the site of the last official meeting of the Republican parliament (on February 1, 1939) before it surrendered to Franco's forces. Ironically, it was here that Lt. Colonel Antonio Tejero was imprisoned after his failed 1981 coup d'état in Madrid. ✉ *Pujada al Castell s/n* ☎ *972/506094* ⊕ *www.castillosanfernando.org* ☜ *€3* ⊙ *Mar.–June and mid-Sept.–Oct., daily 10:30–2 and 4–6; July–mid-Sept., daily 10:30–8; Nov.–Feb., daily 10:30–2. Last admission 1 hr before closing.*

Museu de l'Empordà. The collections here range from the Roman era to the Catalan Renaixença. ✉ *Rambla 217600* ☎ *972/502305* ⊕ *www.museuemporda.org* ☜ *€3* ⊙ *July–Sept., Tues.–Sat. 11–7, Sun. 11–2.*

ⓒ **Museu del Joguet de Catalunya.** Displaying childhood playthings pre–Toys 'R' Us, this is Spain's only toy museum. Hundreds of antique dolls are on display. The museum has collections of toys owned by, among others, Salvador Dalí, Federico García Lorca, and Joan Miró. It also hosts Catalonia's only *caganer* exhibit, from mid-December to mid-January on odd-numbered years. These playful little figures of guys (and gals) answering nature's call have long had a special spot in the Catalan *pessebre* (Nativity scene). Farmers are the most traditional figures, squatting discreetly behind the animals, but these days you'll find Barça soccer players and politicians, too. Check with the museum for exact dates. ✉ *Hotel de Figueres, Carrer de Sant Pere 1* ☎ *972/504508* ⊕ *www.mjc.cat* ☜ *€5* ⊙ *June–Sept., daily 10–1 and 4–7; Oct.–May, Tues.–Sat. 10–6, Sun. 11–2.*

★ **Teatre-Museu Dalí.** "Museum" was not a big enough word for Dalí, so he christened his monument a "Theater." It was, indeed, once the Old Town theater, reduced to a ruin in the Spanish civil war. Now topped with a glass geodesic dome and studded with Dalí's iconic egg shapes, the multilevel museum pays homage to his fertile imagination and artistic creativity. It includes gardens, ramps, and a spectacular drop cloth Dalí painted for Les Ballets de Monte Carlo. Don't look for his greatest paintings here, although there are some memorable images, including *Gala at the Mediterranean,* which takes the body of Gala (Dalí's wife) and morphs it into the image of Abraham Lincoln once you look through coin-operated viewfinders. The sideshow theme continues with other coin-operated pieces, including *Taxi Plujós* (Rainy Taxi), in which water gushes over the snail-covered occupants sitting in a Cadillac once owned by Al Capone, or *Sala de Mae West,* a trompe-l'oeil vision in which a pink sofa, two fireplaces, and two paintings morph into the face of Hollywood sex symbol Mae West. Fittingly, another "exhibit" on view is Dalí's own crypt. When his friends considered what flag to lay over his coffin, they decided to cover it with an embroidered heirloom tablecloth instead. Dalí would have liked this unconventional touch, if not the actual site: he wanted to be buried at his castle of Púbol next to his wife Gala, but the then mayor of Figueres took matters into his own hands. All in all, the museum is a piece of Dalí dynamite. The summer night session is a perfect time for a postprandial browse through the world's largest Surrealist museum. ⊠ *Pl. Gala-Salvador Dalí 5* ☎ *972/677500* ⊕ *www.salvador-dali.org* ⊠€*12* ☉ *Oct.–June, Tues.–Sun. 10:30–5:15; July–Sept., daily 9–7:15; special summer nighttime visits July 28–Sept. 2, 10* PM–1AM.

WHERE TO STAY

$ ⊡ **Hotel Duràn.** Once a stagecoach relay station, the Duràn is now a well-known hotel and restaurant. Salvador Dalí had his own private dining room here, and you can still have dinner ($–$$) with the great Surrealist, or at least with pictures of him. Try the *mandonguilles amb sèpia a l'estil Anna* (meatballs and cuttlefish), a *mar i muntanya* (surf-and-turf) specialty of the house. The elegant, classic guest rooms are outfitted with wooden furniture; some rooms overlook the Rambla. A relaxing spot is the good-size sitting room on the first floor. **Pros:** handy location at the nerve center of pretty rural town. **Cons:** both rooms and public spaces are somewhat over-cluttered with rustic furnishings and artifacts. ⊠ *Carrer Lasauca 5* ☎ *972/501250* ⊕ *www.hotelduran.com* ⊅ *65 rooms* ⚒ *In-room: Wi-Fi. In-hotel: restaurant, bar, parking (paid)* ⊟ *AE, MC, V* ⊙|*EP.*

$–$$ ⊡ **Hotel Empordà.** Just a mile north of town, this hotel and elegant restaurant ($$–$$$) run by Jaume Subirós is hailed as the birthplace of modern Catalan cuisine, and has become a beacon for gourmands seeking superb Catalan cooking. Try the *terrina calenta de lluerna a l'oli de cacauet* (hot pot of gurnard fish in peanut oil) or, if it's winter, *llebre a la Royal* (boned hare cooked in red wine). Guest rooms have parquet floors and sparkling bathrooms, and you can sit in the sun and have a drink on the terrace. The hotel is 1½ km (1 mi) north of town. **Pros:** historic culinary destination and, of course, great cuisine. **Cons:** the hotel occupies an unprepossessing roadside lot beside the busy NII highway. ⊠ *Ctra. NII, Km 1.5,* ☎ *972/500562* ⊕ *www.hotelemporda.com* ⊅ *42*

Fodor's Choice
★

rooms ♿ *In-room: Wi-Fi. In-hotel: restaurant, bar, some pets allowed* ▤ *AE, DC, MC, V* ⦿| *BP.*

PERALADA

12 km (7 mi) northeast of Figueres, 47 km (29 mi) north of Girona.

This small, quiet village has a fine glassware museum, a noted summer music festival, and—of all things—a casino. The village's history goes back at least to the 9th century, and the counts of Peralada, one of the noblest titles of Catalonia, originated here. Ramon Muntaner, the great 13th-century Catalan chronicler, was from Peralada; his *Chronicle* describes how the town was put to the torch in 1285 by the Almogàvers, Catalan soldiers of fortune who carved out an empire in Greece. Archaeological excavations have uncovered signs of this great fire.

EXPLORING

Museu del Castell de Peralada. In the old Convent del Carme, this space houses the best glassware museum in Spain, a library with more than 70,000 volumes, and a wine museum. The park is one of the finest English-style gardens in the region, with a lake in which swans glide back and forth. The guided tours take 55 minutes and end with a tasting of cava. ⊠ *Pl. del Carme s/n* ☎ *972/538125* 🖳 *www.museucastellperalada. com* €6 ⊗ *July–Aug., tours (in English) daily on the hr 10–noon and 5–8; Sept.–June, tours Tues.–Sat. on the hr 10–noon and 4:30–6:30, Sun. 10–noon.*

WHERE TO EAT AND STAY

$-$$ ✕**Cal Sagristà.** This neo-rustic space greets you warmly with aged
SPANISH brick walls and contemporary paintings. A former convent-school of Augustinian nuns, the restaurant has an arbored terrace with a view encompassing the Alberes range. For openers, the *amanida amb bolets confitats* (salad with preserved mushrooms) is a treat. Other delights include *magret de anec amb salsa de gerds* (duck with raspberry jam) and *cua de bou amb cebetes* (oxtail with shallots), all accompanied by the local Castell de Peralada Blanco Seco. ⊠ *Rodona 2* ☎ *972/538301* ▤ *AE, MC, V* ⊗ *Closed last 2 wks of Nov. and last 2 wks of Jan. No dinner Sun. or Tues. Sept.–June.*

$$$$ ▦ **Golf Peralada.** Surrounded by an often windswept 18-hole golf course, this graceful upper Empordà refuge has become a point of reference in Peralada. Equipped with every luxury, from hydrotherapy to state-of-the-art fitness and sauna equipment, this pleasure palace is a little redolent of a Las Vegas spa dropped into northern Catalonia, but if that's what you're looking for, here it is. **Pros:** impeccable and encyclopedic list of amenities, resources, and comforts. **Cons:** excessively ultramodern and impersonal. ⊠ *Av. Rocaberti s/n* ☎ *972/538830* ⊕ *www. golfperalada.com* ⤶*53 rooms, 2 suites* ♿ *In-room: Wi-Fi. In-hotel: restaurant, bar, Internet terminal, Wi-Fi hotspot, golf course, pool, gym, spa, parking (paid), some pets allowed* ▤ *AE, DC, MC, V* ⦿|*EP.*

$ ▦ **Hostal de la Font.** This solid stone house in the center of town was once a convent. Enric Serraplana, the proprietor, is also an antiques dealer, to the hotel's benefit. Rooms have wooden floors and handsome, sometimes antique, furnishings, with contemporary, renovated baths. The interior patio was once the convent cloister. The dining room is wood paneled and gracefully decorated with antiques, and has a communal table where guests have breakfast together. **Pros:** the midtown location allows you to get the feel of life in this small rural town. **Cons:** rooms are not spacious and sometimes overfurnished. ✉ *Carrer de la Font 15–19* ☎ *972/538507* ⊕ *www.hostaldelafont.com.es* ⊊*12 rooms* ⚬ *In-room: Wi-Fi. In-hotel: Internet terminal, Wi-Fi hotspot, some pets allowed* ═ *AE, DC, MC, V* ⍥⎮*EP.*

NIGHTLIFE AND THE ARTS

The **Casino Castell de Peralada** occupies the Castell de Perelada, a 19th-century re-creation (complete with crenellated battlements) of an original medieval castle. Games include French and American roulette, blackjack, and slot machines. A valid ID (proving you are over 21) is necessary for admission. ✉ *Carrer Sant Joan s/n* ☎ *972/538125* ⊕ *www. casino-peralada.com* ⊠ *€4* ⊘ *Mon.–Thurs. 7* PM–*4* AM, *Fri. and Sat. 7* PM–*5* AM, *Sun. 5* PM–*4* AM.

The Castell de Peralada is the main site of the **Festival Internacional de Música,** a music festival held in its gardens every July and August. The world's finest artists perform in the town castle, and original works are especially composed for this event. ✉ *Carrer Sant Joan s/n* ☎ *93/280– 5868 or 972/538292* ⊕ *www.festivalperalada.com.*

INLAND TO GIRONA

Much of Girona's charm comes from its narrow medieval streets, historic buildings, fine restaurants, and a community of students and scholars drawn by the local university. To the west you can discover a region that, studded with historic and picturesque towns such as Besalú and Olot, calls to mind Italy's Tuscany or France's Lubéron. Sprinkled across these landscapes are *masies* (farmhouses) with austere, grayish or pinkish staggered-stone rooftops and ubiquitous square towers that make them look like fortresses. Even the tiniest village has its church, arcaded square, and *rambla,* where villagers take their evening stroll. Around Olot, the volcanic region of the Garrotxa, with more than 30 now-extinct volcanoes (the last eruption was at least 9,500 years ago, though experts say new activity cannot be discounted), is a striking landscape, with—amid lush forests of beech, oak, and pine—barren moonscapes worthy of *Star Wars.* Heading back south from Girona, nature lovers can also make a stop at the pristine Montseny wilderness park before entering the tumultuous rhythm of Barcelona once again.

GIRONA

97 km (60 mi) northeast of Barcelona.

Girona (Gerona in Castilian), a city of more than 70,000 inhabitants, keeps intact the magic of its historic past. In fact, with its brooding hilltop castle, soaring cathedral, and dreamy riverside setting it resembles a vision from the Middle Ages. Once called a "Spanish Venice"—although there are no real canals here, just the confluence of four rivers—the city is almost as evocative as that city on the lagoon. With El Call, one of

Europe's best-preserved Jewish communities dating from the Middle Ages, and the Arab Baths, lovely Girona is a reminder that Spain's Jewish and Islamic communities both thrived here for centuries. Today, as a university center, it combines past and vibrant present—art galleries, chic cafés, and trendy boutiques have set up shop in many of the restored buildings of the Old Quarter.

The Romans founded Gerunda in the 1st century AD at a convenient ford that spanned the confluence of four rivers: the Ter, Onyar, Güell, and Galligants. Nearby stone quarries supplied building material, and the mountain on which the Old City sits is known as Les Pedreres (the quarries). The Old Quarter of Girona, called the Força Vella (Old Force, or Fortress), is built on the side of the mountain, and is a tightly packed labyrinth of fine buildings, monuments, and steep, narrow cobblestone streets linked with frequent stairways. You can still see vestiges of the Iberian and Roman walls in the cathedral square and in the patio of the old university. Head over from modern Girona (on the west side of the Onyar) to the Old Quarter on the east side. The main street of the Old Quarter is Carrer de la Força. It follows the old Via Augusta, the Roman road that connected Rome with its provinces.

The best way to get to know Girona is by walking along its streets. As you wander through the Força Vella you will be repeatedly surprised by new discoveries. One of Girona's treasures is its setting, as it rises high above the Riu Onyar, where that river merges with the Ter. (The Ter flows from a mountain waterfall that can be glimpsed in a gorge above the town.) Regardless of your approach to the town, walk first along the west-side banks of the Onyar, between the train trestle and the Plaça de la Independència, to admire the classic view of the Old Town, with its pastel yellow, pink, and orange waterfront facades. Windows and balconies are always draped with colorful drying laundry reflected in the shimmering river and often adorned with fretwork grilles of embossed wood or delicate iron tracery. Cross the Pont de Sant Agustí over to the Old City from under the arcades in the corner of the Plaça de la Independència, and find your way to the tourist office, to the right at Rambla Llibertat 1. Then work your way up through the labyrinth of steep streets, using the cathedral's huge baroque facade as a guide.

A special Girona visitor's card allowing free admission to some museums and monuments and discounts at others can be purchased at the tourist-office welcome station. Look for the **Punt de Benvinguda** (⊠ *Carrer Berenguer Carnicer 3* ☎ *972/211678* ⊕ *www.girona-net.com*), at the entrance to Girona from the town's main parking area on the right bank of the Onyar River.

GETTING HERE AND AROUND
There are more than 20 daily trains from Barcelona to Girona (continuing on to the French border). Girona airport is also a destination for flights from London via the no frills airways, Ryan Air. Getting around the city is easiest by foot or by taxi; several bridges connect the historic old quarter with the more modern town across the river.

ESSENTIALS
Visitor Information Girona (⊠ *Rambla de la Libertat 1* ☎ *972/226575* ⊕ *www. ajuntament.gi*).

EXPLORING
Numbers in the text correspond to numbers in the Girona map.

❹ Banys Arabs. A misnomer, the Banys Arabs were actually built by Morisco (workers of Moorish descent who remained in Spain after the 1492 Expulsion Decree) craftsmen in the late 12th century, long after Girona's Islamic occupation (795–1015) had ended. Following the old Roman model that had disappeared in the West, the custom of bathing publicly may have been brought back from the Holy Land with the Crusaders. These baths are sectioned off into three rooms in descending order; a *frigidarium,* or cold bath, a square room with a central octagonal pool and a skylight with cupola held up by two stories of eight fine columns; a *tepidarium,* or warm bath; and a *caldarium,* or steam room, beneath which is a chamber where a fire was kept burning. Here the inhabitants of the old Girona came to relax, exchange gossip, or do business. It is known from another public bathhouse in Tortosa, Tarragona, that the various social classes came to bathe by sexes on fixed days of the week; Christian men on one day, Christian women on another, Jewish men on still another, Jewish women (and prostitutes) on a fourth, Muslims on others. ⊠ *Carrer Ferran el Catòlic s/n* ☎ *972/213262* ⊕ *www.*

Ninety steps lead up to the massive Cathedral in Girona.

banysarabs.org ⬛ *€2.50* ⊙ *Apr–Sept., Tues.–Sat. 10–2 and 4–7, Sun. 10–2; Nov.–Apr., Tues.–Sun. 10–1.*

❶ Cathedral. At the heart of the Old City, this cathedral looms above 90
Fodor's Choice steps and is famous for its nave—at 75 feet, the widest in the world
★ and the epitome of the spatial ideal of Catalan Gothic architects. Since
Charlemagne founded the original church in the 8th century, it has been
through many fires, changes, and renovations, so you are greeted by a
rococo-era facade—"eloquent as organ music" and impressively set off
by a spectacular flight of 17th-century stairs, which rises from its own
plaça. Inside, three smaller naves were compressed into one gigantic hall
by the famed architect Guillermo Bofill in 1416. The change was typical
of Catalan Gothic "hall" churches, and it was done to facilitate preaching to crowds. Note the famous silver canopy, or *baldaquí* (baldachin).
The oldest part of the cathedral is the 11th-century Romanesque **Torre
de Carlemany** (Charlemagne Tower).

The cathedral has an exquisite 12th-century cloister, which has an obvious affinity with the cloisters in the Roussillon area of France; you can
visit it with a ticket to the cathedral's **Museu Capitular**, or Tresor, indeed
filled with treasures. They include a 10th-century copy of Beatus's manu-
script *Commentary on the Apocalypse*—one of the famous 10th-century
manuscripts illuminated in the dramatically primitive Mozarabic style—
the Bible of Emperor Charles V, and the celebrated *Tapís de la Creació*
(*Tapestry of the Creation*), considered by most experts to be the finest
tapestry surviving from the Romanesque era (and, in fact, thought to
be the needlework of Saxons working in England). It depicts the seven
days of the Creation as told in Genesis in the primitive but powerful

fashion of early Romanesque art, and looks not unlike an Asian mandala. Made of wool, with predominant colors of green, brown, and ocher, the tapestry once hung behind the main altar as a pictorial Bible lesson. The four seasons, the stars, winds, months of the year and days of the week, plants, animals, and elements of nature circle round a central figure, likening paradise to the eternal cosmos presided over by Christ. In addition to its intrinsic beauty, along the bottom band (which appears to have been added at a later date) another significant detail is the depiction of two *iudeis*, or Jews, dressed in the round cloaks they were compelled to wear to set them apart from Christians. This scene is thought to be the earliest portrayal of a Jew (other than biblical figures) known in Christian art.

VERGES : HALLOWEEN MEETS EASTER

The village of Verges, northeast of Girona, holds one of Spain's most macabre and unusual Easter celebrations, La Dansa de la Mort (The Dance of Death), a tribute to mortality that seems more Halloween than Easter. Descended from medieval tradition, the Dance of Death is part of the procession commemorating the life and death of Christ. Five luminous skeletons painted over black leotards create a lifelike (that is, deathlike) effect of dancing bones. Props include a scythe, a handless clock suggesting death's unknowable hour, and a bowl of ashes symbolizing mortal decay.

✉ *Pl. de la Catedral* ☎ *972/214426* ⊕ *www.catedraldegirona.org* 🖼 *€5; free Sun.* ☉ *Nov.–Mar., weekdays 10–7, Sat. 4:30–7, Sun. 10–2, 4:30–7; Apr.–Oct., weekdays 10–8 and 4:30–8, Sat. 4:30–8, Sun. 2–8.*

➒ Centre Bonastruc ça Porta. Housed in a former synagogue and dedicated to the preservation of Girona's Jewish heritage, this center organizes conferences, exhibitions, and seminars. The **Museu de Història dels Jueus** (Museum of Jewish History) contains 21 stone tablets, one of the finest collections in the world of medieval Jewish funerary slabs. These came from the old Jewish cemetery of Montjuïc, revealed when the railroad between Barcelona and France was laid out in the 19th century. Its exact location, about 1½ km (1 mi) north of Girona on the road to La Bisbal and known as La Tribana, is being excavated. The center also holds the **Institut d'Estudis Nahmànides,** with its extensive library of Judaica. ✉ *Carrer de la Força 817004* ☎ *972/216761* ⊕ *www.ajgirona.org/call* 🖼 *€3* ☉ *Mon.–Sat. 10–6, Sun. 10–3.*

➐ El Call. Girona is especially noted for its 13th-century Jewish Quarter, El Call, which can be found branching off Carrer de la Força, south of the Plaça Catedral. The word *call* (pronounced "kyle" in Catalan) may come from an old Catalan word meaning "narrow way" or "passage," derived from the Latin word *callum* or *callis*. Others suggest that it comes from the Hebrew word *Qahal*, meaning "assembly" or "meeting of the community." Owing allegiance to the Spanish king (who exacted tribute for this distinction) and not to the city government, this once prosperous Jewish community—one of the most flourishing in Europe during the Middle Ages—was, at its height, a leading center of learning. An important school of the Kabala was centered here. The most famous teacher of the Kabala from Girona was Rabbi Mossé ben

Nahman (also known as Nahmànides, and by the acronym RMBN—or Ramban—taken from the first letters of his title and name), who is popularly believed to be one and the same as Bonastruc ça Porta. Nahmànides wrote an important religious work based on meditation and the reinterpretation of the Bible and the Talmud.

The earliest presence of Jews in Girona is uncertain, but the first historical mention dates from 982, when a group of 25 Jewish families moved to Girona from nearby Juïgues. Jews may have been already present in the region for several hundred years, however. Today the layout of El Call bears no resemblance to what this area looked like in the 15th century, when Jews last lived here. Space was at a premium inside the city walls in Girona, and houses were destroyed and built higgledy-piggledy one atop the other. The narrow streets, barely wide enough for a single person to pass (they have now been widened slightly), crisscrossed one above the other.

② **Museu d'Art.** The Episcopal Palace near the cathedral contains the wide-ranging collections of Girona's main art museum. You'll see everything from superb Romanesque *majestats* (carved wood figures of Christ) to reliquaries from Sant Pere de Rodes, and illuminated 12th-century manuscripts to works of the 20th-century Olot school of landscape painting. ⊠ *Pujada de la Catedral 12* ☎ *972/203834* ⊕ *www.museuart. com* ✆ *€3.50* ☉ *Tues.–Sat. 10–7, Sun. 10–2.*

NEED A BREAK? Fortify yourself for sightseeing with some superb tea and plump pastries at **La Vienesa** (⊠ *Carrer La Pujada del Pont de Pedra 1 17004* ☎ *972/486046*). One of the town's best-loved gathering points for conversation, this cozy spot is good place to regroup and re-navigate.

⑪ **Museu del Cinema.** An interactive cinema museum, this spot has artifacts and movie-related paraphernalia starting from Chinese shadows, the first rudimentary moving pictures, to Lyon's Lumière brothers. The Cine Nic toy filmmaking machines, originally developed in 1931 by the Nicolau brothers of Barcelona and now being relaunched commercially, allow even novices to put together their own movies. ⊠ *Carrer Sèquia 1* ☎ *972/412777* ⊕ *www.museudelcinema.org* ✆ *€4* ☉ *May–Sept., Mon.–Sat. 10–8, Sun. 10–3; Oct.–Apr., Mon.–Sat. 10–6, Sun. 10–3.*

⑩ **Museu d'Història de la Ciutat.** On Carrer de la Força, this fascinating museum is filled with artifacts from Girona's long and embattled past. From pre-Roman objects to paintings and drawings from the notorious siege at the hands of Napoleonic troops to the early municipal lighting system and the medieval printing press, there is plenty to see here. You will definitely come away with a clearer idea of Girona's past. ⊠ *Carrer de la Força 27* ☎ *972/222229* ⊕ *www.ajuntament.gi/museu_ciutat* ✆ *€3* ☉ *May–Sept., Tues.–Sat. 10–2 and 5–7, Sun. 10–3.*

⑥ **Passeig Arqueològic.** The landscaped gardens of this stepped archaeological walk run below the restored walls of the Old Quarter (which you can walk, in parts) and has good views from belvederes and watchtowers. From there, climb through the Jardins de la Francesa to the highest ramparts for a view of the cathedral's 11th-century Charlemagne Tower.

❽ Placeta del Institut Vell. In this small square on Carrer de la Força you can study a tar-blackened 3-inch-long, half-inch-deep groove carved shoulder-high into the stone of the right-hand door post as you enter the square. It indicates the location of a mezuzah, a small case or tube of metal or wood in which a piece of parchment with verses from the Torah (declaring the essence of Jewish belief in one God) was placed. Anyone passing through the doorway touched the mezuzah as a sign of devotion. Evidence of the labyrinthine layout of a few street ruts in the Old Quarter may still be seen inside the antiques store Antiguitats la Canonja Vella at Carrer de la Força 33.

❸ Sant Feliu. The vast bulk of this structure is landmarked by one of Girona's most distinctive belfries, topped by eight pinnacles. One of Girona's most beloved churches, it was repeatedly rebuilt and altered over four centuries and stands today as an amalgam of Romanesque columns, Gothic nave, and baroque facade. It was founded over the tomb of St. Felix of Africa, a martyr under the Roman emperor Diocletian. ⊠ *Pujada de Sant Feliu* ☎ *972/201407* ☉ *Daily 9–10:30, 11:30–1, and 4–6:30.*

❺ Sant Pere. The church of *St. Peter*, across the Galligants River, was finished in 1131, and is notable for its octagonal Romanesque belfry and the finely detailed capitals atop the columns in the cloister. It now houses the **Museu Arqueològic** (Museum of Archaeology), which documents the region's history since Paleolithic times and includes some artifacts from Roman times. ⊠ *Carrer Santa Llúcia s/n* ☎ *972/202632* ☑ *€3* ☉ *Church and museum daily 10–1 and 4:30–7.*

Torre de Gironella. A five-minute walk uphill behind the cathedral leads to a park and this four-story tower (no entry permitted) dating from the year 1190 that marks the highest point in the Jewish Quarter. Girona's Jewish community took refuge here in early August of 1391, emerging 17 weeks later to find their houses in ruins. Even though Spain's official expulsion decree did not go into effect until 1492, this attack effectively ended the Girona Jewish community. Destroyed in 1404, reconstructed in 1411, and destroyed anew by retreating Napoleonic troops in 1814, the Torre de Gironella was the site of the celebration of the first Hanukkah ceremony in 607 years held on December 20, 1998, with Jerusalem's chief Sephardic rabbi Rishon Letzion presiding. ⊠ *Ctra. Sant Gregori 91.*

8

WHERE TO EAT

$$–$$$ **✕ Albereda.** Excellent Catalan cuisine with exotic touches is served here
CATALAN in an elegant setting under exposed brick arches. Try the *galeta amb llagostins glaçada* (zucchini bisque with prawns) or the *amanida tèbia d'espàrrecs naturals amb bacallà i cansalada ibérica* (warm asparagus salad with codfish and ibérico ham) for a *mar i muntanya* (surf-and-turf) with the garden thrown in as well. Wild mushrooms, truffles, foie gras, and fresh fish vie for space on this rich menu. ⊠ *Carrer Albereda 7 bis* ☎ *972/226002* ⊕ *www.restaurantalbereda. com* ▭ *AE, DC, MC, V* ☉ *Closed Sun.*

$–$$ **✕ Cal Ros.** Tucked under the arcades just behind the north end of Plaça
CATALAN de la Llibertat, this restaurant combines ancient stone arches with crisp,
★

contemporary furnishings and cheerful lighting. The cuisine is flavorful: hot goat-cheese salad with pine nuts and *garum* (black-olive and anchovy paste, a delicacy dating back to Roman times), *oca amb naps* (goose with turnips), and a blackberry sorbet should not to be missed. ⊠ *Carrer Cort Reial 9* ☎ *972/219176* ⊕ *www.calros-restaurant.com* ☐ *AE, DC, MC, V* ☉ *Closed Mon. No dinner Sun.*

$$$–$$$$
LA NUEVA
COCINA
Fodor's Choice
★

✕ **Celler de Can Roca.** Despite the dust-up (a bit too literally) over Joan Roca's eau de dirt (yes, he made a batter of water and dirt—aka mud—and put it on an oyster), this is universally acclaimed as one of the dozen top restaurants below the Pyrenees. A mile and a half northwest of town on the Taialà road, this is a must-stop for any self-respecting foodie. You can survey the kitchen from the dining room and watch the Roca brothers, Joan and Jordi, in the act of creating their masterful *arròs amb garotes i botifarra negre* (rice with sea urchins and black sausage) and *cua de bou farcida amb foie gras* (oxtail with foie gras). For dessert, try the *pastel calent de xocolata i gingebre* (hot-chocolate ginger cake) or jasmine-tea ice cream. Don't be embarrassed to ask the sommelier for guidance through the encyclopedic wine list. ⊠ *Can Sunyer 48* ☎ *972/222157* ⊕ *www.cellercanroca.com* ⚒ *Reservations essential* ☐ *AE, DC, MC, V* ☉ *Closed Sun., Mon., and Aug. 24–31.*

$
LA NUEVA
COCINA

✕ **Mimolet.** Contemporary architecture and cuisine in the old part of Girona make for interesting dining at this sleek and streamlined restaurant just below the Colegiata de Sant Feliu and the Monastery of Sant Pere de Galligants. *Croquetes casolanes* (homemade croquettes) of onion, shrimp, and black sausage or *carpaccio de vedella amb poma, nous i cingles de bertí* (beef carpaccio with apple, walnuts, and a local blue cheese) are typical starters on this rapidly changing seasonal menu. Entrées star grass-fed beef from Girona, lamb, duck, and an anthology of Mediterranean fish and seafood. ⊠ *Pou Rodó 12* ☎ *972/202124* ⊕ *www.mimolet.net* ☐ *AE, DC, MC* ☉ *Closed Sun., Mon., Dec. 23–Jan. 7.*

WHERE TO STAY

¢–$

⊺ **Bellmirall.** This pretty little hostel across the Onyar in the Jewish Quarter, despite its scarcity of amenities, offers top value in the heart of Girona's most historic section. **Pros:** a budget choice, this hostel provides the basics with perfect aesthetic taste as well. **Cons:** rooms are small, and—without the Internet, TV, and telephone—can feel isolating. ⊠ *Carrer Bellmirall 3* ☎ *972/204009* ⊕ *www.grn.es/bellmirall* ⤳ *7 rooms* ⚐ *In-room: no a/c, no phone, no TV. In-hotel: Wi-Fi hotspot* ☐ *No credit cards* ☉ *Closed Jan. and Feb.* ⑩ *EP.*

$–$$
★

⊺ **Hotel Històric y Apartaments Històric Girona.** This boutique hotel has one room (the suite) with views of the cathedral and Gothic vaulting overhead. The apartment accommodations are in a 9th-century house, with remnants of a 3rd-century Roman wall and a Roman aqueduct on the ground floor and in one of the apartments. One dining room even contains a wall made in the pre-Roman *opus spicatum* herringbone pattern. Wooden furniture fills the simply but pleasantly furnished rooms. Casilda Cruz rents these good-value apartments in the Old Quarter for as many days as you'd like, from one day to one month. **Pros:** ideal environment for a visit to Europe's best-preserved medieval Jewish

CLOSE UP

Farmhouse Stays

Dotted throughout Catalonia are farmhouses (*casas rurales* in Spanish, and *cases de pagès* or *masies* in Catalan), where you can spend a weekend or longer. Accommodations vary from small, rustic homes to spacious, luxurious farmhouses with fireplaces and pools. Sometimes you stay in a guest room, as at a B&B; in other places you rent the entire house and do your own cooking. Most tourist offices, including the main Catalonia Tourist Office in Barcelona, have info and listings for the *cases de pagès*

of the region. You can peruse listings of farmhouses on ⊕ *www.gencat.net.* Several organizations in Spain also have detailed listings and descriptions of Catalonia's farmhouses, and it's best to book through one of these.

LOCAL AGENTS
Federació d'Agroturisme i Turisme Rural Comarques de Tarragona (✉ *Sant Francesc 1 Cornudella de Montsant* ☎ *977/821082* ⊕ *www. agroturisme.org*). **Tural** (✉ *Carrer Aragó 359 Eixample, Barcelona* ☎ *93/539–4678* ⊕ *www.tural.org*).

Quarter; top technology and comforts. **Cons:** rooms and apartments are a little cramped. ✉ *Carrer Bellmirall 4A, 17004* ☎ *972/223583* ⊕ *www. hotelhistoric.com* 🛏 *8 rooms, 7 apartments, 1 junior suite, 1 suite* ⚉ *In-room: Wi-Fi, kitchen* ⊟ *AE, DC, MC, V* ⦿ *EP.*

¢ 🖼 **Hotel Peninsular.** In a handsomely restored early 20th-century building
★ across the Onyar River with views into Girona's historic Old Quarter, this modest but useful hotel occupies a strategic spot at the end of the Pont de Pedra (Stone Bridge), a Girona landmark in the center of the shopping district. **Pros:** a good location over the Onyar at the hub of Girona life; near the bus stop from Girona airport. **Cons:** smallish rooms and sometimes noisy on Friday and Saturday nights. ✉ *Av. Sant Francesc 6* ☎ *902/734541* ⊕ *www.novarahotels.com* 🛏 *68 rooms* ⚉ *In-room: Wi-Fi, safe. In-hotel: bar, Internet terminal* ⊟ *AE, DC, MC, V* ⦿ *EP.*

8

NIGHTLIFE AND THE ARTS

Girona is a university town, so the night scene is especially lively during the school year. Trendy young people flock to **Accés 21** (✉ *Carrer Carreras Peralta 7* ☎ *972/213708*). **Babel** (✉ *Carrer Nord 14* ☎ *972/213179*) provides another hot nocturnal address. The older crowd goes to **Cadillac Café** (✉ *Barcelona 130* ☎ *972/228452*), on the road going to Palamós. A popular nightspot for the young, hip set is **Platea** (✉ *Carrer Real de Fontclara 4* ☎ *972/227288*).

In summer, nighttime action centers on **Les Carpes de la Devesa** (✉ *Passeig de la Devesa*), a park on the west side of the Onyar River in the modern city. From June to September 15, three awnings, or *carpes*, are set up here so that people can sit outside in the warm weather until the wee hours, enjoying drinks and listening to music.

SHOPPING

If it's jewelry you're looking for, head to **Anna Casals** (✉ *Carrer Ballesteries 33* ☎ *972/410227*). For interior decoration, plastic arts, religious paintings, and sculptures, stop at **Dolors Turró** (✉ *Ballesteries 19* ☎ *972/410193*). **Gluki** (✉ *Carrer Argenteria 26* ☎ *972/201989*) has made chocolate since 1880. Candles are the specialty at **Karla** (✉ *Carrer Ballesteries 22* ☎ *972/227210*). All manner of masks, dolls, pottery, and crafts are available at **La Carpa** (✉ *Carrer Ballesteries 37* ☎ *972/212002*). **Torrons Victoria Candela** (✉ *Carrer Anselm Clavé 3* ☎ *972/211103*) specializes in tasty nougat.

Codina (✉ *Carrer Nord 20* ☎ *972/219880*) sells jazzy women's clothes. Young people stock up on threads at **Desideratum** (✉ *Carrer Migdia 30* ☎ *972/221448*). Men will find fine plumage at **Falcó** (✉ *Carrer Josep Maluquer Salvador 16* ☎ *972/207156*). For shoes, go to one of the three locations for **Peacock** (✉ *Carrer Nou 15* ☎ *972/226848*) ✉ *Carrer de Santa Clare 31* ☎ *972/201–420* ✉ *Carrer Migdia 18* ☎ *972/216115* ⊕ *www.peacock.cat*).

Girona's best bookstore, with a large travel-guide section and a small section of English fiction, is **Llibreria 22** (✉ *Carrer Hortes 22 17001* ☎ *972/212395* ⊕ *www.llibreria22.net*). For travel books and other editions in English, try **Ulysus** (✉ *Carrer Ballesteries 29 17004* ☎ *972/221773*).

BANYOLES

19 km (12 mi) north of Girona, 116 km (72 mi) northeast of Barcelona.

If Girona has cosmopolitan pleasures, Banyoles, with its lovely lake, makes a pleasant escape into the Catalan countryside. The town itself has a graceful historic quarter, complete with the Monestir de Sant Esteve (usually locked, but ask around for admittance) and an arcaded Plaça Major.

EXPLORING

Cuevas de Serinyà. You can visit the *Serinyà Caves*, 8 km (5 mi) north of Banyoles, where many of the artifacts in the local archaeological museum were unearthed. In July and August guided tours (though usually not in English) take you through the series of small caves every hour on the hour; during the rest of the year, guided tours are only on weekends, every hour on the hour. ✉ *Ctra. de Serinyà s/n* ☎ *972/593310* 🎫 *€3 includes archaeology and natural history museums* ⊙ *Mar.–June, Tues.–Fri. 10–4, weekends 11–6; July–Sept., daily 11–7; Oct.–Feb., Tues.–Fri. 10–3, weekends 11–5.*

Estany de Banyoles. This spring-fed lake, where rowing contests were held for the 1992 Olympic Games, is known for its natural beauty. Swimming, rowing, picnicking, and fishing for the lake's famous carp draw many people here. Although there is no Loch Ness monster here, some say the lake holds a fabled carp called *La Ramona*, which weighs more than 33 pounds and eats peanuts from your hand. You can try to spot her by renting a rowboat for €3 per hour per person, or taking the scenic cruiser around the lake for the same price.

Museu Arqueològic Comarcal. Displayed here are the intriguing finds from the archaeological site of La Draga, next to the lake and a 10-minute walk from town. Catalan archaeologists working at the Neolithic lakeshore site found a wooden tool at least 7,000 years old, the oldest wooden artifact ever found in the Mediterranean area, and one of the oldest in the world. You can also see the bones of ancient mastadons found in the area, and a copy of the famous Banyoles Jaw, discovered in 1887 and believed to be more than 100,000 years old, making it one of the earliest known human jawbones. Finds from the Serinyà Caves are exhibited as well. ⊠ *Pl. de Font 1117820* ☎ *972/572361* ⊕ *www.banyolescultura.net* ☜ *€2 includes natural history museum, €3 includes natural history museum and Serinyà Caves* ☉ *Sept.–June, Tues.–Sat. 10:30–1:30 and 4–6:30, Sun. 10:30–2; July and Aug., Tues.–Sat. 11–1:30 and 4–8, Sun. 10:30–2.*

Museu Municipal Darder d'Història Natural. Regional treasures of natural history are on view here, near the archaeology museum. Stuffed animals from the area (and the world) are on display, including crocodiles, ducks, bears, and sheep. The flora section of the museum displays regional plant life. ⊠ *Pl. dels Estudis s/n* ☎ *972/574467* ☜ *€2 includes archaeology museum, €3 includes archaeology museum and Serinyà Caves* ☉ *Sept.–June, Tues.–Sat. 10:30–1:30 and 4–6:30, Sun. 10:30–2; July and Aug., Tues.–Sat. 11–1:30 and 4–8, Sun. 10:30–2.*

WHERE TO EAT

$$–$$$
CATALAN

✕ **Ca l'Arpa.** The best restaurant in Banyoles also offers eight elegant rooms to guests who are wise enough to request a bed within crawling distance of the dinner table. Traditional cuisine with contemporary and innovative touches is the rule here, with roast suckling pig, risotto with Palamós jumbo shrimp, and fine products from the land and sea of this fertile northeastern corner of Iberia. ⊠ *Passeig Industria 5* ☎ *972/572353* ⊕ *www.calarpa.com* ☜ *Reservations essential* ═ *AE, DC, MC, V* ☉ *Closed Dec. 15–31 and Mon. No dinner Sun.*

BESALÚ

25 km (15 mi) north of Banyoles, 34 km (21 mi) north of Girona.

Besalú, once the capital of a feudal county until power was transferred to Barcelona at the beginning of the 12th century, remains one of the best-preserved and most evocative medieval towns in Catalonia. Among its main sights are two churches, Sant Vicenç (set on an attractive, café-lined plaza) and Sant Pere, and the ruins of the convent of Santa Maria on the hill above town.

GETTING HERE AND AROUND

With a population of just over 2,000, the village is certainly small enough to stroll, with all the restaurants and sights within easy distance of each other. There is bus service to Besalú from Figueres and the surrounding Costa Brava resorts.

ESSENTIALS
Visitor Information Besalú (✉ *Pl. de la Libertat 1* ☎ *972/591240*).

To visit the *mikvah* (Jewish ritual baths) and the churches (usually closed otherwise), there are guided tours organized by the tourist office. During the Jewish Festival (first week of March) and the Medieval Festival (first weekend in September) there are special visits to the historic quarter led by residents and costumed actors. The 11th century seems little more than a heartbeat away as a rabbi (an actor) from the old Jewish community shows the mikvah. A walk through the Call, or Jewish Quarter, follows. At the church of Sant Pere, with its 13th-century ambulatory, you may hear Gregorian chant. Book at the **tourist office.** ✉ *Pl. de la Llibertat* ☎ *972/591240* 🎫 *€3* ⊙ *Tours July and Aug., Wed. at 11.*

EXPLORING
Convent de Santa Maria. The ruins of the Santa Maria Convent on a hill just outside of town make a good walk and offer a panoramic view over Besalú.

Església de Sant Pere. The 12th-century Romanesque Sant Pere church, part of a 10th-century monastery, is a cavernous yet intimate medieval wonder. ✉ *Pl. de Sant Pere s/n*

Església de Sant Vicenç. Founded in 977, this pre-Romanesque gem contains the relics of Saint Vincent as well as the tomb of their benefactor, Pere de Rovira. La Capella de la Veracreu (Chapel of the True Cross) displays a reproduction of an alleged fragment of the True Cross brought from Rome by Bernat Tallafer in 977 and stolen in 1899. ✉ *Carrer de Sant Vicens s/n*

Pont Fortificat. The town's most emblematic feature is this Romanesque 11th-century fortified bridge with crenellated battlements spanning the Fluvià River.

Jewish ritual baths. Besalú's most unusual sight is the mikvah, 13th-century baths discovered in the 1960s. See the tourist office for keys.

WHERE TO EAT
$$–$$$ ✕**Els Fogons de Can Llaudes.** A faithfully restored 11th-century
CATALAN Romanesque chapel holds proprietor Jaume Soler's outstanding res-
★ taurant, one of Catalonia's best. A typical main dish is *confitat de bou amb patates al morter i raïm glacejat* (beef confit with glacé grapes, served with mashed potatoes). The *menú de degustació* (tasting menu) is recommended; call at least one day in advance to reserve it. ✉ *Prat de Sant Pere 6* ☎ *972/590858* 🍴 *Reservations essential* ⊟ *AE, MC, V* ⊙ *Closed Tues. and last 2 wks of Nov.*

OLOT

21 km (13 mi) west of Besalú, 55 km (34 mi) northwest of Girona.

Capital of the Garrotxa area, Olot is famous for its 19th-century school of landscape painters and has several excellent Art Nouveau buildings, including the Casa Solà-Morales, which has a facade by Palau de la Música Catalana architect Lluís Domènech i Montaner. The Sant Esteve

Besalú contains astonishingly well preserved medieval buildings.

church at the southeastern end of Passeig d'en Blay is famous for its El Greco painting *Christ Carrying the Cross* (1605).

EXPLORING

Museu Comarcal de la Garrotxa. *This County Museum of La Garrotxa* contains works of Catalan Modernisme (Art Nouveau), as well as sculptures by Miquel Blay, creator of the long-tressed maidens who support the balconies along Olot's main boulevard, Passeig d'en Blay. ⊠ *Carrer Hospici 8* ☏ *972/279130* ⊠ *€3.50* ⊘ *Mon. and Wed.–Sat. 10–1 and 4–7, Sun. 10–1:30.*

WHERE TO EAT AND STAY

$$–$$$

CATALAN

✗ **Ca l'Enric.** Chefs Jordi and Isabel Juncà have become legends in the town of La Vall de Bianya just north of Olot, where symposiums on culinary matters such as woodcock preparation have inspired prize-winning books. Cuisine firmly rooted in local products, starring game of all sorts, is taken to another level here. Woodcock in four servings (soup, risotto with wings, drumstick, breast) is the house specialty, but wild boar and local mini-vegetables roasted over coals are all exquisitely prepared. ⊠ *Ctra. C 26* ☏ *972/290015* ⊕ *www.calenric.net* ⊠ *Reservations essential* ⊟ *AE, DC, MC, V* ⊘ *Closed Mon. No dinner Sun., Tues., Wed. Closed Dec. 24–Jan. 18 and July 1–14.*

$$–$$$

CATALAN

✗ **Les Cols.** Off the road east to Figueres, Fina Puigdevall has made this ancient masia (Catalan farmhouse), with five rooms for overnight stays, a design triumph. The sprawling 18th-century rustic structure is filled with glassed-in halls, intimate gardens, and wrought-iron and steel details. The cuisine is seasonal and based on locally grown products, from wild mushrooms to the extraordinarily flavorful legumes and vegetables grown in the rich, volcanic soil of La Garrotxa. ⊠ *Mas les Cols, Ctra. de la Canya* ☎ *972/261001* ⊕ *www.lescols.com* ⌨ *Reservations essential* ☰ *AE, DC, MC, V* ⊘ *Closed Jan. 2–22 and July 28–Aug. 14.*

¢ 🖫 **La Perla d'Olot.** Known for its friendly family ambience, this hotel is always the first in Olot to fill up. On the edge of town toward the Vic road, it's within walking distance of two parks. Rooms are classic and unsurprising, though well equipped and comfortable. **Pros:** relaxed and unpretentious; an easy stop with comfortable rooms and personalized service. **Cons:** a little far from the center of Olot where the locals live. ⊠ *Ctra. La Deu 9* ☎ *972/262326* ⊕ *www.laperlahotels.com* ⇗ *32 rooms, 30 apartments* ⌂ *In-room: Wi-Fi. In-hotel: restaurant, bar, Internet terminal, some pets allowed* ☰ *AE, DC, MC, V* ⧖ *EP.*

▌ EN
ROUTE

The villages of **Vall d'En Bas** lie south of Olot off Route A153. A freeway cuts across this countryside to Vic, but you'll miss a lot by taking it. The twisting old road leads you through rich farmland past farmhouses with dark wooden balconies bedecked with bright flowers. Turn off for Sant Privat d'En Bas and Els Hostalets d'En Bas. Farther on, the picturesque medieval village of Rupit has excellent restaurants serving the famous patata de Rupit, potato stuffed with duck and beef, while the rugged Collsacabra mountains offer some of Catalonia's most pristine landscapes.

MONTSENY

75 km (47 mi) south of Olot, 60 km (37 mi) northeast of Barcelona.

Montseny is Barcelona's mountain retreat and refuge, a highland forest less than an hour north of the city, and the highest mountain range in Catalonia aside from the Pyrenees. Its softly undulating slopes sweep up to the massif's main peaks at Turó de l'Home (5,656 feet), les Agudes (5,633 feet), Matagalls (5,590 feet), and Calma i Puigdrau (4,455 feet). In summer and in good weather they are a fairly easy climb. The almost overwhelming view at the top of the Turó de l'Home stretches to the Pyrenees in the north and far past Barcelona in the south. Known as one of the great *pulmons* (lungs) of Europe for its forests of oxygen-producing beech, pine, oak, and fir trees, Montseny may, in the long run, be even more important to Catalonia's spiritual health than to its physical well-being. Montseny's mountain villages, such as Montseny itself, or Mosqueroles, Riells, Campins, Viladrau, and El Brull, are rustic sanctuaries with delightful little inns and farmhouses to admire and to dine at or stay in. It has been a protected park area since 1978, and is also part of UNESCO's world network of biosphere reserves.

ESSENTIALS

The **Servei de Parcs Naturals** (☎ *93/340–2541* ⊕ *www.diba.es/parcs/montseny/montseny.htm*) organizes excursions along the many rivers and streams draining the Montseny massif.

WHERE TO STAY

$ ⚿ **Can Barrina.** Splendid views over the Montseny massif enhance this comfortable stone country house built in 1620 and reconstructed in 1988. The restaurant here ($$–$$$) focuses on local products, ranging from wild mushrooms such as *rossinyols* (chanterelles) and *múrgules* (morels) to wild boar, rabbit, duck, and venison. A roaring fireplace in the dining room can be complemented by another in your room (if you can manage to secure either Room D or F). In summer you can relax in the garden or on the terraces after a day of hiking the crests. **Pros:** comfortable and rustic base camp for hiking in the Montseny massif. **Cons:** can get overpopulated if a wedding reception happens to be scheduled while you are there. ⊠ *Ctra. Palautordera, Km 1.2,* ☏ *93/847–3065* ⊕ *www.canbarrina.com* ⌁ *14 rooms* ♿ *In-room: Wi-Fi. In-hotel: restaurant, pool* ⊟ *AE, DC, MC, V* ��ⓄⓁ *EP.*

$$$$ ⚿ **Hotel Monestir de Sant Marçal.** Jordi Tell runs this small, very exclusive hotel high up in the Montseny massif. In an 11th-century monastery with adjacent chapel (where mass can be celebrated), it offers a personalized sanctum sanctorum with cozy, rustic rooms. Some people will appreciate its library; others, its private honey-based cosmetic line, Sant Marçal del Montseny. You can arrange guided excursions on foot or by bike. **Pros:** exquisite rustic and aristocratic highland refuge. **Cons:** weekends can be crowded, better during the week when you have the hotel, and the Montseny, to yourself. ⊠ *Ctra. de Sant Celoni a Sant Marçal, Km 28,* ☏ *93/847–3043* ⊕ *www.hotel-santmarcal.com* ⌁ *12 rooms* ♿ *In-room: no a/c, Wi-Fi. In-hotel: restaurant, Wi-Fi hotspot, bar, pool* ⊟ *AE, DC, MC, V* ⓄⓁ *BP.*

8

SOUTHERN CATALONIA: MONTSERRAT TO TARRAGONA

Barcelona is surrounded by scenic landscapes and ancient architecture—Sant Cugat del Vallés, with a lovely Benedictine abbey; Terrassa with its notable examples of Romanesque architecture; Martorell, with its Puente del Diablo Roman bridge. The world-famous monastery of Montserrat is where medieval legend placed the Holy Grail (a claim contested by many other places). From Montserrat you can move south of Barcelona and continue backward in time, with a pleasure stop in Sitges, the prettiest and most popular resort in Barcelona's immediate environs, with an excellent beach, an attractive Old Quarter, and some interesting Moderniste details. In from the coast lies the "Cistercian triangle," with celebrated historic monasteries at Poblet, Santes Creus, and Vallbona de les Monges. The walled town at Montblanc is also a lovely sight. Farther south, along the coast, the time machine zooms back to the days of ancient Rome when you arrive in Tarragona, in Roman times regarded as one of the empire's finest creations. Its wine was already famous and its population was the first *gens togata* (literally, the toga-clad race) in Spain, which conferred on them equality with the citizens of Rome. Roman relics, with the Circus Maximus heading the list, are still the evidence of Tarragona's grandeur, and to this the Middle Ages added wonderful city walls and citadels.

MONTSERRAT

★ *50 km (31 mi) northwest of Barcelona.*

You don't have to be a believer to visit the Benedictine monastery of Montserrat. A traditional side trip from Barcelona is the shrine of La Moreneta, the Black Virgin of Montserrat, high in the crags of the Montserrat massif. These jagged, sawtooth peaks have given rise to countless legends: here St. Peter left a statue of the Virgin Mary carved by St. Luke, Parsifal found the Holy Grail, and Wagner sought inspiration for his opera. Whatever the truth of such mysteries, Montserrat has long been considered Catalonia's spiritual heart. A monastery has stood on this site since the early Middle Ages, though the present 19th-century building replaced the rubble left by Napoléon's troops in 1812. Honeymooning couples flock here by the thousands seeking La Moreneta's blessing. Twice a year, on April 27, Our Lady of Montserrat's name day, and September 8 (which celebrates the *verges trobades*, or found virgins, of Catalonia, statues of Our Lady discovered by shepherds in remote places and venerated all over the country), the diminutive statue of Montserrat's Black Virgin becomes the object of one of Spain's greatest pilgrimages.

While the Montserrat complex is vast, most architectural historians have little praise for its modern renovation. Note, however, the Gothic portal of the Twelve Apostles. At the monastery, only the basilica and museum are regularly open to the public. The **basilica** is dark and ornate, its blackness pierced by the glow of hundreds of votive lamps. Above the high altar stands the famous polychrome statue of the Virgin and Child, to which the faithful can pay their respects by way of a separate door. The statue is black thanks to centuries of incense and candle smoke, not because the face and hands were ever painted black. Another treasure found here is the **Escolania,** the monastery's famous boys' choir, founded in the 13th century and now known internationally through concert tours and recordings. The boys receive intense musical training and a general education from an early age; some of them later enter the monastery as monks. At 1 PM daily they sing the *Salve regina* and the *Virolai,* the hymn of Our Lady of Montserrat. In the evening after vespers, at 7:10 PM, they sing, together with the monks, the *Salve montserratina,* alternating between polyphony and Gregorian chant. On Sunday and holidays they take part in the mass at Montserrat and in vespers. In July and at Christmas the choir is away from Montserrat.

The monastery's **museum** has two sections: the Secció Antiga (open Tuesday–Saturday 10:30–2) contains old masters, among them paintings by El Greco, Correggio, and Caravaggio, and the amassed gifts to the Virgin; the Secció Moderna (open Tuesday–Saturday 3–6) concentrates on more recent artists. This impressive art collection is the result of private bequests. Xavier Busquets, one of Barcelona's most important architects, left many impressionist and Moderniste paintings to Montserrat on his death in 1990, including works by Monet, Sisley, Degas, Pissarro, Rouault, Sargent, Sorolla, and Zuloaga. Other donors have left examples by lesser-known masters of 19th- and 20th-century Catalan painting: Martí Alsina, Joaquim Vayreda, Francesc Gimeno,

Santiago Rusiñol, Ramon Casas, Isidre Nonell, Joaquim Mir, Hermen Anglada-Camarasa, plus works by Picasso and Dalí.

Montserrat is as memorable for its setting as for its artistic and religious treasures, so be sure to explore its strange pink hills, many of whose crests are dotted with hermitages. The hermitage of **Sant Joan** can be reached by funicular. The views over the mountains to the Mediterranean and, on a clear day, to the Pyrenees are breathtaking. Montserrat's rocky masses are of stone conglomerate, which, over thousands of years, has been molded into bizarre shapes by tectonic movements, climatic changes, and erosion. In the deep, humid shade between the stony outcroppings, vegetation thrives. Many trails and paths crisscross these formations; there are also routes good for short walks of a half-day or more. Expert climbers will be challenged by the difficulty of the pinnacles and spires, but play it safe—every year climbers are killed or injured. The countless legends that surround the monastery are undoubtedly rooted in the strangely unreal appearance of these peaks of San Jerónimo, some of which jut up abruptly 3,725 feet above the valley of the Llobregat River and are outlined with monoliths, which, from a distance, look like immense stone figures. Look especially for La Momia and her "daughter," La Momieta. El Massif de Sant Salvador crowns all. Also remarkable are the six colossal rocks called Les Santes Magdalenes, which have been compared to everything from Henry Moore sculptures to a Victorian tea party. In 1987 Montserrat's mountain range was declared a national park.

GETTING HERE
Overnight stays in the monastery's simple lodgings are an option. To get to Montserrat from Barcelona, follow the AP2/AP7 *autopista* on the upper ring road (Ronda de Dalt), or from the western end of the Diagonal as far as Sortida (Exit) 25 to Martorell. Bypass this industrial center and follow AP18 and the signs to Montserrat. You can also take a train from Barcelona's Plaça Espanya metro station, which takes you to Monistrol de Montserrat (where you can catch the funicular up to the monastery), or a guided tour with Pullmantur or Julià. ☎ 93/877–7777, 93/877–7701 *for accommodations* ⊕ *www.visitmontserrat.com.*

SITGES

81 km (50 mi) south of Montserrat, 43 km (27 mi) southwest of Barcelona.

Sitges is the prettiest and most popular resort in Barcelona's immediate environs, with an excellent beach, an attractive Old Quarter, and some interesting Moderniste architecture. It's also one of Europe's premier gay resorts. In summer this action-packed town never sleeps—its nightlife, especially along Primer de Maig Street, known as Carrer del Pecat (Street of Sin), is famous. The old part of Sitges still retains its narrow streets and fishermen's houses, although apartment developments spread in all directions. Beautiful but overgrown, the village has long been nicknamed Blanca Subur for its whitewashed houses. The easily recognizable 18th-century parish church of Sant Bartomeu and Santa Tecla, sitting on the promontory of La Punta over the sea, is a scene endlessly painted by artists. Today Sitges has almost become a suburb of Barcelona, just 30 minutes away from the city via the C32 tunnel.

There's always been an artistic climate in Sitges. At the end of the 19th century followers of the Moderniste movement flocked here, led by Santiago Rusiñol, to celebrate the Festes Modernistes, a bonding of like-minded artists. American millionaire Charles Deering, heir to the farm-machinery fortune of his father, William Deering, stayed here from 1910 to 1921, and was a friend of the Modernistes, playing a leading role in stimulating the arts in Sitges.

Natives of Sitges emigrated to the Americas in the 19th century, especially to Cuba and Puerto Rico, many returning with great fortunes that they quickly spent on splendid homes that are still standing. You can see the elegant Vidal-Quadras homes at Carrer del Port Alegre 9 and Carrer Davallada 12, as well as many others around the town. February is Carnival time, and Sitges hosts thousands of people who come to see the parades and outrageous costumes.

If you're traveling to Sitges by car from Barcelona, head southwest along Gran Via or Passeig Colom to the Ronda Litoral and the freeway that passes the airport on its way to Castelldefels. From here, the AP16 freeway and C32 tunnel will get you to Sitges in about 30 minutes. Regular trains leave Sants and Passeig de Gràcia for Sitges; the ride takes half an hour. To get from Montserrat to Sitges you don't have to go back to Barcelona; take local road C1411 south from Montserrat to get on the AP7. Continue south on the AP7 to Vilafranca del Penedès, where you exit and take local road C15 to Sitges.

EXPLORING

Cau Ferrat. Of the three Sitges museums (the other two are Maricel de Mar, exhibiting Gothic and Renaissance works, and the Museu Romàntic–Can Llopis, a look at 18th- and 19th-century bourgeois family life), the most interesting is Cau Ferrat, founded by the artist Santiago Rusiñol (1861–1931). The museum is a compendium of Rusiñol's Arte Total philosophy and covers ceramics, wrought iron, stained glass, carvings, furniture, and works by Rusiñol contemporaries Casas, Utrillo, Clarasó, Mas i Fondevila, Regoyos, Zuloaga, Picasso, Pitchot, and Anglada-Camarasa, as well as several Rusiñols and two El Grecos. Connoisseurs of wrought iron will appreciate the beautiful collection of *creus terminals,* crosses that once marked town boundaries. ⊠ *Fonollar s/n* ☎ *93/894–0364* ⊕ *www.diba.es* ⬛*€4; combined ticket €6.40, valid for all 3 museums; free 1st Wed. of month* ☻ *June 14–Sept. 30, Tues.–Sat. 9:30–2 and 4–7; Oct. 1–June 13, Tues.–Sat. 9:30–2 and 3:30–6:30, Sun. 10–2.*

OFF THE BEATEN PATH

Fodor's Choice
★

Museu Pau Casals. The family house of renowned cellist Pablo (Pau in Catalan) Casals (1876–1973) is on the beach at Sant Salvador, just east of the town of El Vendrell. Casals, who abandoned Spain in self-imposed exile after Franco's rise to power in 1939, left a museum here with his belongings, including several of his cellos, original musical manuscripts, personal letters, and works of (mostly Moderniste) art. Other exhibits describe the Casals campaign for world peace. (Coincidentally, Pau, in

Whitewashed buildings dominate the landscape in Sitges.

Catalan, is the word for both Paul and peace). Across the street, the Auditori Pau Casals holds frequent concerts and, in July and August, a classical music festival. In El Vendrell, 18 km (11 mi) west of Sitges, you can also visit the **Casa Nadiua (Natal House) Pau Casals** (⊠ Carrer Santana 6 ☎ 977/665642). ⊠ *Av. Palfuriana 67 El Vendrell* ☎ *977/684276* ⊕ *www.paucasals.org* 🎫 *€6* ☉ *Mid-June–mid-Sept., Tues.–Sat. 10–2 and 5–9, Sun. 10–2; mid-Sept.–mid-June, Tues.–Sat. 10–2 and 4–6, Sun. 10–2.*

WHERE TO EAT

$–$$ ✕ **Can Pagès.** Snug and family-owned, this restaurant in the heart of
SPANISH the old part of town serves hearty regional fare in a setting of color-ful tiles, sturdy wooden tables and chairs, and brick-red walls lined with works by local artists. The menu, adorned with the painting of a grizzled *pagès* (farmer), created by Aragonese artist and longtime Sitges resident Manuel Blesa, promises down-home Catalan cuisine, includ-ing the restaurant's signature dish, *bacallà Can Pagès* (cod with lobster and aioli) and *carxofes a la brasa* (grilled artichoke). ⊠ *Sant Pere 24–26* ☎ *93/894–1195* ▤ *AE, DC, MC, V* ☉ *Closed Mon. in Dec.*

$–$$ ✕ **La Nansa.** Now in its fifth generation and run by Antoni Rafecas,
SPANISH this family restaurant on a narrow street in the old quarter is famous for having brought back traditional recipes such as *arròs a la sitgetana* (Sitges-style rice, a rice broth with meats and seafood). La Nansa (named for the basket fish traps seen adorning the restaurant) also makes an outstanding *suquet de lluerna* (stew of gurnard fish). For openers, try their homegrown tangy *escabetx de bonítol* (pickled bonito). ⊠ *Carrer*

de la Carreta 24 ☎ *93/894–1927* ▤ *AE, DC, MC, V* ⊘ *Closed Tues. and Wed. in Jan.*

$–$$ ✕ **La Torreta.** An understated waterfront gem, this longtime favorite

SPANISH beckons with its excellent seafood, low whitewashed ceilings, and pale yellow walls hung with maritime paintings and old maps. Owner Josep Amigo, whose mother opened the restaurant in 1962, delivers a menu based on the freshest seasonal ingredients and "fruits of the sea," including such dishes as *cargols de puntxes* (sea snails in a vinaigrette sauce) and *calamars a la planxa amb all i julivert* (grilled squid with garlic and parsley). In summer, diners flock to the outdoor patio that overlooks the teeming boardwalk and a beach. ⊠ *Port Alegre 17* ☎ *93/894–5253* ▤ *AE, DC, MC, V* ⊘ *Closed Tues. and Nov.; no dinner Mon.*

WHERE TO STAY

$$$–$$$$ 🏨 **San Sebastián Playa.** At center stage directly over the Platja de Sant Sebastiá, this alabaster elephant is widely recognized as the best place to stay in Sitges. Ample windows with vistas of frothy waves and the beach adorn this gleaming facade. Rooms, done in bright white with wood trimming and furnishings, have elegant white-balustraded balconies, where you can soak up the rays before joining the milling crowds in summer or, in winter, spreading out in lonely splendor on the sand. **Pros:** dead center in the middle of the action; top technology; nonpareil views. **Cons:** corporate groups favor this hotel; bookings can be hard to get. ⊠ *Port Alegre 53* ☎ *93/894–8676* ⊕ *www.hotelsansebastian.com* ⇱ *48 rooms, 3 suites* ⚬ *In-room: Wi-Fi. In-hotel: restaurant, bar, Wi-Fi hotspot, Internet terminal, pool* ▤ *AE, DC, MC, V* ⎈ *EP.*

$$ 🏨 **Terramar.** This once-splendid hotel built in the 1930s sits at the end of the long beachside promenade. Some rooms, with drab orange-and-brown color schemes, still show the effects of a 1960s renovation. Ongoing refurbishment is producing a brighter look, so do ask for a new room. The terrace is great for people-watching. Guests have a 50% discount at the excellent golf course behind the hotel. **Pros:** good-size balconied rooms with large windows and panoramic views out to sea. **Cons:** some rooms have dated decor. ⊠ *Passeig Marítim 80* ☎ *93/894–0050* ⊕ *www.hotelterramar.com* ⇱ *204 rooms* ⚬ *In-room: Wi-Fi. In-hotel: restaurant, Wi-Fi hotspot, tennis courts, pool* ▤ *AE, DC, MC, V* ⎈ *BP.*

■ EN ROUTE

Upon leaving Sitges, make straight for the AP2 *autopista* by way of Vilafranca del Penedès, where you can taste the excellent Penedès wines and tour the **Bodega Miguel Torres** (⊠ *Comercio 2208720* ☎ *93/890–0100 www.torres.es*).

The interesting **Vinseum–Museu des les Cultures del Vi de Catalunya** (Museum of Wine Cultures of Catalunya) in the 14th-century former royal palace at Vilafranca del Penedès explores wine-making history. ⊠ *Pl. Jaume I, 5 08720* ☎ *93/890–0582* ⊕ *www.vinseum.cat* ⊠ *€6* ⊘ *Tues.–Sun. 10–2 and 4–7.*

SANTES CREUS

50 km (31 mi) southwest of Sitges, 95 km (59 mi) west of Barcelona.

Founded in 1157 by Ramon Berenguer IV, the Cistercian monastery of Santes Creus has three austere aisles and an unusual 14th-century apse that connects with the cloisters and the courtyard of the royal palace. The cloister was designed by Reinard des Fonoll, probably an Englishman, who stayed on to live for 30 years at the monastery. The columns, originally a symbol of simplicity with leaf or plain motifs, are here a veritable zoo in stone: griffins, mermaids, and all types of mythological animals accompany Adam and Eve, elephants, monkeys, dogs, and lions. There are even the exotic faces of a Viking and the Green Man, a Celtic representation of nature. From Sitges, drive inland toward Vilafranca del Penedès and the A7 freeway; then take the A2 (Lleida). To get to Santes Creus by train from Sitges, take the Lleida line to L'Espluga de Francolí, 4 km (2½ mi) from Poblet. ⊠ *Off the A2* ☎ *977/638329* 🎟 *€6* ⊙ *Mid-Mar.–mid-Sept., Tues.–Sun. 10–1:30 and 3–7; mid-Sept.–mid-Jan., Tues.–Sun. 10–1:30 and 3–5:30; mid-Jan.– mid-Mar., Tues.–Sun. 10–1:30 and 3–6.*

▌EN ROUTE The walled town of **Montblanc** is off the A2 at Salida (Exit) 9, its ancient gates too narrow for cars. A walk through its tiny streets takes you past Gothic churches, a 16th-century hospital, and medieval mansions.

SANTA MARIA DE POBLET

Fodor'sChoice *25 km (19 mi) west of Santes Creus.*

★ This splendid Cistercian foundation at the foot of the Prades Mountains is one of the great masterpieces of Spanish monastic architecture. The cloister is a stunning combination of lightness and size; on sunny days the shadows on the yellow sandstone are extraordinary. Founded in 1150 by Ramon Berenguer IV in gratitude for the Christian Reconquest, the monastery first housed a dozen Cistercians from Narbonne. Later, the Crown of Aragón used Santa Maria de Poblet for religious retreats and burials. The building was damaged in an 1836 anticlerical revolt, and monks of the reformed Cistercian Order have managed the difficult task of restoration since 1940.

Today monks and novices again pray before the splendid retable over the tombs of Aragonese rulers, restored to their former glory by sculptor Frederic Marés; sleep in the cold, barren dormitory; and eat frugal meals in the stark refectory. If you would like to join the monks— 18 comfortable rooms are available, for men only—call **Pare Benito** (☎ *977/870089*) to arrange a stay of up to 10 days within the stones and silence of one of Catalonia's gems. There has always been a sharp rivalry between the monasteries of Montserrat and Poblet, which often took opposing sides in the many quarrels that plagued Catalonia in its history. The last coup may have been won by Poblet. In 1980 Josep Tarradellas, the first president of the restored Generalitat, Catalonia's autonomous government, left his library and papers to Poblet and not to Montserrat. To get to Poblet from Sitges by train, take the Lleida

An impressive example of Spanish monastic architecture: Santa Maria de Poblet.

line to L'Espluga de Francolí, 4 km (2½ mi) from Poblet. You can also take the **train** (✉ *Autotransports Perelada* ☎ *973/202058*) to Tarragona and catch a bus to the monastery. Be sure to reserve your one-hour guided tour of the monastery at least a few days in advance. ✉ *Off A2* ☎ *977/870254* 🎫 *€6* 🕒 *Guided tours by reservation Apr.–Sept., daily 10–12:30 and 3–6; Oct.–Mar., daily 10–12:30 and 3–5:30.*

TARRAGONA

50 km (30 mi) southeast of Poblet, 98 km (61 mi) southwest of Barcelona.

Set on a rocky hill overlooking the sea, the ancient Roman stronghold of Tarragona is a bracing architectural mix of past and present. Roman pillars rise amid modern apartment buildings, and a Roman amphitheater shares the city coastline with trawlers and tugboats. Though the modern city is very much an industrial town, with a large port and thriving fishing industry, it has preserved its heritage superbly. Stroll along the town's cliff-side perimeter and you'll see why the Romans set up shop here: Tarragona is strategically positioned at land's edge, its lookout points commanding unobstructed sea views. As capital of the Roman province of Tarraconensis (from 218 BC), Tarraco, as it was then called, formed the empire's principal stronghold in Spain, and by the 1st century BC the city was regarded as one of the empire's finest urban creations. Its wine was already famous, and its people were the first in Spain to become Roman citizens. St. Paul preached here in AD 58, and Tarragona became the seat of the Christian church in Spain until it was superseded by Toledo in the 11th century.

Entering the city from Barcelona, you'll pass the **Triumphal Arch of Berà,** dating from the 3rd century BC, 19 km (12 mi) north of Tarragona; and from the Lleida (Lérida) road, or *autopista,* you can see the 1st-century **Roman aqueduct** that helped carry fresh water 32 km (19 mi) from the Gaià River. Tarragona is divided clearly into old and new by the Rambla Vella; the Old Town and most of the Roman remains are to the north, while modern Tarragona spreads out to the south. You could start your visit to Tarragona at the acacia-lined Rambla Nova, at the end of which is a balcony overlooking the sea, the **Balcó del Mediterrània.** Then walk uphill along the Passeig de les Palmeres; below it is the ancient amphitheater, and the modern, semicircular Imperial Tarraco hotel on the passeig artfully echoes the amphitheater's curve.

GETTING HERE AND AROUND

Tarragona is well connected by train: there are hourly trains from Barcelona and regular train service from other major cities, including Madrid. There are bus connections with the main Andalusian cities, plus Alicante, Madrid, and Valencia.

The €14 Tarragona Card, valid for 24 hours (€19 for 48 hours), gives free entry to all the city's museums and historical sites, free passes on municipal buses, and discounts at more than 100 shops, restaurants, and bars. It's sold at the main tourist office and at most hotels.

Tarragona is divided clearly into old and new by the Rambla Vella. Tours of the cathedral and archaeological sites are conducted by the tourist office.

ESSENTIALS

Visitor Information Tarragona (⊠ *Carrer Major 39 [just below the cathedral]* ☏ *977/245203*).

EXPLORING

★ **Amphitheater.** The remains of Tarragona's Roman amphitheater, built in the 2nd century AD, have a spectacular view of the sea. This arena with tiered seats was the site of gladiatorial and other contests. You're free to wander through the access tunnels and along the seating rows. Sitting with your back to the sea, you might understand why Augustus favored Tarragona as a winter resort. In the center of the theater are the remains of two superimposed churches, the earlier of which was a Visigothic basilica built to mark the bloody martyrdom of St. Fructuós and his deacons in AD 259. ■TIP➔ **€10 buys a combination ticket card valid for all Tarragona museums and sites.** ⊠ *Passeig de les Palmeres* ☏ *€3, €10 combination ticket valid for all Tarragona museums and sites* ☉ *June–Sept., Tues.–Sat. 9–9, Sun. 9–3; Oct.–May, Tues.–Sat. 9–5, Sun. 10–3.*

Casa Castellarnau. Now a museum, this Gothic *palauet,* or town house, built by Tarragona nobility in the 18th century, includes stunning furnishings from the 18th and 19th centuries. The last member of the Castellarnau family vacated the house in 1954. ⊠ *Carrer Cavallers* ☏ *977/242220* ☏ *€3, €10 combination ticket* ☉ *June–Sept., Tues.–Sat. 9–9, Sun. 9–3; Oct.–May, Tues.–Sat. 9–7, Sun. 10–3.*

Catedral. Built between the 12th and 14th centuries on the site of a Roman temple and a mosque, this cathedral shows the changes from

8

the Romanesque to Gothic style. The initial rounded placidity of the Romanesque apse, begun in the 12th century, later gave way to the spiky restlessness of the Gothic; the result is somewhat confused. If no mass is in progress, enter the cathedral through the cloister. The main attraction here is the 15th-century Gothic alabaster altarpiece of St. Tecla by Pere Joan, a richly detailed depiction of the life of Tarragona's patron saint. Converted by St. Paul and subsequently persecuted by local pagans, St. Tecla was repeatedly saved from demise through divine intervention. ⊠ *Pla de la Seu* ☎ *977/221736* ⊠ *€3.50* ☉ *July–mid-Sept., Mon.–Sat. 10–7; mid-Sept.–mid-Nov., Mon.–Sat. 10–5; mid-Nov.–mid-Mar., Mon.–Sat. 10–2; mid-Mar.–June, Mon.–Sat. 10–1 and 4–7; Sun. open for services only.*

Circus Maximus. Students have excavated the vaults of the 1st-century Roman arena, near the amphitheater. The plans just inside the gate show that the vaults now visible formed only a small corner of a vast space (350 yards long), where 23,000 spectators gathered to watch chariot races. As medieval Tarragona grew, the city gradually swamped the circus. ⊠ *Pl. del Rei* ⊠ *€3, €10 combination ticket* ☉ *June–Sept., Tues.–Sat. 9–9, Sun. 9–3; Oct.–May, Tues.–Sat. 9–5, Sun. 10–3.*

El Serrallo. The always entertaining fishing quarter and harbor are below the city near the bus station and the mouth of the Francolí River. Attending the afternoon fish auction is a golden opportunity to see how choice seafood starts its journey toward your table in Barcelona or Tarragona. For seafood closer to its source, restaurants in the port such as **Estació Marítima** (⊠ *Moll de Costa, Tinglado 4* ☎ *977/232100*) or **Manolo** (⊠ *Carrer Gravina 61* ☎ *977/223484*) are excellent choices for no-frills fresh fish in a rollicking environment.

Passeig Arqueològic. A 1½-km (1-mi) circular path skirting the surviving section of the 3rd-century BC Ibero-Roman ramparts, this walkway was built on even earlier walls of giant rocks. On the other side of the path is a glacis, a fortification added by English military engineers in 1707 during the War of the Spanish Succession. Look for the rusted bronze of Romulus and Remus. ⊠ *Access from Via de l'Imperi Romà.*

Praetorium. This towering building was Augustus's town house, and is reputed to be the birthplace of Pontius Pilate. Its Gothic appearance is the result of extensive alterations in the Middle Ages, when it housed the kings of Catalonia and Aragón during their visits to Tarragona. The Praetorium is now the city's **Museu d'Història** (History Museum), with plans showing the evolution of the city. The museum's highlight is the **Hippolytus Sarcophagus,** which bears a bas-relief depicting the legend of Hippolytus and Fraeda. You can also access the remains of the Circus Maximus from the Praetorium. ⊠ *Pl. del Rei* ☎ *977/241952* ⊠ *€3, €10 combination ticket* ☉ *June–Sept., Tues.–Sat. 9–9, Sun. 9–3; Oct.–May, Tues.–Sat. 9–7, Sun. 10–3.*

★ **Museu Nacional Arqueològic de Tarragona.** A 1960s neoclassical building contains this museum housing the most significant collection of Roman artifacts in Catalonia. Among the items are Roman statuary and domestic fittings such as keys, bells, and belt buckles. The beautiful mosaics include a head of Medusa, famous for its piercing stare. Don't miss the video on Tarragona's history. ⊠ *Pl. del Rei 5* ☎ *977/236209* 🖾 *€3.50; free Tues.* ⊙ *June–Sept., Tues.–Sat. 10–8, Sun. 10–2; Oct.–May, Tues.–Sat. 10–1:30 and 4–7, Sun. 10–2.*

Necrópolis i Museu Paleocristià. Just uphill from the fish market is the fascinating early Christian necropolis and museum. ⊠ *Av. Ramon y Cajal 80* ☎ *977/211175* 🖾 *€3, €10 combination ticket; free Tues.* ⊙ *June–Sept., Tues.–Sat. 10–1 and 4:30–8, Sun. 10–2; Oct.–May, Tues.–Sat. 10–1:30 and 3–5:30, Sun. 10–2.*

WHERE TO EAT AND STAY

$$$–$$$$
CATALAN
★

✕ **Joan Gatell.** A short 15-minute hop down the coast to Cambrils will give you a memorable chance to try one of the most famous restaurants in southern Catalonia. The Gatell sisters used to run two restaurants side by side; Fanny now carries on the tradition of exquisite local meals by herself in this one, named after their founding father Joan. Try the *fideus negres amb sepionets* (noodle paella with baby squid cooked in squid ink) or *lubina al horno con cebolla y patata* (roast sea bass with onion and potato). Cambrils is 18 km (11 mi) southwest of Tarragona. ⊠ *Passeig Miramar 26 Cambrils* ☎ *977/360057* ▬ *AE, DC, MC, V* ⊙ *Closed Mon., Oct., and late Dec.–Jan. No dinner Sun.*

$–$$
MEDITERRANEAN

✕ **Les Coques.** If you have time for only one meal in the city, take it at this elegant little restaurant in the heart of historic Tarragona. The menu is bursting with both mountain and Mediterranean fare. Meat lovers should try the *costelles de xai* (lamb chops in a dark burgundy sauce); seafood fans should ask for *calamarsets amb favetes* (baby calamari sautéed in olive oil and garlic and served with legumes). ⊠ *Baixada Nova del Patriarca 2 bis* ☎ *977/228300* ▬ *AE, DC, MC, V* ⊙ *Closed Sun., 10 days in Feb., and mid-July–mid-Aug.*

$–$$
SPANISH
★

✕ **Les Voltes.** Built into the vaults of the Roman Circus Maximus, this out-of-the-way spot serves a hearty cuisine. You'll find Tarragona specialties, mainly fish dishes, as well as international recipes, with *calçotada* (spring onions) in winter. (If you want to try calçotadas, you must call to order them a day in advance.) ⊠ *Carrer Trinquet Vell 12* ☎ *977/230651* ▬ *MC, V* ⊙ *Closed July and Aug. No dinner Sun., no lunch Mon.*

$–$$

🛏 **Imperial Tarraco.** Large and white, this half-moon-shape hotel has a superb position overlooking the Mediterranean. The large public rooms have cool marble floors, black-leather furniture, marble-top tables, and Oriental rugs. Guest rooms are plain but comfortable, and each has a private balcony. Insist on a sea view. **Pros:** facing the Mediterrranean, looking over the fishing port and the Roman amphitheater, a privileged spot. **Cons:** occupies a very busy Tarragona intersection with heavy traffic. ⊠ *Passeig Palmeres,* ☎ *977/233040* ⊕ *www.husa.es* 🛏 *170 rooms* ⚬ *In-room: Wi-Fi. In-hotel: restaurant, bar, tennis court, Internet terminal, pool* ▬ *AE, DC, MC, V* ⦿ *EP.*

¢

🛏 **Plaça de la Font.** The central location and the cute rooms at this budget choice just off the Rambla Vella in the leafy Plaça de la Font make for a comfortable home base in downtown Tarragona. A public parking lot under the square is a boon for those with rental cars, while the rooms with balconies afford a sense of being part of the street life. **Pros:** easy on the budget and comfortable, with charming rooms. **Cons:** rooms are on the small side, the best rooms over the square with balconies can be noisy on weekends. ⊠ *Plaça de la Font 26* ☎ *977/246134* ⊕ *www. hotelpdelafont.com* ⤵ *20 rooms* ⚒ *In room: Wi-Fi. In-hotel: restaurant, bar, Internet terminal, pool* ⊟ *AE, DC, MC, V* ⦿ *EP.*

NIGHTLIFE AND THE ARTS

Nightlife in Tarragona takes two forms: older and quieter in the upper city, younger and more raucous down below. There are some lovely rustic bars in the Casc Antic, the upper section of Old Tarragona. Port Esportiu, a pleasure-boat harbor separate from the working port, has another row of dining and dancing establishments; young people flock here on weekends and summer nights. For a dose of culture with your cocktail, try **Antiquari** (⊠ *Santa Anna 3* ☎ *977/241843*), a laid-back bar that hosts readings, art exhibits, and occasional screenings of classic or contemporary films. At **Museum** (⊠ *Carrer Sant Llorenç s/n* ☎ *977/240612*) you can relax and have a peaceful drink.

The **Teatre Metropol** (⊠ *Rambla Nova 46* ☎ *977/244795*) is Tarragona's center for music, dance, theater, and cultural events ranging from *castellers* (human-castle formations), usually performed in August and September, to folk dances.

SHOPPING

Antigüedades Ciria (⊠ *Pla de la Seu 2* ☎ *977/248541*), like other shops in front of the cathedral and in the Pla de la Seu, has an interesting selection of antiques. You have to haggle for bargains, but **Carrer Major** has some exciting antiques stores. They're worth a thorough rummage, as the gems tend to be hidden away.

Excursion to Bilbao

WORD OF MOUTH

"We did one day and an overnight in Bilbao specifically to go to the Guggenheim, and I thought that was perfect. [We] spent most of the day at the museum and then took the tram into town. . . . Be sure to check the museum's Web site in advance as they can close down major portions of the museum at one time for installations."

—venturegirl

WELCOME TO BILBAO

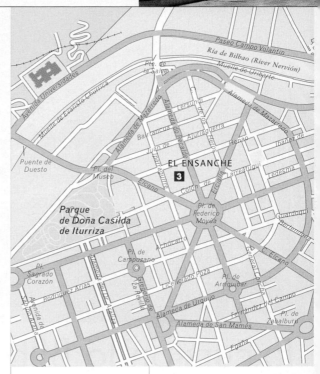

TOP REASONS TO GO

★ **The Guggenheim:** it's unthinkable to come to Bilbao and not admire Frank Gehry's masterpiece.

★ **Siete Calles:** a joyous street party with happy Basques out *de txiquiteo* (barhopping).

★ **Mercado de la Ribera:** a triple-decker market resembles an ocean liner parked in the Nervión.

★ **Museo de Bellas Artes:** Bilbao's superb fine-arts museum provides a traditional counterpoint to the Guggenheim's postmodern glitter.

★ **San Mamés:** Bilbao's soccer stadium offers top European teams in an emotion-charged and historic environment.

★ **Cider Houses:** cider houses and their typical fare are a must for visitors.

1 **Along the Nervión River.** From the Euskalduna Palace at the downstream end of the Nervión to the Mercado de la Ribera at the upstream edge, the river is increasingly becoming the city's spinal column and forum. The Abandoibarra shopping and leisure center leads up past the Torre Abandoibarra skyscraper (under construction) to the Guggenheim, through gardens and past sculptures to Santiago Calatrava's Zubi-Zuri foot ridge, on past the Teatro Arriaga, and up to the vast triple-triered food market: a good walk or tram ride.

2 **El Casco Viejo.** Siete Calles (seven streets) was the original Bilbao, an echo chamber and (on weekends) rolling street party filled with taverns, tapas bars, and restaurants. The Museo Vasco and the Bidebarrieta library provide cultural interest, while five churches and convents ensure architectural incentives.

GETTING ORIENTED

The Basque Country's bright "must-see" industrial city of Bilbao is centered around the stunning Museo Guggenheim, but that's just the first course this city has to offer. With a second standout arts museum, a dozen culinary standouts, and an Old Quarter that's getting better every day, Bilbao provides a feast for the culturally starved.

3 El Ensanche. The post-1876 new Bilbao or, as in Barcelona, "expansion," is filled with shops, department stores, restaurants, and cafés and all the fruits of a late 19th-century steel-making and boatbuilding boom that made the Basque industrial capital one of Spain's most important cities.

9

BILBAO PLANNER

When to Go

Mid-April through June and September and October are the best times to enjoy the temperate climate and both the coastal and upland landscapes of this wet and grassy corner of Spain—though any time of year except August, when Europeans are on vacation, is nearly as good. The Basque Country is rainy in winter, but the wet Atlantic weather is always invigorating and—as if anyone needed it in this culinary paradise—appetite enhancing. Much of the classically powerful Basque cuisine evolved with the northern maritime climate in mind.

Planning Your Time

If You Have 1 Day

Begin at the Guggenheim in the morning and continue by taking a stroll (or a tram ride) up the river to the Mercado de la Ribera for a look at the vast and spectacular triple-tier display of food products. With a whetted appetite, allow yourself a light midday *tapeo* and *txikiteo* run through the Casco Viejo's taverns followed by lunch at El Perro Chico. The next move is to walk across the Ensanche to the Museo de Bellas Artes for a look at the Zurbaráns and El Grecos and the Basque collection of Zuloaga. Dinner might take you through a Licenciado Poza tavern or two on your way to Guria or Etxanobe, or back to the Guggenheim for some serious Bilbao cuisine.

If You Have 3 Days

For the three-day Bilbao tour, start with the Guggenheim in the morning on Day 1, visit the Mercado de la Ribera, and dive into the Casco Viejo for a tapa at Xukela and another at Victor Montes in Plaza Nueva before crossing the Puente del Mercado footbridge to Perro Chico for lunch. In the afternoon, see more of the Guggenheim and eventually have dinner at Guria or Zortziko or Etxanobe. On Day 2 see the Museo de Bellas Artes and walk across the Ensanche for one of Ander Calvo's designer sandwiches at his Taberna de los Mundos before hopping the Eusko Tren from Estación de Atxuri to Mundaka and Bermeo for sunset over the Urdaibai nature preserve at the mouth of the Ría de Gernika. The relentless will find a way to swing a late dinner at Goizeko Kabi. Day 3 would start with a walk through the Doña Casilda de Iturrizar Park, a look through the fascinating Museo Vasco in the Casco Viejo, and a funicular ride to Artxanda and the Txakolí de Artxanda for lunch overlooking the city. Visit the Museo Marítimo in the afternoon and have dinner in the excellent Casa Rufo or the postmodern Aizian in the Meliá Bilbao.

About the Restaurants

Though top restaurants are expensive in Bilbao, some of what is undoubtedly Europe's finest cuisine is served here in settings that range from the traditional hewn beams and stone walls to sleekly contemporary international restaurants all the way up to the Guggenheim itself, where San Sebastián superstar Martín Berasategui runs a dining room as superb as its habitat.

Word of Mouth

"The Guggenheim museum has put Bilbao on the map, and I have to be thankful to Mr. Gehry for that. When it was just a project, there were by far more people opposing to this museum than supporters. Today, everybody admits that it was the best idea ever to revitalize this former gray city, [that's] now a great place to live." —mikelg

About the Hotels

Ever since the Guggenheim reinvented Bilbao as a design darling, the city's hotel fleet has expanded and reflected (in the case of the Gran Hotel Domine, literally) the glitter and panache of Gehry's museum. Boutique hotels such as the Miró, design hotels such as the Gran Hotel Domine, and high-rise mammoths such as the Meliá Bilbao have made the classic Carlton begin to seem small and quaint by comparison. Despite new developments, the López de Haro remains the city's best lodging option, and many longtime Bilbao visitors prefer the memory-encrusted halls of the Carlton to the glass and steel labyrinths overlooking Abandoibarra and the Nervión estuary. Some of the hotels in the Casco Viejo are charming, while others are merely economical. Nocturnal reverberations in the Casco Viejo, a festive part of town, can pose serious sleeping problems for those in rooms over the street.

Getting Around

Bilbao is a scenic and easy drive from Barcelona that can be accomplished in five hours or less. Thanks to the prohibition on highway advertising and the lack of forestation along major highways, driving in Spain is a superb way to see the geography of the Iberian Peninsula.

Once here, getting around Bilbao is easily accomplished on foot, though the occasional subway from, say, San Mamés at the western edge of town to the Casco Viejo at the other edge can be useful and save a 30-minute walk. The Euskotram, Bilbao's tramway, runs from the Basurto hospital downriver from (southwest of) San Mamés soccer stadium along a grassy track past the Guggenheim and along the river to Atxuri Station just upriver from the Casco Viejo. ⇨ *For more information see the Planning section.*

9

DINING & LODGING PRICE CATEGORIES (IN EUROS)					
	¢	$	$$	$$$	$$$$
Restaurants	€8 or less	€9–€11	€12–€18	€19–€25	over €25
Hotels	under €75	€75–€100	€101–€150	€151–€190	over €190

Restaurant prices are per person for a main course at dinner. Hotel prices are for a standard double room for two people, excluding service and tax.

By George
Semler

When Frank O. Gehry's Museo Guggenheim Bilbao opened in 1997, few would have predicted that an art museum would be able to singlehandly transform Bilbao's character and economy from a dreary post-industrial pit to a dazzling cultural tourism and design destination. No single art and architecture monument has ever so radically changed a city as the Guggenheim did with Bilbao.

Even the Basque Country's longtime political and social conflict came to a temporary halt after the Guggenheiming of Bilbao. The city once known as a steel and boatbuilding giant reinvented itself as a cultural capital not only with this art museum, but with a sleek subway system by Norman Foster, a glass footbridge by Santiago Calatrava, and the urban landscape of César Pelli's Abandoibarra project. Residents of the inner city recently numbered 353,168, but greater Bilbao (Bilbo, in Euskera, the Basque language) now encompasses almost 1 million inhabitants. That gives Bilbao, the capital of the province of Vizcaya, nearly half the total population of the Basque Country and makes it the fourth-largest urban population in Spain. Until relatively recently a smoke-stained industrial soot bowl—though never lacking a sparkling cultural and culinary tradition—Bilbao has made a brilliant investment in art and tourism and led the entire Basque Country into a new era of economic and spiritual regeneration, suggesting that life can indeed, to some degree, imitate art (or at least an art museum).

Gehry's gleaming titanium whale of a museum hovers alongside the estuary of the Nervión River, connecting Bilbao's 700-year-old Casco Viejo (Old Quarter) with the 19th-century Ensanche (Widening), and it seems to collect and reflect light throughout Bilbao. For starters, from the central atrium of the Guggenheim you can look both east up into Bilbao's most urban streets or above to the hills to the west, where farmers and grazing livestock continue about their age-old business. Meanwhile, churches in Bilbao's Casco Viejo are emerging from centuries of industrial grime, while parks and gardens are being reclaimed from what were once rusting shipyards and steel mills. Bilbao now seems a happy version of Hieronymous Bosch's *Garden of Earthly Delights* triptych, on view in Madrid's Prado, a virtual anthill of commerce and endeavor. And as the saying goes, "As Bilbao goes, so goes Euskadi."

PLANNING

GETTING HERE AND AROUND
AIR TRAVEL

Bilbao's airport terminal is a snowy pterodactyl-like structure, designed by flying-bridge specialist Santiago Calatrava, 12 km (7 mi) northeast of the city in Loiu. Iberia has regular connections with Madrid, Barcelona, the United Kingdom, France, and Belgium. Iberia, Spanair, and Air Europa flights from Barcelona arrive, on average, eight times a day and take just under an hour. The bus from the airport to Bilbao leaves every 30 minutes, takes 15–20 minutes, and costs about €1.50. Taxis cost about €24 and get you to town in under 15 minutes.

Airport Information Aeropuerto Internacional de Bilbao (☎ 94/486–9663 ⊕ www.aena.es).

BUS TRAVEL

Viacarsa Buses (⊕ *www.alsa.es*) connect Barcelona and Bilbao, a seven- to eight-hour trip. Viacarsa's buses from Barcelona to Bilbao leave from Barcelona Nord station at 7 AM, 10:15 AM, 3:15 PM, 10:45 PM, and 11:30 PM, arriving at, respectively, 3:15 PM, 5:30 PM, 10:45 PM, 7 AM, and 6:45 AM.

Buses from Bilbao to Barcelona leave from the Termibus station (metro: San Mamés) at 7 AM, 10:30 AM, 3:15 PM, and 10:30 PM, arriving at, respectively, 2:15 PM, 5:45 PM, 10:45 PM, and 6:15 AM.

A one-way ticket costs €41.90; round-trip is €79.61.

Bus Information Estación d'autobuses de Barcelona Nord (⊠ Ali Bei 80 Eixample ☎ 902/260606 ⊕ www.barcelonanord.com Ⓜ Arc de Triomf). **Termibus Bilbao** (⊠ Gurtubay 1, San Mamés ☎ 94/439–5077 ⊕ www.termibus.es Ⓜ San Mamés).

CAR TRAVEL

Bilbao is a scenic drive from Barcelona that can be accomplished in five hours or less. The drive from Barcelona through Zaragoza and Logroño is 613 km (368 mi) on the AP7–A68 freeway. Traveling at normal Spanish freeway speeds (120 kph–140 kph [72 mph–87 mph]), this is under five hours. Plan on averaging about half that speed when you drive on non-freeways. Between construction, cycling events, herds of sheep, slow trucks, and curves, it's difficult (and dangerous) to do much better.

Car rentals from national or cheaper local agencies are available in town. At the airport are Avis, Hertz, Budget, and the European agency Europcar. National companies work through the Spanish agency Atesa. All agencies have a wide range of models, but cars with automatic transmission are less common. Rates begin at €75 a day and €195 a week for an economy car with air-conditioning, manual transmission, and unlimited mileage. This does not include the tax on car rentals, which is 16%. Look for cheaper arrangements through ⊕ *www.spaincarrental.com*.

Agencies Alquibilbo (✉ *General Eguía 20 El Ensanche* ☎ *94/441–2012*
⊕ *www.alquibilbo.com*). **A-Rental** (✉ *Pérez Galdós 24 El Ensanche* ☎ *94/427–*
0781 ⊕ *www.a-rental.es*). **Atesa** (✉ *Plaza Circular 1 El Ensanche* ☎ *94/423–*
4285 ⊕ *www.atesa.es*). **Europcar** (✉ *Estación del Abando, El Ensanche*
☎ *94/423–9390* ⊕ *www.europcar.es*). **Hertz** (✉ *Doctor Achocarro 10 El*
Ensanche ☎ *94/415–3677* ⊕ *www.hertz.es*).

TAXI TRAVEL

In Bilbao taxis are normally hailed on the street. A taxi across the center of the city from Palacio de Euskalduna to Atxuri Station will rarely
exceed €10. A taxi stand is called a *parada de taxis*; taxis charge extra
for airport drop-offs and pick-ups as well as for baggage, and tipping
is entirely optional.

TRAIN TRAVEL

Trains from Barcelona's Sants station to Bilbao leave twice daily at
7:30 AM (arriving at 1:48 PM) and at 4:30 PM (arriving at 11:03 PM).
Both trains cost €62.30. Call RENFE for information or reserve online
(see phone number and Web site below).

Within and around Bilbao there are four railroad options as well as
the subway system. Cercanías RENFE (local trains) will take you up
and down the left bank of the river, notably to Santurtzi with its excellent Hogar del Pescador sardine sanctuary. The regional train company
FEVE runs a narrow-gauge train to Santander. Euskotram sends a narrow-gauge railway to San Sebastián from Atxuri station near the Casco
Viejo as well as trains to Gernika, Mundaka, and Bermeo.

Train Information Bilbao (✉ *Estación del Abando, Calle Hurtado de Amézaga*
☎ *94/423–8623 or 94/423–8636*). **FEVE** (✉ *Estación de FEVE, next to Estación*
del Abando ☎ *94/423–2266* ⊕ *www.feve.es*). **RENFE** (☎ *902/240202* ⊕ *www.*
renfe.es). **Euskotren** (✉ *Estación de Atxuri, north of Mercado de la Ribera, Bil-*
bao ☎ *94/433–8007* ⊕ *www.euskotren.es*).

TRAVEL BY PUBLIC TRANSPORTATION

The Creditrans ticket is good for tram, metro, and bus travel and is
available in values of €5, €10, and €15, though the €5 ticket should suf-
fice for the few subway hops you might need to get around town. Creditrans can be purchased at newspaper stands, bus stops, metro stations,
and from some drivers. The ticket is passed through a machine getting
on and off metros, tramways, or buses, and your Creditrans is charged
according to the length of your trip. Transfers cost extra. A single in-
town (Zone 1) ride costs about €1 and can be purchased from a driver;
with a Creditrans transaction the cost is reduced to about €0.93

Bilbobus provides bus service 6 AM–10:20 PM. Plaza Circular and Plaza
Moyúa are the principal hubs for all lines. Once the metro and normal
bus routes stop service, take a night bus, known as a *Gautxori* ("night
bird" in Euskera). Six lines run radially between Plaza Circular and
Plaza Moyúa and the city limits 11:30 PM–2 AM weekdays and until
6 AM on Saturday.

Metro Bilbao is lineal, running down the Nervión estuary from Basauri,
above, or east of, the Casco Viejo, all the way to the mouth of the Nervión at Getxo, before continuing on to the beach town of Plentzia. There

is no main hub, but the Moyúa station is the most central stop and lies in the middle of Bilbao's Ensanche, or modern (post-1860) part. The second subway line runs down the left bank of the Nervión to Santurtzi.

Contacts Bilbobus (☎ 94/448–4080). **Euskotram** (✉ Atxuri 6 Casco Viejo ☎ 902/543210). **Metro Bilbao** (✉ Atxuri 10 Casco Viejo ☎ 94/425–4000).

VISITOR INFORMATION

Tourist offices are found at Plaza Ensanche 11 and Avenida de Abandoibarra 2. There are two other offices, one in the airport at Loiu and the other, with no telephone, in the Teatro Arriaga at the edge of the Casco Viejo.

Municipal Tourist Offices Bilbao Iniciativas Turísticas (✉ Plaza Ensanche 11 El Ensanche ☎ 94/479–5760 ⊕ www.bilbao.net ✉ Aeropuerto de Loiu ☎ 94/471–0310 ✉ Av. de Abandoibarra 2 ☎ 94/479–5760 ✉ Teatro Arriaga office, Plaza Arriaga 1 Casco Viejo ☎ No phone).

TOURS

Bilbao's tourist office, Iniciativas Turísticas, conducts weekend guided tours in English and Spanish. The Casco Viejo tour starts at 10 AM at the tourist office on the ground floor of the Teatro Arriaga. The Ensanche and Abandoibarra tour begins at noon at the tourist office located to the left of the Guggenheim entrance. The tours last 90 minutes and cost €4.50.

Bilbao Paso a Paso arranges custom-designed visits and tours of Bilbao throughout the week. Stop Bilbao leads visits and tours of Bilbao and the province of Vizcaya.

Contacts Bilbao Paso a Paso (✉ Calle Mitxel Labegerie 1 [5–1] ☎ 94/415–3892 ⊕ www.bilbaopasoapaso.com). **Iniciativas Turísticas** (✉ Plaza Ensanche 11 ☎ 94/479–5760 ⊕ www.bilbao.net). **Stop Bilbao** (✉ Gran Vía 80 ☎ 94/442–4689 ⊕ www.stop.es).

9

EXPLORING BILBAO

Post-Guggenheim Bilbao has become more famous for its "Bilbao blue" skies than for its traditional *siri-miri* drizzle. Once a gloomy industrial seaport, the city is now known for green parks, riverside strolls, dazzling art museums, and poetic footbridges.

Bilbao's old treasures still line the banks of the Nervión: the Casco Viejo (Old Quarter) is a charming jumble of shops, bars, and restaurants on the river's right bank, while the late-19th-century Ensanche (Expansion) on the left bank has wide and elegant boulevards such as Gran Vía and Alameda Mazarredo.

ALONG THE NERVIÓN RIVER

Walking the banks of the Nervión is a satisfying jaunt. After all, this was how—while out on a morning jog—the Guggenheim's director, Thomas Krens, first discovered the perfect spot for his project, nearly opposite the right bank's Deusto University. From the Palacio de Euskalduna upstream to the colossal Mercado de la Ribera, parks and green zones line either

The whimsical art of the Museo de Bellas Artes is appreciated by all ages.

side of the river. An amble here will offer even more when César Pelli's Abandoibarra project fills in the half mile between the Guggenheim and the Euskalduna bridge with a series of parks, the Deusto University library, the Meliá Bilbao Hotel, and a major shopping center.

WHAT TO SEE

㉖ Mercado de la Ribera. This triple-decker ocean liner with its prow headed down the estuary toward the open sea is one of the best markets of its kind in Europe, as well as one of the biggest, with more than 400 retail stands covering 37,950 square feet. Like the architects of the Guggenheim and the Palacio de Euskalduna nearly 75 years later, the architect here was not unplayful with this well-anchored ocean-going grocery store in the river. From the stained-glass entryway over Calle de la Ribera to the tiny catwalks over the river or the diminutive restaurant on the second floor, the market is an inviting place. Look for the farmers' market on the top floor, and down on the bottom floor ask how fresh a fish is some morning and you might hear, "Oh, that one's not too fresh: caught last night." ⊠ *Calle de la Ribera 20 Casco Viejo* ☎ *94/415–3136* ⊙ *Mon.–Sat. 8 AM–1 PM* Ⓜ *Casco Viejo.*

④ **Museo de Bellas Artes** *(Museum of Fine Arts).* Considered one of the top five museums in a country that has a staggering number of museums and great paintings, the Museo de Bellas Artes is like a mini-Prado, with representatives from every Spanish school and movement from the 12th through the 20th centuries. The museum's fine collection of Flemish, French, Italian, and Spanish paintings includes works by El Greco, Goya, Velázquez, Zurbarán, Ribera, Gauguin, and Tàpies. One large and excellent section traces developments in 20th-century Spanish and Basque art

CLOSE UP

Habla Euskera?

Although the Basque people speak French north of the border and Spanish south of the border, they consider Euskera their first language and identify themselves as the Euskaldunak (the "Basque speakers"). Euskera remains one of the great enigmas of linguistic scholarship. Theories connect it with everything from Sanskrit to Japanese to Finnish. What is certain is where Euskera did not come from, namely the Indo-European family of languages that includes the Germanic, Italic, and Hellenic language groups. Currently used by about a million people in northern Spain and southwestern France, Euskera sounds like a consonant-ridden version of Spanish, with its five pure vowels, rolled "r," and palatal "n" and "l." Basque has survived two millennia of cultural and political pressure, and is the only remaining language of those spoken in southwestern Europe before the Roman conquest.

alongside works by better-known European contemporaries, such as Léger and Bacon. Look especially for Zuloaga's famous portrait of La Condesa Mathieu de Moailles and Sorolla's portrait of Basque philosopher Miguel de Unamuno. A statue of Basque painter Ignacio de Zuloaga outside greets visitors to this sparkling collection at the edge of Doña Casilda Park and on the left bank end of the Deusto bridge, five minutes from the Guggenheim. Three hours might be barely enough to fully appreciate this international and pan-chronological painting course. The museum's excellent Arbolagaña restaurant offers a stellar lunch break to break up the visit. ⊠ *Museo Plaza 2D Parque de Doña Casilda de Iturrizar, El Ensanche* ☎ *94/439–6060* ⊕ *www.museobilbao.com* ☒ *€5.50; Bono Artean combined ticket with Guggenheim (valid 1 yr) €15; free Wed.* ☉ *Tues.–Sat. 10–1:30 and 4–7:30, Sun. 10–2* Ⓜ *Moyúa.*

⑤ **Museo Guggenheim Bilbao.** Described by the late Spanish novelist Manuel
Fodor's Choice Vázquez Montalbán as a "meteorite," the Guggenheim, with its erup-
★ tion of light in the ruins of Bilbao's failed shipyards and steelworks, has dramatically reanimated this onetime industrial city. How Bilbao and the Guggenheim met is in itself a saga: Guggenheim director Thomas Krens was looking for a venue for a major European museum, having found nothing acceptable in Paris, Madrid, or elsewhere, and glumly accepted an invitation to Bilbao. Krens was out for a morning jog when he found it—the empty riverside lot once occupied by the Altos Hornos de Vizcaya steel mills. The site, at the heart of Bilbao's traditional steel and shipping port, was the perfect place for a metaphor for Bilbao's macro-reconversion from steel to titanium, from heavy industry to art, as well as a nexus between the early-14th-century Casco Viejo and the new 19th-century Ensanche and between the wealthy right bank and working-class left bank of the Nervión River.

Frank Gehry's gleaming brainchild, opened in 1997 and hailed as "the greatest building of our time" by architect Philip Johnson and "a miracle" by Herbert Muschamp of the *New York Times*, has sparked an economic renaissance in the Basque Country after more than a half

9

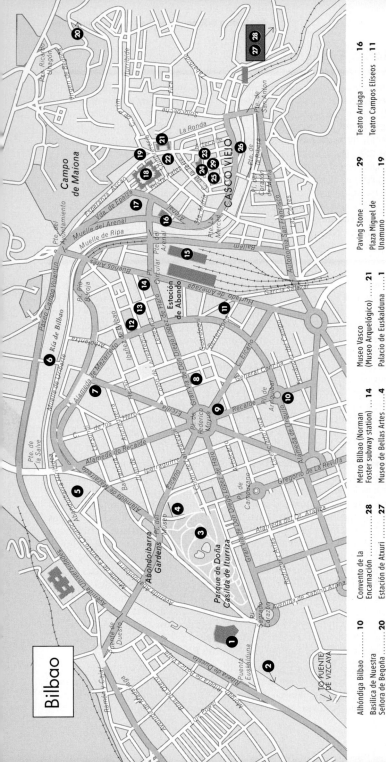

Bilbao

century of troubles. In its first year, the Guggenheim attracted 1.4 million visitors, three times the number expected and more than both Guggenheim museums in New York during the same period.

At once suggestive of a silver-scaled fish and a mechanical heart, Gehry's sculpture in titanium, limestone, and glass is the perfect habitat for the contemporary and postmodern artworks it contains. The smoothly rounded jumble of surfaces and cylindrical shapes recalls Bilbao's shipbuilding and steel-manufacturing past, whereas the transparent and reflective materials create a shimmering, futuristic luminosity. With the final section of the La Salve bridge over the Nervión folded into the structure, the Guggenheim is both a doorway to Bilbao and an urban forum: the atrium looks up into the center of town and across the river to the Old City and the green hillsides of Artxanda where livestock graze tranquilly. Gehry's intent to build something as moving as a Gothic cathedral in which "you can feel your soul rise up," and to make it as poetically playful and perfect as a fish—as per Schubert's ichthyological homage in his famous "Trout Quintet"—is patent: "I wanted it to be more than just a dumb building; I wanted it to have a plastic sense of movement!"

Covered with 30,000 sheets of titanium, the Guggenheim became Bilbao's main attraction overnight. Despite unexpected cleaning problems (Bilbao's industrial grime knows no equal), which was solved in 2002 using a customized procedure, the museum's luster endures. The enormous atrium, more than 150 feet high, is connected to the 19 galleries by a system of suspended metal walkways and glass elevators. Vertical windows reveal the undulating titanium flukes and contours of this beached whale. With most of its modern art drawn from New York's Solomon R. Guggenheim Museum, the Bilbao Guggenheim is a magnet for visitors from all over the world. The free Audio Guía explains everything you always wanted to know about modern art, contemporary art, and the Guggenheim. Frank Gehry talks of his love of fish and how his creative process works, while the pieces in the collection are presented one by one (a Kokoschka painting includes a description of Alma Mahler's lethal romance with the painter).

The collection, described by Krens as "a daring history of the art of the 20th century," consists of more than 250 works, most from the New York Guggenheim and the rest acquired by the Basque government. The second and third floors reprise the original Guggenheim collection of abstract expressionist, cubist, surrealist, and geometrical works. Artists whose names are synonymous with the art of the 20th century (Kandinsky, Picasso, Ernst, Braque, Miró, Pollock, Calder, Malevich) and European artists of the '50s and '60s (Chillida, Tàpies, Iglesias, Clemente, and Kiefer) are joined by contemporary figures (Nauman, Muñoz, Schnabel, Badiola, Barceló, Basquiat). The ground floor is dedicated to large-format and installation work, some of which—like Richard Serra's *Serpent*—were created specifically for the spaces they occupy. Claes Oldenburg's *Knife Ship,* Robert Morris's walk-in *Labyrinth,* and pieces by Beuys, Boltansky, Long, Holzer, and others round out the heavyweight division in one of the largest galleries in the world.

On holidays and weekends lines may develop, though between the playful clarinetist making a well-deserved killing on the front steps and the general spell of the place (who can be irked in the shadow of Jeff Koons's flower-covered, 40-foot-high Westmoreland Terrier, *Puppy?*), no one seems too impatient. Advance tickets from Servicaixa ATM machines or, in the Basque Country, the BBK bank machines are the way to miss the line. Failing that (sometimes they run out), go around at closing time and buy tickets for the next few days. The museum has no parking of its own, but underground lots throughout the area provide alternatives; check the Web site for information. ⊠ *Abandoibarra Etorbidea 2 El Ensanche* ☎ *94/435–9080* ⊕ *www.guggenheim-bilbao. es* ⤢€13; *Bono Artean combined ticket with Museo de Bellas Artes €15* ۵ *Tues.–Sun. 11–8* Ⓜ *Moyúa.*

> **BILBAO BLUE**
>
> The Guggenheim office building near the Jeff Koons *Puppy* is startlingly, deeply, enormously blue. While working on the Guggenheim, Frank Gehry fell in love with this "Bilbao blue," so-called for the vivid blue sky seen on rare days over Bilbao when the Atlantic drizzle–the famous Basque *siri-miri*–permits. Curiously, as a result of either the Guggenheim's reflected light, less industrial smog, or climate change, Bilbao's blue skies have become more frequent but less intense, leaving the Guggenheim offices and the Perro Chico restaurant, Gehry's favorite, among the few surviving outbursts of the city's emblematic color.

❷ **Museo Marítimo Ría de Bilbao** *(Maritime Museum of Bilbao).* This interesting nautical museum on the left bank of the Ría de Bilbao reconstructs the history of the Bilbao waterfront and shipbuilding industry beginning with medieval times. Temporary exhibits range from visits by extraordinary seacraft such as tall ships or traditional fishing vessels to thematic displays on 17th- and 18th-century clipper ships or the sinking of the *Titanic.* ⊠ *Muelle Ramón de la Sota, San Mamés* ☎ *902/131000* ⊕ *www. museomaritimobilbao.org* ⤢€5. ۵ *Tues.–Sun. 10–8* Ⓜ *San Mamés.*

❶ **Palacio de Euskalduna.** In homage to the Astilleros Euskalduna (Basque Country shipbuilders) that operated shipyards here beside the Euskalduna bridge into the late 20th century, this music venue and convention hall resembles a rusting ship, a stark counterpoint to Frank Gehry's shimmering titanium fantasy just up the Nervión. Designed by architects Federico Soriano and Dolores Palacios, Euskalduna opened in 1999 and is Bilbao's main opera venue and home of the Bilbao Symphony Orchestra. The auditorium has a 2,200-person capacity, three smaller music halls, eight practice rooms, seven lecture halls and press conference spaces, as well as a restaurant, a cafeteria, and a shopping center. A 71-stop organ, Spain's largest, offers quite a different tune from the past pitched battles waged here between workers, Basque nationalists, management, and police as the shipyards laid off thousands in the mid-1980s. ⊠ *Av. Abandoibarra 4 El Ensanche* ☎ *94/403–5000* ⊕ *www. euskalduna.net* ⤢ *Tour €3* ۵ *Office weekdays 9–2 and 4–7; box office Mon.–Sat. noon–2 and 5–8:30, Sun. noon–2; guided tours Sat. at noon or by appointment (fax Departamento Comercial)* Ⓜ *San Mamés.*

A swirling masterpiece of architecture—the Museo Guggenheim Bilbao.

❸ Parque de Doña Casilda de Iturrizar. Bilbao's main park, this lush collection of exotic trees, ducks and geese, fountains, falling water, and great expanses of lawns usually dotted with lovers is a delight and a sanctuary from the hard-edged Ensanche, Bilbao's modern, post-1876 expansion. As for the name, Doña Casilda de Iturrizar was a well-to-do 19th-century Bilbao matron who married a powerful banker and used his wealth to support various cultural and beneficent institutions in the city, including this grassy refuge. ⊠ *El Ensanche* Ⓜ *San Mamés*.

❻ Puente de Zubi-Zuri. Santiago Calatrava's signature span (the name means "white bridge" in Euskera) connects Campo Volantín on the right bank with the Ensanche on the left. Just a few minutes east of the Guggenheim, the playful seagull-shape bridge swoops brightly over the dark Nervión. The Plexiglas walkway suggests walking on water, though wear and tear has reduced the surface from transparent to a mere translucent. The airport just west of Bilbao at Loiu, also designed by Calatrava, resembles a massive, white Concorde plane and has been dubbed *La Paloma* (The Dove), despite more closely resembling a snow goose poised for takeoff. Calatrava's third Vizcaya creation, the bridge at Ondarroa, completes this troika of gleaming white suspension bridges exploring the theme of flight. ⊠ *El Ensanche 48007* Ⓜ *Moyúa*.

⓰ Teatro Arriaga.
★ A hundred years ago, this 1,500-seat theater was as exciting a source of Bilbao pride as the Guggenheim is today. Built between 1886 and 1890, when Bilbao's population was a mere 35,000, the Teatro Arriaga represented a gigantic per-capita cultural investment. Always a symbol of Bilbao's industrial might and cultural vibrancy, the original "Nuevo Teatro" (New Theater) de Bilbao was a lavish

Belle Époque, neo-baroque spectacular modeled after the Paris Opéra by architect Joaquín Rucoba (1844–1909). The theater was renamed in 1902 for the Bilbao musician thought of as "the Spanish Mozart," Juan Crisóstomo de Arriaga (1806—26).

After a 1914 fire, the new version of the theater opened in 1919. Following years of splendor, the Teatro Arriaga (along with Bilbao's economy) gradually lost vigor; it closed down in 1978 for restoration work that was finally concluded in 1986. Now largely eclipsed by the splendid and more spacious Palacio de Euskalduna, the Arriaga stages opera, theater, concerts, and dance events from September through June. Walk around the building to see the stained glass on its rear facade and the exuberant caryatids holding up the arches facing the river. ⊠ *Plaza Arriaga 1 Casco Viejo* ☎ *94/416–3333* ⊕ *www.teatroarriaga.com* Ⓜ *Casco Viejo.*

EL CASCO VIEJO

Walled until the 19th century, Bilbao's Casco Viejo (Old Quarter, the city's oldest nucleus) is often synonymous with Siete Calles, so called for the original "seven streets" of proto-Bilbao in 1442. A finer distinction separates the Casco Viejo per se—the newer part of the old part of town around the 19th-century Plaza Nueva (New Square)—from the original 15th-century Siete Calles, the seven streets between the Santiago cathedral and the Mercado de la Ribera. Both parts of this warren of antiquity are filled with some of Bilbao's oldest and most charming architecture. It's all miraculously connected to modern Bilbao, and even the beach at Getxo, by Norman Foster's spotless "*fosterito*," the streamlined subway stop across the square from the outstanding Museo Vasco.

WHAT TO SEE

㉠ Ascensor de Begoña *(Begoña Elevator).* This popular Bilbao landmark is an elevator that connects the Casco Viejo with points overlooking the city. La Basilica de la Begoña is the classic pilgrimage and site of weddings and christenings. ⊠ *Entrance at Calle Esperanza 6 Casco Viejo* ⌦ *€0.40* Ⓜ *Casco Viejo.*

㉠ Basílica de Nuestra Señora de Begoña. Bilbao's most cherished religious sanctuary, dedicated to the patron saint of Vizcaya, can be reached by the 313 stairs from Plaza de Unamuno or by the gigantic elevator (the Ascensor de Begoña) looming over Calle Esperanza 6 behind the San Nicolás church. The church's Gothic nave was begun in 1519 on the site of an early hermitage, where the Virgin Mary was alleged to have appeared long before. Finished in 1620, the basilica was completed with the economic support of the shipbuilders and merchants of Bilbao, many of whose businesses are commemorated on the inner walls of the church. The high ground the basilica occupies was strategically important during the Carlist Wars of 1836 and 1873, and as a result La Begoña suffered significant damage that was not restored until the beginning of the 20th century. Comparable in importance (if not in geographical impact) to Barcelona's Virgen de Montserrat, the Basílica de la Begoña is where the Athletic de Bilbao soccer team makes its pilgrimage, some of the players often barefoot, in gratitude for triumphs. ⊠ *Calle*

CLOSE UP

Abandoibarra: Bilbao's New Heart

The Abandoibarra project covers nearly a full square mile along the Nervión estuary. Formerly occupied by docks, warehouses, and shipyards, two-thirds of this new urban center are now parks and open spaces. Javier López Chollet's 280,000-square-foot Ribera Park borders the Parque de Doña Casilda between the Guggenheim and Palacio de Euskalduna. This green space joins the quais of La Naja, Ripa, and Uribitarte to connect with the Olabeaga park downriver, creating a riverside promenade over 3 km (2 mi) long.

The head architect for the project is the Connecticut-based César Pelli, designer of New York's World Financial Center and its Winter Garden fronting the Hudson River. Offices are also part of the project, as well as five apartment blocks and a residential

building by Basque architect Luis Peña Ganchegui. Other buildings include the Meliá Bilbao Hotel (formerly the Sheraton Bilbao) by the Mexican architect Ricardo Legorreta; and American Robert Stern's shopping and leisure center, Zubiarte. Flanking the riverside thoroughfare named for Bilbao businessman and benefactor Ramón Rubial are the auditorium of the University of the Basque Country and the Deusto University library. Pedro Arrupe's footbridge, an exercise in rationalism with a simple geometrical form, connects Abandoibarra and Deusto University. The footbridge creates a complete urban promenade joining the Avenue of the Universities, the riverside walk, and the new streets of Abandoibarra, the culminating act of the revitalized, 21st-century Bilbao.

Virgen de Begoña 38 Begoña ☎ *94/412–7091* ⊕ *www.basilicadebegona. com* ✉ *Free* ☉ *Weekdays 9:30–1:30 and 4:30–8:30* Ⓜ *Casco Viejo.*

㉕ ★ **Biblioteca de Bidebarrieta.** This historic library and intellectual club was originally called "El Sitio" (The Siege) in memory of Bilbao's successful resistance to the Carlist siege of 1876 (Carlists were supporters of Fernando VII's brother, Don Carlos, over his daughter Isabella II as rightful heir to the Spanish throne). Now a municipal library, the Bidebarrieta has a music auditorium that is one of Bilbao's most beautiful venues and a spot to check for the infrequent performances held there. The reading rooms are open to the public, a good place to read newspapers, make notes, or just enjoy the historical echoes of the place. ⊠ *Calle Bidebarrieta 4 Casco Viejo* ☎ *94/415–6930* ☉ *Weekdays 8:30–8:30, Sat. 8:30–2* Ⓜ *Casco Viejo.*

㉔ **Catedral de Santiago** *(St. James's Cathedral).* Bilbao's earliest church was a pilgrimage stop on the coastal route to Santiago de Compostela. Work on the structure began in 1379, but fire delayed completion until the early 16th century. The florid Gothic style with Isabelline elements features a nave in the form of a Greek cross, with ribbed vaulting resting on cylindrical columns. The notable outdoor arcade, or *pórtico*, was used for public meetings of the early town's governing bodies. ⊠ *Plaza de Santiago 1 Casco Viejo* ☎ *94/415–3627* ✉ *Free* ☉ *Tues.–Sat. 10–1:30 and 4–7, Sun. 10:30–1:30* Ⓜ *Casco Viejo.*

9

28 Convento de la Encarnación. The Basque Gothic architecture of this early-16th-century convent, church, and museum gives way to Renaissance and baroque ornamentation high on the main facade. The **Museo Diocesano de Arte Sacro** (Diocesan Museum of Sacred Art) occupies a carefully restored 16th-century cloister. The inner patio alone, ancient and intimate, more than amortizes the visit. On display are religious silverwork, liturgical garments, sculptures, and paintings dating back to the 12th century. The convent is across from the Atxuri station just upstream from the Puente de San Antón. ⊠ *Plaza de la Encarnación 9 Casco Viejo* ☎ *94/432–0125* ☎ *Free* ⊘ *Tues.–Sat. 10:30–1:30 and 4–7, Sun. 10:30–1* Ⓜ *Casco Viejo.*

27 Estación de Atxuri. Bilbao's narrow-gauge railroad station at Atxuri connects with Gernika, Mundaka, and Bermeo on the Basque coast, a spectacular ride through the Ría de Gernika that allows the best available views of the Urdaibai natural park (unless you're in a boat). The train to San Sebastián is another favorite excursion, chugging through villages such as Zumaya and Zarautz. You can even get off and walk for a few hours, catching a later train. Narrow-gauge railways were the standard in Vizcaya and in much of northern Spain owing to steep grades and tight quarters, as well as economics. Today only a few remain. Check with **FEVE** (*Ferrocarriles Españoles de Via Estrecha* ☎ *94/423–2266* ⊕ *www.transcantabrico.feve.es*) for information about the luxury Cantabrican Express that runs from San Sebastián to Santiago de Compostela, with stops for wining, dining, and sightseeing. ⊠ *Calle Atxuri s/n, Casco Viejo* ☎ *902/543210* Ⓜ *Casco Viejo.*

**OFF THE
BEATEN
PATH**

Funicular de Artxanda. The panorama from the hillsides of Artxanda is the most comprehensive view of Bilbao, and the various typical *asadors* (roasters) here serve delicious beef or fish cooked over coals. ⊠ *Entrance on Plaza de Funicular s/n, Matiko* ☎ *94/445–4956* ☎ *€0.90* Ⓜ *Casco Viejo.*

21 ★ Museo Vasco (Museo Arqueológico, Etnográfico e Histórico Vasco) (*Basque Museum; Museum of Basque Archaeology, Ethnology, and History*). One of the stand-out, not-to-miss visits in Bilbao, this museum occupies an austerely elegant 16th-century convent. The collection centers on Basque ethnography, Bilbao history, and comprehensive displays from the lives of Basque shepherds, fishermen, and farmers. Highlights include *El Mikeldi* in the cloister, a pre-Christian iron-age stone animal representation that may be 4,000 years old; the room dedicated to Basque shepherds and the pastoral way of life; the Mar de los Vascos (Se of the Basques) exhibit featuring whaling, fishing, and maritime activities; the second-floor prehistoric exhibit featuring a wooden harpoon, recovered in the Santimamiñe caves at Kortezubi, that dates from the 10th century BC; and the third-floor scale model of Vizcaya province with the *montes bocineros* (bugling mountains), showing the five peaks of Vizcaya used for calling the different *anteiglesias* (parishes) with bonfires or *txalaparta* (percussive sticks) to the general assemblies held in Gernika. ⊠ *Calle Cruz 4 Casco Viejo* ☎ *94/415–5423* ⊕ *www.euskal-museoa.org* ☎ *€3.50; free Thurs.* ⊘ *Tues.–Sat. 11–5, Sun. 11–2* Ⓜ *Casco Viejo.*

㉔ Palacio Yohn. Now used for the Centro Cívico de la Bolsa, a municipal cultural center, the palace has medieval ceilings that are covered with graceful vaulting. This ancient building, oddly and erroneously known as "La Bolsa" (The Stock Exchange)—though no exchange of stock has ever taken place here—is thought to have been built over a 14th-century structure. Immigrants from Central Europe moved here in the 18th century and apparently set up such a thriving commercial enterprise that it became known as "The Exchange." The building takes its name from Leandro Yohn, one of the successful merchants. ⊠ *Calle Pelota 10 Casco Viejo* ☎ *94/416–3199* ✆ *Oct.–May, Mon.–Sat. 9–1:30 and 4–9; June–Sept., Mon.–Sat. 9–1:30* Ⓜ *Casco Viejo.*

⑲ Plaza Miguel de Unamuno. Named for Bilbao's all-time greatest intellectual, figure of fame and fable throughout Spain and beyond, this bright and open space at the upper edge of the Casco Viejo honors Miguel de Unamuno (1864–1936)—a philosopher, novelist, professor, and wit, as well as a man of character and temperament. De Unamuno wrote some of Spain's most seminal works, including *Del sentimiento trágico de la vida en los hombres y los pueblos* (*The Tragic Sense of Life in Men and Nations*); his *Niebla* (*Mist*) has been generally accepted as the first existentialist novel, published in 1914 when Jean-Paul Sartre was but nine years old. Remembrances to Unamuno in the Casco Viejo include the philosopher's bust here, his birthplace at No. 7 Calle de la Cruz, and the nearby Filatelia Unamuno, a rare stamp emporium that is a favorite of collectors. Ⓜ *Casco Viejo.*

⑱ Plaza Nueva. This 64-arch neoclassical plaza seems to be typical of every Spanish city from San Sebastián to Salamanca to Seville. With its Sunday-morning market, its December 21 natural-produce Santo Tomás market, and its permanent tapas and restaurant offerings, Plaza Nueva is an easy place in which to spend a lot of time. It was finished in 1851 as part of an ambitious housing project designed to ease the pressure on limited mid-19th-century Bilbao space. Note the size of the houses' balconies: it was the measure—the bigger, the better—of the social clout of their inhabitants. The tiny windows near the top of the facades were servants' quarters. The building behind the powerful coat of arms at the head of the square was originally the Diputación, or provincial government office, but is now the **Academia de la Lengua Vasca** (Academy of the Basque Language). The coat of arms shows the tree of Gernika, symbolic of Basque autonomy, with the two wolves representing Don Diego López de Haro (López derives from *lupus*, meaning wolf). The bars and shops around the arcades include two versions of **Victor Montes** establishments, one for tapas at Plaza Nueva 8 and the other for more serious sit-down dining at Plaza Nueva 2. The **Café Bar Bilbao,** at Plaza Nueva 6, also known as Casa Pedro, has photos of early Bilbao, while the **Argoitia** at No. 15 across the square has a nice angle on the midday sun and a coat of arms inside with the *zatzpiakbat* ("seven-one" in Basque), referring to the cultural unity of the three French and four Spanish Basque provinces. Ⓜ *Casco Viejo.*

⑰ San Nicolás de Bari. Honoring the patron saint of mariners, San Nicolás de Bari, the city's early waterfront church, was built over an earlier eponymous hermitage and opened in 1756. With a powerful facade

The streets of El Casco Viejo.

over the Arenal, originally a sandy beach, San Nicolás was much abused by French and Carlist troops throughout the 19th century. Sculptures by Juan Pascual de Mena adorn the inside of the church. Look for the oval plaque to the left of the door marking the high-water mark of the flood of 1983. ⊠ *Plaza de San Nicolás 1 Casco Viejo* ☎ *94/416–3424* Ⓜ *Casco Viejo.*

㉒ Santos Juanes. Distinguished for accumulating the deepest water of any building in the Casco Viejo during the disastrous 1983 flood, as can be witnessed by the water mark more than 14 feet above the floor in the back of the church (to the left as you come in), this simple baroque church was the first Jesuit building in Bilbao, built in 1604. Originally the home of the Colegio de San Andrés de la Compañía de Jesús (St. Andrew's School of the Order of Jesuits), the original school is now divided between the Museo Vasco and the church dedicated to both St. Johns, the Evangelist and the Baptist. The church's most important relic is the *Relicario de la Vera Cruz* (Relic of the True Cross), a silver-plated cross containing what is widely believed to be the largest existing fragment of the cross used at Calvary to execute Jesus in AD 33. ⊠ *Calle de la Cruz 4 Casco Viejo* ☎ *94/415–3997* Ⓜ *Casco Viejo.*

EL ENSANCHE

Bilbao's busy Ensanche (Widening) has a rhythm and timbre more redolent of Manhattan or London than of Paris or Barcelona. Once Bilbao *saltó el río* (jumped the river) from the Casco Viejo in 1876, the new city center became Plaza Moyúa—at the heart of the Ensanche—with the Gran Vía as the district's most important thoroughfare. The late-

19th-century and early-20th-century architecture typical of this part of town is colossal, ornate, and formal, with only a few eruptions into Art Nouveau. Bilbao expressed its euphoria and wealth in the Ensanche as Barcelona did in its famous Art Nouveau neighborhood, the Eixample, though the distinct tastes and sensibilities of Basques and Catalans are nowhere more manifest than in these two wildly divergent turn-of-the-20th-century urban developments.

WHAT TO SEE

⑩ AlhóndigaBilbao. Once an early-20th-century municipal wine storage facility used by Bilbao's Rioja wine barons, this city block-sized, Philippe Starck–designed civic center is filled with shops, cafés, restaurants, movie theaters, swimming pools, fitness centers, and nightlife opportunities at the very heart of the city. Conceived as a hub for entertainment, culture, wellness, and civic coexistence AlhóndigaBilbao's opening in spring of 2010 added another star to Bilbao's cosmos of architectural and cultural offerings. ⊠ *Alameda Recalde 56 El Ensanche* ☎ *94/470–3458* ⊕ *www.alhondigabilbao.com* Ⓜ *Moyúa.*

⑬ Café Iruña. Famous for its decor and its boisterous and ebullient ambience, the Iruña is an essential Bilbao haunt on the Ensanche's most popular garden and square, Los Jardines de Albia. The neo-Mudéjar dining room overlooking the square is the place to be (if they try to stuff you in the back dining room, resist or come back another time). The bar has two distinct sections: the elegant side near the dining room, where sculptor Lorenzo Quinn's bronze arm hoists a beer tankard at the center of the counter; and the older, more bare-bones Spanish side on the Calle Berástegui side, with its plain marble counters and *pinchos morunos de carne de cordero* (lamb brochettes) as the house specialty. This place was founded by a Navarran restaurateur (Iruña is Euskera for Pamplona) in 1903; the Moorish decor in the dining room has been understood as an echo of the town hall's Salón Árabe (Arabian Hall). Jumping from dawn until after midnight, the Iruña is Bilbao's most cosmopolitan café. ⊠ *Calle Berástegui 5 El Ensanche* ☎ *94/423–7021* Ⓜ *Moyúa.*

⑮ Estación de la Concordia. Designed by the engineer Valentín Gorbeña in 1893 and finished by architect Severino Achúcarro in 1898, this colorful railroad station looks across the Nervión River to the Paris Opéra–inspired Teatro Arriaga, responding with its own references to the colonnaded Parisian Louvre. The peacock-fan-shape, yellow-and-green-tiled entrance is spectacular, along with the immense stained-glass window over the access to the tracks in which facets of Vizcayan life and work are represented, from farmers and fishermen to factory workers and jai alai players. Meanwhile, the graceful arch of the hangar over the tracks is typical of traditional railroad terminals around Europe. ⊠ *Calle Bailén 2 El Ensanche* ☎ *94/423–2266* Ⓜ *Abando.*

❾ Hotel Carlton. Bilbao's grande-dame favorite has hosted top-tier celebrities over the last century, from Orson Welles and Ernest Hemingway to Ava Gardner, casting giant Gretchen Rennell, and music czar John Court, not to mention Francis Ford Coppola. Architect Manuel María de Smith based this project on the London hotel of the same name, although the stained glass in the oval reception area is a reduced version

9

of the one in Nice's Hotel Negresco. The hotel's bar, the Grill, has a clubby English feel to it, with murals painted by client Martinez Ortiz in 1947. The murals, representing an equestrian scene and some 10 bourgeois figures, are remarkable for the detailed painting of every hand and finger. ⊠ *Plaza Federico Moyúa 2 El Ensanche* ☏ *944/162200* ⊕ *www.hotelcarlton.es* Ⓜ *Moyúa.*

⑫ **Los Jardines de Albia.** One of the two or three places all *bilbainos* will insist you see is this welcoming green space in the concrete and asphalt surfaces of this part of town. Overlooking the square is the lovely Basque Gothic **Iglesia de San Vicente Mártir,** its Renaissance facade facing its own Plaza San Vicente. The amply robed sculpture of the Virgin on the main facade, as the story goes, had to be sculpted a second time after the original version was deemed too scantily clad. The Jardines de Albia are centered on the bronze effigy of writer Antonio de Trueba by the famous Spanish sculptor Mariano Benlliure (1866–1947), creator of monuments to the greatest national figures of the epoch. ⊠ *Calle Colón de Larreátegui s/n, El Ensanche* Ⓜ *Moyúa.*

⑭ **Metro Bilbao (Norman Foster subway station).** The city's much-cherished subway system opened in 1995, and was designed by British architect Sir Norman Foster, winner of the 1999 Pritzker Architecture Prize and author of Barcelona's 1992 Collserola Communications tower, and, most recently, of the world's highest bridge, the Millau viaduct over the French Tarn valley. Bilbao's first metro has become a source of great pride for *bilbainos.* Only a necessity when Bilbao began to spread up and down the Nervión estuary, the Bilbao subway now connects Bolueta, upstream from the Casco Viejo, with Plentzia, a run of 30 km (19 mi). The metro is invariably spotless, graffiti is scarce, and most of its passengers are well dressed and ride in a respectful silence. A new line running down the left bank of the Nervión to Portugalete and Santurtzi is presently under construction.

Winner of the railway architecture Brunel Prize of 1996, the metro in general and the Sarriko station in particular were designated as the prizewinning elements. The Sarriko station, the largest of all of the 23 stops, is popularly known as *El Fosterazo* (the Big Foster); the others are *Fosteritos* (Little Fosters). The most spectacular are segmented glass tubes curving up from underground, such as those at Plaza Circular and Plaza Moyúa, widely thought to resemble transparent snails. ⊠ *Plaza Circular, El Ensanche* ⊕ *www.metrobilbao.net* Ⓜ *Abando.*

❼ **Palacio de Ibaigane.** This graceful manor-house design is the only one of its kind left in Bilbao. It is an elegant and sweeping country estate with classic *caserío* (farmhouse) details surrounded by the generally hard-edged Ensanche. Now the official seat of the Athletic de Bilbao soccer club, the house was originally the residence of the de la Sota family, whose most outstanding member, Ramón de la Sota, founded the company Euskalduna and became one of the most important shipbuilders in Europe. His company specialized in ship repair and opened shipyards in New York, London, Rotterdam, and Paris. Awarded the title "sir" by Great Britain for his services to the Allied cause in World War I, de la Sota went on to found the Euskalerria Basque rights organization, which later joined forces with the Basque Nationalist party. Because of his affiliation with Basque nationalism, Sir Ramón de la Sota's properties and businesses were seized by the Franco regime in 1939 and not returned to the family until 1973. ⊠ *Alameda de Mazarredo 15 El Ensanche* Ⓜ *Moyúa.*

⑧ Palacio Foral. Architect Luis Aladrén created this intensely decorated facade just two blocks from Plaza Moyúa for the seat of the Diputación (provincial government) in 1900. A manifestation of the bullish economic moment Bilbao was experiencing as the 20th century kicked off, the building was much criticized for its combination of overwrought aesthetic excess on the outside and minimally practical use of the interior space. The 19th-century Venetian motifs of its halls and salons, the chapel, and the important collection of paintings and sculptures are the best reasons to see the inside of the building. ⊠ *Gran Vía 45 El Ensanche* 🕭 *Free* 🕙 *Weekdays 9–2 and 4–8* Ⓜ *Moyúa.*

OFF THE BEATEN PATH

Puente de Vizcaya. Commonly called the **Puente Colgante** (Hanging Bridge), this has been one of Bilbao's most extraordinary sights ever since it was built in 1893. The bridge, a transporter hung from cables, ferries cars and passengers across the Nervión, uniting two distinct worlds: exclusive, bourgeois Las Arenas and Portugalete, a much older, working-class town. (Dolores Ibarruri, the famous Republican orator of the Spanish civil war, known as *La Pasionaria* for her ardor, was born here.) Portugalete is a 15-minute walk from Santurce, where the quayside Hogar del Pescador serves simple fish specialties. *Besugo* (sea bream) is the traditional choice, but the grilled sardines are hard to surpass. To reach the bridge, take the subway to Areeta, or drive across the Puente de Deusto, turn left on Avenida Lehendakari Aguirre, and follow signs for Las Arenas; it's a 10- or 15-minute drive from downtown. 🕭 *94/480–1012* ⊕ *www.puente-colgante.com* 🕭 *€0.30 to cross on foot, €1.20 by car between 5 AM and 10 PM (after 10 PM prices are higher); €5 for visit to observation deck* Ⓜ *Areeta.*

⑪ Teatro Campos Elíseos. If you've come from Barcelona, this extraordinary facade built in 1901 by architects Alfredo Acebal and Jean Baptiste Darroquy may seem familiar. The wild Moderniste (Art Nouveau) excitement of the intensely ornate circular arch—nearly plateresque in its intricate decorative detail—is a marked contrast to the more sober Bilbao interpretation of the turn-of-the-20th-century Art Nouveau euphoria. Predictably, *bilbainos* don't think very highly of this—to the Basque eye—exaggerated ornamentation. The theater is called Campos Elíseos after Paris's Champs-Elysées (a brief spasm of Francophilia in a town of Anglophiles), as this area of town was a favorite for early-20th-century promenades. During most of the 20th century Bilbao's theatrical life had two poles: the Casco Viejo's Teatro Arriaga and the Ensanche's Campos Elíseos. Known as *la bombonera de Bertendona* (the candy box of Bertendona) for its intimate and vertical distribution of stage and boxes, the 742-seat theater was recently restored and reopened in 2010. ⊠ *Calle Bertendona 3 El Ensanche* Ⓜ *Moyúa.*

9

WHERE TO EAT

$$$–$$$$
CONTEMPORARY

✗ **Aizian.** Euskera for "in the wind," the hotel restaurant for the Meliá Bilbao (formerly Sheraton Bilbao), under the direction of chef José Miguel Olazabalaga, has in record time become one of the city's most respected dining establishments. Typical Bilbaino culinary classicism doesn't keep Mr. Olazabalaga from creating surprising reductions and contemporary interpretations of traditional dishes such as *vieiras sobre risotto crujiente de hongos* (scallops on a crunchy wild mushroom risotto), or *la marmita de chipirón,* a stew of sautéed cuttlefish with a topping of whipped potatoes covering the sauce of squid ink. The clean-lined contemporary dining room and the streamlined, polished cuisine are a perfect match. ⊠ *C. Lehendakari Leizaola 29 El Ensanche* ☎ *94/428–0039* ⊕ *www.restaurante-aizian.com* ▤ *AE, DC, MC, V* ⊘ *Closed Sun. and Aug. 1–15* Ⓜ *San Mamés.*

$$$–$$$$
CONTEMPORARY
Fodor'sChoice
★

✗ **Arbolagaña.** On the top floor of the Museo de Bellas Artes, this elegant space has bay windows overlooking the lush Parque de Doña Casilda. Chef Aitor Basabe's cuisine is modern and streamlined, offering innovative versions of Basque classics such as codfish on toast, venison with wild mushrooms, or rice with truffles and shallots. The €42 *menú de degustación* (tasting menu) is a superb affordable luxury, while the abbreviated menú de trabajo (work menu) provides a perfect light lunch. ⊠ *Alameda Conde Arteche s/n El Ensanche* ☎ *94/442–4657* ⩘ *Reservations essential* ▤ *AE, DC, MC, V* ⊘ *Closed Easter Week, July 15–30, Mon. No dinner Tues., Wed., Sun.* Ⓜ *Moyúa.*

$–$$
BASQUE

✗ **Arriaga.** The cider-house experience is a must in the Basque Country. Cider *al txotx* (poured straight out of the barrel), sausage stewed in apple cider, codfish omelets, *txuleton de buey* (beefsteaks), and Idiazabal cheese with quince jelly are the classic fare. Reserving a table is a good idea, on weekends especially. ⊠ *Santa Maria 13 Casco Viejo* ☎ *94/416–5670* ▤ *AE, DC, MC, V* ⊘ *No dinner Sun.* Ⓜ *Casco Viejo.*

$$$$
SEAFOOD

✗ **Bermeo.** Named after and decorated in the style of the coastal fishing village to the north, this perennially top Bilbao restaurant housed in the Hotel Ercilla specializes in fresh market cuisine and traditional Basque interpretations of fish, shellfish, and seafood of all kinds. The *rodaballo* (turbot) in vinaigrette sauce is a good choice. ⊠ *Calle Ercilla 37 El Ensanche* ☎ *94/470–5700* ⩘ *Reservations essential* ▤ *AE, DC, MC, V* ⊘ *Closed Aug. 1–15. No lunch Sat. No dinner Sun.* Ⓜ *Moyúa.*

$$
BASQUE

✗ **Berton.** Dinner is served until 11:30 in this sleek, contemporary bistro in the Casco Viejo. Fresh wood tables with a green-tint polyethylene finish and exposed ventilation pipes give the dining room an industrialoid designer look, while the classic cuisine ranges from Iberian ham to smoked salmon, foie gras, cod, beef, and lamb. ⊠ *Jardines 11 Casco Viejo* ☎ *94/416–7035* ▤ *AE, DC, MC, V* ⊘ *No dinner Sun.* Ⓜ *Casco Viejo.*

$$$–$$$$
BASQUE
Fodor'sChoice
★

✗ **Casa Rufo.** Charming and cozy, this series of nooks and crannies tucked into a fine food, wine, olive-oil, cheese, and ham emporium has become famous for its *txuleta de buey* (beef chops). Let the affable owners size you up and bring on what you crave. The house wine is an excellent *crianza* (two years in oak, one in bottle) from La Rioja, but the wine list offers a good selection of wines from Ribera de Duero,

Somantano, and El Priorat as well. ⊠ *Calle Hurtado de Amézaga 5 El Ensanche* ☎ *94/443–2172* ⌕ *Reservations essential* ═ *AE, DC, MC, V* ☺ *Closed Sun.* Ⓜ *Abando.*

$$$–$$$$
SPANISH
Fodor's Choice
★

✕ **El Perro Chico.** The global glitterati who adopted post-Guggenheim Bilbao favor this spot across the Puente de la Ribera footbridge below the market. Frank Gehry discovered, on the walls here, the color "Bilbao blue"—the azure of the skies over (usually rainy) Bilbao—and used it for the Guggenheim's office building. Chef Rafael García Rossi and owner Santiago Diez Ponzoa run a happy ship. Noteworthy are the *alcachofas con almejas* (artichokes with clams), the extraordinarily light *bacalao con berenjena* (cod with eggplant), and the dark and fresh *pato a la naranja* (duck à l'orange). ⊠ *Calle Aretxaga 2 El Ensanche* ☎ *94/415–0519* ⌕ *Reservations essential* ═ *AE, DC, MC, V* ☺ *Closed Sun. No lunch Mon.* Ⓜ *Casco Viejo.*

$$$–$$$$
CONTEMPORARY

✕ **Etxanobe.** This luminous corner of the Euskalduna palace overlooks the Nervión River, the hills of Artxanda, and Bilbao. Fernando Canales creates sleek, homegrown contemporary cuisine using traditional ingredients. Standouts are the five codfish recipes, the duckling with Pedro Ximenez sherry, poached eggs with lamb kidneys and foie gras, and the braised scallops with shallot vinaigrette. ⊠ *Av. de Abandoibarra 4 El Ensanche* ☎ *94/442–1071* ═ *AE, DC, MC, V* ☺ *Closed Sun. and Aug. 1–20* Ⓜ *San Mamés.*

$$$–$$$$
BASQUE

✕ **Goizeko Kabi.** You can choose your own crab or crayfish at this excellent and famous sanctuary for first-rate Basque cuisine. The dining rooms are of brick and wood accented by plush Persian rugs and chairs upholstered with tapestries. Chef Fernando Canales's standout creations include *láminas de bacalao en ensalada con pimientos rojos asados* (sliced cod in green salad with roasted red peppers) and *hojaldre de verdura a la plancha con manito de cordero* (grilled vegetables in puff pastry with leg of lamb). ⊠ *Particular de Estraunza 4–6 El Ensanche* ☎ *94/442–1129* ⌕ *Reservations essential* ═ *AE, DC, MC, V* ☺ *Closed Sun. and July 31–Aug. 20* Ⓜ *Indautxu.*

$$$–$$$$
ECLECTIC

✕ **Gorrotxa.** Carmelo Gorrotxategui's fine eclectic menu mixes Basque, French, and Castilian cuisines. The man can do anything from *foie gras con uvas* (goose liver with grapes) to lobster Thermidor to *txuleta de buey* (beef chops). The *costillar*, roast rack of lamb with potatoes, is beyond satisfying. Enjoy it in English decor, complete with wood paneling. ⊠ *Alameda Urquijo 30, El Ensanche* ☎ *94/443–4937* ═ *AE, DC, MC, V* ☺ *Closed Sun., Holy Week, last wk in July, and first wk in Aug.* Ⓜ *Indautxu.*

$$$–$$$$
BASQUE

✕ **Guetaria.** A longtime local favorite for fresh fish and meats cooked over coals, this family operation is known for first-rate ingredients lovingly prepared. Named for the famous fishing village just west of San Sebastián long known as la cocina de Guipúzcoa (the kitchen of Guipúzcoa province), Bilbao's Guetaria does its namesake justice. The kitchen, open to the clientele, cooks *lubina* (sea bass), *besugo* (sea bream), *dorada* (gilthead bream), *txuletas de buey* (beef steaks), and *chuletas de cordero*(lamb chops) to perfection in a classic *asador* (barbecue) setting. ⊠ *Colón de Larreátegui 12 El Ensanche* ☎ *94/424–3923* ⊕ *www. guetaria.com* ⌕ *Reservations essential* ═ *AE, DC, MC, V* ☺ *Closed Easter Week* Ⓜ *Moyúa.*

9

$$$–$$$$
BASQUE

✕ **Guggenheim Bilbao.** Complementing the Guggenheim's visual feast with more sensorial elements, this spot overseen by Martín Berasategui is on everyone's short list of Bilbao restaurants. Try the *lomo de bacalao asado en aceite de ajo con txangurro a la donostiarra i pil-pil* (cod flanks in garlic oil with crab San Sebastián–style and emulsified juices)—a postmodern culinary pun on Bilbao's traditional codfish addiction. A lobster salad with lettuce-heart shavings and tomatoes at a table overlooking the Nervión, the University of Deusto, and the heights of Artxanda qualifies as a perfect 21st-century Bilbao moment. ✉ *Av. Abandoibarra 2 El Ensanche* ☎ *94/423–9333* ⌕ *Reservations essential* ▬ *AE, DC, MC, V* ⊗ *Closed Mon. and late Dec.–early Jan. No dinner Sun. or Tues.* Ⓜ *Moyúa.*

> **MACHISMO AND MATRIARCHY**
>
> Basque men-only eating societies may seem just another example of misogyny. But ethnologists have long defined Basque society as a matriarchy wherein the authority of the *etxekoandre* (female house honcho) has been so absolute that men were forced out of the home to cook, play cards, or imbibe spirits. The exiles formed drinking clubs. Food came later, and with the Basque passion for competition, cooking contests followed. Today there are mixed and even all-women's eating clubs, to which men are rarely, if ever, invited.

$$$$
BASQUE
Fodor's Choice
★

✕ **Guria.** Born in the smallest village in Vizcaya, Arakaldo, Guria's founder, the late Genaro Pildain, learned cooking from his mother and focused more on potato soup than truffles and caviar. Don Genaro's influence is still felt here in Guria's streamlined traditional Basque cooking that dazzles with simplicity. Every ingredient and preparation is perfect, from *alubias "con sus sacramentos"* (fava beans, chorizo, and blood sausage) are deconstructed to a puree. The *crema de puerros y patatas* (cream of potato and leek soup) is as perfect as the lobster salad with, in season, *perretxikos de Orduña* (wild mushrooms). ✉ *Gran Vía 66 El Ensanche* ☎ *94/441–5780* ⌕ *Reservations essential* ▬ *AE, DC, MC, V* ⊗ *No dinner Sun.* Ⓜ *Indautxu.*

$$$–$$$$
BASQUE

✕ **Jolastoki.** Begoña Beaskoetxea's graceful mansion, the setting for one of Bilbao's finest restaurants, is 20 minutes from downtown (and then a 7-minute walk) on the city's Norman Foster subway. At Jolastoki ("place to play" in Basque), wild salmon from the Cares River; dark, red Bresse pigeon roasted in balsamic vinegar; *lubina al vapor* (steamed sea bass) as light as a soufflé; becada estofada a los nabos o flambeada al Armagnac (woodcock stuffed with turnips or flambé in Armagnac); and encyclopedic salads are all done to perfection. The red fruit dessert includes 11 varieties with sorbet in raspberry coulis. Afterward, digest with a walk through the fishing quarter or a swim at the beach. ✉ *Los Chopos 24 Getxo* ☎ *94/491–2031* ⊕ *www.restaurantejolastoki.com* ⌕ *Reservations essential* ▬ *AE, DC, MC, V* ⊗ *Closed Sun.* Ⓜ *Gobela, Neguri.*

$–$$
CONTEMPORARY
Fodor's Choice
★

✕ **Kiskia.** A modern take on the traditional cider house, this rambling tavern near the San Mamés soccer stadium serves the classical *sidrería* menu of chorizo sausage cooked in cider, codfish omelet, *txuleta de buey* (beef chops), Idiazabal (Basque smoked cheese) with quince jelly and

Tapas bars provide a quick meal on the go.

nuts, and as much cider as you can drink, all for €25. Actors, sculptors, writers, soccer stars, and Spain's who's who frequent this boisterous marvel. ⊠ *Pérez Galdós 51 San Mamés* ☎ *94/441–3469* ⊟ *AE, DC, MC, V* ⊘ *No dinner Sun.–Tues.* Ⓜ *San Mamés.*

$–$$
CONTEMPORARY
✕ **La Deliciosa.** For carefully prepared food at friendly prices, this simply designed, intimate space is one of the best values in the Casco Viejo. The *crema de puerros* (cream of leeks) is as good as any in town, and the *dorada al horno* (roast gilthead bream) is fresh from the nearby La Ribera market. ⊠ *Jardines 1 Casco Viejo* ☎ *94/415–0944* ⊟ *AE, DC, MC, V* Ⓜ *Casco Viejo.*

$$–$$$
CONTEMPORARY
✕ **La Gallina Ciega.** With some of Bilbao's finest *pintxos* (morsels impaled on toothpicks) at the bar and a single table serving the chef's daily whim, this modern, clean-lined tavern decorated in eclectic patterns of wood, glass, and marble is one of Bilbao's favorite foodie haunts. The table, as might be expected, is rarely empty and must be reserved well in advance. ⊠ *Máximo Aguirre 2 El Ensanche* ☎ *94/442–3943* ⊟ *AE, DC, MC, V* Ⓜ *Moyúa.*

$–$$
ECLECTIC
✕ **La Taberna de los Mundos.** Sandwich-maker Ander Calvo is famous throughout Spain, and his masterpiece is a slipper bread sandwich of melted goat cheese with garlic, wild mushrooms, organic tomatoes, and sweet red piquillo peppers on a bed of acorn-fed wild Iberian ham. Calvo's two restaurants in Bilbao and one in Vitoria include creative interpretations of the sandwich along with photography, art exhibits, travel lectures, and a global interest reflected in his obsession with early maps and navigational techniques. ⊠ *Calle Lutxana 1 El Ensanche* ☎ *94/416–8181* ⊕ *www.delosmundos.com* ⊟ *AE, DC, MC, V* ⊘ *Closed Mon. mid-Sept.–mid-June* Ⓜ *Moyúa.*

9

$$$–$$$$ ✕ **Matxinbenta.** Mixing Basque cooking with an international flair, this
ECLECTIC cozy spot presents innovative seafood dishes and roasts. Best in show goes
to the *bacalao Matxinbenta con base vizcaina* (cod prepared on a red-
pepper base), and the wine list is comprehensive. The *delicia de verduras
con foie gras* (vegetables with goose liver) displays broccoli, spinach, car-
rots, and zucchini with a cream-of-tomato sauce. The train decor includes
separate glass compartments allowing you to study fellow diners freely
without eavesdropping at the same time. ⊠ *Ledesma 26 El Ensanche*
☎ *94/424–8495* ⊟ *AE, DC, MC, V* ☺ *Closed Sun.* Ⓜ *Moyúa.*

$$ ✕ **Txakolí de Artxanda.** The funicular from the end of Calle Múgica y
BASQUE Butrón up to the mountain of Artxanda deposits you next to an excel-
lent spot for a roast of one kind or another after a hike around the
heights. Whether ordering lamb, beef, or the traditional Basque *besugo*
(sea bream), you can't go wrong at this picturesque spot with unbeatable
panoramas over Bilbao. ⊠ *Monte Artxanda, El Arenal* ☎ *94/445–5015*
⊟ *AE, DC, MC, V* ☺ *Closed Mon. mid-Sept.–mid-June* Ⓜ *Abando.*

¢–$ ✕ **Txiriboga Taberna.** Specialists in *croquetas* (croquettes) made of ham,
BASQUE chicken, or wild mushrooms, this little hole-in-the-wall, a simple no-
frills local favorite and semi-secret hideout, also has a back room for
sit-down dining. The historic photographs on the walls add to the
authenticity, but the croquetas (in Euskera *kroketak*) speak for themselves. ⊠ *Santa Maria Kalea 13, Casco Viejo* ☎ *94/415–7874* ⊟ *AE,
DC, MC, V* ☺ *Closed Mon.* Ⓜ *Casco Viejo.*

$–$$ ✕ **Victor Montes.** A hot spot for the daily *tapeo* (tapas tour), this place
TAPAS is always crowded with congenial grazers. The well-stocked counter
might offer anything from wild mushrooms to *txistorra* (spicy sausages), Idiazabal (Basque smoked cheese), or, for the adventurous, *hue-
vas de merluza* (hake roe), all taken with splashes of Rioja, *txakolí* (a
young, white brew made from tart green grapes), or cider. ⊠ *Pl. Nueva
8 Casco Viejo* ☎ *94/415–7067* ⊕ *www.victormontesbilbao.com* ⟡ *Reservations essential* ⊟ *AE, DC, MC, V* ☺ *Closed Sun. and Aug. 1–15*
Ⓜ *Casco Viejo.*

¢–$ ✕ **Xukela.** Amid bright lighting and a vivid palette of green and crim-
TAPAS son morsels of ham and bell peppers lining his bar, chef Santiago Ruíz
Bombin creates some of the tastiest and most interesting and varied
pintxos (miniature cuisine presented on toothpicks) in all of tapas-
dom. The tavern has the general feel of a small library: it is lined with
books, magazines, paintings, and little reading nooks. Drinks range
from beer to the acidic Basque txakoli to a handsome selection of red
and white wines from all over Spain. ⊠ *Calle del Perro 2 Casco Viejo*
☎ *94/415–9772* ⊟ *AE, DC, MC, V* Ⓜ *Casco Viejo.*

$$$$ ✕ **Zortziko.** An ultramodern kitchen contrasts with this restaurant's his-
BASQUE toric building. Try the *langostinos con risotto de perretxikos* (prawns
with wild mushroom risotto) or the *suprema de pintada asada a la
salsa de trufas* (guinea hen in truffle sauce). Chef Daniel García, one of
the Basque Country's culinary stars, also offers a cooking exhibition
for groups of 10 or more at a special table where diners can watch the
chef in action, as well as another exclusive table surrounded by historic
vintages in the wine cellar. ⊠ *Calle Alameda Mazarredo 17 El Ensanche*

☎ *94/423–9743* ⊕ *www.zortziko.es* ⟶ *Reservations essential* ≡ *AE, DC, MC, V* ⊘ *Closed Sun., Mon., and late Aug.–mid-Sept.* Ⓜ *Moyúa.*

CAFÉS

Bar los Fueros. As much a watering hole as a café, this is one of Bilbao's most authentic enclaves, perfect for an *aperitivo* or a nightcap. ✉ *Calle de los Fueros 6 Casco Viejo* ☎ *94/415–0614* Ⓜ *Casco Viejo.*

★ **Café Boulevard.** This is Bilbao's oldest café, dating back to 1871 and occupying a privileged position across from the Teatro Arriaga. Behind its colorful 1929 Art Deco facade, the Boulevard is known for its literary *tertulias* (semiformal intellectual get-togethers). ✉ *Calle Arenal 3 Casco Viejo* ☎ *94/415–3128* Ⓜ *Casco Viejo.*

Café El Tilo. Named for the linden tree typical of Bilbao, this may be the best of all the cafés, featuring original frescoes by Basque painter Juan de Aranoa (1901–73). ✉ *Calle Arenal 1 Casco Viejo* ☎ *94/415–0282* Ⓜ *Casco Viejo.*

Fodor's Choice **Café Iruña.** One of Bilbao's most beloved architectural gems combines ★ neo-Mudéjar fantasy and retro-saloon reality. The enormous turn-of-the-20th-century classic is a perfect place to dine, read, graze, tipple, or just people-watch. ✉ *Jardines de Albia, El Ensanche* ☎ *94/423–7021* Ⓜ *Moyúa.*

Café La Granja. First opened in 1926, this landmark serves up Bilbao panache as well as fine beers, coffees, and food, with the lunch menu a reasonably priced delight. ✉ *Biribila Plaza (Plaza Circular) 3 El Ensanche* ☎ *94/423–1813* Ⓜ *Moyúa.*

WHERE TO STAY

¢–$ ⊡ **Artetxe.** With rooms overlooking Bilbao from the heights of Artxanda, this Basque farmhouse with wood trimmings and eager young owners offers excellent value and quiet. It's surrounded by the green hills and meadows you see from the Guggenheim museum, so what you lose here in big-city ambience you gain in good air and peace. Local *asadores* (restaurants specializing in meat or fish cooked over coals) are good dining options. You'll need a car to connect easily with downtown Bilbao. **Pros:** a peaceful, grassy place from which to enjoy Bilbao and the Basque countryside. **Cons:** far from the center, the museums, and the action. ✉ *C. de Berriz 112 (off Ctra. Enékuri–Artxanda, Km 7), Artxanda,* ☎ *94/474–7780* ⊕ *www.hotelartetxe.com* ⇆ *12 rooms* ⌂ *In-hotel: parking (free)* ≡ *AE, DC, MC, V* ⦿ *EP* Ⓜ *Sarriko.*

$$–$$$ ⊡ **Castillo de Arteaga.** Built in the mid-19th-century for Empress Eugenia
Fodor's Choice de Montijo, wife of Napoleon III, this neogothic limestone castle with
★ rooms in the watchtowers and defensive walls is one of the most extraordinary lodging options in or around Bilbao. Overlooking the Urdaibai Nature Reserve wetlands 30 minutes north of Bilbao near Guernica, Torre Arteaga is a favorite for bird watchers, with excursions by canoe available for exploring the marshes. The excellent restaurant and interaction with local products from seafood to *txakolí* (young white wine) producers make this a culinary destination as well. Rooms are palatial and equipped with contemporary technology. **Pros:** excellent wine and local food product tastings; views over the wetlands. **Cons:** somewhat

9

isolated from village life and a half hour drive to Bilbao. ⊠ *Calle Gaztelubide, Barrio Basetxeta 7, Gautegiz Arteaga* ☎ *94/627–0440* ⊕ *www.panaiv.com* ⬎ *13 rooms, 1 suite* ⚘ *In-room: Wi-Fi. In-hotel: restaurant, bar, spa, parking (free)* ☰ *AE, DC, MC, V* ⦿*EP*

$$$ ⬚ **Gran Hotel Domine.** As much modern design celebration as hotel, this
Fodor'sChoice   Silken chain establishment directly across the street from the Guggen-
★   heim showcases the conceptual wit of Javier Mariscal, creator of Barcelo-
na's 1992 Olympic mascot Cobi, and the structural know-how of Bilbao
architect Iñaki Aurrekoetxea. With adjustable windowpanes reflecting
Gehry's titanium leviathan and every lamp and piece of furniture reflect-
ing Mariscal's playful whimsy, this is the brightest star in Bilbao's design
firmament. Comprehensively equipped and comfortable, it's the next best
thing to moving into the Guggenheim. **Pros:** at the very epicenter and,
indeed, part of Bilbao's art and architecture excitement; the place to cross
paths with Catherine Zeta-Jones or Antonio Banderas. **Cons:** hard on
the wallet and a little full of its own glamour. ⊠ *Alameda de Mazarredo
61 El Ensanche,* ☎ *94/425–3300* ⊕ *www.granhoteldominebilbao.com*
⬎ *139 rooms, 6 suites* ⚘ *In-room: Wi-Fi. In-hotel: restaurant, bar, gym,
parking (paid)* ☰ *AE, DC, MC, V* ⦿*EP* Ⓜ *Moyúa.*

$$$ ⬚ **Hesperia Zubialde.** Overlooking the San Mamés soccer stadium, also
known as "La Catedral," and with views of the Nervión River, this for-
mer schoolhouse is just a 15-minute walk through the lush Parque de
Doña Casilda gardens from the Museo de Bellas Artes and the Guggenheim. Rooms are contemporary in decor and outfitted with all the latest
technology, from flat-screen TVs to Wi-Fi. The restaurant, El Botxo,
serves carefully prepared Basque and international cuisine. **Pros:** views
over the Nervión, good for hiking the river but also handy to the sleek
and quiet tramway and the metro. **Cons:** when national-league soccer games erupt in the nearby San Mamés stadium, the neighborhood
is bedlam, a long hike (or short metro ride) from the Casco Viejo.
⊠ *Camino de la Ventosa 34, El Ensanche* ☎ *94/400–8100* ⊕ *www.hesperioa-zubialde.com* ⬎ *82 rooms* ⚘ *In-room: Wi-Fi. In-hotel: restaurant, bar* ☰ *AE, DC, MC, V* ⦿*EP* Ⓜ *San Mamés.*

¢   ⬚ **Hostal Mendez.** This may be the best value in town, with small but
impeccable and well-appointed rooms, some of which (nos. 1 and 2)
overlook the facade of the Palacio Yohn (pretty views but noisy at
night). A brace of handsome sculpted setters stands vigil at the bottom
of lovely, creaky wooden stairs. Fourth-floor rooms are even less expensive in this century-old walk-up building. **Pros:** excellent value and location in the middle of the Casco Viejo. **Cons:** with no air-conditioning;
summer on the street side with the windows can be very noisy. ⊠ *Santa
María Kalea 13 Casco Viejo,* ☎ *94/416–0364* ⊕ *www.pensionmendez.com* ⬎ *12 rooms* ⚘ *In-room: no a/c* ☰ *AE, DC, MC, V* ⦿*EP* Ⓜ *Casco
Viejo.*

$$$ ⬚ **Hotel Carlton.** Luminaries who have trod the halls of this elegant white
elephant of a hotel include Orson Welles, Ava Gardner, Ernest Heming-
way, Lauren Bacall, Federico García Lorca, Albert Einstein, and Alfonso
XIII, grandfather of Spain's King Juan Carlos I. During the Spanish
civil war it was the seat of the Republican Basque government; later it
housed a number of Nationalist generals. The hotel exudes old-world

grace and charm along with a sense of history. Squarely in the middle of the Ensanche, the Carlton is equidistant from the Casco Viejo and Abandoibarra area. **Pros:** historic, old-world surroundings that remind you that Bilbao has an illustrious past. **Cons:** also surrounded by plenty of concrete and urban frenzy. ⊠ *Plaza Federico Moyúa 2 El Ensanche,* ☎ *94/416–2200* ⊕ *www.hotelcarlton.es* ⤳ *135 rooms, 7 suites* ⌂ *In-room: Wi-Fi. In-hotel: restaurant, bar, parking (paid)* ☰ *AE, DC, MC, V* ⦿❘ *EP* Ⓜ *Moyúa.*

¢–$
Fodor's Choice
★
Iturrienea Ostatua. Extraordinarily beautiful, this traditional Basque town house one flight above the street in Bilbao's Old Quarter has charm to spare. With wooden ceiling beams, stone floors, and ethnographical and historical objects including a portable Spanish civil war combat confessional, there is plenty to learn and explore without leaving the hotel. The staff is extraordinarily friendly and helpful. **Pros:** budget friendly and exquisite rustic decor. **Cons:** nocturnal noise on the front side, especially on Friday and Saturday nights in summer; try for a room in the back or bring earplugs. ⊠ *Santa María Kalea 14 Casco Viejo,* ☎ *94/416–1500* ⊕ *www.iturrieneaostatua.com* ⤳ *21 rooms* ⌂ *In-room: no a/c* ☰ *AE, DC, MC, V* ⦿❘ *EP* Ⓜ *Casco Viejo.*

$$$–$$$$
Fodor's Choice
★
López de Haro. This luxury hotel, five minutes from the Guggenheim, is becoming quite a scene now that the city is a bona fide nexus for contemporary art. A converted 19th-century building, López de Haro has an English feel and all the comforts your heart desires. Rooms are classical in design and feel, yet contemporary in equipment and comfort. The excellent restaurant, the Club Náutico, serves modern Basque dishes created by Alberto Vélez—a handy alternative on one of Bilbao's many rainy evenings. **Pros:** state-of-the-art comfort, service, and cuisine in a traditional and aristocratic setting. **Cons:** a less than relaxing, slightly hushed and stuffy scene; not for the shorts and tank tops set. ⊠ *Obispo Orueta 2 El Ensanche,* ☎ *94/423–5500* ⊕ *www.hotellopezdeharo.com* ⤳ *49 rooms, 4 suites* ⌂ *In-room: Wi-Fi. In-hotel: restaurant, bar, parking (paid)* ☰ *AE, DC, MC, V* ⦿❘ *EP* Ⓜ *Moyúa.*

$$$$
Meliá Bilbao Hotel. This colossus erected in 2004 (as the Sheraton Bilbao) over what was once the nerve center of Bilbao's shipbuilding industry feels like a futuristic ocean liner. Designed by architect Ricardo Legorreta and inspired by the work of Basque sculptor Eduardo Chillida (1920–2002), the Meliá is filled with contemporary art and a collection of Spanish ship models, many of which were constructed in Bilbao's historic shipyards. Rooms are high, wide, and handsome, with glass, steel, stone, and wood trimmings. Although massive in scope, the comforts and the views from upper floors are superb. Both the Chillida café and the restaurant, Aizian, are excellent. **Pros:** great views over the whole shebang if you can get a room facing the Guggenheim. **Cons:** a high-rise colossus that might be more at home in Miami or Malibu. ⊠ *C. Lehendakari Leizaola 29, El Ensanche,* ☎ *94/428–0000* ⊕ *www.solmelia.com* ⤳ *199 rooms, 12 suites* ⌂ *In-room: Wi-Fi. In-hotel: 2 restaurants, bar, gym, parking (paid)* ☰ *AE, DC, MC, V* ⦿❘ *EP* Ⓜ *San Mamés.*

$$–$$$
Miró Hotel. Perfectly placed between the Guggenheim and Bilbao's excellent Museo de Bellas Artes, this boutique hotel refurbished by Barcelona fashion designer Toni Miró competes with the reflecting facade

9

of Javier Mariscal's Domine just up the street. Comfortable and daringly innovative, it is one of the city's sleek new fleet of hotels inspired by the world's most talked-about and architecturally revolutionary art museum. Rooms are spacious, lavishly draped in subdued mauves and salmon-hued fabrics, and very-high-tech contemporary. **Pros:** a design refuge that places you in the eye of Bilbao's art and architecture hurricane. **Cons:** not unpretentious, a hint of preciosity pervades these ultrachic halls. ⊠ *Alameda de Mazarredo 77 El Ensanche,* ☎ *94/661–1880* ⊕ *www.mirohotelbilbao.com* ⌨ *50 rooms* ⟁ *In-room: Wi-Fi. In-hotel: restaurant, bar, gym, spa, parking (fee)* ⊟ *AE, DC, MC, V* ⎮❍⎮ *EP* Ⓜ *Moyúa.*

$$ ⛫ **Petit Palace Arana.** Next to the Teatro Arriaga in the Casco Viejo, this contemporary-antique design has a blended style: centenary limestone blocks, exposed brickwork, hand-hewn beams, and spiral wooden staircases are juxtaposed with clean new surfaces of glass and steel. The standard rooms and the showers are a tight fit, and the street below can be noisy on weekends, depending on your location. Fifteen executive rooms have exercise bikes and computers, while all rooms have hot tubs with hydromassage and computer hookups. **Pros:** being next to the Casco Viejo and the Mercado de la Ribera places you in the heart of traditional Bilbao. **Cons:** the night can be noisy on the Casco Viejo side of the building; ask for a room overlooking the Teatro Arriaga and the Nervión for the views and for less night racket. ⊠ *Bidebarrieta 2 Casco Viejo,* ☎ *94/415–6411* ⊕ *www.petitpalacearana.com* ⌨ *64 rooms* ⟁ *In-room: Wi-Fi. In-hotel: bar* ⊟ *AE, DC, MC, V* ⎮❍⎮ *EP* Ⓜ *Abando, Casco Viejo.*

$ ⛫ **Sirimiri.** A small, attentively run hotel near the Atxuri station, this modest spot has modern rooms with views over some of Bilbao's oldest architecture. The buffet-style breakfast is excellent, and the owner and manager offer helpful with advice about Bilbao. **Pros:** handy to the Mercado de la Ribera, Casco Viejo, and the Atxuri train station. **Cons:** tight quarters and noisy on weekends. ⊠ *Plaza de la Encarnación, Casco Viejo,* ☎ *94/433–0759* ⊕ *www.hotelsirimiri.com* ⌨ *28 rooms* ⟁ *In-hotel: restaurant, bar, gym, parking (paid)* ⊟ *AE, DC, MC, V* ⎮❍⎮ *EP* Ⓜ *Casco Viejo.*

SPORTS AND THE OUTDOORS

"Sports" in Bilbao means the Athletic de Bilbao soccer team, traditionally one of Spain's top *fútbol* powers during the city's heyday as an industrial power. While it has been 30 years or so since Bilbao has won a league title, "the lions" are often in the top half of the league standings and seem to take special pleasure in tormenting powerhouses Madrid and Barcelona. The local rivalry with San Sebastián's Real Sociedad is as bitter as baseball's Yankees–Red Sox feud. Athletic de Bilbao's headquarters on Alameda de Mazarredo occupy a lovely mansion, while **San Mamés Stadium** (⊠ *Rafael Moreno Pichichi s/n, San Mamés* ☎ *94/441–3954* Ⓜ *San Mamés*) is the place to buy tickets to games and have a look through the Museo del Athletic de Bilbao. The stadium has always been known as *La Catedral* (The Cathedral).

SHOPPING

The main stores for clothing are found around Plaza Moyúa in the Ensanche, along streets such as Calle Iparraguirre and Calle Rodríguez Arias. The Casco Viejo has dozens of smaller shops, many of them handsomely restored early houses with gorgeous wooden beams and ancient stones, specializing in an endless variety of products from crafts to antiques. Wool items, foodstuffs, and wood carvings from around the Basque Country can be found throughout Bilbao. *Txapelas* (berets or Basque boinas) are famous worldwide and make fine gifts. Best when waterproofed, they'll keep you remarkably warm in rain and mist.

The city is home to international fashion names from Coco Chanel to Zara to Toni Miró, Calvin Klein, and Adolfo Domínguez. The ubiquitous department store Corte Inglés is an easy one-stop shop, if a bit massified and routine. Benetton and Marks & Spencer grace Bilbao's Gran Vía.

9

SPANISH VOCABULARY

WORDS AND PHRASES

When touring from Barcelona to Bilbao, you can be faced with a daunting number of languages, from Barcelona's Catalan to Bilbao's pre–Indo-European Basque, or Euskera. Whereas an effort to use phrases in the most universal and widely known form of Spanish (Castilian), which you will find in the following vocabulary pages, will be appreciated, a word or two of Catalan or Euskera will immediately make you into a local hero and elicit an entirely different (and much warmer) response.

From Galicia in Spain's northwestern corner to Catalonia's Cap de Creus, the Iberian Peninsula's easternmost point, some 13 recognized languages and dialects are spoken: Gallego; Lengua Asturiana (Bable); Basque (Euskera); Pyrenean dialects such as Béarnais and Toy on the French side of the border; Aragonese dialects such as Belsetan, Chistavino, and Patués; Castilian Spanish; Occitanian, Gascon French, Aranés, and Catalan.

If you wish to make a start in the languages of Barcelona and Bilbao—Catalan and Euskera—here are some words and phrases to keep in mind. After the English meaning, the Catalan and Euskera equivalencies are given.

My name is . . . (*Em dic . . . /Ni . . . naiz*); Hello, how are you? (*Hola! Com va això?/Kaixo, zer moduz?*); I'm very well, and you? (*Molt bé, i vostè?/Ni oso ondo, ta su?*); Good morning (*Bon dia/Egun on*); Good afternoon (*Bona tarda/Arratsalde on*); Goodnight (*Bona nit/Gabon*); Welcome (*Benvingut(s)/Ongi etorri*); Hello (*Hola!/Kaixó!*); Bye (*Adéu/ Agur*); See you later (*fins ara/Gero arte*); Thank you (*Gràcies/Eskerrik asko*); Don't mention it (*De res/Es horregatik*); Please (*Si us plau/ Mesedez*); Excuse me (*Perdó/Barkatu*); Yes (*Sí/Bai*); No (*No/Ez*); What is this? (*Que es això?/Zer da Hau?*); How much is this? (Cuan val?/ Zenbat da?); One red wine (*Un vi negre/Beltza bat*); Good morning, where is the tourist office? (*Bon dia, on es l'oficina de Turisme?/Egun on, non dago turismo bulegoa?*); Straight (*Tot recte/Zuzen*); To the left (*A l'esquerre/Ezkerretara*); To the right (*A la dreta/Eskubitara*); Bank (*Banc/Banketxea*); Bookshop (*Llibreria/Liburudenda*); Art gallery (*Sala d'Exposicions/Erakusgela*); Bus stop (*Parada d'autobus/ Autobus geltokia*); Train station (*Estació de tren/Tren geltokia*); Hospital (*Hospital/Ospitalea*); Hotel (*Hôtel/Hotela*).

	ENGLISH	SPANISH	PRONUNCIATION
BASICS			
	Yes/no	Sí/no	see/no
	Please	Por favor	pohr fah-vohr
	May I?	¿Me permite?	meh pehr-mee-teh
	Thank you (very much)	(Muchas) gracias	(moo-chas) grah-see-as

ENGLISH	SPANISH	PRONUNCIATION
You're welcome	De nada	deh nah-dah
Excuse me	Con permiso/perdón	con pehr-mee-so/ pehr-dohn
Pardon me/ what did you say?	¿Perdón?/Mande?	pehr-dohn/mahn-deh
Could you tell me . . . ?	¿Podría decirme . . . ?	po-dree-ah deh-seer-meh
I'm sorry	Lo siento	lo see-en-to
Good morning!	¡Buenos días!	bway-nohs dee-ahs
Good afternoon!	¡Buenas tardes!	bway-nahs tar-dess
Good evening!	¡Buenas noches!	bway-nahs no-chess
Goodbye!	¡Adiós!/ ¡Hasta luego!	ah-dee-ohss/ ah-stah-lwe-go
Mr./Mrs.	Señor/Señora	sen-yor/sen-yohr-ah
Miss	Señorita	sen-yo-ree-tah
Pleased to meet you	Mucho gusto	moo-cho goose-to
How are you?	¿Cómo está usted?	ko-mo es-tah oo-sted
Very well, thank you.	Muy bien, gracias.	moo-ee bee-en, grah-see-as
And you?	¿Y usted?	ee oos-ted
Hello (on the phone)	Diga	dee-gah

NUMBERS

1	un, uno	oon, oo-no
2	dos	dohs
3	tres	tress
4	cuatro	kwah-tro
5	cinco	sink-oh
6	seis	saice
7	siete	see-et-eh
8	ocho	o-cho
9	nueve	new-eh-veh
10	diez	dee-es

ENGLISH	SPANISH	PRONUNCIATION
11	once	ohn-seh
12	doce	doh-seh
13	trece	treh-seh
14	catorce	ka-tohr-seh
15	quince	keen-seh
16	dieciséis	dee-es-ee-saice
17	diecisiete	dee-es-ee-see-et-eh
18	dieciocho	dee-es-ee-o-cho
19	diecinueve	dee-es-ee-new-ev-eh
20	veinte	vain-teh
21	veinte y uno/ veintiuno	vain-te-oo-noh
30	treinta	train-tah
32	treinta y dos	train-tay-dohs
40	cuarenta	kwah-ren-tah
50	cincuenta	seen-kwen-tah
60	sesenta	sess-en-tah
70	setenta	set-en-tah
80	ochenta	oh-chen-tah
90	noventa	no-ven-tah
100	cien	see-en
200	doscientos	doh-see-en-tohss
500	quinientos	keen-yen-tohss
1,000	mil	meel
2,000	dos mil	dohs meel

DAYS OF THE WEEK

Sunday	domingo	doh-meen-goh
Monday	lunes	loo-ness
Tuesday	martes	mahr-tess
Wednesday	miércoles	me-air-koh-less
Thursday	jueves	hoo-ev-ess

ENGLISH	SPANISH	PRONUNCIATION
Friday	viernes	vee-air-ness
Saturday	sábado	sah-bah-doh

USEFUL PHRASES

Do you speak English?	¿Habla usted inglés?	ah-blah oos-ted in-glehs
I don't speak Spanish	No hablo español	no ah-bloh es-pahn-yol
I don't understand (you)	No entiendo	no en-tee-en-doh
I understand (you)	Entiendo	en-tee-en-doh
I don't know	No sé	no seh
I am American/ British	Soy americano (americana)/ inglés(a)	soy ah-meh-ree-kah- no (ah-meh-ree-kah- nah)/in-glehs(ah)
My name is . . .	Me llamo . . .	meh yah-moh
Yes, please/	Sí, por favor/	see pohr fah-vor/
No, thank you	No, gracias	no grah-see-ahs
Yesterday/today/ tomorrow	Ayer/hoy/mañana	ah-yehr/oy/ mahn- yah-nah
This morning/ afternoon	Esta mañana/tarde	es-tah mahn-yah- nah/ tar-deh
Tonight	Esta noche	es-tah no-cheh
This/Next week	Esta semana/ la semana que entra	es-tah seh-mah- nah/ lah seh-mah-nah keh en-trah
This/Next month	Este mes/el próximo mes	es-teh mehs/el prok-see-moh mehs
How?	¿Cómo?	koh-mo
When?	¿Cuándo?	kwahn-doh
What?	¿Qué?	keh
What is this?	¿Qué es esto?	keh es es-toh
Why?	¿Por qué?	por keh
Who?	¿Quién?	kee-yen
Where is . . . ?	¿Dónde está . . . ?	dohn-deh es-tah

ENGLISH	SPANISH	PRONUNCIATION
the train station?	la estación del tren?	la es-tah-see-on del train
the subway station?	la estación del metro?	la es-ta-see-on del meh-tro
the bus stop?	la parada del autobus?	la pah-rah-dah del oh-toh-boos
the bank?	el banco?	el bahn-koh
the hotel?	el hotel?	el oh-tel
the post office?	la oficina de correos?	la oh-fee-see-nah deh-koh-reh-os
the museum?	el museo?	el moo-seh-oh
the hospital?	el hospital?	el ohss-pee-tal
the bathroom?	el baño?	el bahn-yoh
Here/there	Aquí/allá	ah-key/ah-yah
Open/closed	Abierto/cerrado	ah-bee-er-toh/ ser-ah-doh
Left/right	Izquierda/derecha	iss-key-er-dah/ dare-eh-chah
Straight ahead	Todo recto	toh-doh-rec-toh
Is it near/far?	¿Está cerca/lejos?	es-tah sehr-kah/ leh-hoss
I'd like . . .	Quisiera . . .	kee-see-ehr-ah
a room	una habitación	oo-nah ah-bee-tah-see-on
the key	la llave	lah yah-veh
a newspaper	un periódico	oon pehr-ee-oh-dee-koh
a stamp	un sello	say-oh
How much is this?	¿Cuánto cuesta?	kwahn-toh kwes-tah
A little/a lot	Un poquito/ mucho	oon poh-kee-toh/ moo-choh
More/less	Más/menos	mahss/men-ohss
I am ill	Estoy enfermo(a)	es-toy en-fehr- moh(mah)

ENGLISH	SPANISH	PRONUNCIATION
Please call a doctor	Por favor llame un médico	pohr fah-vor ya- meh oon med-ee-koh
Help!	¡Ayuda!	ah-yoo-dah

ON THE ROAD

Avenue	Avenida	ah-ven-ee-dah
Broad, tree-lined boulevard	Paseo	pah-seh-oh
Highway	Carretera	car-reh-ter-ah
Port; mountain pass	Puerto	poo-ehr-toh
Street	Calle	cah-yeh
Waterfront promenade	Paseo marítimo	pah-seh-oh mahr-ee-tee-moh

IN TOWN

Cathedral	Catedral	cah-teh-dral
Church	Iglesia	tem-plo/ ee-glehs- see-ah
City hall, town hall	Ayuntamiento	ah-yoon-tah-me- yen-toh
Door, gate	Puerta	poo-ehr-tah
Main square	Plaza mayor	plah-thah mah-yohr
Market	Mercado	mer-kah-doh
Neighborhood	Barrio	bahr-ree-o
Tavern, rustic restaurant	Mesón	meh-sohn
Traffic circle, roundabout	Glorieta	glor-ee-eh-tah
Wine cellar, wine bar, wine shop	Bodega	boh-deh-gah

DINING OUT

A bottle of . . .	Una botella de . . .	oo-nah bo-teh-yah deh
A glass of . . .	Un vaso de . . .	oon vah-so deh
Bill/check	La cuenta	lah kwen-tah
Breakfast	El desayuno	el deh-sah-yoon-oh

ENGLISH	SPANISH	PRONUNCIATION
Dinner	La cena	lah seh-nah
Menu of the day	Menú del día	meh-noo del dee-ah
Fork	El tenedor	ehl ten-eh-dor
Is the tip included?	¿Está incluida la propina?	es-tah in-cloo-ee-dahah pro-pee-nah
Knife	El cuchillo	el koo-chee-yo
Large portion of tapas	Ración	rah-see-ohn
Lunch	La comida	lah koh-mee-dah
Menu	La carta, el menú	lah cart-ah, el meh-noo
Napkin	La servilleta	lah sehr-vee-yet-ah
Please give me . . .	Por favor déme . . .	pohr fah-vor deh-meh
Spoon	Una cuchara	oo-nah koo-chah-rah

Travel Smart
Barcelona

WORD OF MOUTH

"The metros in Barcelona are safe and I used them everywhere. Just watch out for pickpockets as you would normally. You shouldn't have any problem and the metros were never overcrowded when I used them."

—Jeannete

GETTING HERE AND AROUND

■ ADDRESSES

Abbreviations used in the book for street names are Av., for *avinguda* (*avenida* in Spanish), and Ctra., for *carreter* (*carretera* in Spanish). The letters *s/n* following an address mean *sin número* (without a street number). *Carrer* (*Calle* in Castilian Spanish) is often dropped entirely or not abbreviated at all. *Camí* (*Camino* in Spanish) is abbreviated to C. *Passeig* (*paseo* in Spanish) is usually written out in full, or sometimes abbreviated as P. Plaça/Plaza is usually not abbreviated (in this book it is abbreviated as Pl.).

■ AIR TRAVEL

Transatlantic flying time to Barcelona is 7 hours from New York. As there are no direct flights from the western United States to Barcelona or Bilbao, an additional flight is required from Madrid or London (for Bilbao), involving a connecting flight lasting 1 hour from Madrid to Barcelona or 40 minutes to Bilbao. A nonstop flight from Chicago to Madrid is 8 hours. Nonstop flights from London to Barcelona are 2¼ hours.

Regular nonstop flights connect the eastern United States with Barcelona. Flying from other cities in North America usually involves a stop. Flights from the United Kingdom to a number of destinations in Spain are frequent and offered at competitive fares, particularly on low-cost carriers such as Ryanair or easyJet. Beware of low-cost flights to "Barcelona" that, in fact, land in Girona, a 45-minute taxi ride north of Barcelona; often the taxi (or even the bus) costs more than the flight.

Iberia operates a shuttle, the *puente aereo*, between Barcelona and Madrid from around 7 AM to 11 PM; planes depart hourly, and more frequently in the morning and afternoon commuter hours. You don't need to reserve ahead; you can buy your tickets at the ticket counter in the airport upon arriving. Note that Terminal C in the Barcelona airport is used exclusively by the shuttle; in Madrid the shuttle departs from Terminal 3.

Airlines and Airports Airline and Airport Links.com (⊕ *www.airlineandairportlinks.com*) has links to many of the world's airlines and airports.

Airline Security Issues Transportation Security Administration (⊕ *www.tsa.gov*) has answers for almost every question.

AIRPORTS

Most flights arriving in Spain from the United States and Canada pass through Madrid's Barajas (MAD), but the major gateway to Catalonia and other regions in this book is Spain's second-largest airport, Barcelona's spectacular glass, steel, and marble El Prat de Llobregat (BCN). BCN opened its new T1 terminal in 2009, a sleek facility that uses solar panels for sustainable energy and offers a spa, a fitness center, excellent restaurants and cafés, and more VIP lounges. This airport is served by numerous international carriers, but Catalonia also has two other airports that handle air traffic, including charter flights. One is just south of Girona, 90 km (56 mi) north of Barcelona and convenient to the resort coast of the Costa Brava. Bus and train connections from Girona to Barcelona work well and cheaply, provided you have the time. The other Catalonia airport is at Reus, 110 km (68 mi) south of Barcelona and a gateway to Tarragona and the coastal towns of the Costa Daurada. Flights to and from the major cities in Europe and Spain also fly into and out of Bilbao's Loiu (BIL) airport. For information about airports in Spain, try ⊕ *www.aena.es*

Airport Information Barcelona: **El Prat de Llobregat** (*BCN* ☎ *902/404704*). Bilbao: **Aeropuerto Internacional de Bilbao** (*BIL* ✉ *Loiu* ☎ *902/404704*). Girona: **Aeroport de Girona-Costa Brava** (*GRO* ☎ *902/404704*).

Madrid: **Barajas Aeropuerto de Madrid** (*MAD* ☎ 902/404704). Reus: **Aeropuerto de Reus** (*REU* ☎ 902/404704).

GROUND TRANSPORTATION

Check first to see if your hotel in Barcelona provides airport-shuttle service; otherwise, you can get into town via train, bus, taxi, or rental car.

The Aerobus leaves the airport for Plaça de Catalunya every 15 minutes (6 AM–11 PM) on weekdays and every 30 minutes (6:30 AM–10:30 PM) on weekends. From Plaça de Catalunya the bus leaves for the airport every 15 minutes (5:30 AM–10 PM) on weekdays and every 30 minutes (6:30 AM–10:30 PM) on weekends. The fare is €4.25 to and from Terminal 2 and €5 for Terminal 1. It is important to remember that Aerobuses for Terminal 1 and for Terminal 2 stop at the same bus stops. If you are traveling to Barcelona Airport, make sure that you take the right Aerobus. The Aerobus for Terminal 1 is two-tone light and dark blue. The Aerobus for Terminal 2 is dark blue and yellow.

Cab fare from the airport into town is about €25, depending on traffic, the part of town you're heading to, and the number of large bags you're carrying (€1 is charged for each large bag). If you're driving your own car, follow signs to the CENTRE CIUTAT and you'll enter the city along Gran Vía. For the port area, follow signs for the Ronda Litoral. The journey to the center of town can take anywhere from 15 to 45 minutes, depending on traffic.

The train's only drawback is that it's a 10- to 15-minute walk from your gate through Terminal 2 over the bridge. From Terminal 1 a shuttle bus drops you at the train. Trains leave the airport every 30 minutes between 6:12 AM and 10:13 PM, stopping at the Estació de Sants, then at the Plaça de Catalunya, later at the Arc de Triomf, and finally at Clot. Trains going to the airport begin at 6 AM from the Clot station, stopping at the Arc de Triomf at 6:05 AM, Plaça de Catalunya at 6:08 AM, and Sants at 6:13 AM. The trip takes 19 minutes. The fare is €2.80 but the best bargain is

the T10 subway card that gives you free connections within Barcelona plus 9 more rides all for €7.70.

TRANSFERS BETWEEN AIRPORTS

To get to Girona Airport from Barcelona Airport by train you have to first catch the RENFE train that leaves from the airport and then change at Barcelona Sants station. From Barcelona Sants station you need to catch the train headed toward Figueres and get off at Girona, which is two stops before. If you are going to Girona Airport you will then have to catch a bus from Girona center or take a taxi to the airport. Allow 30 minutes after arrival in Girona to get to the airport.

The Autocares Julià Bus service leaves three times daily (at 8 AM, 2 PM, and 9 PM) from outside Terminal B and Terminal C of Barcelona Airport and will take you to Girona center. A taxi or bus to Girona airport will take another 30 minutes. Transport time to Girona is approximately 1½ hours. Ticket price is approximately €20. For further information, bookings, timetables, and up-to-date pricing information, call (0034) 93–402–6900 or (0034) 902–400–0080.

Alternatively, call the Barcelona Airport tourist information line and ask for further information on Autocares Julià: Barcelona Airport Tourist information 9 AM–9 PM, call (0034) 93–478–4704.

Contact Transports Metropolitans de Barcelona (TMB) Estació del Nord (✉ *Numero 62, Zona Franca, Eixample* ☎ *93/298-7000*).

FLIGHTS

If you buy a round-trip transatlantic ticket on the Spanish airline Iberia, you might purchase an Iberiabono España pass, good for major discounts on domestic flights during your trip. The pass must be purchased outside Spain at the time you purchase your international ticket. All internal Spain flights must be booked in advance. On certain days of the week, Iberia also offers minifares (*minitarifas*), which can save you 40% on domestic flights. Tickets must be purchased at least two days in advance, and you must stay over at the destination Saturday night.

American, Continental, Delta, and Iberia fly to Madrid and Barcelona; US Airways, Air Europa, and Spanair fly to Madrid. Within Spain, Iberia is the main domestic airline; two independent airlines, Air Europa and Spanair, fly a number of domestic routes at somewhat lower prices.

Airline Contacts Air Europa (☎ 888/238–7672 ⊕ www.air-europa.com). **American Airlines** (☎ 800/433–7300 ⊕ www.aa.com). **British Airways** (☎ 0845/773–3377 ⊕ www.britishairways.com). **Continental Airlines** (☎ 800/523–3273 for U.S. and Mexico reservations, 800/231–0856 for international reservations ⊕ www.continental.com). **Delta Airlines** (☎ 800/221–1212 for U.S. reservations, 800/241–4141 for international reservations ⊕ www.delta.com). **easyJet** (☎ 0870/600–0000 ⊕ www.easyjet.com). **Iberia** (☎ 800/772–4642 ⊕ www.iberia.com). **Ryanair** (☎ 0871/246–0000 in the U.K. ⊕ www.ryanair.com). **Spanair** (☎ 888/545–5757 ⊕ www.spanair.com). **United Airlines** (☎ 800/864–8331 for U.S. reservations, 800/538–2929 for international reservations ⊕ www.united.com). **USAirways** (☎ 800/428–4322 for U.S. and Canada reservations, 800/622–1015 for international reservations ⊕ www.usairways.com).

Within Spain Air Europa (☎ 902/401501 ⊕ www.air-europa.com). **Iberia** (☎ 902/400500 ⊕ www.iberia.com). **Spanair** (☎ 902/131415 ⊕ www.spanair.com).

Air Pass Info FlightPass (EuropebyAir ☎ 888/387–2479 ⊕ www.europebyair.com). **Iberiabono España** (☎ 800/772–4642 in the U.S., 0845/850–9000 in the U.K. ⊕ www.iberia.com).

▮ BOAT TRAVEL

There are regular ferry services between the United Kingdom and northern Spain. Brittany Ferries sails from Portsmouth to Santander, and P&O European Ferries sails from Plymouth to Bilbao. Spain's major ferry line, Trasmediterránea, links mainland Spain (including Barcelona) with the Balearics and the Canary Islands. Trasmediterránea's fast catamaran service takes half the time of the standard ferry, but catamarans are often canceled because they can only navigate in very calm waters.

You can pick up schedules and buy tickets at the ferry ticket office in the port, and also at most travel agencies.

From the U.K. Brittany Ferries (☎ 0871/2440744 ⊕ www.brittany-ferries.com). **P&O European Ferries** (☎ 1870/520–2020 ⊕ www.poferries.com).

In Spain Trasmediterránea (☎ 902/454645 ⊕ www.trasmediterranea.es).

▮ BUS TRAVEL

Barcelona's main bus station for intra-Spain routes is Estació del Nord, a few blocks east of the Arc de Triomf. Buses also depart from the Estació de Sants for long-distance and international routes, as well as from the depots of Barcelona's various private bus companies. Spain's major national long-haul company is Alsa-Enatcar. Grup Sarbus serves Catalonia and, with its subsidiary Sarfa, the Costa Brava. Rather than pound the pavement (or the telephone, usually futile because of overloaded lines) trying to sort out Barcelona's complex and confusing bus system, plan your bus travel through a local travel agent, who can quickly book you the best bus passage to your destination.

Within Spain, private companies provide comfortable and efficient bus services between major cities. Fares are lower than the corresponding train fares, and service is more extensive: if you want to reach a town not served by train, you can be sure a bus will go there. *See the planner section in Chapters 8 and 9 for companies serving the rest of Catalonia.*

You can get to Spain by bus from London, Paris, Rome, Frankfurt, Prague, and other major European cities. It is a long journey, but the buses are modern and inexpensive. Eurolines, the main carrier, connects many European cities with Barcelona.

Alsa-Enatcar, Spain's largest national bus company, has two luxury classes in addition to its regular line. The top of the line is Supra Clase, with roomy leather seats and on-board meals; in this class you also have the option of *asientos individuales*, individual seats (with no other seat next to you) that line one side of the bus. The next class is the Eurobus, with comfy seats and plenty of legroom, but no *asientos individuales* or on-board meals. The Supra Clase and Eurobus cost up to one-third and one-fourth more, respectively, than the regular line.

Some smaller, regional bus lines offer multi-trip bus passes, which are worthwhile if you plan on making multiple trips between two destinations. Generally, these tickets offer a savings of 20% per journey; you can only buy them in the bus station (not on the bus).

In Barcelona you can pick up schedule and fare information at the tourist information offices in Plaça Catalunya, Plaça Sant Jaume, or at the Sants train station. A better and faster solution is to click onto ⊕ *www.barcelonanord.com*.

City buses run daily 5:30 AM–11:30 PM. Route maps are displayed at bus stops. Note that those with a red band always stop at a central square—Catalunya, Universitat, or Urquinaona—and blue indicates a night bus. Barcelona's 30 night buses generally run until about 4:30 AM, though some stop as early as 3:30 AM and others continue until as late as 5:20 AM.

Bus Information Alsa-Enatcar (☏ 902/ 422242 ⊕ *www.alsa.es*) **Alsina–Graells** (✉ *Estació d'Autobusos Barcelona–Nord, Carrer Alí Bei 80, Eixample* ☏ *93/265-6592* ⊕ *www. alsinagraells.es*). **Grup Sarbus** (✉ *Estació d'Autobusos Barcelona–Nord, Carrer d' Alí Bei 80, Eixample* ☏ *93/265-6508, 902/303222 bus ticket delivery to your place of lodging* ⊕ *www. sarfa.com*). **Julià** (✉ *Ronda Universitat 5, Eixample* ☏ *93/342-5180* ⊕ *www.julia.net*).

Bus Terminals Estació del Nord (✉ *Carrer d'Ali Bei 80, Eixample* ☏ *93/265-6508* ⊕ *www. barcelonanord.com*). **Estació de Sants** (✉ *Carrer de Viriat, Eixample* ☏ *93/490-0202*).

From the U.K. Eurolines/National Express (☏ *0870/580-8080* ⊕ *www.nationalexpress.com*).

International Bus Companies Eurolines (✉ *Carrer Viriato, Eixample* ☏ *93/490-4000* ✉ *Estació del Nord, Carrer d'Ali Bei 80, Eixample* ☏ *93/232-1092* ✉ *Ronda Universitat 5, Eixample* ☏ *93/342-5180* ⊕ *www. eurolines.es*). **Linebus** (✉ *Estació d'Autobusos Barcelona–Nord, Carrer d' Alí Bei 80, Eixample* ☏ *93/265-0700*).

▌ CABLE CAR AND FUNICULAR TRAVEL

The Montjuïc Funicular is a cog railway that runs from the junction of Avinguda Paral. lel and Nou de la Rambla (Metro: Paral. lel) to the Miramar station on Montjuïc. It operates weekends and holidays 11 AM– 8 PM in winter, daily 11 AM–9:30 PM in summer; the fare is €1.35, or one ride on a T10 card. A *telefèric* (cable car) then takes you up to Montjuïc Castle. In winter the telefèric runs weekends and holidays 11–2:45 and 4–7:30; in summer, daily 11:30–9. The return fare is €7.50.

A Transbordador Aeri del Port (Harbor Cable Car) runs between Miramar and Montjuïc across the harbor to Torre de Jaume I, on Barcelona's *moll* (quay), and on to Torre de Sant Sebastià, at the end of Passeig Joan de Borbó in Barceloneta. You can board at either stage. The return fare is €13.50, and the car runs October–June, weekdays noon–5:45, weekends noon– 6:15, and July–September, daily 11–9.

To reach the summit of Tibidabo, take the metro to Avinguda de Tibidabo, then the Tramvía Blau (€2.30 one-way) to Peu del Funicular, and finally the Tibidabo Funicular (€3 round-trip) from there to the Tibidabo fairground. It runs every 30 minutes, 7:05 AM–9:35 PM ascending, 7:25 AM–9:55 PM descending.

■ CAR TRAVEL

The country's main cities are well connected by a network of four-lane *autovías* (freeways). The letter N stands for a national route (*carretera nacional*), either four- or two-lane. An *Autopista* (AP) is a toll road. At the toll-booth plazas (the Spanish term is *peaje*; in Catalan, *peatge*), there are three systems to choose from—*Automàtic,* with machines for credit cards or coins; *Manual,* with an attendant; or *Telepago,* an automatic chip-driven system mostly used by native regulars.

GETTING AROUND AND OUT OF BARCELONA

Arriving in Barcelona by car from the north along the AP7 *autopista* (freeway) or from the west along the AP2 autopista, you will encounter signs for the *rondes* (ring roads). Ronda Litoral (beware, it's most prominently marked AEROPORT, which can be misleading) will take you into lower and central Barcelona along the waterfront, while Ronda de Dalt (the upper Ronda) takes you along the edge of upper Barcelona to Horta, the Bonanova, Sarrià, and Pedralbes. For the center of town, take the Ronda Litoral and look for Exit 21 (PARAL.LEL–LES RAMBLES) or 22 (BARCELONETA–VIA LAIETANA–HOSPITAL DE MAR). If you are arriving from the Pyrenees on the C1411/E9 through the Tunel del Cadí, the Tunels de Vallvidrera will place you on the upper Via Augusta next to Sarrià, Pedralbes, and La Bonanova. The Eixample and Ciutat Vella are 10–15 minutes farther if traffic is fluid. Watch out for the new variable speed limits on the approaches to Barcelona. While 80 kph (48 mph) is the maximum speed on the Rondes, flashing signs over the motorway sometimes cut the speed limit down to 40 kph (24 mph) during peak hours.

Barcelona's main crosstown traffic arteries are the Diagonal (running diagonally through the city) and the midtown speedways, Carrer d'Aragó, and Gran Via de les Corts Catalanes, both cutting northeast–southwest through the heart of the city. Passeig de Gràcia, which becomes Gran de Gràcia above the Diagonal, runs all the way from Plaça de Catalunya up to Plaça Lesseps, but the main up-and-down streets, for motorists, are Balmes, Muntaner, Aribau, and Comtes d'Urgell. The general urban speed limit is 50 kph (30 mph).

Leaving Barcelona is not difficult. Follow signs for the *rondes,* do some advance mapping, and you're off. Follow signs for Girona and França for the Costa Brava, Girona, Figueres, and France. Follow Via Augusta and signs for Tunels de Vallvidrera or E9 and Manresa for the Tunel del Cadí and the Pyrenean Cerdanya valley. Follow the Diagonal west and then the freeway AP7 signs for Lleida, Zaragoza, Tarragona, and Valencia to leave the city headed west. Look for airport, Castelldefells, and Sitges signs for heading straight southwest down the coast for these beach points on the Costa Daurada. This C32 freeway to Sitges joins the AP7 to Tarragona and Valencia.

For travel outside Barcelona, the freeways to Girona, Figueres, Sitges, Tarragona, and Lleida are surprisingly fast. The distance to Girona, 97 km (58 mi), is a 45-minute shot. The French border is an hour away. Perpignan is, at 188 km (113 mi), an hour and 20 minutes.

GASOLINE

Gas stations are plentiful and often open 24 hours, especially around Barcelona's *rondas* (ring roads). Most stations are self-service, though prices are the same as those at full-service stations. At the tank, punch in the amount of gas you want (in euros, not in liters), unhook the nozzle, pump the gas, and then pay. At night, however, you must pay before you fill up. Most pumps offer unleaded gas and diesel fuel, so be careful to pick the right one for your car. All cars in Spain use unleaded gas (*gasolina sin plomo*), which is available in two grades, 95 and 98 octane. Prices per liter (*www.elpreciodelagasolina. com*) vary little between stations: €1.13 for *sin plomo* (unleaded; 95 octane); and

€1.24 for unleaded, 98 octane. Diesel fuel, known as *gas-oleo,* is €1.05 a liter and, what's more, gets you farther per liter, so renting a car with a diesel engine will save you major fuel money.

PARKING

Barcelona's underground parking lots (posted PARKING and symbolized by a white P on a blue background) are generally more than adequate to allow you to safely and conveniently park. Garage prices vary; expect close to €2.70 an hour and €16–€31 per 24-hour day. The Diagonal Mar in the Fòrum at the east end of Avinguda Diagonal offers eight-day underground parking for €40. Airport Parking runs from €3.27 up to two hours to €14.40 per day for more than four days (€18 up to four days). The long-term parking located between Terminal 1 (T1) and Terminal 2 (T2) costs €12 per day up to 5 days and €10 per day after that.

Barcelona's street-parking system runs 9 AM–2 PM and 4 PM–8 PM (with on-call attendants) weekdays and all day Saturday. Park in the specially marked blue spaces (about €2.40 per hour), with tickets valid for one, two, or three hours (€4.10), but renewable every half hour for €0.75. The ticket must be displayed on the front dashboard. On the streets, do not park where the pavement edge is yellow or where there is a private entry (*gual* or *vado*). Parking signs marked 1–15 or 15–30 signify you can park on those dates in the month on the side of the street where indicated. Whenever you feel you have found a lucky free parking spot, be alert for triangular yellow stickers on the pavement that indicate a tow-away zone. If your car is towed in Barcelona, you will find one of these yellow stickers, with the address of the municipal car deposit where your vehicle now resides, on the pavement where you left your car. A taxi will know where to take you to get it back.

Towing Contact Information Barcelona (☏ *901/513151*). **Bilbao Ayuntamiento (Town Hall)** (☏ *94/424-1700*).

RENTAL CARS

Generally you'll get a better deal if you book a car before you leave home. Avis, Hertz, Budget, and the European agency Europcar all have agencies at the airports in Barcelona and Bilbao and in other cities. National companies work through the Spanish agency Atesa. Smaller, local companies offer lower rates. Cars with automatic transmission are less common, so specify your need for one in advance. Rates in Barcelona begin at the equivalents of US$55 a day and US$240 a week for an economy car with air-conditioning, manual transmission, and unlimited mileage. This does not include the tax on car rentals, which is 16%.

Your own driver's license is valid in Spain, but you may want to get an International Driver's Permit (IDP) for extra assurance. Permits are available from the American or Canadian Automobile Association, or, in the United Kingdom, from the Automobile Association or Royal Automobile Club. Check the AAA Web site for more info as well as for IDPs ($15) themselves.

Automobile Associations American Automobile Association (*AAA* ☏ *315/797-5000* ⊕ *www.aaa.com*); most contact with the organization is through state and regional members. **National Automobile Club** (☏ *650/294-7000* ⊕ *www.thenac.com*); membership is open to California residents only.

Local Agencies in Barcelona Atesa (✉ *El Prat Airport, El Prat del Llobregat* ☏ *93/298-3433* ✉ *Muntaner 45, Eixample* ☏ *93/323-0266*). **Vanguard** (✉ *Londres 31, Eixample* ☏ *93/439-3880*).

Major Agencies Avis (✉ *Casanova 209, Eixample* ☏ *93/209-9533* ✉ *Aragó 235, Eixample* ☏ *93/487-8754*). **Europcar** (✉ *Viladomat 214, Eixample* ☏ *93/439-8403* ✉ *Estació de Sants, Eixample* ☏ *93/491-4822*). **Hertz** (✉ *Estació de Sants, Eixample* ☏ *93/490-8662* ✉ *Tuset 10, Eixample* ☏ *93/217-3248*).

ROAD CONDITIONS

Traffic jams (*atascos*) can be a problem in and around Barcelona, where the *rondas* (ring roads) slow to a standstill at peak hours. If possible, avoid the rush hours, which can last from 8 AM until 9:30 AM and 7 PM to 9 PM.

ROADSIDE EMERGENCIES

The rental agencies Hertz and Avis have 24-hour breakdown service. If you belong to an auto club (AAA or CAA), you can get emergency assistance from their Catalan counterpart, the Reial Automovil Club de Catalunya (RACC), or the Spanish branch Real Automovil Club de España (RACE). There are emergency telephones on all *autopistas,* every 2 km (1 mi), with service stations generally found every 40 km (25 mi).

Emergency Services Real Automovil Club de Catalunya (*RACC* ✉ *Diagonal 687, Barcelona* ☎ *93/495-5000, 902/106106 for emergency aid* ⊕ *www.racc.es*). **Real Automovil Club de España** (*RACE* ✉ *Muntaner 81-bajo, Barcelona* ☎ *93/451-1551, 902/300505 for emergency aid* ⊕ *www.race.com*).

RULES OF THE ROAD

Children under 10 may not ride in the front seat, and seat belts are compulsory. Speed limits are 50 kph (31 mph) in cities; 100 kph (62 mph) on N roads; 120 kph (74 mph) on the *autopistas* (toll highways) and *autovías* (freeways); and, unless otherwise signposted, 90 kph (56 mph) on other roads, such as *carreteras nacionales* (main roads) and *carreteras comarcales* (secondary roads). Barcelona's *rondas* (ring roads) now limit motorists to 80 kph (48 mph) and sometimes, at peak hours, cut the speed limit down to 40 kph (24 mph).

Right turns on red are not permitted. In the cities people are more often stopped for petty rule-breaking such as crossing a solid line or doing a U-turn than for speeding. However, Spanish highway police are especially vigilant regarding speeding and illegal passing, generally interpreted as crossing the solid line; fines

start at €100 and, in the case of foreign drivers, police are empowered to demand payment on the spot.

On freeway ramps, expect to come to a full stop at the red stop (not yield) triangle at the end of the on-ramp and wait for a break in the traffic; expect no merging to the left lane, especially from trucks, which, by law, must remain in the right lane.

■ METRO TRAVEL

In Barcelona the underground metro, or subway, is the fastest, cheapest, and easiest way to get around. Lines 2, 3, and 5 run weekdays 5 AM–midnight. Lines 1 and 4 close at 11. On Friday, Saturday, and holiday evenings all trains run 24 hours. The FGC trains run 5 AM–12:30 AM on weekdays and all night on weekends and the eves of holidays. Sunday trains run on weekday schedules.

When switching from the metro line to the FGC (or vice-versa), merely insert the card through the slot and the turnstile will open without charging you for a second ride provided less than an hour has elapsed since you punched in initially. Maps showing bus and metro routes are available free from booths in the Plaça de Catalunya.

TICKET/PASS	PRICE
Single Fare	€1.35
10-Ride Pass	€7.70

Subway Info Transports Metropolitans de Barcelona (*TMB*) (☎ *93/298-7000* ⊕ *www.tmb.net*).

■ TAXI TRAVEL

In Barcelona taxis are black and yellow and show a green rooftop light on the front right corner when available for hire. The meter currently starts at €2 (€2.10 at night) and rises in increments of €0.11 every 100 meters or 1.10 per kilometer.

These rates apply 6 AM–10 PM weekdays. At hours outside of these, the rates rise 20%. There are official supplements of €1 per bag for luggage.

Trips from a train station or to the airport entail a supplemental charge of €3.10, as do trips to or from the bullring or a football match. There are cabstands (*parades*, in Catalan) all over town, and you can also hail cabs on the street, though if you are too close to an official stand they may not stop. You can call for a cab 24 hours a day. Drivers do not expect a tip, though rounding up in their favor is the norm.

Taxi Companies Barna Taxi (☎ 93/357-7755). **Cooperativa Radio-Taxi Metropolitana Barcelona** (☎ 93/225-0000). **Radio Taxi** (☎ 93/303-3033). **Taxi Class Rent** (☎ 93/307-0707). **Teocar Mercedes** (☎ 93/308-8434).

▌ TRAIN TRAVEL

International overnight trains to Barcelona arrive from many European cities, including Paris, Grenoble, Geneva, Zurich, and Milan; the route from Paris takes 11½ hours. Almost all long-distance trains arrive at and depart from Estació de Sants, though many make a stop at Passeig de Gràcia that comes in handy for hotels in the Eixample or in the Ciutat Vella. The Estació de França, near the port, handles only a few regional trains within Catalonia. Train service connects Barcelona with most other major cities in Spain; in addition a high-speed Euromed route connects Barcelona to Tarragona and Valencia.

Spain's intercity services (along with some of Barcelona's *rodalies,* or local train routes) are handled by the government-run railroad system—RENFE (Red Nacional de Ferrocarriles Españoles). The high-speed AVE train now connects Barcelona and Madrid (via Lleida and Zaragoza) in under 3 hours. The fast TALGO and ALTARIA trains are efficient, though local trains remain slow and tedious. In addition to RENFE, the Catalan government's FGC (Ferrocarril de la Generalitat

de Catalunya) also provides train service, notably to Barcelona's commuter suburbs of Sant Cugat, Terrassa, and Sabadell.

Information on the local/commuter lines (*rodalies* in Catalan, *cercanias* in Spanish) can be found at www.renfe.es/cercanias. Rodalies go to, for example, Sitges from Barcelona, whereas you would take a regular RENFE train to, say, Tarragona. It's important to know whether you are traveling RENFE or rodalies, distinguished by a stylized C, so you don't end up in the wrong line.

First-class train service in Spain, with the exception of the *coche-cama* (Pullman) overnight service, barely differs from second class or *turista*. First-class trains, on the other hand, such as the TALGO or the AVE, are wildly faster than second-class carriers such as the slowpoke Estrella overnight from Barcelona to Madrid. Legroom and general comforts are about the same (that is, mediocre). The AVE is the exception, however. Between Barcelona and Madrid or between Madrid and Sevilla, these sleek bullets with their tinted windows are superlative moving observation platforms. Over two dozen AVE trains leaving on the hours and half hours connect Barcelona and Madrid daily with departures from 5:45 AM to 9 PM. Ticket prices in tourist class range from €110 to €130 depending on peak hours. Trips take about 2 hours and 45 minutes.

After buses, trains are the most economical way to travel. Within the RENFE pricing system, there are 20% discounts on long-distance tickets if you buy a round-trip ticket, and there are 20% discounts for students and senior citizens (though they usually have to carry cards issued by the local government, the Generalitat, so they are not intended for tourists).

If you're planning extensive train travel, look into rail passes. If Spain is your only destination, consider a Spain Flexipass. Prices begin at U.S. €153 for three days of second-class travel within a two-month period and €191 for first class. Other passes cover more days and longer periods. The 10-day pass costs €313 in second class, €391 in first class.

Spain is one of 17 European countries in which you can use Eurail Global Passes, which buy you unlimited first-class rail travel in all participating countries for the duration of the pass. If you plan to rack up the miles and go between countries, get a standard pass; these are available for 15 days (€511), 21 days (€662), one month (€822), two months (€1,161), and 3 months (€1,432). Eurail passes are also available for 10 days of travel within two months (€603) or for 15 days within two months (€792). If your needs are more limited, look into a Regional Pass, which costs less than a Eurail Pass and buys you a limited number of travel days in a limited number of countries (France, Italy, and Spain, for example), during a specified time period.

In addition to standard Eurail Passes, Rail Europe sells the Eurail Youthpass (for those under age 26), the Eurail Saverpass (which gives a discount for two or more people traveling together), a Eurail Flexipass (which allows a certain number of travel days within a set period), the Euraildrive Pass (4 days of train travel and 2 days of Avis or Hertz car rental), and the Europass Drive (which combines 3 days travel by train and 2 by rental car). Whichever pass you choose, remember that you must buy your pass before you leave for Europe.

Many travelers assume that rail passes guarantee them seats on the trains they wish to ride. Not so: you need to reserve seats in advance even if you're using a rail pass. Seat reservations are required on some European trains, particularly high-speed trains, and are wise on any train that might be crowded. You'll also need a reservation if you want sleeping accommodations. All reservations require an extra fee.

For schedules and fares, call RENFE. The easiest way for non–Spanish speakers to obtain schedule information is to go the RENFE Web site, (www.renfe.es).

Train services to Barcelona from the United Kingdom are not as frequent, fast, or affordable as flights, and you have to change trains (and stations) in Paris. From Paris it's worth paying extra for a TALGO express to avoid having to change trains again at the Spanish border. Journey time to Paris (from London via Eurostar through the Channel Tunnel) is around three hours; from Paris to Barcelona, it's an additional seven hours. Allow at least two hours in Paris for changing trains.

Although overnight trains have comfortable sleeper cars for two or four in coche-cama class, first-class fares that include a sleeping compartment are comparable to airfares.

The overnight Costa Brava train from Barcelona to Madrid takes eight hours. A tourist-class seat costs €41.20. A bunk in a compartment with three other people, called *clase turista damas-caballeros* (tourist class), separates travelers by gender and costs €52.80, but the windows do not open and the heat can be suffocating. The air shuttle (or a scheduled flight) between Madrid and Barcelona can, if all goes well, get you door to door in under three hours for only about €40 more than the overnight train costs, and certain off-hour flights are available for as low as €20.

For shorter, regional train trips, you can often buy your tickets directly from machines in the main train stations. For a one-way ticket, ask for, in Catalan, *anada* (in Spanish it's *ida*); or for a round-trip ticket, *anada i tornada*. In Castilian Spanish, it's *ida y vuelta*.

In Barcelona a handy secret is the Passeig de Gràcia ticket office, where there is rarely a line. Lines at Sants can be long, though, with a separate line (marked *salida inmediata*), where same-day tickets can be obtained more quickly.

You can make reservations over the phone by calling RENFE, by Internet, or, for the cyber-challenged, by waiting at the station ticket counter, preferably in Barcelona's Passeig de Gràcia, where lines are shorter or nonexistent.

The easiest way to make reservations is to use the TIKNET service on the RENFE Web site. TIKNET involves registering and providing your credit card information. When you make the reservation, you will be given a car and seat assignment and a *localizador* (translated as "localizer" on the English version of the site). Print out the reservations page or write down car number, seat number, and localizer. When traveling, go to your assigned seat on the train. When the conductor comes round, give him the localizer, and he will issue the ticket on the spot. You will need your passport and, in most cases, the credit card you used for the reservation. The AVE trains check you in at the gate to the platform, where you provide the localizer. You can review your pending reservations online at any time.

Caveats: The first time you use TIKNET, you must pick up the tickets at a RENFE station; you can go to a RENFE booth at the airport as you get off your plane. A 15% cancellation fee is charged if you cancel more than two hours after making the reservation. You cannot buy tickets online for certain regional lines or for commuter lines (*cercanias*). Station agents cannot alter TIKNET reservations: you must do this yourself online. If a train is booked, the TIKNET process doesn't reveal this until the final stage of the reservation attempt. Then it gives you a cryptic error message in a little box, though if you reserve a few days in advance it's unlikely you'll encounter this problem except at Easter or Christmas or in the first week of August.

There is no line per se at the train station for advance tickets (and often for information); you take a number and wait until it is called. Ticket clerks at stations rarely speak English, so if you need help or advice in planning a more complex train journey, you may be better off going to a

travel agency that displays the blue-and-yellow RENFE sign. A small commission (American Express Viajes charges €3.50) should be expected.

General Information Estació de França (⊠ *Marquès de l'Argentera s/n, Born-Ribera*). **Estació de Sants** (⊠ *Pl. dels Països Catalans s/n, Eixample*). **Estació de Passeig de Gràcia** (⊠ *Passeig de Gràcia at corner of Carrer Aragó, Eixample*). **Ferrocarrils de la Generalitat de Catalunya (FGC)** (☎ *93/205-1515* ⊕ *www.fgc.es*). **RENFE** (☎ *902/240202* ⊕ *www.renfe.es*).

Information and Passes CIT Tours Corp. (⊠ *342 Madison Ave., Suite 207, New York, NY* ☎ *212/697-2100, 800/248-8687, 800/248-7245 in western U.S.* ⊕ *www.cit-tours.com*). **DER Tours** (⌖ *Box 1606, Des Plaines, IL 60017* ☎ *800/782-2424*). **Eurail.** (⊕ *www.eurail.com*). **Rail Europe** (⊠ *226–230 Westchester Ave., White Plains, NY 10604* ☎ *914/682-5172 or 800/438-7245* ⌖ *2087 Dundas E, Suite 105, Mississauga, Ontario L4X 1M2, Canada* ☎ *416/602-4195* ⊕ *www.raileurope.com*).

From the U.K. Eurostar (☎ *01233/617575 or 0870/518-6186* ⊕ *www.eurostar.co.uk*). **National Rail Enquiries** (☎ *0845/748-4950* ⊕ *www.nationalrail.co.uk*). **Rail Europe** (☎ *800/942-4866 or 800/274-8724, 0870/584-8848 credit-card bookings* ⊕ *www.raileurope.com*).

Channel Tunnel Car Transport Eurotunnel (☎ *0870/535-3535 in the U.K., 070/223210 in Belgium, 03-21-00-61-00 in France* ⊕ *www.eurotunnel.com*). **French Motorail/Rail Europe** (☎ *0870/241-5415 in the U.K.* ⊕ *www.raileurope.co.uk/frenchmotorail*).

Channel Tunnel Passenger Service Eurostar (☎ *0870/518-6186 in the U.K.* ⊕ *www.eurostar.co.uk*). **Rail Europe** (☎ *888/382-7245 in the U.S., 0870/584-8848 in the U.K. inquiries and credit-card bookings* ⊕ *www.raileurope.com*).

ESSENTIALS

■ COMMUNICATIONS

INTERNET

Internet access via Wi-Fi is available in all virtually Barcelona hotels. In addition, many cafés and bars are Internet hot spots and have signs indicating it in their windows. Easy Internet Café near the top of the Rambla is one of the citys's most complete and convenient cyber-cafés, with 300 computers available from 8:30 AM to 2:30 AM daily.

Easy Internet Café (✉ *Rambla 31, Rambla* ☎ *93/268-8787*).

PHONES

Calling from a hotel is almost always the most expensive option; hotels usually add huge surcharges to all calls. In some countries you can phone from call centers or even the post office. Calling cards usually keep costs to a minimum, but only if you purchase them locally. And then there are mobile phones, which are usually a much cheaper option than calling from your hotel.

The country code for Spain is 34. To phone home from Spain, 00 gets you an international line; country codes are 1 for the United States and Canada, 61 for Australia, 64 for New Zealand, and 44 for the United Kingdom.

CALLING WITHIN SPAIN

Spain's telephone system is efficient, and direct dialing is the norm everywhere. Only cell phones conforming to the European GSM standard will work in Spain.

All Spanish area codes begin with a 9; for instance, Barcelona is 93 and Bilbao is 94. The 900 code indicates a toll-free number. Numbers starting with a 6 indicate a cellular phone; note that calls to cell phones are significantly more expensive.

For general information in Spain, dial 1-18-18. The operator for international information and assistance is at 1-18-25 (some operators speak English). Barcelona information of all kinds, including telephone information, is available by dialing 010, where many operators speak English.

Calls within Spain require dialing 8, 9, or 10 digits (beginning with a 2- or 3-digit regional code), even within the same area code.

Making a long-distance call within Spain simply requires dialing the 8, 9, or 10-digit number including the provincial area code and number.

Between phone booths in the street (ask for a *cabina telefónica*) and public phones in bars and restaurants, telephone communication in Spain functions as well as anyplace in the world. Many phones have digital readout screens, so you can see your money ticking away. If using coins, you need at least €0.20 for a local call, €1 to call another province. Pick up the phone, wait for the dial tone, and only then insert coins before dialing. Rates are reduced on weekends and after 8 PM on weekdays.

CALLING OUTSIDE SPAIN

International calls are easiest from public pay phones using a phone card. The best way to phone home is to use a public phone that accepts phone cards (available from tobacconists and most newsagents) or go to the local telephone office or *locutorio,* a phone center. The best thing about the locutorio is the quiet, private booth. If the call costs over €5, you can often pay with Visa or MasterCard.

To make an international call yourself, dial 00, then the country code, then the area code and number. Ask at a tourist office for a list of locutorios and Internet centers that include phone service.

Before you go, find out your long-distance company's access code in Spain.

Access Codes AT&T (☎ *900/990011*). **MCI WorldPhone** (☎ *900/990014*). **Sprint International Access** (☎ *900/990013*).

CALLING CARDS

Pay phones work with a phone card (*tarjeta telefónica*), of which there are several varieties that you can buy at any tobacco shop (Tabac) or newsagent. The Euro Hours Card, sold at many tobacco shops for €6, gives three hours of international phone calls.

MOBILE PHONES

If you have a multiband phone (some countries use different frequencies from what's used in the United States) and your service provider uses the world-standard GSM network (as do T-Mobile, Cingular, and Verizon), you can probably use your phone abroad. Roaming fees can be steep, however: 99¢ a minute is considered reasonable. And overseas you normally pay the toll charges for incoming calls. It's almost always cheaper to send a text message than to make a call, since text messages have a very low set fee (often less than 5¢).

If you just want to make local calls, consider buying a new SIM card (note that your provider may have to unlock your phone for you to use a different SIM card) and a prepaid service plan in the destination. You'll then have a local number and can make local calls at local rates. If your trip is extensive, you could also simply buy a new cell phone in your destination, as the initial cost will be offset over time.

Cell Phone Rentals Rentaphone Taxi (☎ *93/280-2131*). **Telecon Iberica** (☎ *93/228-9110*). **Telenisa** (☎ *93/414-1966*). **Walkie Talkie** (☎ *93/238-0360*).

Contacts Cellular Abroad (☎ *800/287-5072* ⊕ *www.cellularabroad.com*) rents and sells GMS phones and sells SIM cards that work in many countries. **Mobal** (☎ *888/888-9162* ⊕ *www.mobalrental.com*) rents mobiles and sells GSM phones (starting at $49) that will operate in 140 countries. Per-call rates vary throughout the world. **Planet Fone** (☎ *888/988-4777* ⊕ *www.planetfone.com*) rents cell phones, but the per-minute rates are expensive.

■ ELECTRICITY

The electrical current in Spain is 220 volts, 50 cycles alternating current (AC); wall outlets take continental-type plugs, with two round prongs. An adapter from flat to round prongs is a must for computers and hair dryers.

■ EMERGENCIES

You can expect local residents to be helpful if you have an emergency. For assistance, dial the pan-European emergency phone number 112, which is operative in northern Spain, but not all parts of Spain. Otherwise, dial the emergency numbers below for national police, local police, fire department, or medical services. On the road, there are emergency phones at frequent regular intervals on freeways (*autovías*) and toll highways (*autopistas*). They are marked S.O.S.

■ MAIL

Post offices are usually open 8:30–2:30 on weekdays, and 10–2 on Saturday, though hours vary. Some main post offices, including Barcelona's, which is on Plaça Antonio López, are open all day, 8:30 AM–8:30 PM Monday–Saturday, and 9–2:30 on Sunday.

Main Branches Oficina Carrer Aragó (⊠ *Aragó 282, Eixample* ☎ *93/216-0453* Ⓜ *Passeig de Gràcia*).

■ MONEY

CREDIT CARDS

Throughout this guide, the following abbreviations are used: **AE**, American Express; **DC**, Diners Club; **MC**, MasterCard; and **V**, Visa.

It's a good idea to inform your credit-card company before you travel. Otherwise, the credit-card company might put a hold on your card owing to unusual activity. Record all your credit-card numbers—as well as the phone numbers to call if your cards are lost or stolen—in a safe place.

Both MasterCard and Visa have general numbers you can call (collect if you're abroad) if your card is lost, but you're better off calling the number of your issuing bank; your bank's number is usually printed on your card.

If you plan to use your credit card for cash advances, you'll need to apply for a PIN at least two weeks before your trip. Although it's usually cheaper (and safer) to use a credit card abroad for large purchases, note that some credit-card companies *and* the banks that issue them add substantial percentages to all foreign transactions, whether they're in a foreign currency or not. Check on these fees before leaving home.

■TIP➔ Before you charge something, ask the merchant whether or not he or she plans to do a dynamic currency conversion (DCC). In such a transaction the credit-card processor (shop, restaurant, or hotel, not Visa or MasterCard) converts the currency and charges you in dollars. In most cases you'll pay the merchant a 3% fee for this service in addition to any credit-card company and issuing-bank foreign-transaction surcharges.

Dynamic currency conversion programs are becoming increasingly widespread. Merchants who participate in them are supposed to ask whether you want to be charged in dollars or the local currency, but they don't always do so. And even if they do offer you a choice, they may well avoid mentioning the additional surcharges. The good news is that you *do* have a choice. And if this practice really gets your goat, you can avoid it entirely: with American Express cards, DCC simply isn't an option.

But note that in Spain, many restaurants don't accept American Express.

Reporting Lost Cards American Express (☎ 800/528–4800 in the U.S., 336/393–1111 collect from abroad ⊕ www.americanexpress. com). **Diners Club** (☎ 800/234–6377 in the U.S., 303/799–1504 collect from abroad ⊕ www.dinersclub.com). **MasterCard**

(☎ 800/627–8372 in the U.S., 636/722–7111 collect from abroad ⊕ www.mastercard.com). **Visa** (☎ 800/847–2911 in the U.S., 410/581–9994 collect from abroad ⊕ www.visa.com).

Toll-free Numbers in Spain American Express (☎ 900/941413). **Diners Club** (☎ 901/101011). **MasterCard** (☎ 900/974445). **Visa** (☎ 900/971231).

CURRENCY AND EXCHANGE

On January 1, 2002, the European monetary unit, the euro (€), went into circulation in Spain and the other countries that have adopted it (Austria, Belgium, Finland, France, Germany, Greece, Ireland, Italy, Luxembourg, the Netherlands, and Portugal). Euro notes come in denominations of 5, 10, 20, 50, 100, 200, and 500 euros; coins are worth 1 cent of a euro, 2 cents, 5 cents, 10 cents, 20 cents, 50 cents, 1 euro, and 2 euros. All coins have one side with the value of the euro on it; the other side has each country's own national symbol. There are seven banknotes, or bills, in denominations of 5, 10, 20, 50, 100, 200, and 500 euros. Banknotes are the same for all European Union countries. At press time exchange rates were U.S. $1.42, U.K. £0.86, Australian $1.69, Canadian $1.54, New Zealand $2.09, and 11.48 South African rands to the euro.

Currency Conversion Google (⊕ www. google.com). **Oanda.com** (⊕ www.oanda.com) **XE.com** (⊕ www.xe.com).

TRAVELER'S CHECKS

Avoid taking traveler's checks to Barcelona, because few vendors accept them.

▋ PASSPORTS

Visitors from the United States, Australia, Canada, New Zealand, and the United Kingdom need a valid passport to enter Spain. No visa is required for U.S. passport holders for a stay of up to three months; for stays exceeding three months, contact the Consulate of Spain nearest you. Australians require a visa for stays of over a month. You should obtain it from the Spanish Embassy before you leave.

TAXES

Value-added tax (similar to sales tax) is called IVA (for *Impuesto sobre el valor añadido*) in Spain. It is levied on services, such as hotels and restaurants, and on consumer products. When in doubt about whether tax is included, ask, *"Está incluido el IVA ("ee-vah")?"*

The IVA rate for hotels and restaurants is 7%. Menus will generally say at the bottom whether tax is included (*IVA incluido*) or not (*más 7% IVA*). While food and basic necessities are taxed at the lowest rate, most consumer goods are taxed at 16%. Non–EU citizens can request a Tax-Free Cheque on purchases of €90.15 and over in shops displaying the Tax-Free Shopping sticker. This Cheque must be stamped at the customs office to the right of the arrivals exit in Barcelona Airport's Terminal A. After this is done, present it to one of the Caixa or Banco de España offices in the airport. The bank issues a certified check or credits the amount to your credit card.

Global Refund is a Europe-wide service with 225,000 affiliated stores and more than 700 refund counters at major airports and border crossings. Its refund form, called a Tax-Free Cheque, is the most common across the European continent. The service issues refunds in the form of cash, check, or credit-card adjustment.

V.A.T. Refunds Global Refund (☏ *800/566–9828* ⊕ *www.globalrefund.com*).

TIPPING

Restaurant checks always include service. The bill may not tell you that the service is included, but it is. An extra tip of 5% to 10% of the bill is icing on the cake. Leave tips in cash, even if paying by credit card. If you eat tapas or sandwiches at a bar—just round up the bill to the nearest

euro. Tip cocktail servers €0.20 a drink, depending on the bar. In a fancy establishment, leave no more than a 10% tip even though service is included—likewise if you had a great time.

Taxi drivers expect no tip at all and are happy if you round up in their favor. A tip of 5% of the total fare is considered generous. Long rides or extra help with luggage may merit a tip, but if you're short of change, you'll never hear a complaint. On the contrary, your taxi driver may round down in *your* favor.

Tip hotel porters €1 a bag, and the bearer of room service €1. A doorman who calls a taxi for you gets €1. If you stay in a hotel for more than two nights, tip the maid about €1 per night. A concierge should receive a tip for service, from €1 for basic help to €5 or more for special assistance such as getting reservations at a popular restaurant.

Tour guides should be tipped about €2, barbers €0.50, and women's hairdressers at least €2 for a wash and style. Restroom attendants are tipped €0.50 or whatever loose change is at hand.

TOURS

SPECIAL-INTEREST TOURS
ART TOURS

The Ruta del Modernisme (Moderniste Route), a self-guided tour, provides an excellent guidebook (available in English) that interprets 100 Moderniste sites from the Sagrada Família and the Palau de la Música Catalana to Art Nouveau building facades, lampposts, and paving stones. Tickets (books of coupons valid for a year) and manuals are sold at the Plaça Catalunya Tourist Office, Pavellons Güell, and Hospital de Sant Pau.

The Palau de la Música Catalana offers guided tours in English every hour on the hour from 10 to 3. Sagrada Família guided tours cost extra. Casa Milà offers one guided tour daily (6 PM weekdays, 11 AM weekends). The ticket price, €18, gets you 50% discounts at numerous sites around town, as well as free guided tours (in English at specified hours) at Pavellons Güell, Hospital de Sant Pau, and the Manzana de la Discòrdia (at 11,12,1, 2:30, and 5).

Contacts Centre del Modernisme, Centre d'Informació de Turisme de Barcelona (✉ *Pl. Catalunya, 17, soterrani, The Rambla*). **Centre del Modernisme, Hospital de la Santa Creu i Sant Pau** (✉ *C. Sant Antoni Maria Claret, 167, Eixample*). **Centre del Modernisme, Pavellons Güell** (✉ *Av. de Pedralbes 7, Pedralbes* ☎ *34-902-076621* |*cultura-impuqv@bcn.cat*).**Centre d'Informació de Turisme de Barcelona** (✉ *Pl. Catalunya 17, soterrani, Eixample* ☎ *93/488-0139*). **Urbancultours** (☎ *93/417-1191*).

CULINARY

Aula Gastronómica del Mercat de la Boqueria (Cooking Lessons at the Boqueria Market) includes tours of the market with breakfast, cooking classes, and tastings, but they're not in English. Jane Gregg, founder of Epicureanways, offers peerless gourmet and wine tours of Barcelona, Catalonia, and the rest of Spain. Teresa Parker of Spanish Journeys organizes cooking classes, seasonal specials, custom cultural or culinary tours, corporate cooking retreats, or off-the-beaten-path travel in Spain.

Contacts Aula Gastronómica del Mercat de la Boqueria (✉ *La Rambla 91, Rambla* ☎ *93/304-0272* ⊕ *www.barcelonaculinaria. com*). **Epicureanways** (✉ *507 Nottingham Rd., Charlottesville, VA* ☎ *866/642-2917* ⊕ *www.epicureanways.com*). **Spanish Journeys** (✉ *805 Long Pond Rd., Wellfleet, MA* ☎ *508/349-9769* ⊕ *www.spanishjourneys. com*).

DAY TOURS AND GUIDES
BOAT TOURS

Golondrina harbor boats make short trips from the Portal de la Pau, near the Columbus monument. The fare is €6 for a 35-minute tour of the harbor and €12.50 for a 90-minute ride out past the beaches and up the coast to the Fòrum at the eastern end of the Diagonal. Departures are spring and summer (Easter week–September), daily 11–7; fall and winter,

weekends and holidays only, 11–5. It's closed mid-December–early January.

Fees and Schedules Las Golondrinas and Trimar y Ómnibus (✉ *Plaza Portal de la Pau s/n, Rambla* ☎ *93/442-3106* ⊕ *www. lasgolondrinas.com* Ⓜ *Drassanes*).

BUS TOURS

The Bus Turístic (9:30–7:30 every 10 to 30 minutes, depending on the season), sponsored by the tourist office, runs on three circuits that pass all the important sights. One covers upper Barcelona; another tours lower Barcelona; and a third runs from the Olympic Port to the Fòrum at the eastern end of the Diagonal. A day's ticket, which you can buy on the bus, costs €21 (a two-day ticket is €27) and also covers the fare for the Tramvía Blau, funicular, and Montjuïc cable car across the port. You receive a booklet with discount vouchers for various attractions. Rides for Buses 1 and 2 start at the Plaça de Catalunya; Bus 3 starts at the Olympic Port. Each bus stops a dozen times, allowing visitors to jump off and catch a later bus after visiting each monument. A live narrator explains the sites and monuments. Julià Tours and Pullmantur run day and half-day excursions outside the city. The most popular trips are those to Montserrat and the Costa Brava resorts, the latter including a cruise to the Medes Isles.

Contacts Bus Turístic (☎ *93/368-9700* ⊕ *www.barcelonaturisme.com*). **Julià Tours** (✉ *Ronda Universitat 5, Eixample* ☎ *93/317-6454*). **Pullmantur** (✉ *Gran Vía 645, Eixample* ☎ *93/317-1297*).

PRIVATE GUIDES

Nicholas Law of Spain Step by Step can take you on brilliantly planned and guided treks all over Spain, including walks through Barcelona, the Costa Brava, or the Catalan Pyrenees. Guides from the other organizations listed below are generally competent and encyclopedic, though the quality of language skills and general showmanship may vary wildly. For customized tours including access to some of Barcelona's leading chefs, architects, art historians, and artists, Heritage Tours will set it all up from New York.

Contacts Associació Professional d'Informadors Turístics (☎ *93/319-8416*). **Barcelona Guide Bureau** (☎ *93/268-2422*). **City Guides Barcelona** (☎ *93/412-0674*). **Heritage Tours** (☎ *800/378-4555 or 212/206-8400 in the U.S.* ⊕ *www. heritagetoursonline.com*). **Spain Step by Step** (☎ *93/217-9395*).

WALKING TOURS

Turisme de Barcelona offers weekend walking tours of the Gothic Quarter, the Waterfront, Picasso's Barcelona, Modernisme, a shopping circuit, and Gourmet Barcelona in English (at 10:30 AM) for €16.21. The Picasso tour, a real bargain, includes the entry free for the Picasso Museum (€9). Tours depart from the Plaça de Catalunya tourist office. For private tours, Julià Tours and Pullmantur (➪ *Bus Tours*) both lead walks around Barcelona. Tours leave from their offices, but you may be able to arrange a pickup at your hotel. Prices per person are €35 for half a day and €90 for a full day, including lunch.

For the best English-language walking tour of the medieval Jewish Quarter (or Gaudí's Sagrada Família), contact Dominique Blinder at Urbancultours (➪ *Art Tours*).

Contact Turisme de Barcelona (✉ *Pl. de Catalunya 17 bis, La Rambla 99, Eixample* ☎ *93/368-9700* ⊕ *www.barcelonaturisme.com*).

∎ VISITOR INFORMATION

The Tourist Office of Spain (and its Web site) provides valuable practical information about visiting the country. Turisme de Barcelona has two main locations, both open Monday–Saturday 9–9 and Sunday 10–2: Plaça de Catalunya, in the center of town; and Plaça Sant Jaume, in the Gothic Quarter. Other tourist information stands are near the top of the Rambla just below Carrer Tallers, at the port end of

the Rambla (just beyond the Columbus monument) and at the main entrance of the Sagrada Família. There are smaller facilities at the Sants train station, open daily 8–8; the Palau de la Virreina, open Monday–Saturday 9–9 and Sunday 10–2; and the Palau de Congressos, open daily 10–8 during trade fairs and conventions only. For general information in English, dial ☎ 010 between 8 AM and 10 PM any day but Sunday.

El Prat Airport has an office with information on Catalonia and the rest of Spain, open Monday–Saturday 9:30–8 and Sunday 9:30–3. The tourist office in Palau Robert, open Monday–Saturday 10–7, specializes in provincial Catalonia. From June to mid-September, tourist-information aides patrol the Gothic Quarter and Ramblas area 9 AM–9 PM. They travel in pairs and are recognizable by their uniforms of red shirts, white trousers or skirts, and badges.

Barcelona Tourist Offices Sants Estació (✉ *Pl. dels Països Catalans s/n, Eixample* ☎ *93/285-3834*). **Palau de Congressos** (✉ *Av. Reina María Cristina 2-16, Eixample*). **Plaça de Catalunya** (✉ *Pl. de Catalunya 17-S, Eixample,* ☎ *93/285-3834* ⊕ *www.barcelonaturisme. com*). **Plaça Sant Jaume** (✉ *Ciutat 2, Barri Gòtic* ☎ *93/285-3834*). **Servei d'Informació Cultural–Palau de la Virreina** (✉ *Rambla 99, Rambla* ☎ *93/301-7775* ⊕ *www.bcn.cat/ cultura*).

Regional Tourist Offices El Prat Airport (✉ *Terminal B* ☎ *93/478-0565*). **Palau Robert** (✉ *Passeig de Gràcia 107, at Diagonal, Eixample* ☎ *93/238-8091* ⊕ *www.gencat.net/ probert*).

INDEX

PHOTO CREDITS